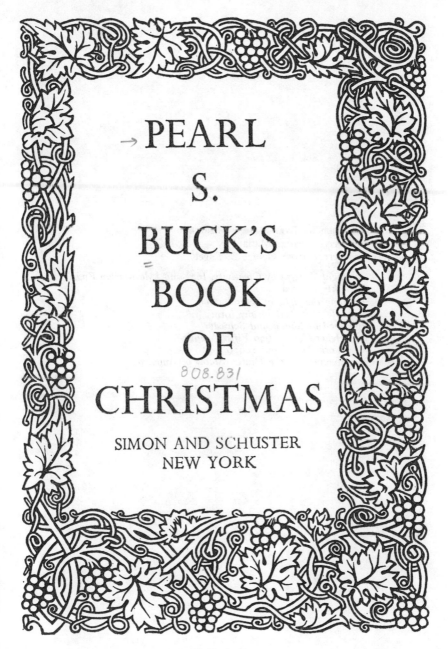

PEARL S. BUCK'S BOOK OF CHRISTMAS

SIMON AND SCHUSTER
NEW YORK

PRODUCED BY LYLE KENYON ENGEL
EXECUTIVE EDITOR: Marla Ray
ASSOCIATE EDITOR: George S. Engel

Contents

Introduction

I first met Pearl Buck in 1961 when we recorded her children's book *The Chinese Children Next Door*.

Miss Buck did the narration in a soundproofed studio while I as producer sat with my staff of engineers in the control room and directed her efforts. At the end of the session Miss Buck joined us and listened to the master tapes. Everyone could see that she was quite pleased with having her literary efforts in yet another medium.

It was four more weeks before I again saw Miss Buck. Those weeks were spent in recording an original music background. When Miss Buck heard the recording with the music and special effects, she was charmed and asked me to call upon her again if I had any other ways of working with her.

I said that I would be quite interested in working with her in producing a book called *Fairy Tales of the Orient*. I would use my organization in collecting and researching material for the book, which I would turn over to her to select those stories that she was most interested in, and she would do an introduction.

The book was quite successful, and it led to our working together on *The People of Japan*, *The Story Bible*, *China: Past and Present*, *The Oriental Cookbook*, and *America*.

The above books covered a span of twelve years during which period we met many times and discussed many projects including a book that consisted of Christmas stories written by some of the world's greatest writers.

"Have you ever read Sir Walter Scott's *Christmas in the Olden Time?*" Miss Buck would say, and "What about *Christmas at Thompson Hall* by Anthony Trollope?"

I would counter with "How about *A Christmas Carol* by Charles Dickens and *The Gift of the Magi* by O. Henry?"

This went on for years until we had a great list of material written by famous authors. All that remained was for Miss Buck to write the introduction into which she felt must be incorporated two excerpts from the Bible dealing with the birth of Christ. One from St. Matthew 2 : 1, 2, 11, because it tells of the Three Wise Men with their gifts of gold, frankincense and myrrh.

Now when Jesus was born in Bethlehem of Judea in the days of Herod the king, behold, there came wise men from the east to Jerusalem.

Saying, Where is he that is born King of the Jews? for we have seen his star in the east, and are come to worship him.

And when they were come into the house, they saw the young child with Mary his mother, and fell down, and worshipped him: and when they had opened their treasures, they presented unto him gifts; gold, and frankincense, and myrrh.

The other from St. Luke 2 : 1–14 because it mentions peace on earth and good will toward men.

And it came to pass in those days, that there went out a decree from Caesar Augustus, that all the world should be taxed.

(And this taxing was first made when Cyrenius was governor of Syria.)

And all went to be taxed, every one into his own city.

And Joseph also went up from Galilee, out of the city of Nazareth,

into Judea, unto the city of David, which is called Bethlehem;
(because he was of the house and lineage of David:)

To be taxed with Mary his espoused wife, being great with child.

And so it was, that, while they were there, the days were accomplished that she should be delivered.

And she brought forth her firstborn son, and wrapped him in swaddling clothes, and laid him in a manger; because there was no room for them in the inn.

And there were in the same country shepherds abiding in the field, keeping watch over their flock by night.

And, lo, the angel of the Lord came upon them, and the glory of the Lord shone round about them: and they were sore afraid.

And the angel said unto them, Fear not: for, behold, I bring you good tidings of great joy, which shall be to all people.

For unto you is born this day in the city of David a Saviour, which is Christ the Lord.

And this shall be a sign unto you; Ye shall find the babe wrapped in swaddling clothes, lying in a manger.

And suddenly there was with the angel a multitude of the heavenly host praising God, and saying,

Glory to God in the highest, and on earth peace, good will toward men.

This grand lady, Pearl S. Buck, beloved by millions of readers and winner of the Pulitzer Prize (1932) and the Nobel Prize for Literature (1938), passed from our scene in 1973, leaving me with the material for the Christmas book but no introduction.

I feel everyone will enjoy her intention of making available in one volume a selection of Christmas stories, some of which were written by the world's greatest authors as their contribution toward the holiday spirit.

Lyle Kenyon Engel
Canaan, New York
1974

CHRISTMAS AT THOMPSON HALL

by Anthony Trollope

from *Christmas at Thompson Hall, A Tale*

Chapter I

MRS. BROWN'S SUCCESS

Every one remembers the severity of the Christmas of 187–. I will
not designate the year more closely, lest I should enable those who are
too curious to investigate the circumstances of this story, and inquire
into details which I do not intend to make known. That winter, however, was especially severe, and the cold of the last ten days of
December was more felt, I think, in Paris than in any part of England.
It may, indeed, be doubted whether there is any town in any country
in which thoroughly bad weather is more afflicting than in the French
capital. Snow and hail seem to be colder there, and fires certainly are
less warm, than in London. And then there is a feeling among visitors
to Paris that Paris ought to be gay; that gayety, prettiness, and
liveliness are its aims, as money, commerce, and general business are
the aims of London, which, with its outside sombre darkness, does
often seem to want an excuse for its ugliness. But on this occasion, at
this Christmas of 187–, Paris was neither gay, nor pretty, nor lively.

You could not walk the streets without being ankle-deep, not in snow, but in snow that had just become slush; and there was falling throughout the day and night of the 23d of December a succession of damp, half-frozen abominations from the sky which made it almost impossible for men and women to go about their business.

It was at ten o'clock on that evening that an English lady and gentleman arrived at the Grand Hôtel on the Boulevard des Italiens. As I have reasons for concealing the names of this married couple, I will call them Mr. and Mrs. Brown. Now, I wish it to be understood that in all the general affairs of life this gentleman and this lady lived happily together, with all the amenities which should bind a husband and a wife. Mrs. Brown was one of a wealthy family, and Mr. Brown, when he married her, had been relieved from the necessity of earning his bread. Nevertheless, she had at once yielded to him when he expressed a desire to spend the winters of their life in the South of France; and he, though he was by disposition somewhat idle, and but little prone to the energetic occupations of life, would generally allow himself, at other periods of the year, to be carried hither and thither by her, whose more robust nature delighted in the excitement of travelling. But on this occasion there had been a little difference between them.

Early in December an intimation had reached Mrs. Brown at Pau that on the coming Christmas there was to be a great gathering of all the Thompsons in the Thompson family hall at Stratford-le-Bow, and that she, who had been a Thompson, was desired to join the party with her husband. On this occasion her only sister was desirous of introducing to the family generally a most excellent young man to whom she had recently become engaged. The Thompsons—the real name, however, is in fact concealed—were a numerous and a thriving people. There were uncles and cousins and brothers who had all done well in the world, and who were all likely to do better still. One had lately been returned to Parliament for the Essex Flats, and was at the time of which I am writing a conspicuous member of the gallant Conservative majority. It was partly in triumph at this success that the great Christmas gathering of the Thompsons was to be held, and an opinion had been expressed by the legislator himself that, should Mrs. Brown, with her husband, fail to join the family on this happy occasion, she and he would be regarded as being but *fainéant* Thompsons.

Since her marriage, which was an affair now nearly eight years old, Mrs. Brown had never passed a Christmas in England. The desirability of doing so had often been mooted by her. Her very soul craved the festivities of holly and mince-pies. There had ever been meetings of the Thompsons at Thompson Hall, though meetings not so significant, not so important to the family, as this one which was now to be collected. More than once had she expressed a wish to see old Christmas again in the old house among the old faces. But her husband had always pleaded a certain weakness about his throat and chest as a reason for remaining among the delights of Pau. Year after year she had yielded, and now this loud summons had come.

It was not without considerable trouble that she had induced Mr. Brown to come as far as Paris. Most unwillingly had he left Pau; and then, twice on his journey—both at Bordeaux and Tours—he had made an attempt to return. From the first moment he had pleaded his throat, and when at last he had consented to make the journey, he had stipulated for sleeping at those two towns and at Paris. Mrs. Brown, who, with no slightest feeling of fatigue, could have made the journey from Pau to Stratford without stopping, had assented to everything, so that they might be at Thompson Hall on Christmas eve. When Mr. Brown uttered his unavailing complaints at the first two towns at which they stayed, she did not, perhaps, quite believe all that he said of his own condition. We know how prone the strong are to suspect the weakness of the weak—as the weak are to be disgusted by the strength of the strong. There were, perhaps, a few words between them on the journey, but the result had hitherto been in favor of the lady. She had succeeded in bringing Mr. Brown as far as Paris.

Had the occasion been less important, no doubt she would have yielded. The weather had been bad even when they left Pau, but as they had made their way northward it had become worse and still worse. As they left Tours, Mr. Brown, in a hoarse whisper, had declared his conviction that the journey would kill him. Mrs. Brown, however, had unfortunately noticed half an hour before that he had scolded the waiter on the score of an overcharged franc or two with a loud and clear voice. Had she really believed that there was danger, or even suffering, she would have yielded; but no woman is satisfied in such a matter to be taken in by false pretences. She observed that he ate a good dinner on his way to Paris, and that he took a small glass of cognac with complete relish, which a man really suffering from bronchitis surely would not do. So she persevered, and brought him into Paris, late in the evening, in the midst of all that slush and snow. Then, as they sat down to supper, she thought he did speak hoarsely, and her loving feminine heart began to misgive her.

But this now was, at any rate, clear to her—that he could not be worse off by going on to London than he would be should he remain in Paris. If a man is to be ill, he had better be ill in the bosom of his family than at a hotel. What comfort could he have, what relief, in that huge barrack? As for the cruelty of the weather, London could not be worse than Paris, and then she thought she had heard that sea air is good for a sore throat. In that bedroom which had been allotted to them *au quatrième* they could not even get a decent fire. It would in every way be wrong now to forgo the great Christmas gathering when nothing could be gained by staying in Paris.

She had perceived that, as her husband became really ill, he became also more tractable and less disputatious. Immediately after that little glass of cognac he had declared that he would be ——— if he would go beyond Paris, and she began to fear that, after all, everything would have been done in vain. But as they went down to supper between ten and eleven he was more subdued, and merely remarked that this journey would, he was sure, be the death of him. It was half past eleven when they got back to their bedroom, and then he seemed to speak with good sense, and also with much real apprehension. "If I can't get something to relieve me, I know I shall never make my way on," he said. It was intended that they should leave the hotel at half past five the next morning, so as to arrive at Stratford, travelling by the tidal train, at half past seven on Christmas-eve. The early hour, the long journey, the infamous weather, the prospect of that horrid gulf between Boulogne and Folkestone, would have been as nothing to Mrs. Brown, had it not been for that settled look of anguish which had now pervaded her husband's face. "If you don't find something to relieve me, I shall never live through it," he said again, sinking back into the questionable comfort of a Parisian hotel arm-chair.

"But, my dear, what can I do?" she asked, almost in tears, standing over him and caressing him. He was a thin, genteel-looking man, with a fine long soft brown beard, a little bald at the top of the head, but certainly a genteel-looking man. She loved him dearly, and in her softer moods was apt to spoil him with her caresses. "What can I do, my dearie? You know I would do anything if I could. Get into bed, my pet, and be warm, and then to-morrow morning you will be all right." At this moment he was preparing himself for his bed, and she was assisting him. Then she tied a piece of flannel around his throat, and kissed him, and put him in beneath the bedclothes.

"I'll tell you what you can do," he said, very hoarsely. His voice was so bad now that she could hardly hear him. So she crept close to him, and bent over him. She would do anything if he would only say what. Then he told her what was his plan. Down in the salon he had seen a large jar of mustard standing on a sideboard. As he left the room he had observed that this had not been withdrawn with the other appurtenances of the meal. If she could manage to find her way down there, taking with her a handkerchief folded for the purpose, and if she could then appropriate a part of the contents of that jar, and, returning with her prize, apply it to his throat, he thought that he could get some relief, so that he might be able to leave his bed the next morning at five. "But I am afraid it will be very disagreeable for you to go down all alone at this time of night," he croaked out in a piteous whisper.

"Of course I'll go," said she. "I don't mind going in the least. Nobody will bite me"; and she at once began to fold a clean handkerchief. "I won't be two minutes, my darling; and if there is a grain of mustard in the house, I'll have it on your chest almost immediately." She was a woman not easily cowed, and the journey down into the salon was nothing to her. Before she went she tucked the clothes carefully up to his ears, and then she started.

To run along the first corridor till she came to a flight of stairs was easy enough, and easy enough to descend them. Then there was another corridor and another flight, and a third corridor and a third flight, and she began to think that she was wrong. She found herself in a part of the hotel which she had not hitherto visited, and soon discovered by looking through an open door or two that she had found her way among a set of private sitting-rooms which she had not seen before. Then she tried to make her way back, up the same stairs and through the same passages, so that she might start again. She was beginning to think that she had lost herself altogether, and that she would be able to find neither the salon nor her bedroom, when she happily met the night porter. She was dressed in a loose white dressing-gown, with a white net over her loose hair, and with white worsted slippers. I ought, perhaps, to have described her personal appearance sooner. She was a large woman with a commanding bust, thought by some to be handsome, after the manner of Juno. But with strangers there was a certain severity of manner about her—a fortification, as it were, of her virtue against all possible attacks—a declared determination to maintain, at all points, the beautiful character of a British matron, which, much as it had been appreciated at Thompson Hall, had met with some ill-natured criticism among French men and women. At Pau she had been called La Fière Anglaise. The name had reached her own ears and those of her husband. He had been much annoyed, but she had taken it in good part—had, indeed, been somewhat proud of the title—and had endeavored to live up to it. With her husband she could, on occasion, be soft, but she was of opinion that with other men a British matron should be stern. She was now greatly in want of assistance; but, nevertheless, when she met the porter she remembered her character. "I have lost my way wandering through these horrid passages," she said in her severest tone. This was in answer to some question from him—some question to which her reply was given very slowly. Then, when he asked where madame wished to go, she paused, again thinking what destination she would announce. No doubt the man could take her back to her bedroom, but if so, the mustard must be renounced, and with the mustard, as she now feared, all hope of reaching Thompson Hall on Christmas-eve. But she, though she was in many respects a brave woman, did not dare to tell the man that she was prowling about the hotel in order that she might make a midnight raid upon the mustard pot. She paused, therefore, for a moment, that she might collect her thoughts, erecting her head as she did so in her best Juno fashion, till the porter was lost in admiration. Thus she gained time to fabricate a tale. She had, she said, dropped her handkerchief under the supper-table; would he show her the way to the salon, in order that she might pick it up? But the porter did more than that, and accompanied her to the room in which she had supped.

Here, of course, there was a prolonged and, it need hardly be said, a vain search. The good-natured man insisted on emptying an enormous receptacle of soiled table napkins, and on turning them over one by one, in order that the lady's property might be found. The lady stood by unhappy, but still patient, and as the man was stooping to his work, her eye was on the mustard pot. There it was, capable of containing enough to blister the throats of a score of sufferers. She edged off a little toward it while the man was busy, trying to persuade herself that he would surely forgive her if she took the mustard and told him her whole story. But the descent from her Juno bearing would have been so great! She must have owned, not only to the quest for mustard, but also to a fib—and she could not do it. The porter was at last of opinion that madame must have made a mistake, and madame acknowledged that she was afraid it was so.

With a longing, lingering eye, with an eye turned back, oh! so sadly to the great jar, she left the room, the porter leading the way. She assured him that she would find it by herself, but he would not leave her till he had put her on to the proper passage. The journey seemed to be longer now even than before; but as she ascended the many stairs she swore to herself that she would not even yet be balked of her object. Should her husband want comfort for his poor throat, and the comfort be there within her reach, and he not have it? She counted every stair as she went up, and marked every turn well. She was sure now that she would know the way, and that she could return to the room without fault. She would go back to the salon. Even though the man should encounter her again, she would go boldly forward and seize the remedy which her poor husband so grievously required.

"Ah, yes," she said, when the porter told her that her room, No. 333, was in the corridor which they had then reached, "I know it all now. I am so much obliged. Do not come a step farther." He was anxious to accompany her up to the very door, but she stood in the passage, and prevailed. He lingered awhile—naturally. Unluckily, she had brought no money with her, and could not give him the two-franc piece which he had earned. Nor could she fetch it from her room, feeling that, were she to return to her husband without the mustard, no second attempt would be possible. The disappointed man turned on his heel at last, and made his way down the stairs and along the passage. It seemed to her to be almost an eternity while she listened to his still audible footsteps. She had gone on, creeping noiselessly up to the very door of her room, and there she stood, shading the candle in her hand, till she thought that the man must have wandered away into some farthest corner of that endless building. Then she turned once more and retraced her steps.

There was no difficulty now as to the way. She knew it, every stair. At the head of each flight she stood and listened, but not a sound was to be heard, and then she went on again. Her heart beat high with anxious desire to achieve her object, and at the same time with fear. What might have been explained so easily at first would now be as difficult of explanation. At last she was in the great public vestibule, which she was now visiting for the third time, and of which, at her last visit, she had taken the bearings accurately. The door was there—closed, indeed, but it opened easily to the hand. In the hall and on the stairs and along the passages there had been gas, but here there was no light beyond that given by the little taper which she carried. When accompanied by the porter she had not feared the darkness, but now there was something in the obscurity which made her dread to walk the length of the room up to the mustard jar. She paused, and listened, and trembled. Then she thought of the glories of Thompson Hall, of the genial warmth of a British Christmas, of that proud legislator who was her first cousin, and with a rush she made good the distance, and laid her hand upon the copious delf. She looked round, but there was no one there; no sound was heard; not the distant creak of a shoe, not a rattle from one of those thousand doors. As she paused with her fair hand upon the top of the jar, while the other held the white cloth on which the medicinal compound was to be placed, she looked like Lady Macbeth as she listened at Duncan's chamber door.

There was no doubt as to the sufficiency of the contents. The jar was full nearly up to the lips. The mixture was, no doubt, very different from that good, wholesome English mustard which your cook makes fresh for you, with a little water, in two minutes. It was impregnated with a sour odor, and was, to English eyes, unwholesome of color. But still it was mustard. She seized the horn spoon, and without further delay spread an ample sufficiency on the folded square of the handkerchief. Then she commenced to hurry her return.

But still there was a difficulty, no thought of which had occurred to her before. The candle occupied one hand, so that she had but the other for the sustenance of her treasure. Had she brought a plate or saucer from the salon, it would have been all well. As it was, she was obliged to keep her eye intent on her right hand, and to proceed very slowly on her return journey. She was surprised to find what an aptitude the thing had to slip from her grasp. But still she progressed slowly, and was careful not to miss a turning. At last she was safe at her chamber door. There it was, No. 333.

Chapter II

MRS. BROWN'S FAILURE

With her eye still fixed upon her burden, she glanced up at the number of the door—333. She had been determined all through not to forget that. Then she turned the latch and crept in. The chamber also was dark after the gaslight on the stairs, but that was so much the better. She herself had put out the two candles on the dressing-table before she had left her husband. As she was closing the door behind her she paused, and could hear that he was sleeping. She was well aware that she had been long absent—quite long enough for a man to fall into slumber who was given that way. She must have been gone, she thought, fully an hour. There had been no end to that turning over of napkins which she had so well known to be altogether vain. She paused at the centre-table of the room, still looking at the mustard, which she now delicately dried from off her hand. She had had no idea that it would have been so difficult to carry so light and so small an affair. But there it was, and nothing had been lost. She took some small instrument from the washing-stand, and with the handle collected the flowing fragments into the centre. Then the question occurred to her whether, as her husband was sleeping so sweetly, it would be well to disturb him. She listened again, and felt that the slight murmur of a snore with which her ears were regaled was altogether free from any real malady in the throat. Then it occurred to her that, after all, fatigue perhaps had only made him cross. She bethought herself how, during the whole journey, she had failed to believe in his illness. What meals he had eaten! How thoroughly he had been able to enjoy his full complement of cigars! And then that glass of brandy, against which she had raised her voice slightly in feminine opposition. And now he was sleeping there like an infant, with full, round, perfected, almost sonorous workings of the throat. Who does not know that sound, almost of two rusty bits of iron scratching against each other, which comes from a suffering windpipe? There was no semblance of that here. Why disturb him when he was so thoroughly enjoying that rest which, more certainly than anything else, would fit him for the fatigue of the morrow's journey?

I think that, after all her labor, she would have left the pungent cataplasm on the table and have crept gently into bed beside him, had not a thought suddenly struck her of the great injury he had been doing her if he were not really ill. To send her down there, in a strange hotel, wandering among the passages, in the middle of the night, subject to the contumely of any one who might meet her, on a commission which, if it were not sanctified by absolute necessity, would be so thoroughly objectionable! At this moment she hardly did believe that he had ever really been ill. Let him have the cataplasm; if not as a remedy, then as a punishment. It could, at any rate, do him no harm. It was with an idea of avenging rather than of justifying the past labors of the night that she proceeded at once to quick action.

Leaving the candle on the table, so that she might steady her right hand with the left, she hurried stealthily to the bedside. Even though he was behaving badly to her, she would not cause him discomfort by waking him roughly. She would do a wife's duty to him as a British matron should. She would not only put the warm mixture on his neck, but would sit carefully by him for twenty minutes, so that she might relieve him from it when the proper period should have come for removing the counter-irritation from his throat. There would doubtless be some little difficulty in this—in collecting the mustard after it had served her purpose. Had she been at home, surrounded by her own comforts, the application would have been made with some delicate linen bag, through which the pungency of the spice would have penetrated with strength sufficient for the purpose. But the circumstance of the occasion had not admitted this. She had, she felt, done wonders in achieving so much success as this which she had obtained. If there should be anything disagreeable in the operation, he must submit to it. He had asked for mustard for his throat, and mustard he should have.

As these thoughts passed quickly through her mind, leaning over him in the dark, with her eye fixed on the mixture lest it should slip, she gently raised his flowing beard with her left hand, and with her other inverted rapidly, steadily but very softly fixed the handkerchief on his throat. From the bottom of his chin to the spot at which the collar-bones meeting together form the orifice of the chest, it covered the whole noble expanse. There was barely time for a glance, but never had she been more conscious of the grand proportions of that manly throat. A sweet feeling of pity came upon her, causing her to determine to relieve his sufferings in the shorter space of fifteen minutes. He had been lying on his back, with his lips apart, and as she held back his beard, that and her hand nearly covered the features of his face. But he made no violent effort to free himself from the encounter. He did not even move an arm or a leg. He simply emitted a snore louder than any that had come before. She was aware that it was not his wont to be so loud—that there was generally something more delicate and perhaps more querulous in his nocturnal voice, but then the present circumstances were exceptional. She dropped the beard very softly—and there on the pillow before her lay the face of a stranger. She had put the mustard plaster on the wrong man.

Not Priam wakened in the dead of night, not Dido when first she learned that Æneas had fled, not Othello when he learned that Desdemona had been chaste, not Medea when she became conscious of her slaughtered children, could have been more struck with horror than was this British matron as she stood for a moment gazing with awe on that stranger's bed. One vain, half-completed, snatching grasp she made at the handkerchief, and then drew back her hand. If she were to touch him, would he not wake at once, and find her standing there in his bedroom? And then how could she explain it? By what words could she so quickly make him know the circumstances of that strange occurrence that he should accept it all before he had said a word that might offend her? For a moment she stood all but paralyzed after that faint ineffectual movement of her arm. Then he stirred his head uneasily on the pillow, opened wider his lips, and twice in rapid succession snored louder than before. She started back a couple of paces, and with her body placed between him and the candle, with her face averted, but with her hand still resting on the foot of the bed, she endeavored to think what duty required of her.

She had injured the man. Though she had done it most unwittingly, there could be no doubt but that she had injured him. If for a moment she could be brave, the injury might in truth be little; but how disastrous might be the consequences if she were now in her cowardice to leave him, who could tell? Applied for fifteen or twenty minutes, a mustard plaster may be the salvation of a throat ill at ease; but if left there throughout the night, upon the neck of a strong man, ailing nothing, only too prone in his strength to slumber soundly, how sad, how painful, for aught she knew how dangerous, might be the effects! And surely it was an error which any man with a heart in his bosom might pardon! Judging from what little she had seen of him, she thought that he must have a heart in his bosom. Was it not her duty to wake him, and then quietly to extricate him from the embarrassment which she had brought upon him?

But in doing this what words should she use? How should she wake him? How should she make him understand her goodness, her beneficence, her sense of duty, before he should have jumped from the bed and rushed to the bell, and have summoned all above, and all below, to the rescue? "Sir, sir, do not move, do not stir, do not scream. I have put a mustard plaster on your throat, thinking that you were my husband. As yet no harm has been done. Let me take it off, and then hold your peace forever." Where is the man of such native constancy and grace of spirit that, at the first moment of waking with a shock, he could hear these words from the mouth of an unknown woman by his bedside, and at once obey them to the letter? Would he not surely jump from his bed, with that horrid compound falling about him—from which there could be no complete relief unless he would keep his present attitude without a motion. The picture which presented itself to her mind as to his probable conduct was so terrible that she found herself unable to incur the risk.

Then an idea presented itself to her mind. We all know how in a moment quick thoughts will course through the subtle brain. She would find that porter and send him to explain it all. There should be no concealment now. She would tell the story and would bid him to find the necessary aid. Alas! as she told herself that she would do so, she knew well that she was only running from the danger which it was her duty to encounter. Once again she put out her hand as though to return along the bed. Then thrice he snorted louder than before, and moved up his knee uneasily beneath the clothes as though the sharpness of the mustard were already working upon his skin. She watched him for a moment longer, and then, with the candle in her hand, she fled.

Poor human nature! Had he been an old man, even a middle-aged man, she would not have left him to his unmerited sufferings. As it was, though she completely recognized her duty, and knew what justice and goodness demanded of her, she could not do it. But there was still left to her that plan of sending the night porter to him. It was not till she was out of the room and had gently closed the door behind her that she began to bethink herself how she had made the mistake. With a glance of her eye she looked up, and then saw the number on the door—353. Remarking to herself, with a Briton's natural criticism on things French, that those horrid foreigners do not know how to make their figures, she scudded rather than ran along the corridor, and then down some stairs and along another passage—so that she might not be found in the neighborhood should the poor man in his agony rush rapidly from his bed.

In the confusion of her first escape she hardly ventured to look for her own passage—nor did she in the least know how she had lost her way when she came up-stairs with the mustard in her hand. But at the present moment her chief object was the night porter. She went on descending till she came again to that vestibule, and looking up at the clock saw that it was now past one. It was not yet midnight when she left her husband, but she was not at all astonished at the lapse of time. It seemed to her as though she had passed a night among these miseries. And, oh, what a night! But there was yet much to be done. She must find that porter, and then return to her own suffering husband. Ah! what now should she say to him? If he should really be ill, how should she assuage him? And yet how more than ever necessary was it that they should leave that hotel early in the morning—that they should leave Paris by the very earliest and quickest train that would take them as fugitives from their present dangers! The door of the salon was open, but she had no courage to go in search of a second supply. She would have lacked strength to carry it up the stairs. Where, now, oh! where was that man? From the vestibule she made her way into the hall, but everything seemed to be deserted. Through the glass she could see a light in the court beyond, but she could not bring herself to endeavor even to open the hall doors.

And now she was very cold—chilled to her very bones. All this had been done at Christmas, and during such severity of weather as had never before been experienced by living Parisians. A feeling of great pity for herself gradually came upon her. What wrong had she done, that she should be so grievously punished? Why should she be driven to wander about in this way till her limbs were failing her? And then so absolutely important as it was that her strength should support her in the morning! The man would not die even though he were left there without aid, to rid himself of the cataplasm as best he might. Was it absolutely necessary that she should disgrace herself?

But she could not even procure the means of disgracing herself, if that telling her story to the night porter would have been a disgrace. She did not find him, and at last resolved to make her way back to her own room without further quest. She began to think that she had done all that she could do. No man was ever killed by a mustard plaster on his throat. His discomfort at the worst would not be worse than hers had been—or, too probably, than that of her poor husband. So she went back up the stairs and along the passages, and made her way on this occasion to the door of her room without any difficulty. The way was so well known to her that she could not but wonder that she had failed before. But now her hands had been empty, and her eyes had been at her full command. She looked up, and there was the number, very manifest on this occasion—333. She opened the door most gently, thinking that her husband might be sleeping as soundly as that other man had slept, and she crept into the room.

Chapter III

MRS. BROWN ATTEMPTS TO ESCAPE

But her husband was not sleeping. He was not even in bed, as she had left him. She found him sitting there before the fireplace, on which one half-burned log still retained a spark of what had once pretended to be a fire. Nothing more wretched than his appearance could be imagined. There was a single lighted candle on the table, on which he was leaning with his two elbows, while his head rested between his hands. He had on a dressing-gown over his nightshirt, but otherwise was not clothed. He shivered audibly, or rather shook himself with the cold, and made the table to chatter, as she entered the room. Then he groaned, and let his head fall from his hands on to the table. It occurred to her at the moment, as she recognized the tone of his querulous voice, and as she saw the form of his neck, that she must have been deaf and blind when she had mistaken that stalwart stranger for her husband. "O my dear," she said, "why are you not in bed?" He answered nothing in words, but only groaned again. "Why did you get up? I left you warm and comfortable."

"Where have you been all night?" he half whispered, half croaked, with an agonizing effort.

"I have been looking for the mustard."

"Have been looking all night, and haven't found it? Where have you been?"

She refused to speak a word to him till she had got him into bed, and then she told her story. But, alas! that which she told was not the true story. As she was persuading him to go back to his rest, and while she arranged the clothes again around him, she with difficulty made up her mind as to what she would do and what she would say. Living or dying, he must be made to start for Thompson Hall at half past five on the next morning. It was no longer a question of the amenities of Christmas, no longer a mere desire to satisfy the family ambition of her own people, no longer an anxiety to see her new brother-in-law. She was conscious that there was in that house one whom she had deeply injured, and from whose vengeance—even from whose aspect—she must fly. How could she endure to see that face which she was so well sure that she would recognize, or to hear the slightest sound of that voice which would be quite familiar to her ears, though it had never spoken a word in her hearing? She must certainly fly on the wings of the earliest train which would carry her toward the old house; but in order that she might do so, she must propitiate her husband.

So she told her story. She had gone forth, as he had bade her, in search of the mustard, and then had suddenly lost her way. Up and down the house she had wandered, perhaps nearly a dozen times. "Had she met no one?" he asked, in that raspy, husky whisper. "Surely there must have been some one about the hotel! Nor was it possible that she could have been roaming about all those hours." "Only one hour, my dear," she said. Then there was a question about the duration of time, in which both of them waxed angry; and as she became angry, her husband waxed stronger, and as he became violent beneath the clothes, the comfortable idea returned to her that he was not perhaps so ill as he would seem to be. She found herself driven to tell him something about the porter, having to account for that lapse of time by explaining how she had driven the poor man to search for the handkerchief which she had never lost.

"Why did you not tell him you wanted the mustard?"

"My dear!"

"Why not? There is nothing to be ashamed of in wanting mustard."

"At one o'clock in the morning! I couldn't do it. To tell you the truth, he wasn't very civil, and I thought that he was—perhaps a little tipsy. Now, my dear, do go to sleep."

"Why didn't you get the mustard?"

"There was none there—nowhere at all about the room. I went down again and searched everywhere. That's what took me so long. They always lock up those kind of things at these French hotels. They are too close-fisted to leave anything out. When you first spoke of it I knew that it would be gone when I got there. Now, my dear, do go to sleep, because we positively must start in the morning."

"That is impossible," said he, jumping up in the bed.

"We must go, my dear. I say that we must go. After all that has passed, I wouldn't not be with Uncle John and my cousin Robert to-morrow evening for more—more—more than I would venture to say."

"Bother!" he exclaimed.

"It's all very well for you to say that, Charles, but you don't know. I say that we must go to-morrow, and we will."

"I do believe you want to kill me, Mary."

"That is very cruel, Charles, and most false, and most unjust. As for making you ill, nothing could be so bad for you as this wretched place, where nobody can get warm either day or night. If anything will cure your throat for you at once, it will be the sea air. And only think how much more comfortable they can make you at Thompson Hall than anywhere in this country. I have so set my heart upon it, Charles, that I will do it. If we are not there to-morrow night, Uncle John won't consider us as belonging to the family."

"I don't believe a word of it."

"Jane told me so in her letter. I wouldn't let you know before because I thought it so unjust. But that has been the reason why I've been so earnest about it all through."

It was a thousand pities that so good a woman should have been driven by the sad stress of circumstances to tell so many fibs. One after another she was compelled to invent them, that there might be a way open to her of escaping the horrors of a prolonged sojourn in that hotel. At length, after much grumbling, he became silent, and she trusted that he was sleeping. He had not as yet said that he would start at the required hour in the morning, but she was perfectly determined in her own mind that he should be made to do so. As he lay there motionless, and as she wandered about the room pretending to pack her things, she more than once almost resolved that she would tell him everything. Surely then he would be ready to make any effort. But there came upon her an idea that he might perhaps fail to see all the circumstances, and that, so failing, he would insist on remaining that he might tender some apology to the injured gentleman. An apology might have been very well had she not left him there in his misery; but what apology would be possible now? She would have to see him and speak to him, and every one in the hotel would know every detail of the story. Every one in France would know that it was she who had gone to the strange man's bedside and put the mustard plaster on the strange man's throat in the dead of night! She could not tell the story even to her husband, lest even her husband should betray her.

Her own sufferings at the present moment were not light. In her perturbation of mind she had foolishly resolved that she would not herself go to bed. The tragedy of the night had seemed to her too deep for personal comfort. And then, how would it be were she to sleep, and have no one to call her? It was imperative that she should have all her powers ready for thoroughly arousing him. It occurred to her that the servant of the hotel would certainly run her too short of time. She had to work for herself and for him too, and therefore she would not sleep. But she was very cold, and she put on first a shawl over her dressing-gown and then a cloak. She could not consume all the remaining hours of the night in packing one bag and one portmanteau; so that at last she sat down on the narrow red cotton velvet sofa, and, looking at her watch, perceived that as yet it was not much past two o'clock. How was she to get through those other three long, tedious, chilly hours?

Then there came a voice from the bed—"Ain't you coming?"

"I hoped you were asleep, my dear."

"I haven't been asleep at all. You'd better come, if you don't mean to make yourself as ill as I am."

"You are not so very bad, are you, darling?"

"I don't know what you call bad. I never felt my throat so choked in my life before." Still as she listened she thought that she remembered his throat to have been more choked. If the husband of her bosom could play with her feelings and deceive her on such an occasion as this—then—then—then she thought that she would rather not have any husband of her bosom at all. But she did creep into bed, and lay down beside him without saying another word.

Of course she slept, but her sleep was not the sleep of the blest. At every striking of the clock in the quadrangle she would start up in alarm, fearing that she had let the time go by. Though the night was so short, it was very long to her. But he slept like an infant. She could hear from his breathing that he was not quite so well as she could wish him to be, but still he was resting in beautiful tranquillity. Not once did he move when she started up, as she did so frequently. Orders had been given and repeated over and over again that they should be called at five. The man in the office had almost been angry as he assured Mrs. Brown for the fourth time that monsieur and madame would most assuredly be wakened at the appointed time. But still she would trust to no one, and was up and about the room before the clock had struck half past four.

In her heart of hearts she was very tender toward her husband. Now, in order that he might feel a gleam of warmth while he was dressing himself, she collected together the fragments of half-burned wood, and endeavored to make a little fire. Then she took out from her bag a small pot and a patent lamp and some chocolate, and prepared for him a warm drink, so that he might have it instantly as he was awakened. She would do anything for him in the way of ministering to his comfort—only he must go! Yes, he certainly must go!

And then she wondered how that strange man was bearing himself at the present moment. She would fain have ministered to him too had it been possible; but, ah! it was so impossible! Probably before this he would have been aroused from his troubled slumbers. But then —how aroused? At what time in the night would the burning heat upon his chest have awakened him to a sense of torture which must have been so altogether incomprehensible to him? Her strong imagination showed to her a clear picture of the scene—clear, though it must have been done in the dark. How he must have tossed and hurled himself under the clothes! how those strong knees must have worked themselves up and down before the potent god of sleep would allow him to return to perfect consciousness! how his fingers, restrained by no reason, would have trampled over his feverish throat, scattering everywhere that unhappy poultice! Then when he should have sat up wide awake, but still in the dark—with her mind's eye she saw it all—feeling that some fire as from the infernal regions had fallen upon him, but whence he would know not, how fiercely wild would be the working of his spirit! Ah, now she knew, now she felt, now she acknowledged, how bound she had been to awaken him at the moment, whatever might have been the personal inconvenience to herself! In such a position what would he do—or rather what had he done? She could follow much of it in her own thoughts: how he would scramble madly from his bed, and, with one hand still on his throat, would snatch hurriedly at the matches with the other. How the light would come, and how then he would rush to the mirror. Ah, what a sight he would behold! She could see it all, to the last widespread daub.

But she could not see, she could not tell herself, what in such a position a man would do; at any rate, not what that man would do. Her husband, she thought, would tell his wife, and then the two of them, between them, would—put up with it.

There are misfortunes which, if they be published, are simply aggravated by ridicule. But she remembered the features of the stranger as she had seen them at that instant in which she had dropped his beard, and she thought that there was a ferocity in them, a certain tenacity of self-importance, which would not permit their owner to endure such treatment in silence. Would he not storm and rage, and ring the bell, and call all Paris to witness his revenge?

But the storming and the raging had not reached her yet, and now it wanted but a quarter to five. In three-quarters of an hour they would be in that demi-omnibus which they had ordered for themselves, and in half an hour after that they would be flying toward Thompson Hall. Then she allowed herself to think of those coming comforts of those comforts so sweet, if only they would come! That very day now present to her was the 24th December, and on that very evening she would be sitting in Christmas joy among all her uncles and cousins, holding her new brother-in-law affectionately by the hand. Oh, what a change from Pandemonium to Paradise! from that wretched room, from that miserable house in which there was such ample cause for fear, to all the domestic Christmas bliss of the home of the Thompsons! She resolved that she would not, at any rate, be deterred by any light opposition on the part of her husband. "It wants just a quarter to five," she said, putting her hand steadily upon his shoulder, "and I'll get a cup of chocolate for you, so that you may get up comfortably."

"I've been thinking about it," he said, rubbing his eyes with the back of his hands. "It will be so much better to go over by the mail-train to-night. We should be in time for Christmas just the same."

"That will not do at all," she answered, energetically. "Come, Charles, after all the trouble, do not disappoint me."

"It is such a horrid grind."

"Think what I have gone through—what I have done for you! In twelve hours we shall be there, among them all. You won't be so little like a man as not to go on now." He threw himself back upon the bed, and tried to re-adjust the clothes around his neck. "No, Charles, no," she continued; "not if I know it. Take your chocolate and get up. There is not a moment to be lost." With that she laid her hand upon his shoulder, and made him clearly understand that he would not be allowed to take further rest in that bed.

Grumbling, sulky, coughing continually, and declaring that life under such circumstances was not worth having, he did at last get up and dress himself. When once she knew that he was obeying her, she became again tender to him, and certainly took much more than her own share of the trouble of the proceedings. Long before the time was up she was ready, and the porter had been summoned to take the luggage down-stairs. When the man came, she was rejoiced to see that it was not he whom she had met among the passages during her nocturnal rambles. He shouldered the box, and told them that they would find coffee and bread and butter in the small *salle à manger* below.

"I told you that it would be so, when you would boil that stuff," said the ungrateful man, who had nevertheless swallowed the hot chocolate when it was given to him.

They followed their luggage down into the hall; but as she went, at every step, the lady looked around her. She dreaded the sight of that porter of the night; she feared lest some potential authority of the hotel should come to her and ask her some horrid question; but of all her fears her greatest fear was that there should arise before her an apparition of that face which she had seen recumbent on its pillow.

As they passed the door of the great salon, Mr. Brown looked in. "Why, there it is still!" said he.

"What?" said she, trembling in every limb.

"The mustard pot."

"They have put it in there since," she exclaimed, energetically, in her despair. "But never mind. The omnibus is here. Come away." And she absolutely took him by the arm.

But at that moment a door behind them opened, and Mrs. Brown heard herself called by her name. And there was the night porter— with a handkerchief in his hand. But the further doings of that morning must be told in a further chapter.

Chapter IV

MRS. BROWN DOES ESCAPE

It had been visible to Mrs. Brown from the first moment of her arrival on the ground floor that "something was the matter," if we may be allowed to use such a phrase; and she felt all but convinced that this something had reference to her. She fancied that the people of the hotel were looking at her as she swallowed, or tried to swallow, her coffee. When her husband was paying the bill there was something disagreeable in the eye of the man who was taking the money. Her sufferings were very great, and no one sympathized with her. Her husband was quite at his ease, except that he was complaining of the cold. When she was anxious to get him out into the carriage, he still stood there, leisurely arranging shawl after shawl around his throat. "You can do that quite as well in the omnibus," she had just said to him, very crossly, when there appeared upon the scene through a side door that very night porter whom she dreaded with a soiled pocket-handkerchief in his hand.

Even before the sound of her own name met her ears, Mrs. Brown knew it all. She understood the full horror of her position from that man's hostile face, and from the little article which he held in his hand. If during the watches of the night she had had money in her pocket, if she had made a friend of this greedy fellow by well-timed liberality, all might have been so different! But she reflected that she had allowed him to go unfed after all his trouble, and she knew that he was her enemy. It was the handkerchief that she feared. She thought that she might have brazened out anything but that. No one had seen her enter or leave that strange man's room. No one had seen her dip her hands in that jar. She had, no doubt, been found wandering about the house while the slumberer had been made to suffer so strangely, and there might have been suspicion, and perhaps accusation. But she would have been ready with frequent protestations to deny all charges made against her, and though no one might have believed her, no one could have convicted her. Here, however, was evidence against which she would be unable to stand for a moment. At the first glance she acknowledged the potency of that damning morsel of linen.

During all the horrors of the night she had never given a thought to the handkerchief, and yet she ought to have known that the evidence it would bring against her was palpable and certain. Her name, "M. Brown," was plainly written on the corner. What a fool she had been not to have thought of this! Had she but remembered the plain marking which she, as a careful, well-conducted British matron, had put upon all her clothes, she would at any hazard have recovered the article. Oh that she had waked the man, or bribed the porter, or even told her husband! But now she was, as it were, friendless, without support, without a word that she could say in her own defence, convicted of having committed this assault upon a strange man as he slept in his own bedroom, and then of having left him! The thing must be explained by the truth; but how to explain such truth, how to tell such story in a way to satisfy injured folk, and she with only barely time sufficient to catch the train! Then it occurred to her that they could have no legal right to stop her because the pocket-handkerchief had been found in a strange gentleman's bedroom. "Yes, it is mine," she said, turning to her husband, as the porter, with a loud voice, asked if she were not Madame Brown. "Take it, Charles, and come on." Mr. Brown naturally stood still in astonishment. He did put out his hand, but the porter would not allow the evidence to pass so readily out of his custody.

"What does it all mean?" asked Mr. Brown.

"A gentleman has been—eh—eh— Something has been done to a gentleman in his bedroom," said the clerk.

"Something done to a gentleman!" repeated Mr. Brown.

"Something very bad indeed," said the porter. "Look here"; and he showed the condition of the handkerchief.

"Charles, we shall lose the train," said the affrighted wife.

"What the mischief does it all mean?" demanded the husband.

"Did madame go into the gentleman's room?" asked the clerk. Then there was an awful silence, and all eyes were fixed upon the lady.

"What does it all mean?" demanded the husband. "Did you go into anybody's room?"

"I did," said Mrs. Brown with much dignity, looking round upon her enemies as a stag at bay will look upon the hounds which are attacking him. "Give me the handkerchief." But the night porter quickly put it behind his back. "Charles, we cannot allow ourselves to be delayed. You shall write a letter to the keeper of the hotel explaining it all." Then she essayed to swim out through the front door into the courtyard, in which the vehicle was waiting for them. But three or four men and women interposed themselves, and even her husband did not seem quite ready to continue his journey. "To-night is Christmas-eve," said Mrs. Brown, "and we shall not be at Thompson Hall. Think of my sister!"

"Why did you go into the man's bedroom, my dear?" whispered Mr. Brown in English.

But the porter heard the whisper, and understood the language—the porter who had not been "tipped." "Ye'es—vy?" asked the porter.

"It was a mistake, Charles; there is not a moment to lose. I can explain it all to you in the carriage." Then the clerk suggested that madame had better postpone her journey a little. The gentleman upstairs had certainly been very badly treated, and had demanded to know why so great an outrage had been perpetrated. The clerk said that he did not wish to send for the police (here Mrs. Brown gasped terribly, and threw herself on her husband's shoulder), but he did not think he could allow the party to go till the gentleman up-stairs had received some satisfaction. It had now become clearly impossible that the journey could be made by the early train. Even Mrs. Brown gave it up herself, and demanded of her husband that she should be taken back to her bedroom.

"But what is to be said to the gentleman?" asked the porter.

Of course it was impossible that Mrs. Brown should be made to tell her story there in the presence of them all. The clerk, when he found he had succeeded in preventing her from leaving the house, was satisfied with a promise from Mr. Brown that he would inquire from his wife what were these mysterious circumstances, and would then come down to the office and give some explanation. If it were necessary, he would see the strange gentleman—whom he now ascertained to be a certain Mr. Jones, returning from the east of Europe. He learned also that this Mr. Jones had been most anxious to travel by that very morning train which he and his wife had intended to use; that Mr. Jones had been most particular in giving his orders accordingly; but that at the last moment he had declared himself to be unable even to dress himself, because of the injury which had been done him during the night. When Mr. Brown heard this from the clerk just before he was allowed to take his wife up stairs, while she was sitting on a sofa in a corner with her face hidden, a look of awful gloom came over his own countenance. What could it be that his wife had done to the man, of so terrible a nature? "You had better come up with me," he said to her, with marital severity; and the poor cowed woman went with him tamely as might have done some patient Grizel. Not a word was spoken till they were in the room and the door was locked. "Now," said he, "what does it all mean?"

It was not till nearly two hours had passed that Mr. Brown came down the stairs very slowly, turning it all over in his mind. He had now gradually heard the absolute and exact truth, and had very gradually learned to believe it. It was first necessary that he should understand that his wife had told him many fibs during the night; but, as she constantly alleged to him when he complained of her conduct in this respect, they had all been told on his behalf. Had she not struggled to get the mustard for his comfort, and when she had secured the prize had she not hurried to put it on—as she had fondly thought—his throat? And though she had fibbed to him afterward, had she not done so in order that he might not be troubled? "You are not angry with me because I was in that man's room?" she asked, looking full into his eyes, but not quite without a sob. He paused a moment, and then declared, with something of a true husband's confidence in his tone, that he was not in the least angry with her on that account. Then she kissed him, and bade him remember that, after all, no one could really injure them. "What harm has been done, Charles? The gentleman won't die because he has had a mustard plaster on his throat. The worst is about Uncle John and dear Jane. They do think so much of Christmas-eve at Thompson Hall!"

Mr. Brown, when he again found himself in the clerk's office, requested that his card might be taken up to Mr. Jones. Mr. Jones had sent down his own card, which was handed to Mr. Brown: "Mr. Barnaby Jones." "And how was it all, sir?" asked the clerk, in a whisper—a whisper which had at the same time something of authoritative demand and something also of submissive respect. The clerk, of course, was anxious to know the mystery. It is hardly too much to say that every one in that vast hotel was by this time anxious to have the mystery unravelled. But Mr. Brown would tell nothing to any one. "It is merely a matter to be explained between me and Mr. Jones," he said. The card was taken up-stairs, and after a while he was ushered into Mr. Jones's room. It was, of course, that very 353 with which the reader is already acquainted. There was a fire burning, and the remains of Mr. Jones's breakfast were on the table. He was sitting in his dressing-gown and slippers, with his shirt open in the front, and a silk handkerchief very loosely covering his throat. Mr. Brown, as he entered the room, of course looked with considerable anxiety at the gentleman of whose condition he had heard so sad an account; but he could only observe some considerable stiffness of movement and demeanor as Mr. Jones turned his head round to greet him.

"This has been a very disagreeable accident, Mr. Jones," said the husband of the lady.

"Accident! I don't know how it could have been an accident. It has been a most—most—most—a most monstrous—er—er—I must say, interference with a gentleman's privacy and personal comfort."

"Quite so, Mr. Jones, but—on the part of the lady, who is my wife—"

"So I understand. I myself am about to become a married man, and I can understand what your feelings must be. I wish to say as little as possible to harrow them." Here Mr. Brown bowed. "But—there's the fact. She did do it."

"She thought it was—me!"

"What!"

"I give you my word as a gentleman, Mr. Jones. When she was putting that mess upon you, she thought it was me! She did indeed."

Mr. Jones looked at his new acquaintance and shook his head. He did not think it possible that any woman would make such a mistake as that.

"I had a very bad sore throat," continued Mr. Brown, "and indeed you may perceive it still"—in saying this he perhaps aggravated a little the sign of his distemper—"and I asked Mrs. Brown to go down and get one—just what she put on you."

"I wish you'd had it," said Mr. Jones, putting his hand up to his neck.

"I wish I had, for your sake as well as mine, and for hers, poor woman. I don't know when she will get over the shock."

"I don't know when I shall. And it has stopped me on my journey. I was to have been to-night, this very night, this Christmas-eve, with the young lady I am engaged to marry. Of course I couldn't travel. The extent of the injury done nobody can imagine at present."

"It has been just as bad to me, sir. We were to have been with our family this Christmas-eve. There were particular reasons—most particular. We were only hindered from going by hearing of your condition."

"Why did she come into my room at all? I can't understand that. A lady always knows her own room at a hotel."

"353—that's yours; 333—that's ours. Don't you see how easy it was? She had lost her way, and she was a little afraid lest the thing should fall down."

"I wish it had with all my heart."

"That's how it was. Now I'm sure, Mr. Jones, you'll take a lady's apology. It was a most unfortunate mistake—most unfortunate; but what more can be said?"

Mr. Jones gave himself up to reflection for a few moments before he replied to this. He supposed that he was bound to believe the story as far as it went. At any rate, he did not know how he could say that he did not believe it. It seemed to him to be almost incredible, especially incredible in regard to that personal mistake, for, except that they both had long beards and brown beards, Mr. Jones thought that there was no point of resemblance between himself and Mr. Brown. But still, even that, he felt, must be accepted. But then why had he been left, deserted, to undergo all those torments? "She found out her mistake at last, I suppose?" he said.

"Oh, yes."

"Why didn't she wake a fellow and take it off again?"

"Ah!"

"She can't have cared very much for a man's comfort, when she went away and left him like that."

"Ah! there was the difficulty, Mr. Jones."

"Difficulty! Who was it that had done it? To come to me in my bedroom in the middle of the night and put that thing on me, and then leave it there and say nothing about it! It seems to me deuced like a practical joke."

"No, Mr. Jones."

"That's the way I look at it," said Mr. Jones, plucking up his courage.

"There isn't a woman in all England or in all France less likely to do such a thing than my wife. She's as steady as a rock, Mr. Jones, and would no more go into another gentleman's bedroom in joke than— Oh dear no! You're going to be a married man yourself."

"Unless all this makes a difference," said Mr. Jones, almost in tears. "I had sworn that I would be with her this Christmas-eve."

"Oh Mr. Jones, I cannot believe that will interfere with your happiness. How could you think that your wife, as is to be, would do such a thing as that in joke?"

"She wouldn't do it at all, joke or any way."

"How can you tell what accident might happen to any one?"

"She'd have wakened the man, then, afterward. I'm sure she would. She would never have left him to suffer in that way. Her heart is too soft. Why didn't she send you to wake me and explain it all? That's what my Jane would have done; and I should have gone and wakened him. But the whole thing is impossible," he said, shaking his head as he remembered that he and his Jane were not in a condition as yet to undergo any such mutual trouble. At last Mr. Jones was brought to acknowledge that nothing more could be done. The lady had sent her apology and told her story, and he must bear the trouble and inconvenience to which she had subjected him. He still, however, had his own opinion about her conduct generally, and could not be brought to give any sign of amity. He simply bowed when Mr. Brown was hoping to induce him to shake hands, and sent no word of pardon to the great offender.

The matter, however, was so far concluded that there was no further question of police interference, nor any doubt but that the lady, with her husband, was to be allowed to leave Paris by the night train. The nature of the accident probably became known to all. Mr. Brown was interrogated by many, and though he professed to declare that he would answer no question, nevertheless he found it better to tell the clerk something of the truth than to allow the matter to be shrouded in mystery. It is to be feared that Mr. Jones, who did not once show himself through the day, but who employed the hours in endeavoring to assuage the injury done him, still lived in the conviction that the lady had played a practical joke on him. But the subject of such a joke never talks about it, and Mr. Jones could not be induced to speak even by the friendly adherence of the night porter.

Mrs. Brown also clung to the seclusion of her own bedroom, never once stirring from it till the time came in which she was to be taken down to the omnibus. Up-stairs she ate her meals, and up-stairs she passed her time in packing and unpacking, and in requesting that telegrams might be sent repeatedly to Thompson Hall. In the course of the day two such telegrams were sent, in the latter of which the Thompson family were assured that the Browns would arrive probably in time for breakfast on Christmas-day, certainly in time for church. She asked more than once tenderly after Mr. Jones's welfare, but could obtain no information. "He was very cross, and that's all I know about it," said Mr. Brown. Then she made a remark as to the gentleman's Christian name, which appeared on the card as "Barnaby." "My sister's husband's name will be Burnaby," she said. "And this man's Christian name is Barnaby; that's all the difference," said her husband, with ill-timed jocularity.

We all know how people under a cloud are apt to fail in asserting their personal dignity. On the former day a separate vehicle had been ordered by Mr. Brown to take himself and his wife to the station, but now, after his misfortunes, he contented himself with such provision as the people at the hotel might make for him. At the appointed hour he brought his wife down, thickly veiled. There were many strangers, as she passed through the hall, ready to look at the lady who had done that wonderful thing in the dead of night, but none could see a feature of her face as she stepped across the hall and was hurried into the omnibus. And there were many eyes also on Mr. Jones, who followed her very quickly, for he also, in spite of his sufferings, was leaving Paris on the evening in order that he might be with his English friends on

Christmas-day. He, as he went through the crowd, assumed an air of great dignity, to which, perhaps, something was added by his endeavors as he walked to save his poor throat from irritation. He, too, got into the same omnibus, stumbling over the feet of his enemy in the dark. At the station they got their tickets, one close after the other, and then were brought into each other's presence in the waiting-room. I think it must be acknowledged that here Mr. Jones was conscious not only of her presence, but of her consciousness of his presence, and that he assumed an attitude as though he should have said, "Now do you think it possible for me to believe that you mistook me for your husband?" She was perfectly quiet, but sat through that quarter of an hour with her face continually veiled. Mr. Brown made some little overture of conversation to Mr. Jones, but Mr. Jones, though he did mutter some reply, showed plainly enough that he had no desire for further intercourse. Then came the accustomed stampede, the awful rush, the internecine struggle in which seats had to be found. Seats, I fancy, are regularly found, even by the most tardy, but it always appears that every British father and every British husband is actuated at these stormy moments by a conviction that unless he proves himself a very Hercules he and his daughters and his wife will be left desolate in Paris. Mr. Brown was quite Herculean, carrying two bags and a hatbox in his own hands, besides the cloaks, the coats, the rugs, the sticks, and the umbrellas. But when he had got himself and his wife well seated, with their faces to the engine, with a corner seat for her—there was Mr. Jones immediately opposite to her. Mr. Jones, as soon as he perceived the inconvenience of his position, made a scramble for another place, but he was too late. In that contiguity the journey as far as Calais had to be made. She, poor woman, never once took up her veil. There he sat, without closing an eye, stiff as a ramrod, sometimes showing by little uneasy gestures that the trouble at his neck was still there, but never speaking a word, and hardly moving a limb.

Crossing from Calais to Dover the lady was, of course, separated from her victim. The passage was very bad, and she more than once reminded her husband how well it would have been with them now had they pursued their journey as she had intended—as though they had been detained in Paris by his fault! Mr. Jones, as he laid himself down on his back, gave himself up to wondering whether any man before him had ever been made subject to such absolute injustice. Now and again he put his hand up to his own beard, and began to doubt whether it could have been moved, as it must have been moved, without waking him. What if chloroform had been used? Many such suspicions crossed his mind during the misery of that passage.

They were again together in the same railway carriage from Dover to London. They had now got used to the close neighborhood, and knew how to endure each the presence of the other. But as yet Mr. Jones had never seen the lady's face. He longed to know what were the features of the woman who had been so blind—if indeed that story were true. Or if it were not true, of what like was the woman who would dare in the middle of the night to play such a trick as that? But still she kept her veil close over her face.

From Cannon Street the Browns took their departure in a cab for the Liverpool Street Station, whence they would be conveyed by the Eastern Counties Railway to Stratford. Now, at any rate, their troubles were over. They would be in ample time not only for Christmas-day church, but for Christmas-day breakfast. "It will be just the same as getting in there last night," said Mr. Brown, as he walked across the platform to place his wife in the carriage for Stratford. She entered it the first, and as she did so, there she saw Mr. Jones seated in the corner! Hitherto she had borne his presence well, but now she could not restrain herself from a little start and a little scream. He bowed his head very slightly, as though acknowledging the compliment, and then down she dropped her veil. When they arrived at Stratford, the journey being over in a quarter of an hour, Jones was out of the carriage even before the Browns.

"There is Uncle John's carriage," said Mrs. Brown, thinking that now, at any rate, she would be able to free herself from the presence of this terrible stranger. No doubt he was a handsome man to look at, but on no face so sternly hostile had she ever before fixed her eyes. She did not, perhaps, reflect that the owner of no other face had ever been so deeply injured by herself.

Chapter V

MRS. BROWN AT THOMPSON HALL

"Please, sir, we were to ask for Mr. Jones," said the servant, putting his head into the carriage after both Mr. and Mrs. Brown had seated themselves.

"Mr. Jones!" exclaimed the husband.

"Why ask for Mr. Jones?" demanded the wife. The servant was about to tender some explanation, when Mr. Jones stepped up and said that he was Mr. Jones. "We are going to Thompson Hall," said the lady, with great vigor.

"So am I," said Mr. Jones, with much dignity. It was, however, arranged that he should sit with the coachman, as there was a rumble behind for the other servant. The luggage was put into a cart, and away all went for Thompson Hall.

"What do you think about it, Mary?" whispered Mr. Brown, after a pause. He was evidently awe-struck by the horror of the occasion.

"I cannot make it out at all. What do you think?"

"I don't know what to think. Jones going to Thompson Hall!"

"He's a very good-looking young man," said Mrs. Brown.

"Well—that's as people think. A stiff, stuck-up fellow, I should say. Up to this moment he has never forgiven you for what you did to him."

"Would you have forgiven his wife, Charles, if she'd done it to you?"

"He hasn't got a wife—yet."

"How do you know?"

"He is coming home now to be married," said Mr. Brown. "He expects to meet the young lady this very Christmas-day. He told me so. That was one of the reasons why he was so angry at being stopped by what you did last night."

"I suppose he knows Uncle John, or he wouldn't be going to the Hall," said Mrs. Brown.

"I can't make it out," said Mr. Brown, shaking his head.

"He looks quite like a gentleman," said Mrs. Brown, "though he has been so stiff. Jones! Barnaby Jones! You're sure it was Barnaby?"

"That was the name on the card."

"Not Burnaby?" asked Mrs. Brown.

"It was Barnaby Jones on the card—just the same as 'Barnaby Rudge'; and as for looking like a gentleman, I'm by no means quite so sure. A gentleman takes an apology when it's offered."

"Perhaps, my dear, that depends on the condition of his throat. If you had had a mustard plaster on all night, you might not have liked it. But here we are at Thompson Hall at last."

Thompson Hall was an old brick mansion, standing within a huge iron gate, with a gravel sweep before it. It had stood there before Stratford was a town, or even a suburb, and had then been known by the name of Bow Place. But it had been in the hands of the present family for the last thirty years, and was now known far and wide as Thompson Hall—a comfortable, roomy, old-fashioned place, perhaps a little dark and dull to look at, but much more substantially built than most of our modern villas. Mrs. Brown jumped with alacrity from the carriage, and with a quick step entered the home of her forefathers. Her husband followed her more leisurely; but he too felt that he was at home at Thompson Hall. Then Mr. Jones walked in also; but he looked as though he were not at all at home. It was still very early, and no one of the family was as yet down. In these circumstances it was almost necessary that something should be said to Mr. Jones.

"Do you know Mr. Thompson?" asked Mr. Brown.

"I never had the pleasure of seeing him—as yet," answered Mr. Jones, very stiffly.

"Oh—I didn't know. Because you said you were coming here."

"And I have come here. Are you friends of Mr. Thompson?"

"Oh dear yes," said Mrs. Brown. "I was a Thompson myself before I married."

"Oh—indeed!" said Mr. Jones. "How very odd!—very odd indeed."

During this time the luggage was being brought into the house, and two old family servants were offering them assistance. Would the new-comers like to go up to their bedrooms? Then the housekeeper, Mrs. Green, intimated with a wink that Miss Jane would, she was sure, be down quite immediately. The present moment, however, was still very unpleasant. The lady probably had made her guess as to the mystery, but the two gentlemen were still altogether in the dark. Mrs. Brown had no doubt declared her parentage, but Mr. Jones, with such a multitude of strange facts crowding on his mind, had been slow to understand her. Being somewhat suspicious by nature, he was beginning to think whether possibly the mustard had been put by this lady on his throat with some reference to his connection with Thompson Hall. Could it be that she, for some reason of her own, had wished to prevent his coming, and had contrived this untoward stratagem out of her brain? or had she wished to make him ridiculous to the Thompson family, to whom, as a family, he was at present unknown? It was becoming more and more improbable to him that the whole thing should have been an accident. When, after the first horrid torments of that morning in which he had in his agony invoked the assistance of the night porter, he had begun to reflect on his situation, he had determined that it would be better that nothing further should be said about it. What would life be worth to him if he were to be known wherever he went as the man who had been mustard-plastered in the middle of the night by a strange lady? The worst of a practical joke is that the remembrance of the absurd condition sticks so long to the sufferer. At the hotel that night porter, who had possessed himself of the handkerchief, and had read the name, who had connected that name with the occupant of 333, whom he had found wandering about the house with some strange purpose, had not permitted the thing to sleep. The porter had pressed the matter home against the Browns, and had produced the interview which has been recorded. But during the whole of that day Mr. Jones had been resolving that he would never again either think of the Browns or speak of them. A great injury had been done to him—a most outrageous injustice; but it was a thing which had to be endured. A horrid woman had come across him like a nightmare. All he could do was to endeavor to forget the terrible visitation. Such had been his resolve, in making which he had passed that long day in Paris. And now the Browns had stuck to him from the moment of his leaving his room! He had been forced to travel with them, but had travelled with them as a stranger. He had tried to comfort himself with the reflection that at every fresh stage he would shake them off. In one railway after another the vicinity had been bad—but still they were strangers. Now he found himself in the same house with them, where of course the story would be told. Had not the thing been done on purpose that the story might be told there at Thompson Hall?

Mrs. Brown had acceded to the proposition of the housekeeper, and was about to be taken to her room, when there was heard a sound of footsteps along the passage above and on the stairs, and a young lady came bounding on to the scene. "You have all of you come a quarter of an hour earlier than we thought possible," said the young lady. "I did so mean to be up to receive you!" With that she passed her sister on the stairs—for the young lady was Miss Jane Thompson, sister to our Mrs. Brown—and hurried down into the hall. Here Mr. Brown, who had ever been on affectionate terms with his sister-in-law, put himself forward to receive her embraces; but she, apparently not noticing him in her ardor, rushed on and threw herself on to the breast of the other gentleman. "This is my Charles," she said. "Oh, Charles, I thought you never would be here!"

Mr. Charles Burnaby Jones—for such was his name since he had inherited the Jones property in Pembrokeshire—received into his arms the ardent girl of his heart with all that love and devotion to which she was entitled, but could not do so without some external shrinking from her embrace. "Oh, Charles, what is it?" she said.

"Nothing, dearest—only—only—" Then he looked piteously up into Mrs. Brown's face, as though imploring her not to tell the story.

"Perhaps, Jane, you had better introduce us," said Mrs. Brown.

"Introduce you! I thought you had been travelling together, and staying at the same hotel, and all that."

"So we have; but people may be in the same hotel without knowing each other. And we have travelled all the way home with Mr. Jones without in the least knowing who he was."

"How very odd! Do you mean you have never spoken?"

"Not a word," said Mrs. Brown.

"I do so hope you'll love each other," said Jane.

"It sha'n't be my fault if we don't," said Mrs. Brown.

"I'm sure it sha'n't be mine," said Mr. Brown, tendering his hand to the other gentleman. The various feelings of the moment were too much for Mr. Jones, and he could not respond quite as he should have done. But as he was taken up-stairs to his room, he determined that he would make the best of it.

The owner of the house was old Uncle John. He was a bachelor, and with him lived various members of the family. There was the great Thompson of them all, Cousin Robert, who was now member of Parliament for the Essex Flats; and young John, as a certain enterprising Thompson of the age of forty was usually called; and then there was old Aunt Bess; and among other young branches there was Miss Jane Thompson, who was now engaged to marry Mr. Charles Burnaby Jones. As it happened, no other member of the family had as yet seen Mr. Burnaby Jones, and he, being by nature of a retiring disposition, felt himself to be ill at ease when he came into the breakfast parlor among all the Thompsons. He was known to be a gentleman of good family and ample means, and all the Thompsons had approved of the match; but during that first Christmas breakfast he did not seem to accept his condition jovially. His own Jane sat beside him, but then on the other side sat Mrs. Brown. She assumed an immediate intimacy—as women know how to do on such occasions—being determined from the very first to regard her sister's husband as a brother; but he still feared her. She was still to him the woman who had come to him in the dead of night with that horrid mixture—and had then left him.

"It was so odd that both of you should have been detained on the very same day," said Jane.

"Yes, it was odd," said Mrs. Brown, with a smile, looking round upon her neighbor.

"It was abominably bad weather, you know," said Brown.

"But you were both so determined to come," said the old gentleman. "When we got the two telegrams at the same moment, we were sure that there had been some agreement between you."

"Not exactly an agreement," said Mrs. Brown; whereupon Mr. Jones looked as grim as death.

"I'm sure there is something more than we understand yet," said the member of Parliament.

Then they all went to church, as a united family ought to do on Christmas-day, and came home to a fine old English early dinner at three o'clock—a sirloin of beef a foot and a half broad, a turkey as big as an ostrich, a plum-pudding bigger than the turkey, and two or three dozen mince-pies. "That's a very large bit of beef," said Mr. Jones, who had not lived much in England latterly.

"It won't look so large," said the old gentleman, "when all our friends down-stairs have had their say to it." "A plum-pudding on Christmas-day can't be too big," he said again, "if the cook will but take time enough over it. I never knew a bit to go to waste yet."

By this time there had been some explanation as to past events between the two sisters. Mrs. Brown had, indeed, told Jane all about it—how ill her husband had been, how she had been forced to go down and look for the mustard, and then what she had done with the mustard.

"I don't think they are a bit alike, you know, Mary, if you mean that," said Jane.

"Well, no; perhaps not quite alike. I only saw his beard, you know. No doubt it was stupid, but I did it."

"Why didn't you take it off again?" asked the sister.

"Oh, Jane, if you'd only think of it! Could you?" Then, of course, all that occurred was explained—how they had been stopped on their journey, how Brown had made the best apology in his power, and how Jones had travelled with them and had never spoken a word. The gentleman had only taken his new name a week since, but of course he had had his new card printed immediately. "I'm sure I should have thought of it, if they hadn't made a mistake of the first name. Charles said it was like Barnaby Rudge."

"Not at all like Barnaby Rudge," said Jane: "Charles Burnaby Jones is a very good name."

"Very good indeed—and I'm sure that after a little bit he won't be at all the worse for the accident."

Before dinner the secret had been told no further, but still there had crept about among the Thompsons, and, indeed, down-stairs also among the retainers, a feeling that there was a secret. The old house-keeper was sure that Miss Mary, as she still called Mrs. Brown, had something to tell, if she could only be induced to tell it, and that this something had reference to Mr. Jones's personal comfort. The head of the family, who was a sharp old gentleman, felt this also, and the member of Parliament, who had an idea that he especially should never be kept in the dark, was almost angry. Mr. Jones, suffering from some kindred feeling throughout the dinner, remained silent and unhappy. When two or three toasts had been drunk—the Queen's health, the old gentleman's health, the young couple's health, Brown's health, and the general health of all the Thompsons—then tongues were loosened and a question was asked. "I know that there has been something doing in Paris between these young people that we haven't heard as yet," said the uncle. Then Mrs. Brown laughed, and Jane, laughing too, gave Mr. Jones to understand that she, at any rate, knew all about it.

"If there is a mystery, I hope it will be told at once," said the member of Parliament angrily.

"Come, Brown, what is it?" asked another male cousin.

"Well, there was an accident. I'd rather Jones should tell," said he.

Jones's brow became blacker than thunder, but he did not say a word. "You mustn't be angry with Mary," Jane whispered into her lover's ear.

"Come, Mary, you never were slow at talking," said the uncle.

"I do hate this kind of thing," said the member of Parliament.

"I will tell it all," said Mrs. Brown, very nearly in tears, or else pre-tending to be very nearly in tears. "I know I was very wrong, and I do beg his pardon; and if he won't say that he forgives me, I never shall be happy again." Then she clasped her hands, and, turning round, looked him piteously in the face.

"Oh, yes; I do forgive you," said Mr. Jones.

"My brother," said she, throwing her arms round him and kissing him. He recoiled from the embrace, but I think that he attempted to return the kiss. "And now I will tell the whole story," said Mrs.

Brown. And she told it, acknowledging her fault with true contrition, and swearing that she would atone for it by life-long sisterly devotion.

"And you mustard-plastered the wrong man!" said the old gentleman, almost rolling off his chair with delight.

"I did," said Mrs. Brown, sobbing; "and I think that no woman ever suffered as I suffered."

"And Jones wouldn't let you leave the hotel?"

"It was the handkerchief stopped us," said Brown.

"If it had turned out to be anybody else," said the member of Parliament, "the results might have been most serious—not to say discreditable."

"That's nonsense, Robert," said Mrs. Brown, who was disposed to resent the use of so severe a word, even from the legislator cousin.

"In a strange gentleman's bedroom!" he continued. "It only shows that what I have always said is quite true. You should never go to bed in a strange house without locking your door."

Nevertheless it was a very jovial meeting and before the evening was over Mr. Jones was happy, and had been brought to acknowledge that the mustard plaster would probably not do him any permanent injury.

THE STAGE COACH

by Washington Irving

from *Christmas at Bracebridge Hall*

> *Omne bene*
> *Sine pœna*
> *Tempus est ludendi,*
> *Venit hora*
> *Absque mora*
> *Libros deponendi.*
> OLD HOLIDAY SCHOOL SONG

In the course of a December tour in Yorkshire, I rode for a long distance in one of the public coaches, on the day preceding Christmas. The coach was crowded, both inside and out, with passengers, who, by their talk, seemed principally bound to the mansions of relations or friends, to eat the Christmas dinner. It was loaded also with hampers of game, and baskets and boxes of delicacies; and hares hung dangling their long ears about the coachman's box, presents from distant friends for the impending feast. I had three fine rosy-cheeked school-boys for my fellow-passengers inside, full of the buxom health and manly spirit which I have observed in the children of this country. They were returning home for the holidays in high glee, and promising themselves a world of enjoyment. It was delightful to hear the gigantic plans of the little rogues, and the impracticable feats they were to perform during their six weeks' emancipation from book, birch, and pedagogue. They were full of anticipations of the meeting with the family and household, down to the very cat and dog; and of the joy they were to give their little sisters by the presents with which their pockets were crammed: but the meeting to which they seemed to look forward with the greatest impatience was with Bantam, which I found to be a pony, and according to their talk, possessed of more virtues than any steed since the days of Bucephalus. How he could trot! how he could run! and then such leaps as he would take —there was not a hedge in the whole country that he could not clear.

They were under the particular guardianship of the coachman, to whom, whenever an opportunity presented, they addressed a host of questions, and pronounced him one of the best fellows in the world. Indeed, I could not but notice the more than ordinary air of bustle and importance of the coachman, who wore his hat a little on one side, and had a large bunch of Christmas greens stuck in the buttonhole of his coat. He is always a person full of mighty care and business, but he is particularly so during this season, having so many commissions to execute in consequence of the interchange of presents. And here, perhaps, it may not be unacceptable to my untravelled readers, to have a sketch that may serve as a general representation of this very numerous and important class of functionaries, who have a dress, a manner, a language, an air, peculiar to themselves, and prevalent throughout the fraternity; so that, wherever an English stage-coachman may be seen, he cannot be mistaken for one of any other craft or mystery.

He has commonly a broad, full face, curiously mottled with red, as if the blood had been forced by hard feeding into every vessel of the skin; he is swelled into jolly dimensions by frequent potations of malt liquors, and his bulk is still further increased by a multiplicity of coats, in which he is buried like a cauliflower, the upper one reaching to his heels. He wears a broad-brimmed, low-crowned hat; a huge roll of coloured handkerchief about his neck, knowingly knotted and tucked in at the bosom; and has in summer-time a large bouquet of flowers in his buttonhole; the present, most probably, of some enamoured country lass. His waistcoat is probably of some bright colour, striped, and his small clothes extend far below the knees, to meet a pair of jockey boots which reach about half way up his legs.

All this costume is maintained with much precision: he has a pride in having his clothes of excellent materials; and, notwithstanding the seeming grossness of his appearance, there is still discernible that neatness and propriety of person which is almost inherent in an Englishman. He enjoys great consequence and consideration along the road;

has frequent conferences with the village housewives, who look upon him as a man of great trust and dependence; and he seems to have a good understanding with every bright-eyed country lass. The moment he arrives where the horses are to be changed, he throws down the reins with something of an air, and abandons the cattle to the care of an ostler; his duty being merely to drive from one stage to another. When off the box, his hands are thrust into the pockets of his great coat, and he rolls about the inn yard with an air of the most absolute lordliness. Here he is generally surrounded by an admiring throng of ostlers, stableboys, shoe-blacks, and those nameless hangers-on that infest inns and taverns, and run errands, and do all kinds of odd jobs, for the privilege of battening on the drippings of the kitchen and the leakage of the taproom.

These all look up to him as to an oracle; treasure up his cant phrases; echo his opinions about horses, and other topics of jockey lore; and above all, endeavour to imitate his air and carriage. Every ragamuffin that has a coat to his back thrusts his hands in the pockets, rolls in his gait, talks slang, and is an embryo Coachey.

Perhaps it might be owing to the pleasing serenity that reigned in my own mind, that I fancied I saw cheerfulness in every countenance throughout the journey. A stage coach, however, carries animation always with it, and puts the world in motion as it whirls along. The horn, sounded at the entrance of a village, produces a general bustle. Some hasten forth to meet friends, some with bundles and bandboxes to secure places, and in the hurry of the moment can hardly take leave of the group that accompanies them. In the meantime the coachman has a world of small commissions to execute. Sometimes he delivers a hare or a pheasant; sometimes jerks a small parcel or newspaper to the door of a public house; and sometimes, with knowing leer and words of sly import, hands to some half-blushing, half-laughing housemaid, an odd-shaped billet-doux from some rustic admirer. As the coach rattles through the village, everyone runs to the window, and you have glances on every side of fresh country faces and blooming giggling girls. At the corners are assembled juntos of village idlers and wise men, who take their stations there for the purpose of seeing company pass; but the sagest knot is generally at the blacksmith's, to whom the passing of the coach is an event fruitful of much speculation. The smith, with the horse's heel in his lap, pauses as the vehicle whirls by; the cyclops round the anvil suspend their ringing hammers, and suffer the iron to grow cool; and the sooty spectre in brown paper cap, labouring at the bellows, leans on the handle for a few moments, and permits the asthmatic engine to heave a long-drawn sigh, while he glares through the murky smoke and sulphurous gleams of the smithy.

Perhaps the impending holiday might have given a more than usual animation to the country, for it seemed to me as if everybody was in good looks and good spirits. Game, poultry, and other luxuries of the table, were in brisk circulation in the villages; the grocers', butchers', and fruiterers' shops were thronged with customers. The housewives were stirring briskly about, putting their dwellings in order; and the glossy branches of holly, with their bright red berries, began to appear at the windows. The scene brought to mind an old writer's account of Christmas preparations: "Now capons and hens, besides turkeys, geese, and ducks, with beef and mutton—must all die—for in twelve days a multitude of people will not be fed with a little. Now plums and spice, sugar and honey, square it among pies and broth. Now or never must music be in tune, for the youth must dance and sing to get them a heat, while the aged sit by the fire. The country maid leaves half her market, and must be sent again, if she forgets a pack of cards on Christmas Eve. Great is the contention of holly and ivy, whether master or dame wears the breeches. Dice and cards benefit the butler; and if the cook do not lack wit, he will sweetly lick his fingers."

I was roused from this fit of luxurious meditation by a shout from my little travelling companions. They had been looking out of the coach windows for the last few miles, recognizing every tree and cottage as they approached home, and now there was a general burst of joy—"There's John! and there's old Carlo! and there's Bantam!" cried the happy little rogues, clapping their hands.

At the end of the lane there was an old sober-looking servant in livery, waiting for them; he was accompanied by a superannuated pointer, and by the redoubtable Bantam, a little old rat of a pony, with a shaggy mane and old rusty tail, who stood dozing quietly by the road-side, little dreaming of the bustling times that awaited him.

I was pleased to see the fondness with which the little fellows leaped about the steady old footman, and hugged the pointer, who wriggled his whole body for joy. But Bantam was the great object of interest; all wanted to mount at once, and it was with some difficulty that John arranged that they should ride by turns, and the eldest should ride first.

Off they set at last; one on the pony, with the dog hounding and barking before him, and the other holding John's hands; both talking at once, and overpowering him with questions about home, and with school anecdotes. I looked after them with a feeling in which I do not know whether pleasure or melancholy predominated: for I was reminded of those days when, like them, I had neither known care nor sorrow, and a holiday was the summit of earthly felicity. We stopped a few moments afterwards to water the horses, and on resuming our route, a turn of the road brought us in sight of a neat country seat. I could just distinguish the forms of a lady and two young girls in the portico, and I saw my little comrades, with Bantam, Carlo, and old John, trooping along the carriage road. I leaned out of the coach window, in hopes of witnessing the happy meeting, but a grove of trees shut it from my sight.

In the evening we reached a village where I had determined to pass the night. As we drove into the great gateway of the inn, I saw on one side the light of a rousing kitchen fire beaming through a window. I entered, and admired, for the hundredth time, that picture of convenience, neatness, and broad, honest enjoyment, the kitchen of an English inn. It was of spacious dimensions, hung round with copper and tin vessels highly polished, and decorated here and there with a Christmas green. Hams, tongues, and flitches of bacon, were suspended from the ceiling; a smoke-jack made its ceaseless clanking beside the fireplace, and a clock ticked in one corner. A well-scoured deal table extended along one side of the kitchen, with a cold round of beef and other hearty viands upon it, over which two foaming tankards of ale seemed mounting guard. Travellers of inferior order were preparing to attack this stout repast, while others sat smoking and gossiping over their ale on two high-backed oaken settles beside the fire. Trim housemaids were hurrying backwards and forwards under the directions of a fresh bustling landlady; but still seizing an occasional moment to exchange a flippant word, and have a rallying laugh with the group round the fire. The scene completely realized Poor Robin's humble idea of the comforts of mid-winter:

> Now trees their leafy hats do bare
> To reverance winter's silver hair;
> A handsome hostess, merry host,
> A pot of ale now and a toast,
> Tobacco and a good coal fire,
> Are things this season doth require.*

* Poor Robin's Almanac, 1684.

I had not been long at the inn when a post-chaise drove up to the door. A young gentleman stepped out, and by the light of the lamps I caught a glimpse of a countenance which I thought I knew. I moved forward to get a nearer view, when his eye caught mine. I was not mistaken; it was Frank Bracebridge, a sprightly good-humoured young fellow, with whom I had once travelled on the Continent. Our meeting was extremely cordial, for the countenance of an old fellow-traveller always brings up the recollection of a thousand pleasant scenes, odd adventures, and excellent jokes. To discuss all these in a transient interview at an inn was impossible; and finding that I was not pressed for time, and was merely making a tour of observation, he insisted that I should give him a day or two at his father's country seat, to which he was going to pass the holidays, and which lay at a few miles' distance. "It is better than eating a solitary Christmas dinner at an inn," said he, "and I can assure you of a hearty welcome in something of the old-fashioned style." His reasoning was cogent, and I must confess the preparation I had seen for universal festivity and social enjoyment had made me feel a little impatient of my loneliness. I closed, therefore, at once, with his invitation; the chaise drove up to the door, and in a few moments I was on my way to the family mansion of the Bracebridges.

CHRISTMAS EVE

by Washington Irving

from *Christmas at Bracebridge Hall*

Saint Francis and Saint Benedight
Blesse this house from wicked wight;
From the night-mare and the goblin,
That is hight good fellow Robin:
Keep it from all evil spirits,
Fairies, weezels, rats, and ferrets:
   From curfew time
   To the next prime.

CARTWRIGHT

It was a brilliant moonlight night, but extremely cold; our chaise whirled rapidly over the frozen ground; the postboy smacked his whip incessantly, and a part of the time his horses were on a gallop. "He knows where he is going," said my companion, laughing, "and is eager to arrive in time for some of the merriment and good cheer of the servants' hall. My father, you must know, is a bigoted devotee of the old school, and prides himself upon keeping up something of old English hospitality. He is a tolerable specimen of what you will rarely meet with nowadays in its purity, the old English country gentleman; for our men of fortune spend so much of their time in town, and fashion is carried so much into the country, that the strong rich peculiarities of ancient rural life are almost polished away. My father, however, from early years, took honest Peacham* for his textbook, instead of Chesterfield; he determined, in his own mind, that there

* *Peacham's Complete Gentleman, 1622.*

was no condition more truly honourable and enviable than that of a country gentleman on his paternal lands, and therefore passes the whole of his time on his estate. He is a strenuous advocate for the revival of the old rural games and holiday observances, and is deeply read in the writers, ancient and modern, who have treated on the subject. Indeed, his favourite range of reading is among the authors who flourished at least two centuries since; who, he insists, wrote and thought more like true Englishmen than any of their successors. He even regrets sometimes that he had not been born a few centuries earlier, when England was itself, and had its peculiar manners and customs. As he lives at some distance from the main road, in rather a lonely part of the country, without any rival gentry near him, he has that most enviable of all blessings to an Englishman, the opportunity of indulging the bent of his own humour without molestation. Being representative of the oldest family in the neighbourhood, and a great part of the peasantry being his tenants, he is much looked up to, and, in general, is known simply by the appellation of 'The Squire'; a title which has been accorded to the head of the family since time immemorial. I think it best to give you these hints about my worthy old father, to prepare you for any eccentricities that might otherwise appear absurd."

We had passed for some time along the wall of a park, and at length the chaise stopped at the gate. It was in a heavy magnificent old style, of iron bars, fancifully wrought at top into flourishes and flowers. The huge square columns that supported the gate were surmounted by the family crest. Close adjoining was the porter's lodge, sheltered under dark fir-trees, and almost buried in shrubbery.

The postboy rang a large porter's bell, which resounded through the still frosty air, and was answered by the distant barking of dogs, with which the mansion-house seemed garrisoned. An old woman immediately appeared at the gate. As the moonlight fell strongly upon her, I had a full view of a little primitive dame, dressed very much in the antique taste, with a neat kerchief and stomacher, and her silver hair peeping from under a cap of snowy whiteness. She came curtseying forth, with many expressions of simple joy at seeing her young master. Her husband, it seemed, was up at the house keeping Christmas Eve in the servants' hall; they could not do without him, as he was the best hand at a song and story in the household.

My friend proposed that we should alight and walk through the park to the hall, which was at no great distance, while the chaise should follow on. Our road wound through a noble avenue of trees, among the naked branches of which the moon glittered as she rolled through the deep vault of a cloudless sky. The lawn beyond was sheeted with a slight covering of snow, which here and there sparkled as the moonbeams caught a frosty crystal; and at a distance might be seen a thin transparent vapour stealing up from the low grounds and threatening gradually to shroud the landscape.

My companion looked around him with transport. "How often," said he, "have I scampered up this avenue, on returning home on school vacations! How often have I played under these trees when a boy! I feel a degree of filial reverence for them, as we look up to those who have cherished us in childhood. My father was always scrupulous in exacting our holidays, and having us around him on family festivals. He used to direct and superintend our games with the strictness that some parents do the studies of their children. He was very particular that we should play the old English games according to their original form; and consulted old books for precedent and authority for every 'merrie sport'; yet I assure you there never was pedantry so delightful. It was the policy of the good old gentleman to make his children feel that home was the happiest place in the world, and I value this delicious home-feeling as one of the choicest gifts a parent could bestow."

We were interrupted by the clamour of a troop of dogs of all sorts and sizes, "mongrel, puppy, whelp and hound, and curs of low degree," that, disturbed by the ring of the porter's bell, and the rattling of the chaise, came bounding, open-mouthed, across the lawn. " 'The little dogs and all—Tray, Blanch, and Sweetheart—see, they bark at me!' " cried Bracebridge, laughing. At the sound of his voice, the bark was changed into a yelp of delight, and in a moment he was surrounded and almost overpowered by the caresses of the faithful animals.

We had now come in full view of the old family mansion, partly thrown in deep shadow, and partly lit up by the cold moonshine. It was an irregular building, of some magnitude, and seemed to be of the architecture of different periods. One wing was evidently very ancient, with heavy stone-shafted bow windows, jutting out and overrun with ivy, from among the foliage of which the small diamond-shaped panes of glass glittered with the moonbeams. The rest of the house was in the French taste of Charles the Second's time, having been repaired and altered, as my friend told me, by one of his ancestors, who returned with that monarch at the Restoration. The grounds about the house were laid out in the old formal manner of artificial flower-beds, clipped shrubberies, raised terraces, and heavy stone balustrades, ornamented with urns, a leaden statue or two, and a jet of water. The old gentleman, I was told, was extremely careful to preserve this obsolete finery in all its original state. He admired this fashion in gardening: it had an air of magnificence, was courtly and noble, and befitting good old family style. The boasted imitation of nature in modern gardening had sprung up with modern republican notions, but did not suit a monarchical government; it smacked of the levelling system. I could not help smiling at this introduction of politics into gardening, though I expressed some apprehension that I should find the old gentleman rather intolerant in his creed. Frank assured me, however, that it was almost the only instance in which he had ever heard his father meddle with politics; and he believed that he had got this notion from a member of parliament who once passed a few weeks with him. The squire was glad of any argument to defend his clipped yew trees and formal terraces which had been occasionally attacked by modern landscape-gardeners.

As we approached the house, we heard the sound of music, and now and then a burst of laughter from one end of the building. This, Bracebridge said, must proceed from the servants' hall, where a great deal of revelry was permitted, and even encouraged, by the squire, throughout the twelve days of Christmas, provided everything was done conformably to ancient usage. Here were kept up the old games of hoodman blind, shoe the wild mare, hot cockles, steal the white loaf, bob apple, and snap dragon: the Yule clog and Christmas candle were regularly burnt, and the mistletoe, with its white berries, hung up, to the imminent peril of all the pretty housemaids.*

So intent were the servants upon their sports, that we had to ring repeatedly before we could make ourselves heard. On our arrival being announced, the squire came out to receive us, accompanied by his two other sons; one a young officer in the army, home on leave of absence; the other an Oxonian, just from the University. The squire was a fine healthy-looking old gentleman, with silver hair curling lightly round an open florid countenance; in which the physiognomist, with the ad-

---

* The mistletoe is still hung up in farmhouses and kitchens at Christmas, and the young men have the privilege of kissing the girls under it, plucking each time a berry from the bush. When the berries are all plucked, the privilege ceases.

vantage, like myself, of a previous hint or two, might discover a singular mixture of whim and benevolence.

The family meeting was warm and affectionate; as the evening was far advanced, the squire would not permit us to change our travelling dresses, but ushered us at once to the company, which was assembled in a large old-fashioned hall. It was composed of different branches of a numerous family connection, where there were the usual proportion of old uncles and aunts, comfortably married dames, superannuated spinsters, blooming country cousins, half-fledged striplings, and bright-eyed boarding-school hoydens. They were variously occupied; some at a round game of cards; others conversing around the fireplace; at one end of the hall was a group of the young folks, some nearly grown up, others of a more tender and budding age, fully engrossed by a merry game; and a profusion of wooden horses, penny trumpets, and tattered dolls, about the floor, showed traces of a troop of little fairy beings, who, having frolicked through a happy day, had been carried off to slumber through a peaceful night.

While the mutual greetings were going on between young Bracebridge and his relatives, I had time to scan the apartment. I have called it a hall, for so it had evidently been in old times, and the squire had evidently endeavoured to restore it to something of its primitive state. Over the heavy projecting fireplace was suspended a picture of a warrior in armour, standing by a white horse, and on the opposite wall hung a helmet, buckler, and lance. At one end an enormous pair of antlers were inserted in the wall, the branches serving as hooks in which to suspend hats, whips, and spurs; and in the corner of the apartment were fowling-pieces, fishing-rods, and other sporting implements. The furniture was of the cumbrous workmanship of former days, though some articles of modern convenience had been added, and the oaken floor had been carpeted; so that the whole presented an odd mixture of parlour and hall.

The grate had been removed from the wide overwhelming fireplace, to make way for a fire of wood, in the midst of which was an enormous log glowing and glazing, and sending forth a vast volume of light and heat; this I understood was the Yule clog, which the squire was particular in having brought in and illumined on a Christmas Eve, according to ancient custom.*

* *The Yule clog is a great log of wood, sometimes the root of a tree, brought into the house with great ceremony, on Christmas Eve, laid in the fireplace, and lighted with the brand of last year's clog. While it lasted, there was great drinking, singing,*

It was really delightful to see the old squire seated in his hereditary elbow chair, by the hospitable fireplace of his ancestors, and looking round him like the sun of a system, beaming warmth and gladness to every heart. Even the very dog that lay stretched at his feet, as he lazily shifted his position and yawned, would look fondly up in his master's face, wag his tail against the floor, and stretch himself again to sleep, confident of kindness and protection. There is an emanation from the heart in genuine hospitality which cannot be described, but is immediately felt, and puts the stranger at once at his ease. I had not been seated many minutes by the comfortable hearth of the worthy old cavalier, before I found myself as much at home as if I had been one of the family.

Supper was announced shortly after our arrival. It was served up in a spacious oaken chamber, the panels of which shone with wax, and around which were several family portraits decorated with holly and ivy. Besides the accustomed lights, two great wax tapers, called Christmas candles, wreathed with greens, were placed on a highly polished beaufet among the family plate. The table was abundantly spread with substantial fare; but the squire made his supper of frumenty, a dish made of wheat cakes boiled in milk, with rich spices, being a standing dish in old times for Christmas Eve. I was happy to find my old friend, minced pie, in the retinue of the feast; and finding him to be perfectly orthodox, and that I need not be ashamed of my predilection, I greeted him with all the warmth wherewith we usually greet an old and very genteel acquaintance.

---

and telling of tales. Sometimes it was accompanied by Christmas candles; but in the cottages the only light was from the ruddy blaze of the great wood fire. The Yule clog was to burn all night; if it went out, it was considered a sign of ill luck. Herrick mentions it in one of his songs—

> Come, bring with a noise,
> My merrie, merrie boys,
> The Christmas log to the firing;
> While my good dame, she
> Bids ye all be free,
> And drink to your heart's desiring.

The Yule clog is still burnt in many farmhouses and kitchens in England, particularly in the north, and there are several superstitions connected with it among the peasantry. If a squinting person comes to the house while it is burning, or a person barefooted, it is considered an ill omen. The brand remaining from the Yule clog is carefully put away to light the next year's Christmas fire.

The mirth of the company was greatly promoted by the humours of an eccentric personage whom Mr. Bracebridge always addressed with the quaint appellation of Master Simon. He was a tight brisk little man, with the air of an arrant old bachelor. His nose was shaped like the bill of a parrot; his face slightly pitted with the small-pox, with a dry perpetual bloom on it, like a frost-bitten leaf in autumn. He had an eye of great quickness and vivacity, with a drollery and lurking waggery of expression that was irresistible. He was evidently the wit of the family, dealing very much in sly jokes and innuendoes with the ladies, and making infinite merriment by harping upon old themes; which unfortunately, my ignorance of the family chronicles did not permit me to enjoy. It seemed to be his great delight during supper to keep a young girl next him in a continual agony of stifled laughter, in spite of her awe of the reproving looks of her mother who sat opposite. Indeed, he was the idol of the younger part of the company, who laughed at everything he said or did, and at every turn of his countenance. I could not wonder at it; for he must have been a miracle of accomplishments in their eyes. He could imitate Punch and Judy; make an old woman of his hand, with the assistance of a burnt cork and pocket-handkerchief; and cut an orange into such a ludicrous caricature, that the young folks were ready to die with laughing.

I was let briefly into his history by Frank Bracebridge. He was an old bachelor, of a small independent income, which, by careful management, was sufficient for all his wants. He revolved through the family system like a vagrant comet in its orbit; sometimes visiting one branch, and sometimes another quite remote; as is often the case with gentlemen of extensive connections and small fortunes in England. He had a chirping buoyant disposition, always enjoying the present moment; and his frequent change of scene and company prevented his acquiring those rusty unaccommodating habits with which old bachelors are so uncharitably charged. He was a complete family chronicle, being versed in the genealogy, history, and intermarriages of the whole house of Bracebridge, which made him a great favourite with the old folks; he was the beau of all the elder ladies and superannuated spinsters, among whom he was habitually considered rather a young fellow, and he was master of the revels among the children; so that there was not a more popular being in the sphere in which he moved than Mr. Simon Bracebridge. Of late years he had resided almost entirely with the squire, to whom he had become a factotum, and whom he particularly delighted by jumping with his humour in respect to old times, and by having a scrap of an old song to suit every occasion. We had presently a specimen of his last-mentioned talent, for no sooner was supper removed, and spiced wines and other beverages peculiar to the season introduced, than Master Simon was called on for a good old Christmas song. He bethought himself for a moment, and then, with a sparkle of the eye, and a voice by no means bad, excepting that it ran occasionally into a falsetto, like the notes of a split reed, he quavered forth a quaint old ditty.

> Now Christmas is come,
> Let us beat up the drum,
> And call all our neighbours together,
> And when they appear,
> Let us make them such cheer,
> As will keep out the wind and the weather, &c.

The supper had disposed every one to gaiety, and an old harper was summoned from the servants' hall, where he had been strumming all the evening, and to all appearance comforting himself with some of the squire's home-brewed. He was a kind of hanger-on, I was told, of the establishment, and, though ostensibly a resident of the village, was oftener to be found in the squire's kitchen than his own home, the old gentleman being fond of the sound of "harp in hall."

The dance, like most dances after supper, was a merry one; some of the older folks joined in it, and the squire himself figured down several couple with a partner, with whom he affirmed he had danced at every Christmas for nearly half a century. Master Simon, who seemed to be a kind of connecting link between the old times and the new, and to be withal a little antiquated in the taste of his accomplishments, evidently piqued himself on his dancing, and was endeavouring to gain credit by the heel and toe, rigadoon, and other graces of the ancient school; but he had unluckily assorted himself with a little romping girl from boarding-school, who by her wild vivacity, kept him continually on the stretch, and defeated all his sober attempts at elegance: such are the ill-assorted matches to which antique gentlemen are unfortunately prone!

The young Oxonian, on the contrary, had led out one of his maiden aunts, on whom the rogue played a thousand little knaveries with impunity; he was full of practical jokes, and his delight was to tease his aunt and cousins; yet, like all madcap youngsters, he was a universal favourite among the women. The most interesting couple in the dance was the young officer and a ward of the squire's, a beautiful blushing girl of seventeen. From several sly glances which I had noticed in the course of the evening, I suspected there was a little kindness growing up between them; and, indeed, the young soldier was just the hero to captivate a romantic girl. He was tall, slender, and handsome, and like most young British officers of late years, had picked up various small accomplishments on the Continent—he could talk French and Italian—draw landscapes, sing very tolerably, dance divinely; but, above all, he had been wounded at Waterloo—what girl of seventeen, well read in poetry and romance, could resist such a mirror of chivalry and perfection!

The moment the dance was over, he caught up a guitar, and lolling against the old marble fireplace, in an attitude which I am half inclined to suspect was studied, began the little French air of the Troubadour. The squire, however, exclaimed against having anything on Christmas Eve but good old English; upon which the young minstrel, casting up his eye for a moment, as if in an effort of memory, struck into another strain, and, with a charming air of gallantry, gave Herrick's "Night-Piece to Julia."

> Her eyes the glow-worm lend thee,
> The shooting stars attend thee,
> And the elves also,
> Whose little eyes glow
> Like the sparks of fire befriend thee.
>
> No Will-o'-the-Wisp mislight thee;
> Nor snake nor slow-worm bite thee;
> But on, on the way,
> Not making a stay,
> Since ghost there is none to affright thee.
>
> Then let not the dark thee cumber;
> What tho' the moon does slumber,
> The stars of the night
> Will lend thee their light,
> Like tapers clear without number;

Then, Julia, let me woo thee,
Thus, thus to come unto me,
And when I shall meet
Thy silvery feet,
My soul I'll pour into thee.

The song might or might not have been intended in compliment to the fair Julia, for so I found his partner was called; she, however, was certainly unconscious of any such application, for she never looked at the singer, but kept her eyes cast upon the floor. Her face was suffused, it is true, with a beautiful blush, and there was a gentle heaving of the bosom, but all that was doubtless caused by the exercise of the dance; indeed, so great was her indifference, that she amused herself with plucking to pieces a choice bouquet of hot-house flowers, and by the time the song was concluded the nosegay lay in ruins on the floor.

The party now broke up for the night, with the kind-hearted old custom of shaking hands. As I passed through the hall, on my way to my chamber, the dying embers of the Yule clog still sent forth a dusky glow, and had it not been the season when "no spirit dares stir abroad," I should have been half tempted to steal from my room at midnight, and peep whether the fairies might not be at their revels about the hearth.

My chamber was in the old part of the mansion, the ponderous furniture of which might have been fabricated in the days of the giants. The room was panelled, with cornices of heavy carved work, in which flowers and grotesque faces were strangely intermingled; and a row of black-looking portraits stared mournfully at me from the walls. The bed was of rich though faded damask, with a lofty tester, and stood in a niche opposite a bow window. I had scarcely got into bed when a strain of music seemed to break forth in the air just below the window. I listened, and found it proceeded from a band, which I concluded to be the waits from some neighbouring village. They went round the house, playing under the windows. I drew aside the curtains to hear them more distinctly. The moonbeams fell through the upper part of the casement, partially lighting up the antiquated apartment. The sounds, as they receded, became more soft and aerial, and seemed to accord with the quiet and moonlight. I listened and listened—they became more and more tender and remote, and, as they gradually died away, my head sunk upon the pillow, and I fell asleep.

THE CHRISTMAS DINNER

by Washington Irving

from *The Sketch Book of Geoffrey Crayon, Gent.*

Lo, now is come our joyful'st feast!
    Let every man be jolly,
Eache roome with yvie leaves is drest,
    And every post with holly.
Now all our neighbours' chimneys smoke,
    And Christmas blocks are burning;
Their ovens they with bak't meats choke
    And all their spits are turning.
      Without the door let sorrow lie,
      And if, for cold, it hap to die,
      Wee'le bury 't in a Christmas pye,
      And evermore be merry.
              WITHERS' JUVENILIA

I had finished my toilet, and was loitering with Frank Bracebridge in the library, when we heard a distant thwacking sound, which he informed me was a signal for the serving up of the dinner. The squire kept up old customs in kitchen as well as hall; and the rolling-pin, struck upon the dresser by the cook, summoned the servants to carry in the meats.

Just in this nick the cook knock'd thrice,
And all the waiters in a trice
    His summons did obey;
Each serving man, with dish in hand,
March'd boldly up, like our train band,
    Presented, and away.*

* *Sir John Suckling.*

The dinner was served up in the great hall, where the squire always held his Christmas banquet. A blazing, crackling fire of logs had been heaped on to warm the spacious apartment, and the flame went sparkling and wreathing up the wide-mouthed chimney. The great picture of the crusader and his white horse had been profusely decorated with greens for the occasion; and holly and ivy had likewise been wreathed round the helmet and weapons on the opposite wall, which I understood were the arms of the same warrior. I must own, by the by, I had strong doubts about the authenticity of the painting and armour as having belonged to the crusader, they certainly having the stamp of more recent days; but I was told that the painting had been so considered time out of mind; and that, as to the armour, it had been found in a lumber-room, and elevated to its present situation by the squire, who at once determined it to be the armour of the family hero; and as he was absolute authority on all such subjects in his own household, the matter had passed into current acceptation. A sideboard was set out just under this chivalric trophy, on which was a display of plate that might have vied (at least in variety) with Belshazzar's parade of the vessels of the temple: "flagons, cans, cups, beakers, goblets, basins, and ewers"; the gorgeous utensils of good companionship that had gradually accumulated through many generations of jovial housekeepers. Before these stood the two Yule candles, beaming like two stars of the first magnitude; other lights were distributed in branches, and the whole array glittered like a firmament of silver.

We were ushered into this banqueting scene with the sound of minstrelsy, the old harper being seated on a stool beside the fireplace, and twanging his instrument with a vast deal more power than melody. Never did Christmas board display a more goodly and gracious assemblage of countenances; those who were not handsome were, at least, happy; and happiness is a rare improver of your hard-favoured visage. I always consider an old English family as well worth studying as a collection of Holbein's portraits or Albert Durer's prints. There is much antiquarian lore to be acquired; much knowledge of the physiognomies of former times. Perhaps it may be from having continually before their eyes those rows of old family portraits, with which the mansions of this country are stocked; certain it is, that the quaint features of antiquity are often most faithfully perpetuated in these ancient lines; and I have traced an old family nose through a whole picture gallery, legitimately handed down from generation to generation, almost from the time of the Conquest. Something of the kind was to be observed in the worthy company around me. Many of their faces had evidently originated in a Gothic age, and been merely copied by succeeding generations; and there was one little girl in particular, of staid demeanour, with a high Roman nose, and an antique, vinegar aspect, who was a great favourite of the squire's, being, as he said, a Bracebridge all over, and the very counterpart of one of his ancestors who figured in the court of Henry VIII.

The parson said grace, which was not a short, familiar one, such as is commonly addressed to the Deity in these unceremonious days; but a long, courtly, well-worded one of the ancient school. There was now a pause, as if something was expected; when suddenly the butler entered the hall with some degree of bustle: he was attended by a servant on each side with a large wax-light, and bore a silver dish, on which was an enormous pig's head, decorated with rosemary, with a lemon in its mouth, which was placed with great formality at the head of the table. The moment this pageant made its appearance, the harper struck up a flourish; at the conclusion of which the young Oxonian, on receiving a hint from the squire, gave, with an air of the most comic gravity, an old carol, the first verse of which was as follows:

> *Caput apri defero*
> *Reddens laudes domino.*
> *The boar's head in hand bring I,*
> *With garlands gay and rosemary.*
> *I pray you all synge merrily*
> *Qui estis in convivio.*

Though prepared to witness many of these little eccentricities, from being apprised of the peculiar hobby of mine host; yet, I confess, the parade with which so odd a dish was introduced somewhat perplexed me, until I gathered from the conversation of the squire and the parson, that it was meant to represent the bringing in of the boar's head; a dish formerly served up with much ceremony and the sound of minstrelsy and song, at great tables, on Christmas day. "I like the old custom," said the squire, "not merely because it is stately and pleasing in itself, but because it was observed at the college at Oxford at which I was educated. When I hear the old song chanted, it brings to mind the time when I was young and gamesome—and the noble old college hall—and my fellow-students loitering about in their black gowns; many of whom, poor lads, are now in their graves!"

The parson, however, whose mind was not haunted by such associations, and who was always more taken up with the text than the sentiment, objected to the Oxonian's version of the carol; which he affirmed was different from that sung at college. He went on, with the dry perseverance of a commentator, to give the college reading, accompanied by sundry annotations; addressing himself at first to the company at large; but finding their attention gradually diverted to other talk and other objects, he lowered his tone as his number of auditors diminished, until he concluded his remarks in an under voice, to a fat-headed old gentleman next him, who was silently engaged in the discussion of a huge plateful of turkey.*

The table was literally loaded with good cheer, and presented an epitome of country abundance, in this season of overflowing larders. A distinguished post was allotted to "ancient sirloin," as mine host termed it; being, as he added, "the standard of old English hospitality, and a joint of goodly presence, and full of expectation." There were several dishes quaintly decorated, and which had evidently something traditional in their embellishments; but about which, as I did not like to appear over-curious, I asked no questions.

* The old ceremony of serving up the boar's head on Christmas day is still observed in the hall of Queen's College, Oxford. I was favored by the parson with a copy of the carol as now sung, and as it may be acceptable to such of my readers as are curious in these grave and learned matters, I give it entire.

> The boar's head in hand bear I,
> Bedeck'd with bays and rosemary;
> And I pray you, my masters, be merry
>   Quot estis in convivio.
>   Caput apri defero,
>   Reddens laudes domino.
>
> The boar's head, as I understand,
> Is the rarest dish in all this land,
> Which thus bedeck'd with a gay garland
>   Let us servire cantico.
>   Caput apri defero, etc.
>
> Our steward hath provided this
> In honour of the King of Bliss,
> Which on this day to be served is
>   In Reginensi Atrio.
>   Caput apri defero,
>   etc., etc., etc.

I could not, however, but notice a pie, magnificently decorated with peacock's feathers, in imitation of the tail of that bird, which overshadowed a considerable tract of the table. This, the squire confessed, with some little hesitation, was a pheasant pie, though a peacock pie was certainly the most authentical; but there had been such a mortality among the peacocks this season, that he could not prevail upon himself to have one killed.*

It would be tedious, perhaps, to my wiser readers, who may not have that foolish fondness for odd and obsolete things to which I am a little given, were I to mention the other makeshifts of this worthy old humorist, by which he was endeavouring to follow up, though at humble distance, the quaint customs of antiquity. I was pleased, however, to see the respect shown to his whims by his children and relatives; who, indeed, entered readily into the full spirit of them, and seemed all well versed in their parts; having doubtless been present at many a rehearsal. I was amused, too, at the air of profound gravity with which the butler and other servants executed the duties assigned them, however eccentric. They had an old-fashioned look; having, for the most part, been brought up in the household, and grown into keeping with the antiquated mansion, and the humours of its lord; and most probably looked upon all his whimsical regulations as the established laws of honourable housekeeping.

When the cloth was removed, the butler brought in a huge silver vessel of rare and curious workmanship, which he placed before the squire. Its appearance was hailed with acclamation; being the Wassail Bowl, so renowned in Christmas festivity. The contents had been prepared by the squire himself; for it was a beverage in the skilful mixture of which he particularly prided himself: alleging that it was too abstruse and complex for the comprehension of an ordinary servant. It

* The peacock was anciently in great demand for stately entertainments. Sometimes it was made into a pie, at one end of which the head appeared above the crust in all its plumage, with the beak richly gilt; at the other end the tail was displayed. Such pies were served up at the solemn banquets of chivalry, when knights-errant pledged themselves to undertake any perilous enterprise, whence came the ancient oath, used by Justice Shallow, "by cock and pie."

The peacock was also an important dish for the Christmas feast; and Massinger, in his "City Madam," gives some idea of the extravagance with which this, as well as other dishes, was prepared for the gorgeous revels of the olden times:

"Men may talk of Country Christmasses,
Their thirty pound butter'd eggs, their pies of carps' tongues;
Their pheasants drench'd with ambergris; the carcases of three fat wethers
bruised for gravy to make sauce for a single peacock."

was a potation, indeed, that might well make the heart of a toper leap within him; being composed of the richest and raciest wines, highly spiced and sweetened, with roasted apples bobbing about the surface.*

The old gentleman's whole countenance beamed with a serene look of indwelling delight, as he stirred this mighty bowl. Having raised it to his lips, with a hearty wish of a merry Christmas to all present, he sent it brimming round the board, for every one to follow his example, according to the primitive style; pronouncing it "the ancient fountain of good feeling, where all hearts met together."†

There was much laughing and rallying as the honest emblem of Christmas joviality circulated, and was kissed rather coyly by the ladies. When it reached Master Simon, he raised it in both hands, and with the air of a boon companion struck up an old Wassail chanson.

> *The brown bowle,*
> *The merry brown bowle,*
> *As it goes round about-a,*
> *Fill*
> *Still,*
> *Let the world say what it will,*
> *And drink your fill all out-a.*
>
> *The deep canne,*
> *The merry deep canne,*

* The Wassail Bowl was sometimes composed of ale instead of wine; with nutmeg, sugar, toast, ginger, and roasted crabs; in this way the nut-brown beverage is still prepared in some old families, and round the hearths of substantial farmers at Christmas. It is also called Lamb's Wool, and is celebrated by Herrick in his "Twelfth Night":

> Next crowne the bowle full
> With gentle Lamb's Wool;
> Add sugar, nutmeg, and ginger
> With store of ale too;
> And thus ye must doe
> To make the Wassaile a swinger.

† "The custom of drinking out of the same cup gave place to each having his cup. When the steward came to the doore with the Wassel, he was to cry three times, Wassel, Wassel, Wassel, and then the chappell (chaplein) was to answer with a song."—ARCHÆOLOGIA

As thou dost freely quaff-a,
Sing
Fling,
Be as merry as a king,
And sound a lusty laugh-a.*

Much of the conversation during dinner turned upon family topics, to which I was a stranger. There was, however, a great deal of rallying of Master Simon about some gay widow, with whom he was accused of having a flirtation. This attack was commenced by the ladies; but it was continued throughout the dinner by the fat-headed old gentleman next the parson, with the persevering assiduity of a slow hound; being one of those long-winded jokers, who, though rather dull at starting game, are unrivalled for their talents in hunting it down. At every pause in the general conversation, he renewed his bantering in pretty much the same terms; winking hard at me with both eyes, whenever he gave Master Simon what he considered a home thrust. The latter, indeed, seemed fond of being teased on the subject, as old bachelors are apt to be; and he took occasion to inform me, in an under-tone, that the lady in question was a prodigiously fine woman, and drove her own curricle.

The dinner-time passed away in this flow of innocent hilarity, and, though the old hall may have resounded in its time with many a scene of broader rout and revel, yet I doubt whether it ever witnessed more honest and genuine enjoyment. How easy it is for one benevolent being to diffuse pleasure around him; and how truly is a kind heart a fountain of gladness, making everything in its vicinity to freshen into smiles! The joyous disposition of the worthy squire was perfectly contagious; he was happy himself, and disposed to make all the world happy; and the little eccentricities of his humour did but season, in a manner, the sweetness of his philanthropy.

When the ladies had retired, the conversation, as usual, became still more animated; many good things were broached which had been thought of during dinner, but which would not exactly do for a lady's ear; and though I cannot positively affirm that there was much wit uttered, yet I have certainly heard many contests of rare wit produce much less laughter. Wit, after all, is a mighty tart, pungent ingredient, and much too acid for some stomachs; but honest good

* From Poor Robin's Almanac.

humour is the oil and wine of a merry meeting, and there is no jovial companionship equal to that where the jokes are rather small, and the laughter abundant.

The squire told several long stories of early college pranks and adventures, in some of which the parson had been a sharer; though in looking at the latter, it required some effort of imagination to figure such a little, dark anatomy of a man into the perpetrator of a madcap gambol. Indeed, the two college chums presented pictures of what men may be made by their different lots in life. The squire had left the university to lie lustily on his paternal domains, in the vigorous enjoyment of prosperity and sunshine, and had flourished on to a hearty and florid old age; whilst the poor parson, on the contrary, had dried and withered away, among dusty tomes, in the silence and shadows of his study. Still there seemed to be a spark of almost extinguished fire, feebly glimmering in the bottom of his soul; and as the squire hinted at a sly story of the parson and a pretty milkmaid, whom they once met on the banks of the Isis, the old gentleman made an "alphabet of faces," which as far as I could decipher his physiognomy, I verily believe was indicative of laughter; indeed, I have rarely met with an old gentleman that took absolute offence at the imputed gallantries of his youth.

I found the tide of wine and wassail fast gaining on the dry land of sober judgment. The company grew merrier and louder as their jokes grew duller. Master Simon was in as chirping a humour as a grasshopper filled with dew; his old songs grew of a warmer complexion, and he began to talk maudlin about the widow. He even gave a long song about the wooing of a widow, which he informed me he had gathered from an excellent black-letter work, entitled "Cupid's Solicitor for Love," containing a store of good advice for bachelors, and which he promised to lend me: the first verse was to this effect:

> He that will woo a widow must not dally,
>   He must make hay while the sun doth shine.
> He must not stand with her, shall I, shall I,
>   But boldly say, Widow, thou must be mine.

This song inspired the fat-headed old gentleman, who made several attempts to tell a rather broad story out of Joe Miller, that was pat to the purpose; but he always stuck in the middle, everybody recollecting the latter part excepting himself. The parson, too, began to show the effects of good cheer, having gradually settled down into a doze, and his wig sitting most suspiciously on one side. Just at this juncture we were summoned to the drawing-room, and, I suspect at the private instigation of mine host, whose joviality seemed always tempered with a proper love of decorum.

After the dinner-table was removed, the hall was given up to the younger members of the family, who, prompted to all kind of noisy mirth by the Oxonian and Master Simon, made its old walls ring with their merriment, as they played at romping games. I delight in witnessing the gambols of children, and particularly at this happy holiday season, and could not help stealing out of the drawing room on hearing one of their peals of laughter. I found them at the game of blindman's-buff. Master Simon, who was the leader of their revels, and seemed on all occasions to fulfil the office of that ancient potentate, the Lord of Misrule,* was blinded in the midst of the hall. The little beings were as busy about him as the mock fairies about Falstaff; pinching him, plucking at the skirts of his coat, and tickling him with straws. One fine blue-eyed girl of about thirteen, with her flaxen hair all in beautiful confusion, her frolic face in a glow, her frock half torn off her shoulders, a complete picture of a romp, was the chief tormentor; and, from the slyness with which Master Simon avoided the smaller game, and hemmed this wild little nymph in corners, and obliged her to jump shrieking over chairs, I suspected the rogue of being not a whit more blinded than was convenient.

When I returned to the drawing-room, I found the company seated round the fire, listening to the parson, who was deeply ensconced in a high-backed oaken chair, the work of some cunning artificer of yore, which had been brought from the library for his particular accommodation. From this venerable piece of furniture, with which his shadowy figure and dark, weazen face so admirably accorded, he was dealing out strange accounts of the popular superstitions and legends of the surrounding country, with which he had become acquainted in the course of his antiquarian researches. I am half inclined to think that the old gentleman was himself somewhat tinctured with superstition, as men are very apt to be who live a recluse and studious life in a sequestered part of the country, and pore over black-letter tracts, so

* "At Christmasse there was in the Kinge's house, wheresoever hee was lodged, a lorde of misrule, or mayster of merie disportes, and the like had ye in the house of every nobleman of honour, or good worshippe, were he spirituall or temporall." —STOWE

often filled with the marvellous and supernatural. He gave us several anecdotes of the fancies of the neighbouring peasantry, concerning the effigy of the crusader, which lay on the tomb by the church altar. As it was the only monument of the kind in that part of the country, it had always been regarded with feelings of superstition by the good wives of the village. It was said to get up from the tomb and walk the rounds of the churchyard in stormy nights, particularly when it thundered; and one old woman, whose cottage bordered on the churchyard, had seen it through the windows of the church, when the moon shone, slowly pacing up and down the aisles. It was the belief that some wrong had been left unredressed by the deceased, or some treasure hidden, which kept the spirit in a state of trouble and restlessness. Some talked of gold and jewels buried in the tomb, over which the spectre kept watch; and there was a story current of a sexton in old times, who endeavoured to break his way to the coffin at night, but, just as he reached it, received a violent blow from the marble hand of the effigy, which stretched him senseless on the pavement. These tales were often laughed at by some of the sturdier among the rustics, yet, when night came on, there were many of the stoutest unbelievers that were shy of venturing alone in the foot-path that led across the churchyard.

From these and other anecdotes that followed, the crusader appeared to be the favourite hero of ghost stories throughout the vicinity. His picture, which hung up in the hall, was thought by the servants to have something supernatural about it; for they remarked that, in whatever part of the hall you went, the eyes of the warrior were still fixed on you. The old porter's wife, too, at the lodge, who had been born and brought up in the family, and was a great gossip among the maid-servants, affirmed, that in her young days she had often heard say, that on Midsummer eve, when it was well known all kinds of ghosts, goblins, and fairies become visible and walk abroad, the crusader used to mount his horse, come down from his picture, ride about the house, down the avenue, and so to the church to visit the tomb; on which occasion the church door most civilly swung open of itself; not that he needed it; for he rode through closed gates and even stone walls, and had been seen by one of the dairy maids to pass between two bars of the great park gate, making himself as thin as a sheet of paper.

All these superstitions, I found had been very much countenanced by the squire, who, though not superstitious himself, was very fond of seeing others so. He listened to every goblin tale of the neighbouring gossips with infinite gravity, and held the porter's wife in high favour on account of her talent for the marvellous. He was himself a great reader of old legends and romances, and often lamented that he could not believe in them; for a superstitious person, he thought, must live in a kind of fairy land.

Whilst we were all attention to the parson's stories, our ears were suddenly assailed by a burst of heterogeneous sounds from the hall, in which were mingled something like the clang of rude minstrelsy, with the uproar of many small voices and girlish laughter. The door suddenly flew open, and a train came trooping into the room, that might almost have been mistaken for the breaking up of the court of Fairy. That indefatigable spirit, Master Simon, in the faithful discharge of his duties as Lord of Misrule, had conceived the idea of a Christmas mummery or masking; and having called in to his assistance the Oxonian and the young officer, who were equally ripe for anything that should occasion romping and merriment, they had carried it into instant effect. The old housekeeper had been consulted; the antique clothes-presses and wardrobes rummaged, and made to yield up the relics of finery that had not seen the light for several generations; the younger part of the company had been privately convened from the parlour and hall, and the whole had been bedizened out, into a burlesque imitation of an antique mask.*

Master Simon led the van, as "Ancient Christmas," quaintly apparelled in a ruff, a short cloak, which had very much the aspect of one of the old housekeeper's petticoats, and a hat that might have served for a village steeple, and must indubitably have figured in the days of the Covenanters. From under this his nose curved boldly forth, flushed with a frost-bitten bloom, that seemed the very trophy of a December blast. He was accompanied by the blue-eyed romp, dished up as "Dame Mince Pie," in the venerable magnificence of a faded brocade, long stomacher, peaked hat, and high-heeled shoes. The young officer appeared as Robin Hood, in a sporting dress of Kendal green, and a foraging cap with a gold tassel.

The costume, to be sure, did not bear testimony to deep research, and there was an evident eye to the picturesque, natural to a young

* Maskings or mummeries were favourite sports at Christmas in old times; and the wardrobes at halls and manor-houses were often laid under contribution to furnish dresses and fantastic disguisings. I strongly suspect Master Simon to have taken the idea of his from Ben Jonson's "Masque of Christmas."

gallant in the presence of his mistress. The fair Julia hung on his arm in a pretty rustic dress as "Maid Marian." The rest of the train had been metamorphosed in various ways; the girls trussed up in the finery of the ancient belles of the Bracebridge line, and the striplings bewhiskered with burnt cork, and gravely clad in broad skirts, hanging sleeves, and full-bottomed wigs, to represent the character of Roast Beef, Plum Pudding, and other worthies celebrated in ancient maskings. The whole was under the control of the Oxonian, in the appropriate character of Misrule; and I observed that he exercised rather a mischievous sway with his wand over the smaller personages of the pageant.

The irruption of this motley crew, with beat of drum, according to ancient custom, was the consummation of uproar and merriment. Master Simon covered himself with glory by the stateliness with which, as Ancient Christmas, he walked a minuet with the peerless, though giggling, Dame Mince Pie. It was followed by a dance of all the characters, which from its medley of costumes, seemed as though the old family portraits had skipped down from their frames to join in the sport. Different centuries were figuring at cross hands and right and left; the dark ages were cutting pirouettes and rigadoons; and the days of Queen Bess jigging merrily down the middle, through a line of succeeding generations.

The worthy squire contemplated these fantastic sports, and this resurrection of his old wardrobe, with the simple relish of childish delight. He stood chuckling and rubbing his hands, and scarcely hearing a word the parson said, notwithstanding that the latter was discoursing most authentically on the ancient and stately dance at the Paon, or peacock, from which he conceived the minuet to be derived.* For my part, I was in a continual excitement from the varied scenes of whim and innocent gayety passing before me. It was inspiring to see wild-eyed frolic and warm-hearted hospitality breaking out from among the chills and glooms of winter, and old age throwing off his apathy, and catching once more the freshness of youthful enjoyment. I felt also an interest in the scene, from the consideration that these fleeting customs were posting fast into oblivion, and that this was,

---

* Sir John Hawkins, speaking of the dance called the Pavon, from pavo, a peacock, says, "It is a grave and majestic dance; the method of dancing it anciently was by gentlemen dressed with caps and swords, by those of the long robe in their gowns, by the peers in their mantles, and by the ladies in gowns with long trains, the motion whereof, in dancing, resembled that of a peacock."—HISTORY OF MUSIC

perhaps, the only family in England in which the whole of them was still punctiliously observed. There was a quaintness, too, mingled with all this revelry, that gave it a peculiar zest: it was suited to the time and place; and as the old manor-house almost reeled with mirth and wassail, it seemed echoing back the joviality of long departed years.*

But enough of Christmas and its gambols; it is time for me to pause in this garrulity. Methinks I hear the questions asked by my graver readers, "To what purpose is all this—how is the world to be made wiser by this talk?" Alas! is there not wisdom enough extant for the instruction of the world? And if not, are there not thousands of abler pens labouring for its improvement? It is so much pleasanter to please than to instruct—to play the companion rather than the preceptor.

What, after all, is the mite of wisdom that I could throw into the mass of knowledge; or how am I sure that my sagest deductions may be safe guides for the opinions of others? But in writing to amuse, if I fail, the only evil is in my own disappointment. If, however, I can by any lucky chance, in these days of evil, rub out one wrinkle from the brow of care, or beguile the heavy heart of one moment of sorrow; if I can now and then penetrate through the gathering film of misanthropy, prompt a benevolent view of human nature, and make my reader more in good humour with his fellow-beings and himself, surely, surely, I shall not then have written entirely in vain.

* At the time of the first publication of this paper, the picture of an old-fashioned Christmas in the country was pronounced by some as out of date. The author had afterwards an opportunity of witnessing almost all the customs above described, existing in unexpected vigour in the skirts of Derbyshire and Yorkshire, where he passed the Christmas holidays. The reader will find some notice of them in the author's account of his sojourn at Newstead Abbey.

THE LITTLE BOY AT CHRIST'S CHRISTMAS TREE

by Feodor Dostoyevsky

from *The Little Boy at Christ's Christmas Tree*

A boy still very small, six years old or even less, awoke in the morning in a damp cold cellar. He was dressed in a sort of little long coat, and he shivered. His breath flew away in white steam, and as he sat on a chest in the corner, out of boredom he purposely blew this steam from his mouth, and amused himself by watching how it flew away. But he was very hungry. Several times since morning he had gone up to the cot where his sick mother lay on a mattress thin as a pancake, with a sort of bundle under her head instead of a pillow. How did she feel now? Apparently she had come with her little boy from a strange city and suddenly fallen ill. The tenants of the corners had scattered, for it was a festival, and the only remaining person, dressed in a long coat, had already lain dead-drunk for whole days, without waiting for the holiday. In another corner of the room lay groaning with rheumatism a certain little old woman of eighty, who had lived sometime and somewhere as a nurse, but now, as she slowly died in loneliness, sighed and muttered and grumbled at the little boy so that he had already begun to be afraid to go close to her corner.

He had succeeded in getting a drink somewhere in the halls, but he could not find any crusts of bread anywhere, and already for almost the tenth time he went close to waken his mother. He finally felt afraid in the dark; evening had long since come on, and they had not kindled a fire. As he touched his mother's face, he wondered that she did not move, and that she had become just as cold as the wall. "It's already very cold here," he thought and paused a little, unconsciously resting his hand on the shoulder of the dead woman. Then he blew on his fingers to warm them, and suddenly, after reaching for his poor little cap on the cot, very quietly groping his way, he went out of the cellar. He would have gone still sooner, but he was always afraid of the big dog up above on the stairs, which howled all day long by the neighbors' doors. But there wasn't any dog, and he suddenly came out on the street.

Heavens, what a city! Never before had he seen anything like it. Where he has come from, there is such black darkness at night, and only one lamp for the whole street. The low wooden cottages have their shutters closed; scarcely has it grown dark, before there is no one on the street at all, everyone shuts himself up in his house, and only whole troops of dogs howl—hundreds and thousands of them howl and bark all night. But just the same, it was warm there, and they gave him something to eat, while here—heavens, if he only could eat just a little! And what a noise and tumult there is here, what lights, and horses, and carriages, and the frost—the terrible frost! The frozen steam rolls from the heated horses, out of their hot-breathing mouths. Through the brittle snow the horseshoes ring on the pavement, and everyone jostles one another so, and heavens! he is so eager to eat something, even just some little bit of a piece, and suddenly his fingers have begun to hurt so.

Here's another street again—oh, what a broad one! Now he will surely be run over; how the people all shout, run, and rush about, and it is so light, so light! But what is that? Ah, what a great glass! And behind the glass a room, and in the room a tree reaching to the ceiling; that is a Christmas tree, and on the Christmas tree there are so many lights, so many little gold papers and apples, and around it, too, dolls and little horses. Children, dressed up and clean, run about the room, laugh and play, and are eating and drinking something. See, that girl has begun to dance with a boy—such a pretty little girl! The boy looks in, wonders, and even smiles, but his fingers and his feet pain him, and his hands have grown all red, and he cannot bend them any more, and it hurts them to move.

And suddenly the little boy remembered that his fingers ached, and he burst into tears and ran further on; and again he sees through another windowpane a room and again there are trees within, but on the tables there are cakes—all sorts of cakes—almond cakes, red ones and yellow ones, and four rich ladies sit there, and give cakes to whoever comes, and the door opens every moment for many people to go in from the street. The little boy stole up, suddenly opened the door, and went in. My, how they began to cry out and motion to him! One lady came quickly over to him and put a penny in his hand, and herself opened the street door for him. How frightened he was! But the penny just then dropped and clinked down the steps; he could not bend his red fingers and stop it.

The little boy ran off and went away so quickly, so very quickly, but he himself did not know whither. He wants to burst out crying again, but he is afraid, and he runs and runs, and blows on his hands. And sadness comes over him because he suddenly has begun to feel lonely and solitary, and all of a sudden—heavens! what is that now? People are standing in a crowd and wondering; in a window behind the glass, are three dolls, little ones, clad in red and green dresses and just exactly as if they are alive! A sort of little old man sits there and it looks as if he is playing on a big fiddle, the other two stand there and move their little heads in time to the music, and look at each other, and their lips move—indeed they are talking, only you see it can't be heard outside the glass. And at first the boy thought they were alive, but when he discovered they were dolls, all at once he burst out laughing. Never had he seen such dolls, and he did not know there were any like them! He wants to cry, but the dolls are so awfully funny.

Suddenly it seemed to him that behind him someone pulled at his coat; a big bad boy stood beside him, and struck him on the head, tore off his cap, and gave him a kick with his foot. The little boy fell to the ground, people cried out, he fainted; then he sprang up, and ran and ran, and suddenly arrived he knew not where, at a doorstep in a strange courtyard, and he sat down behind the woodpile. "Here they won't find me," he thought, "and it's dark too."

He sat there and hunched himself together, and could not recover from his terror, when suddenly, quite suddenly, he began to feel so comfortable; his hands and feet ceased to ache, and it got so warm; just as warm as on the stove; he trembled all over; oh, but he had only fallen asleep! "I'll sit here awhile, and then go look at the dolls again," thought the little boy, and he smiled as he remembered them; just as if they were alive! And suddenly he thought he heard his mother above him, singing a little song. "Mama, I'm asleep. Oh, how nice it is to sleep here!"

"Let's go to my Christmas tree, little boy," a soft voice above him suddenly whispered.

He thought first that it was his mother all the time, but no, it was not she. Who was it that called him? He does not see, but someone bent over him and embraced him in the darkness, and stretched out his hand to him and . . . and suddenly—oh, what a light! Oh, what a Christmas tree! That can't be a Christmas tree, why, he had never seen any such trees! Where he is now, everything is so bright, everything shines, and there are dolls around everywhere—but no, those are all little boys and girls, only such bright ones—they all crowd around him, fly to him, they all kiss him, and take him and carry him with them, and he even flies himself, and he sees that his mother is looking at him and smiling joyfully.

"Mama, Mama! Oh, how nice it is here, Mama!" the little boy cries to her, and again he kisses the children, and he is eager to tell them quickly about those dolls behind the glass. "Who are you, boys, who are you, girls?" he asks, smiling and loving them.

"This is Christ's Christmas tree," they answered him. "Christ always has a Christmas tree on this day for little children who haven't any tree of their own at home."

And he recognized that all the little boys and girls were just such children as he, but some had frozen to death in the baskets in which they had been abandoned on the doorsteps of Petrograd officials. Others, sent out from the orphanage to be brought up, had been smothered at their Finnish nurses'. Others had died at the dried-up breasts of their mothers during the Samara famine. Still more had choked with the stench in third-class cars. But now all of them are here, all are here like angels, all are with Christ, and he himself is among them, and stretches out his hands to them, and blesses them and their mothers. But the mothers of these children all stand there at one side, and weep; each one recognizes her little boy or girl, and the children fly to them and kiss them, and wipe away the tears with their little hands, and beg them not to weep, because they are so happy here. . . .

But below, in the morning, the doormen found behind the wood-pile the little body of the boy who had run away and frozen to death.

CHRISTMAS EVERY DAY

by William Dean Howells

from *Christmas Every Day and Other Stories Told for Children*

The little girl came into her papa's study, as she always did Saturday morning before breakfast, and asked for a story. He tried to beg off that morning, for he was very busy, but she would not let him. So he began:

"Well, once there was a little pig—"

She put her hand over his mouth and stopped him at the word. She said she had heard little pig-stories till she was perfectly sick of them.

"Well, what kind of story *shall* I tell, then?"

"About Christmas. It's getting to be the season. It's past Thanksgiving already."

"It seems to me," her papa argued, "that I've told as often about Christmas as I have about little pigs."

"No difference! Christmas is more interesting."

"Well!" Her papa roused himself from his writing by a great effort.

"Well, then, I'll tell you about the little girl that wanted it Christmas every day in the year. How would you like that?"

"First-rate!" said the little girl; and she nestled into comfortable shape in his lap, ready for listening.

"Very well, then, this little pig— Oh, what are you pounding me for?"

"Because you said little pig instead of little girl."

"I should like to know what's the difference between a little pig and a little girl that wanted it Christmas every day!"

"Papa," said the little girl, warningly, "if you don't go on, I'll *give* it to you!" And at this her papa darted off like lightning, and began to tell the story as fast as he could.

Well, once there was a little girl who liked Christmas so much that she wanted it to be Christmas every day in the year; and as soon as Thanksgiving was over she began to send postal-cards to the old Christmas Fairy to ask if she mightn't have it. But the old Fairy never answered any of the postals; and after a while the little girl found out that the Fairy was pretty particular, and wouldn't notice anything but letters—not even correspondence cards in envelopes; but real letters on sheets of paper, and sealed outside with a mono-gram—or your initial, anyway. So, then, she began to send her letters; and in about three weeks—or just the day before Christmas, it was —she got a letter from the Fairy, saying she might have it Christmas every day for a year, and then they would see about having it longer.

The little girl was a good deal excited already, preparing for the old-fashioned, once-a-year Christmas that was coming the next day, and perhaps the Fairy's promise didn't make such an impression on her as it would have made at some other time. She just resolved to keep it to herself, and surprise everybody with it as it kept coming true; and then it slipped out of her mind altogether.

She had a splendid Christmas. She went to bed early, so as to let Santa Claus have a chance at the stockings, and in the morning she was up the first of anybody and went and felt them, and found hers all lumpy with packages of candy, and oranges and grapes, and pocket-books and rubber balls, and all kinds of small presents, and her big brother's with nothing but the tongs in them, and her young lady sister's with a new silk umbrella, and her papa's and mamma's with potatoes and pieces of coal wrapped up in tissue-paper, just as they always had every Christmas. Then she waited around till the rest of the family were up, and she was the first to burst into the library, when the doors were opened, and look at the large presents laid out on the library-table—books, and portfolios, and boxes of stationery, and breastpins, and dolls, and little stoves, and dozens of handkerchiefs, and inkstands, and skates, and snow-shovels, and photograph-frames, and little easels, and boxes of water-colors, and Turkish paste, and nougat, and candied cherries, and dolls' houses, and waterproofs—and the big Christmas-tree, lighted and standing in a waste-basket in the middle.

She had a splendid Christmas all day. She ate so much candy that she did not want any breakfast; and the whole forenoon the presents kept pouring in that the expressman had not had time to deliver the night before; and she went round giving the presents she had got for other people, and came home and ate turkey and cranberry for dinner, and plum-pudding and nuts and raisins and oranges and more candy, and then went out and coasted, and came in with a stomach-ache, crying; and her papa said he would see if his house was turned into that sort of fool's paradise another year; and they had a light supper, and pretty early everybody went to bed cross.

Here the little girl pounded her papa in the back, again.
"Well, what now? Did I say pigs?"
"You made them *act* like pigs."
"Well, didn't they?"
"No matter; you oughtn't to put it into a story."
"Very well, then, I'll take it all out."
Her father went on:

The little girl slept very heavily, and she slept very late, but she was wakened at last by the other children dancing round her bed with their stockings full of presents in their hands.
"What is it?" said the little girl, and she rubbed her eyes and tried to rise up in bed.
"Christmas! Christmas! Christmas!" they all shouted, and waved their stockings.
"Nonsense! It was Christmas yesterday."
Her brothers and sisters just laughed. "We don't know about that. It's Christmas to-day, anyway. You come into the library and see."
Then all at once it flashed on the little girl that the Fairy was keeping her promise, and her year of Christmases was beginning. She was

dreadfully sleepy, but she sprang up like a lark—a lark that had over-eaten itself and gone to bed cross—and darted into the library. There it was again! Books, and portfolios, and boxes of stationery, and breastpins—

"You needn't go over it all, papa; I guess I can remember just what was there," said the little girl.

Well, and there was the Christmas-tree blazing away, and the family picking out their presents, but looking pretty sleepy, and her father perfectly puzzled, and her mother ready to cry. "I'm sure I don't see how I'm to dispose of all these things," said her mother, and her father said it seemed to him they had had something just like it the day before, but he supposed he must have dreamed it. This struck the little girl as the best kind of a joke; and so she ate so much candy she didn't want any breakfast, and went round carrying presents, and had turkey and cranberry for dinner, and then went out and coasted, and came in with a—

"Papa!"
"Well, what now?"
"What did you promise, you forgetful thing?"
"Oh! oh yes!"

Well, the next day, it was just the same thing over again, but everybody getting crosser; and at the end of a week's time so many people had lost their tempers that you could pick up lost tempers anywhere; they perfectly strewed the ground. Even when people tried to recover their tempers they usually got somebody else's, and it made the most dreadful mix.

The little girl began to get frightened, keeping the secret all to herself; she wanted to tell her mother, but she didn't dare to; and she was ashamed to ask the Fairy to take back her gift, it seemed ungrateful and ill-bred, and she thought she would try to stand it, but she hardly knew how she could, for a whole year. So it went on and on, and it was Christmas on St. Valentine's Day and Washington's Birthday, just the same as any day, and it didn't skip even the First of April, though everything was counterfeit that day, and that was some *little* relief.

After a while coal and potatoes began to be awfully scarce, so many had been wrapped up in tissue-paper to fool papas and mammas with. Turkeys got to be about a thousand dollars apiece—

"Papa!"

"Well, what?"

"You're beginning to fib."

"Well, *two* thousand, then."

And they got to passing off almost anything for turkeys—half-grown humming-birds, and even rocs out of the *Arabian Nights*—the real turkeys were so scarce. And cranberries—well, they asked a diamond apiece for cranberries. All the woods and orchards were cut down for Christmas-trees, and where the woods and orchards used to be it looked just like a stubble-field, with the stumps. After a while they had to make Christmas-trees out of rags, and stuff them with bran, like old-fashioned dolls; but there were plenty of rags, because people got so poor, buying presents for one another, that they couldn't get any new clothes, and they just wore their old ones to tatters. They got so poor that everybody had to go to the poor-house, except the confectioners, and the fancy-store keepers, and the picture-book sellers, and the expressmen; and *they* all got so rich and proud that they would hardly wait upon a person when he came to buy. It was perfectly shameful!

Well, after it had gone on about three or four months, the little girl, whenever she came into the room in the morning and saw those great ugly, lumpy stockings dangling at the fireplace, and the disgusting presents around everywhere, used to just sit down and burst out crying. In six months she was perfectly exhausted; she couldn't even cry any more; she just lay on the lounge and rolled her eyes and panted. About the beginning of October she took to sitting down on dolls wherever she found them—French dolls, or any kind—she hated the sight of them so; and by Thanksgiving she was crazy, and just slammed her presents across the room.

By that time people didn't carry presents around nicely any more. They flung them over the fence, or through the window, or anything; and, instead of running their tongues out and taking great pains to write "For dear Papa," or "Mamma," or "Brother," or "Sister," or "Susie," or "Sammie," or "Billie," or "Bobbie," or "Jimmie," or "Jennie," or whoever it was, and troubling to get the spelling right, and then signing their names, and "Xmas, 18—," they used to write in the gift-books, "Take it, you horrid old thing!" and then go and bang it against the front door. Nearly everybody had built barns to hold their presents, but pretty soon the barns overflowed, and then they used to let them lie out in the rain, or anywhere. Sometimes the police used to come and tell them to shovel their presents off the sidewalk, or they would arrest them.

"I thought you said everybody had gone to the poor-house," interrupted the little girl.

"They did go, at first," said her papa; "but after a while the poor-houses got so full that they had to send the people back to their own houses. They tried to cry, when they got back, but they couldn't make the least sound."

"Why couldn't they?"

"Because they had lost their voices, saying 'Merry Christmas' so much. Did I tell you how it was on the Fourth of July?"

"No; how was it?" And the little girl nestled closer, in expectation of something uncommon.

Well, the night before, the boys stayed up to celebrate, as they always do, and fell asleep before twelve o'clock, as usual, expecting to be wakened by the bells and cannon. But it was nearly eight o'clock before the first boy in the United States woke up, and then he found out what the trouble was. As soon as he could get his clothes on he ran out of the house and smashed a big cannon-torpedo down on the pavement; but it didn't make any more noise than a damp wad of paper; and after he tried about twenty or thirty more, he began to pick them up and look at them. Every single torpedo was a big raisin! Then he just streaked it upstairs, and examined his firecrackers and toy pistol and two-dollar collection of fireworks, and found that they were nothing but sugar and candy painted up to look like fireworks! Before ten o'clock every boy in the United States found out that his Fourth of July things had turned into Christmas things; and then they just sat down and cried—they were so mad. There are about twenty million boys in the United States, and so you can imagine what a noise they made. Some men got together before night, with a little powder that hadn't turned into purple sugar yet, and they said they would fire off *one* cannon, anyway. But the cannon burst into a thousand pieces, for it was nothing but rock-candy, and some of the men nearly got killed. The Fourth of July orations all turned into Christmas carols, and when anybody tried to read the Declaration, instead of saying, "When in the course of human events it becomes necessary," he was sure to sing, "God rest you, merry gentlemen." It was perfectly awful.

The little girl drew a deep sigh of satisfaction.

"And how was it at Thanksgiving?"

Her papa hesitated. "Well, I'm almost afraid to tell you. I'm afraid you'll think it's wicked."

"Well, tell, anyway," said the little girl.

Well, before it came Thanksgiving it had leaked out who had caused all these Christmases. The little girl had suffered so much that she had talked about it in her sleep; and after that hardly anybody would play with her. People just perfectly despised her, because if it had not been for her greediness it wouldn't have happened; and now, when it came Thanksgiving, and she wanted them to go to church, and have squash-pie and turkey, and show their gratitude, they said that all the turkeys had been eaten up for her old Christmas dinners, and if she would stop the Christmases, they would see about the gratitude. Wasn't it dreadful? And the very next day the little girl began to send letters to the Christmas Fairy, and then telegrams, to stop it. But it didn't do any good; and then she got to calling at the Fairy's house, but the girl that came to the door always said, "Not at home," or "Engaged," or "At dinner," or something like that; and so it went on till it came to the old once-a-year Christmas Eve. The little girl fell asleep, and when she woke up in the morning—

"She found it was all nothing but a dream," suggested the little girl.

"No, indeed!" said her papa. "It was all every bit true!"

"Well, what *did* she find out, then?"

"Why, that it wasn't Christmas at last, and wasn't ever going to be, any more. Now it's time for breakfast."

The little girl held her papa fast around the neck.

"You sha'n't go if you're going to leave it *so!*"

"How do you want it left?"

"Christmas once a year."

"All right," said her papa; and he went on again.

Well, there was the greatest rejoicing all over the country, and it extended clear up into Canada. The people met together everywhere, and kissed and cried for joy. The city carts went around and gathered up all the candy and raisins and nuts, and dumped them into the river; and it made the fish perfectly sick; and the whole United States, as far out as Alaska, was one blaze of bonfires, where the children were burning up their gift-books and presents of all kinds. They had the greatest *time!*

The little girl went to thank the old Fairy because she had stopped its being Christmas, and she said she hoped she would keep her promise and see that Christmas never, never came again. Then the Fairy frowned, and asked her if she was sure she knew what she meant; and the little girl asked her, Why not? and the old Fairy said that now she was behaving just as greedily as ever, and she'd better look out. This made the little girl think it all over carefully again, and she said she would be willing to have it Christmas about once in a thousand years; and then she said a hundred, and then she said ten, and at last she got down to one. Then the Fairy said that was the good old way that had pleased people ever since Christmas began, and she was agreed. Then the little girl said, "What're your shoes made of?" And the Fairy said, "Leather." And the little girl said, "Bargain's done forever," and skipped off, and hippity-hopped the whole way home, she was so glad.

"How will that do?" asked the papa.

"First-rate!" said the little girl; but she hated to have the story stop, and was rather sober.

However, her mamma put her head in at the door, and asked her papa, "Are you never coming to breakfast? What have you been telling that child?"

"Oh, just a moral tale."

The little girl caught him around the neck again.

"We know! Don't you tell *what*, papa! Don't you tell *what!*"

CHRISTMAS
IN THE OLDEN TIME

by Sir Walter Scott

from *Christmas in the Olden Time*

Heap on more wood! The wind is chill;
But let it whistle as it will,
We'll keep our Christmas merry still.
Each age has deemed the new-born year
The fittest time for festal cheer.
And well our Christian sires of old
Loved when the year its course had rolled,
And brought blithe Christmas back again,
With all his hospitable train.
Domestic and religious rite
Gave honor to the holy night:
On Christmas eve the bells were rung;
On Christmas eve the mass was sung;
That only night, in all the year,
Saw the stoled priest the chalice rear.

The damsel donned her kirtle sheen;
The hall was dressed with holly green;
Forth to the wood did merry-men go,
To gather in the mistletoe.
Then opened wide the baron's hall
To vassal, tenant, serf, and all;
Power laid his rod of rule aside,
And Ceremony doffed his pride.
The heir, with roses in his shoes,
That night might village partner choose;
The lord, underogating, share
The vulgar game of "post and pair."
All hailed, with uncontrolled delight,
And general voice, the happy night,
That to the cottage, as the crown,
Brought tidings of salvation down.
The fire, with well-dried logs supplied,
Went roaring up the chimney wide;
The huge hall table's oaken face,
Scrubbed till it shone the day to grace,
Bore then upon its massive board
No mark to part the squire and lord.
Then was brought in the lusty brawn
By old blue-coated serving-man;
Then the grim boar's-head frowned on high,
Crested with bays and rosemary.
Well can the green-garbed ranger tell,
How, when, and where the monster fell;
What dogs before his death he tore,
And all the baiting of the boar.
The wassail round in good brown bowls,
Garnished with ribbons, blithely trowls.
There the huge sirloin reeked; hard by
Plum-porridge stood, and Christmas pie;
Nor failed old Scotland to produce,
At such high tide, her savory goose.
Then came the merry masquers in,
And carols roared with blithesome din;
If unmelodious was the song,
It was a hearty note, and strong.

Who lists may in their mumming see
Traces of ancient mystery;
White shirts supplied the masquerade,
And smutted cheeks the visors made;
But, oh! what masquers richly dight
Can boast of bosoms half so light!
England was merry England, when
Old Christmas brought his sports again.
'Twas Christmas broached the mightiest ale,
'Twas Christmas told the merriest tale;
A Christmas gambol oft could cheer
The poor man's heart through half the year.

THE LOUIS-d'OR

from the French of François Coppée

from Christmas Stories from French and Spanish Writers
by Antoinette Ogden

When Lucien de Hem saw his last bill for a hundred francs clawed by the banker's rake, when he rose from the roulette table where he had just lost the debris of his little fortune scraped together for this supreme battle, he experienced something like vertigo, and thought that he should fall. His brain was muddled; his legs were limp and trembling. He threw himself upon the leather lounge that circumscribed the gambling table. For a few moments he mechanically followed the clandestine proceedings of that hell in which he had sullied the best years of his youth, recognized the worn profiles of the gamblers under the merciless glare of the three great shadeless lamps, listened to the clicking and the sliding of the gold over the felt, realized that he was bankrupt, lost, remembered that in the top drawer of his dressing table lay a pair of pistols—the very pistols of which General de Hem, his father, had made noble use at the attack of Zaatcha; then, overcome by exhaustion, he sank into a heavy sleep.

When he awoke, his mouth was clammy, and his tongue stuck to his palate. He realized by a hasty glance at the clock that he had scarcely slept a half hour, and he felt the imperious necessity of going out to get a breath of the fresh night air. The hands on the dial pointed exactly to a quarter of twelve. As he rose and stretched his arms it occurred to him that it was Christmas Eve, and by one of those ironical freaks of the memory, he felt as though he were once more a child, ready to stand his little boot on the hearth before going to bed. Just then old Dronski, one of the pillars of the trade, the traditional Pole, wrapped in the greasy worn cloak adorned with frogs and passementerie, came up to Lucien muttering something behind his dirty grayish beard.

"Lend me five francs, will you, monsieur? I haven't stirred from this place for two days, and for two whole days seventeen hasn't come out once. You may laugh at me all you like, but I'll bet you my fist that when the clock strikes twelve, seventeen will be the winning number."

Lucien de Hem shrugged his shoulders; and fumbling through his pockets, he found that he had not even money enough to comply with that feature of gambling etiquette known among the frequenters of the establishment as "the Pole's hundred cents." He passed into the antechamber, put on his hat and cloak, and disappeared down the narrow stairway with the agility of people who have a fever. During the four hours which Lucien had spent in the den it had snowed heavily, and the street, one of those narrow wedges between two rows of high buildings in the very heart of Paris, was intensely white. Above, in the calm blue-black of the sky, cold stars glittered. The exhausted gambler shivered under his furs and hurried along with a blank despair in his heart, thinking of the pistols that awaited him in the top drawer of his dressing table. He had not gone a hundred feet when he stopped suddenly before a heart-rending spectacle.

On a stone bench, near the monumental doorway of a wealthy residence, sat a little girl six or seven years old, barely covered by a ragged black gown. She had fallen asleep there in spite of the bitter cold, her body bent forward in a pitiful posture of resigned exhaustion. Her poor little head and her dainty shoulder had molded themselves into the angle of the freezing wall. One of her worn slippers had fallen from her dangling foot and lay in the snow before her. Lucien de Hem mechanically thrust his hand into his vest pocket, but he remembered that he had not even been able to fee the club waiter. He went up to the child, however, impelled by an instinct of pity. He meant, no doubt, to pick her up and take her home with him, to give her shelter for the night, when suddenly he saw something glitter in the little slipper at his feet. He stooped. It was a louis-d'or.

Some charitable soul—a woman, no doubt—had passed there, and at the pathetic sight of that little shoe in the snow had remembered the poetic Christmas legend, and with discreet fingers had dropped a splendid gift, so that the forsaken little one might still believe in the presents of the Child Christ, and might awake with renewed faith in the midst of her misery.

A gold louis! That meant many days of rest and comfort for the little beggar. Lucien was just about to awaken her and surprise her with her good fortune when, in a strange hallucination, he heard a voice in his ear, which whispered with the drawling inflection of the old Pole, "I haven't stirred from this place for two days, and for two whole days seventeen hasn't come out once. I'll bet you my fist that when the clock strikes twelve, seventeen will be the winning number."

Then this youth, who was twenty-three years of age, the descendant of a race of honest men—this youth who bore a great military name, and had never been guilty of an unmanly act—conceived a monstrous thought; an insane desire took possession of him. He looked anxiously up and down the street, and having assured himself that he had no witness, he knelt and, reaching out cautiously with trembling fingers, stole the treasure from the little shoe, then rose with a spring and ran breathlessly down the street. He rushed like a madman up the stairs of the gambling house, flung open the door with his fist, and burst into the room at the first stroke of midnight. He threw the gold piece on the table and cried, "Seventeen!"

Seventeen won. He then pushed the whole pile on the "red." The red won. He left the seventy-two louis on the same color. The red came out again. He doubled the stakes, twice, three times, and always with the same success. Before him was a huge pile of gold and banknotes. He tried the "twelve," the "column"—he worked every combination. His luck was something unheard of, something almost supernatural. One might have believed that the little ivory ball, in its frenzied dance around the table, had been bewitched, magnetized by this feverish gambler, and obeyed his will. With a few bold strokes he had won back the bundle of banknotes which he had lost in the early part of the evening. Then he staked two and three hundred louis at a time, and as his fantastic luck never failed him, he soon won back the whole capital that had constituted his inherited fortune.

In his haste to begin the game he had not even thought of taking off his fur-lined coat, the great pockets of which were now swollen with the rolls of banknotes, and heavy with the weight of the gold. Not knowing where to put the money that was steadily accumulating before him, he stuffed it away in the inside and outside pockets of his coat, his vest, his trousers, in his cigar case, his handkerchief. Everything became a recipient. And still he played and still he won, his brain whirling the while like that of a drunkard or a madman. It was amazing to see him stand there throwing gold on the table by the handful, with that haughty gesture of absolute certainty and disdain. But withal there was a gnawing at his heart, something that felt like a red-hot iron there, and he could not rid himself of the vision of the child asleep in the snow—the child whom he had robbed.

"In just a few minutes," said he, "I will go back to her. She must be there in the same place. Of course she must be there. It is no crime, after all. I will make it right to her—it will be no crime. Quite the contrary. I will leave here in a few moments, when the clock strikes again. I swear it. Just as soon as the clock strikes again I will stop, I will go straight to where she is, I will take her up in my arms and will carry her home with me asleep. I have done her no harm; I have made a fortune for her. I will keep her with me and educate her; I will love her as I would a child of my own, and I will take care of her—always, as long as she lives!"

But the clock struck one, a quarter past, half past, and Lucien was still there. Finally, a few minutes before two the man opposite him rose brusquely and said in a loud voice, "The bank is broken, gentlemen; this will do for tonight."

Lucien started and, wedging his way brutally through the group of gamblers who pressed around him in envious admiration, hurried out into the street and ran as fast as he could toward the stone bench. In a moment he saw by the light of the gas that the child was still there.

"God be praised!" said he, and his heart gave a great throb of joy. Yes, here she was! He took her little hand in his. Poor little hand, how cold it was! He caught her under the arms and lifted her. Her head fell back, but she did not awake. "The happy sleep of childhood!" thought he. He pressed her close to his breast to warm her, and with a vague presentiment he tried to rouse her from this heavy sleep by kissing her eyelids. But he realized then with horror that through the child's half-open lids her eyes were dull, glassy, fixed. A distracting suspicion flashed through his mind. He put his lips to the child's mouth; he felt no breath.

While Lucien had been building a fortune with the louis stolen from this little one, she, homeless and forsaken, had perished with cold.

Lucien felt a suffocating knot at his throat. In his anguish he tried to cry out; and in the effort which he made he awoke from his nightmare, and found himself on the leather lounge in the gambling room, where he had fallen asleep a little before midnight. The *garçon* of the den had gone home at about five o'clock, and out of pity had not wakened him.

A misty December dawn made the windowpanes pale. Lucien went out, pawned his watch, took a bath, then went over to the Bureau of Recruits and enlisted as a volunteer in the First Regiment of the Chasseurs d'Afrique.

Lucien de Hem is now a lieutenant. He has not a cent in the world but his pay. He manages to make that do, however, for he is a steady officer, and never touches a card. He even contrives to economize, it would seem; for a few days ago a comrade, who was following him up one of the steep streets of the Kasba, saw him stop to lay a piece of money in the lap of a little Spanish girl who had fallen asleep in a doorway. His comrade was startled at the poor lieutenant's generosity, for this piece of money was a gold louis.

THE THREE LOW MASSES

from the French of Alphonse Daudet

from *Christmas Stories from French and Spanish Writers*

by Antoinette Ogden

I

"Two truffled turkeys, did you say, Garrigou?"

"Yes, my reverend, two great, glorious turkeys stuffed with truffles. I ought to know something about it, considering I helped stuff them myself. I thought their skins would crack while they were roasting, they were stretched so tight."

"Merciful Saints! And I'm so fond of truffles too! Hurry there, Garrigou, hand me my surplice. And what else did you see in the kitchen besides the turkeys?"

"Oh, all sorts of good things. Ever since twelve o'clock we have been plucking pheasants, hoopoes, hazel hens, and heath cocks. From the pond they brought in eels, goldfish, trouts, and—"

"About how big were the trouts, Garrigou?"

"Oh, about so big, my reverend; simply enormous."

"Holy Fathers! I can just see them. Did you put the wine in the vases?"

"Yes, my reverend, I filled them; but mercy! that isn't anything like the wine you'll have later, after midnight Mass. You ought to see the dining hall at the castle—all the decanters glittering with the many-colored wines, and the silver, the plate, the chased center-pieces, the flowers, the candelabrum; I don't suppose there has ever been such a Christmas supper! The Lord Marquis has invited all the lords of the neighboring estates. There will be over forty at the table, leaving out the bailiff and the notary. Ah, my reverend, you are very lucky to be invited! The smell of the truffles haunts me now, simply from having sniffed at those turkeys—meuh!"

"Come, come, my child, let us beware of the sin of greediness—particularly on the night of the Nativity. Hurry off now and light the tapers, and ring the first call for Mass; it will soon be midnight, and we can't afford to lose time."

This conversation occurred one Christmas night in the year of our Lord sixteen hundred and something, between the reverend Dom Balaguère, formerly prior of the Barnabites, and present chaplain of the Sires of Trinquelague, and his little clerk, or rather what he believed to be his little clerk Garrigou—for let me tell you that the Devil on that particular night had assumed the round face and uncertain features of the young sacristan, the better to lead the reverend father into temptation and make him commit a great sin of greediness. So while the would-be Garrigou (hem! hem!) rang out the chimes with all his might from the seigniorial chapel, the reverend father was slipping on his chasuble in the little vestry; and as his imagination was somewhat excited by Garrigou's gastronomic accounts, he repeated mechanically as he got into his vestments, "Two roast turkeys, goldfish, trouts about so big!"

Without, the night wind blew, and scattered the music of the bells. Gradually lights began to pierce the gloom along the roads of Mount Ventoux, on whose summit the old towers of Trinquelague reared their mighty heads. The neighboring farmers and their families were on their way to the castle to hear midnight Mass. They climbed the mountain singing gayly, in little groups of five or six—the father ahead carrying the lantern, the women following, wrapped in great dark cloaks under which the children snuggled to keep warm. In spite of the cold and the advanced hour of the night, all these good people walked along merrily, cheered by the thought that a great supper was awaiting them as usual, below, in the castle kitchens, after Mass. Every now and then on the rough declivity some fine lord's coach, preceded by torchbearers, showed its glimmering windowpanes in the moonlight; or then a mule trotted along shaking its bells; or again, by the light of their lanterns wrapped in mist, the farmers recognized their bailiff and hailed him as they passed.

"Good night, good night, Master Arnoton!"

"Good night; good night, my children!"

It was a clear night; the stars seemed brightened by the cold; the wind was nipping; and a fine sleet powdered all these cloaks without wetting them, just in order to preserve the tradition that requires Christmas to be white with snow.

On the very crest of the mountain the castle appeared like a goal, with its huge mass of towers and gables, the chapel steeple rising straight into the blue-black sky, while a thousand little lights moved rapidly hither and thither, blinking at all the windows, and looking, against the intense black of the building, like the tiny sparks that glimmer in a pile of burnt paper.

After passing the drawbridge and the postern, in order to reach the chapel one had to cross the first court, crowded with coaches, footmen, sedan chairs, and bright with the flame of torches and the glare from the kitchens. One could hear the clicking of the spits, the rattling of pots, the tinkling of crystal and silver, as they were laid out for the banquet; and above it all floated a warm vapor smelling of roasted meats and the pungent herbs of complicated sauces, which made the farmers, as well as the chaplain, the bailiff, and everybody say, "What a good supper we shall have after Mass!"

II

Ding, ling, ling! Ding, ling, ling!

Midnight Mass has begun. In the chapel of the castle, which is a miniature cathedral, with intercrossed arches and oaken wainscoting up to the ceiling, all the tapestries are hung, all the tapers lighted. What a crowd of people, and what sumptuous costumes! Here, in one of the carven stalls that surround the choir, sits the Sire of Trinquelague, clad in salmon-colored silk, and around him all the noble lords, his guests. Opposite them, on velvet prie-dieus, kneel the old dowager Marchioness, in a gown of flame-colored brocade, and the young lady of Trinquelague, wearing on her pretty head a great tower of lace puffed and quilled according to the latest fashion at the court of France. Farther down the aisle, all dressed in black, with vast pointed wigs and cleanly shaven chins, sit Thomas Arnoton the bailiff, and the notary, Master Ambroy, two somber spots amid the high colors of silks and brocaded damasks. Then come the fat major-domos, the pages, outriders, the stewards, Dame Barbe with her great bunch of keys dangling from her side on a ring of fine silver. On the benches in the rear is the lower service—butlers, maids, the farmers and their families. And last of all, far back against the doors, which they discreetly open and close, come the cooks, between two sauces, to catch a little whiff of the Mass, bringing with them into the bedecked church, warm with the light of so many tapers, odoriferous sugges-tions of the Christmas supper.

Can it be the sight of these crisp white caps that diverts the rever-end father's attention? Or is it not rather Garrigou's bell?—that fiendish little bell that tinkles away at the foot of the altar with such infernal haste, and seems to be saying, "Come, come, let us hurry! The sooner we dispatch the service, the sooner we go to supper."

The fact of the matter is that at every peal from this little devil of a bell, the chaplain forgets his Mass and allows his mind to wander to the Christmas supper. He evokes visions of busy kitchens, with ovens glowing like furnaces, warm vapors rising from under tin lids, and through these vapors, two superb turkeys, stuffed, crammed, mottled with truffles. Or then again, he sees long files of little pages carrying great dishes wrapped in their tempting fumes, and with them he is about to enter the dining hall. What ecstasy! Here stands the im-mense table, laden and dazzling with peacocks dressed in their feathers, pheasants spreading their bronzed wings, ruby-colored decanters, pyramids of luscious fruit amid the foliage, and those won-derful fish that Garrigou spoke of (Garrigou, forsooth!) reclining on a bed of fennel, their pearly scales looking as if they were just from the pond, and a bunch of pungent herbs in their monsterlike nostrils. This beatific vision is so vivid that Dom Balaguère actually fancies that the glorious dishes are being served before him, on the very em-broideries of the altar cloth, and instead of saying *Dominus vobis-cum*, he catches himself saying the *Benedicite*.

With the exception of these slight mistakes the worthy man rattled off the service conscientiously, without skipping a line or omitting a genuflection, and all went well to the end of the first Mass. For you must know that on Christmas the same officiating priest is obliged to say three Masses consecutively.

"So much for one!" thought the chaplain, with a sigh of relief; and without losing a second, he motioned his clerk, or him whom he believed to be his clerk, and—

Ding, ling, ling! Ding, ling, ling!

The second Mass had begun—and with it Dom Balaguère's sin. "Come, let us hurry!" says Garrigou's bell, in a shrill, devilish little voice, at the mere sound of which the unfortunate priest pounces upon the missal and devours its pages with all the avidity of his overexcited brain. He kneels and rises frantically, barely sketches the sign of the cross and the genuflections, and shortens all of his gestures in order to get through sooner. He scarcely extends his arms at the Gospel, or strikes his breast at the *Confileor*. Between him and his little clerk it is hard to tell who mumbles the faster. The words, half uttered between their teeth—for it would take them too long to open their lips every time—die out into unintelligible murmurs.

Oremus—ps—ps—ps—

Mea culpa—pa—pa—

Like hurried vintagers crushing the grapes in the mash tuns, they both splashed about in the Latin of the service, spattering it in every direction.

"Dom—scum!" says Balaguère.

"Stutuo!" responds Garrigou, while the infernal little bell jingles in their ears like the sleighbells that are put on stage horses to hasten their speed. You may well imagine that at such a rate a Low Mass is soon rattled off.

"So much for the second," says the panting chaplain, with scarlet face, in a full perspiration; and without taking time to breathe, he goes tumbling down the altar steps, and—

Ding, ling, ling! Ding, ling, ling!

The third Mass is under way. Only a few minutes stand between them and the supper. But alas! as the time approaches, Dom Balaguère's fever of impatience and greediness increases. His vision grows more and more vivid; the fish, the roasted turkeys, are there before him; he touches them; he—great heavens!—he breathes the perfume of the wines and the savory fumes of the dishes, and the frantic little bell calls out to him, "Hurry, hurry! Faster, faster!"

But how on earth can he go faster? His lips barely move; he has given up enunciating altogether—unless, forsooth, he chooses to cheat the Lord, and swindle him out of his Mass. And that is just what he is doing, the wretched man! Yielding first to one temptation, then another, he skips one verse, then two; then, the Epistle being very long, he omits part of it, skims over the Gospel, passes the Creed unnoticed, skips the *Pater*, hails the preface from afar, and thus with a skip and a jump plunges into eternal damnation, followed by that infamous Garrigou (*Vade retro, Satanas!*), who seconds him with marvelous sympathy, upholds his chasuble, turns the pages two at a time, jostles the lectern, and upsets the vases, while the little bell rings constantly, ever faster and louder.

It would be impossible to describe the bewildered expression of the congregation. Compelled to follow, mimicking the priest, through this Mass, of which they can make neither head nor tail, some stand while others kneel, some sit while others stand; and all the phases of this singular service are jumbled together along the benches in the greatest confusion of varied postures. The Christmas star on the celestial road, journeying toward the little manger yonder, grows pale at the very thought.

"The abbé reads too fast; it is impossible to follow him," whispers the old dowager Marchioness, whose voluminous headdress shakes wildly. Master Arnoton, with his great steel spectacles on his nose, loses his place every minute and fingers his prayer book nervously. Still, at heart all these good people, whose minds are equally bent upon the Christmas supper, are not at all disturbed at the idea of following Mass at such breakneck speed; and when Dom Balaguère, facing them radiantly, exclaims in a thundering voice, "Ite missa est," the response, "Deo gracias," is so unanimous, joyous, and spirited, that anyone might take it for the first toast of the supper.

III

Five minutes later the assembled lords, and the chaplain among them, had taken their seats in the great hall. The castle, brilliantly illumined, echoed with songs and laughter; and the venerable Dom Balaguère drove his fork resolutely into a capon's wing, drowning the remorse for his sin in the savory juice of meats and the soothing drafts of old wine. He ate and drank so heartily, the dear good man, that he died of a spasm that very night, without even having had time to repent. By morning he reached heaven, where the thrills of the past night's ecstasies lingered still in the air, and I leave you to imagine how he was received.

"Get thee gone, thou wretched Christian!" said Saint Peter; "thy sin is great enough to wipe out the virtues of a lifetime! Ah, so thou wouldst swindle us out of a Mass! Very well, then, three hundred Masses shalt thou say, nor shalt thou enter into Paradise until three hundred Christmas Masses have been celebrated in thine own chapel, and in the presence of all those who sinned with thee and through thee."

And this is the true legend of Dom Balaguère, as it is told in the land of the olive tree. The castle of Trinquelague has long ceased to exist; but the chapel stands erect on the crest of Mount Ventoux, in a clump of evergreen oaks. The wind sways its unhinged door; the grass grows over the threshold; there are nests in the angles of the altar, and on the sills of the high ogive windows, whose jeweled panes have long since disappeared. Still, it seems that every year at Christmas supernatural, mysterious lights hover among the ruins; and on their way to midnight Mass and the Christmas supper, the peasants see this specter of a chapel lighted by invisible tapers, which burn in the open air, even in the wind and under the snow. You may laugh if you will, but a wine dresser of the district, named Garrigue, a descendant of Garrigou, no doubt, has often told me that on one particular Christmas night, being somewhat in liquor, he had lost his way on the mountain somewhere near Trinquelague, and this is what he saw: until eleven o'clock nothing. Everything was silent and dark. Suddenly at midnight the chimes rang out from the old steeple—strange, uncanny chimes, that seemed to be ringing a thousand miles away. Soon lights began to tremble along the road, and vague shadows moved about. Under the portal of the chapel there were sounds of footsteps and muffled voices: "Good night, Master Arnoton!"

"Good night, good night, my children!"

When they had all gone in, my wine dresser, who was a courageous fellow, crawled up to the door and there beheld a most marvelous spectacle. All these good shadows sat around the choir in the ruined nave just as though the benches were still there. There were fine ladies in brocades and lace headdresses, lords gayly bedizened, peasants in flowered coats like those our grandfathers wore, all of them dusty, faded, weary. Every now and then, some night bird, a habitual lodger in the chapel, awakened by all these lights, began to flutter about the tapers, whose flames rose erect and vague as though they were burning behind a strip of gauze. Garrigue was particularly amused at a gentleman with great steel spectacles who constantly shook his huge black wig, upon which perched one of these birds with entangled claws and beating wings.

A little old man with a childlike figure knelt in the center of the choir and frantically shook a tiny bell which had lost its voice, while a priest clad in old-gold vestments moved hither and thither before the altar repeating orisons of which not a syllable could be heard.

Who could this have been but Dom Balaguère, saying his third Low Mass?

I TAKE SUPPER WITH MY WIFE

from the French of Antoine Gustave Droz

from *Christmas Stories from French and Spanish Writers*

by Antoinctte Ogden

It was Christmas Eve, and a devilishly cold night. The snow fell in great flakes, which the wind beat against the windowpanes. The distant chimes reached us, confused and faint through the heavy, cottony atmosphere. The passers-by, muffled in their cloaks, glided along hurriedly, brushing by the walls of the houses, bending their heads before the wind. Wrapped in my dressing gown, I smiled as I drummed on the windowpane, smiled at the passers-by, at the north wind and the snow, with the smile of a happy man who is in a warm room with his feet in a pair of flannel-lined slippers which sink into a thick, soft carpet.

My wife sat in a corner of the hearth with a great piece of cloth before her which she cut and trimmed off; and every now and then she raised her eyes, which met mine. A new book lay on the mantelpiece awaiting me, and a log in the fireplace whistled as it spit out those little blue flames which tempt one to poke it.

"There is nothing so stupid as a man trudging along in the snow. Is there?" said I.

"Sh-h-h!" said my wife, laying down her scissors. Then she stroked her chin thoughtfully with her tapering pink fingers, slightly plump at the extremities, and looked over very carefully the pieces she had just cut out.

"I say that it is absurd to go out into the cold when it is so easy to stay at home by the fire."

"Sh-h-h!"

"What the deuce are you doing that is so important?"

"I—I am cutting out a pair of suspenders for you"; and she resumed her task. Her hair was coiled a little higher than usual; and where I stood, behind her, I could just see, as she leaned over her work, the nape of her neck, white and velvety. Innumerable soft little locks curled there gracefully, and this pretty down reminded me of those ripe peaches into which we drive our teeth greedily. I leaned nearer to see and—kissed my wife on the neck.

"Monsieur!" exclaimed Louise, turning suddenly around.

"Madame!" and we both burst into a laugh.

"Come, come; on Christmas Eve!"

"Monsieur apologizes?"

"Madame complains?"

"Yes, madame complains. Madame complains of your not being more moved, more thrilled by the spirit of Christmas. The ding-ding-dong from the bells of Notre Dame awakens no emotion in you; and when the magic lantern went by under your very window, you were perfectly unmoved, utterly indifferent. I watched you attentively, though I pretended to work."

"Unmoved? Indifferent? I? When the magic lantern went by! Ah, my dear! you judge me very severely, and really—"

"Yes, yes; laugh if you will. It is nevertheless true that the pretty memories of your childhood are lost."

"Come, my pet, would you like me to stand my boots in the fireplace tonight before I go to bed? Would you like me to stop the magic-lantern man and go and get him a sheet and a candle end, as my mother used to do? I can almost see her as she handed him the sheet. 'Be careful you don't tear it, now,' she would say; and we all clapped our hands in the mysterious obscurity. I remember all those joys, dear; but, you see, so many things have happened since. Other pleasures have obliterated those."

"Yes, I understand—the pleasures of your bachelorhood! Come, now, I am sure this is the first Christmas Eve that has ever found you by your own fireside, in your dressing gown and without a supper, because you always had supper; that goes without saying—"

"Why, I don't know—"

"Yes, yes; I wager you always had a supper."

"Well, perhaps I did, once or twice, although I scarcely remember; I may have had supper with a few old friends. And what did it all amount to? Two pennies' worth of chestnuts and—"

"And a glass of sugar and water."

"Well, just about. Oh, it was nothing much, I can assure you! It sounds great at a distance. We talked awhile, and then we went to bed."

"And he says all that with the straightest face! You have never breathed a word of these simple pleasures to me."

"But, my dear, what I tell you is the absolute truth. I remember once, however, at Ernest's, when I was in rather high spirits, we had a little music afterwards— Will you push me that log? Well, never mind; it is almost midnight, and time for all reasonable people to—"

(Louise, rising and throwing her arms around me.) "Well, I don't choose to be reasonable, and I mean to eclipse the memory of those penny chestnuts and all that sugar and water!" (Pushing me hastily into my study and locking the door.)

"What the deuce is the matter with you, my dear?" I cried from the other side of the partition.

"Give me ten minutes, no more. Your paper is on the mantelpiece; you have not seen it tonight. You will find the matches in the corner."

Then I heard the rattle of china, the rustle of silky stuffs. Could my wife have gone crazy? At the end of about ten minutes she unlocked the door.

"Don't scold me for shutting you out," said she, embracing me. "Look at me. Have I not made myself beautiful? See! My hair just as you like it, high, and my neck uncovered. But my poor neck is so extremely shy that it never could have displayed itself in the broad light, if I had not encouraged it a little by wearing a low-necked gown. After all, it is only right to be in full-dress uniform at a supper with the authority."

"What supper?"

"Why, our supper. My supper with you, of course. Don't you see my illumination and the table covered with flowers and good things to eat? I had it all ready in the alcove; but, you see, to push the table before the fire and make something of a toilet, I had to be alone. I have a big drop of old Chambertin for you. Come, monsieur, come to supper; I am as hungry as a bear! May I offer you this chicken wing?"

"This is a charming idea of yours, my love, but I really feel ashamed of myself—in my dressing gown."

"Take it off, sir, if you are uncomfortable, but do not leave me with this chicken wing on my hands. Wait a minute; I want to wait upon you myself." And rising, she swung her napkin over her arm and pulled up her sleeve to her elbow. "Isn't that the way the waiters do at the restaurants, tell me?"

"Exactly. But stop a moment, waiter; will you permit me to kiss your hand?"

"I haven't time," she said, smiling, and she drove the corkscrew bravely into the neck of a bottle. "Chambertin—a pretty name! And, besides, do you remember, before we were married—*sapristi*, what a hard cork!—you told me you liked it on account of a play by Alfred de Musset?—which you never gave me to read, by the way. Do you see those little Bohemian glass tumblers that I bought especially for tonight? We will drink each other's health in them."

"And his too, eh?"

"The heir's, you mean? Poor little love of an heir, I should think so! Then I shall hide the two glasses and bring them out again this day next year, eh, dear? They will be the Christmas supper glasses, and we will have supper every year before the hearth, you and I alone, until our very old, old age."

"Yes; but when we shall have lost all our teeth—"

"Never mind; we shall have nice little soups, and it will nonetheless be very sweet. Another piece for me, please, with a little jelly, thank you."

As she held out her plate to me, I caught a glimpse of her arm, the pretty contours of which disappeared in the lace.

"What are you looking up my sleeve for instead of eating?"

"I am looking at your arm, dear. You are exquisitely pretty tonight; do you know it? Your hair is wonderfully becoming, and that gown—I had never seen that gown before."

"*Dame!* When a person starts out to make a conquest!"

"You are adorable!"

"Are you quite sure that I am adorable tonight, charming, ravishing?" Then, looking at her bracelet attentively, "In that case I don't see why—I don't see—"

"What is it that you don't see, dear?"

"I don't see why you don't come and kiss me."

And as the kiss was prolonged, she threw her head back, showing the double row of her pretty white teeth, exclaiming between her pearls of laughter, "Give me some more *pâté!* I want some more *pâté!* Take care! You are going to break my Bohemian glass, the fruit of my economy! There is always some disaster when you try to kiss me. You remember at Madame de Brill's ball, two nights before we were married, how you tore my gown while we were waltzing in the little parlor?"

"Well, but it is very difficult to do two things at once—keep time with the music and kiss your partner."

"I remember when mamma asked me how I tore my gown, I felt that I was blushing up to the roots of my hair. And Madame D., that old yellow witch, said to me with her lenten smile, 'What a brilliant color you have tonight, my child!' I could have choked her! I said I had caught my gown on a nail in the door. I was watching you out of the corner of my eye. You were twirling your mustache, and you seemed quite vexed. You keep all the truffles for yourself—how nice of you! Not that one; I want that big black one there—in the corner. Well, after all, it was nonetheless very wrong, because—no, no, don't fill my glass; I don't want to get tipsy—because if we had not married (that might have happened, you know; they say that marriages hang by a thread), well, if the thread had not been strong enough, here I was left with that kiss on my shoulder—a pretty plight!"

"Nonsense! It does not stain."

"Yes, sir, it does; I beg your pardon, but it does stain, and so much so that there are husbands, I am told, who spill their blood to wash out those little stains."

"I was only jesting, dear. Heavens! I should think it did! Fancy! Why—"

"Ah, I am glad to hear you say so. I like to see you get angry. You are just a wee bit jealous, tell me, are you not? Well, upon my word! I asked you for the big black one, and you are quietly eating it!"

"I am very sorry, my love; I beg your pardon. I forgot all about it."

"Yes, just as you did when we were being married. I was obliged to touch your elbow to make you answer yes to Monsieur the Mayor's kind words!"

"Kind words?"

"Yes, kind words. I thought the Mayor was charming. No one could have been more happy than he was in addressing me. 'Mademoiselle, do you consent to take this great big ugly little man who stands beside you for your lawful—' [Laughing with her mouth full.] I was about to say to him, 'Let us understand each other, Monsieur; there is much to be said for and against.' Heavens! I am choking! [Bursts into great peals of laughter.] I was wrong in not making some restrictions. There! I am teasing you, and that is stupid. I said yes with my whole heart, I assure you, my darling, and the word was only too weak. When I think that all women, even the bad ones, use that same word, I feel ashamed of not having invented a better one. [Holding up her glass.] Here is to our golden wedding!"

"And here is to his christening, little mother!"

In an undertone: "Tell me, dear, are you sorry you married me?"

(Laughing.) "Yes. [Kissing her on the shoulder.] I think I have found the stain. Here it is."

"Do you realize that it is two o'clock. The fire is out. I am—you won't laugh? Well, I am just a little dizzy!"

"That was a famous *pâté!*"

"A famous *pâté!* We will have a cup of tea in the morning, eh, dear?"

SOLANGE, THE WOLF-GIRL

from the French of Marcel Prévost

from *Christmas Stories from French and Spanish Writers*
by Antoinette Ogden

All that afternoon we had walked through the forest, stick in hand, our bags slung over our shoulders, through that magnificent forest of Tronsays, which covers one half the St. Amand country, and one half of Nevers. The little village of Ursay, squatting on the bank of the Cher, in the rent of the valley which cuts through the center of the forest, was our last halting place for the day. We dined with an old friend, the modest doctor of five or six neighboring communes; and after dinner we sat musing on the stoop, with our cherry pipes between our lips.

The shadows fell around us, over the dense blue mass of forest that encircled the horizon, with all the solemn slowness of night in June. The sky was streaked with flights of swallows. The nine o'clock Angelus scattered its notes with intervals of silence from the height of a snufferlike steeple which emerged from among the roofs. From distant farms came the barking of dogs calling and answering one another.

A woman, still young, in a red woolen skirt and a white linen shirt, came out of a house near by, and walked down toward the river. With her left arm she pressed a baby against her bosom. A little boy held her other hand, and gave his in turn to a still smaller brother. When they reached the bank of the Cher, the young woman sat upon a great stone; and while the two boys, hastily undressed, were paddling and splashing about like ducks in the stream, she nursed her last-born.

One of our party, who was a painter, said, "There is a picture that would be popular at the Salon. How splendidly built and well lighted that woman is! And what a pretty bright spot that red skirt forms in the blue landscape!"

A voice behind us called out, "The girl you see there, young men, is Solange, the wolf-girl." And our host, who had been detained by a consultation, came out to join us. As we asked him who was this wolf-girl, and how she had come by so strange a nickname, he told us this story:

"This Solange, the wolf-girl, whose real name is Solange Tournier, wife of Grillet, was the prettiest girl in the whole Tronsays country about ten years ago. Now, of course, working in the fields as she does, and having had five children, she looks hardened and worn. Still, considering her thirty years, she is handsome enough, as you see. At the time of the adventure whence she derived her strange nickname she was living with her parents, who were farmers of the Rein-du-Bois, some fifteen kilometers from here. Although very poor, she was much sought by all the boys, even by the well-to-do; but she accepted the addresses of only one—a certain Laurent Grillet, on whom she had set her heart when she was a wee bit of a girl, when the two kept the sheep together in the neighborhood of Rein-du-Bois.

"Laurent Grillet was a foundling, who had nothing in the world but his two arms for a fortune. Solange's parents felt no inclination to add poverty to poverty, especially as the girl had so many wealthy suitors.

"So Solange was forbidden to see her friend. Naturally, the girl never failed at a tryst. Living in the same commune, with the forest at hand, they never lost an opportunity of meeting there. When the father and mother Tournier realized that scoldings and blows were of no avail, they determined upon a radical step. Solange was accordingly sent out to work at Ursay, on the model farm of M. Roger Duflos, our deputy.

"Perhaps you think our two lovers ceased to see each other. Not in the least. They now met at night; they slept no more. After nightfall they both left the farms where they were employed and started toward each other; and then they remained together until nearly dawn in the maternal forest, the accomplice of their young love.

"This was in 1879. In this manner the summer and autumn went by. Then came the winter, and a fierce winter it was. The Cher carried ice drifts, and finally froze from bank to bank. The Tronsays forests, covered with snow, were bent like the weak supports of an overladen roof. The roads were almost impassable. The forest, deserted by man, was gradually being reconquered by beasts. It was soon invaded by wolves, which had neither been seen nor heard of since the Terrible year.

"Yes, sir, wolves! They haunted the isolated farms around Lurcy-Lévy and Ursay. They even ventured into the streets of St. Bonnet le Désert—a little village in the heart of the forest on the banks of a pond. It reached such a point that men were organized into bands to beat the woods. A reward of fifty francs was offered for the head of a wolf.

"Neither winter nor wolves, however, daunted Solange and Laurent, or interfered with their nocturnal meetings. They continued their expeditions in the face of a thousand dangers. This was the dead season in the fields, the time when the land lies fallow. Every night Laurent left Lurcy-Lévy, a gun over his shoulder, and penetrated with a lively step into the black and white forest. Solange, on the other hand, started from Ursay at about nine o'clock, and they met near a glade some three kilometers from here, traversed by a road, and known as the Découverte.

"It so happened that one night, which, by the way, was Christmas Eve, Laurent Grillet, as he reached the rendezvous, slipped on the hardened snow and fell, breaking his right leg and spraining his right wrist. Solange tried to raise him, but could only drag him to a great elm, against which she propped him, after wrapping him in her own cloak.

" 'Wait for me here, my poor Laurent,' said she; 'I will run to Ursay for the doctor, and get him to come for you in his carryall.'

"She started off, but had not reached the first turn in the road when she heard a report and the cry, 'Help!'

"She ran back and found her friend in an agony of pain and fear, his trembling hand on the gun which lay beside him. She said, 'What is it, Laurent? Was it you who fired?'

"He answered, 'It was I. I saw a beast about the size of a large dog, and with great red eyes. I believe, on my word, it was a wolf.'

" 'Was it at him you fired?'

" 'No. I cannot lift my gun on account of my arm. I fired on the ground to scare him. He has gone now.'

"Solange reflected for a moment. 'Will he come back?'

" 'I am afraid he will,' answered the lad. 'Solange, you will have to stay, or that beast will eat me.'

" 'Well,' she said, 'I will stay. Let me have the gun.'

"She took it, put in a fresh cartridge, and they both waited.

"An hour passed. The moon, as yet invisible, had risen, however, above the horizon, for the zenith reflected a confused light, which was gradually growing more intense. Laurent felt the fever coming upon him. He shivered and moaned. Solange, half frozen, as she stood leaning against the tree, was beginning to feel drowsy. Suddenly a bark—a sort of howl like that of a dog at night when it is tied—made her start. In the faint light she saw two red eyes fixed upon her. It was the wolf. Laurent tried to rise and take his gun, but the pain flung him back with a cry.

" 'Load, Solange,' said he. 'Do not fire too soon, and aim between the eyes.'

"She shouldered, aimed, and fired, but the gun recoiled and missed aim. The beast was untouched. It ran off a short way down the road. Then it was heard howling at a distance, and other howls came in answer.

"The moon was climbing the sky. It suddenly passed the dark mass of the thickets and flooded the entire forest as the footlights illumine the scenery on the stage. Then Solange and Laurent saw this horrible sight: at a few feet from them five wolves were seated on their haunches, drawn in line across the road, while another, bolder than the rest, was walking slowly toward them.

" 'Listen,' said Laurent. 'Aim at that one that is coming. If you bring him down, the others will eat him, and they will leave us in peace in the meantime.'

"The wolf continued to advance with short, cautious steps. They could now see his bloodshot eyeballs distinctly, the protruding rings of his spine, the sharp bones of his carcass, his dull hair and his open jaw, with the long tongue hanging out. 'Hold the butt end well in the hollow of your shoulder. Now fire.'

"There was a report; the beast leaped to one side and fell dead without a groan. The whole band galloped off and disappeared in the copse.

" 'Run, Solange!' cried Laurent; 'drag him as far as you can along the road. There is no danger; the others will not come back for a while yet.'

"She had started, when he called her back. 'It might be just as well to cut off that beast's head on account of the reward.'

" 'Have you a knife?' asked Solange.

" 'Yes; in my belt.'

"It was a short-handled, broad-bladed hunter's knife. She took it and ran to the dead wolf. She made a great effort and drove it in his throat, the warm blood trickling down her hands and along her skirt; she turned her knife around, cut deep, then hacked, and finally severed the head from the trunk, which she dragged by one leg over the slippery snow as far as she could. Then she returned to her lover with the bloody, bristly head of the beast in her hand.

"What Laurent had foreseen occurred. The wolves, at first frightened by the death of their leader, were soon brought back by the smell of the blood. In the white light of the moon, reflected by the snow like the fantastic light of a fairy scene, the two young people saw the group of lean, ravenous beasts rubbing their backs against one another, crowding around the fresh prey, tearing it limb from limb, growling and snarling over it, wrenching off the flesh, until nothing was left of it, not even a tuft of hair.

"Meanwhile the boy was suffering greatly from his injuries. Solange, whose nerves were beginning to relax, struggled vainly against exhaustion and sleep. Twice her gun fell from her hands. The wolves, having finished their meal, began to draw nearer. The girl fired twice in the lot, but her benumbed fingers trembled and she missed her aim. At each report the band turned tail, trotted about a hundred meters down the road, waited a moment and came back.

"Then the two poor children were convinced that it was all over with them, and that they must die. Solange dropped her gun. It never once occurred to her that she might save herself. She threw herself down beside her lover, clasped her arms around him, laid her cheek against his, and there under the same cloak they awaited death, half frozen with the cold, half burning with fever. Their confused brains conjured strange visions. Now they thought they had gone back to the balmy nights of June when the forest, clad in deep green, sheltered their peaceful meetings, then suddenly the wood was bare, lighted with a weird snowy light, peopled with shifting forms, eyes like burning embers, great open jaws that multiplied, and came nearer, ever nearer.

"But neither Solange nor Laurent was destined to die so horrible a death. Providence—yes, young men, I believe in a Providence—had decreed that I, on that Christmas morning, should find myself on that particular road on my way home in my carryall from St. Bonnet le Désert. I managed the lines; my man held the gun and inspected the road. No doubt our sleigh bells frightened away the wolves, for we saw none. As we drove near the elm at the foot of which the lovers lay, my mare shied, and so drew our attention to them. I jumped down from the seat. My man and I settled them in the carryall as best as we could, covering them with what wraps we had along. They were unconscious and almost frozen. We took the bloody head of the wolf with us too.

"It was about seven o'clock in the morning when we reached Ursay. The day was breaking over a landscape of spun glass and white velvet. M. Roger Duflos' farmers and at least one half of the inhabitants of the borough, having heard of Solange's disappearance, came out to meet us; and in the very kitchen where we dined this evening, in front of a great fire of crackling heather, Laurent and his friend warmed themselves and told us the story of their terrible Christmas."

One of us said, "And what followed, Doctor? Did they marry?"

"Yes; they were married," answered our host. "The will of Providence is sometimes so plainly indicated by events that the most obtuse cannot fail to perceive it. After the adventure with the wolves, Solange's parents consented to her marriage with Laurent Grillet. The marriage took place in the spring. The reward of fifty francs for the wolf's head paid for the wedding dress."

The doctor was silent. Night was full upon us. The sky, of a turquoise blue, reflected its first stars in the river. The mass of forest, dense and inky, shut off the horizon. We saw Solange, the wolf-girl, dress her two boys and start homeward with them, the youngest asleep on her shoulder. She passed very near us, and looking up, smiled at the doctor. The doctor said, "Good night, Solange!"

THE TORN CLOAK

from the French of Maxime Du Camp

from *Christmas Stories from French and Spanish Writers*
by Antoinette Ogden

I

High in the steeple the bells were conversing. Two of the younger ones were vexed and spoke angrily, "Is it not time we were asleep? It is almost midnight, and twice have we been shaken, twice have we been forced to cry out through the gloom just as though it were day, and we were singing the call for Sunday Mass. There are people moving about in the church; are we going to be tormented again, I wonder? Might they not leave us in peace?"

At this the oldest bell in the steeple said indignantly, in a voice which though cracked had lost none of its solemnity, "Hush, little ones! Are you not ashamed to speak so foolishly? When you went to Rome to be blessed, did you not take an oath, did you not swear to fulfill your duty? Do you not know that in a few minutes it will be Christmas, and that you will then celebrate the birth of Him whose resurrection you have already celebrated?"

"But it is so cold!" whimpered a young bell.

"And do you not think that He was cold, when He came into the world, naked and weak? Would He not have suffered on the heights of Bethlehem had not the ass and the ox warmed Him with their breath? Instead of grumbling and complaining, let your voices be sweet and tender in memory of the canticles with which His mother lulled Him to sleep. Come, hold yourselves in readiness. I can see them lighting the tapers; they have constructed a little manger before the Virgin's altar; the banner is unfurled; the beadle is bustling about. He has a bad cold, the poor man; how he sneezes! Monsieur le Curé has put on his embroidered alb. I hear the approaching sound of wooden shoes; the peasants are coming to pray. The clock is about to strike the hour—now—Christmas! Christmas! Ring out with all your heart and all your might! Let no man say that he has not been summoned to midnight Mass."

II

It had been snowing for three days. The sky was black, the ground white; the north wind howled through the trees; the ponds were frozen; and the little birds were hungry. Women, wrapped in long mantles of brown wool, and men in heavy cloaks slowly made their way into the church. They knelt and with bent brows murmured the answer as the priest said, "And the Lord said unto me, 'Thou art my Son, whom this day I have begotten.' " The incense was smoking, and blossoms of hellebore, which are the roses of Christmas, lay before the tabernacle in the light of the tapers. Behind one of the pillars, near the door of the church, knelt a child. His feet were bare. He had slipped off his wooden shoes on account of the noise they made. His cap lay on the floor before him and with clasped hands he prayed, "For the soul of my father who is dead, for the life of my mother, and for me, for your little Jacques, who loves you, O my God, I implore you!" And he knelt all through Mass, lost in the fervor of his devotion, and rose only when he heard the words "Ite missa est."

The people crowded together under the exterior porch. Every man lighted his lantern and pulled up the collar of his cloak; and the women drew their mantles closely around them. Brrr! how cold it was! A little boy called out to Jacques, "Are you coming with us?"

"No," said he, "I have not time"; and he started off on a run. He could hear the village people far away singing the favorite carol of olden France as they walked home:

> *He is born, the Heavenly Child.*
> *Ring out, hautbois! ring out, bagpipes!*
> *He is born, the Heavenly Child;*
> *Let all voices sing his advent!*

III

Jacques reached the thatched cottage at the far end of the hamlet nestling in a rocky hollow at the foot of the hill. He opened the door carefully and tiptoed into a room in which there was neither light nor fire.

"Is that you, little one?"

"Yes, mother."

"I prayed while you were praying. You must be half asleep; go to bed, child. I do not need anything. If I am thirsty, I have the water jug here where I can reach it."

In a corner of the room near Marguerite's bed, Jacques turned over a litter of ferns and dry grasses, stretched himself upon it, drew the ragged end of a blanket over him, and fell asleep. Marguerite, however, did not sleep. She was thinking, and her thoughts wrung tears from her eyes. She was evoking the happy days when her husband was with her, and life seemed so full of hope. She lay still, so as not to waken her boy, her head thrown back on the bolster, the tears trickling off her bony cheeks, her hand pressed to her hot chest.

Marguerite's husband had been the pride of his village, a hard worker and an upright man. At the call of the Conscription he went to the wagon train, for he was a good driver, kind to his horses, a man who made his own bed only after having prepared their litter. He spoke with pleasure of the time when he had been "in the army of the war," and would say laughingly, "I carted heaps of glory in the Crimea and in Italy." His return to the village was a source of rejoicing. He had known Marguerite as a child; he now found her a woman and married her. They were poor, Marguerite's trousseau consisting of a three-franc cap, which she bought in order to make a good appearance at the church ceremony. They owned the cottage—a miserable, dilapidated hut; but they were happy in it because they worked hard and loved each other. The village people said, "Marguerite is no simpleton. She knew what she was about when she married Grand-Pierre. The sun does not find him abed. He is strong, saving too, and no drunkard."

Yes, Grand-Pierre was a good workman, spry, punctual—a man of much action and few words. He had resumed his old trade, and drove his teams through the mountains for a man who was quarrying granite. He drove four stout-haunched, wide-chested horses, and excelled in maneuvering the screw-jack, in balancing the heaviest blocks, and driving down the steep declivities that opened into the plain. When he came home after his day's work, he found the soup and a jug of cider on the table, and Marguerite waiting for him. Everything smiled upon them in the poor little home, where there was soon a willow cradle.

But happiness is short-lived. There is an Arab proverb that says, "As soon as a man paints his house in pink, fate hastens to daub it black." For eleven years Pierre and Marguerite lived happily together and laid their plans with no fear of the future. Then misfortune came and made its home with them. One raw, foggy winter's day Grand-Pierre went out to the mountain. He loaded his wagon; and after having left the dangerous passes of the road behind, he sat on the shaft for a rest, and leaned against a great block of granite. He was tired; and lulled by the swaying of the vehicle and the monotonous jingle of the bells, he involuntarily closed his eyes. After a little the left wheel went over a great limb that lay across the road. The shock was violent. Pierre was pitched from his seat; and before he could move, the heavy wheels rolled slowly over him and crushed in his chest.

The horses went their way unconscious of the fact that their driver, their oldest friend, lay dead behind them. They reached the quarriers and stopped at the door.

"Where is Grand-Pierre?"

Inquiries were made at once. Men were sent to the cottage. Marguerite grew anxious. As the light failed, they took torches and went up the mountain, shouting, "Hello there, Grand-Pierre!" but no voice answered. At last they came upon the poor man lying in the middle of the road on his back with outstretched arms. The wheels had cut through the cloak and the edge of the rent was crushed into his chest and black with blood.

All the villagers followed the corpse to the church and the cemetery and held out their hands to Marguerite, who stood white and immobile, like a statue of wax, muttering mechanically under her breath, "O God, have pity! have pity!" Jacques was then in his tenth year. He could not appreciate the greatness of his mother's sorrow, and only cried because she did.

Then misfortune had followed misfortune—poverty, illness, misery. And so through this Christmas night Marguerite lay stifling her sobs as she recalled the past.

IV

Jacques rose at dawn, shook off the dry grasses that stuck to his hair, and went over to his mother. Her eyes were half closed, her lips very white, and there were warm red spots on her cheeks. When she saw the boy, she made a faint movement with her head.

"Did you sleep, mother? Do you feel well?"

"Yes, but I am very cold. Make a little fire, will you?"

Jacques searched every corner of the hut, looked in the old cupboard, went through the cellar which had formerly contained their supplies, and said, "There is no wood left, and there are no roots either."

"Never mind then. It is not so very cold after all."

Jacques picked up a stone, hammered at the nail that secured the strap of his wooden shoe, slipped his foot into it, pulled his cap down over his ears, and said resolutely, "I am going out to the mountain to get some dead wood."

"Why, you forget that today is Christmas, my child!"

"I know, but Monsieur le Curé will forgive me."

"No, no, you must not go; it has been prohibited."

"I will see that the rural guard does not catch me. Please let me go; I will be back soon."

"Well, go then."

Jacques put his pruning knife in his pocket, threw a rope over his shoulder, and opened the door. A gust of wind thick with snow dashed him back and whirled through the room.

"What a storm!"

"Holy angels!" cried Marguerite, "it is the white deluge! Listen, little one, you are not warm enough. Open the old chest where your father's things are, and get his cloak—the cloak he had on when they brought him home. Wrap it around you, and see that you do not take cold. One sick person in the house is enough."

Jacques took the cloak, upon which a twig of blessed box had been laid. It was one of those great black and white cloaks of thick wool and goat hair, with a small velvet collar and brass clasps. There was a gaping black rent in it, and here and there an ugly dark spot. It was very long for Jacques, so Marguerite pinned the edges up under the collar. When he was halfway out of the door she called out to him, "Jacques, if you pass the Trèves do not forget to say a prayer."

V

Jacques started off at a brisk pace. There was not a human being to be seen anywhere. The fields were gloomy and desolate. The snow seemed to shoot along horizontally, so violently was it lashed by the north wind. On the high, frosted limb of a poplar a raven was croaking. Jacques stopped every now and again to knock off the snow which gathered and hardened on the soles of his wooden shoes. He was not cold, but he found his cloak very heavy. He had gone a long way and had reached the first undulations of the mountain, the edge of the forest, when he stopped petrified before the rural guard, who appeared suddenly at a turn in the road, imposing with his cocked hat, his sword, and the word "Law" glittering on his belt.

This Father Monhache, who had been a sapper before he became a rural guard, was greatly dreaded in the land. He was the terror of the village boys, for whenever he found any of them stealing apples, shaking the plum trees, or knocking down nuts, he swore at them terribly, and then led them by the ear to Monsieur le Maire, who sentenced the delinquents to a paternal spanking. Jacques was therefore aghast when he found himself face to face with this merciless representative of the authority.

"Where are you going, Jacques, in this devil of a storm?"

Jacques tried to concoct some story to explain his expedition; and before he had decided which would be the most effective, he caught himself saying simply, "I am going to the mountain, Father

Monhache, to get some dead wood. We have none at home, and my mother is ill."

The old guard dropped an oath and said in a voice which was by no means harsh, "Ah, so you are going to the mountain for dead wood, are you? Well, if I meet you in the village this evening with your fagot, I will close one eye and wink the other, do you understand? And if you ever tell anybody what I said, I will pull your ears." And he walked off with a shrug. He had not gone ten feet when he turned and shouted, "There is more dead wood in the copse of the Prévoté than anywhere else."

VI

"He is not such a bad man, after all," thought Jacques.

He was now climbing the mountain, and it was a hard struggle for his little legs. Every now and then he heard what he thought was a moan in the distance—the breaking of a limb under the weight of the snow. Look as he would through all those branches, he could not see a single blackbird, nor even a jay. Not a little mouse ran along the slope. A few intrepid sparrows alone, black spots on the white ground, hopped about in search of food.

Measuring his steps to the time, Jacques began to sing in a low tone, "He is born, the Heavenly Child," and walked along with a great effort, leaning forward. He sank into hollows where the snow was deep. He knew that he was not far from the copse of the Prévoté, so he took courage, though he stubbed his foot against the hard, concealed ruts, and tumbled into holes. Father Monhache was right; there was surely no lack of dead wood at the copse of the Prévoté.

Over the shivering heather and the crouching brier lay the fallen branches in their furrows. Jacques fell to work, and how he toiled! He had taken off his cloak that his movements might be freer. His legs sunk deep in the snow. His hands and his arms were drenched and chilled, while his face was hot and wet with perspiration. He would stop every minute or two to look at his pile of wood and think of the bright flame it would make in the hut.

When he had all he could carry, he tied it in a fagot, threw his cloak over his shoulders, and started along the shortest cut to the village. His legs trembled. Now and then he was compelled to stop and lean against a tree.

VII

After a little he came to a crossroad. This was Trèves. In the days of the Romans it had been called Trivium, because of the three roads that met there. On that spot had formerly stood an altar to Mercury, the protector of roads, the god of travelers, and the patron of thieves. Christianity had torn down the pagan altar and replaced it by a crucifix of granite. On the pedestal, gnawed by lichens, one may still find the date A.D. 1314. During the Hundred Years' War the statue was shattered, and the crossroad strewn with its fragments. Then, when the foreign element which sullied our land had been cast out, when "Joan, the good maid of Lorraine," had returned the kingdom of France to the little king of Bourges, the statue was raised, and from that time it has been the object of special veneration through the country. Every peasant bows before it, and even the veterinary, who delights in laughing at priests, would not dare pass the Trèves without raising his hat.

With his hands nailed to the cross, his brow encircled with thorns, the Christ hangs as though he were calling the whole world to take refuge in his outstretched arms. He seems enormous. In the folds of the cloth which girds his loins wrens have built nests that have never been disturbed. His face is turned toward the East; and his hollow, suffering gaze is fixed upon the sky, as though he were looking for the star that guided the Magi and led the shepherds to the stable in Bethlehem.

VIII

Jacques did not forget his mother's instruction. He laid down his fagot, took off his cap, and there, on his knees, began a prayer, to which the wind moaned a dreary accompaniment. He repeated some prayers which he had learned at the Catechism class; he said others too—fervent words that rose of themselves from his heart. And as he prayed, he looked up at the Christ, lashed by the storm. Its parted lips and upturned eyes gave it an expression of infinite pain. Two little icicles, like congealed tears, hung on its eyelids, and the emaciated body stretched itself upon the cross in a last spasm of agony. Jacques began to suffer with the suffering embodied there, and he was moved to console the One whom he had come to invoke.

When his prayers were said, he took up his fagot and started on his way; but before he had left the crossroad behind him, he turned and looked back. The Christ's eyes seemed to follow him. The face was less somber; the features seemed to have relaxed into an expression of infinite gentleness. A gust of wind shook the snow that had accumulated on its outstretched arms. One might have believed that the statue had shivered. Jacques stopped. "Oh, my poor God," said he, "how cold you are!" and he went back and stood before the crucifix. Then with a sudden impulse he took off his cloak. He climbed upon the pedestal, then putting his foot upon the projection of the loincloth, and reaching about the shoulders, he threw the cloak around the statue.

When he had reached the ground again, "Now, at least, you will not be so cold!" said he; and the two little icicles that had hung on the eyelids of the divine image melted and ran slowly down the granite cheeks like tears of gratitude.

Jacques started off at a rapid pace. The cruel north wind blew through his cotton blouse. He began to run, and the fagot beat against his shoulders and bruised them. At last he reached the foot of a declivity and stopped, panting, by a ravine sheltered from the snow and the wind by a wall of pines. How tired he was! He descended into the ravine and sat down to rest, only for a minute, thought he—just a minute more, and he would be up again and on his way to his mother. How tired he was! His head too was very hot and felt heavy. He lay down and leaned his head against the fagot. "I must not go to sleep," he said. "Oh, no, I will not go to sleep"; and as he said this, his eyelids drooped, and he became suddenly engulfed in a great flood of unconsciousness.

IX

When Jacques awoke he was greatly surprised. The ravine, the snow, the forest, the mountain, the gray sky, the freezing wind—all had disappeared. He looked for his fagot, but could find it nowhere. He had never seen or even heard of this new country; and he was unable to define its substance, to circumscribe its immensity, or appreciate its splendors. The air was balmy, saturated with exquisite perfumes, and it exhaled soft harmonies that made his heart quiver with delight.

He rose. The ground beneath his feet was elastic, and seemed to rise to meet his step, so that walking became restful. A luminous halo hovered about him. Instead of the old torn cloak, he wore a mantle strewn with stars, and it was seamless, like the one for which dice were cast on the heights of Calvary. His hands—his poor little hands, tumefied with chilblains, and which the cold had chapped and creviced—were now white and soft like the tips of a swan's wings. Jacques was amazed, but no feeling of fear agitated him. He was calm and felt strangely confident. A great burden seemed to have been lifted from his shoulders; he was as light as the air, and aglow with beatitude.

"Where am I?" he asked.

And a voice more harmonious than the whispering of the breeze answered, "In my Father's House, which is the home of the Just."

Then through a veil of azure and light a great granite crucifix arose before him. It was the crucifix of the Trèves. Grand-Pierre's cloak, with the rent across it, floated from the shoulders of the Christ. The coarse wool had grown as diaphanous as a cloud, and through it the light radiated as from a sun. The thorns on his brow glittered like carbuncles, and a superhuman beauty lighted his countenance. From fields of space which the sight could now explore came aerial chants. Jacques fell upon his knees and prostrated himself.

The Christ said, "Rise, little one; you were moved to pity by the sufferings of your God; you stripped yourself of your cloak to shield him from the cold, and this is why he has given you his cloak in exchange for yours; for of all the virtues, the highest and rarest is charity, which surpasses wisdom and knowledge. Hereafter you will be the host of your God."

Jacques took a few steps toward the dazzling vision and held out his arms in supplication.

"What do you want?" said the Christ.

The child said, "I want my mother."

"The angels who carried Mary into Egypt will bring her to you."

There was a great rustle of wings, and a smile shone on the face of the granite Christ.

Jacques was praying, but his prayer was unlike any that he had ever said before. It was a chant of ecstasy, which rose to his lips in words so beautiful that he experienced a sense of ineffable happiness in listening to himself.

Far away, on the brink of the horizon, pure and clear as crystal, he saw Marguerite borne toward him on billows of white. She was no longer pale, worn, and sad. She was radiant, and glowed with that internal light which is the beauty of the soul, and is alone imperishable. The angels laid her at the foot of the crucifix, and she prostrated herself and adored. When she raised her head there were two souls beside her, and their essences blended in one kiss, in one burst of gratitude. The granite Christ wept.

X

High in the steeple the bells are conversing. The two younger ones are sullen. "The people in this village are mad. Why can they never be quiet? Were not yesterday's duties sufficiently tiresome?—midnight Mass, Matins, the Mass of the Aurora, the third Mass, High Mass, Vespers, the Angelus, to say nothing of supplementary chimes. There was no end to it! And now today we must begin all over again. They pull us, they shake us—first the toll for the dead, the funeral service next, then the burial. It is really too much! Why will they never leave us in peace on our frames? Our clappers are weary, and our sides are bruised with the repeated strokes. What can be the matter with these peasants? Here they come to church again in their holiday clothes. Father Monhache wears his most forbidding scowl; his beard bristles fiercely; every now and then he brushes something from his eyes with the back of his hand. His cocked hat has a defiant tilt. The boys had better be on their guard this day. Far down the road there, I see two coffins, one large and one small. They are lifting them on the oxcart; see! But what is that to us, and why are we expected to ring?"

The old bell, full of wisdom and experience, reproved them, saying, "Be still, and do not shame me with your ignorance. You have no conception of the dignity of your functions. You have been blessed; you are church bells. To men you say, 'Keep vigil over your immortal souls!' and to God, 'O Father, have pity on human weakness!' Instead of being proud of your exalted mission, and meditating upon what you see, you chatter like hand-bells and reason like sleigh bells. Your bright color and your clear voices need not make you vain, for age will tarnish you and the fatigues of your duty will crack your voices. When years have passed; when you shall have proclaimed church festivals, weddings, births, christenings, and funerals; after having raised the alarms for conflagrations, and rung the tocsin at the invasion of the enemy, you will no longer complain of your fate; you will begin to comprehend the things of this world and divine the secrets of the other; you will come to understand how tears on earth can become smiles in heaven.

"So ring gently, gently, without sadness or fear. Let your voices sound like the cooing of doves. A torn cloak in this world may be a mantle of eternal blessedness in the next."

A BIRD IN THE SNOW

from the Spanish of Armando Palacio Valdés

from *Christmas Stories from French and Spanish Writers*
by Antoinette Ogden

He was born blind, and had been taught the one thing which the blind generally learn—music; for this art he was specially gifted. His mother died when he was little more than a child, and his father, who was the first cornetist of a military band, followed her to the grave a few years later. He had a brother in America from whom he had never heard; still, through indirect sources he knew him to be well off, married, and the father of two fine children. To the day of his death the old musician, indignant at his son's ingratitude, would not allow his name to be mentioned in his presence; but the blind boy's affection for his brother remained unchanged. He could not forget that this elder brother had been the support of his childhood, the defense of his weakness against the other boys, and that he had always spoken to him with kindness. The recollection of Santiago's voice as he entered his room in the morning, shouting, "Hey there, Juanito! get up, man; don't sleep so!" rang in the blind boy's ears with a more pleasing harmony than could ever be drawn from the keys of a piano or the strings of a violin. Was it probable that such a kind heart had grown cold? Juan could not believe it, and was always striving to justify him. At times the fault was with the mail, or it might be that his brother did not wish to write until he could send them a good deal of money; then again, he fancied that he meant to surprise them by presenting himself some fine day, laden with gold, in the modest *entresol* in which they lived. But he never dared communicate any of these fancies to his father; only when the old man, wrought to an unusual pitch of exasperation, bitterly apostrophized the absent one, he found the courage to say: "You must not despair, father. Santiago is good, and my heart tells me that we shall hear from him one of these days."

The father died, however, without hearing from his son, between a priest, who exhorted him, and the blind boy, who clung convulsively to his hand, as if he meant to detain him in this world by main force. When the old man's body was removed from the house, the boy seemed to have lost his reason, and in a frenzy of grief he struggled with the undertaker's men. Then he was left alone. And what loneliness was his! No father, no mother, no relatives, no friends; he was even deprived of the sunlight, which is the friend of all created things. He was two whole days in his room pacing the floor like a caged wolf, without tasting food. The chambermaid, assisted by a compassionate neighbor, succeeded in saving him from this slow process of suicide. He was prevailed upon to eat. He spent the rest of his life praying, and working at his music.

His father, shortly before his death, had obtained for him a position as organist in one of the churches of Madrid, with a salary of seventy cents a day. This was scarcely sufficient to meet the running expenses of a house, however modest; so within a fortnight Juan sold all that had constituted the furniture of his humble home, dismissed his servant, and took a room at a boardinghouse, for which he paid forty cents a day; the remaining thirty cents covered all his other expenses. He lived thus for several months without leaving his room except to fulfill his obligations. His only walks were from the house to the church, and from the church back again. His grief weighed upon him so heavily that he never opened his lips. He spent the long hours of the day composing a grand requiem Mass for the repose of his father's soul, depending upon the charity of the parish for its execution; and although it would be incorrect to say that he strained his five senses—

on account of his having but four—it can at least be said that he threw all the energies of his body and soul into his work.

The ministerial crisis overtook him before his task was half finished. I do not remember who came into power, whether the Radicals, Conservatives, or Constitutionals; at any rate, there was some great change. The news reached Juan late, and to his sorrow. The new cabinet soon judged him, in his capacity as an organist, to be a dangerous citizen, and felt that from the heights of the choir, at vespers or in the solemnity of the Mass, with the swell and the roar from all the stops of the organ, he was evincing sentiments of opposition which were truly scandalous. The new ministers were ill disposed, as they declared in Congress through the lips of one of their authorized members, "to tolerate any form of imposition," so they proceeded with praiseworthy energy to place Juan on the retired list, and to find for him a substitute whose musical maneuvers might offer a better guarantee—a man, in a word, who would prove more loyal to the institutions. On being officially informed of this, the blind one experienced no emotion beyond surprise. In the deep recesses of his heart he was pleased, as he was thus left more time in which to work at his Mass. The situation appeared to him in its real light only when his landlady, at the end of the month, came to him for money. He had none to give her, naturally, as his salary had been withdrawn; and he was compelled to pawn his father's watch, after which he resumed his work with perfect serenity and without a thought of the future. But the landlady came again for money at the end of another month, and he once more pawned a jewel of the scant paternal legacy; this was a small diamond ring. In a few months there was nothing left to pawn. So the landlady, in consideration of his helplessness, kept him two or three days beyond the time and then turned him out, with the self-congratulatory feeling of having acted generously in not claiming his trunk and clothes, from which she might have realized the few cents that he still owed her.

He looked for another lodging but was unable to rent a piano, which was a sore trial to him; evidently he could not finish his Mass. He knew a shopkeeper who owned a piano and who permitted him to make use of it. But Juan soon noticed that his visits grew more and more inopportune, so he left off going. Shortly, too, he was turned out of his new lodgings, only this time they kept his trunk. Then came a period of misery and anguish—of that misery of which it is hard to conceive. We know that life has few joys for the homeless and the poor, but if in addition they be blind and alone, surely they have found the limit of human suffering. Juan was tossed about from lodging to lodging, lying in bed while his only shirt was being washed, wandering through the streets of Madrid with torn shoes, his trousers worn to a fringe about his feet, his hair long, and his beard unshaven. Some compassionate fellow lodger obtained a position for him in a café, from which, however, he was soon turned out, for its frequenters did not relish his music. He never played popular dances or peteneras, no fandangos, not even an occasional polka. His fingers glided over the keys in dreamy ecstasies of Beethoven and Chopin, and the audience found some difficulty in keeping time with their spoons. So out he went again through the byways of the capital. Every now and then some charitable soul, accidentally brought in contact with his misery, assisted him indirectly, for Juan shuddered at the thought of begging. He took his meals in some tavern or other in the lowest quarter of Madrid, ate just enough to keep from starving, and for two cents he was allowed to sleep in a hovel between beggars and evildoers. Once they stole his trousers while he was asleep, and left him a pair of cotton ones in their stead. This was in November.

Poor Juan, who had always cherished the thought of his brother's return, now in the depths of his misery nursed his chimera with redoubled faith. He had a letter written and sent to Havana. As he had no idea how his brother could be reached, the letter bore no direction. He made all manner of inquiries, but to no effect, and he spent long hours on his knees, hoping that Heaven might send Santiago to his rescue. His only happy moments were those spent in prayer, as he knelt behind a pillar in the far-off corner of some solitary church, breathing the acrid odors of dampness and melting wax, listening to the flickering sputter of the tapers and the faint murmur rising from the lips of the faithful in the nave of the temple. His innocent soul then soared above the cruelties of life and communed with God and the Holy Mother. From his early childhood, devotion to the Virgin had been deeply rooted in his heart. As he had never known his mother, he instinctively turned to the mother of God for that tender and loving protection which only a woman can give a child. He had composed a number of hymns and canticles in her honor, and he never fell asleep without pressing his lips to the image of the Carmen, which he wore on his neck.

There came a day, however, when Heaven and earth forsook him. Driven from his last shelter, without a crust to save him from starvation, or a cloak to protect him from the cold, he realized with terror that the time had come when he would have to beg. A great struggle took place in his soul. Shame and suffering made a desperate stand against necessity. The profound darkness which surrounded him increased the anguish of the strife; but hunger conquered in the end. He prayed for strength with sobs, and resigned himself to his fate. Still wishing to disguise his humiliation, he determined to sing in the streets at night only. His voice was good, and he had a rare knowledge of the art of singing. It occurred to him that he had no means of accompaniment. But he soon found another unfortunate, perhaps a trifle less wretched than himself, who lent him an old and broken guitar. He mended it as best he could, and with a voice hoarse with tears he went out into the street on a frosty December night. His heart beat violently; his knees trembled under him. When he tried to sing in one of the central thoroughfares, he found he could not utter a sound. Suffering and shame seemed to have tied a knot in his throat. He groped about until he had found a wall to lean against. There he stood for a while, and when he felt a little calmer he began the tenor's aria from the first act of *Favorita*. A blind singer who sang neither couplets nor popular songs soon excited some curiosity among the passers-by, and in a few minutes a crowd had gathered around him. There was a murmur of surprise and admiration at the art with which he overcame the difficulties of the composition, and many a copper was dropped in the hat that dangled from his arm. After this he sang the aria of the fourth act of *Africana*. But too many had stopped to listen, and the authorities began to fear that this might be a cause of disturbance; for it is a well-established fact with officials of the police force that people who congregate in the streets to hear a blind man sing are always prompted by motives of rebellion—it means a peculiar hostility to the institutions; in a word, an attitude thoroughly incompatible with the peace of society and the security of the State. Accordingly, a policeman caught Juan energetically by the arm and said, "Here, here! go straight home now, and don't let me catch you stopping at any more street corners."

"I'm doing no harm!"

"You are blocking the thoroughfare. Come, move on, move on, if you don't want to go to the lock-up."

It is really encouraging to see how careful our authorities are in clearing the streets of blind singers; and I really believe, in spite of all that has been said to the contrary, that if they could keep them equally free from thieves and murderers, they would do so with pleasure. Juan went back to his hovel with a heavy heart, for he was by nature shrinking and timid, and was grieved at having disturbed the peace and given rise to the interference of the executive power. He had made twenty-seven cents. With this he bought something to eat on the following day, and paid rent for the little pile of straw on which he slept. The next night he went out again and sang a few more operatic arias; but the people again crowded around him, and once more a policeman felt himself called upon to interfere, shouting at him to move on. But how could he? If he kept moving on, he would not make a cent. He could not expect the people to follow him. Juan moved on, however, on and on, because he was timid, and the mere thought of infringing the laws, of disturbing even momentarily the peace of his native land, was worse than death to him. So his earnings rapidly decreased. The necessity of moving on, on the one hand, and the fact that his performances had lost the charm of novelty, which in Spain always commands its price, daily deprived him of a few coppers. With what he brought home at night he could scarcely buy enough food to keep him alive. The situation was desperate. The poor boy saw but one luminous point in the clouded horizon of his life, and that was his brother's return to Madrid. Every night as he left his hovel with his guitar swinging from his shoulder he thought, "If Santiago should be in Madrid and hear me sing, he would know me by my voice." And this hope, or rather this chimera, alone gave him the strength to endure life. However, there came again a day in which his anguish knew no limit. On the preceding night he had earned only six coppers. It had been so cold! This was Christmas Eve. When the morning dawned upon the world, it found Madrid wrapped in a sheet of snow six inches thick. It snowed steadily all day long, which was a matter of little consequence to the majority of people, and was even a cause of much rejoicing among æsthetes generally. Those poets in particular who enjoy what is called easy circumstances spent the greater part of the day watching the flakes through the plate glass of their study windows, meditating upon and elaborating those graceful and ingenious similes that cause the audiences at the theater to shout, "Bravo, bravo!" or those who read their verses to exclaim, "What a genius that young fellow is!"

Juan's breakfast had been a crust of stale bread and a cup of watery coffee. He could not divert his hunger by contemplating the beauty of the snow—in the first place, because he was blind, and in the second,

because, even had he not been blind, he would have had some
difficulty in seeing it through the patched and filthy panes of his
hovel. He spent the day huddled in a corner on his straw mattress,
evoking scenes of his childhood and caressing the sweet dream of his
brother's return. At nightfall he grew very faint, but necessity drove
him into the streets to beg. His guitar was gone. He had sold it for
sixty cents on a day of similar hardship. The snow fell with the same
persistence. His legs trembled as they had when he sang for the first
time, but now it was from hunger rather than shame. He groped
about as best he could, with great lumps of mud above his ankles. The
silence told him that there was scarcely a soul on the street. The carriages rolled noiselessly along, and he once came near being run over.
In one of the central thoroughfares he began to sing the first thing
that came to his lips. His voice was weak and hoarse. Nobody stopped
to listen. "Let us try another street," thought he; and he went down
the Avenue of San Jeronimo, walking awkwardly in the snow, with a
white coating on his shoulders and water squirting from his shoes.
The cold had begun to penetrate into his very bones, and hunger gave
him a violent pain. For a moment with the cold and the pain came a
feeling of faintness which made him think that he was about to die,
and lifting his spirit to the Virgin of the Carmen, his protectress, he
exclaimed in his anguish, "Mother, have pity!" And after pronouncing these words he felt relieved and walked, or rather dragged
himself, to the Plaza de las Cortes. There he grasped a lamppost, and
under the impression of the Virgin's protection sang Gounod's "Ave
Maria." Still nobody stopped to hear him. The people of Madrid were
at the theaters, at the cafés, or at home, dancing their little ones on
their knees in the glow of the hearth—in the warmth of their love.
The snow continued to fall steadily, copiously, with the evident purpose of furnishing a topic for the local column of the morning paper,
where it would be described in a thousand delicate phrases. The occasional passers-by hurried along muffled up to their ears under their
umbrellas. The lampposts had put on their white nightcaps, from
under which escaped thin rays of dismal light. The silence was broken
only by the vague and distant rumble of carriages and by the light fall
of the snowflakes, that sounded like the faint and continuous rustle
of silk. The voice of Juan alone vibrated in the stillness of the night,
imploring the mother of the unprotected; and his chant seemed a cry
of anguish rather than a hymn of praise, a moan of sadness and resignation falling dreary and chill, like snow upon the heart.

And his cry for pity was in vain. In vain he repeated the sweet name of Mary, adjusting it to the modulations of every melody. Heaven and the Virgin were far away, it seemed, and could not hear him. The neighbors of the plaza were near at hand, but they did not choose to hear. Nobody came down to take him in from the cold; no window was thrown open to drop him a copper. The passers-by, pursued, as it were, by the fleet steps of pneumonia, scarcely dared stop. Juan's voice at last died in his throat; he could sing no more. His legs trembled under him; his hands lost their sense of touch. He took a few steps, then sank on the sidewalk at the foot of the grating that surrounds the square. He sat with his elbows on his knees and buried his head in his hands. He felt vaguely that it was the last moment of his life, and he again prayed, imploring the divine pity.

At the end of a few minutes he was conscious of being shaken by the arm and knew that a man was standing before him. He raised his head, and taking for granted it was the old story about moving on, inquired timidly, "Are you an officer?"

"No, I am no officer. What is the matter with you? Get up."

"I don't believe I can, sir."

"Are you very cold?"

"Yes, sir; but it isn't exactly that. I haven't had anything to eat today."

"I will help you, then. Come, up with you."

The man took Juan by both arms and stood him on his feet. He seemed very strong.

"Now lean on me, and let us see if we can find a cab."

"But where are you going to take me?"

"Nowhere where you wouldn't want to go. Are you afraid?"

"No, I feel in my heart that you will help me."

"Come along, then. Let's see how soon I can get you something hot to drink."

"God will reward you for this, sir; the Virgin will reward you. I thought I was going to die there, against that grating."

"Don't talk about dying, man. The question now is to find a cab; if we can only move along fast enough— What is the matter? Are you stumbling?"

"Yes, sir. I think I struck a lamppost. You see—as I am blind—"

"Are you blind?" asked the stranger anxiously.

"Yes, sir."

"Since when?"

"I was born blind."

Juan felt his companion's arm tremble in his, and they walked along in silence. Suddenly the man stopped and asked in a voice husky with emotion, "What is your name?"

"Juan."

"Juan what?"

"Juan Martinez."

"And your father was Manuel Martinez, wasn't he—musician of the third artillery band?"

"Yes, sir."

The blind one felt the tight clasp of two powerful arms that almost smothered him, and heard a trembling voice exclaim, "My God, how horrible, and how happy! I am a criminal, Juan! I am your brother Santiago!"

And the two brothers stood sobbing together in the middle of the street. The snow fell on them lightly. Suddenly Santiago tore himself from his brother's embrace, and began to shout, intermingling his words with interjections, "A cab! A cab! Isn't there a cab anywhere around? Curse my luck! Come, Juanillo, try; make an effort, my boy; we are not so very far. But where in the name of sense are all the cabs? Not one has passed us. Ah, I see one coming, thank God! No, the brute is going in the other direction. Here is another. This one is mine. Hello there, driver! Five dollars if you take us flying to Number 13 Castellana."

And taking his brother in his arms as though he had been a mere child, he put him in the cab and jumped in after him. The driver whipped his horse, and off they went, gliding swiftly and noiselessly over the snow. In the meantime Santiago, with his arms still around Juan, told him something of his life. He had been in Costa Rica, not Cuba, and had accumulated a respectable fortune. He had spent many years in the country, beyond mail service and far from any point of communication with Europe. He had written several letters to his father, and had managed to get these on some steamer trading with England, but had never received any answer. In the hope of returning shortly to Spain, he had made no inquiries. He had been in Madrid for four months. He learned from the parish record that his father was dead; but all he could discover concerning Juan was vague and contradictory. Some believed that he had died, while others said that, reduced to the last stages of misery, he went through the streets singing and playing on the guitar. All his efforts to find him had been fruitless; but fortunately Providence had thrown him into his arms. Santiago laughed and cried alternately, showing himself to be the same frank, open-hearted, jovial soul that Juan had loved so in his childhood. The cab finally came to a stop. A man-servant opened the door, and Juan was fairly lifted into the house. When the door closed behind him, he breathed a warm atmosphere full of that peculiar aroma of comfort which wealth seems to exhale. His feet sank in the soft carpet. Two servants relieved him of his dripping clothes and brought him clean linen and a warm dressing gown. In the same room, before a crackling wood fire, he was served a comforting bowl of hot broth, followed by something more substantial, which he was made to take very slowly and with all the precautions which his critical condition required. Then a bottle of old wine was brought up from the cellar. Santiago was too restless to sit still. He came and went, giving orders, interrupting himself every minute to say, "How do you feel now, Juan? Are you warm enough? Perhaps you don't care for this wine."

When the meal was over, the two brothers sat silently side by side before the fire. Santiago then inquired of one of the servants if the Señora and the children had already retired. On learning that they had, he said to Juan, beaming with delight, "Can you play on the piano?"

"Yes."

"Come into the parlor, then. Let us give them a surprise."

He accordingly led him into an adjoining room and seated him at the piano. He raised the top so as to obtain the greatest possible vibration, threw open the doors, and went through all the maneuvers peculiar to a surprise—tiptoeing, whispering, speaking in a falsetto, and so much absurd pantomime that Juan could not help laughing as he realized how little his brother had changed.

"Now, Juanillo, play something startling, and play it loud, with all your might."

The blind boy struck up a military march. A quiver ran through the silent house like that which stirs a music box while it is being wound up. The notes poured from the piano, hurrying, jostling one another, but never losing their triumphant rhythm. Every now and then Santiago exclaimed, "Louder, Juanillo! Louder!"

And the blind boy struck the notes with all his spirit and might.

"I see my wife peeping in from behind the curtains. Go on, Juanillo. She is in her nightgown—he, he! I am pretending not to see her. I have no doubt she thinks I am crazy—he, he! Go on, Juanillo."

Juan obeyed, although he thought the jest had been carried far enough. He wanted to know his sister-in-law and kiss his nephew.

"Now I can just see Manolita. Hello! Paquito is up too. Didn't I tell you we should surprise them? But I am afraid they will take cold. Stop a minute, Juanito!"

And the infernal clamor was silenced.

"Come, Adela, Manolita, and Paquito, get on your things and come in to see your uncle Juan. This is Juanillo, of whom you have heard me speak so often. I have just found him in the street almost frozen to death. Come, hurry and dress, all of you."

The whole family was soon ready and rushed in to embrace the blind boy. The wife's voice was soft and harmonious. To Juan it sounded like the voice of the Virgin. He discovered, too, that she was weeping silently at the thought of all his sufferings. She ordered a foot warmer to be brought in. She wrapped his legs in a cloak and put a soft cushion behind his head. The children stood around his chair, caressing him, and all listened with tears to the accounts of his past misery. Santiago struck his forehead; the children stroked his hands, saying, "You will never be hungry again, will you, uncle? Or go out without a cloak and an umbrella? I don't want you to, neither does Manolita, nor mamma, nor papa."

"I wager you will not give him your bed, Paquito," said Santiago, trying to conceal his tears under his affected merriment.

"My bed won't fit him, papa! But he can have the bed in the guests' chamber. It is a great bed, uncle, a big, big bed!"

"I don't believe I care to go to bed," said Juan. "Not just now at any rate, I am so comfortable here."

"That pain has gone, hasn't it, uncle?" whispered Manolita, kissing and stroking his hand.

"Yes, dear, yes. God bless you! Nothing pains me now. I am happy, very happy! Only I feel sleepy, so sleepy that I can hardly raise my eyelids."

"Never mind us; sleep if you feel like it," said Santiago.

"Yes, uncle, sleep," repeated the children.

And Juan fell asleep—but he wakened in another world.

The next morning, at dawn, two policemen stumbled against a

corpse in the snow. The doctor of the charity hospital pronounced it a case of congealing of the blood.

As one of the officers turned him over, face upward, "Look, Jimenez," said he; "he seems to be laughing."

A CHRISTMAS CAROL IN PROSE

by Charles Dickens

from *Christmas Books, Tales and Sketches*

Stave One

MARLEY'S GHOST

Marley was dead, to begin with. There is no doubt whatever about that. The register of his burial was signed by the clergyman, the clerk, the undertaker, and the chief mourner. Scrooge signed it. And Scrooge's name was good upon 'Change for anything he chose to put his hand to.

Old Marley was as dead as a door-nail.

Mind! I don't mean to say that I know, of my own knowledge, what there is particularly dead about a door-nail. I might have been inclined, myself, to regard a coffin-nail as the deadest piece of ironmongery in the trade. But the wisdom of our ancestors is in the simile; and my unhallowed hands shall not disturb it, or the Country's done for. You will therefore permit me to repeat, emphatically, that Marley was as dead as a door-nail.

Scrooge knew he was dead? Of course he did. How could it be otherwise? Scrooge and he were partners for I don't know how many years. Scrooge was his sole executor, his sole administrator, his sole assign, his sole residuary legatee, his sole friend, and sole mourner. And even Scrooge was not so dreadfully cut up by the sad event, but that he was an excellent man of business on the very day of the funeral, and solemnised it with an undoubted bargain.

The mention of Marley's funeral brings me back to the point I started from. There is no doubt that Marley was dead. This must be distinctly understood, or nothing wonderful can come of the story I am going to relate. If we were not perfectly convinced that Hamlet's Father died before the play began, there would be nothing more remarkable in his taking a stroll at night, in an easterly wind, upon his own ramparts, than there would be in any other middle-aged gentleman rashly turning out after dark in a breezy spot—say St. Paul's Churchyard, for instance—literally to astonish his son's weak mind.

Scrooge never painted out old Marley's name. There it stood, years afterwards, above the warehouse door: Scrooge and Marley. The firm was known as Scrooge and Marley. Sometimes people new to the business called Scrooge Scrooge, and sometimes Marley, but he answered to both names. It was all the same to him.

Oh! But he was a tight-fisted hand at the grindstone, Scrooge! A squeezing, wrenching, grasping, scraping, clutching, covetous, old sinner! Hard and sharp as flint, from which no steel had ever struck out generous fire; secret, and self-contained, and solitary as an oyster. The cold within him froze his old features, nipped his pointed nose, shrivelled his cheek, stiffened his gait; made his eyes red, his thin lips blue; and spoke out shrewdly in his grating voice. A frosty rime was on his head, and on his eyebrows, and his wiry chin. He carried his own low temperature always about with him; he iced his office in the dog-days; and didn't thaw it one degree at Christmas.

External heat and cold had little influence on Scrooge. No warmth could warm, no wintry weather chill him. No wind that blew was bitterer than he, no falling snow was more intent upon its purpose, no pelting rain less open to entreaty. Foul weather didn't know where to have him. The heaviest rain, and snow, and hail, and sleet, could boast of the advantage over him in only one respect. They often "came down" handsomely, and Scrooge never did.

Nobody ever stopped him in the street to say, with gladsome looks, "My dear Scrooge, how are you? When will you come to see me?" No beggars implored him to bestow a trifle, no children asked him what it was o'clock, no man or woman ever once in all his life inquired the way to such and such a place, of Scrooge. Even the blindmen's dogs appeared to know him; and when they saw him coming on would tug their owners into doorways and up courts; and then would wag their tails as though they said, "No eye at all is better than an evil eye, dark master!"

But what did Scrooge care! It was the very thing he liked. To edge his way along the crowded paths of life, warning all human sympathy to keep its distance, was what the knowing ones call "nuts" to Scrooge.

Once upon a time—of all the good days in the year, on Christmas Eve—old Scrooge sat busy in his counting-house. It was cold, bleak, biting weather—foggy withal; and he could hear the people in the court outside go wheezing up and down, beating their hands upon their breasts, and stamping their feet upon the pavement stones to warm them. The city clocks had only just gone three, but it was quite dark already—it had not been light all day—and candles were flaring in the windows of the neighbouring offices, like ruddy smears upon the palpable brown air. The fog came pouring in at every chink and keyhole, and was so dense without that, although the court was of the narrowest, the houses opposite were mere phantoms. To see the dingy cloud come dropping down, obscuring everything, one might have thought that Nature lived hard by, and was brewing on a large scale.

The door of Scrooge's counting-house was open, that he might keep his eye upon his clerk, who in a dismal little cell beyond, a sort of tank, was copying letters. Scrooge had a very small fire, but the clerk's fire was so very much smaller that it looked like one coal. But he couldn't replenish it, for Scrooge kept the coal-box in his own room; and so surely as the clerk came in with the shovel, the master predicted that it would be necessary for them to part. Wherefore the clerk put on his white comforter, and tried to warm himself at the candle; in which effort, not being a man of strong imagination, he failed.

"A merry Christmas, uncle! God save you!" cried a cheerful voice. It was the voice of Scrooge's nephew, who came upon him so quickly that this was the first intimation he had of his approach.

"Bah!" said Scrooge. "Humbug!"

He had so heated himself with rapid walking in the fog and frost, this nephew of Scrooge's, that he was all in a glow; his face was ruddy and handsome; his eyes sparkled, and his breath smoked again.

"Christmas a humbug, uncle?" said Scrooge's nephew. "You don't mean that, I am sure!"

"I do," said Scrooge. "Merry Christmas! What right have you to be merry? What reason have you to be merry? You're poor enough."

"Come, then," returned the nephew gaily. "What right have you to be dismal? What reason have you to be morose? You're rich enough."

Scrooge, having no better answer ready on the spur of the moment, said, "Bah!" again; and followed it up with "Humbug!"

"Don't be cross, uncle!" said the nephew.

"What else can I be," returned the uncle, "when I live in such a world of fools as this? Merry Christmas! Out upon merry Christmas! What's Christmas-time to you but a time for paying bills without money; a time for finding yourself a year older, and not an hour richer; a time for balancing your books and having every item in 'em through a round dozen of months presented dead against you? If I could work my will," said Scrooge indignantly, "every idiot who goes about with 'Merry Christmas' on his lips should be boiled with his own pudding, and buried with a stake of holly through his heart. He should!"

"Uncle!" pleaded the nephew.

"Nephew!" returned the uncle sternly, "keep Christmas in your own way, and let me keep it in mine."

"Keep it!" repeated Scrooge's nephew. "But you don't keep it."

"Let me leave it alone, then," said Scrooge. "Much good may it do you! Much good it has ever done you!"

"There are many things from which I might have derived good, by which I have not profited, I dare say," returned the nephew, "Christmas among the rest. But I am sure I have always thought of Christmas-time, when it has come round—apart from the veneration due to its sacred name and origin, if anything belonging to it can be apart from that—as a good time; a kind, forgiving, charitable, pleasant time; the only time I know of, in the long calendar of the year, when men and women seem by one consent to open their shut-up hearts freely, and to think of people below them as if they really were fellow-passengers to the grave, and not another race of creatures bound on other journeys. And therefore, uncle, though it has never put a scrap of gold or silver in my pocket, I believe that it *has* done me good, and *will* do me good; and I say, God bless it!"

The clerk in the tank involuntarily applauded. Becoming immediately sensible of the impropriety, he poked the fire, and extinguished the last frail spark for ever.

"Let me hear another sound from *you*," said Scrooge, "and you'll keep your Christmas by losing your situation. You're quite a powerful speaker, sir," he added, turning to his nephew. "I wonder you don't go into Parliament."

"Don't be angry, uncle. Come! Dine with us tomorrow."

Scrooge said that he would see him—yes, indeed, he did. He went the whole length of the expression, and said that he would see him in that extremity first.

"But why?" cried Scrooge's nephew. "Why?"

"Why did you get married?" said Scrooge.

"Because I fell in love."

"Because you fell in love!" growled Scrooge, as if that were the only one thing in the world more ridiculous than a merry Christmas. "Good afternoon!"

"Nay, uncle, but you never came to see me before that happened. Why give it as a reason for not coming now?"

"Good afternoon," said Scrooge.

"I want nothing from you; I ask nothing of you; why cannot we be friends?"

"Good afternoon," said Scrooge.

"I am sorry, with all my heart, to find you so resolute. We have never had any quarrel to which I have been a party. But I have made the trial in homage to Christmas, and I'll keep my Christmas humour to the last. So A Merry Christmas, uncle!"

"Good afternoon!" said Scrooge.

"And A Happy New Year!"

"Good afternoon," said Scrooge.

His nephew left the room without an angry word, notwithstanding. He stopped at the outer door to bestow the greetings of the season on the clerk, who, cold as he was, was warmer than Scrooge; for he returned them cordially.

"There's another fellow," muttered Scrooge, who overheard him; "my clerk, with fifteen shillings a week, and a wife and family, talking about a merry Christmas. I'll retire to Bedlam."

This lunatic, in letting Scrooge's nephew out, had let two other people in. They were portly gentlemen, pleasant to behold, and now stood, with their hats off, in Scrooge's office. They had books and papers in their hands, and bowed to him.

"Scrooge and Marley's, I believe," said one of the gentlemen, referring to his list. "Have I the pleasure of addressing Mr. Scrooge, or Mr. Marley?"

"Mr. Marley has been dead these seven years," Scrooge replied. "He died seven years ago, this very night."

"We have no doubt his liberality is well represented by his surviving partner," said the gentleman, presenting his credentials.

It certainly was; for they had been two kindred spirits. At the ominous word "liberality," Scrooge frowned, and shook his head, and handed the credentials back.

"At this festive season of the year, Mr. Scrooge," said the gentleman, taking up a pen, "it is more than usually desirable that we should make some slight provision for the Poor and destitute, who suffer greatly at the present time. Many thousands are in want of common necessaries; hundreds of thousands are in want of common comforts, sir."

"Are there no prisons?" asked Scrooge.

"Plenty of prisons," said the gentleman, laying down the pen again.

"And the Union workhouses?" demanded Scrooge. "Are they still in operation?"

"They are. Still," returned the gentleman, "I wish I could say they were not."

"The Treadmill and the Poor Law are in full vigour, then?" said Scrooge.

"Both very busy, sir."

"Oh! I was afraid, from what you said at first, that something had occurred to stop them in their useful course," said Scrooge. "I am very glad to hear it."

"Under the impression that they scarcely furnish Christian cheer of mind or body to the multitude," returned the gentleman, "a few of us are endeavouring to raise a fund to buy the Poor some meat and drink, and means of warmth. We choose this time, because it is a time, of all others, when Want is keenly felt, and Abundance rejoices. What shall I put you down for?"

"Nothing!" Scrooge replied.

"You wish to be anonymous?"

"I wish to be left alone," said Scrooge. "Since you ask me what I wish, gentlemen, that is my answer. I don't make merry myself at Christmas, and I can't afford to make idle people merry. I help to support the establishments I have mentioned—they cost enough; and those who are badly off must go there."

"Many can't go there; and many would rather die."

"If they would rather die," said Scrooge, "they had better do it, and decrease the surplus population. Besides—excuse me—I don't know that."

"But you might know it," observed the gentleman.

"It's not my business," Scrooge returned. "It's enough for a man to understand his own business, and not to interfere with other people's. Mine occupies me constantly. Good afternoon, gentlemen!"

Seeing clearly that it would be useless to pursue their point, the gentlemen withdrew. Scrooge resumed his labours with an improved opinion of himself, and in a more facetious temper than was usual with him.

Meanwhile the fog and darkness thickened so that people ran about with flaring links, proffering their services to go before horses and carriages, and conduct them on their way. The ancient tower of a church, whose gruff old bell was always peeping slily down at Scrooge out of a gothic window in the wall, became invisible, and struck the hours and quarters in the clouds, with tremulous vibrations afterwards, as if its teeth were chattering in its frozen head up there. The cold became intense. In the main street, at the corner of the court, some labourers were repairing the gas-pipes, and had lighted a great fire in a brazier, round which a party of ragged men and boys were gathered, warming their hands and winking their eyes before the blaze in rapture. The water-plug being left in solitude, its overflowings suddenly congealed, and turned to misanthropic ice. The brightness of the shops where holly sprigs and berries crackled in the lamp heat of the windows made pale faces ruddy as they passed. Poulterers' and grocers' trades became a splendid joke; a glorious pageant, with which it was next to impossible to believe that such dull principles as bargain and sale had anything to do. The Lord Mayor, in the stronghold of the mighty Mansion House, gave orders to his fifty cooks and butlers to keep Christmas as a Lord Mayor's household should; and even the little tailor whom he had fined five shillings on the previous Monday for being drunk and bloodthirsty in the streets stirred up tomorrow's pudding in his garret, while his lean wife and the baby sallied out to buy the beef.

Foggier yet, and colder! Piercing, searching, biting cold. If the good St. Dunstan had but nipped the Evil Spirit's nose with a touch of such weather as that, instead of using his familiar weapons, then indeed he would have roared to lusty purpose. The owner of one scant young nose, gnawed and mumbled by the hungry cold as bones are gnawed by dogs, stooped down at Scrooge's keyhole to regale him with a Christmas carol; but at the first sound of

> *God bless you, merry gentleman,*
> *May nothing you dismay!*

Scrooge seized the ruler with such energy of action that the singer fled in terror, leaving the keyhole to the fog, and even more congenial frost.

At length the hour of shutting up the counting-house arrived. With an ill-will Scrooge dismounted from his stool, and tacitly admitted the fact to the expectant clerk in the tank, who instantly snuffed his candle out, and put on his hat.

"You'll want all day tomorrow, I suppose?" said Scrooge.

"If quite convenient, sir."

"It's not convenient," said Scrooge, "and it's not fair. If I was to stop half a crown for it, you'd think yourself ill-used, I'll be bound?"

The clerk smiled faintly.

"And yet," said Scrooge, "you don't think *me* ill-used, when I pay a day's wages for no work."

The clerk observed that it was only once a year.

"A poor excuse for picking a man's pocket every twenty-fifth of December!" said Scrooge, buttoning his great-coat to the chin. "But I suppose you must have the whole day. Be here all the earlier next morning."

The clerk promised that he would; and Scrooge walked out with a growl. The office was closed in a twinkling, and the clerk, with the long ends of his white comforter dangling below the waist (for he boasted no great-coat), went down a slide on Cornhill, at the end of a lane of boys, twenty times, in honour of its being Christmas Eve, and then ran home to Camden Town as hard as he could pelt, to play at blindman's buff.

Scrooge took his melancholy dinner in his usual melancholy tavern; and having read all the newspapers, and beguiled the rest of the evening with his banker's book, went home to bed. He lived in chambers which had once belonged to his deceased partner. They were a gloomy suite of rooms, in a lowering pile of building up a yard, where it had so little business to be that one could scarcely help fancying it must have run there when it was a young house, playing at hide-and-seek with other houses, and have forgotten the way out again. It was old enough now, and dreary enough; for nobody lived in it but Scrooge, the other rooms being all let out as offices. The yard was so dark that even Scrooge, who knew its every stone, was fain to grope with his hands. The fog and frost so hung about the black old gateway of the house that it seemed as if the Genius of the Weather sat in mournful meditation on the threshold.

Now it is a fact that there was nothing at all particular about the knocker on the door, except that it was very large. It is also a fact that Scrooge had seen it, night and morning, during his whole residence in that place; also that Scrooge had as little of what is called fancy about him as any man in the city of London, even including —which is a bold word—the corporation, aldermen, and livery. Let it also be borne in mind that Scrooge had not bestowed one thought on Marley since his last mention of his seven-years' dead partner that afternoon. And then let any man explain to me, if he can, how it happened that Scrooge, having his key in the lock of the door, saw in the knocker, without its undergoing any intermediate process of change—not a knocker, but Marley's face.

Marley's face. It was not in impenetrable shadow, as the other objects in the yard were, but had a dismal light about it, like a bad lobster in a dark cellar. It was not angry or ferocious, but looked at Scrooge as Marley used to look; with ghostly spectacles turned up on its ghostly forehead. The hair was curiously stirred, as if by breath or hot air; and though the eyes were wide open, they were perfectly motionless. That, and its livid colour, made it horrible; but its horror seemed to be in spite of the face, and beyond its control, rather than a part of its own expression.

As Scrooge looked fixedly at this phenomenon, it was a knocker again.

To say that he was not startled, or that his blood was not conscious of a terrible sensation to which it had been a stranger from infancy, would be untrue. But he put his hand upon the key he had relinquished, turned it sturdily, walked in, and lighted his candle.

He *did* pause, with a moment's irresolution, before he shut the door; and he *did* look cautiously behind it first, as if he half expected to be terrified with the sight of Marley's pig-tail sticking out into the hall. But there was nothing on the back of the door, except the screws and nuts that held the knocker on, so he said, "Pooh, pooh!" and closed it with a bang.

The sound resounded through the house like thunder. Every room above, and every cask in the wine-merchant's cellars below, appeared to have a separate peal of echoes of its own. Scrooge was not a man to be frightened by echoes. He fastened the door, and walked across the hall, and up the stairs; slowly, too, trimming his candle as he went.

You may talk vaguely about driving a coach-and-six up a good old flight of stairs, or through a bad young Act of Parliament; but I mean to say you might have got a hearse up that staircase, and taken it broadside, with the splinter-bar towards the wall and the door towards the balustrades, and done it easy. There was plenty of width for that, and room to spare; which is perhaps the reason why Scrooge thought he saw a locomotive hearse going on before him in the gloom. Half a dozen gas-lamps out of the street wouldn't have lighted the entry too well, so you may suppose that it was pretty dark with Scrooge's dip.

Up Scrooge went, not caring a button for that. Darkness is cheap, and Scrooge liked it. But before he shut his heavy door, he walked through his rooms to see that all was right. He had just enough recollection of the face to desire to do that.

Sitting-room, bedroom, lumber-room. All as they should be. Nobody under the table, nobody under the sofa; a small fire in the grate; spoon and basin ready; and the little saucepan of gruel (Scrooge had a cold in his head) upon the hob. Nobody under the bed; nobody in the closet; nobody in his dressing-gown, which was hanging up in a suspicious attitude against the wall. Lumber-room as usual. Old fire-guard, old shoes, two fish-baskets, washing-stand on three legs, and a poker.

Quite satisfied, he closed his door, and locked himself in; double-locked himself in, which was not his custom. Thus secured against surprise, he took off his cravat; put on his dressing-gown and slippers, and his nightcap; and sat down before the fire to take his gruel.

It was a very low fire, indeed; nothing on such a bitter night. He was obliged to sit close to it, and brood over it, before he could extract the least sensation of warmth from such a handful of fuel. The fireplace was an old one, built by some Dutch merchant long ago, and paved all round with quaint Dutch tiles, designed to illustrate the Scriptures. There were Cains and Abels, Pharaoh's daughters, Queens of Sheba, Angelic messengers descending through the air on clouds like feather-beds, Abrahams, Belshazzars, Apostles putting off to sea in butter-boats, hundreds of figures to attract his thoughts; and yet that face of Marley, seven years dead, came like the ancient prophet's rod, and swallowed up the whole. If each smooth tile had been a blank at first, with power to shape some picture on its surface from the disjointed fragments of his thoughts, there would have been a copy of old Marley's head on every one.

"Humbug!" said Scrooge; and walked across the room.

After several turns, he sat down again. As he threw his head back in the chair, his glance happened to rest upon a bell, a disused bell, that hung in the room, and communicated for some purpose now forgotten with a chamber in the highest story of the building. It was with great astonishment, and with a strange, inexplicable dread, that, as he looked, he saw this bell begin to swing. It swung so softly in the outset that it scarcely made a sound; but soon it rang out loudly, and so did every bell in the house.

This might have lasted half a minute, or a minute, but it seemed an hour. The bells ceased as they had begun, together. They were succeeded by a clanking noise, deep down below, as if some person were dragging a heavy chain over the casks in the wine-merchant's cellar. Scrooge then remembered to have heard that ghosts in haunted houses were described as dragging chains.

The cellar door flew open with a booming sound, and then he heard the noise much louder, on the floors below; then coming up the stairs; then coming straight towards his door.

"It's humbug still!" said Scrooge. "I won't believe it."

His colour changed, though, when, without a pause, it came on through the heavy door, and passed into the room before his eyes. Upon its coming in, the dying flame leaped up, as though it cried, "I know him! Marley's ghost!" and fell again.

The same face—the very same. Marley in his pig-tail, usual waistcoat, tights, and boots; the tassels on the latter bristling like his pig-tail, and his coat-skirts, and the hair upon his head. The chain he drew was clasped about his middle. It was long and wound about him like a tail; and it was made (for Scrooge observed it closely) of cashboxes, keys, padlocks, ledgers, deeds, and heavy purses wrought in steel. His body was transparent; so that Scrooge, observing him, and looking through his waistcoat, could see the two buttons on his coat behind.

Scrooge had often heard it said that Marley had no bowels, but he had never believed it until now.

No, nor did he believe it even now. Though he looked the phantom through and through, and saw it standing before him; though he felt the chilling influence of its death-cold eyes; and marked the very texture of the folded kerchief bound about its head and chin, which wrapper he had not observed before—he was still incredulous, and fought against his senses.

"How now!" said Scrooge, caustic and cold as ever. "What do you want with me?"

"Much!"—Marley's voice, no doubt about it.

"Who are you?"

"Ask me who I *was*."

"Who *were* you, then?" said Scrooge, raising his voice. "You're particular for a shade." He was going to say "*to* a shade," but substituted this, as more appropriate.

"In life I was your partner, Jacob Marley."

"Can you—can you sit down?" asked Scrooge, looking doubtfully at him.

"I can."

"Do it, then."

Scrooge asked the question, because he didn't know whether a ghost so transparent might find himself in a condition to take a chair; and felt that, in the event of its being impossible, it might involve the necessity of an embarrassing explanation. But the Ghost sat down on the opposite side of the fireplace, as if he were quite used to it.

"You don't believe in me," observed the Ghost.

"I don't," said Scrooge.

"What evidence would you have of my reality beyond that of your own senses?"

"I don't know," said Scrooge.

"Why do you doubt your senses?"

"Because," said Scrooge, "a little thing affects them. A slight disorder of the stomach makes them cheats. You may be an undigested bit of beef, a blot of mustard, a crumb of cheese, a fragment of an underdone potato. There's more of gravy than of grave about you, whatever you are!"

Scrooge was not much in the habit of cracking jokes, nor did he feel in his heart by any means waggish then. The truth is that he tried to be smart, as a means of distracting his own attention, and keeping down his terror; for the spectre's voice disturbed the very marrow in his bones.

To sit staring at those fixed, glazed eyes, in silence for a moment, would play, Scrooge felt, the very deuce with him. There was something very awful, too, in the spectre's being provided with an infernal atmosphere of his own. Scrooge could not feel it himself, but this was clearly the case; for though the Ghost sat perfectly motionless, its hair, and skirts, and tassels, were still agitated as by the hot vapour from an oven.

"You see this toothpick?" said Scrooge, returning quickly to the charge, for the reason just assigned; and wishing, though it were only for a second, to divert the vision's stony gaze from himself.

"I do," replied the Ghost.

"You are not looking at it," said Scrooge.

"But I see it," said the Ghost, "notwithstanding."

"Well!" returned Scrooge; "I have but to swallow this, and be for the rest of my days persecuted by a legion of goblins, all of my own creation. Humbug, I tell you; humbug!"

At this the spirit raised a frightful cry, and shook its chain with such a dismal and appalling noise that Scrooge held on tight to his chair, to save himself from falling in a swoon. But how much greater was his horror, when the phantom, taking off the bandage round his head, as if it were too warm to wear indoors, its lower jaw dropped down upon its breast!

Scrooge fell upon his knees, and clasped his hands before his face.

"Mercy!" he said. "Dreadful apparition, why do you trouble me?"

"Man of the worldly mind," replied the Ghost, "do you believe in me or not?"

"I do," said Scrooge. "I must. But why do spirits walk the earth, and why do they come to me?"

"It is required of every man," the Ghost returned, "that the spirit within him should walk abroad among his fellow-men, and travel far and wide; and if that spirit goes not forth in life, it is condemned to do so after death. It is doomed to wander through the world—oh, woe is me!—and witness what it cannot share, but might have shared on earth, and turned to happiness!"

Again the spectre raised a cry, and shook its chain and wrung its shadowy hands.

"You are fettered," said Scrooge, trembling. "Tell me why?"

"I wear the chain I forged in life," replied the Ghost. "I made it link by link, and yard by yard; I girded it on of my own free will, and of my own free will I wore it. Is its pattern strange to *you?*"

Scrooge trembled more and more.

"Or would you know," pursued the Ghost, "the weight and length of the strong coil you bear yourself? It was full as heavy and as long as this, seven Christmas Eves ago. You have laboured on it since. It is a ponderous chain!"

Scrooge glanced about him on the floor, in the expectation of finding himself surrounded by some fifty or sixty fathoms of iron cable; but he could see nothing.

"Jacob," he said imploringly. "Old Jacob Marley, tell me more. Speak comfort to me, Jacob!"

"I have none to give," the Ghost replied. "It comes from other regions, Ebenezer Scrooge, and is conveyed by other ministers, to other kinds of men. Nor can I tell you what I would. A very little more is all permitted to me. I cannot rest, I cannot stay, I cannot linger anywhere. My spirit never walked beyond our counting-house—mark me!—in life my spirit never roved beyond the narrow limits of our money-changing hole; and weary journeys lie before me!"

It was a habit with Scrooge, whenever he became thoughtful, to put his hands in his breeches' pockets. Pondering on what the Ghost had said, he did so now, but without lifting up his eyes, or getting off his knees.

"You must have been very slow about it, Jacob," Scrooge observed, in a business-like manner, though with humility and deference.

"Slow!" the Ghost repeated.

"Seven years dead," mused Scrooge. "And travelling all the time?"

"The whole time," said the Ghost. "No rest, no peace. Incessant torture of remorse."

"You travel fast?" said Scrooge.

"On the wings of the wind," replied the Ghost.

"You might have got over a great quantity of ground in seven years," said Scrooge.

The Ghost, on hearing this, set up another cry, and clanked its chain so hideously in the dead silence of the night that the Ward would have been justified in indicting it for a nuisance.

"Oh! captive, bound, and double-ironed," cried the phantom, "not to know that ages of incessant labour, by immortal creatures, for this earth must pass into eternity before the good of which it is susceptible is all developed. Not to know that any Christian spirit working kindly in its little sphere, whatever it may be, will find its mortal life too short for its vast means of usefulness. Not to know that no space of regret can make amends for one life's opportunities misused! Yet such was I! Oh! such was I!"

"But you were always a good man of business, Jacob," faltered Scrooge, who now began to apply this to himself.

"Business!" cried the Ghost, wringing its hands again. "Mankind was my business. The common welfare was my business; charity, mercy, forbearance, and benevolence were, all, my business. The dealings of my trade were but a drop of water in the comprehensive ocean of my business!"

It held up its chain at arm's length, as if that were the cause of all its unavailing grief, and flung it heavily upon the ground again.

"At this time of the rolling year," the spectre said, "I suffer most. Why did I walk through crowds of fellow-beings with my eyes turned down, and never raise them to that blessed Star which led the Wise Men to a poor abode! Were there no poor homes to which its light would have conducted *me!*"

Scrooge was very much dismayed to hear the spectre going on at this rate, and began to quake exceedingly.

"Hear me!" cried the Ghost. "My time is nearly gone."

"I will," said Scrooge. "But don't be hard upon me! Don't be flowery, Jacob! Pray!"

"How is it that I appear before you in a shape that you can see, I may not tell. I have sat invisible beside you many and many a day."

It was not an agreeable idea. Scrooge shivered, and wiped the perspiration from his brow.

"That is no light part of my penance," pursued the Ghost. "I am here tonight to warn you, that you have yet a chance and hope of escaping my fate. A chance and hope of my procuring, Ebenezer."

"You were always a good friend to me," said Scrooge. "Thankee!"

"You will be haunted," resumed the Ghost, "by Three Spirits."

Scrooge's countenance fell almost as low as the Ghost's had done.

"Is that the chance and hope you mentioned, Jacob?" he demanded, in a faltering voice.

"It is."

"I—I think I'd rather not," said Scrooge.

"Without their visits," said the Ghost, "you cannot hope to shun the path I tread. Expect the first tomorrow, when the bell tolls One."

"Couldn't I take 'em all at once, and have it over, Jacob?" hinted Scrooge.

"Expect the second on the next night at the same hour. The third, upon the next night when the last stroke of Twelve has ceased to vibrate. Look to see me no more; and look that, for your own sake, you remember what has passed between us!"

When it had said these words, the spectre took its wrapper from the table, and bound it round its head, as before. Scrooge knew this by the smart sound its teeth made, when the jaws were brought together by the bandage. He ventured to raise his eyes again, and found his supernatural visitor confronting him in an erect attitude, with its chain wound over and about its arm.

The apparition walked backwards from him; and at every step it took, the window raised itself a little, so that when the spectre reached it, it was wide open. It beckoned Scrooge to approach, which he did. When they were within two paces of each other, Marley's Ghost held up its hand, warning him to come no nearer. Scrooge stopped.

Not so much in obedience, as in surprise and fear; for on the raising of the hand, he became sensible of confused noises in the air; incoherent sounds of lamentation and regret; wailings inexpressibly sorrowful and self-accusatory. The spectre, after listening for a moment, joined in the mournful dirge, and floated out upon the bleak, dark night.

Scrooge followed to the window, desperate in his curiosity. He looked out.

The air was filled with phantoms, wandering hither and thither in restless haste, and moaning as they went. Every one of them wore chains like Marley's Ghost; some few (they might be guilty governments) were linked together; none were free. Many had been personally known to Scrooge in their lives. He had been quite familiar with one old ghost in a white waistcoat, with a monstrous iron safe attached to its ankle, who cried piteously at being unable to assist a wretched woman with an infant, whom it saw below upon a doorstep. The misery with them all was, clearly, that they sought to interfere, for good, in human matters and had lost the power for ever.

Whether these creatures faded into mist, or mist enshrouded them, he could not tell. But they and their spirit voices faded together; and the night became as it had been when he walked home.

Scrooge closed the window, and examined the door by which the Ghost had entered. It was double-locked, as he had locked it with his own hands, and the bolts were undisturbed. He tried to say "Humbug!" but stopped at the first syllable. And being, from the emotion he had undergone, or the fatigues of the day, or his glimpse of the Invisible World, or the dull conversation of the Ghost, or the lateness of the hour, much in need of repose, went straight to bed, without undressing, and fell asleep upon the instant.

Stave Two

THE FIRST OF THE THREE SPIRITS

When Scrooge awoke, it was so dark, that, looking out of bed, he could scarcely distinguish the transparent window from the opaque walls of his chamber. He was endeavouring to pierce the darkness with his ferret eyes, when the chimes of a neighbouring church struck the four quarters. So he listened for the hour.

To his great astonishment, the heavy bell went on from six to seven, and from seven to eight, and regularly up to twelve; then stopped. Twelve! It was past two when he went to bed. The clock was wrong. An icicle must have got into the works. Twelve!

He touched the spring of his repeater to correct this most preposterous clock. Its rapid little pulse beat twelve, and stopped.

"Why, it isn't possible," said Scrooge, "that I can have slept through a whole day and far into another night. It isn't possible that anything has happened to the sun, and this is twelve at noon!"

The idea being an alarming one, he scrambled out of bed, and groped his way to the window. He was obliged to rub the frost off with the sleeve of his dressing-gown before he could see anything; and could see very little then. All he could make out was, that it was still very foggy and extremely cold, and that there was no noise of people running to and fro, and making a great stir, as there unquestionably would have been if night had beaten off bright day, and taken possession of the world. This was a great relief, because "Three days after sight of this First of Exchange pay to Mr. Ebenezer Scrooge or his order," and so forth, would have become a mere United States' security if there were no days to count by.

Scrooge went to bed again, and thought, and thought, and thought it over and over, and could make nothing of it. The more he thought, the more perplexed he was; and the more he endeavoured not to think, the more he thought.

Marley's Ghost bothered him exceedingly. Every time he resolved within himself after mature inquiry, that it was all a dream, his mind flew back again, like a strong spring released, to its first position, and presented the same problem to be worked all through, "Was it a dream or not?"

Scrooge lay in this state until the chime had gone three quarters more, when he remembered, on a sudden, that the Ghost had warned him of a visitation when the bell tolled one. He resolved to lie awake until the hour was passed; and, considering that he could no more go to sleep than go to Heaven, this was perhaps the wisest resolution in his power.

The quarter was so long, that he was more than once convinced he must have sunk into a doze unconsciously, and missed the clock. At length it broke upon his listening ear.

"Ding, dong!"

"A quarter past," said Scrooge, counting.

"Ding, dong!"

"Half-past!" said Scrooge.

"Ding, dong!"

"A quarter to it," said Scrooge.

"Ding, dong!"

"The hour itself," said Scrooge triumphantly, "and nothing else!"

He spoke before the hour bell sounded, which it now did with a deep, dull, hollow, melancholy ONE. Light flashed up in the room upon the instant, and the curtains of his bed were drawn.

The curtains of his bed were drawn aside, I tell you, by a hand. Not the curtains at his feet, nor the curtains at his back, but those to which his face was addressed. The curtains of his bed were drawn aside; and Scrooge, starting up into a half-recumbent attitude, found himself face to face with the unearthly visitor who drew them—as close to it as I am now to you, and I am standing in the spirit at your elbow.

It was a strange figure—like a child; yet not so like a child as like an old man, viewed through some supernatural medium, which gave him the appearance of having receded from the view, and being diminished to a child's proportions. Its hair, which hung about its neck and down its back, was white as if with age; and yet the face had not a wrinkle in it, and the tenderest bloom was on the skin. The arms were very long and muscular; the hands the same, as if its hold were of uncommon strength. Its legs and feet, most delicately formed, were, like those upper members, bare. It wore a tunic of the purest white; and round its waist was bound a lustrous belt, the sheen of which was beautiful. It held a branch of fresh green holly in its hand; and, in singular contradiction of that wintry emblem, had its dress trimmed with summer flowers. But the strangest thing about it was, that from the crown of its head there sprung a bright clear jet of light, by which all this was visible; and which was doubtless the occasion of its using, in its duller moments, a great extinguisher for a cap, which it now held under its arm.

Even this, though, when Scrooge looked at it with increasing steadiness, was *not* its strangest quality. For as its belt sparkled and glittered now in one part and now in another, and what was light one instant at another time was dark, so the figure itself fluctuated in its distinctness, being now a thing with one arm, now with one leg, now with twenty legs, now a pair of legs without a head, now a head without a body, of which dissolving parts, no outline would be visible in the dense gloom wherein they melted away. And in the very wonder of this, it would be itself again; distinct and clear as ever.

"Are you the Spirit, sir, whose coming was foretold to me?" asked Scrooge.

"I am!"

The voice was soft and gentle. Singularly low, as if instead of being so close beside him, it were at a distance.

"Who and what are you?" Scrooge demanded.

"I am the Ghost of Christmas Past."

"Long Past?" inquired Scrooge, observant of its dwarfish stature.

"No. Your past."

Perhaps Scrooge could not have told anybody why, if anybody could have asked him; but he had a special desire to see the Spirit in his cap, and begged him to be covered.

"What!" exclaimed the Ghost, "would you so soon put out, with worldly hands, the light I give? Is it not enough that you are one of those whose passions made this cap, and force me through whole trains of years to wear it low upon my brow!"

Scrooge reverently disclaimed all intention to offend or any knowledge of having wilfully "bonneted" the Spirit at any period of his life. He then made bold to inquire what business brought him there.

"Your welfare!" said the Ghost.

Scrooge expressed himself much obliged, but could not help thinking that a night of unbroken rest would have been more conducive to that end. The Spirit must have heard him thinking, for it said immediately: "Your reclamation, then. Take heed!"

It put out its strong hand as it spoke, and clasped him gently by the arm.

"Rise! and walk with me!"

It would have been in vain for Scrooge to plead that the weather and the hour were not adapted to pedestrian purposes; that bed was warm, and the thermometer a long way below freezing; that he was clad but lightly in his slippers, dressing-gown, and nightcap; and that he had a cold upon him at that time. The grasp, though gentle as a woman's hand, was not to be resisted. He rose; but finding that the Spirit made towards the window, clasped its robe in supplication.

"I am a mortal," Scrooge remonstrated, "and liable to fall."

"Bear but a touch of my hand *there*," said the Spirit, laying it upon his heart, "and you shall be upheld in more than this."

As the words were spoken, they passed through the wall, and stood upon an open country road, with fields on either hand. The city had entirely vanished. Not a vestige of it was to be seen. The darkness and the mist had vanished with it, for it was a clear, cold, winter day, with snow upon the ground.

"Good Heaven!" said Scrooge, clasping his hands together, as he looked about him. "I was bred in this place. I was a boy here!"

The Spirit gazed upon him mildly. Its gentle touch, though it had been light and instantaneous, appeared still present to the old man's sense of feeling. He was conscious of a thousand odours floating in the air, each one connected with a thousand thoughts, and hopes, and joys, and cares long, long forgotten!

"Your lip is trembling," said the Ghost. "And what is that upon your cheek?"

Scrooge muttered, with an unusual catching in his voice, that it was a pimple; and begged the Ghost to lead him where he would.

"You recollect the way?" inquired the Spirit.

"Remember it!" cried Scrooge, with fervour; "I could walk it blindfold."

"Strange to have forgotten it for so many years!" observed the Ghost. "Let us go on."

They walked along the road, Scrooge recognising every gate, and post, and tree; until a little market-town appeared in the distance, with its bridge, its church, and winding river. Some shaggy ponies now were seen trotting towards them with boys upon their backs, who called to other boys in country gigs and carts, driven by farmers. All these boys were in great spirits, and shouted to each other, until the broad fields were so full of merry music that the crisp air laughed to hear it.

"These are but shadows of the things that have been," said the Ghost. "They have no consciousness of us."

The jocund travellers came on; and as they came, Scrooge knew and named them every one. Why was he rejoiced beyond all bounds to see them! Why did his cold eye glisten, and his heart leap up as they went past! Why was he filled with gladness when he heard them give each other Merry Christmas, as they parted at cross-roads and byways for their several homes? What was Merry Christmas to Scrooge? Out upon Merry Christmas! What good had it ever done to him?

"The school is not quite deserted," said the Ghost. "A solitary child, neglected by his friends, is left there still."

Scrooge said he knew it. And he sobbed.

They left the high-road, by a well-remembered lane, and soon approached a mansion of dull red brick, with a little weathercock-surmounted cupola on the roof, and a bell hanging in it. It was a large house, but one of broken fortunes; for the spacious offices were little used, their walls were damp and mossy, their windows broken, and their gates decayed. Fowls clucked and strutted in the stables; and the coach-houses and sheds were overrun with grass. Nor was it more retentive of its ancient state within; for entering the dreary hall, and glancing through the open doors of many rooms, they found them poorly furnished, cold, and vast. There was an earthy savour in the air, a chilly bareness in the place which associated itself somehow with too much getting up by candle-light, and not too much to eat.

They went, the Ghost and Scrooge, across the hall, to a door at the back of the house. It opened before them, and disclosed a long, bare, melancholy room, made barer still by lines of plain deal forms and desks. At one of these a lonely boy was reading near a feeble fire; and Scrooge sat down upon a form, and wept to see his poor forgotten self as he had used to be.

Not a latent echo in the house, not a squeak and scuffle from the mice behind the panelling, not a drip from the half-thawed waterspout in the dull yard behind, not a sigh among the leafless boughs of one despondent poplar, not the idle swinging of an empty storehouse door, no, not a clicking in the fire, but fell upon the heart of Scrooge with softening influence, and gave a freer passage to his tears.

The Spirit touched him on the arm, and pointed to his younger self, intent upon his reading. Suddenly a man in foreign garments, wonderfully real and distinct to look at, stood outside the window, with an axe stuck in his belt, and leading by the bridle an ass laden with wood.

"Why, it's Ali Baba!" Scrooge exclaimed in ecstasy. "It's dear old honest Ali Baba! Yes, yes, I know. One Christmas-time, when yonder solitary child was left here all alone, he *did* come, for the first time, just like that. Poor boy! And Valentine," said Scrooge, "and his wild brother, Orson; there they go! And what's his name, who was put down in his drawers, asleep, at the gate of Damascus; don't you see him! And the Sultan's Groom turned upside down by the Genii, there he is upon his head! Serve him right. I'm glad of it. What business had *he* to be married to the Princess!"

To hear Scrooge expending all the earnestness of his nature on such subjects, in a most extraordinary voice between laughing and crying, and to see his heightened and excited face, would have been a surprise to his business friends in the city, indeed.

"There's the Parrot!" cried Scrooge. "Green body and yellow tail, with a thing like a lettuce growing out of the top of his head; there he is! Poor Robin Crusoe, he called him, when he came home again after sailing round the island. 'Poor Robin Crusoe, where have you been, Robin Crusoe?' The man thought he was dreaming, but he wasn't. It was the Parrot, you know. There goes Friday, running for his life to the little creek! Halloa! Hoop! Halloo!"

Then, with a rapidity of transition very foreign to his usual character, he said, in pity for his former self, "Poor boy!" and cried again.

"I wish," Scrooge muttered, putting his hand in his pocket, and looking about him, after drying his eyes with his cuff—"but it's too late now."

"What is the matter?" asked the Spirit.

"Nothing," said Scrooge. "Nothing. There was a boy singing a Christmas carol at my door last night. I should like to have given him something; that's all."

The Ghost smiled thoughtfully, and waved its hand; saying as it did so, "Let us see another Christmas!"

Scrooge's former self grew larger at the words, and the room became a little darker and more dirty. The panels shrunk, the windows cracked; fragments of plaster fell out of the ceiling, and the naked laths were shown instead; but how all this was brought about, Scrooge knew no more than you do. He only knew that it was quite correct; that everything had happened so; that there he was, alone again, when all the other boys had gone home for the jolly holidays.

He was not reading now, but walking up and down despairingly. Scrooge looked at the Ghost, and, with a mournful shaking of his head, glanced anxiously towards the door.

It opened; and a little girl, much younger than the boy, came darting in, and putting her arms about his neck, and often kissing him, addressed him as her "Dear, dear brother."

"I have come to bring you home, dear brother!" said the child, clapping her tiny hands, and bending down to laugh. "To bring you home, home, home!"

"Home, little Fan?" returned the boy.

"Yes!" said the child, brimful of glee. "Home, for good and all. Home, for ever and ever. Father is so much kinder than he used to be that home's like Heaven! He spoke so gently to me one dear night when I was going to bed that I was not afraid to ask him once more if you might come home; and he said Yes, you should; and sent me in a coach to bring you. And you're to be a man!" said the child, opening her eyes; "and are never to come back here; but first, we're to be together all the Christmas long, and have the merriest time in all the world."

"You are quite a woman, little Fan!" exclaimed the boy.

She clapped her hands and laughed, and tried to touch his head; but being too little, laughed again, and stood on tiptoe to embrace him. Then she began to drag him, in her childish eagerness, towards the door; and he, nothing loth to go, accompanied her.

A terrible voice in the hall cried, "Bring down Master Scrooge's box, there!" and in the hall appeared the schoolmaster himself, who glared on Master Scrooge with a ferocious condescension, and threw him into a dreadful state of mind by shaking hands with him. He then conveyed him and his sister into the veriest old well of a shivering best parlour that ever was seen, where the maps upon the wall, and the celestial and terrestrial globes in the windows were waxy with cold. Here he produced a decanter of curiously light wine, and a block of curiously heavy cake, and administered instalments of those dainties to the young people; at the same time sending out a meagre servant to offer a glass of "something" to the postboy, who answered that he thanked the gentleman, but if it was the same tap as he had tasted before he had rather not. Master Scrooge's trunk being by this time tied on to the top of the chaise, the children bade the schoolmaster good-bye right willingly; and getting into it, drove gaily down the garden-sweep, the quick wheels dashing the hoar-frost and snow from off the dark leaves of the evergreens like spray.

"Always a delicate creature, whom a breath might have withered," said the Ghost. "But she had a large heart!"

"So she had," cried Scrooge. "You're right. I will not gainsay it, Spirit. God forbid!"

"She died a woman," said the Ghost, "and had, as I think, children."

"One child," Scrooge returned.

"True," said the Ghost. "Your nephew!"

Scrooge seemed uneasy in his mind; and answered briefly, "Yes."

Although they had but that moment left the school behind them, they were now in the busy thoroughfares of a city, where shadowy passengers passed and repassed; where shadowy carts and coaches battled for the way, and all the strife and tumult of a real city were. It was made plain enough, by the dressing of the shops, that here, too, it was Christmas-time again; but it was evening, and the streets were lighted up.

The Ghost stopped at a certain warehouse door, and asked Scrooge if he knew it.

"Know it!" said Scrooge. "I was apprenticed here!"

They went in. At sight of an old gentleman in a Welsh wig, sitting behind such a high desk that if he had been two inches taller he must have knocked his head against the ceiling, Scrooge cried in great excitement: "Why, it's old Fezziwig! Bless his heart; it's Fezziwig alive again!"

Old Fezziwig laid down his pen, and looked up at the clock, which pointed to the hour of seven. He rubbed his hands; adjusted his capacious waistcoat; laughed all over himself, from his shoes to his organ of benevolence, and called out in a comfortable, oily, rich, fat, jovial voice: "Yo ho, there! Ebenezer! Dick!"

Scrooge's former self, now grown a young man, came briskly in, accompanied by his fellow-'prentice.

"Dick Wilkins, to be sure!" said Scrooge to the Ghost. "Bless me, yes. There he is. He was very much attached to me, was Dick. Poor Dick! Dear, dear!"

"Yo ho, my boys!" said Fezziwig. "No more work tonight. Christmas Eve, Dick. Christmas, Ebenezer! Let's have the shutters up," cried old Fezziwig, with a sharp clap of his hands, "before a man can say Jack Robinson!"

You wouldn't believe how those two fellows went at it! They charged into the street with the shutters—one, two, three—had 'em up in their places—four, five, six—barred 'em and pinned 'em—seven, eight, nine—and came back before you could have got to twelve, panting like race-horses.

"Hilli-ho!" cried old Fezziwig, skipping down from the high desk, with wonderful agility. "Clear away, my lads, and let's have lots of room here! Hilli-ho, Dick! Chirrup, Ebenezer!"

Clear away! There was nothing they wouldn't have cleared away, or couldn't have cleared away, with old Fezziwig looking on. It was done in a minute. Every movable was packed off, as if it were dismissed from public life for evermore; the floor was swept and watered, the lamps were trimmed, fuel was heaped upon the fire; and the warehouse was as snug, and warm, and dry, and bright a ballroom, as you would desire to see upon a winter's night.

In came fiddler with a music-book, and went up to the lofty desk, and made an orchestra of it, and tuned like fifty stomach-aches. In came Mrs. Fezziwig, one vast substantial smile. In came the three Miss Fezziwigs, beaming and lovable. In came the six young followers whose hearts they broke. In came all the young men and women employed in the business. In came the housemaid, with her cousin the baker. In came the cook, with her brother's particular friend, the milkman. In came the boy from over the way, who was suspected of not having board enough from his master; trying to hide himself behind the girl from next door but one, who was proved to have had her ears pulled by her mistress. In they all came, one after another; some shyly, some boldly, some gracefully, some awkwardly, some pushing, some pulling—in they all came, anyhow and everyhow. Away they all went, twenty couple at once; hands half round and back again the other way; down the middle and up again, round and round in various stages of affectionate groupings; old top couple always turning up in the wrong place; new top couple starting off again, as soon as they got there; all top couples at last, and not a bottom one to help them! When this result was brought about, old Fezziwig, clapping his hands to stop the dance, cried out, "Well done!" and the fiddler plunged his hot face into a pot of porter, especially provided for that purpose. But scorning rest upon his reappearance, he instantly began again, though there were no dancers yet, as if the other fiddler had been carried home, exhausted, on a shutter, and he were a brand-new man resolved to beat him out of sight or perish.

There were more dances, and there were forfeits, and more dances, and there was cake, and there was negus, and there was a great piece of Cold Roast, and there was a great piece of Cold Boiled, and there were mince-pies, and plenty of beer. But the great effect of the evening came after the Roast and Boiled, when the fiddler (an artful dog, mind! The sort of man who knew his business better than you or I could have told it him!) struck up "Sir Roger de Coverley." Then old Fezziwig stood out to dance with Mrs. Fezziwig. Top couple, too; with a good stiff piece of work cut out for them; three or four and twenty pair of partners; people who were not to be trifled with; people who *would* dance, and had no notion of walking.

But if they had been twice as many—ah, four times—old Fezziwig would have been a match for them, and so would Mrs. Fezziwig. As to *her*, she was worthy to be his partner in every sense of the term. If that's not high praise, tell me higher, and I'll use it. A positive light appeared to issue from Fezziwig's calves. They shone in every part of the dance like moons. You couldn't have predicted, at any given time, what would become of them next. And when old Fezziwig and Mrs. Fezziwig had gone all through the dance; advance and retire, both hands to your partner, bow and curtsey, corkscrew, thread-the-needle, and back again to your place; Fezziwig "cut"—cut so deftly that he appeared to wink with his legs, and came upon his feet again without a stagger.

When the clock struck eleven, this domestic ball broke up. Mr. and Mrs. Fezziwig took their stations, one on either side the door, and shaking hands with every person individually as he or she went out, wished him or her a Merry Christmas. When everybody had retired but the two 'prentices, they did the same to them; and thus the cheerful voices died away, and the lads were left to their beds; which were under a counter in the back shop.

During the whole of this time Scrooge had acted like a man out of his wits. His heart and soul were in the scene, and with his former self. He corroborated everything, remembered everything, enjoyed everything, and underwent the strangest agitation. It was not until now, when the bright faces of his former self and Dick were turned from them, that he remembered the Ghost, and became conscious that it was looking full upon him, while the light upon its head burnt very clear.

"A small matter," said the Ghost, "to make these silly folks so full of gratitude."

"Small!" echoed Scrooge.

The Spirit signed to him to listen to the two apprentices, who were pouring out their hearts in praise of Fezziwig, and when he had done so said: "Why! Is it not? He has spent but a few pounds of your mortal money: three or four, perhaps. Is that so much that he deserves this praise?"

"It isn't that," said Scrooge, heated by the remark, and speaking unconsciously like his former, not his latter self. "It isn't that, Spirit. He has the power to render us happy or unhappy; to make our service light or burdensome; a pleasure or a toil. Say that his power lies in words and looks; in things so slight and insignificant that it is impossible to add and count 'em up; what, then? The happiness he gives is quite as great as if it cost a fortune."

He felt the Spirit's glance, and stopped.

"What is the matter?" asked the Ghost.

"Nothing particular," said Scrooge.

"Something, I think?" the Ghost insisted.

"No," said Scrooge, "no. I should like to be able to say a word or two to my clerk just now. That's all."

His former self turned down the lamps as he gave utterance to the wish; and Scrooge and the Ghost again stood side by side in the open air.

"My time grows short," observed the Spirit. "Quick!"

This was not addressed to Scrooge, or to any one whom he could see, but it produced an immediate effect. For again Scrooge saw himself. He was older now; a man in the prime of life. His face had not the harsh and rigid lines of later years; but it had begun to wear the signs of care and avarice. There was an eager, greedy, restless motion in the eye, which showed the passion that had taken root, and where the shadow of the growing tree would fall.

He was not alone, but sat by the side of a fair young girl in a mourning-dress; in whose eyes there were tears, which sparkled in the light that shone out of the Ghost of Christmas Past.

"It matters little," she said softly. "To you, very little. Another idol has displaced me; and if it can cheer and comfort you in time to come as I would have tried to do, I have no just cause to grieve."

"What idol has displaced you?" he rejoined.

"A golden one."

"This is the even-handed dealing of the world!" he said. "There is nothing on which it is so hard as poverty; and there is nothing it professes to condemn with such severity as the pursuit of wealth!"

"You fear the world too much," she answered gently. "All your other hopes have merged into the hope of being beyond the chance of its sordid reproach. I have seen your nobler aspirations fall off one by one, until the master-passion, Gain, engrosses you. Have I not?"

"What then?" he retorted. "Even if I have grown so much wiser, what then? I am not changed towards you."

She shook her head.

"Am I?"

"Our contract is an old one. It was made when we were both poor and content to be so, until, in good season, we could improve our worldly fortune by our patient industry. You *are* changed. When it was made, you were another man."

"I was a boy," he said impatiently.

"Your own feeling tells you that you were not what you are," she returned. "I am. That which promised happiness when we were one in heart is fraught with misery now that we are two. How often and how keenly I have thought of this, I will not say. It is enough that I *have* thought of it, and can release you."

"Have I ever sought release?"

"In words—no. Never."

"In what, then?"

"In a changed nature; in an altered spirit; in another atmosphere of life; another Hope as its great end. In everything that made my love of any worth or value in your sight. If this had never been between us," said the girl, looking mildly, but with steadiness, upon him, "tell me, would you seek me out and try to win me now? Ah, no!"

He seemed to yield to the justice of this supposition, in spite of himself. But he said, with a struggle, "You think not."

"I would gladly think otherwise if I could," she answered, "Heaven knows! When I have learned a Truth like this, I know how strong and irresistible it must be. But if you were free today, tomorrow, yesterday, can even I believe that you would choose a dowerless girl—you who, in your very confidence with her, weigh everything by Gain; or choosing her, if for a moment you were false enough to your one guiding principle to do so, do I not know that your repentance and regret would surely follow? I do; and I release you. With a full heart, for the love of him you once were."

He was about to speak; but with her head turned from him, she resumed: "You may—the memory of what is past half makes me hope you will—have pain in this. A very, very brief time, and you will dismiss the recollection of it, gladly, as an unprofitable dream, from which it happened well that you awoke. May you be happy in the life you have chosen!"

She left him and they parted.

"Spirit!" said Scrooge, "show me no more! Conduct me home. Why do you delight to torture me?"

"One shadow more!" exclaimed the Ghost.

"No more!" cried Scrooge. "No more. I don't wish to see it. Show me no more!"

But the relentless Ghost pinioned him in both his arms, and forced him to observe what happened next.

They were in another scene and place; a room, not very large or handsome, but full of comfort. Near to the winter fire sat a beautiful young girl, so like that last that Scrooge believed it was the same, until he saw her, now a comely matron, sitting opposite her daughter. The noise in this room was perfectly tumultuous, for there were more children there than Scrooge in his agitated state of mind could count; and, unlike the celebrated herd in the poem, they were not forty children conducting themselves like one, but every child was conducting itself like forty. The consequences were uproarious beyond belief; but no one seemed to care; on the contrary, the mother and daughter laughed heartily, and enjoyed it very much; and the latter, soon beginning to mingle in the sports, got pillaged by the young brigands most ruthlessly. What would I not have given to be one of them! Though I never could have been so rude, no, no! I wouldn't for the wealth of all the world have crushed that braided hair, and torn it down; and for the precious little shoe, I wouldn't have plucked it off, God bless my soul! to save my life. As to measuring her waist in sport, as they did, bold young brood, I couldn't have done it; I should have expected my arm to have grown round it for a punishment, and never come straight again. And yet I should have dearly liked, I own, to have touched her lips; to have questioned her, that she might have opened them; to have looked upon the lashes of her downcast eyes, and never raised a blush; to have let loose waves of hair, an inch of which would be a keepsake beyond price; in short, I should have liked, I do confess, to have had the slightest licence of a child, and yet to have been man enough to know its value.

But now a knocking at the door was heard, and such a rush immediately ensued that she with laughing face and plundered dress was borne towards it in the centre of a flushed and boisterous group, just in time to greet the father, who came home attended by a man laden with Christmas toys and presents. Then the shouting and the struggling, and the onslaught that was made on the defenceless porter! The scaling him, with chairs for ladders, to dive into his pockets, despoil him of brown-paper parcels, hold on tight by his cravat, hug him round the neck, pommel his back, and kick his legs in irrepressible affection! The shouts of wonder and delight with which the development of every package was received! The terrible announcement that the baby had been taken in the act of putting a doll's frying-pan into his mouth, and was more than suspected of having swallowed a fictitious turkey, glued on a wooden platter! The immense relief of finding this a false alarm! The joy, and gratitude, and ecstasy! They are all indescribable alike. It is enough that, by degrees, the children and their emotions got out of the parlour, and, by one stair at a time, up to the top of the house, where they went to bed and so subsided.

And now Scrooge looked on more attentively than ever, when the master of the house, having his daughter leaning fondly on him, sat down with her and her mother at his own fireside; and when he thought that such another creature, quite as graceful and as full of promise, might have called him father, and been a spring-time in the haggard winter of his life, his sight grew very dim indeed.

"Belle," said the husband, turning to his wife with a smile, "I saw an old friend of yours this afternoon."

"Who was it?"

"Guess!"

"How can I? Tut, don't I know," she added, in the same breath, laughing as he laughed. "Mr. Scrooge."

"Mr. Scrooge it was. I passed his office window; and as it was not shut up, and he had a candle inside, I could scarcely help seeing him. His partner lies upon the point of death, I hear; and there he sat alone. Quite alone in the world, I do believe."

"Spirit!" said Scrooge, in a broken voice, "remove me from this place."

"I told you these were shadows of the things that have been," said the Ghost. "That they are what they are, do not blame me!"

"Remove me!" Scrooge exclaimed. "I cannot bear it!"

He turned upon the Ghost, and seeing that it looked upon him with a face in which in some strange way there were fragments of all the faces it had shown him, wrestled with it.

"Leave me! Take me back. Haunt me no longer!"

In the struggle—if that can be called a struggle in which the Ghost, with no visible resistance on its own part, was undisturbed by any effort of its adversary—Scrooge observed that its light was burning high and bright; and dimly connecting that with its influence over him, he seized the extinguisher cap, and by a sudden action pressed it down upon its head.

The Spirit dropped beneath it, so that the extinguisher covered its whole form; but though Scrooge pressed it down with all his force, he could not hide the light, which streamed from under it, in an unbroken flood upon the ground.

He was conscious of being exhausted, and overcome by an irresistible drowsiness; and further, of being in his own bedroom. He gave the cap a parting squeeze, in which his hand relaxed; and had barely time to reel to bed, before he sank into a heavy sleep.

Stave Three

THE SECOND OF THE THREE SPIRITS

Awaking in the middle of a prodigiously tough snore, and sitting up in bed to get his thoughts together, Scrooge had no occasion to be told that the bell was again upon the stroke of One. He felt that he was restored to consciousness in the right nick of time, for the especial purpose of holding a conference with the second messenger despatched to him through Jacob Marley's intervention. But finding that he turned uncomfortably cold when he began to wonder which of his curtains this new spectre would draw back, he put them every one aside with his own hands, and lying down again, established a sharp look-out all round the bed. For he wished to challenge the Spirit on the moment of its appearance, and did not wish to be taken by surprise and made nervous.

Gentlemen of the free and easy sort, who plume themselves on being acquainted with a move or two, and being usually equal to the time of day, express the wide range of their capacity for adventure by observing that they are good for anything from pitch and toss to man-slaughter; between which opposite extremes, no doubt, there lies a tolerably wide and comprehensive range of subjects. Without ventur-ing for Scrooge quite as hardily as this, I don't mind calling on you to believe that he was ready for a good broad field of strange appear-ances, and that nothing between a baby and rhinoceros would have as-tonished him very much.

Now being prepared for almost anything, he was not by any means prepared for nothing; and consequently, when the bell struck One, and no shape appeared, he was taken with a violent fit of trembling. Five minutes, ten minutes, a quarter of an hour went by, yet nothing came. All this time, he lay upon his bed, the very core and centre of a blaze of ruddy light, which streamed upon it when the clock proclaimed the hour; and which, being only light, was more alarming than a dozen ghosts, as he was powerless to make out what it meant, or would be at; and was sometimes apprehensive that he might be at that very moment an interesting case of spontaneous combustion, without having the consolation of knowing it. At last, however, he began to think—as you or I would have thought at first; for it is always the person not in the predicament who knows what ought to have been done in it, and would unquestionably have done it too—at last, I say, he began to think that the source and secret of this ghostly light might be in the adjoining room, from whence, on further tracing it, it seemed to shine. This idea taking full possession of his mind, he got up softly and shuffled in his slippers to the door.

The moment Scrooge's hand was on the lock, a strange voice called him by his name, and bade him enter. He obeyed.

It was his own room. There was no doubt about that. But it had un-dergone a surprising transformation. The walls and ceiling were so hung with living green, that it looked a perfect grove; from every part of which, bright gleaming berries glistened. The crisp leaves of holly, mistletoe, and ivy reflected back the light, as if so many little mirrors had been scattered there; and such a mighty blaze went roaring up the chimney as that dull petrifaction of a hearth had never known in Scrooge's time, or Marley's, or for many and many a winter season gone. Heaped up on the floor, to form a kind of throne, were turkeys, geese, game, poultry, brawn, great joints of meat, sucking-pigs, long wreaths of sausages, mince-pies, plum-puddings, barrels of oysters, red-hot chestnuts, cherry-cheeked apples, juicy oranges, luscious pears, immense twelfth-cakes, and seething bowls of punch, that made the chamber dim with their delicious steam. In easy state upon this couch there sat a jolly Giant, glorious to see; who bore a glowing torch, in shape not unlike Plenty's horn, and held it up, high up, to shed its light on Scrooge, as he came peeping round the door.

"Come in!" exclaimed the Ghost. "Come in! and know me better, man!"

Scrooge entered timidly, and hung his head before this Spirit. He was not the dogged Scrooge he had been; and though the Spirit's eyes were clear and kind, he did not like to meet them.

"I am the Ghost of Christmas Present," said the Spirit. "Look upon me!"

Scrooge reverently did so. It was clothed in one simple deep green robe, or mantle, bordered with white fur. This garment hung so loosely on the figure, that its capacious breast was bare, as if disdaining to be warded or concealed by any artifice. Its feet, observable beneath the ample folds of the garment, were also bare; and on its head it wore no other covering than a holly wreath, set here and there with shining icicles. Its dark brown curls were long and free; free as its genial face, its sparkling eye, its open hand, its cheery voice, its unconstrained demeanour, and its joyful air. Girded round its middle was an antique scabbard; but no sword was in it, and the ancient sheath was eaten up with rust.

"You have never seen the like of me before!" exclaimed the Spirit.

"Never," Scrooge made answer to it.

"Have never walked forth with the younger members of my family; meaning (for I am very young) my elder brothers born in these later years?" pursued the Phantom.

"I don't think I have," said Scrooge. "I am afraid I have not. Have you had many brothers, Spirit?"

"More than eighteen hundred," said the Ghost.

"A tremendous family to provide for," muttered Scrooge.

The Ghost of Christmas Present rose.

"Spirit," said Scrooge submissively, "conduct me where you will. I went forth last night on compulsion, and I learnt a lesson which is working now. Tonight, if you have aught to teach me, let me profit by it."

"Touch my robe!"

Scrooge did as he was told, and held it fast.

Holly, mistletoe, red berries, ivy, turkeys, geese, game, poultry, brawn, meat, pigs, sausages, oysters, pies, puddings, fruit, and punch, all vanished instantly. So did the room, the fire, the ruddy glow, the hour of night, and they stood in the city streets on Christmas morning, where (for the weather was severe) the people made a rough, but brisk and not unpleasant kind of music, in scraping the snow from the pavement in front of their dwellings, and from the tops of their houses, whence it was mad delight to the boys to see it come plumping down into the road below, and splitting into artificial little snowstorms.

The house fronts looked black enough, and the windows blacker, contrasting with the smooth white sheet of snow upon the roofs, and with the dirtier snow upon the ground; which last deposit had been ploughed up in deep furrows by the heavy wheels of carts and wagons; furrows that crossed and recrossed each other hundreds of times where the great streets branched off; and made intricate channels, hard to trace, in the thick yellow mud and icy water. The sky was gloomy, and the shortest streets were choked up with a dingy mist, half thawed, half frozen, whose heavier particles descended in a shower of sooty atoms, as if all the chimneys in Great Britain had, by one consent, caught fire, and were blazing away to their dear hearts' content. There was nothing very cheerful in the climate or the town, and yet was there an air of cheerfulness abroad that the clearest summer air and brightest summer sun might have endeavoured to diffuse in vain.

For the people who were shovelling away on the housetops were jovial and full of glee; calling out to one another from the parapets, and now and then exchanging a facetious snowball—better-natured missile far than many a wordy jest—laughing heartily if it went right, and not less heartily if it went wrong. The poulterers' shops were still half open, and the fruiterers' were radiant in their glory. There were great, round, pot-bellied baskets of chestnuts, shaped like the waistcoats of jolly old gentlemen, lolling at the doors, and tumbling out into the street in their apoplectic opulence. There were ruddy, brown-faced, broad-girthed Spanish onions, shining in the fatness of their growth like Spanish Friars, and winking from their shelves in wanton slyness at the girls as they went by, and glanced demurely at the hung-up mistletoe. There were pears and apples, clustered high in blooming pyramids; there were bunches of grapes, made, in the shopkeepers' benevolence, to dangle from conspicuous hooks, that people's mouths might water gratis as they passed; there were piles of filberts, mossy and brown, recalling, in their fragrance, ancient walks among the woods, and pleasant shufflings ankle-deep through withered leaves; there were Norfolk Biffins, squab and swarthy, setting off the yellow of the oranges and lemons, and in the great compactness of their juicy persons, urgently entreating and beseeching to be carried home in paper bags and eaten after dinner. The very gold and silver fish, set forth among these choice fruits in a bowl, though members of a dull and stagnant-blooded race, appeared to know that there was something going on; and, to a fish, went gasping round and round their little world in slow and passionless excitement.

The Grocers'! oh, the Grocers'! nearly closed, with perhaps two shutters down, or one; but through those gaps such glimpses! It was not alone that the scales descending on the counter made a merry sound, or that the twine and roller parted company so briskly, or that the canisters were rattled up and down like juggling tricks, or even that the blended scents of tea and coffee were so grateful to the nose, or even that the raisins were so plentiful and rare, the almonds so extremely white, the sticks of cinnamon so long and straight, the other spices so delicious, the candied fruits so caked and spotted with molten sugar as to make the coldest lookers-on feel faint and subsequently bilious. Nor was it that the figs were moist and pulpy, or that the French plums blushed in modest tartness from their highly decorated boxes, or that everything was good to eat and in its Christmas dress; but the customers were all so hurried and so eager in the hopeful promise of the day, that they tumbled up against each other at the door, crashing their wicker baskets wildly, and left their purchases upon the counter, and came running back to fetch them, and committed hundreds of the like mistakes, in the best humour possible; while the Grocer and his people were so frank and fresh that the polished hearts with which they fastened their aprons behind might have been their own, worn outside for general inspection, and for Christmas daws to peck at if they chose.

But soon the steeples called good people all to church and chapel, and away they came, flocking through the streets in their best clothes, and with their gayest faces. And at the same time there emerged from scores of by-streets, lanes, and nameless turnings, innumerable people, carrying their dinners to the bakers' shops. The sight of these poor revellers appeared to interest the Spirit very much, for he stood with Scrooge beside him in a baker's doorway, and, taking off the covers as their bearers passed, sprinkled incense on their dinners from his torch. And it was a very uncommon kind of torch, for once or twice when there were angry words between some dinner-carriers who had jostled each other, he shed a few drops of water on them from it, and their good-humour was restored directly. For they said, it was a shame to quarrel upon Christmas Day. And so it was! God love it, so it was!

In time the bells ceased, and the bakers were shut up; and yet there was a genial shadowing forth of all these dinners and the progress of their cooking, in the thawed blotch of wet above each baker's oven, where the pavement smoked as if its stones were cooking, too.

"Is there a peculiar flavour in what you sprinkle from your torch?" asked Scrooge.

"There is. My own."

"Would it apply to any kind of dinner on this day?" asked Scrooge.

"To any kindly given. To a poor one most."

"Why to a poor one most?" asked Scrooge.

"Because it needs it most."

"Spirit," said Scrooge, after a moment's thought, "I wonder you, of all the beings in the many worlds about us, should desire to cramp these people's opportunities of innocent enjoyment."

"I!" cried the Spirit.

"You would deprive them of their means of dining every seventh day, often the only day on which they can be said to dine at all," said Scrooge; "wouldn't you?"

"I!" cried the Spirit.

"You seek to close these places on the Seventh Day!" said Scrooge. "And it comes to the same thing."

"I seek!" exclaimed the Spirit.

"Forgive me if I am wrong. It has been done in your name, or at least in that of your family," said Scrooge.

"There are some upon this earth of yours," returned the Spirit, "who lay claim to know us, and who do their deeds of passion, pride, ill-will, hatred, envy, bigotry, and selfishness in our name, who are as strange to us and all our kith and kin as if they had never lived. Remember that, and charge their doings on themselves, not us."

Scrooge promised that he would; and they went on, invisible, as they had been before, into the suburbs of the town. It was a remarkable quality of the Ghost (which Scrooge had observed at the baker's) that, notwithstanding his gigantic size, he could accommodate himself to any place with ease, and that he stood beneath a low roof quite as gracefully and like a supernatural creature as it was possible he could have done in any lofty hall.

And perhaps it was the pleasure the good Spirit had in showing off this power of his, or else it was his own kind, generous, hearty nature, and his sympathy with all poor men, that led him straight to Scrooge's clerk's; for there he went, and took Scrooge with him, holding to his robe; and on the threshold of the door the Spirit smiled, and stopped to bless Bob Cratchit's dwelling with the sprinklings of his torch. Think of that! Bob had but fifteen "Bob" a week himself; he pocketed on Saturdays but fifteen copies of his Christian name; and yet the Ghost of Christmas Present blessed his four-roomed house!

Then up rose Mrs. Cratchit, Cratchit's wife, dressed out but poorly in a twice-turned gown, but brave in ribbons, which are cheap and make a goodly show for sixpence; and she laid the cloth, assisted by Belinda Cratchit, second of her daughters, also brave in ribbons; while Master Peter Cratchit plunged a fork into the saucepan of potatoes, and, getting the corners of his monstrous shirt-collar (Bob's private property, conferred upon his son and heir in honour of the day) into his mouth, rejoiced to find himself so gallantly attired, and yearned to show his linen in the fashionable Parks. And now two smaller Cratchits, boy and girl, came tearing in, screaming that outside the baker's they had smelt the goose, and known it for their own; and basking in luxurious thoughts of sage and onion, these young Cratchits danced about the table, and exalted Master Peter Cratchit to the skies, while he (not proud, although his collars near choked him) blew the fire, until the slow potatoes, bubbling up, knocked loudly at the saucepan lid to be let out and peeled.

"What has ever got your precious father, then?" said Mrs. Cratchit. "And your brother Tiny Tim! And Martha warn't as late last Christmas Day by half an hour!"

"Here's Martha, mother!" said a girl, appearing as she spoke.

"Here's Martha, mother!" cried the two young Cratchits. "Hurrah! There's *such* a goose, Martha!"

"Why, bless your heart alive, my dear, how late you are!" said Mrs. Cratchit, kissing her a dozen times, and taking off her shawl and bonnet for her with officious zeal.

"We'd a deal of work to finish up last night," replied the girl, "and had to clear away this morning, mother!"

"Well! never mind so long as you are come," said Mrs. Cratchit.

"Sit ye down before the fire, my dear, and have a warm, Lord bless ye!"

"No, no! There's father coming," cried the two young Cratchits, who were everywhere at once. "Hide, Martha, hide!"

So Martha hid herself, and in came little Bob, the father, with at least three feet of comforter exclusive of the fringe hanging down before him; and his threadbare clothes darned up and brushed, to look seasonable; and Tiny Tim upon his shoulder. Alas for Tiny Tim, he bore a little crutch, and had his limbs supported by an iron frame!

"Why, where's our Martha?" cried Bob Cratchit, looking round.

"Not coming," said Mrs. Cratchit.

"Not coming!" said Bob, with a sudden declension in his high spirits; for he had been Tim's blood horse all the way from church, and had come home rampant. "Not coming upon Christmas Day!"

Martha didn't like to see him disappointed, if it were only in joke; so she came out prematurely from behind the closet door, and ran into his arms, while the two young Cratchits hustled Tiny Tim, and bore him off into the wash-house, that he might hear the pudding singing in the copper.

"And how did little Tim behave?" asked Mrs. Cratchit, when she had rallied Bob on his credulity, and Bob had hugged his daughter to his heart's content.

"As good as gold," said Bob, "and better. Somehow he gets thoughtful, sitting by himself so much, and thinks the strangest things you ever heard. He told me, coming home, that he hoped the people saw him in the church, because he was a cripple, and it might be pleasant to them to remember upon Christmas Day who made lame beggars walk and blind men see."

Bob's voice was tremulous when he told them this, and trembled more when he said that Tiny Tim was growing strong and hearty.

His active little crutch was heard upon the floor, and back came Tiny Tim before another word was spoken, escorted by his brother and sister to his stool beside the fire; and while Bob, turning up his cuffs—as if, poor fellow, they were capable of being made more shabby—compounded some hot mixture in a jug with gin and lemons, and stirred it round and round and put it on the hob to simmer, Master Peter and the two ubiquitous young Cratchits went to fetch the goose, with which they soon returned in high procession.

Such a bustle ensued that you might have thought a goose the rarest of all birds; a feathered phenomenon, to which a black swan was a matter of course—and in truth it was something very like it in that house. Mrs. Cratchit made the gravy (ready beforehand in a little saucepan) hissing hot; Master Peter mashed the potatoes with incredible vigour; Miss Belinda sweetened up the apple sauce; Martha dusted the hot plates; Bob took Tiny Tim beside him in a tiny corner at the table; the two young Cratchits set chairs for everybody, not forgetting themselves, and mounting guard upon their posts, crammed spoons into their mouths, lest they should shriek for goose before their turn came to be helped. At last the dishes were set on, and grace was said. It was succeeded by a breathless pause, as Mrs. Cratchit, looking slowly all along the carving-knife, prepared to plunge it in the breast; but when she did, and when the long expected gush of stuffing issued forth, one murmur of delight arose all round the board, and even Tiny Tim, excited by the two young Cratchits, beat on the table with the handle of his knife, and feebly cried Hurrah!

There never was such a goose. Bob said he didn't believe there ever was such a goose cooked. Its tenderness and flavour, size and cheapness, were the themes of universal admiration. Eked out by apple sauce and mashed potatoes, it was a sufficient dinner for the whole family; indeed, as Mrs. Cratchit said with great delight (survey ing one small atom of a bone upon the dish), they hadn't ate it all at last! Yet every one had had enough, and the youngest Cratchits in particular were steeped in sage and onion to the eyebrows! But now the plates were changed by Miss Belinda, Mrs. Cratchit left the room alone—too nervous to bear witnesses—to take the pudding up, and bring it in.

Suppose it should not be done enough! Suppose it should break in turning out! Suppose somebody should have got over the wall of the backyard, and stolen it, while they were merry with the goose—a supposition at which the two young Cratchits became livid! All sorts of horrors were supposed.

Hallo! A great deal of steam! The pudding was out of the copper. A smell like a washing-day! That was the cloth. A smell like an eating-house and a pastry-cook's next door to each other, with a laundress's next door to that! That was the pudding! In half a minute Mrs. Cratchit entered—flushed, but smiling proudly—with the pudding, like a speckled cannon ball, so hard and firm, blazing in half of half a quartern of ignited brandy, and bedight with Christmas holly stuck into the top.

Oh, a wonderful pudding! Bob Cratchit said, and calmly, too, that he regarded it as the greatest success achieved by Mrs. Cratchit since their marriage. Mrs. Cratchit said that, now the weight was off her mind, she would confess she had her doubts about the quantity of flour. Everybody had something to say about it, but nobody said or thought it was at all a small pudding for a large family. It would have been flat heresy to do so. Any Cratchit would have blushed to hint at such a thing.

At last the dinner was all done, the cloth was cleared, the hearth swept, and the fire made up. The compound in the jug being tasted, and considered perfect, apples and oranges were put upon the table, and a shovelful of chestnuts on the fire. Then all the Cratchit family drew round the hearth, in what Bob Cratchit called a circle, meaning half a one; and at Bob Cratchit's elbow stood the family display of glass. Two tumblers and a custard-cup without a handle.

These held the hot stuff from the jug, however, as well as golden goblets would have done; and Bob served it out with beaming looks, while the chestnuts on the fire sputtered and cracked noisily. Then Bob proposed: "A Merry Christmas to us all, my dears. God bless us!" Which all the family re-echoed.

"God bless us every one!" said Tiny Tim, the last of all.

He sat very close to his father's side, upon his little stool. Bob held his withered little hand in his, as if he loved the child, and wished to keep him by his side, and dreaded that he might be taken from him.

"Spirit," said Scrooge, with an interest he had never felt before, "tell me if Tiny Tim will live."

"I see a vacant seat," replied the Ghost, "in the poor chimney corner, and a crutch without an owner, carefully preserved. If these shadows remain unaltered by the Future the child will die."

"No, no," said Scrooge. "Oh, no, kind Spirit! say he will be spared."

"If these shadows remain unaltered by the Future, none other of my race," returned the Ghost, "will find him here. What, then? If he be like to die, he had better do it, and decrease the surplus population."

Scrooge hung his head to hear his own words quoted by the Spirit, and was overcome with penitence and grief.

"Man," said the Ghost, "if man you be in heart, not adamant, forbear that wicked cant until you have discovered What the surplus is, and Where it is. Will you decide what men shall live, what men shall die? It may be that in the sight of Heaven you are more worthless and less fit to live than millions like this poor man's child. O God! to hear the Insect on the leaf pronouncing on the too much life among his hungry brothers in the dust!"

Scrooge bent before the Ghost's rebuke, and trembling cast his eyes upon the ground. But he raised them speedily, on hearing his own name.

"Mr. Scrooge!" said Bob; "I'll give you Mr. Scrooge, the Founder of the Feast!"

"The Founder of the Feast, indeed!" cried Mrs. Cratchit, reddening. "I wished I had him here. I'd give him a piece of my mind to feast upon, and I hope he'd have a good appetite for it."

"My dear," said Bob, "the children! Christmas Day."

"It should be Christmas Day, I am sure," said she, "on which one drinks the health of such an odious, stingy, hard, unfeeling man as Mr. Scrooge. You know he is, Robert! Nobody knows it better than you do, poor fellow!"

"My dear," was Bob's mild answer. "Christmas Day."

"I'll drink his health for your sake and the Day's," said Mrs. Cratchit, "not for his. Long life to him! A Merry Christmas and a Happy New Year! He'll be very merry and very happy, I have no doubt!"

The children drank the toast after her. It was the first of their proceedings which had no heartiness in it. Tiny Tim drank it last of all, but he didn't care twopence for it. Scrooge was the Ogre of the family. The mention of his name cast a dark shadow on the party, which was not dispelled for full five minutes.

After it had passed away, they were ten times merrier than before, from the mere relief of Scrooge the Baleful being done with. Bob Cratchit told them how he had a situation in his eye for Master Peter, which would bring in, if obtained, full five-and-sixpence weekly. The two young Cratchits laughed tremendously at the idea of Peter's being a man of business; and Peter himself looked thoughtfully at the fire from between his collars, as if he were deliberating what particular investment he should favour when he came into the receipt of that bewildering income. Martha, who was a poor apprentice at a milliner's, then told them what kind of work she had to do, and how many hours she worked at a stretch, and how she meant to lie abed tomorrow morning for a good long rest; tomorrow being a holiday she passed at home. Also how she had seen a countess and a lord some days before, and how the lord was much about as tall as Peter; at which Peter pulled up his collars so high that you couldn't have seen his head if you had been there. All this time the chestnuts and the jug went round and round; and by and by they had a song, about a lost child travelling in the snow, from Tiny Tim, who had a plaintive little voice, and sang it very well, indeed.

There was nothing of high mark in this. They were not a handsome family; they were not well dressed; their shoes were far from being waterproof; their clothes were scanty; and Peter might have known, and very likely did, the inside of a pawnbroker's. But they were happy, grateful, pleased with one another, and contented with the time; and when they faded, and looked happier yet in the bright sprinklings of the Spirit's torch at parting, Scrooge had his eye upon them, and especially on Tiny Tim, until the last.

By this time it was getting dark and snowing pretty heavily; and as Scrooge and the Spirit went along the streets, the brightness of the roaring fires in kitchens, parlours, and all sorts of rooms was wonderful. Here the flickering of the blaze showed preparations for a cosy dinner, with hot plates baking through and through before the fire, and deep red curtains, ready to be drawn to shut out cold and darkness. There all the children of the house were running out into the snow to meet their married sisters, brothers, cousins, uncles, aunts, and be the first to greet them. Here, again, were shadows on the window-blinds of guests assembling; and there a group of handsome girls, all hooded and fur-booted, and all chattering at once, tripped lightly off to some near neighbour's house; where woe upon the single man who saw them enter—artful witches, well they knew it—in a glow!

But if you had judged from the numbers of people on their way to friendly gatherings, you might have thought that no one was at home to give them welcome when they got there, instead of every house expecting company, and piling up its fires half-chimney high. Blessings on it, how the Ghost exulted! How it bared its breadth of breast, and opened its capacious palm, and floated on, outpouring with a generous hand its bright and harmless mirth on everything within its reach! The very lamplighter, who ran on before, dotting the dusky street with specks of light, and who was dressed to spend the evening somewhere, laughed out loudly as the Spirit passed, though little kenned the lamplighter that he had any company but Christmas!

And now, without a word of warning from the Ghost, they stood upon a bleak and desert moor, where monstrous masses of rude stone were cast about, as though it were the burial-place of giants; and water spread itself wheresoever it listed; or would have done so, but for the frost that held it prisoner; and nothing grew but moss and furze, and coarse, rank grass. Down in the west the setting sun had left a streak of fiery red, which glared upon the desolation for an instant, like a sullen eye, and, frowning lower, lower, lower yet, was lost in the thick gloom of darkest night.

"What place is this?" asked Scrooge.

"A place where Miners live, who labour in the bowels of the earth," returned the Spirit. "But they know me. See!"

A light shone from the window of a hut, and swiftly they advanced towards it. Passing through the wall of mud and stone, they found a cheerful company assembled round a glowing fire. An old, old man and woman, with their children and their children's children, and another generation beyond that, all decked out gaily in their holiday attire. The old man, in a voice that seldom rose above the howling of the wind upon the barren waste, was singing them a Christmas song— it had been a very old song when he was a boy—and from time to time they all joined in the chorus. So surely as they raised their voices, the old man got quite blithe and loud; and so surely as they stopped, his vigour sank again.

The Spirit did not tarry here, but bade Scrooge hold his robe, and, passing on above the moor, sped whither? Not to sea? To sea. To Scrooge's horror, looking back, he saw the last of the land, a frightful range of rocks, behind them; and his ears were deafened by the thundering of water, as it rolled, and roared, and raged, among the dreadful caverns it had worn, and fiercely tried to undermine the earth.

Built upon a dismal reef of sunken rocks, some league or so from shore, on which the waters chafed and dashed, the wild year through, there stood a solitary lighthouse. Great heaps of sea-weed clung to its base, and storm-birds—born of the wind one might suppose, as sea-weed of the water—rose and fell about it, like the waves they skimmed.

But even here, two men who watched the light had made a fire, that through the loophole in the thick stone wall shed out a ray of brightness on the awful sea. Joining their horny hands over the rough table at which they sat, they wished each other Merry Christmas in their can of grog; and one of them—the elder, too, with his face all damaged and scarred with hard weather, as the figure-head of an old ship might be—struck up a sturdy song that was like a gale in itself.

Again the Ghost sped on, above the black and heaving sea—on, on —until, being far away, as he told Scrooge, from any shore, they lighted on a ship. They stood beside the helmsman at the wheel, the look-out in the bow, the officers who had the watch—dark, ghostly figures in their several stations—but every man among them hummed a Christmas tune, or had a Christmas thought, or spoke below his breath to his companion of some bygone Christmas Day, with home-ward hopes belonging to it. And every man on board, waking or sleep-ing, good or bad, had had a kinder word for one another on that day than on any day in the year; and had shared to some extent in its fes-tivities; and had remembered those he cared for at a distance, and had known that they delighted to remember him.

It was a great surprise to Scrooge, while listening to the moaning of the wind, and thinking what a solemn thing it was to move on through the lonely darkness over an unknown abyss, whose depths were secrets as profound as Death—it was a great surprise to Scrooge, while thus engaged, to hear a hearty laugh. It was a much greater surprise to Scrooge to recognize it as his own nephew's, and to find himself in a bright, dry, gleaming room, with the Spirit standing smiling by his side, and looking at that same nephew with approving affability!

"Ha, ha!" laughed Scrooge's nephew. "Ha, ha, ha!"

If you should happen, by any unlikely chance, to know a man more blest in a laugh than Scrooge's nephew, all I can say is I should like to know him, too. Introduce him to me, and I'll cultivate his ac-quaintance.

It is a fair, even-handed, noble adjustment of things that, while there is infection in disease and sorrow, there is nothing in the world so irresistibly contagious as laughter and good-humour. When Scrooge's nephew laughed in this way, holding his sides, rolling his head, and twisting his face into the most extravagant contortions, Scrooge's niece, by marriage, laughed as heartily as he. And their as-sembled friends, being not a bit behindhand, roared out lustily.

"Ha, ha! Ha, ha, ha, ha!"

"He said that Christmas was a humbug, as I live!" cried Scrooge's nephew. "He believed it, too!"

"More shame for him, Fred!" said Scrooge's niece indignantly. Bless those women! They never do anything by halves. They are always in earnest.

She was very pretty; exceedingly pretty. With a dimpled, surprised-looking, capital face; a ripe little mouth, that seemed made to be kissed—as no doubt it was; all kinds of good little dots about her chin, that melted into one another when she laughed; and the sunniest pair of eyes you ever saw in any little creature's head. Altogether she was what you would have called provoking, you know; but satisfactory, too. Oh, perfectly satisfactory.

"He's a comical old fellow," said Scrooge's nephew, "that's the truth; and not so pleasant as he might be. However, his offences carry their own punishment, and I have nothing to say against him."

"I'm sure he is very rich, Fred," hinted Scrooge's niece. "At least, you always tell *me* so."

"What of that, my dear!" said Scrooge's nephew. "His wealth is of no use to him. He don't do any good with it. He don't make himself comfortable with it. He hasn't the satisfaction of thinking—ha, ha, ha!—that he is ever going to benefit Us with it."

"I have no patience with him," observed Scrooge's niece. Scrooge's niece's sisters, and all the other ladies, expressed the same opinion.

"Oh, I have!" said Scrooge's nephew. "I am sorry for him; I couldn't be angry with him if I tried. Who suffers by his ill whims! Himself, always. Here he takes it into his head to dislike us, and he won't come and dine with us. What's the consequence? He don't lose much of a dinner."

"Indeed, I think he loses a very good dinner," interrupted Scrooge's niece. Everybody else said the same, and they must be allowed to have been competent judges, because they had just had dinner; and with the dessert upon the table, were clustered round the fire, by lamplight.

"Well! I am very glad to hear it," said Scrooge's nephew, "because I haven't any great faith in these young housekeepers. What do *you* say, Topper?"

Topper had clearly got his eye upon one of Scrooge's niece's sisters, for he answered that a bachelor was a wretched outcast, who had no right to express an opinion on the subject. Whereat Scrooge's niece's sister—the plump one with the lace tucker, not the one with the roses —blushed.

"Do go on, Fred," said Scrooge's niece, clapping her hands. "He never finishes what he begins to say! He is such a ridiculous fellow!"

Scrooge's nephew revelled in another laugh, and as it was impossible to keep the infection off, though the plump sister tried hard to do it with aromatic vinegar, his example was unanimously followed.

"I was only going to say," said Scrooge's nephew, "that the consequence of his taking a dislike to us, and not making merry with us, is, as I think, that he loses some pleasant moments, which could do him no harm. I am sure he loses pleasanter companions than he can find in his own thoughts, either in his mouldy old office or his dusty chambers. I mean to give him the same chance every year, whether he likes it or not, for I pity him. He may rail at Christmas till he dies, but he can't help thinking better of it—I defy him—if he finds me going there, in good temper, year after year, and saying, 'Uncle Scrooge, how are you?' If it only puts him in the vein to leave his poor clerk fifty pounds, *that's* something; and I think I shook him yesterday."

It was their turn to laugh now, at the notion of his shaking Scrooge. But being thoroughly good-natured, and not much caring what they laughed at, so that they laughed at any rate, he encouraged them in their merriment, and passed the bottle joyously.

After tea, they had some music. For they were a musical family, and knew what they were about, when they sung a Glee or Catch, I can assure you; especially Topper, who could growl away in the bass like a good one, and never swell the large veins in his forehead, or get red in the face over it. Scrooge's niece played well upon the harp; and played among other tunes a simple little air (a mere nothing, you might learn to whistle it in two minutes), which had been familiar to the child who fetched Scrooge from the boarding-school, as he had been reminded by the Ghost of Christmas Past. When this strain of music sounded, all the things that Ghost had shown him came upon his mind; he softened more and more; and thought that if he could have listened to it often, years ago, he might have cultivated the kindnesses of life for his own happiness with his own hands, without resorting to the sexton's spade that buried Jacob Marley.

But they didn't devote the whole evening to music. After a while they played at forfeits; for it is good to be children sometimes, and never better than at Christmas, when its mighty Founder was a child himself. Stop! There was first a game at blindman's buff. Of course there was. And I no more believe Topper was really blind than I believe he had eyes in his boots. My opinion is that it was a done thing between him and Scrooge's nephew; and that the Ghost of Christmas Present knew it. The way he went after that plump sister in the lace tucker was an outrage on the credulity of human nature. Knocking down the fire-irons, tumbling over the chairs, bumping up against the piano, smothering himself amongst the curtains, wherever she went, there went he! He always knew where the plump sister was. He wouldn't catch anybody else. If you had fallen up against him (as some of them did) on purpose, he would have made a feint of endeavouring to seize you which would have been an affront to your understanding, and would instantly have sidled off in the direction of the plump sister. She often cried out that it wasn't fair; and it really was not. But when at last he caught her; when, in spite of all her silken rustlings, and her rapid flutterings past him, he got her into a corner whence there was no escape, then his conduct was the most execrable. For his pretending not to know her, his pretending that it was necessary to touch her head-dress, and further to assure himself of her identity by pressing a certain ring upon her finger, and a certain chain about her neck, was vile, monstrous! No doubt she told him her opinion of it, when, another blindman being in office, they were so very confidential together, behind the curtains.

Scrooge's niece was not one of the blindman's buff party, but was made comfortable with a large chair and a footstool, in a snug corner where the Ghost and Scrooge were close behind her. But she joined in the forfeits, and loved her love to admiration with all the letters of the alphabet. Likewise at the game of How, When, and Where, she was very great, and, to the secret joy of Scrooge's nephew, beat her sisters hollow, though they were sharp girls too, as Topper could have told you. There might have been twenty people there, young and old, but they all played, and so did Scrooge; for wholly forgetting, in the interest he had in what was going on, that his voice made no sound in their ears, he sometimes came out with his guess quite loud, and very often guessed right, too; for the sharpest needle, best Whitechapel, warranted not to cut in the eye, was not sharper than Scrooge, blunt as he took it in his head to be.

The Ghost was greatly pleased to find him in this mood, and looked upon him with such favour, that he begged like a boy to be allowed to stay until the guests departed. But this the Spirit said could not be done.

"Here is a new game," said Scrooge. "One half hour, Spirit, only one!"

It was a Game called Yes and No, where Scrooge's nephew had to think of something, and the rest must find out what; he only answering to their questions yes or no, as the case was. The brisk fire of questioning to which he was exposed elicited from him that he was thinking of an animal, a live animal, rather a disagreeable animal, a savage animal, an animal that growled and grunted sometimes, and talked sometimes, and lived in London, and walked about the streets, and wasn't made a show of, and wasn't led by anybody, and didn't live in a menagerie, and was never killed in a market, and was not a horse, or an ass, or a cow, or a bull, or a tiger, or a dog, or a pig, or a cat, or a bear. At every fresh question that was put to him this nephew burst into a fresh roar of laughter, and was so inexpressibly tickled, that he was obliged to get up off the sofa and stamp. At last the plump sister, falling into a similar state, cried out: "I have found it out! I know what it is, Fred! I know what it is!"

"What is it?" cried Fred.

"It's your uncle Scro-o-o-o-oge!"

Which it certainly was. Admiration was the universal sentiment, though some objected that the reply to "Is it a bear?" ought to have been "Yes"; inasmuch as an answer in the negative was sufficient to have diverted their thoughts from Mr. Scrooge, supposing they had ever had any tendency that way.

"He has given us plenty of merriment, I am sure," said Fred, "and it would be ungrateful not to drink his health. Here is a glass of mulled wine ready to our hand at the moment; and I say, 'Uncle Scrooge!' "

"Well! Uncle Scrooge!" they cried.

"A Merry Christmas and a Happy New Year to the old man, whatever he is!" said Scrooge's nephew. "He wouldn't take it from me, but may he have it, nevertheless. Uncle Scrooge!"

Uncle Scrooge had imperceptibly become so gay and light of heart, that he would have pledged the unconscious company in return, and thanked them in an inaudible speech if the Ghost had given him time. But the whole scene passed off in the breath of the last word spoken by his nephew; and he and the Spirit were again upon their travels.

Much they saw, and far they went, and many homes they visited, but always with a happy end. The Spirit stood beside sick beds, and they were cheerful; on foreign lands, and they were close at home; by struggling men, and they were patient in their greater hope; by poverty, and it was rich. In almshouse, hospital, and jail, in misery's every refuge, where vain man in his little brief authority had not made fast the door, and barred the Spirit out, he left his blessing, and taught Scrooge his precepts.

It was a long night, if it were only a night; but Scrooge had his doubts of this, because the Christmas Holidays appeared to be condensed into the space of time they passed together. It was strange, too, that while Scrooge remained unaltered in his outward form, the

Ghost grew older, clearly older. Scrooge had observed this change, but never spoke of it, until they left a children's Twelfth Night party, when, looking at the Spirit as they stood together in an open place, he noticed that its hair was grey.

"Are spirits' lives so short?" asked Scrooge.

"My life upon this globe is very brief," replied the Ghost. "It ends tonight."

"Tonight!" cried Scrooge.

"Tonight at midnight. Hark! The time is drawing near."

The chimes were ringing the three quarters past eleven at that moment.

"Forgive me if I am not justified in what I ask," said Scrooge, looking intently at the Spirit's robe, "but I see something strange, and not belonging to yourself, protruding from your skirts. Is it a foot, or a claw?"

"It might be a claw, for the flesh there is upon it," was the Spirit's sorrowful reply. "Look here."

From the foldings of its robe it brought two children; wretched, abject, frightful, hideous, miserable. They knelt down at its feet, and clung upon the outside of its garment.

"Oh, Man! look here. Look, look, down here!" exclaimed the Ghost.

They were a boy and girl. Yellow, meagre, ragged, scowling, wolfish; but prostrate, too, in their humility. Where graceful youth should have filled their features out, and touched them with its freshest tints, a stale and shrivelled hand, like that of age, had pinched, and twisted them, and pulled them into shreds. Where angels might have sat enthroned, devils lurked, and glared out menacing. No change, no degradation, no perversion of humanity, in any grade, through all the mysteries of wonderful creation, has monsters half so horrible and dread.

Scrooge started back, appalled. Having them shown to him in this way, he tried to say they were fine children, but the words choked themselves, rather than be parties to a lie of such enormous magnitude.

"Spirit! are they yours?" Scrooge could say no more.

"They are Man's," said the Spirit, looking down upon them. "And they cling to me, appealing from their fathers. This boy is Ignorance. This girl is Want. Beware of them both, and all of their degree, but most of all beware this boy, for on his brow I see that written which is

Doom, unless the writing be erased. Deny it!" cried the Spirit, stretching out its hand towards the city. "Slander those who tell it ye! Admit it for your factious purposes, and make it worse! And bide the end!"

"Have they no refuge or resource?" cried Scrooge.

"Are there no prisons!" said the Spirit, turning on him for the last time with his own words. "Are there no workhouses?"

The bell struck twelve.

Scrooge looked about him for the Ghost, and saw it not. As the last stroke ceased to vibrate, he remembered the prediction of old Jacob Marley, and, lifting up his eyes, beheld a solemn Phantom, draped and hooded, coming like a mist along the ground towards him.

Stave Four

THE LAST OF THE SPIRITS

The Phantom slowly, gravely, silently, approached. When it came near him, Scrooge bent down upon his knee; for in the very air through which this Spirit moved it seemed to scatter gloom and mystery.

It was shrouded in a deep black garment, which concealed its head, its face, its form, and left nothing of it visible, save one outstretched hand. But for this it would have been difficult to detach its figure from the night, and separate it from the darkness by which it was surrounded.

He felt that it was tall and stately when it came beside him, and that its mysterious presence filled him with a solemn dread. He knew no more, for the Spirit neither spoke nor moved.

"I am in the presence of the Ghost of Christmas Yet To Come?" said Scrooge.

The Spirit answered not, but pointed onward with its hand.

"You are about to show me shadows of the things that have not happened, but will happen in the time before us," Scrooge pursued. "Is that so, Spirit?"

The upper portion of the garment was contracted for an instant in its folds, as if the Spirit had inclined its head. That was the only answer he received.

Although well used to ghostly company by this time, Scrooge feared the silent shape so much that his legs trembled beneath him, and he found that he could hardly stand when he prepared to follow it. The Spirit paused a moment, as observing his condition, and giving him time to recover.

But Scrooge was all the worse for this. It thrilled him with a vague uncertain horror, to know that behind the dusky shroud there were ghostly eyes intently fixed upon him, while he, though he stretched his own to the utmost, could see nothing but a spectral hand and one great heap of black.

"Ghost of the Future!" he exclaimed, "I fear you more than any spectre I have seen. But as I know your purpose is to do me good, and as I hope to live to be another man from what I was, I am prepared to bear you company, and do it with a thankful heart. Will you not speak to me?"

It gave him no reply. The hand was pointed straight before them.

"Lead on!" said Scrooge. "Lead on! The night is waning fast, and it is precious time to me, I know. Lead on, Spirit!"

The Phantom moved away as it had come towards him. Scrooge followed in the shadow of its dress, which bore him up, he thought, and carried him along.

They scarcely seemed to enter the city; for the city rather seemed to spring up about them, and encompass them of its own act. But there they were in the heart of it; on 'Change, amongst the merchants; who hurried up and down, and chinked the money in their pockets, and conversed in groups, and looked at their watches, and trifled thoughtfully with their great gold seals, and so forth as Scrooge had seen them often.

The Spirit stopped beside one little knot of business men. Observing that the hand was pointed to them, Scrooge advanced to listen to their talk.

"No," said a great fat man with a monstrous chin, "I don't know much about it either way. I only know he's dead."

"When did he die?" inquired another.

"Last night, I believe."

"Why, what was the matter with him?" asked a third, taking a vast quantity of snuff out of a very large snuff-box. "I thought he'd never die."

"God knows," said the first, with a yawn.

"What has he done with his money?" asked a red-faced gentleman with a pendulous excrescence on the end of his nose, that shook like the gills of a turkey-cock.

"I haven't heard," said the man with the large chin, yawning again. "Left it to his company, perhaps. He hasn't left it to *me*. That's all I know."

This pleasantry was received with a general laugh.

"It's likely to be a very cheap funeral," said the same speaker; "for upon my life I don't know of anybody to go to it. Suppose we make up a party and volunteer?"

"I don't mind going if a lunch is provided," observed the gentleman with the excrescence on his nose. "But I must be fed if I make one."

Another laugh.

"Well, I am the most disinterested among you, after all," said the first speaker, "for I never wear black gloves, and I never eat lunch. But I'll offer to go, if anybody else will. When I come to think of it, I'm not at all sure that I wasn't his most particular friend; for we used to stop and speak whenever we met. Bye, bye!"

Speakers and listeners strolled away, and mixed with other groups. Scrooge knew the men, and looked towards the Spirit for an explanation.

The Phantom glided on into a street. Its finger pointed to two persons meeting. Scrooge listened again, thinking that the explanation might lie here.

He knew these men, also, perfectly. They were men of business, very wealthy and of great importance. He had made a point always of standing well in their esteem; in a business point of view, that is; strictly in a business point of view.

"How are you?" said one.

"How are you?" returned the other.

"Well!" said the first. "Old Scratch has got his own at last, hey?"

"So I am told," returned the second. "Cold, isn't it?"

"Seasonable for Christmas-time. You are not a skater, I suppose?"

"No. No. Something else to think of. Good morning!"

Not another word. That was their meeting, their conversation, and their parting.

Scrooge was at first inclined to be surprised that the Spirit should attach importance to conversations apparently so trivial; but feeling assured that they must have some hidden purpose, he set himself to consider what it was likely to be. They could scarcely be supposed to have any bearing on the death of Jacob, his old partner, for that was

Past, and this Ghost's province was the Future. Nor could he think of any one immediately connected with himself to whom he could apply them. But nothing doubting that to whomsoever they applied they had some latent moral for his own improvement, he resolved to treasure up every word he heard, and everything he saw; and especially to observe the shadow of himself when it appeared. For he had an expectation that the conduct of his future self would give him the clue he missed, and would render the solution of these riddles easy.

He looked about in that very place for his own image; but another man stood in his accustomed corner, and though the clock pointed to his usual time of day for being there, he saw no likeness of himself among the multitudes that poured in through the Porch. It gave him little surprise, however; for he had been revolving in his mind a change of life, and thought and hoped he saw his new-born resolutions carried out in this.

Quiet and dark, beside him stood the Phantom, with its outstretched hand. When he roused himself from his thoughtful quest, he fancied from the turn of the hand, and its situation in reference to himself, that the Unseen Eyes were looking at him keenly. It made him shudder, and feel very cold.

They left the busy scene, and went into an obscure part of the town, where Scrooge had never penetrated before, although he recognised its situation and its bad repute. The ways were foul and narrow; the shops and houses wretched; the people half-naked, drunken, slipshod, ugly. Alleys and archways, like so many cesspools, disgorged their offences of smell, and dirt, and life, upon the straggling streets; and the whole quarter reeked with crime, with filth and misery.

Far in this den of infamous resort, there was a low-browed, beetling shop, below a pent-house roof, where iron, old rags, bottles, bones, and greasy offal were bought. Upon the floor within were piled up heaps of rusty keys, nails, chains, hinges, files, scales, weights, and refuse iron of all kinds. Secrets that few would like to scrutinise were bred and hidden in mountains of unseemly rags, masses of corrupted fat, and sepulchres of bones. Sitting in among the wares he dealt in, by a charcoal stove, made of old bricks, was a grey-haired rascal, nearly seventy years of age; who had screened himself from the cold air without by a frowsy curtaining of miscellaneous tatters hung upon a line, and smoked his pipe in all the luxury of calm retirement.

Scrooge and the Phantom came into the presence of this man, just as a woman with a heavy bundle slunk into the shop. But she had scarcely entered, when another woman, similarly laden, came in, too; and she was closely followed by a man in faded black, who was no less startled by the sight of them than they had been upon the recognition of each other. After a short period of blank astonishment, in which the old man with the pipe had joined them, they all three burst into a laugh.

"Let the charwoman alone to be the first!" said she who had entered first. "Let the laundress alone to be the second; and let the undertaker's man alone to be the third. Look here, old Joe, here's a chance! If we haven't all three met here without meaning it!"

"You couldn't have met in a better place," said old Joe, removing his pipe from his mouth. "Come into the parlour. You were made free of it long ago, you know; and the other two ain't strangers. Stop till I shut the door of the shop. Ah! How it skreeks! There ain't such a rusty bit of metal in the place as its own hinges, I believe; and I'm sure there's no such old bones here as mine. Ha, ha! We're all suitable to our calling, we're well matched. Come into the parlour. Come into the parlour."

The parlour was the space behind the screen of rags. The old man raked the fire together with an old stair-rod, and, having trimmed his smoky lamp (for it was night) with the stem of his pipe, put it into his mouth again.

While he did this the woman who had already spoken threw her bundle on the floor and sat down in a flaunting manner on a stool; crossing her elbows on her knees, and looking with a bold defiance at the other two.

"What odds, then! What odds, Mrs. Dilber?" said the woman. "Every person has a right to take care of themselves. *He* always did!"

"That's true, indeed!" said the laundress. "No man more so."

"Why, then, don't stand staring as if you was afraid, woman; who's the wiser? We're not going to pick holes in each other's coats, I suppose?"

"No, indeed!" said Mrs. Dilber and the man together. "We should hope not."

"Very well, then!" cried the woman. "That's enough. Who's the worse for the loss of a few things like these? Not a dead man, I suppose?"

"No, indeed," said Mrs. Dilber, laughing.

"If he wanted to keep 'em after he was dead, a wicked old screw," pursued the woman, "why wasn't he natural in his lifetime? If he had been, he'd have had somebody to look after him when he was struck with Death, instead of lying gasping out his last there, alone by himself."

"It's the truest word that ever was spoke," said Mrs. Dilber. "It's a judgment on him."

"I wish it was a little heavier judgment," replied the woman; "and it should have been, you may depend upon it, if I could have laid my hands on anything else. Open that bundle, old Joe, and let me know the value of it. Speak out plain. I'm not afraid to be the first, nor afraid for them to see it. We knew pretty well that we were helping ourselves, before we met here, I believe. It's no sin. Open the bundle, Joe."

But the gallantry of her friends would not allow of this; and the man in faded black, mounting the breach first, produced *his* plunder. It was not extensive. A seal or two, a pencil-case, a pair of sleeve-buttons, and a brooch of no great value, were all. They were severally examined and appraised by old Joe, who chalked the sums he was disposed to give for each, upon the wall, and added them up into a total when he found that there was nothing more to come.

"That's your account," said Joe, "and I wouldn't give another sixpence, if I was to be boiled for not doing it. Who's next?"

Mrs. Dilber was next. Sheets and towels, a little wearing apparel, two old-fashioned silver teaspoons, a pair of sugar-tongs, and a few boots. Her account was stated on the wall in the same manner.

"I always give too much to ladies. It's a weakness of mine, and that's the way I ruin myself," said old Joe. "That's your account. If you asked me for another penny and made it an open question, I'd repent of being so liberal and knock off half a crown."

"And now undo *my* bundle, Joe," said the first woman.

Joe went down on his knees for the greater convenience of opening it, and having unfastened a great many knots, dragged out a large heavy roll of some dark stuff.

"What do you call this?" said Joe. "Bed-curtains!"

"Ah!" returned the woman, laughing, and leaning forward on her crossed arms. "Bed-curtains!"

"You don't mean to say you took 'em down rings and all, with him lying there?" said Joe.

"Yes, I do," replied the woman. "Why not?"

"You were born to make your fortune," said Joe, "and you'll certainly do it."

"I certainly shan't hold my hand, when I can get anything in it by reaching it out, for the sake of such a man as he was, I promise you, Joe," returned the woman coolly. "Don't drop that oil upon the blankets, now."

"His blankets?" asked Joe.

"Whose else's do you think?" replied the woman. "He isn't likely to take cold without 'em, I dare say."

"I hope he didn't die of anything catching? Eh?" said old Joe, stopping in his work, and looking up.

"Don't you be afraid of that," returned the woman. "I ain't so fond of his company that I'd loiter about him for such things, if he did. Ah! You may look through that shirt till your eyes ache, but you won't find a hole in it, nor a threadbare place. It's the best he had, and a fine one too. They'd have wasted it, if it hadn't been for me."

"What do you call wasting of it?" asked old Joe.

"Putting it on him to be buried in, to be sure," replied the woman, with a laugh. "Somebody was fool enough to do it, but I took it off again. If calico ain't good enough for such a purpose, it isn't good enough for anything. It's quite as becoming to the body. He can't look uglier than he did in that one."

Scrooge listened to this dialogue in horror. As they sat grouped about their spoil, in the scanty light afforded by the old man's lamp, he viewed them with a detestation and disgust, which could hardly have been greater, though they had been obscene demons, marketing the corpse itself.

"Ha, ha!" laughed the same woman, when old Joe, producing a flannel bag with money in it, told out their several gains upon the ground. "This is the end of it, you see? He frightened every one away from him when he was alive, to profit us when he was dead! Ha, ha, ha!"

"Spirit!" said Scrooge, shuddering from head to foot. "I see, I see. The case of this unhappy man might be my own. My life tends that way, now. Merciful Heaven, what is this!"

He recoiled in terror, for the scene had changed, and now he almost touched a bed—a bare, uncurtained bed, on which, beneath a ragged sheet, there lay a something covered up, which, though it was dumb, announced itself in awful language.

The room was very dark, too dark to be observed with any accuracy, though Scrooge glanced round it in obedience to a secret impulse, anxious to know what kind of room it was. A pale light rising in the outer air, fell straight upon the bed; and on it, plundered and bereft, unwatched, unwept, uncared for, was the body of this man.

Scrooge glanced towards the Phantom. Its steady hand was pointed to the head. The cover was so carelessly adjusted that the slightest raising of it, the motion of a finger upon Scrooge's part, would have disclosed the face. He thought of it, felt how easy it would be to do, and longed to do it; but had no more power to withdraw the veil than to dismiss the spectre at his side.

Oh, cold, cold, rigid, dreadful Death, set up thine altar here, and dress it with such terrors as thou hast at thy command, for this is thy dominion! But of the loved, revered, and honoured head, thou canst not turn one hair to thy dread purposes, or make one feature odious. It is not that the hand is heavy and will fall down when released; it is not that the heart and pulse are still; but that the hand was open, generous, and true; the heart brave, warm, and tender; and the pulse a man's. Strike, Shadow, strike! And see his good deeds springing from the wound, to sow the world with life immortal!

No voice pronounced these words in Scrooge's ears, and yet he heard them when he looked upon the bed. He thought, if this man could be raised up now, what would be his foremost thoughts? Avarice, hard-dealing, griping cares? They have brought him to a rich end, truly!

He lay, in the dark, empty house, with not a man, a woman, or a child, to say he was kind to me in this or that, and for the memory of one kind word I will be kind to him. A cat was tearing at the door, and there was a sound of gnawing rats beneath the hearthstone. What *they* wanted in the room of death, and why they were so restless and disturbed, Scrooge did not dare to think.

"Spirit!" he said, "this is a fearful place. In leaving it, I shall not leave its lesson, trust me. Let us go!"

Still the Ghost pointed with an unmoved finger to the head.

"I understand you," Scrooge returned, "and I would do it if I could. But I have not the power, Spirit. I have not the power."

Again it seemed to look upon him.

"If there is any person in the town who feels emotion caused by this man's death," said Scrooge, quite agonised, "show that person to me, Spirit, I beseech you!"

The Phantom spread its dark robe before him for a moment, like a wing; and withdrawing it, revealed a room by daylight, where a mother and her children were.

She was expecting some one, and with anxious eagerness; for she walked up and down the room; started at every sound; looked out from the window; glanced at the clock; tried, but in vain, to work with her needle; and could hardly bear the voices of her children in their play.

At length the long, expected knock was heard. She hurried to the door and met her husband; a man whose face was care-worn and depressed, though he was young. There was a remarkable expression in it now; a kind of serious delight of which he felt ashamed, and which he struggled to repress.

He sat down to the dinner that had been hoarding for him by the fire, and when she asked him faintly what news (which was not until after a long silence), he appeared embarrassed how to answer.

"Is it good," she said, "or bad?"—to help him.

"Bad," he answered.

"We are quite ruined?"

"No. There is hope yet, Caroline."

"If *he* relents," she said, amazed, "there is! Nothing is past hope, if such a miracle has happened."

"He is past relenting," said her husband. "He is dead."

She was a mild and patient creature, if her face spoke truth; but she was thankful in her soul to hear it, and she said so, with clasped hands. She prayed forgiveness the next moment, and was sorry; but the first was the emotion of her heart.

"What the half-drunken woman, whom I told you of last night, said to me, when I tried to see him and obtain a week's delay, and what I thought was a mere excuse to avoid me, turns out to have been quite true. He was not only very ill, but dying, then."

"To whom will our debt be transferred?"

"I don't know. But before that time we shall be ready with the money; and even though we were not, it would be bad fortune indeed to find so merciless a creditor in his successor. We may sleep tonight with light hearts, Caroline!"

Yes. Soften it as they would, their hearts were lighter. The children's faces, hushed and clustered round to hear what they so little understood, were brighter; and it was a happier house for this man's death! The only emotion that the Ghost could show him, caused by the event, was one of pleasure.

"Let me see some tenderness connected with a death," said

Scrooge; "or that dark chamber, Spirit, which we left just now, will be for ever present to me."

The Ghost conducted him through several streets familiar to his feet; and as they went along, Scrooge looked here and there to find himself, but nowhere was he to be seen. They entered poor Bob Cratchit's house, the dwelling he had visited before, and found the mother and the children seated round the fire.

Quiet. Very quiet. The noisy little Cratchits were as still as statues in one corner, and sat looking up at Peter, who had a book before him. The mother and her daughters were engaged in sewing. But surely they were very quiet!

" 'And he took a child, and set him in the midst of them.' "

Where had Scrooge heard those words? He had not dreamed them. The boy must have read them out, as he and the Spirit crossed the threshold. Why did he not go on?

The mother laid her work upon the table, and put her hand up to her face.

"The colour hurts my eyes," she said.

The colour? Ah, poor Tiny Tim!

"They're better now again," said Cratchit's wife. "It makes them weak by candle-light; and I wouldn't show weak eyes to your father when he comes home, for the world. It must be near his time."

"Past it rather," Peter answered, shutting up his book. "But I think he has walked a little slower than he used, these few last evenings, mother."

They were very quiet again. At last she said, and in a steady, cheerful voice, that only faltered once: "I have known him walk with—I have known him walk with Tiny Tim upon his shoulder, very fast indeed."

"And so have I," cried Peter. "Often."

"And so have I," exclaimed another. So had all.

"But he was very light to carry," she resumed, intent upon her work, "and his father loved him so, that it was no trouble; no trouble. And there is your father at the door!"

She hurried out to meet him; and little Bob in his comforter—he had need of it, poor fellow—came in. His tea was ready for him on the hob, and they all tried who should help him to it most. Then the two young Cratchits got upon his knees and laid, each child, a little cheek against his face, as if they said, "Don't mind it, father." "Don't be grieved!"

Bob was very cheerful with them, and spoke pleasantly to all the family. He looked at the work upon the table, and praised the industry and speed of Mrs. Cratchit and the girls. They would be done long before Sunday, he said.

"Sunday! You went today, then, Robert?" said his wife.

"Yes, my dear," returned Bob. "I wish you could have gone. It would have done you good to see how green a place it is. But you'll see it often. I promised him that I would walk there on a Sunday. My little, little child!" cried Bob. "My little child!"

He broke down all at once. He couldn't help it. If he could have helped it, he and his child would have been farther apart perhaps than they were.

He left the room, and went up stairs into the room above, which was lighted cheerfully, and hung with Christmas. There was a chair set close beside the child, and there were signs of someone having been there, lately. Poor Bob sat down in it, and when he had thought a little and composed himself, he kissed the little face. He was reconciled to what had happened, and went down again quite happy.

They drew about the fire, and talked; the girls and mother working still. Bob told them of the extraordinary kindness of Mr. Scrooge's nephew, whom he had scarcely seen but once, and who, meeting him in the street that day, and seeing that he looked a little—"just a little down you know," said Bob, inquired what had happened to distress him. "On which," said Bob, "for he is the pleasantest-spoken gentleman you ever heard, I told him. 'I am heartily sorry for it, Mr. Cratchit,' he said, 'and heartily sorry for your good wife.' By the bye, how he ever knew *that* I don't know."

"Knew what, my dear?"

"Why, that you were a good wife," replied Bob.

"Everybody knows that!" said Peter.

"Very well observed, my boy!" cried Bob. "I hope they do. 'Heartily sorry,' he said, 'for your good wife. If I can be of service to you in any way,' he said, giving me his card, 'that's where I live. Pray come to me.' Now, it wasn't," cried Bob, "for the sake of anything he might be able to do for us, so much as for his kind way, that this was quite delightful. It really seemed as if he had known our Tiny Tim, and felt with us."

"I'm sure he's a good soul!" said Mrs. Cratchit.

"You would be sure of it, my dear," returned Bob, "if you saw and spoke to him. I shouldn't be at all surprised—mark what I say!—if he got Peter a better situation."

"Only hear that, Peter," said Mrs. Cratchit.

"And then," cried one of the girls, "Peter will be keeping company with some one, and setting up for himself."

"Get along with you!" retorted Peter, grinning.

"It's just as likely as not," said Bob, "one of these days; though there's plenty of time for that, my dear. But however and whenever we part from one another, I am sure we shall none of us forget poor Tiny Tim—shall we—or this first parting that there was among us?"

"Never, father!" cried they all.

"And I know," said Bob—"I know, my dears, that when we recollect how patient and how mild he was, although he was a little, little child, we shall not quarrel easily among ourselves, and forget poor Tiny Tim in doing it."

"No, never, father!" they all cried again.

"I am very happy," said little Bob, "I am very happy!"

Mrs. Cratchit kissed him, his daughters kissed him, the two young Cratchits kissed him, and Peter and himself shook hands. Spirit of Tiny Tim, thy childish essence was from God!

"Spectre," said Scrooge, "something informs me that our parting moment is at hand. I know it, but I know not how. Tell me what man that was whom we saw lying dead?"

The Ghost of Christmas Yet To Come conveyed him, as before—though at a different time, he thought; indeed, there seemed no order in these latter visions, save that they were in the Future—into the resorts of business men, but showed him not himself. Indeed, the Spirit did not stay for anything, but went straight on, as to the end just now desired, until besought by Scrooge to tarry for a moment.

"This court," said Scrooge, "through which we hurry now, is where my place of occupation is, and has been for a length of time. I see the house. Let me behold what I shall be, in days to come."

The Spirit stopped; the hand was pointed elsewhere.

"The house is yonder," Scrooge exclaimed. "Why do you point away?"

The inexorable finger underwent no change.

Scrooge hastened to the window of his office, and looked in. It was an office still, but not his. The furniture was not the same, and the figure in the chair was not himself. The Phantom pointed as before.

He joined it once again, and wondering why and whither he had gone, accompanied it until they reached an iron gate. He paused to look round before entering.

A churchyard. Here, then, the wretched man whose name he had now to learn lay underneath the ground. It was a worthy place. Walled in by houses; overrun by grass and weeds, the growth of vegetation's death, not life; choked up with too much burying; fat with repleted appetite. A worthy place!

The Spirit stood among the graves, and pointed down to One. He advanced towards it trembling. The Phantom was exactly as it had been, but he dreaded that he saw new meaning in its solemn shape.

"Before I draw nearer to that stone to which you point," said Scrooge, "answer me one question. Are these the shadows of the things that Will be, or are they shadows of the things that May be, only?"

Still the Ghost pointed downward to the grave by which it stood.

"Men's courses will foreshadow certain ends, to which, if persevered in, they must lead," said Scrooge. "But if the courses be departed from, the ends will change. Say it is thus with what you show me!"

The Spirit was immovable as ever.

Scrooge crept towards it, trembling as he went; and following the finger, read upon the stone of the neglected grave his own name, EBENEZER SCROOGE.

"Am I that man who lay upon the bed?" he cried, upon his knees.

The finger pointed from the grave to him, and back again.

"No, Spirit! Oh, no, no!"

The finger still was there.

"Spirit!" he cried, tight clutching at its robe, "hear me! I am not the man I was. I will not be the man I must have been but for this intercourse. Why show me this, if I am past all hope!"

For the first time the hand appeared to shake.

"Good Spirit," he pursued, as down upon the ground he fell before it; "your nature intercedes for me, and pities me. Assure me that I yet may change these shadows you have shown me, by an altered life?"

The kind hand trembled.

"I will honor Christmas in my heart, and try to keep it all the year. I will live in the Past, the Present, and the Future. The Spirits of all Three shall strive within me. I will not shut out the lessons that they teach. Oh, tell me I may sponge away the writing on this stone?"

In his agony, he caught the spectral hand. It sought to free itself, but he was strong in his entreaty, and detained it. The Spirit, stronger yet, repulsed him.

Holding up his hands in a last prayer to have his fate reversed, he saw an alteration in the Phantom's hood and dress. It shrunk, collapsed, and dwindled down into a bedpost.

Stave Five

THE END OF IT

Yes! and the bedpost was his own. The bed was his own, the room was his own. Best and happiest of all, the Time before him was his own, to make amends in!

"I will live in the Past, the Present, and the Future!" Scrooge repeated, as he scrambled out of bed. "The Spirits of all Three shall strive within me. O Jacob Marley! Heaven, and the Christmas-time be praised for this! I say it on my knees, old Jacob; on my knees!"

He was so fluttered and so glowing with his good intentions that his broken voice would scarcely answer to his call. He had been sobbing violently in his conflict with the Spirit, and his face was wet with tears.

"They are not torn down," cried Scrooge, folding one of his bedcurtains in his arms, "they are not torn down, rings and all. They are here —I am here—the shadows of the things that would have been may be dispelled. They will be. I know they will!"

His hands were busy with his garments all this time; turning them inside out, putting them on upside down, tearing them, mislaying them, making them parties to every kind of extravagance.

"I don't know what to do!" cried Scrooge, laughing and crying in the same breath; and making a perfect Laocoön of himself with his stockings. "I am as light as a feather, I am as happy as an angel, I am as merry as a school-boy. I am as giddy as a drunken man. A merry Christmas to everybody! A happy New Year to all the world! Hallo here! Whoop! Hallo!"

He had frisked into the sitting-room, and was now standing there, perfectly winded.

"There's the saucepan that the gruel was in!" cried Scrooge, starting off again, and going round the fireplace. "There's the door by which the Ghost of Jacob Marley entered! There's the corner where the

Ghost of a Christmas Present sat! There's the window where I saw the wandering Spirits! It's all right, it's all true, it all happened. Ha, ha, ha!"

Really, for a man who had been out of practice for so many years, it was a splendid laugh, a most illustrious laugh. The father of a long, long line of brilliant laughs!

"I don't know what day of the month it is," said Scrooge. "I don't know how long I have been among the Spirits. I don't know anything. I'm quite a baby. Never mind; I don't care. I'd rather be a baby. Hallo! Whoop! Hallo here!"

He was checked in his transports by the churches ringing out the lustiest peals he had ever heard. Clash, clash, hammer; ding, dong, bell. Bell, dong, ding; hammer, clang, clash! Oh, glorious, glorious!

Running to the window, he opened it, and put out his head. No fog, no mist; clear, bright, jovial, stirring, cold; cold, piping for the blood to dance to; golden sunlight; Heavenly sky; sweet fresh air; merry bells. Oh, glorious, glorious!

"What's today?" cried Scrooge, calling downward to a boy in Sunday clothes, who perhaps had loitered in to look about him.

"Eh?" returned the boy, with all his might of wonder.

"What's today, my fine fellow?" said Scrooge.

"Today!" replied the boy. "Why, CHRISTMAS DAY."

"It's Christmas Day!" said Scrooge to himself. "I haven't missed it. The Spirits have done it all in one night. They can do anything they like. Of course they can. Of course they can. Hallo, my fine fellow!"

"Hallo!" returned the boy.

"Do you know the poulterer's, in the next street but one, at the corner?" Scrooge inquired.

"I should hope I did," replied the lad.

"An intelligent boy!" said Scrooge. "A remarkable boy! Do you know whether they've sold the prize Turkey that was hanging up there?—not the little prize Turkey; the big one?"

"What, the one as big as me?" returned the boy.

"What a delightful boy!" said Scrooge. "It's a pleasure to talk to him. Yes, my buck!"

"It's hanging there now," replied the boy.

"Is it?" said Scrooge. "Go and buy it."

"Walk-ER!" exclaimed the boy.

"No, no," said Scrooge, "I am in earnest. Go and buy it, and tell 'em to bring it here, that I may give them the directions where to take it. Come back with the man, and I'll give you a shilling. Come back with him in less than five minutes, and I'll give you half a crown!"

The boy was off like a shot. He must have had a steady hand at a trigger who could have got a shot off half so fast.

"I'll send it to Bob Cratchit's," whispered Scrooge, rubbing his hands, and splitting with a laugh. "He shan't know who sends it. It's twice the size of Tiny Tim. Joe Miller never made such a joke as sending it to Bob's will be!"

The hand in which he wrote the address was not a steady one; but write it he did, somehow, and went down stairs to open the street door, ready for the coming of the poulterer's man. As he stood there, waiting his arrival, the knocker caught his eye.

"I shall love it as long as I live!" cried Scrooge, patting it with his hand. "I scarcely ever looked at it before. What an honest expression it has in its face! It's a wonderful knocker!—Here's the Turkey. Hallo! Whoop! How are you! Merry Christmas!"

It *was* a Turkey! He never could have stood upon his legs, that bird. He would have snapped 'em short off in a minute, like sticks of sealing-wax.

"Why, it's impossible to carry that to Camden Town," said Scrooge. "You must have a cab."

The chuckle with which he said this, and the chuckle with which he paid for the Turkey, and the chuckle with which he paid for the cab, and the chuckle with which he recompensed the boy were only to be exceeded by the chuckle with which he sat down breathless in his chair again, and chuckled till he cried.

Shaving was not an easy task, for his hand continued to shake very much; and shaving requires attention, even when you don't dance while you are at it. But if he had cut the end of his nose off, he would have put a piece of sticking plaster over it, and been quite satisfied.

He dressed himself "all in his best," and at last got out into the streets. The people were by this time pouring forth, as he had seen them with the Ghost of Christmas Present; and walking with his hands behind him, Scrooge regarded every one with a delighted smile. He looked so irresistibly pleasant, in a word, that three or four good-humoured fellows said, "Good morning, sir! A merry Christmas to you!" And Scrooge said often afterwards that, of all the blithe sounds he had ever heard, those were the blithest in his ears.

He had not gone far, when coming on towards him he beheld the portly gentleman who had walked into his counting-house the day before, and said "Scrooge and Marley's, I believe?" It sent a pang across his heart to think how this old gentleman would look upon him when they met; but he knew what path lay straight before him, and he took it.

"My dear sir," said Scrooge, quickening his pace, and taking the old gentleman by both his hands. "How do you do? I hope you succeeded yesterday. It was very kind of you. A merry Christmas to you, sir!"

"Mr. Scrooge?"

"Yes," said Scrooge. "That is my name, and I fear it may not be pleasant to you. Allow me to ask your pardon. And will you have the goodness"—here Scrooge whispered in his ear.

"Lord bless me!" cried the gentleman, as if his breath were taken away. "My dear Mr. Scrooge, are you serious?"

"If you please," said Scrooge. "Not a farthing less. A great many back-payments are included in it, I assure you. Will you do me that favour?"

"My dear sir," said the other, shaking hands with him, "I don't know what to say to such munifi—"

"Don't say anything, please," retorted Scrooge. "Come and see me. Will you come and see me?"

"I will!" cried the old gentleman. And it was clear he meant to do it.

"Thankee," said Scrooge. "I am much obliged to you. I thank you fifty times. Bless you!"

He went to church, and walked about the streets, and watched the people hurrying to and fro, and patted the children on the head, and questioned beggars, and looked down into the kitchens of houses, and up to the windows; and found that everything could yield him pleasure. He had never dreamed that any walk—that any thing—could give him so much happiness. In the afternoon he turned his steps towards his nephew's house.

He passed the door a dozen times, before he had the courage to go up and knock. But he made a dash, and did it.

"Is your master at home, my dear?" said Scrooge to the girl. Nice girl! Very.

"Yes, sir."

"Where is he, my love?" said Scrooge.

"He's in the dining-room, sir, along with mistress. I'll show you up stairs, if you please."

"Thankee. He knows me," said Scrooge, with his hand already on the dining-room lock. "I'll go in here, my dear."

He turned it gently, and sidled his face in, round the door. They were looking at the table (which was spread out in great array); for these young housekeepers are always nervous on such points, and like to see that everything is right.

"Fred!" said Scrooge.

Dear heart alive, how his niece by marriage started! Scrooge had forgotten, for the moment, about her sitting in the corner with the footstool, or he wouldn't have done it, on any account.

"Why, bless my soul!" cried Fred, "who's that?"

"It's I. Your uncle Scrooge. I have come to dinner. Will you let me in, Fred?"

Let him in! It is a mercy he didn't shake his arm off. He was at home in five minutes. Nothing could be heartier. His niece looked just the same. So did Topper when *he* came. So did the plump sister, when *she* came. So did every one when *they* came. Wonderful party, wonderful games, wonderful unanimity, won-der-ful happiness!

But he was early at the office next morning. Oh, he was early there. If he could only be there first, and catch Bob Cratchit coming late! That was the thing he had set his heart upon.

And he did it; yes, he did! The clock struck nine. No Bob. A quarter past. No Bob. He was full eighteen minutes and a half behind his time. Scrooge sat with his door wide open, that he might see him come into the tank.

His hat was off, before he opened the door; his comforter too. He was on his stool in a jiffy; driving away with his pen as if he were trying to overtake nine o'clock.

"Hallo!" growled Scrooge, in his accustomed voice as near as he could feign it. "What do you mean by coming here at this time of day?"

"I am very sorry, sir," said Bob. "I *am* behind my time."

"You are!" repeated Scrooge. "Yes. I think you are. Step this way, sir, if you please."

"It's only once a year, sir," pleaded Bob, appearing from the tank. "It shall not be repeated. I was making rather merry yesterday, sir."

"Now, I'll tell you what, my friend," said Scrooge. "I am not going to stand this sort of thing any longer. And therefore," he continued, leaping from his stool, and giving Bob such a dig in the waistcoat that he staggered back into the tank again; "and therefore I am about to raise your salary!"

Bob trembled, and got a little nearer to the ruler. He had a momentary idea of knocking Scrooge down with it, holding him, and calling to the people in the court for help and a strait-waistcoat.

"A merry Christmas, Bob!" said Scrooge, with an earnestness that could not be mistaken, as he clapped him on the back. "A merrier Christmas, Bob, my good fellow, than I have given you for many a year! I'll raise your salary, and endeavour to assist your struggling family, and we will discuss your affairs this very afternoon, over a Christmas bowl of smoking bishop, Bob! Make up the fires, and buy another coal-scuttle before you dot another i, Bob Cratchit!"

Scrooge was better than his word. He did it all, and infinitely more; and to Tiny Tim, who did NOT die, he was a second father. He became as good a friend, as good a master, and as good a man, as the good old city knew, or any other good old city, town, or borough, in the good old world. Some people laughed to see the alteration in him, but he let them laugh, and little heeded them; for he was wise enough to know that nothing ever happened on this globe, for good, at which some people did not have their fill in laughter in the outset; and knowing that such as these would be blind anyway, he thought it quite as well that they should wrinkle up their eyes in grins, as have the malady in less attractive forms. His own heart laughed; and that was quite enough for him.

He had no further intercourse with Spirits, but lived upon the Total Abstinence Principle, ever afterwards; and it was always said of him that he knew how to keep Christmas well, if any man alive possessed the knowledge. May that be truly said of us, and all of us! And so, as Tiny Tim observed, God Bless Us, Every One!

THE GHOST OF CHRISTMAS EVE

by J. M. Barrie

from *My Lady Nicotine*

A few years ago, as some may remember, a startling ghost paper appeared in the monthly organ of the Society for Haunting Houses. The writer guaranteed the truth of his statement, and even gave the name of the Yorkshire manor-house in which the affair took place. The article and the discussion to which it gave rise agitated me a good deal, and I consulted Pettigrew about the advisability of clearing up the mystery. The writer wrote that he "distinctly saw his arm pass through the apparition and come out at the other side," and indeed I still remember his saying so next morning. He had a scared face, but I had presence of mind to continue eating my rolls and marmalade as if my briar had nothing to do with the miraculous affair.

Seeing that he made a "paper" of it, I suppose he is justified in touching up the incidental details. He says, for instance, that we were told the story of the ghost which is said to haunt the house, just before going to bed. As far as I remember, it was only mentioned at luncheon, and then sceptically. Instead of there being snow falling outside and an eerie wind wailing through the skeleton trees, the night was still and muggy. Lastly, I did not know, until the journal reached my hands, that he was put into the room known as the Haunted Chamber, nor that in that room the fire is noted for casting weird shadows upon the walls. This, however, may be so. The legend of the manor-house ghost he tells precisely as it is known to me. The tragedy dates back to the time of Charles I., and is led up to by a pathetic love-story, which I need not give. Suffice it that for seven days and nights the old steward had been anxiously awaiting the return of his young master and mistress from their honeymoon. On Christmas Eve, after he had gone to bed, there was a great clanging of the door-bell. Flinging on a dressing-gown, he hastened downstairs. According to the story, a number of servants watched him, and saw by the light of his candle that his face was an ashy white. He took off the chains of the door, unbolted it, and pulled it open. What he saw no human being knows; but it must have been something awful, for without a cry the old steward fell dead in the hall. Perhaps the strangest part of the story is this: that the shadow of a burly man, holding a pistol in his hand, entered by the open door, stepped over the steward's body, and, gliding up the stairs, disappeared, no one could say where. Such is the legend. I shall not tell the many ingenious explanations of it that have been offered. Every Christmas Eve, however, the silent scene is said to be gone through again; and tradition declares that no person lives for twelve months at whom the ghostly intruder points his pistol.

On Christmas Day the gentleman who tells the tale in the scientific journal created some sensation at the breakfast-table by solemnly asserting that he had seen the ghost. Most of the men present scouted his story, which may be condensed into a few words. He had retired to his bedroom at a fairly early hour, and as he opened the door his candle-light was blown out. He tried to get a light from the fire, but it was too low, and eventually he went to bed in the semi-darkness. He was wakened—he did not know at what hour—by the clanging of a bell. He sat up in bed, and the ghost-story came in a rush to his mind. His fire was dead, and the room was consequently dark; yet by and by he knew, though he heard no sound, that his door had opened. He cried out, "Who is that?" but got no answer. By an effort he jumped up and went to the door, which was ajar. His bedroom was on the first floor, and looking up the stairs he could see nothing.

He felt a cold sensation at his heart, however, when he looked the other way. Going slowly and without a sound down the stairs, was an old man in a dressing-gown. He carried a candle. From the top of the stairs only part of the hall is visible, but as the apparition disappeared the watcher had the courage to go down a few steps after him. At first nothing was to be seen, for the candle-light had vanished. A dim light, however, entered by the long narrow windows which flank the hall-door, and after a moment the onlooker could see that the hall was empty. He was marvelling at this sudden disappearance of the steward, when, to his horror, he saw a body fall upon the hall-floor within a few feet of the door. The watcher cannot say whether he cried out, nor how long he stood there trembling. He came to himself with a start as he realized that something was coming up the stairs. Fear prevented his taking flight, and in a moment the thing was at his side. Then he saw indistinctly that it was not the figure he had seen descend. He saw a younger man in a heavy over-coat, but with no hat on his head. He wore on his face a look of extravagant triumph. The guest boldly put out his hand towards the figure. To his amazement his arm went through it. The ghost paused for a moment and looked behind it. It was then the watcher realized that it carried a pistol in its right hand. He was by this time in a highly strung condition, and he stood trembling lest the pistol should be pointed at him. The apparition, however, rapidly glided up the stairs and was soon lost to sight. Such are the main facts of the story; none of which I contradicted at the time.

I cannot say absolutely that I can clear up this mystery; but my suspicions are confirmed by a good deal of circumstantial evidence. This will not be understood unless I explain my strange infirmity. Wherever I went I used to be troubled with a presentiment that I had left my pipe behind. Often even at the dinner-table, I paused in the middle of a sentence as if stricken with sudden pain. Then my hand went down to my pocket. Sometimes, even after I felt my pipe, I had a conviction that it was stopped, and only by a desperate effort did I keep myself from producing it and blowing down it. I distinctly remember once dreaming three nights in succession that I was on the Scotch express without it. More than once, I know, I have wandered in my sleep, looking for it in all sorts of places, and after I went to bed I generally jumped out, just to make sure of it. My strong belief, then, is that I was the ghost seen by the writer of the paper. I fancy that I rose in my sleep, lighted a candle and wandered down to the hall to feel if my pipe was safe in my coat, which was hanging there. The light had gone out when I was in the hall. Probably the body seen to fall on the hall floor was some other coat which I had flung there to get more easily at my own. I cannot account for the bell; but perhaps the gentleman in the Haunted Chamber dreamt that part of the affair. I had put on the overcoat before reascending; indeed, I may say that next morning I was surprised to find it on a chair in my bedroom, also to notice that there were several long streaks of candle-grease on my dressing-gown. I conclude that the pistol, which gave my face such a look of triumph, was my briar, which I found in the morning beneath my pillow. The strangest thing of all, perhaps, is that when I awoke there was a smell of tobacco-smoke in the bedroom.

CAPTAIN ELI'S BEST EAR

by Frank R. Stockton

from *The Novels and Stories of Frank R. Stockton*

The little seaside village of Sponkannis lies so quietly upon a protected spot on our Atlantic coast that it makes no more stir in the
world than would a pebble which, held between one's finger and
thumb, should be dipped below the surface of a millpond and then
dropped. About the post-office and the store—both under the same
roof—the greater number of the houses cluster, as if they had come for
their week's groceries, or were waiting for the mail, while toward the
west the dwellings become fewer and fewer, until at last the village
blends into a long stretch of sandy coast and scrubby pine-woods.
Eastward the village ends abruptly at the foot of a wind-swept bluff,
on which no one cares to build.

Among the last houses in the western end of the village stood two
neat, substantial dwellings, one belonging to Captain Eli Bunker, and
the other to Captain Cephas Dyer. These householders were two very
respectable retired mariners, the first a widower about fifty, and the

other a bachelor of perhaps the same age, a few years more or less making but little difference in this region of weather-beaten youth and seasoned age.

Each of these good captains lived alone, and each took entire charge of his own domestic affairs, not because he was poor, but because it pleased him to do so. When Captain Eli retired from the sea he was the owner of a good vessel, which he sold at a fair profit; and Captain Cephas had made money in many a voyage before he built his house in Sponkannis and settled there.

When Captain Eli's wife was living she was his household manager. But Captain Cephas had never had a woman in his house, except during the first few months of his occupancy, when certain female neighbors came in occasionally to attend to little matters of cleaning which, according to popular notions, properly belong to the sphere of woman.

But Captain Cephas soon put an end to this sort of thing. He did not like a woman's ways, especially her ways of attending to domestic affairs. He liked to live in sailor fashion, and to keep house in sailor fashion. In his establishment everything was ship-shape, and everything which could be stowed away was stowed away, and, if possible, in a bunker. The floors were holystoned nearly every day, and the whole house was repainted about twice a year, a little at a time, when the weather was suitable for this marine recreation. Things not in frequent use were lashed securely to the walls, or perhaps put out of the way by being hauled up to the ceiling by means of blocks and tackle. His cooking was done sailor fashion, like everything else, and he never failed to have plum-duff on Sunday. His well was near his house, and every morning he dropped into it a lead and line, and noted down the depth of water. Three times a day he entered in a little note-book the state of the weather, the height of the mercury in barometer and thermometer, the direction of the wind, and special weather points when necessary.

Captain Eli managed his domestic affairs in an entirely different way. He kept house woman fashion—not, however, in the manner of an ordinary woman, but after the manner of his late wife, Miranda Bunker, now dead some seven years. Like his friend, Captain Cephas, he had had the assistance of his female neighbors during the earlier days of his widowerhood. But he soon found that these women did not do things as Miranda used to do them, and, although he frequently suggested that they should endeavor to imitate the methods of his late consort, they did not even try to do things as she used to do them, preferring their own ways. Therefore it was that Captain Eli determined to keep house by himself, and to do it, as nearly as his nature would allow, as Miranda used to do it. He swept his floors and he shook his door-mats; he washed his paint with soap and hot water; he dusted his furniture with a soft cloth, which he afterwards stuck behind a chest of drawers. He made his bed very neatly, turning down the sheet at the top, and setting the pillow upon edge, smoothing it carefully after he had done so. His cooking was based on the methods of the late Miranda. He had never been able to make bread rise properly, but he had always liked ship-biscuit, and he now greatly preferred them to the risen bread made by his neighbors. And as to coffee, and the plainer articles of food with which he furnished his table, even Miranda herself would not have objected to them had she been alive and very hungry.

The houses of the two captains were not very far apart, and they were good neighbors, often smoking their pipes together and talking of the sea. But this was always on the little porch in front of Captain Cephas's house, or by his kitchen fire in the winter. Captain Eli did not like the smell of tobacco smoke in his house, or even in front of it in summer-time, when the doors were open. He had no objection himself to the odor of tobacco, but it was contrary to the principles of woman housekeeping that rooms should smell of it, and he was always true to those principles.

It was late in a certain December, and through the village there was a pleasant little flutter of Christmas preparations. Captain Eli had been up to the store, and he had stayed there a good while, warming himself by the stove, and watching the women coming in to buy things for Christmas. It was strange how many things they bought for presents or for holiday use—fancy soap and candy, handkerchiefs and little woolen shawls for old people, and a lot of pretty little things which he knew the use of, but which Captain Cephas would never have understood at all had he been there.

As Captain Eli came out of the store he saw a cart in which were two good-sized Christmas trees, which had been cut in the woods, and were going, one to Captain Holmes's house, and the other to Mother Nelson's. Captain Holmes had grandchildren, and Mother Nelson, with never a child of her own, good old soul, had three little orphan nieces who never wanted for anything needful at Christmas-time or any other time.

Captain Eli walked home very slowly, taking observations in his mind. It was more than seven years since he had had anything to do with Christmas, except that on that day he had always made himself a mince-pie, the construction and the consumption of which were equally difficult. It is true that neighbors had invited him, and they had invited Captain Cephas, to their Christmas dinners, but neither of these worthy seamen had ever accepted any of these invitations. Even holiday food, when not cooked in sailor fashion, did not agree with Captain Cephas, and it would have pained the good heart of Captain Eli if he had been forced to make believe to enjoy a Christmas dinner so very inferior to those which Miranda used to set before him.

But now the heart of Captain Eli was gently moved by a Christmas flutter. It had been foolish, perhaps, for him to go up to the store at such a time as this, but the mischief had been done. Old feelings had come back to him, and he would be glad to celebrate Christmas this year if he could think of any good way to do it. And the result of his mental observations was that he went over to Captain Cephas's house to talk to him about it.

Captain Cephas was in his kitchen, smoking his third morning pipe. Captain Eli filled his pipe, lighted it, and sat down by the fire.

"Cap'n," said he, "what do you say to our keepin' Christmas this year? A Christmas dinner is no good if it's got to be eat alone, and you and me might eat ourn together. It might be in my house, or it might be in your house—it won't make no great difference to me which. Of course, I like woman housekeepin', as is laid down in the rules of service fer my house. But next best to that I like sailor housekeepin', so I don't mind which house the dinner is in, Cap'n Cephas, so it suits you."

Captain Cephas took his pipe from his mouth. "You're pretty late thinkin' about it," said he, "fer day after to-morrow's Christmas."

"That don't make no difference," said Captain Eli. "What things we want that are not in my house or your house we can easily get either up at the store or else in the woods."

"In the woods!" exclaimed Captain Cephas. "What in the name of thunder do you expect to get in the woods for Christmas?"

"A Christmas tree," said Captain Eli. "I thought it might be a nice thing to have a Christmas tree fer Christmas. Cap'n Holmes has got one, and Mother Nelson's got another. I guess nearly everybody's got one. It won't cost anything—I can go and cut it."

Captain Cephas grinned a grin, as if a great leak had been sprung in the side of a vessel, stretching nearly from stem to stern.

"A Christmas tree!" he exclaimed. "Well, I am blessed! But look here, Cap'n Eli. You don't know what a Christmas tree's fer. It's fer children, and not fer grown-ups. Nobody ever does have a Christmas tree in any house where there ain't no children."

Captain Eli rose and stood with his back to the fire. "I didn't think of that," he said, "but I guess it's so. And when I come to think of it, a Christmas isn't much of a Christmas, anyway, without children."

"You never had none," said Captain Cephas, "and you've kept Christmas."

"Yes," replied Captain Eli, reflectively, "we did do it, but there was always a lackment—Miranda has said so, and I have said so."

"You didn't have no Christmas tree," said Captain Cephas.

"No, we didn't. But I don't think that folks was as much set on Christmas trees then as they 'pear to be now. I wonder," he continued, thoughtfully gazing at the ceiling, "if we was to fix up a Christmas tree—and you and me's got a lot of pretty things that we've picked up all over the world, that would go miles ahead of anything that could be bought at the store fer Christmas trees—if we was to fix up a tree real nice, if we couldn't get some child or other that wasn't likely to have a tree to come in and look at it, and stay awhile, and make Christmas more like Christmas. And then, when it went away, it could take along the things that was hangin' on the tree, and keep 'em fer its own."

"That wouldn't work," said Captain Cephas. "If you get a child into this business, you must let it hang up its stockin' before it goes to bed, and find it full in the mornin', and then tell it an all-fired lie about Santa Claus if it asks any questions. Most children think more of stockin's than they do of trees—so I've heard, at least."

"I've got no objections to stockin's," said Captain Eli. "If it wanted to hang one up, it could hang one up either here or in my house, wherever we kept Christmas."

"You couldn't keep a child all night," sardonically remarked Captain Cephas, "and no more could I. Fer if it was to get up a croup in the night, it would be as if we was on a lee shore with anchors draggin' and a gale a-blowin'."

"That's so," said Captain Eli. "You've put it fair. I suppose if we did keep a child all night, we'd have to have some sort of a woman within hail in case of a sudden blow."

Captain Cephas sniffed. "What's the good of talkin'?" said he. "There ain't no child, and there ain't no woman that you could hire to sit all night on my front step or on your front step, a-waitin' to be piped on deck in case of croup."

"No," said Captain Eli. "I don't suppose there's any child in this village that ain't goin' to be provided with a Christmas tree or a Christmas stockin', or perhaps both—except, now I come to think of it, that little gal that was brought down here with her mother last summer, and has been kept by Mrs. Crumley sence her mother died."

"And won't be kept much longer," said Captain Cephas, "fer I've hearn Mrs. Crumley say she couldn't afford it."

"That's so," said Captain Eli. "If she can't afford to keep the little gal, she can't afford to give no Christmas trees nor stockin's, and so it seems to me, cap'n, that that little gal would be a pretty good child to help us keep Christmas."

"You're all the time forgettin'," said the other, "that nuther of us can keep a child all night."

Captain Eli seated himself, and looked ponderingly into the fire. "You're right, cap'n," said he. "We'd have to ship some woman to take care of her. Of course, it wouldn't be no use to ask Mrs. Crumley?"

Captain Cephas laughed. "I should say not."

"And there doesn't seem to be anybody else," said his companion. "Can you think of anybody, cap'n?"

"There ain't anybody to think of," replied Captain Cephas, "unless it might be Eliza Trimmer. She's generally ready enough to do anything that turns up. But she wouldn't be no good—her house is too far away for either you or me to hail her in case a croup came up suddint."

"That's so," said Captain Eli. "She does live a long way off."

"So that settles the whole business," said Captain Cephas. "She's too far away to come if wanted, and nuther of us couldn't keep no child without somebody to come if they was wanted, and it's no use to have a Christmas tree without a child. A Christmas without a Christmas tree don't seem agreeable to you, cap'n, so I guess we'd better get along just the same as we've been in the habit of doin', and eat our Christmas dinner, as we do our other meals, in our own houses."

Captain Eli looked into the fire. "I don't like to give up things if I can help it. That was always my way. If wind and tide's ag'in' me, I can wait till one or the other, or both of them, serve."

"Yes," said Captain Cephas, "you was always that kind of a man."

"That's so. But it does 'pear to me as if I'd have to give up this time, though it's a pity to do it, on account of the little gal, fer she ain't likely to have any Christmas this year. She's a nice little gal, and takes as natural to navigation as if she'd been born at sea. I've given her two or three things because she's so pretty, but there's nothing she likes so much as a little ship I gave her."

"Perhaps she was born at sea," remarked Captain Cephas.

"Perhaps she was," said the other; "and that makes it the bigger pity."

For a few moments nothing was said. Then Captain Eli suddenly exclaimed, "I'll tell you what we might do, cap'n! We might ask Mrs. Trimmer to lend a hand in givin' the little gal a Christmas. She ain't got nobody in her house but herself, and I guess she'd be glad enough to help give that little gal a regular Christmas. She could go and get the child, and bring her to your house or to my house, or wherever we're goin' to keep Christmas, and—"

"Well," said Captain Cephas, with an air of scrutinizing inquiry, "what?"

"Well," replied the other a little hesitatingly, "so far as I'm concerned—that is, I don't mind one way or the other—she might take her Christmas dinner along with us and the little gal, and then she could fix her stockin' to be hung up, and help with the Christmas tree, and—"

"Well," demanded Captain Cephas, "what?"

"Well," said Captain Eli, "she could—that is, it doesn't make any difference to me one way or the other—she might stay all night at whatever house we kept Christmas in, and then you and me might spend the night in the other house, and then she could be ready there to help the child in the mornin', when she came to look at her stockin'."

Captain Cephas fixed upon his friend an earnest glare. "That's pretty considerable of an idea to come upon you so suddint," said he. "But I can tell you one thing: there ain't a-goin' to be any such doin's in my house. If you choose to come over here to sleep, and give up your house to any woman you can find to take care of the little gal, all right. But the thing can't be done here."

There was a certain severity in these remarks, but they appeared to affect Captain Eli very pleasantly.

"Well," said he, "if you're satisfied, I am. I'll agree to any plan you choose to make. It doesn't matter to me which house it's in, and if you say my house, I say my house. All I want is to make the business agreeable to all concerned. Now it's time fer me to go to my dinner, and this afternoon we'd better go and try to get things straightened out, because the little gal, and whatever woman comes with her, ought to be at my house to-morrow before dark. S'posin' we divide up this business: I'll go and see Mrs. Crumley about the little gal, and you can go and see Mrs. Trimmer."

"No, sir," promptly replied Captain Cephas, "I don't go to see no Mrs. Trimmer. You can see both of them just the same as you can see one—they're all along the same way. I'll go cut the Christmas tree."

"All right," said Captain Eli. "It don't make no difference to me which does which. But if I was you, cap'n, I'd cut a good big tree, because we might as well have a good one while we're about it."

When he had eaten his dinner, and washed up his dishes, and had put everything away in neat, housewifely order, Captain Eli went to Mrs. Crumley's house, and very soon finished his business there. Mrs. Crumley kept the only house which might be considered a boarding-house in the village of Sponkannis; and when she had consented to take charge of the little girl who had been left on her hands she had hoped it would not be very long before she would hear from some of her relatives in regard to her maintenance. But she had heard nothing, and had now ceased to expect to hear anything, and in consequence had frequently remarked that she must dispose of the child some way or other, for she couldn't afford to keep her any longer. Even an absence of a day or two at the house of the good captain would be some relief, and Mrs. Crumley readily consented to the Christmas scheme. As to the little girl, she was delighted. She already looked upon Captain Eli as her best friend in the world.

It was not so easy to go to Mrs. Trimmer's house and put the business before her. "It ought to be plain sailin' enough," Captain Eli said to himself, over and over again, "but, fer all that, it don't seem to be plain sailin'."

But he was not a man to be deterred by difficult navigation, and he walked straight to Eliza Trimmer's house.

Mrs. Trimmer was a comely woman about thirty-five, who had come to the village a year before, and had maintained herself, or at least had tried to, by dressmaking and plain sewing. She had lived at Stetford, a seaport about twenty miles away, and from there, three years before, her husband, Captain Trimmer, had sailed away in a good-sized schooner, and had never returned. She had come to Sponkannis because she thought that there she could live cheaper and get more work than in her former home. She had found the first quite possible, but her success in regard to the work had not been very great.

When Captain Eli entered Mrs. Trimmer's little room, he found her busy mending a sail. Here fortune favored him. "You turn your hand to 'most anything, Mrs. Trimmer," said he, after he had greeted her.

"Oh, yes," she answered, with a smile, "I am obliged to do that. Mending sails is pretty heavy work, but it's better than nothing."

"I had a notion," said he, "that you was ready to turn your hand to any good kind of business, so I thought I would step in and ask you if you'd turn your hand to a little bit of business I've got on the stocks."

She stopped sewing on the sail, and listened while Captain Eli laid his plan before her. "It's very kind in you and Captain Cephas to think of all that," said she. "I have often noticed that poor little girl, and pitied her. Certainly I'll come, and you needn't say anything about paying me for it. I wouldn't think of asking to be paid for doing a thing like that. And besides"—she smiled again as she spoke—"if you are going to give me a Christmas dinner, as you say, that will make things more than square."

Captain Eli did not exactly agree with her, but he was in very good humor, and she was in good humor, and the matter was soon settled, and Mrs. Trimmer promised to come to the captain's house in the morning and help about the Christmas tree, and in the afternoon to go to get the little girl from Mrs. Crumley's and bring her to the house.

Captain Eli was delighted with the arrangements. "Things now seem to be goin' along before a spankin' breeze," said he. "But I don't know about the dinner. I guess you will have to leave that to me. I don't believe Captain Cephas could eat a woman-cooked dinner. He's accustomed to livin' sailor fashion, you know, and he has declared over and over again to me that woman-cookin' doesn't agree with him."

"But I can cook sailor fashion," said Mrs. Trimmer, "just as much sailor fashion as you or Captain Cephas, and if he don't believe it, I'll prove it to him; so you needn't worry about that."

When the captain had gone, Mrs. Trimmer gayly put away the sail. There was no need to finish it in a hurry, and no knowing when she would get her money for it when it was done. No one had asked her to a Christmas dinner that year, and she had expected to have a lonely time of it. But it would be very pleasant to spend Christmas with the little girl and the two good captains. Instead of sewing any more on the sail, she got out some of her own clothes to see if they needed anything done to them.

The next morning Mrs. Trimmer went to Captain Eli's house, and finding Captain Cephas there, they all set to work at the Christmas tree, which was a very fine one, and had been planted in a box. Captain Cephas had brought over a bundle of things from his house, and Captain Eli kept running here and there, bringing, each time that he returned, some new object, wonderful or pretty, which he had brought from China or Japan or Korea, or some spicy island of the Eastern seas; and nearly every time he came with these treasures Mrs. Trimmer declared that such things were too good to put upon a Christmas tree, even for such a nice little girl as the one for which that tree was intended. The presents which Captain Cephas brought were much more suitable for the purpose; they were odd and funny, and some of them pretty, but not expensive, as were the fans and bits of shell-work and carved ivories which Captain Eli wished to tie upon the twigs of the tree.

There was a good deal of talk about all this, but Captain Eli had his own way.

"I don't suppose, after all," said he, "that the little gal ought to have all the things. This is such a big tree that it's more like a family tree. Cap'n Cephas can take some of my things, and I can take some of his things, and, Mrs. Trimmer, if there's anything you like, you can call it your present and take it for your own, so that will be fair and comfortable all round. What I want is to make everybody satisfied."

"I'm sure I think they ought to be," said Mrs. Trimmer, looking very kindly at Captain Eli.

Mrs. Trimmer went home to her own house to dinner, and in the afternoon she brought the little girl. She had said there ought to be an early supper, so that the child would have time to enjoy the Christmas tree before she became sleepy.

This meal was prepared entirely by Captain Eli, and in sailor fashion, not woman fashion, so that Captain Cephas could make no excuse for eating his supper at home. Of course they all ought to be together the whole of that Christmas eve. As for the big dinner on the morrow, that was another affair, for Mrs. Trimmer undertook to make Captain Cephas understand that she had always cooked for Captain

Trimmer in sailor fashion, and if he objected to her plum-duff, or if anybody else objected to her mince-pie, she was going to be very much surprised.

Captain Cephas ate his supper with a good relish, and was still eating when the rest had finished. As to the Christmas tree, it was the most valuable, if not the most beautiful, that had ever been set up in that region. It had no candles upon it, but was lighted by three lamps and a ship's lantern placed in the four corners of the room, and the little girl was as happy as if the tree were decorated with little dolls and glass balls. Mrs. Trimmer was intensely pleased and interested to see the child so happy, and Captain Eli was much pleased and interested to see the child and Mrs. Trimmer so happy, and Captain Cephas was interested, and perhaps a little amused in a superior fashion, to see Captain Eli and Mrs. Trimmer and the little child so happy.

Then the distribution of the presents began. Captain Eli asked Captain Cephas if he might have the wooden pipe that the latter had brought for his present. Captain Cephas said he might take it, for all he cared, and be welcome to it. Then Captain Eli gave Captain Cephas a red bandanna handkerchief of a very curious pattern, and Captain Cephas thanked him kindly. After which Captain Eli bestowed upon Mrs. Trimmer a most beautiful tortoise-shell comb, carved and cut and polished in a wonderful way, and with it he gave a tortoise-shell fan, carved in the same fashion, because he said the two things seemed to belong to each other and ought to go together; and he would not listen to one word of what Mrs. Trimmer said about the gifts being too good for her, and that she was not likely ever to use them.

"It seems to me," said Captain Cephas, "that you might be giving something to the little gal."

Then Captain Eli remembered that the child ought not to be forgotten, and her soul was lifted into ecstasy by many gifts, some of which Mrs. Trimmer declared were too good for any child in this wide, wide world. But Captain Eli answered that they could be taken care of by somebody until the little girl was old enough to know their value.

Then it was discovered that, unbeknown to anybody else, Mrs. Trimmer had put some presents on the tree, which were things which had been brought by Captain Trimmer from somewhere in the far East or the distant West. These she bestowed upon Captain Cephas and Captain Eli. And the end of all this was that in the whole of

Sponkannis, from the foot of the bluff to the east, and to the very last house on the shore to the west, there was not one Christmas eve party so happy as this one.

Captain Cephas was not quite so happy as the three others were, but he was very much interested. About nine o'clock the party broke up, and the two captains put on their caps and buttoned up their pea-jackets, and started for Captain Cephas's house, but not before Captain Eli had carefully fastened every window and every door except the front door, and had told Mrs. Trimmer how to fasten that when they had gone, and had given her a boatswain's whistle, which she might blow out of the window if there should be a sudden croup and it should be necessary for any one to go anywhere. He was sure he could hear it, for the wind was exactly right for him to hear a whistle from his house. When they had gone Mrs. Trimmer put the little girl to bed, and was delighted to find in what a wonderfully neat and womanlike fashion that house was kept.

It was nearly twelve o'clock that night when Captain Eli, sleeping in his bunk opposite that of Captain Cephas, was aroused by hearing a sound. He had been lying with his best ear uppermost, so that he should hear anything if there happened to be anything to hear. He did hear something, but it was not a boatswain's whistle; it was a prolonged cry, and it seemed to come from the sea.

In a moment Captain Eli was sitting on the side of his bunk, listening intently. Again came the cry. The window toward the sea was slightly open, and he heard it plainly.

"Cap'n!" said he, and at the word Captain Cephas was sitting on the side of his bunk, listening. He knew from his companion's attitude, plainly visible in the light of a lantern which hung on a hook at the other end of the room, that he had been awakened to listen. Again came the cry.

"That's distress at sea," said Captain Cephas. "Harken!"

They listened again for nearly a minute, when the cry was repeated.

"Bounce on deck, boys!" said Captain Cephas, getting out on the floor. "There's some one in distress off shore."

Captain Eli jumped to the floor, and began to dress quickly.

"It couldn't be a call from land?" he asked hurriedly. "It don't sound a bit to you like a boatswain's whistle, does it?"

"No," said Captain Cephas, disdainfully. "It's a call from sea." Then, seizing a lantern, he rushed down the companionway.

As soon as he was convinced that it was a call from sea, Captain Eli was one in feeling and action with Captain Cephas. The latter hastily opened the draughts of the kitchen stove, and put on some wood, and by the time this was done Captain Eli had the kettle filled and on the stove. Then they clapped on their caps and their pea-jackets, each took an oar from a corner in the back hall, and together they ran down to the beach.

The night was dark, but not very cold, and Captain Cephas had been to the store that morning in his boat.

Whenever he went to the store, and the weather permitted, he rowed there in his boat rather than walk. At the bow of the boat, which was now drawn up on the sand, the two men stood and listened. Again came the cry from the sea.

"It's something ashore on the Turtle-back Shoal," said Captain Cephas.

"Yes," said Captain Eli, "and it's some small craft, fer that cry is down pretty nigh to the water."

"Yes," said Captain Cephas. "And there's only one man aboard, or else they'd take turns a-hollerin'."

"He's a stranger," said Captain Eli, "or he wouldn't have tried, even with a cat-boat, to get in over that shoal on ebb-tide."

As they spoke they ran the boat out into the water and jumped in, each with an oar. Then they pulled for the Turtle-back Shoal.

Although these two captains were men of fifty or thereabout, they were as strong and tough as any young fellows in the village, and they pulled with steady strokes, and sent the heavy boat skimming over the water, not in a straight line toward the Turtle-back Shoal, but now a few points in the darkness this way, and now a few points in the darkness that way, then with a great curve to the south through the dark night, keeping always near the middle of the only good channel out of the bay when the tide was ebbing.

Now the cries from seaward had ceased, but the two captains were not discouraged.

"He's heard the thumpin' of our oars," said Captain Cephas.

"He's listenin', and he'll sing out again if he thinks we're goin' wrong," said Captain Eli. "Of course he doesn't know anything about that."

And so when they made the sweep to the south the cry came again, and Captain Eli grinned. "We needn't to spend no breath hollerin'," said he. "He'll hear us makin' fer him in a minute."

When they came to head for the shoal they lay on their oars for a moment, while Captain Cephas turned the lantern in the bow, so that its light shone out ahead. He had not wanted the shipwrecked person to see the light when it would seem as if the boat were rowing away from him. He had heard of castaway people who became so wild when they imagined that a ship or boat was going away from them that they jumped overboard.

When the two captains reached the shoal, they found there a cat-boat aground, with one man aboard. His tale was quickly told. He had expected to run into the little bay that afternoon, but the wind had fallen, and in trying to get in after dark, and being a stranger, he had run aground. If he had not been so cold, he said, he would have been willing to stay there till the tide rose; but he was getting chilled, and seeing a light not far away, he concluded to call for help as long as his voice held out.

The two captains did not ask many questions. They helped anchor the cat-boat, and then they took the man on their boat and rowed him to shore. He was getting chilled sitting out there doing nothing, and so when they reached the house they made him some hot grog, and promised in the morning, when the tide rose, they would go out and help him bring his boat in. Then Captain Cephas showed the stranger to a bunk, and they all went to bed. Such experiences had not enough of novelty to the good captains to keep them awake five minutes.

In the morning they were all up very early, and the stranger, who proved to be a seafaring man with bright blue eyes, said that, as his cat-boat seemed to be riding all right at its anchorage, he did not care to go out after her just yet. Any time during flood-tide would do for him, and he had some business that he wanted to attend to as soon as possible.

This suited the two captains very well, for they wished to be on hand when the little girl discovered her stocking.

"Can you tell me," said the stranger, as he put on his cap, "where I can find a Mrs. Trimmer, who lives in this village?"

At these words all the sturdy stiffness which, from his youth up, had characterized the legs of Captain Eli entirely went out of them, and he sat suddenly upon a bench. For a few moments there was silence.

Then Captain Cephas, who thought some answer should be made to the question, nodded his head.

"I want to see her as soon as I can," said the stranger. "I have come to see her on particular business that will be a surprise to her. I wanted to be here before Christmas began, and that's the reason I took that cat-boat from Stetford, because I thought I'd come quicker that way than by land. But the wind fell, as I told you. If either one of you would be good enough to pilot me to where Mrs. Trimmer lives, or to any point where I can get a sight of the place, I'd be obliged."

Captain Eli rose and with hurried but unsteady steps went into the house (for they had been upon the little piazza), and beckoned to his friend to follow. The two men stood in the kitchen and looked at each other. The face of Captain Eli was of the hue of a clam-shell.

"Go with him, cap'n," he said in a hoarse whisper. "I can't do it."

"To your house?" inquired the other.

"Of course. Take him to my house. There ain't no other place where she is. Take him along."

Captain Cephas's countenance wore an air of the deepest concern, but he thought that the best thing to do was to get the stranger away.

As they walked rapidly toward Captain Eli's house there was very little said by either Captain Cephas or the stranger. The latter seemed anxious to give Mrs. Trimmer a surprise, and not to say anything which might enable another person to interfere with his project.

The two men had scarcely stepped upon the piazza when Mrs. Trimmer, who had been expecting early visitors, opened the door. She was about to call out "Merry Christmas!" but, her eyes falling upon a stranger, the words stopped at her lips. First she turned red, then she turned pale, and Captain Cephas thought she was about to fall. But before she could do this the stranger had her in his arms. She opened her eyes, which for a moment she had closed, and, gazing into his face, she put her arms around his neck. Then Captain Cephas came away, without thinking of the little girl and the pleasure she would have in discovering her Christmas stocking.

When he had been left alone, Captain Eli sat down near the kitchen stove, close to the very kettle which he had filled with water to heat for the benefit of the man he had helped bring in from the sea, and, with his elbows on his knees and his fingers in his hair, he darkly pondered.

"If I'd only slept with my hard-o'-hearin' ear up," he said to himself, "I'd never have heard it."

In a few moments his better nature condemned this thought.

"That's next to murder," he muttered, "fer he couldn't have kept himself from fallin' asleep out there in the cold, and when the tide riz he'd have been blowed out to sea with this wind. If I hadn't heard him, Captain Cephas never would, fer he wasn't primed up to wake, as I was."

But, notwithstanding his better nature, Captain Eli was again saying to himself, when his friend returned, "If I'd only slept with my other ear up!"

Like the honest, straightforward mariner he was, Captain Cephas made an exact report of the facts. "They was huggin' when I left them," he said, "and I expect they went indoors pretty soon, fer it was too cold outside. It's an all-fired shame she happened to be in your house, cap'n, that's all I've got to say about it. It's a thunderin' shame."

Captain Eli made no answer. He still sat with his elbows on his knees and his hands in his hair.

"A better course than you laid down fer these Christmas times was never dotted on a chart," continued Captain Cephas. "From port of sailin' to port of entry you laid it down clear and fine. But it seems there was rocks that wasn't marked on the chart."

"Yes," groaned Captain Eli, "there was rocks."

Captain Cephas made no attempt to comfort his friend, but went to work to get breakfast.

When that meal—a rather silent one—was over, Captain Eli felt better. "There was rocks," he said, "and not a breaker to show where they lay, and I struck 'em bow on. So that's the end of that voyage. But I've tuk to my boats, cap'n, I've tuk to my boats."

"I'm glad to hear you've tuk to your boats," said Captain Cephas, with an approving glance upon his friend.

About ten minutes afterwards Captain Eli said, "I'm goin' up to my house."

"By yourself?" said the other.

"Yes, by myself. I'd rather go alone. I don't intend to mind anything, and I'm goin' to tell her that she can stay there and spend Christmas—the place she lives in ain't no place to spend Christmas—and she can make the little gal have a good time, and go 'long just as we intended to go 'long—plum-duff and mince-pie all the same. I can stay here, and you and me can have our Christmas dinner together, if we choose to give it that name. And if she ain't ready to go tomorrow, she can stay a day or two longer. It's all the same to me, if it's the same to you, cap'n."

Captain Cephas having said that it was the same to him, Captain Eli put on his cap and buttoned up his pea-jacket, declaring that the sooner he got to his house the better, as she might be thinking that she would have to move out of it now that things were different.

Before Captain Eli reached his house he saw something which pleased him. He saw the sea-going stranger, with his back toward him, walking rapidly in the direction of the village store.

Captain Eli quickly entered his house, and in the doorway of the room where the tree was he met Mrs. Trimmer, beaming brighter than any morning sun that ever rose.

"Merry Christmas!" she exclaimed, holding out both her hands. "I've been wondering and wondering when you'd come to bid me 'Merry Christmas'—the merriest Christmas I've ever had."

Captain Eli took her hands and bid her "Merry Christmas" very gravely.

She looked a little surprised. "What's the matter, Captain Eli?" she exclaimed. "You don't seem to say that as if you meant it."

"Oh, yes, I do," he answered. "This must be an all-fired—I mean a thunderin' happy Christmas fer you, Mrs. Trimmer."

"Yes," said she, her face beaming again. "And to think that it should happen on Christmas day—that this blessed morning, before anything else happened, my Bob, my only brother, should—"

"Your what!" roared Captain Eli, as if he had been shouting orders in a raging storm.

Mrs. Trimmer stepped back almost frightened. "My brother," said she. "Didn't he tell you he was my brother—my brother Bob, who sailed away a year before I was married, and who has been in Africa and China and I don't know where? It's so long since I heard that he'd gone into trading at Singapore that I'd given him up as married and settled in foreign parts. And here he has come to me as if he'd tumbled from the sky on this blessed Christmas morning."

Captain Eli made a step forward, his face very much flushed.

"Your brother, Mrs. Trimmer—did you really say it was your brother?"

"Of course it is," said she. "Who else could it be?" Then she paused for a moment and looked steadfastly at the captain.

"You don't mean to say, Captain Eli," she asked, "that you thought it was—"

"Yes, I did," said Captain Eli, promptly.

Mrs. Trimmer looked straight in the captain's eyes, then she looked on the ground. Then she changed color and changed back again.

"I don't understand," she said hesitatingly, "why—I mean what difference it made."

"Difference!" exclaimed Captain Eli. "It was all the difference between a man on deck and a man overboard—that's the difference it was to me. I didn't expect to be talkin' to you so early this Christmas mornin', but things has been sprung on me, and I can't help it. I just want to ask you one thing: Did you think I was gettin' up this Christmas tree and the Christmas dinner and the whole business fer the good of the little gal, and fer the good of you, and fer the good of Captain Cephas?"

Mrs. Trimmer had now recovered a very fair possession of herself. "Of course I did," she answered, looking up at him as she spoke. "Who else could it have been for?"

"Well," said he, "you were mistaken. It wasn't fer any one of you. It was all fer me—fer my own self."

"You yourself?" said she. "I don't see how."

"But I see how," he answered. "It's been a long time since I wanted to speak my mind to you, Mrs. Trimmer, but I didn't ever have no chance. And all these Christmas doin's was got up to give me the chance not only of speakin' to you, but of showin' my colors better than I could show them in any other way. Everything went on a-skimmin' till this mornin', when that stranger that we brought in from the shoal piped up and asked fer you. Then I went overboard—at least, I thought I did—and sunk down, down, clean out of soundin's."

"That was too bad, captain," said she, speaking very gently, "after all your trouble and kindness."

"But I don't know now," he continued, "whether I went overboard or whether I am on deck. Can you tell me, Mrs. Trimmer?"

She looked up at him. Her eyes were very soft, and her lips trembled just a little. "It seems to me, captain," she said, "that you are on deck —if you want to be."

The captain stepped closer to her. "Mrs. Trimmer," said he, "is that brother of yours comin' back?"

"Yes," she answered, surprised at the sudden question. "He's just gone up to the store to buy a shirt and some things. He got himself splashed trying to push his boat off last night."

"Well, then," said Captain Eli, "would you mind tellin' him when he comes back that you and me's engaged to be married? I don't know whether I've made a mistake in the lights or not, but would you mind tellin' him that?"

Mrs. Trimmer looked at him. Her eyes were not so soft as they had been, but they were brighter. "I'd rather you'd tell him that yourself," said she.

The little girl sat on the floor near the Christmas tree, just finishing a large piece of red-and-white candy which she had taken out of her stocking. "People do hug a lot at Christmas-time," said she to herself. Then she drew out a piece of blue-and-white candy and began on that.

Captain Cephas waited a long time for his friend to return, and at last he thought it would be well to go and look for him. When he entered the house he found Mrs. Trimmer sitting on the sofa in the parlor, with Captain Eli on one side of her and her brother on the other, and each of them holding one of her hands.

"It looks as if I was in port, don't it?" said Captain Eli to his astonished friend. "Well, here I am, and here's my fust mate," inclining his head toward Mrs. Trimmer. "And she's in port too, safe and sound. And that strange captain on the other side of her, he's her brother Bob, who's been away for years and years, and is just home from Madagascar."

"Singapore," amended Brother Bob.

Captain Cephas looked from one to the other of the three occupants of the sofa, but made no immediate remark. Presently a smile of genial maliciousness stole over his face, and he asked, "How about the poor little gal? Have you sent her back to Mrs. Crumley's?"

The little girl came out from behind the Christmas tree, her stocking, now but half filled, in her hand. "Here I am," she said. "Don't you want to give me a Christmas hug, Captain Cephas? You and me's the only ones that hasn't had any."

The Christmas dinner was as truly and perfectly a sailor-cooked meal as ever was served on board a ship or off it. Captain Cephas had said that, and when he had so spoken there was no need of further words.

It was nearly dark that afternoon, and they were all sitting around the kitchen fire, the three seafaring men smoking, and Mrs. Trimmer greatly enjoying it. There could be no objection to the smell of tobacco in this house so long as its future mistress enjoyed it. The little girl sat on the floor nursing a Chinese idol which had been one of her presents.

"After all," said Captain Eli, meditatively, "this whole business come out of my sleepin' with my best ear up. Fer if I'd slept with my hard-o'-hearin' ear up—" Mrs. Trimmer put one finger on his lips. "All right," said Captain Eli, "I won't say no more. But it would have been different."

Even now, several years after that Christmas, when there is no Mrs. Trimmer, and the little girl, who has been regularly adopted by Captain Eli and his wife, is studying geography, and knows more about latitude and longitude than her teacher at school, Captain Eli has still a slight superstitious dread of sleeping with his best ear uppermost.

"Of course it's the most all-fired nonsense," he says to himself over and over again. Nevertheless, he feels safer when it is his "hard-o'-hearin' ear" that is not upon the pillow.

OLD APPLEJOY'S GHOST

by Frank R. Stockton

from *Afield and Afloat*

The large and commodious apartments in the upper part of the old Applejoy mansion were occupied exclusively, at the time of our story, by the ghost of the grandfather of the present owner of the estate.

For many, many years old Applejoy's ghost had been in the habit of wandering freely about the grand old house and the fine estate of which he had once been the lord and master; but early in that spring a change had come over the household of his grandson, John Applejoy, an elderly man and a bachelor, a lover of books, and, for the later portion of his life, almost a recluse. A young girl, his niece Bertha, had come to live with him and make part of his very small family, and it was since the arrival of this newcomer that old Applejoy's ghost had confined himself almost exclusively to the upper portions of the house.

This secluded existence, so different from his ordinary habits, was adopted entirely on account of the kindness of his heart. During the lives of two generations of his descendants he knew that he had frequently been seen by members of the family and others, but this did not disturb him, for in life he had been a man who had liked to assert his position, and the disposition to do so had not left him now. His grandson John had seen him, and two or three times had spoken with him; but as old Applejoy's ghost had heard his sceptical descendant declare that these ghostly interviews were only dreams or hallucinations, he cared very little whether John saw him or not. As to other people, it might be a very good thing if they believed that the house was haunted. People with uneasy consciences would not care to live in such a place.

But when this fresh young girl came upon the scene the case was entirely different. She might be timorous and she might not, but old Applejoy's ghost did not want to take any risks. There was nothing the matter with her conscience, he was quite sure; but she was not twenty yet, her character was not formed, and if anything should happen which would lead her to suspect that the house was haunted she might not be willing to live there, and if that should come to pass it would be a great shock to the ghost.

For a long time the venerable mansion had been a quiet, darkened, melancholy house. A few rooms only were opened and occupied, for John Applejoy and his housekeeper, Mrs. Dipperton, who for years had composed the family, needed but little space in which to pass the monotonous days of their lives. Bertha sang; she played on the old piano; she danced by herself on the broad piazza; she wandered through the gardens and brought flowers into the house; and sometimes it almost might have been imagined that the days which were gone had come back again.

One winter evening, when the light of the full moon entered softly through every unshaded window of the house, old Applejoy's ghost sat in a stiff, high-backed chair which on account of an accident to one of its legs had been banished to the garret. It was not at all necessary, either for rest or comfort, that this kind old ghost should seat himself in a chair, for he would have been quite as much at his ease upon a clothes-line; but in other days he had been in the habit of sitting in chairs, and it pleased him to do so now. Throwing one shadowy leg over the other, he clasped the long fingers of his hazy hands, and gazed thoughtfully out into the moonlight.

"Winter has come," he said to himself. "All is hard and cold, and soon it will be Christmas. Yes, in two days it will be Christmas!"

For a few minutes he sat reflecting, and then he suddenly started to his feet.

"Can it be!" he exclaimed. "Can it possibly be that that close-fisted old John, that degenerate son of my noble George, does not intend to celebrate Christmas! It has been years since he has done so; but now that Bertha is in the house, since it is her home, will he dare to pass over Christmas as though it were but a common day? It is almost incredible that such a thing could happen, but so far there have been no signs of any preparations. I have seen nothing, heard nothing, smelt nothing; but this moment will I go and investigate the state of affairs."

Clapping his misty old cocked hat on his head, and tucking under his arm the shade of his faithful cane, he descended to the lower part of the house. Glancing into the great parlors dimly lighted by the streaks of moonlight which came between the cracks of the shutters, he saw that all the furniture was shrouded in ancient linen covers, and that the pictures were veiled with gauzy hangings.

"Humph!" ejaculated old Applejoy's ghost, "he expects no company here!" and forthwith he passed through the dining-room—where in the middle of the wide floor was a little round table large enough for three—and entered the kitchen and pantry. There were no signs in the one that anything extraordinary in the way of cooking had been done or was contemplated, and when he gazed upon the pantry shelves, lighted well enough from without for his keen gaze, he groaned. "Two days before Christmas," he said to himself, "and a pantry furnished thus! How widely different from the olden time when I gave orders for the holidays! Let me see what the old curmudgeon has provided for Christmas!"

So saying, old Applejoy's ghost went around the spacious pantry, looking upon shelves and tables and peering through the doors of a closed closet. "Emptiness! Emptiness! Emptiness!" he ejaculated. "A cold leg of mutton with, I should say, three slices cut out of it; a ham half gone, and the rest of it hardened by exposure to the air; a piece of steak left over from yesterday or nobody knows when, to be made into hash, no doubt! Cold boiled potatoes—it makes me shiver to look at them—to be cut up and fried! Pies? There ought to be rows and rows of them, and there is not one! Cake? Upon my word, there is no sign of any! And Christmas two days off!

"What is this? Is it possible? A fowl! Yes; it is a chicken not full grown, enough for three, no doubt, and the servants can pick the bones. Oh, John, John! how have you fallen! A small-sized fowl for Christmas day!

"And what more, now? Cider? No trace of it! Here is vinegar—that suits John, no doubt"; and then, forgetting the present condition of his organism, he said to himself: "It makes my very blood run cold to look upon a pantry furnished out like this! I must think about it! I must think about it!" And with bowed head he passed out into the great hall.

If it were possible to do anything to prevent the desecration of his old home during the sojourn therein of the young and joyous Bertha, the ghost of old Applejoy was determined to do it; but in order to do anything he must put himself into communication with some living being, and who that being should be he did not know. Still wrapped in revery, he passed up the stairs and into the great chamber where his grandson slept. There lay the old man, his hard features tinged by the moonlight, his eyelids as tightly closed as if there had been money underneath them. The ghost of old Applejoy stood by his bedside.

"I can make him wake up and look at me," he thought, "for very few persons can remain asleep when any one is standing gazing down upon them—even if the gazer be a ghost—and I might induce him to speak to me so that I might open my mind to him and tell him what I think of him; but what impression could I expect my words to make upon the soul of a one-chicken man like John? I am afraid his heart is harder than that dried-up ham. Moreover, if I should be able to speak to him and tell him his duty, he would persuade himself that he had been dreaming, and my words would be of no avail. I am afraid it would be lost time to try to do anything with John!"

Old Applejoy's ghost turned away from the bedside of his sordid descendant, crossed the hall, and passed into the room of Mrs. Dipperton, the elderly housekeeper. There she lay fast asleep, her round face glimmering like a transparent bag filled with milk, and from her slightly parted lips there came at regular intervals a feeble little snore, as if even in her hours of repose she was afraid of disturbing somebody.

The kind-hearted ghost shook his head as he looked down upon her. "It would be of no use," he said; "she hasn't any backbone, and she would never be able to induce old John to turn one inch aside from his parsimonious path. More than that, if she were to see me she would probably scream and go into a spasm—die, for all I know—and that would be a pretty preparation for Christmas!"

Out he went, and into the dreams of the good woman there came no suspicion that the ghost had been standing by her considering her character with a pitying contempt.

Now the kind ghost, getting more and more anxious in this mind, passed to the front of the house and entered the chamber occupied by young Bertha. Once inside the door, he stopped reverently and removed his cocked hat. The head of the little bed was near the uncurtained window, and the bright light of the moon shone upon a face more beautiful in slumber than in the sunny hours of day.

She was not under the influence of the sound, hard sleep which lay upon the master of the house and the mild Mrs. Dipperton. She slept lightly. Her delicate lids, through which might almost be seen the deep blue of her eyes, trembled now and then as if they would open, and sometimes her lips moved as if she would whisper something about her dreams.

Old Applejoy's ghost drew nearer to the maiden, and bent slightly over her. He knew very well that it was mean to be eavesdropping like this, but it was really necessary that he should know this young girl better than he did. If he could hear a few words from that little mouth he might find out what she thought about, where her mind wandered, what she would like him to do for her. At last, faintly whispered, scarcely more audible than her breathing, he heard one word, and that was "Tom!"

"Oh," said old Applejoy's ghost, as he stepped back from the bedside, "she wants Tom! I like that! I do not know anything about Tom, but she ought to want him. It is natural, it is true, it is human, and it is long since there has been anything natural, true, or human in this house! But I wish she would say something else. She can't have Tom for Christmas—at least, not Tom alone. There is a great deal else necessary before this can be made a place suitable for Tom!"

Again he drew near to Bertha and listened, but, instead of speaking, suddenly the maiden opened wide her eyes. The ghost of old Applejoy drew back and made a low, respectful bow. The maiden did not move, but her lovely eyes opened wider and wider, and she fixed them upon the apparition, who trembled as he stood, for fear that she might scream, or faint, or in some way foil his generous purpose. If she did not first address him he could not speak to her.

"Am I asleep?" she murmured; and then, after slightly turning her head from side to side, as if to assure herself that she was in her own room and surrounded by familiar objects, she looked full into the face of old Applejoy's ghost and boldly spoke to him. "Are you a spirit?" said she.

If a flush of joy could redden the countenance of a filmy shade, the face of old Applejoy's ghost would have glowed like a sunlit rose.

"Dear child," he exclaimed, "I am a spirit! I am the ghost of your uncle's grandfather. His sister Maria, the youngest of the family, and much the most charming, I assure you, was your mother, and of course I was her grandfather, and, just as much of course, I am the ghost of your great-grandfather; but I declare to you I never felt prouder at any moment of my existences, previous or present!"

"Then you must be the original Applejoy," said Bertha; "and I think it very wonderful that I am not afraid of you, but I am not. You look as if you would not hurt anybody in this world, especially me!"

"There you have it," he exclaimed, bringing his cane down upon the floor with a violence which, had it been the cane it used to be, would have wakened everybody in the house. "There you have it, my dear! I vow to you there is not a person in this world for whom I have such an affection as I feel for you. You remind me of my dear son George. You are the picture of Maria when she was about your age. Your coming to this house has given me the greatest pleasure; you have brought into it something of the old life. I wish I could tell you how happy I have been since the bright spring day that brought you here."

"I did not suppose I would make any one happy by coming here," said Bertha. "Uncle John does not seem to care much about me, and I suppose I ought to be satisfied with Mrs. Dipperton if she does not object to me. But now the case is different. I did not know about you."

"No, indeed," exclaimed the good ghost; "you did not know about me, but I intend you to know about me. But now we must waste no more words—we must get down to business. I came here tonight with a special object."

"Business?" said Bertha, inquiringly.

"Yes," said the ghost; "it is business, and it is important, and it is about Christmas. Your uncle does not mean to have any Christmas in this house, but I intend, if I can possibly do so, to prevent him from disgracing himself; but I cannot do anything without somebody's help, and there is nobody to help me but you. Will you do it?"

Bertha could not refrain from a smile. "It would be funny to help a ghost to do anything," she said; "but if I can assist you I shall be very glad."

"I want you to go into the lower part of the house," said he; "I have something to show you that I am sure will interest you very much. I shall now go down into the hall, where I shall wait for you, and I should like you to dress yourself as warmly and comfortably as you can. It would be well to put a shawl around your head and shoulders. Have you some warm, soft slippers that will make no noise?"

"Oh, yes," said Bertha, her eyes twinkling with delight at the idea of this novel expedition; "I shall be dressed and with you in no time."

"Do not hurry yourself," said the good ghost, as he left the room; "we have most of the night before us."

When the young girl had descended the great staircase almost as noiselessly as the ghost who had preceded her, she found her venerable companion waiting for her.

"Do you see the lantern on the table?" said he. "John uses it when he goes his round of the house at bedtime. There are matches hanging above it. Please light it. You may be sure I would not put you to this trouble if I were able to do it myself."

She dimly perceived the brass lantern, and when she had lighted it the ghost invited her to enter the study.

"Now," said he, as he led the way to the large desk with the cabinet above it, "will you be so good as to open that glass door? It is not locked."

Bertha hesitated a little, but she opened the door.

"Now please put your hand into the front corner of that middle shelf. You cannot see anything, but you will feel a key hanging upon a little hook."

But Bertha did not obey. "This is my uncle's cabinet," she said, "and I have no right to meddle with his keys and things!"

Now the ghost of old Applejoy drew himself up to the six feet two inches which had been his stature in life; he slightly frowned—his expression was almost severe; but he controlled himself, and spoke calmly to the girl. "This was my cabinet," he said, "and I have never surrendered it to your uncle John! With my own hands I screwed the little hook into that dark corner and hung the key upon it! Now I beg that you will take down that key. You have the authority of your great-grandfather."

Without a moment's hesitation Bertha put her hand into the dark corner of the shelf and took the key from the hook.

"Thank you very much," said the ghost of old Applejoy. "And now please unlock that little drawer—the one at the bottom."

Bertha unlocked and opened the drawer. "It is full of old keys!" she said.

"Yes," said the ghost; "and you will find that they are all tied together in a bunch. Those keys are what we came for! Now, my dear," said he, standing in front of her and looking down upon her very earnestly, but so kindly that she was not in the least afraid of him, "I want you to understand that what we are going to do is strictly correct and proper, without a trace of inquisitive meanness about it. This was once my house—everything in it I planned and arranged. I am now going to take you into the cellars of my old mansion. They are wonderful cellars; they were my pride and glory! I often used to take my visitors to see them, and wide and commodious stairs lead down to them. Are you afraid," he said, "to descend with me into these subterranean regions?"

"Not a bit of it!" exclaimed Bertha, almost too loud for prudence. "I have heard of the cellars and wanted to see them, though Mrs. Dipperton told me that my uncle never allowed any one to enter them; but I think it will be the jolliest thing in the world to go with my great-grandfather into the cellars which he built himself, and of which he was so proud!"

This speech so charmed the ghost of old Applejoy that he would instantly have kissed his great-granddaughter had it not been that he was afraid of giving her a cold.

"You are a girl to my liking!" he exclaimed, "and I wish with all my heart that you had been living at the time I was alive and master of this house. We should have had gay times together—you may believe that!"

"I wish you were alive now, dear great-grandpapa," said she, "and that would be better than the other way! And now let us go on—I am all impatience!"

They then descended into the cellars, which, until the present owner came into possession of the estate, had been famous throughout the neighborhood. "This way," said old Applejoy's ghost. "You will find the floor perfectly dry, and if we keep moving you will not be chilled.

"Do you see that row of old casks nearly covered with cobwebs and dust? Now, my dear, those casks contain some of the choicest spirits ever brought into this country, and most of them are more than half full! The finest rum from Jamaica, brandy from France, and gin from Holland—gin with such a flavor, my dear, that if you were to take out the bung the delightful aroma would fill the whole house! There is port there, too, and if it is not too old it must be the rarest wine in the country! And Madeira, a little glass of which, my dear, is a beverage worthy even of you!

"These things were not stowed away by me, but by my dear son George, who knew their value. But as for John—he drinks water and tea! He is a one-chicken man, and if he has allowed any of these rare spirits to become worthless simply on account of age, he ought to be sent to the county prison!

"But we must move on! Do you see all these bottles—dingy-looking enough, but filled with the choicest wines? Many of these are better than ever they were, although some of them may have spoiled. John would let everything spoil. He is a dog in the manger!

"Come into this little room. Now, then, hold up your lantern and look all around you. Notice that row of glass jars on the shelf. They are filled with the finest mincemeat ever made by mortal man—or woman! It is the same kind of mincemeat I used to eat. George had it put up so that he might have the sort of pies at Christmas which I gave him when he was a boy. That mincemeat is just as good as ever it was! John is a dyspeptic; he wouldn't eat mince-pie! But he will eat fried potatoes, and they are ten times worse for him, if he did but know it!

"There are a lot more jars and cans, all sealed up tightly. I do not know what good things are in them, but I am sure their contents are just what will be wanted to fill out a Christmas table. If Mrs. Dipperton were to come down here and open those jars and bottles she would think she was in heaven!

"But now, my dear, I want to show you the grandest thing in these cellars, the diamond of the collection! Behold that wooden box! Inside of it is another box made of tin, soldered up tightly, so that it is perfectly air-tight. Inside of that tin box is a great plum-cake! And now listen to me, Bertha! That cake was put into that box by me. I intended it to stay there for a long time, for plum-cake gets better and better the longer it is kept, but I did not suppose that the box would not be opened for three generations! The people who eat that cake, my dear Bertha, will be blessed above all their fellow-mortals! that is to say, as far as cake-eating goes.

"And now I think you have seen enough to understand thoroughly that these cellars are the abode of many good things to eat and to drink. It is their abode, but if John could have his way it would be their sepulchre! I was fond of good living, as you may well imagine, and so was my dear son George; but John is a degenerate!"

"But why did you bring me here, great-grandpapa?" said Bertha. "Do you want me to come down here and have my Christmas dinner with you?" And as she said this she unselfishly hoped that when the tin box should be opened it might contain the ghost of a cake, for it was quite plain that her great-grandfather had been an enthusiast in the matter of plum-cake.

"No, indeed," said old Applejoy's ghost. "Come upstairs and let us go into the study. There are some coals left on the hearth, and you will not be chilled while we talk."

When the great cellar door had been locked, the keys replaced in the drawer, the little key hung upon its hook, and the cabinet closed, Bertha sat down before the fireplace and warmed her fingers over the few embers it contained, while the spirit of her great-grandfather stood by her and talked to her.

"Bertha," said he, "it is wicked not to celebrate Christmas—especially when one is able to do so—in the most hospitable and generous way. For years John has taken no notice of Christmas, and it is full time that he should reform, and it is your duty and my duty to reform him if we can! You have seen what he has in the cellars; there are turkeys in the poultry-yard—for I know he has not sold them all—and if there is anything wanting for a grand Christmas celebration he has an abundance of money with which to buy it. There is not much time before Christmas day, but there is time enough to do everything that has to be done, if you and I go to work and set other people to work."

"And how are we to do that?" asked Bertha.

"We haven't an easy task before us," said the ghost, "but I have been thinking a great deal about it, and I believe we can accomplish it. The straightforward thing to do is for me to appear to your uncle, tell him his duty, and urge him to perform it; but I know what will be the result. He would call the interview a dream, and attribute it to too much hash and fried potatoes, and the result would be that he would have a plainer table for a while and half starve you and Mrs. Dipperton. But there is nothing dreamlike about you, my dear. If any one hears you talking he will know he is awake."

"I think that is very true," said Bertha, smiling. "Do you want me to talk to uncle?"

"Yes," said old Applejoy's ghost; "I do want you to talk to him. I want you to go to him immediately after breakfast to-morrow morning, and tell him exactly what has happened this night. He cannot believe dreams are fried potatoes when you tell him about the little key in the corner of the shelf, the big keys in the drawer, the casks of spirits (and you can tell him what is in each one), the jars of mince-meat, and the wooden box nailed fast and tight, with the tin box inside holding the cake. John knows all about that cake, for his father told him; and he knows all about me, too, although he tries not to believe in me; and when you have told him all you have seen, and when you give him my message, I think it will make him feel that you and I are awake, and that he would better keep awake, too, if he knows what's good for him."

"And what is the message?" asked Bertha.

"It is simply this," said old Applejoy's ghost. "When you have told him all the events of this night, and when he sees that they must have happened, for you could not have imagined them, I want you to tell him that it is my wish and desire, the wish and desire of his grandfather, to whom he owes everything he possesses, that there shall be worthy festivities in this house on Christmas day and night—I would say something about Christmas eve, but I am afraid there is not time enough for that. Tell him to kill his turkeys, open his cellars, and spend his money. Tell him to send for at least a dozen good friends and relatives, for they will gladly give up their own Christmas dinner when they know that the great holiday is to be celebrated in this house. There is time enough; messengers and horses can be hired, and you can attend to the invitations. Mrs. Dipperton is a good manager when she has a chance, and I know she will do herself honor this time if John will give her the range.

"Now, my dear," said old Applejoy's ghost, drawing near to the young girl, "I want to ask you a question—a private, personal question. Who is Tom?"

At these words a sudden blush rushed into the cheeks of Bertha.

"Tom?" she said. "What Tom?"

"Now, don't beat about the bush with me," said old Applejoy's ghost; "I am sure you know a young man named Tom, and I want you to tell me who he is. My name was Tom, and for the sake of my past life I am very fond of Toms. But you must tell me about your Tom. Is he a nice young fellow? Do you like him very much?"

"Yes," said Bertha, meaning the answer to cover both questions.

"And does he like you?"

"I think so," said Bertha.

"That means you are in love with each other!" exclaimed old Applejoy's ghost. "And now, my dear, tell me his name. Out with it! You can't help yourself."

"Mr. Burcham," said Bertha, her cheeks now a little pale, for it seemed to her a very bold thing for her to talk in this way even in the company of only a spirit.

"Son of Thomas Burcham of the Meadows? Grandson of the old General Burcham?"

"Yes, sir," said Bertha.

The ghost of old Applejoy gazed down upon his great-granddaughter with pride and admiration.

"My dear Bertha," he exclaimed, "I congratulate you! I knew the old general well, and I have seen young Tom. He is a fine-looking fellow, and if you love him I know he is a good one. Now, I'll tell you what we will do, Bertha. We will have Tom here on Christmas."

"Oh, great-grandfather," exclaimed the girl, "I can't ask uncle to invite him!"

"We will make it all right," said the beaming ghost. "We will have a bigger party than we thought we would. All the guests, when they are invited, will be asked to bring their families. When a big dinner is given at this house, Thomas Burcham, Esq., must not be left out; and don't you see, Bertha, he is bound to bring Tom? And now you must not stay here a minute longer. Skip back to your bed, and immediately after breakfast come to your uncle and tell him everything I have told you to tell him."

Bertha rose to obey, but she hesitated.

"Great-grandfather," she said, "if uncle does allow us to celebrate Christmas, will you be with us?"

"Yes, indeed, my dear," said he. "And you need not be afraid of my frightening anybody. When I choose I can be visible to some and invisible to others. I shall be everywhere and I shall hear everything, but I shall appear only to the loveliest woman who ever graced this mansion. And now be off to bed without another word."

"If she hadn't gone," said old Applejoy's ghost to himself, "I couldn't have helped giving her a good-night kiss."

The next morning, as Bertha told the story of her night's adventures to her uncle, the face of John Applejoy grew paler and paler. He was a hard-headed man, but a superstitious one, and when the story began he wondered if it were a family failing to have dreams about ghosts; but when he heard of the visit to the cellars, and especially when Bertha told him of his grandfather's plum-cake, the existence of which he had believed was not known to any one but himself, he felt it was impossible for the girl to have dreamed these things. When Bertha had finished he actually believed that she had seen and talked with the ghost of her great-grandfather. With all the power of his will he opposed this belief, but it was too much for him, and he surrendered. But he was a proud man and would not admit to his niece that he put any faith in the existence of ghosts.

"My dear," said he, rising and standing before the fire, his face still pale, but his expression under good control, "you have had a very strange dream. Now, don't declare that it wasn't a dream—people always do that—but hear me out. Although there is nothing of weight in what you have told me—for traditions about my cellars have been afloat in the family—still your pretty little story suggests something to me. This is Christmas-time and I had almost overlooked it. You are young and lively and accustomed to the celebration of holidays. Therefore, I have determined, my dear, to consider your dream just as if it had been a real happening, and we will have a grand Christmas dinner, and invite our friends and their families. I know there must be good things in the cellars, although I had almost forgotten them, and they shall be brought up and spread out and enjoyed. Now go and send Mrs. Dipperton to me, and when we have finished our consultation, you and I will make out a list of guests and send off the invitations."

When she had gone, John Applejoy sat down in his big chair and looked fixedly into the fire. He would not have dared to go to bed that night if he had disregarded the message from his grandfather.

Never since the old house had begun to stand upon its foundations had there been such glorious Christmas-times within its walls. The news that old Mr. Applejoy was sending out invitations to a Christmas dinner spread like wild-fire through the neighborhood, and those who were not invited were almost as much excited as those who were asked to be guests. The idea of inviting people by families was considered a grand one, worthy indeed of the times of old Mr. Tom

Applejoy, the grandfather of the present owner, who had been the most hospitable man in the whole country.

For the first time in nearly a century all the leaves of the great dining-table were put into use, and chairs for the company were brought from every part of the house. All the pent-up domestic enthusiasm in the soul of Mrs. Dipperton, the existence of which no one had suspected, now burst out in one grand volcanic eruption, and the great table had as much as it could do to stand up under its burdens brought from cellar, barn, and surrounding country.

In the very middle of everything was the great and wonderful plum-cake which had been put away by the famous grandfather of the host.

But the cake was not cut. "My friends," said Mr. John Applejoy, "we may all look at this cake, but we will not eat it! We will keep it just as it is until a marriage shall occur in this family. Then you are all invited to come and enjoy it!"

At the conclusion of this little speech old Applejoy's ghost patted his degenerate grandson upon the head. "You don't feel that, John," he said to himself, "but it is approbation, and this is the first time I have ever approved of you! You must know of the existence of young Tom! You may turn out to be a good fellow yet, and if you will drink some of that rare old Madeira every day, I am sure you will!"

Late in the evening there was a grand dance in the great hall, which opened with an old-fashioned minuet, and when the merry guests were forming on the floor, a young man named Tom came forward and asked the hand of Bertha.

"No," said she; "not this time. I am going to dance this first dance with—well, we will say by myself!"

At these words the most thoroughly gratified ghost in all space stepped up to the side of the lovely girl, and, with his cocked hat folded flat under his left arm, he made a low bow and held out his hand. With his neatly tied cue, his wide-skirted coat, his long waist-coat trimmed with lace, his tightly drawn stockings, and his buckled shoes, there was not such a gallant figure in the whole company.

Bertha put out her hand and touched the shadowy fingers of her partner, and then, side by side, she and the ghost of her great-grandfather opened the ball. Together they made the coupee, the high step, and the balance. They advanced, they retired, they came together. With all the grace of fresh young beauty and ancient courtliness they danced the minuet.

"What a strange young girl!" said some of the guests, "and what a queer fancy to go through that dance all by herself, but how beautifully she did it!"

"Very eccentric, my dear!" said Mr. John Applejoy, when the dance was over. "But you danced most charmingly. I could not help thinking, as I looked at you, that there was nobody in this room that was worthy to be your partner."

"You are wrong there, old fellow!" was the simultaneous mental ejaculation of young Tom Burcham and of old Applejoy's ghost.

CHRISTMAS BEFORE LAST; OR, THE FRUIT OF THE FRAGILE PALM

by Frank R. Stockton

from *The Novels and Stories of Frank R. Stockton*

The *Horn o' Plenty* was a fine, big, old-fashioned ship, very high in the bow, very high in the stern, with a quarter-deck always carpeted in fine weather, because her captain could not see why one should not make himself comfortable at sea as well as on land. Covajos Maroots was her captain, and a fine, jolly, old-fashioned, elderly sailor he was. The *Horn o' Plenty* always sailed upon one sea, and always between two ports, one on the west side of the sea, and one on the east. The port on the west was quite a large city, in which Captain Covajos had a married son, and the port on the east was another city in which he had a married daughter. In each family he had several grandchildren, and consequently, it was a great joy to the jolly old sailor to arrive at either port. The captain was very particular about his cargo, and the *Horn o' Plenty* was generally laden with good things to eat, or sweet things to smell, or fine things to wear, or beautiful things to look at.

Once a merchant brought to him some boxes of bitter aloes and mustard-plasters, but Captain Covajos refused to take them into his ship.

"I know," said he, "that such things are very useful and necessary at times, but you would better send them over in some other vessel. The *Horn o' Plenty* has never carried anything that, to look at, to taste, or to smell, did not delight the souls of old and young. I am sure you cannot say that of these commodities. If I were to put such things on board my ship, it would break the spell which more than fifty savory voyages have thrown around it."

There were sailors who sailed upon that sea who used to say that sometimes, when the weather was hazy and they could not see far, they would know they were about to meet the *Horn o' Plenty* before she came in sight. Her planks and timbers, and even her sails and masts, had gradually become so filled with the odor of good things that the winds that blew over her were filled with an agreeable fragrance.

There was another thing about which Captain Covajos was very particular: he always liked to arrive at one of his ports a few days before Christmas. Never, in the course of his long life, had the old sailor spent a Christmas at sea, and now that he had his grandchildren to help make the holidays merry, it would have grieved him very much if he had been unable to reach one or the other of his ports in good season. His jolly old vessel was generally heavily laden, and very slow, and there were many days of calm on that sea when she did not sail at all, so that her voyages were usually very, very long. But the captain fixed the days of sailing so as to give himself plenty of time to get to the other end of his course before Christmas came around.

One spring, however, he started too late, and when he was about at the middle of his voyage, he called to him Baragat Bean, his old boatswain. This venerable sailor had been with the captain ever since he had commanded the *Horn o' Plenty*, and on important occasions he was always consulted in preference to the other officers, none of whom had served under Captain Covajos more than fifteen or twenty years.

"Baragat," said the captain, "we have just passed the Isle of Guinea-hens. You can see its one mountain standing up against the sky to the north."

"Ay, ay, sir," said old Baragat. "There she stands, the same as usual."

"That makes it plain," said the captain, "that we are not yet halfway across, and I am very much afraid that I shall not be able to reach my dear daughter's house before Christmas."

"That would be doleful, indeed," said Baragat, "but I've feared something of the kind, for we've had calms nearly every other day, and sometimes, when the wind did blow, it came from the wrong direction, and it's my belief that the ship sailed backward."

"That was very bad management," said the captain. "The chief mate should have seen to it that the sails were turned in such a manner that the ship could not go backward. If that sort of thing happened often, it would become quite a serious affair."

"But what is done can't be helped," said the boatswain, "and I don't see how you are going to get into port before Christmas."

"Nor do I," said the captain, gazing out over the sea.

"It would give me a sad turn, sir," said Baragat, "to see you spend Christmas at sea, a thing you never did before, nor ever shall do, if I can help it. If you'll take my advice, sir, you'll turn around and go back. It's a shorter distance to the port we started from than to the one we are going to, and if we turn back now, I am sure we all shall be on shore before the holidays."

"Go back to my son's house!" exclaimed Captain Covajos, "where I was last winter! Why, that would be like spending last Christmas over again!"

"But that would be better than having none at all, sir," said the boatswain, "and a Christmas at sea would be about equal to none."

"Good!" exclaimed the captain. "I will give up the coming Christmas with my daughter and her children, and go back and spend last Christmas over again with my son and his dear boys and girls. Have the ship turned around immediately, Baragat, and tell the chief mate I do not wish to sail backward if it can possibly be avoided."

For a week or more the *Horn o' Plenty* sailed back upon her track toward the city where dwelt the captain's son. The weather was fine, the carpet was never taken up from the quarter-deck, and everything was going on very well, when a man, who happened to have an errand at one of the topmasts, came down and reported that he had seen, far away to the north, a little open boat with some people in it.

"Ah me!" said Captain Covajos, "it must be some poor fellows who are shipwrecked. It will take us out of our course, but we must not leave them to their fate. Have the ship turned about, so that it will sail northward."

It was not very long before they came up with the boat, and, much to the captain's surprise, he saw that it was filled with boys.

"Who are you?" he cried as soon as he was near enough. "And where do you come from?"

"We are the First Class in Long Division," said the oldest boy, "and we are cast away. Have you anything to eat that you can spare us? We are almost famished."

"We have plenty of everything," said the captain. "Come on board instantly, and all your wants shall be supplied.

"How long have you been without food?" he asked, when the boys were on the deck of the vessel.

"We have had nothing to eat since breakfast," said one of them, "and it is now late in the afternoon. Some of us are nearly dead from starvation."

"It is very hard for boys to go so long without eating," said the good captain, and leading them below, he soon set them to work upon a bountiful meal.

Not until their hunger was fully satisfied did he ask them how they came to be cast away.

"You see, sir," said the oldest boy, "we and the Multiplication Class had a holiday to-day, and each class took a boat and determined to have a race, so as to settle, once for all, which was the highest branch of arithmetic—multiplication or long division. Our class rowed so hard that we entirely lost sight of the Multiplicationers, and found, indeed, that we were out of sight of everything, so that, at last, we did not know which was the way back, and thus we became castaways."

"Where is your school?" asked the captain.

"It is on Apple Island," said the boy. "And although it is a long way off for a small boat with only four oars for nine boys, it can't be very far for a ship."

"That is quite likely," said the captain, "and we shall take you home. Baragat, tell the chief mate to have the vessel turned toward Apple Island, that we may restore these boys to their parents and guardians."

Now, the chief mate had not the least idea in the world where Apple Island was, but he did not like to ask, because that would be confessing his ignorance. So he steered his vessel toward a point where he believed he had once seen an island, which, probably, was the one in question. The *Horn o' Plenty* sailed in this direction all night, and when day broke, and there was no island in sight, she took another course, and so sailed this way and that for six or seven days, without ever seeing a sign of land. All this time, the First Class in Long Division was as happy as it could be, for it was having a perfect holiday, fishing off the sides of the vessel, climbing up the ladders and ropes, and helping the sailors whistle for wind. But the captain now began to grow a little impatient, for he felt he was losing time; so he sent for the chief mate, and said to him mildly but firmly:

"I know it is out of the line of your duty to search for island schools, but if you really think that you do not know where Apple Island lies, I wish you to say so, frankly and openly."

"Frankly and openly," answered the mate, "I don't think I do."

"Very well," said the captain. "Now, that is a basis to work upon, and we know where we stand. You can take a little rest, and let the second mate find the island. But I can only give him three days in which to do it. We really have no time to spare."

The second mate was very proud of the responsibility placed upon him, and immediately ordered the vessel to be steered due south.

"One is just as likely," he said, "to find a totally unknown place by going straight ahead in a certain direction as by sailing here, there, and everywhere. In this way you really get over more water, and there is less wear and tear on the ship and rigging."

So he sailed due south for two days, and at the end of that time they came in sight of land. This was a large island, and when they approached near enough, they saw upon its shores a very handsome city.

"Is this Apple Island?" said Captain Covajos to the oldest boy.

"Well, sir," answered the youth, "I am not sure I can say with certainty that I truly believe it is. But I think, if we were to go on shore, the people there would be able to tell us how to go to Apple Island."

"Very likely," said the good captain. "We will go on shore and make inquiries. And it has struck me, Baragat," he said, "that perhaps the merchants in the city where my son lives may be somewhat annoyed when the *Horn o' Plenty* comes back with all their goods on board, and not disposed of. Not understanding my motives, they may be disposed to think ill of me. Consequently, the idea has come into my head that it might be a good thing to stop here for a time, and to try to dispose of some of our merchandise. The city seems to be prosperous, and I have no doubt there are a number of merchants here."

So the *Horn o' Plenty* was soon anchored in the harbor, and as many of the officers and crew as could be spared went on shore to make inquiries. Of course the First Class in Long Division was not left behind, and, indeed, they were ashore as soon as anybody.

The captain and his companions were cordially welcomed by some of the dignitaries of the city who had come down to the harbor to see the strange vessel, but no one could give any information in regard to Apple Island, the name of which had never been heard on those shores. The captain was naturally desirous of knowing at what place he had landed, and was informed that this was the Island of the Fragile Palm.

"That is rather an odd name," said the old captain. "Why is it so called?"

"The reason is this," said his informant: "Near the center of the island stands a tall and very slender palm-tree, which has been growing there for hundreds of years. It bears large and handsome fruit which is something like the cocoanut, and, in its perfection, is said to be a transcendently delicious fruit."

"Said to be!" exclaimed the captain. "Are you not positive about it?"

"No," said the other. "No one living has ever tasted the fruit in its perfection. When it becomes over-ripe it drops to the ground, and even then it is considered royal property, and is taken to the palace for the king's table. But on fête-days and grand occasions small bits of it are distributed to the populace."

"Why don't you pick the fruit," asked Captain Covajos, "when it is in its best condition to eat?"

"It would be impossible," said the citizen, "for any one to climb up that tree, the trunk of which is so extremely delicate and fragile that the weight of a man would probably snap it, and, of course, a ladder placed against it would produce the same result. Many attempts have been made to secure this fruit at the proper season, but all of them have failed. Another palm-tree of a more robust sort was once planted near this one, in the hope that when it grew high enough men could climb up the stronger tree and get the fruit from the other. But although we waited many years, the second tree never attained sufficient height, and it was cut down."

"It is a great pity," said the captain, "but I suppose it cannot be helped." Then he began to make inquiries about the merchants in the place, and what probability there was of his doing a little trade here.

The captain soon discovered that the cargo of his ship was made up of goods which were greatly desired by the citizens of this place, and for several days he was very busy selling the good things to eat, the sweet things to smell, the fine things to wear, and the beautiful things to look at, with which the hold of the *Horn o' Plenty* was crowded.

During this time the First Class in Long Division roamed, in delight, over the city. The busy streets, the shops, the handsome buildings, and the queer sights with which they occasionally met, interested and amused them greatly. Still the boys were not satisfied. They had heard of the Fragile Palm, and they made up their minds to go and have a look at it. Therefore, taking a guide, they tramped out into the country, and in about an hour they came in sight of the beautiful tree standing in the center of the plain. The trunk was, indeed, exceedingly slender, and, as the guide informed them, the wood was of so very brittle a nature that, if the tree had not been protected from the winds by the high hills which encircled it, it would have been snapped off ages ago. Under the broad tuft of leaves that formed its top, the boys saw hanging large clusters of the precious fruit, great nuts as big as their heads.

"At what time of the year," asked the oldest boy, "is that fruit just ripe enough to eat?"

"Now," answered the guide. "This is the season when it is in the most perfect condition. In about a month it will become entirely too ripe and soft, and will drop. But, even then, the king and all the rest of us are glad enough to get a taste of it."

"I should think the king would be exceedingly eager to get some of it just as it is," said the boy.

"Indeed, he is!" replied the guide. "He and his father, and I don't know how many grandfathers back, have offered large rewards to any one who would procure them this fruit in its best condition. But nobody has ever been able to get any yet."

"The reward still holds good, I suppose?" said the head boy.

"Oh, yes," answered the guide. "There never was a king who so much desired to taste the fruit as our present monarch."

The oldest boy looked up at the top of the tree, shut one eye, and gave his head a little wag. Whereupon every boy in the class looked up, shut one eye, and slightly wagged his head. After which the oldest boy said that he thought it was about time for them to go back to the ship.

As soon as they reached the vessel, and could talk freely together, the boys had an animated discussion. It was unanimously agreed that they would make an attempt to get some of the precious fruit from the Fragile Palm, and the only difference of opinion among them was as to how it should be done. Most of them were in favor of some method of climbing the tree and trusting to its not breaking. But this the oldest boy would not listen to. The trunk might snap, and then somebody would be hurt, and he felt, in a measure, responsible for the rest of the class. At length a good plan was proposed by a boy who had studied mechanics.

"What we ought to do with that tree," said he, "is to put a hinge into her. Then we could let her down gently, pick off the fruit, and set her up again."

"But how are you going to do it?" asked the others.

"This is the way," said the boy who had studied mechanics. "You take a saw, and then, about two feet from the ground, you begin and saw down diagonally, for a foot and a half, to the center of the trunk. Then you go on the other side, and saw down in the same way, the two cuts meeting each other. Now you have the upper part of the trunk ending in a wedge, which fits into a cleft in the lower part of the trunk. Then, about nine inches below the place where you first began to saw, you bore a hole straight through both sides of the cleft and the wedge between them. Then you put an iron bolt through this hole, and you have your tree on a hinge, only she won't be apt to move, because she fits in so snug and tight. Then you get a long rope, and tie one end in a slip-knot loosely around the trunk. Then you get a lot of poles, and fasten them end to end, and push this slip-knot up until it is somewhere near the top, when you pull it tight. Then you take another rope with a slip-knot, and push this a little more than half-way up the trunk. By having two ropes, that way, you prevent too much strain coming on any one part of the trunk. Then, after that, you take a mallet and chisel and round off the lower corners of the wedge, so that it will turn easily in the cleft. Then we take hold of the ropes, let her down gently, pick off the fruit, and haul her up again. That will all be easy enough."

This plan delighted the boys, and they all pronounced in its favor. But the oldest one suggested that it would be better to fasten the ropes to the trunk before they began to saw upon it, and another boy asked how they were going to keep the tree standing when they hauled her up again.

"Oh, that is easy," said the one who had studied mechanics. "You just bore another hole about six inches above the first one, and put in another bolt. Then, of course, she can't move."

This settled all the difficulties, and it was agreed to start out early the next morning, gather the fruit, and claim the reward the king had offered. They accordingly went to the captain and asked him for a sharp saw, a mallet and chisel, an auger, two iron bolts, and two very long ropes. These, having been cheerfully given to them, were put away in readiness for the work to be attempted.

Very early on the next morning, the First Class in Long Division set out for the Fragile Palm, carrying their tools and ropes. Few people were awake as they passed through the city, and, without being observed, they reached the little plain on which the tree stood. The ropes were attached at the proper places, the tree was sawn diagonally, according to the plan, the bolt was put in, and the corners of the wedge were rounded off. Then the eldest boy produced a pound of butter, whereupon his comrades, who had seized the ropes, paused in surprise and asked him why he had brought that.

"I thought it well," was the reply, "to bring along some butter, because, when the tree is down, we can grease the hinge, and then it will not be so hard to pull it up again."

When all was ready, eight of the boys took hold of the long ropes, while another one with a pole pushed against the trunk of the Fragile Palm. When it began to lean over a little, he dropped his pole and ran to help the others with the ropes. Slowly the tree moved on its hinge, descending at first very gradually. But it soon began to move with greater rapidity, although the boys held it back with all their strength, and, in spite of their most desperate efforts, the top came to the ground at last with a great thump. Then they all dropped their ropes and ran for the fruit. Fortunately the great nuts encased in their strong husks were not in the least injured, and the boys soon pulled them off, about forty in all. Some of the boys were in favor of cracking open a few of the nuts and eating them, but this the eldest boy positively forbade.

"This fruit," he said, "is looked upon as almost sacred, and if we were to eat any of it, it is probable that we should be put to death, which would be extremely awkward for fellows who have gone to all the trouble we have had. We must set up the tree and carry the fruit to the king."

According to this advice, they thoroughly greased the hinge in the tree with the butter, and then set themselves to work to haul up the trunk. This, however, was much more difficult than letting it down; and they had to lift up the head of it, and prop it up on poles, before they could pull upon it with advantage. The tree, although tall, was indeed a very slender one, with a small top, and if it had been as fragile as it was supposed to be, the boys' efforts would surely have broken it. At last, after much tugging and warm work, they pulled it into an upright position, and put in the second bolt. They left the ropes on the tree because, as some of them had suggested, the people might want to let the tree down again the next year. It would have been difficult for the boys to carry in their arms the great pile of fruit they had gathered, but having noticed a basket-maker's cottage on their way to the tree, two of them were sent to buy one of his largest baskets or hampers. This was attached to two long poles, and having been filled with the nuts, the boys took the poles on their shoulders, and marched into the city.

On their way to the palace they attracted a great crowd, and when they were ushered into the presence of the king, his surprise and delight knew no bounds. At first he could scarcely believe his eyes, but he had seen the fruit so often that there could be no mistake about it.

"I shall not ask you," he said to the boys, "how you procured this fruit, and thus accomplished a deed which has been the object of the ambition of myself and my forefathers. All I ask is, did you leave the tree standing?"

"We did," said the boys.

"Then all that remains to be done," said his Majesty, "is to give you the reward you have so nobly earned. Treasurer, measure out to each of them a quart of gold coin. And pray be quick about it, for I am wild with desire to have a table spread, and one of these nuts cracked, that I may taste of its luscious contents."

The boys, however, appeared a little dissatisfied. Huddling together, they consulted in a low tone, and then the eldest boy addressed the king.

"May it please your Majesty," he said, "we should very much prefer to have you give each of us one of those nuts instead of a quart of gold."

The king looked grave. "This is a much greater reward," he said, "than I had ever expected to pay. But, since you ask it, you must have it. You have done something which none of my subjects has ever been able to accomplish, and it is right, therefore, that you should be fully satisfied."

So he gave them each a nut, with which they departed in triumph to the ship.

By the afternoon of the next day the captain had sold all his cargo at very good prices, and when the money was safely stored away in the *Horn o' Plenty*, he made ready to sail, for he declared he had really no time to spare. "I must now make all possible haste," he said to old Baragat, "to find Apple Island, put these boys ashore, and then speed away to the city where lives my son. We must not fail to get there in time to spend last Christmas over again."

On the second day after the *Horn o' Plenty* had left the Island of the Fragile Palm, one of the sailors who happened to be aloft noticed a low, black, and exceedingly unpleasant-looking vessel rapidly approaching. This soon proved to be the ship of a band of corsairs who, having heard of the large amount of money on the *Horn o' Plenty*, had determined to pursue her and capture the rich prize. All sails were set upon the *Horn o' Plenty*, but it soon became plain that she could never outsail the corsair vessel.

"What our ship can do better than anything else," said Baragat to the captain, "is to stop short. Stop her short, and let the other one go by."

This maneuvre was executed, but although the corsair passed rapidly by, not being able to stop so suddenly, it soon turned around and came back, its decks swarming with savage men armed to the teeth.

"They are going to board us," cried Baragat. "They are getting out their grappling-irons, and they will fasten the two ships together."

"Let all assemble on the quarter-deck," said the captain. "It is higher there, and we shall not be so much exposed to accidents."

The corsair ship soon ran alongside the *Horn o' Plenty*, and in a moment the two vessels were fastened together, and then the corsairs, every man of them, each with cutlass in hand and a belt full of dirks and knives, swarmed up the side of the *Horn o' Plenty*, and sprang upon its central deck. Some of the ferocious fellows, seeing the officers and crew all huddled together upon the quarter-deck, made a movement in that direction. This so frightened the chief mate that he jumped down upon the deck of the corsair ship. A panic now arose, and he was immediately followed by the officers and crew. The boys, of course, were not to be left behind, and as the captain and Baragat felt themselves bound not to desert the crew, they jumped also. None of the corsairs interfered with this proceeding, for each one of them was anxious to find the money at once.

When the passengers and crew of the *Horn o' Plenty* were all on board the corsair ship, Baragat came to the captain, and said, "If I were you, sir, I'd cast off those grapnels, and separate the vessels. If we don't do that, those rascals, when they have finished robbing our money-chests, will come back here and murder us all."

"That is a good idea," said Captain Covajos. And he told the chief mate to give orders to cast off the grapnels, push the two vessels apart, and set some of the sails.

When this had been done, the corsair vessel began to move away from the other, and was soon many lengths distant from her. When the corsairs came on deck and perceived what had happened, they were infuriated, and immediately began to pursue their own vessel with the one they had captured. But the *Horn o' Plenty* could not, by any possibility, sail as fast as the corsair ship, and the latter easily kept away from her.

"Now, then," said Baragat to the captain, "what you have to do is easy enough. Sail straight for our port, and those sea-robbers will follow you, for, of course, they will wish to get their own vessel back again, and will hope, by some carelessness on our part, to overtake us. In the meantime the money will be safe enough, for they will have no opportunity of spending it, and when we come to port, we can take some soldiers on board, and go back and capture those fellows. They can never sail away from us on the *Horn o' Plenty*."

"That is an admirable plan," said the captain, "and I shall carry it out. But I cannot sail to port immediately. I must first find Apple Island and land these boys, whose parents and guardians are probably growing very uneasy. I suppose the corsairs will continue to follow us wherever we go."

"I hope so," said Baragat. "At any rate, we shall see."

The First Class in Long Division was very much delighted with the change of vessels, and the boys rambled everywhere, and examined with great interest all that belonged to the corsairs. They felt quite easy about the only treasures they possessed, because, when they had first seen the piratical vessel approaching, they had taken the precious nuts which had been given to them by the king, and had hidden them at the bottom of some large boxes in which the captain kept the sailors' winter clothes.

"In this warm climate," said the eldest boy, "the robbers will never meddle with those winter clothes, and our precious fruit will be perfectly safe."

"If you had taken my advice," said one of the other boys, "we should have eaten some of the nuts. Those, at least, we should have been sure of."

"And we should have had that many less to show to the other classes," said the eldest boy. "Nuts like these, I am told, if picked at the proper season, will keep for a long time."

For some days the corsairs on board the *Horn o' Plenty* followed their own vessel, but then they seemed to despair of ever being able to overtake it, and steered in another direction. This threatened to ruin all the plans of Captain Covajos, and his mind became troubled. Then the boy who had studied mechanics came forward and said to the captain:

"I'll tell you what I'd do, sir, if I were you. I'd follow your old ship, and when night came on I'd sail up quite near to her, and let some of your sailors swim quietly over, and fasten a cable to her, and then you could tow her after you wherever you wished to go."

"But they might unfasten the cable, or cut it," said Baragat, who was standing by.

"That could easily be prevented," said the boy. "At their end of the cable must be a stout chain which they cannot cut, and it must be fastened so far beneath the surface of the water that they will not be able to reach it to unfasten it."

"A most excellent plan," said Captain Covajos. "Let it be carried out."

As soon as it became quite dark, the corsair vessel quietly approached the other, and two stout sailors from Finland, who swam very well, were ordered to swim over and attach the chain-end of a long cable to the *Horn o' Plenty*. It was a very difficult operation, for the chain was heavy; but the men succeeded at last, and returned to report.

"We put the chain on fast and strong, sir," they said to the captain, "and six feet under water. But the only place we could find to make it fast to was the bottom of the rudder."

"That will do very well," remarked Baragat, "for the *Horn o' Plenty* sails better backward than forward, and will not be so hard to tow."

For week after week, and month after month, Captain Covajos, in the corsair vessel, sailed here and there in search of Apple Island, always towing after him the *Horn o' Plenty*, with the corsairs on board; but never an island with a school on it could they find, and one day old Baragat came to the captain and said, "If I were you, sir, I'd sail no more in these warm regions. I am quite sure that apples grow in colder latitudes, and are never found so far south as this."

"That is a good idea," said Captain Covajos. "We should sail for the north if we wish to find an island of apples. Have the vessel turned northward."

So, for days and weeks, the two vessels slowly moved on to the north. One day the captain made some observations and calculations, and then he hastily summoned Baragat.

"Do you know," said he, "that I find it is now near the end of November, and I am quite certain that we shall not get to the port where my son lives in time to celebrate last Christmas again. It is dreadfully slow work, towing after us the *Horn o' Plenty*, full of corsairs, wherever we go. But we cannot cast her off and sail straight for our port, for I should lose my good ship, the merchants would lose all their money, and the corsairs would go unpunished. Besides all that, think of the misery of the parents and guardians of those poor boys. No. I must endeavor to find Apple Island. And if I cannot reach port in time to spend last Christmas with my son, I shall certainly get there in season for Christmas before last. It is true that I spent that Christmas with my daughter, but I cannot go on to her now. I am much nearer the city where my son lives. Besides, it is necessary to go back and give the merchants their money. So now we shall have plenty of time, and need not feel hurried."

"No," said Baragat, heaving a vast sigh, "we need not feel hurried."

The mind of the eldest boy now became very much troubled, and he called his companions about him. "I don't like at all," said he, "this sailing to the north. It is now November, and although it is warm enough at this season in the southern part of the sea, it will become colder and colder as we go on. The consequence of this will be that those corsairs will want winter clothes; they will take them out of the captain's chests, and they will find our fruit."

The boys groaned. "That is true," said one of them. "But still we wish to go back to our island."

"Of course," said the eldest boy, "it is quite proper that we should return to Long Division. But think of the hard work we did to get that fruit, and think of the quarts of gold we gave up for it! It would be too bad to lose it now!"

It was unanimously agreed that it would be too bad to lose the fruit, and it was also unanimously agreed that they wished to go back to Apple Island. But what to do about it they did not know.

Day by day the weather grew colder and colder, and the boys became more and more excited and distressed for fear they should lose their precious fruit. The eldest boy lay awake for several nights, and then a plan came into his head. He went to Captain Covajos and proposed that he should send a flag of truce over to the corsairs, offering to exchange winter clothing. He would send over to them the heavy garments they had left on their own vessel, and in return would take the boxes of clothes intended for the winter wear of his sailors. In this way they would get their fruit back without the corsairs knowing anything about it. The captain considered this an excellent plan, and ordered the chief mate to take a boat and a flag of truce, and go over to the *Horn o' Plenty* and make the proposition. The eldest boy and two of the others insisted on going also, in order that there might be no mistake about the boxes. But when the flag-of-truce party reached the *Horn o' Plenty* they found not a corsair there! Every man of them had gone. They had taken with them all the money-chests, but, to the great delight of the boys, the boxes of winter clothes had not been disturbed, and in them still nestled, safe and sound, the precious nuts of the Fragile Palm.

When the matter had been thoroughly looked into, it became quite evident what the corsairs had done. There had been only one boat on board the *Horn o' Plenty*, and that was the one on which the First Class in Long Division had arrived. The night before, the two vessels had passed within a mile or so of a large island, which the captain had approached in the hope it was the one they were looking for, and they passed it so slowly that the corsairs had time to ferry themselves over, a few at a time, in the little boat, taking with them the money—and all without discovery.

Captain Covajos was greatly depressed when he heard of the loss of all the money.

"I shall have a sad tale to tell my merchants," he said, "and Christmas before last will not be celebrated so joyously as it was the first time. But we cannot help what has happened, and we all must endeavor to bear our losses with patience. We shall continue our search for Apple Island, but I shall go on board my own ship, for I have greatly missed my carpeted quarter-deck and my other comforts. The chief mate, however, and a majority of the crew shall remain on board the corsair vessel, and continue to tow us. The *Horn o' Plenty* sails better stern foremost, and we shall go faster that way."

The boys were overjoyed at recovering their fruit, and most of them were in favor of cracking two or three of the great nuts and eating their contents in honor of the occasion; but the eldest boy dissuaded them.

"The good captain," he said, "has been very kind in endeavoring to take us back to our school, and still intends to keep up the search for dear old Apple Island. The least we can do for him is to give him this fruit, which is all we have, and let him do what he pleases with it. This is the only way in which we can show our gratitude to him."

The boys turned their backs on one another, and each of them gave his eyes a little rub, but they all agreed to give the fruit to the captain.

When the good old man received his present, he was much affected. "I will accept what you offer me," he said, "for if I did not, I know your feelings would be wounded. But you must keep one of the nuts for yourselves. And, more than that, if we do not find Apple Island in the course of the coming year, I invite you all to spend Christmas before last over again with me at my son's house."

All that winter the two ships sailed up and down, and here and there, but never could they find Apple Island. When Christmas-time came, old Baragat went around among the boys and the crew, and told them it would be well not to say a word on the subject to the captain, for his feelings were very tender in regard to spending Christmas away from his families, and the thing had never happened before. So nobody made any allusion to the holidays, and they passed over as if they had been ordinary days.

During the spring, and all through the summer, the two ships kept up the unavailing search, but when the autumn began, Captain Covajos said to old Baragat, "I am very sorry, but I feel that I can no longer look for Apple Island. I must go back and spend Christmas before last over again with my dearest son, and if these poor boys never return to their homes, I am sure they cannot say it was any fault of mine."

"No, sir," said Baragat. "I think you have done all that could be expected of you."

So the ships sailed to the city on the west side of the sea, and the captain was received with great joy by his son and his grandchildren. He went to the merchants, and told them how he had lost all their money. He hoped they would be able to bear their misfortune with fortitude, and begged, as he could do nothing else for them, that they would accept the eight great nuts from the Fragile Palm that the boys had given him. To his surprise, the merchants became wild with delight when they received the nuts. The money they had lost was as nothing, they said, compared to the value of this incomparable and precious fruit, picked in its prime, and still in a perfect condition.

It had been many, many generations since this rare fruit, the value of which was like unto that of diamonds and pearls, had been for sale in any market in the world; and kings and queens in many countries were ready to give for it almost any price that might be asked.

When the good old captain heard this he was greatly rejoiced, and, as the holidays were now near, he insisted that the boys should spend Christmas before last over again at his son's house. He found that a good many people there knew where Apple Island was, and he made arrangements for the First Class in Long Division to return to that island in a vessel which was to sail about the first of the year.

The boys still possessed the great nut which the captain had insisted they should keep for themselves, and he now told them that if they chose to sell it they would each have a nice little fortune to take back with them.

The eldest boy consulted the others, and then he said to the captain, "Our class has gone through a good many hardships, and has had a lot of trouble with that palm-tree and other things, and we think we ought to be rewarded. So, if it is all the same to you, I think we will crack the nut on Christmas day, and we all will eat it."

"I never imagined," cried Captain Covajos, as he sat, on that Christmas day, surrounded by his son's family and the First Class in Long Division, the eyes of the whole party sparkling with ecstasy as they tasted the peerless fruit of the Fragile Palm, "that Christmas before last could be so joyfully celebrated over again."

THE CONCILIATOR
OF CHRISTENDOM

by Israel Zangwill

from *Dreamers of the Ghetto*

I

The Red Beadle shook his head. "There is nothing but Nature," he said obstinately, as his hot iron polished the boot between his knees. He was called the Red Beadle because, though his irreligious opinions had long since lost him his synagogue appointment and driven him back to his old work of bootmaking, his beard was still ruddy.

"Yes, but who made Nature?" retorted his new employer, his strange, scholarly face aglow with argument, and the flame of the lamp suspended over his bench by strings from the ceiling. The other clickers and riveters of the Spitalfields workshop, in their shocked interest in the problem of the origin of Nature, ceased for an instant breathing in the odors of burnt grease, cobbler's wax, and a coke fire replenished with scraps of leather.

"Nature makes herself," answered the Red Beadle. It was his declaration of faith—or of war. Possibly it was the familiarity with divine things which synagogue beadledom involves that had bred his contempt for them. At any rate, he was not now to be coerced by Zussmann Herz, even though he was fully alive to the fact that Zussmann's unique book-lined workshop was the only one that had opened to him, when the more pious shoemakers of the Ghetto had professed to be "full up." He was, indeed, surprised to find Zussmann a believer in the Supernatural, having heard whispers that the man was as great an "Epicurean" as himself. Had not Zussmann—ay, and his wigless wife, Hulda, too—been seen emerging from the mighty Church that stood in frowsy majesty amid its tall, neglected box-like tombs, and was to the Ghetto merely a topographical point and the chronometric standard? And yet, here was Zussmann, an assiduous attendant at the synagogue of the first floor—nay, a scholar so conversant with Hebrew, not to mention European, lore, that the Red Beadle felt himself a Man-of-the-Earth, only retaining his superiority by remembering that learning did not always mean logic.

"Nature make herself!" Zussmann now retorted, with a tolerant smile. "As well say this boot made itself! The theory of Evolution only puts the mystery further back, and already in the Talmud we find—"

"*Nature* made the boot," interrupted the Red Beadle. "Nature made you, and you made the boot. But nobody made Nature."

"But what is Nature?" cried Zussmann. "The garment of God, as Goethe says. Call Him Noumenon with Kant or Thought and Extension with Spinoza—I care not."

The Red Beadle was awed into temporary silence by these unknown names and ideas, expressed, moreover, in German words foreign to his limited vocabulary of Yiddish.

The room in which Zussmann thought and worked was one of two that he rented from the Christian corn-factor who owned the tall house—a stout Cockney who spent his life book-keeping in a little office on wheels, but whom the specimens of oats and dog-biscuits in his window invested with an air of roseate rurality. This personage drew a little income from the population of his house, whose staircases exhibited strata of children of different social developments, and to which the synagogue on the first floor added a large floating population. Zussmann's attendance thereat was not the only thing in him that astonished the Red Beadle. There was also a gentle deference of manner not usual with masters, or with pious persons. His consideration for his employes amounted, in the Beadle's eyes, to maladministration, and the grave loss he sustained through one of his hands selling off a crate of finished goods and flying to America was deservedly due to confidence in another pious person.

II

Despite the Red Beadle's Rationalism, which, basing itself on the facts of life, was not to be crushed by high-flown German words, the master-shoemaker showed him marked favor and often invited him to stay on to supper. Although the Beadle felt this was but the due recognition of one intellect by another, if an inferior intellect, he was at times irrationally grateful for the privilege of a place to spend his evenings in. For the Ghetto had cut him—there could be no doubt of that. The worshippers in his old synagogue whom he had once dominated as Beadle now passed him by with sour looks—"a dog one does not treat thus," the Beadle told himself, tugging miserably at his red beard.

"It is not as if I were a Meshummad—a convert to Christianity." Some hereditary instinct admitted *that* as a just excuse for execration. "I can't make friends with the Christians, and so I am cut off from both."

When after a thunderstorm two of the hands resigned their places at Zussmann's benches on the avowed ground that atheism attracts lightning, Zussmann's loyalty to the freethinker converted the Beadle's gratitude from fitfulness into a steady glow.

And, other considerations apart, those were enjoyable suppers after the toil and grime of the day. The Beadle especially admired Zussmann's hands when the black grease had been washed off them, the fingers were so long and tapering. Why had his own fingers been made so stumpy and square-tipped? Since Nature made herself, why was she so uneven a worker? Nay, why could she not have given him white teeth like Zussmann's wife? Not that these were ostentatious—you thought more of the sweetness of the smile of which they were part. Still, as Nature's irregularity was particularly manifest in his own teeth, he could not help the reflection.

If the Red Beadle had not been a widower, the unfeigned success of the Herz union might have turned his own thoughts to that happy state. As it was, the sight of their happiness occasionally shot through his breast renewed pangs of vain longing for his Leah, whose death from cancer had completed his conception of Nature. Lucky Zussmann, to have found so sympathetic a partner in a pretty female! For Hulda shared Zussmann's dreams, and was even copying out his great work for the press, for business was brisk and he would soon have saved up enough money to print it. The great work, in the secret of which the Red Beadle came to participate, was written in Hebrew, and the elegant curves and strokes would have done honor to a Scribe. The Beadle himself could not understand it, knowing only the formal alphabet such as appears in books and scrolls, but the first peep at it which the proud Zussmann permitted him removed his last disrespect for the intellect of his master, without, however, removing the mystery of that intellect's aberrations.

"But you dream with the eyes open," he said, when the theme of the work was explained to him.

"How so?" asked Hulda gently, with that wonderful smile of hers.

"Reconcile the Jews and the Christians! *Meshuggas*—madness." He laughed bitterly. "Do you forget what we went through in Poland? And even here in free England, can you walk in the street without every little *shegetz* calling after you and asking, 'Who killed Christ?'"

"Yes, but herein my husband explains that it was not the Jews who killed Christ, but Herod and Pilate."

"As it says in Corinthians," broke in Zussmann eagerly: "'We speak the wisdom of God in a mystery, which none of the princes of this world knew; for had they known it, they would not have crucified the Lord of Glory.'"

"So," said the Red Beadle, visibly impressed.

"Assuredly," affirmed Hulda. "But, as Zussmann explains here, they threw the guilt upon the Jews, who were too afraid of the Romans to deny it."

The Beadle pondered.

"Once the Christians understand that," said Zussmann, pursuing his advantage, "they will stretch out the hand to us."

The Beadle had a flash. "But how will the Christians read you? No Christian understands Hebrew."

Zussmann was taken momentarily aback. "But it is not so much for the Christians," he explained. "It is for the Jews—that they should stretch out the hand to the Christians."

The Red Beadle stared at him in shocked silent amaze. "Still greater madness!" he gasped at length. "They will treat you worse than they treat me."

"Not when they read my book."

"Just when they read your book."

Hulda was smiling serenely. "They can do nothing to my husband; he is his own master, God be thanked; no one can turn him away."

"They can insult him."

Zussmann shook his head gently. "No one can insult me!" he said simply. "When a dog barks at me I pity it that it does not know I love it. Now draw to the table. The pickled herring smells well."

But the Red Beadle was unconvinced. "Besides, what should we make it up with the Christians for—the stupid people?" he asked, as he received his steaming coffee-cup from Frau Herz.

"It is a question of the Future of the World," said Zussmann gravely, as he shared out the herring, which had already been cut into many thin slices by the vendor and pickler. "This antagonism is a perversion of the principles of both religions. Shall we allow it to continue for ever?"

"It will continue till they both understand that Nature makes herself," said the Red Beadle.

"It will continue till they both understand my husband's book," corrected Hulda.

"Not while Jews live among Christians. Even here they say we take the bread out of the mouths of the Christian shoemakers. If we had our own country now—"

"Hush!" said Zussmann. "Do you share that materialistic dream? Our realm is spiritual. Nationality—the world stinks with it! Germany for the Germans, Russia for the Russians. Foreigners to the devil—pah! Egomania posing as patriotism. Human brotherhood is what we stand for. Have you forgotten how the Midrash explains the verse in the Song of Solomon: 'I charge you, O ye daughters of Jerusalem, by the roes, and by the hinds of the field, that ye stir not up, nor awake my love till he please'?"

The Red Beadle, who had never read a line of the Midrash, did not deny that he had forgotten the explanation, but persisted: "And even if we didn't kill Christ, what good will it do to tell the Jew so? It will only make them angry."

"Why so?" said Zussmann, puzzled.

"They will be annoyed to have been punished for nothing."

"But they have not been punished for nothing!" cried Zussmann, setting down his fork in excitement. "They have denied their greatest son. For, as He said in Matthew, 'I come to fulfil the Law of Moses.' Did not all the Prophets, His predecessors, cry out likewise against mere form and sacrifice? Did not the teachers in Israel who followed Him likewise insist on a pure heart and a sinless soul? Jesus must be restored to His true place in the glorious chain of Hebrew Prophets. As I explain in my chapter on the Philosophy of Religion, which I have founded on Immanuel Kant, the ground-work of Reason is—"

But here the Red Beadle, whose coffee had with difficulty got itself sucked into the right channel, gasped—"You have put that into your book?"

The wife touched the manuscript with reverent pride. "It all stands here," she said.

"What! Quotations from the New Testament?"

"From our Jewish Apostles!" said Zussmann. "Naturally! On every page!"

"Then God help you!" said the Red Beadle.

III

The Brotherhood of the Peoples was published. Though the bill was far heavier than the Hebrew printer's estimate—there being all sorts of mysterious charges for corrections, which took away the last *Groschen* of their savings—Hulda and her husband were happy. They had sown the seed, and waited in serene faith the ingathering, the reconciliation of Israel with the Gentiles.

The book, which was in paper covers, was published at a shilling; five hundred copies had been struck off for the edition. After six months the account stood thus: Sales, eighty-four copies; press notices, two in the jargon papers (printed in the same office as his book and thus amenable to backstairs influence). The Jewish papers written in English, which loomed before Zussmann's vision as world-shaking, did not even mention its appearance; perhaps it had been better if the jargon papers had been equally silent, for, though less than one hundred copies of *The Brotherhood of the Peoples* were in circulation, the book was in everybody's mouth—like a piece of pork to be spat out again shudderingly. The Red Beadle's instinct had been only too sound. The Ghetto, accustomed by this time to insidious attacks on its spiritual citadel, feared writers even bringing Hebrew. Despite the Oriental sandal which the cunning shoemaker had fashioned, his fellow-Jews saw the cloven hoof. They were not to be deceived by the specious sanctity which Darwin and Schopenhauer—probably Bishops of the Established Church—borrowed from their Hebrew lettering. Why, that was the very trick of the Satans who sprinkled the sacred tongue freely about handbills inviting souls that sought for light to come and find it in the Whitechapel Road between three and seven. It had been abandoned as hopeless even by the thin-nosed gentlewomen who had begun by painting a Hebrew designation over their bureau of beneficence. But the fact that the Ghetto was perspicacious did not mitigate the author's treachery to his race and faith. Zussmann was given violently to understand that his presence in the little synagogue would lead to disturbances in the service. "The Jew needs no house of prayer," he said; "his life is a prayer, his workshop a temple."

His workmen deserted him one by one as vacancies occurred elsewhere.

"We will get Christians," he said.

But the work itself began to fail. He was dependent upon a large firm whose head was Parnass of a North London congregation, and when one of Zussmann's workers, anxious to set up for himself, went to him with the tale, the contract was transferred to him, and Zussmann's security deposit returned. But far heavier than all these blows was Hulda's sudden illness, and though the returned trust-money came in handy to defray the expense of doctors, the outlook was not cheerful. But "I will become a hand myself," said Zussmann cheerfully. "The annoyance of my brethren will pass away when they really understand my Idea; meantime it is working in them, for even to hate an Idea is to meditate upon it."

The Red Beadle grunted angrily. He could hear Hulda coughing in the next room, and that hurt his chest.

But it was summer now, and quite a considerable strip of blue sky could be seen from the window, and the mote-laden sun-rays that streamed in encouraged Hulda to grow better. She was soon up and about again, but the doctor said her system was thoroughly upset and she ought to have sea air. But that, of course, was impossible now. Hulda herself declared there was much better air to be got higher up, in the garret, which was fortunately "to let." It is true there was only one room there. Still, it was much cheaper. The Red Beadle's heart was heavier than the furniture he helped to carry upstairs. But the unsympathetic couple did not share his gloom. They jested and laughed, as light of heart as the excited children on the staircases who assisted at the function. "My Idea has raised me nearer heaven," said Zussmann. That night, after the Red Beadle had screwed up the fourposter, he allowed himself to be persuaded to stay to supper. He had given up the habit as soon as Zussmann's finances began to fail.

By way of house-warming, Hulda had ordered in baked potatoes and liver from the cook-shop, and there were also three tepid slices of plum-pudding.

"Plum-pudding!" cried Zussmann in delight, as his nostrils scented the dainty. "What a good omen for the Idea!"

"How an omen?" inquired the Red Beadle.

"Is not plum-pudding associated with Christmas, with peace on earth?"

Hulda's eyes flashed. "Yes, it is a sign—the Brotherhood of the Peoples! The Jew will be the peace-messenger of the world." The Red Beadle ate on sceptically. He had studied *The Brotherhood of the Peoples* to the great improvement of his Hebrew but with little edification. He had even studied it in Hulda's original manuscript, which he had borrowed and never intended to return. But still he could not share his friends' belief in the perfectibility of mankind. Perhaps if they had known how he had tippled away his savings after his wife's death, they might have thought less well of humanity and its potentialities of perfection. After all, Huldas were too rare to make the world sober, much less fraternal. And, charming as they were, honesty demanded one should not curry favor with them by fostering their delusions.

"What put such an idea into your head, Zussmann!" he cried unsympathetically.

Zussmann answered naïvely, as if to a question, "I have had the Idea from a boy. I remember sitting stocking-footed on the floor of the synagogue in Poland on the Fast of Ab, wondering why we should weep so over the destruction of Jerusalem, which scattered us among the nations as fertilizing seeds. How else should the mission of Israel be fulfilled? I remember"—and here he smiled pensively—"I was awakened from my day-dream by a *Patsch* [smack] in the face from my poor old father, who was angry because I wasn't saying the prayers."

"There will be always somebody to give you that *Patsch*," said the Red Beadle gloomily. "But in what way is Israel dispersed? It seems to me our life is everywhere as hidden from the nations as if we were all together in Palestine."

"You touch a great truth! Oh, if I could only write in English! But though I read it almost as easily as the German, I can write it as little. You know how one has to learn German in Poland—by stealth—the Christians jealous on one hand, the Jews suspicious on the other. I could not risk the Christians laughing at my bad German—that would hurt my Idea. And English is a language like the Vale of Siddim—full of pits."

"We ought to have it translated," said Hulda. "Not only for the Christians, but for the rich Jews, who are more liberal-minded than those who live in our quarter."

"But we cannot afford to pay for the translating now," said Zussmann.

"Nonsense; one has always a jewel left," said Hulda.

Zussmann's eyes grew wet. "Yes," he said, drawing her to his breast, "one has always a jewel left."

"More *meshuggas!*" cried the Red Beadle huskily. "Much the English Jews care about ideas! Did they even acknowledge your book in their journals? But probably they couldn't read it," he added with a laugh. "A fat lot of Hebrew little Sampson knows! You know little Sampson—he came to report the boot-strike for *The Flag of Judah*. I got into conversation with him—a rank pork-gorger. He believes with me that Nature makes herself."

But Zussmann was scarcely eating, much less listening.

"You have given me a new scheme, Hulda," he said, with exaltation. "I will send my book to the leading English Jews—yes, especially to the ministers. They will see my Idea, they will spread it abroad, they will convert first the Jews and then the Christians."

"Yes, but they will give it as their own Idea," said Hulda.

"And what then? He who has faith in an Idea, his Idea it is. How great for me to have had the Idea first! Is not that enough to thank God for? If only my Idea gets spread in English! English! Have you ever thought what that means, Hulda? The language of the future! Already the language of the greatest nations, and the most on the lips of men everywhere—in a century it will cover the world." He murmured in Hebrew, uplifting his eyes to the rain-streaked sloping ceiling. "And in that day God shall be One and His name One."

"Your supper is getting cold," said Hulda gently.

He began to wield his knife and fork as if hypnotized by her suggestion, but his vision was inwards.

IV

Fifty copies of *The Brotherhood of the Peoples* went off by post the next day to the clergy and gentry of the larger Jewry. In the course of the next fortnight seventeen of the recipients acknowledged the receipt with formal thanks, four sent the shilling mentioned on the cover, and one sent five shillings. This last depressed Zussmann more than all the others. "Does he take me for a *Schnorrer?*" he said, almost angrily, as he returned the postal order.

He did not foresee the day when, a *Schnorrer* indeed, he would have taken five shillings from anybody who could afford it: had no prophetic intuition of that long, slow progression of penurious days which was to break down his spirit. For though he managed for a time to secure enough work to keep himself and the Red Beadle going, his ruin was only delayed. Little by little his apparatus was sold off, his benches and polishing-irons vanished from the garret, only one indispensable set remaining, and master and man must needs quest each for himself for work elsewhere. The Red Beadle dropped out of the ménage, and was reduced to semi-starvation. Zussmann and Hulda, by the gradual disposition of their bits of jewellery and their Sabbath garments, held out a little longer, and Hulda also got some sewing of children's under-garments. But with the return of winter, Hulda's illness returned, and then the beloved books began to leave bare the nakedness of the plastered walls. At first, Hulda, refusing to be visited by doctors who charged, struggled out bravely through rain and fog to a free dispensary, where she was jostled by a crowd of head-shawled Polish crones, and where a harassed Christian physician, tired of jargon-speaking Jewesses, bawled and bullied. But at last Hulda grew too ill to stir out, and Zussmann, still out of employment, was driven to look about him for help. Charities enough there were in the Ghetto, but to charity, as to work, one requires an apprenticeship. He knew vaguely that there were persons who had the luck to be ill and to get broths and jellies. To others, also, a board of guardian angels doled out payments, though some one had once told him you had scant chance unless you were a Dutchman. But the inexperienced in begging are naturally not so successful as those always at it. 'Twas vain for Zussmann to kick his heels among the dismal crowd in the corridor, the whisper of his misdeeds had been before him, borne by some competitor in the fierce struggle for assistance. What! help a hypocrite to sit on the twin stools of Christendom and Judaism, fed by the bounty of both! In this dark hour he was approached by the thin-nosed gentlewomen, who had got wind of his book and who scented souls. Zussmann wavered. Why, indeed, should he refuse their assistance? He knew their self-sacrificing ways, their genuine joy in salvation. On their generosities he was far better posted than on Jewish—the lurid legend of these Mephistophelian matrons included blankets, clothes, port wine, and all the delicacies of the season. He admitted that Hulda had indeed been brought low, and permitted them to call. Then he went home to cut dry bread for the bedridden, emaciated creature who had once been beautiful, and to comfort her—for it was Friday evening—by reading the Sabbath prayers; winding up, "A virtuous woman who can find? For her price is far above rubies."

On the forenoon of the next day arrived a basket, scenting the air with delicious odors of exquisite edibles.

Zussmann received it with delight from the boy who bore it. "God bless them!" he said. "A chicken—grapes—wine. Look, Hulda!"

Hulda raised herself in bed; her eyes sparkled, a flush of color returned to the wan cheeks.

"Where do these come from?" she asked.

Zussmann hesitated. Then he told her they were the harbingers of a visit from the good sisters.

The flush in her cheek deepened to scarlet.

"My poor Zussmann!" she cried reproachfully. "Give them back— give them back at once! Call after the boy."

"Why?" stammered Zussmann.

"Call after the boy!" she repeated imperatively. "Good God! If the ladies were to be seen coming up here, it would be all over with your Idea. And on the Sabbath, too! People already look upon you as a tool of the missionaries. Quick! quick!"

His heart aching with mingled love and pain, he took up the basket and hurried after the boy. Hulda sank back on her pillow with a sigh of relief.

"Dear heart!" she thought, as she took advantage of his absence to cough freely. "For me he does what he would starve rather than do for himself. A nice thing to imperil his Idea—the dream of his life? When the Jews see he makes no profit by it, they will begin to consider it. If he did not have the burden of me he would not be tempted. He could go out more and find work farther afield. This must end—I must die or be on my feet again soon."

Zussmann came back, empty-handed and heavy-hearted.

"Kiss me, my own life!" she cried. "I shall be better soon."

He bent down and touched her hot, dry lips. "Now I see," she whispered, "why God did not send us children. We thought it was an affliction, but lo! it is that your Idea shall not be hindered."

"The English Rabbis have not yet drawn attention to it," said Zussmann huskily.

"All the better," replied Hulda. "One day it will be translated into English—I know it, I feel it here." She touched her chest, and the action made her cough.

Going out later for a little fresh air, at Hulda's insistence, he was stopped in the broad hall on which the stairs debouched by Cohen, the ground-floor tenant, a black-bearded Russian Jew, pompous in Sabbath broadcloth.

"What's the matter with my milk?" abruptly asked Cohen, who supplied the local trade besides selling retail. "You might have complained, instead of taking your custom out of the house. Believe me, I don't make a treasure heap out of it. One has to be up at Euston to meet the trains in the middle of the night, and the competition is so cut-throat that one has to sell at eighteen pence a barn gallon. And on Sabbath one earns nothing at all. And then the analyst comes poking his nose into the milk."

"You see—my wife—my wife—is ill," stammered Zussmann. "So she doesn't drink it."

"Hum!" said Cohen. "Well, *you* might oblige me then. I have so much left over every day, it makes my reputation turn quite sour. Do, do me a favor and let me send you up a can of the leavings every night. For nothing, of course; would I talk business on the Sabbath? I don't like to be seen pouring it away. It would pay me to pay *you* a penny a pint," he wound up emphatically.

Zussmann accepted unsuspiciously, grateful to Providence for enabling him to benefit at once himself and his neighbor. He bore a can upstairs now and explained the situation to the shrewder Hulda, who, however, said nothing but, "You see the Idea commences to work. When the book first came out, didn't he—though he sells secretly to the trade on Sabbath mornings—call you an Epicurean?"

"Worse," said Zussmann joyously, with a flash of recollection.

He went out again, lightened and exalted. "Yes, the Idea works," he said, as he came out into the gray street. "The Brotherhood of the Peoples will come, not in my time, but it will come." And he murmured again the Hebrew aspiration: "In that day shall God be One and His name One."

"Whoa, where's your —— eyes?"

Awakened by the oath, he just got out of the way of a huge Flemish dray-horse dragging a brewer's cart. Three ragged Irish urchins, who had been buffeting each other with whirling hats knotted into the ends of dingy handkerchiefs, relaxed their enmities in a common rush for the projecting ladder behind the dray and collided with Zussmann on the way. A one-legged, misery-eyed hunchback offered him penny diaries. He shook his head in impotent pity, and passed on, pondering. "In time God will make the crooked straight," he thought.

Jews with tall black hats and badly made frock-coats slouched along, their shoulders bent. Wives stood at the open doors of the old houses, some in Sabbath finery, some flaunting irreligiously their every-day shabbiness, without troubling even to arrange their one dress differently, as a pious Rabbi recommended. They looked used-up and haggard, all these mothers in Israel. But there were dark-eyed damsels still gay and fresh, with artistic bodices of violet and green picked out with gold arabesque.

He turned a corner and came into a narrow street that throbbed with the joyous melody of a piano-organ. His heart leapt up. The roadway bubbled with Jewish children, mainly girls, footing it gleefully in the graying light, inventing complex steps with a grace and an abandon that lit their eyes with sparkles and painted deeper flushes on their olive cheeks. A bounding little bow-legged girl seemed unconscious of her deformity; her toes met each other as though in merry dexterity.

Zussmann's eyes were full of tears. "Dance on, dance on," he murmured. "God shall indeed make the crooked straight."

Fixed to one side of the piano-organ on the level of the handle he saw a little box, in which lay, as in a cradle, what looked like a monkey, then like a doll, but on closer inspection turned into a tiny live child, flaxen-haired, staring with wide gray eyes from under a blue cap, and sucking at a milk-bottle with preternatural placidity, regardless of the music throbbing through its resting-place.

"Even so shall humanity live," thought Zussmann, "peaceful as a babe, cradled in music. God hath sent me a sign."

He returned home, comforted, and told Hulda of the sign.

"Was it an Italian child?" she asked.

"An English child," he answered. "Fair-eyed and fair-haired."

"Then it is a sign that through the English tongue shall the Idea move the world. Your book will be translated into English—I shall live to see it."

V

A few afternoons later the Red Beadle, his patched garments pathetically spruced up, came to see his friends, goaded by the news of Hulda's illness. There was no ruddiness in his face, the lips of which were pressed together in defiance of a cruel and credulous world. That Nature in making herself should have produced creatures who attributed their creation elsewhere, and who refused to allow her one acknowledger to make boots, was indeed a proof, albeit vexatious, of her blind workings.

When he saw what she had done to Hulda and to Zussmann, his lips were pressed tighter, but as much to keep back a sob as to express extra resentment.

But on parting he could not help saying to Zussmann, who accompanied him to the dark spider-webbed landing, "Your God has forgotten you."

"Do you mean that men have forgotten Him?" replied Zussmann. "If I am come to poverty, my suffering is in the scheme of things. Do you not remember what the Almighty says to Eleazar ben Pedos, in the Talmud, when the Rabbi complains of poverty? 'Wilt thou be satisfied if I overthrow the universe, so that perhaps thou mayest be created again in a time of plenty?' No, no, my friend, we must trust the scheme."

"But the fools enjoy prosperity," said the Red Beadle.

"It is only a fool who *would* enjoy prosperity," replied Zussmann. "If the righteous sometimes suffer and the wicked sometimes flourish, that is just the very condition of virtue. What! would you have righteousness always pay and wickedness always fail! Where then would be the virtue in virtue? It would be a mere branch of commerce. Do you forget what the Chassid said of the man who foreknew in his lifetime that for him there was to be no heaven? 'What a unique and enviable chance that man had of doing right without fear of reward!' "

The Red Beadle, as usual, acquiesced in the idea that he had forgotten these quotations from the Hebrew, but to acquiesce in their teachings was another matter. "A man who had no hope of heaven would be a fool not to enjoy himself," he said doggedly, and went downstairs, his heart almost bursting. He went straight to his old synagogue, where he knew a *Hesped* or funeral service on a famous *Maggid* (preacher) was to be held. He could scarcely get in, so dense was the throng. Not a few eyes, wet with tears, were turned angrily on him as on a mocker come to gloat, but he hastened to weep too, which was easy when he thought of Hulda coughing in her bed in the garret. So violently did he weep that the *Gabbai* or treasurer—one of the most pious master-bootmakers—gave him the "Peace" salutation after the service.

"I did not expect to see you weeping," said he.

"Alas!" answered the Red Beadle. "It is not only the fallen Prince in Israel that I weep; it is my own transgressions that are brought home to me by his sudden end. How often have I heard him thunder and lighten from this very pulpit!" He heaved a deep sigh at his own hypocrisy, and the *Gabbai* sighed in response.

"Even from the grave the *Tsaddik* [saint] works good," said the pious master-bootmaker. "May my latter end be like his!"

"Mine, too!" suspired the Red Beadle. "How blessed am I not to have been cut off in my sin, denying the Maker of Nature!" They walked along the street together.

The next morning, at the luncheon hour, a breathless Beadle, with a red beard and a very red face, knocked joyously at the door of the Herz garret.

"I am in work again," he explained.

"*Mazzeltov!* Zussmann gave him the Hebrew congratulation, but softly, with finger on lip, to indicate Hulda was asleep. "With whom?"

"Harris the *Gabbai*."

"Harris! What, despite your opinions?"

The Red Beadle looked away. "So it seems!"

"Thank God!" said Hulda. "The Idea works."

Both men turned to the bed, startled to see her sitting up with a rapt smile.

"How so?" said the Red Beadle uneasily. "I am not a *Goy* [Christian] befriended by a *Gabbai*."

"No, but it is the brotherhood of humanity."

"Bother the brotherhood of humanity, Frau Herz!" said the Red

Beadle gruffly. He glanced round the denuded room. "The important thing is that you will now be able to have a few delicacies."

"*I?*" Hulda opened her eyes wide.

"Who else? What I earn is for all of us."

"God bless you!" said Zussmann; "but you have enough to do to keep yourself."

"Indeed he has!" said Hulda. "We couldn't dream of taking a farthing!" But her eyes were wet.

"I insist!" said the Red Beadle.

She thanked him sweetly, but held firm.

"I will advance the money on loan till Zussmann gets work."

Zussmann wavered, his eyes beseeching her, but she was inflexible.

The Red Beadle lost his temper. "And this is what you call the brotherhood of humanity!"

"He is right, Hulda. Why should we not take from one another? Pride perverts brotherhood."

"Dear husband," said Hulda, "it is not pride to refuse to rob the poor. Besides, what delicacies do I need? Is not this a land flowing with milk?"

"You take Cohen's milk and refuse my honey!" shouted the Red Beadle unappeased.

"Give me of the honey of your tongue and I shall not refuse it," said Hulda, with that wonderful smile of hers which showed the white teeth Nature had made; the smile which, as always, melted the Beadle's mood. That smile could repair all the ravages of disease and give back her memoried face.

After the Beadle had been at work a day or two in the *Gabbai*'s workshop, he broached the matter of a fellow-penitent, one Zussmann Herz, with no work and a bedridden wife.

"That *Meshummad!*" (apostate) cried the *Gabbai*. "He deserves all that God has sent him."

Undaunted, the Red Beadle demonstrated that the man could not be of the missionary camp, else had he not been left to starve, one converted Jew being worth a thousand pounds of fresh subscriptions. Moreover he, the Red Beadle, had now convinced the man of his spiritual errors, and *The Brotherhood of the Peoples* was no longer on sale. Also, being unable to leave his wife's bedside, Zussmann would do the work at home below the Union rates prevalent in public. So, trade being brisk, the *Gabbai* relented and bargained, and the Red Beadle sped to his friend's abode and flew up the four flights of stairs.

"Good news!" he cried. "The *Gabbai* wants another hand, and he is ready to take you."

"Me?" Zussmann was paralyzed with joy and surprise.

"Now will you deny that the Idea works?" cried Hulda, her face flushed and her eyes glittering. And she fell a-coughing.

"You are right, Hulda; you are always right," cried Zussmann, in responsive radiance. "Thank God! Thank God!"

"God forgive me," muttered the Red Beadle.

"Go at once, Zussmann," said Hulda. "I shall do very well here— this has given me strength. I shall be up in a day or two."

"No, no, Zussmann," said the Beadle hurriedly. "There is no need to leave your wife. I have arranged it all. The *Gabbai* does not want you to come there or to speak to him, because, though the Idea works in him, the other hands are not yet so large minded: I am to bring you the orders, and I shall come here to fetch them."

The set of tools to which Zussmann clung in desperate hope made the plan both feasible and pleasant.

And so the Red Beadle's visits resumed their ancient frequency even as his Sabbath clothes resumed their ancient gloss, and every week's end he paid over Zussmann's wages to him—full Union rate.

But Hulda, although she now accepted illogically the Red Beadle's honey in various shapes, did not appear to progress as much as the Idea, or as the new book which she stimulated Zussmann to start for its further propagation.

VI

One Friday evening of December, when miry snow underfoot and grayish fog all around combined to make Spitalfields a malarious marsh, the Red Beadle, coming in with the week's wages, found to his horror a doctor hovering over Hulda's bed like the shadow of death.

From the look that Zussmann gave him he saw a sudden change for the worse had set in. The cold of the weather seemed to strike right to his heart. He took the sufferer's limp chill hand.

"How goes it?" he said cheerily.

"A trifle weak. But I shall be better soon."

He turned away. Zussmann whispered to him that the doctor who had been called in that morning had found the crisis so threatening that he was coming again in the evening.

The Red Beadle, grown very white, accompanied the doctor downstairs, and learned that with care the patient might pull through.

The Beadle felt like tearing out his red beard. "And to think that I have not yet arranged the matter!" he thought distractedly.

He ran through the gray bleak night to the office of *The Flag of Judah;* but as he was crossing the threshold he remembered that it was the eve of the Sabbath, and that neither little Sampson nor anybody else would be there. But little Sampson *was* there, working busily.

"Hullo! Come in," he said, astonished.

The Red Beadle had already struck up a drinking acquaintanceship with the little journalist, in view of the great negotiation he was plotting. Not in vain did the proverbial wisdom of the Ghetto bid one beware of the red-haired.

"I won't keep you five minutes," apologized little Sampson. "But, you see, Christmas comes next week, and the compositors won't work. So I have to invent the news in advance."

Presently little Sampson, lighting an unhallowed cigarette by way of Sabbath lamp, and slinging on his shabby cloak, repaired with the Red Beadle to a restaurant, where he ordered "forbidden" food for himself and drinks for both.

The Red Beadle felt his way so cautiously and cunningly that the negotiation was unduly prolonged. After an hour or two, however, all was settled. For five pounds, paid in five monthly installments, little Sampson would translate *The Brotherhood of the Peoples* into English, provided the Beadle would tell him what the Hebrew meant. This the Beadle, from his loving study of Hulda's manuscript, was now prepared for. Little Sampson also promised to run the translation through *The Flag of Judah,* and thus the Beadle could buy the plates cheap for book purposes, with only the extra cost of printing such passages, if any, as were too dangerous for *The Flag of Judah.* This unexpected generosity, coupled with the new audience it offered the Idea, enchanted the Red Beadle. He did not see that the journalist was getting gratuitous "copy," he saw only the bliss of Hulda and Zussmann, and in some strange exaltation, compact of whisky and affection, he shared in their vision of the miraculous spread of the Idea, once it had got into the dominant language of the world.

In his gratitude to little Sampson he plied him with fresh whisky; in his excitement he drew the paper-covered book from his pocket, and insisted that the journalist must translate the first page then and there, as a hansel. By the time it was done it was near eleven o'clock.

Vaguely the Red Beadle felt that it was too late to return to Zuss-mann's to-night. Besides, he was liking little Sampson very much. They did not separate till the restaurant closed at midnight.

Quite drunk, the Red Beadle staggered towards Zussmann's house. He held the page of the translation tightly in his hand. The Hebrew original he had forgotten on the restaurant table, but he knew in some troubled nightmare way that Zussmann and Hulda must see that paper at once, that he had been charged to deliver it safely, and must die sooner than disobey.

The fog had lifted, but the heaps of snow were a terrible hindrance to his erratic progression. The cold air and the shock of a fall lessened his inebriety, but the imperative impulse of his imaginary mission still hypnotized him. It was past one before he reached the tall house. He did not think it at all curious that the great outer portals should be open; nor, though he saw the milk-cart at the door and noted Cohen's uncomfortable look, did he remember that he had discovered the milk-purveyor nocturnally infringing the Sabbath. He stumbled up the stairs and knocked at the garret door, through the chinks of which light streamed. The thought of Hulda smote him almost sober. Zuss-mann's face, when the door opened, restored him completely to his senses. It was years older.

"She is not dead?" the visitor whispered hoarsely.

"She is dying, I fear—she cannot rouse herself." Zussmann's voice broke in a sob.

"But she must not die—I bring great news—*The Flag of Judah* has read your book—it will translate it into English—it will print it in its own paper—and then it will make a book of it for you. See, here is the beginning!"

"Into English!" breathed Zussmann, taking the little journalist's scrawl. His whole face grew crimson, his eyes shone as with madness. "Hulda! Hulda!" he cried, "the Idea works! God be thanked! English! Through the world! Hulda! Hulda!" He was bending over her, raising her head.

She opened her eyes.

"Hulda! the Idea wins. The book is coming out in English. The great English paper will print it. In that day God shall be One and His name One. Do you understand?" Her lips twitched faintly, but only her eyes spoke with the light of love and joy. His own look met hers, and for a moment husband and wife were one in a spiritual ec-stasy.

Then the light in Hulda's eyes went out, and the two men were left in darkness.

The Red Beadle turned away and left Zussmann to his dead, and, with scalding tears running down his cheek, pulled up the cotton window blind and gazed out unseeing into the night.

Presently his vision cleared: he found himself watching the milk-cart drive off, and, following it towards the frowsy avenue of Brick Lane, he beheld what seemed to be a drunken fight in progress. He saw a policeman, gesticulating females, the nondescript nocturnal crowd of the sleepless city. The old dull hopelessness came over him. "Nature makes herself," he murmured in despairing resignation.

Suddenly he became aware that Zussmann was beside him, looking up at the stars.

CHRISTMAS EVE
ON LONESOME

by John Fox, Jr.

from *Christmas Eve on Lonesome and Other Stories*

It was Christmas Eve on Lonesome. But nobody on Lonesome knew that it was Christmas Eve, although a child of the outer world could have guessed it, even out in those wilds where Lonesome slipped from one lone log-cabin high up the steeps, down through a stretch of jungled darkness to another lone cabin at the mouth of the stream.

There was the holy hush in the gray twilight that comes only on Christmas Eve. There were the big flakes of snow that fell as they never fall except on Christmas Eve. There was a snowy man on horseback in a big coat, and with saddle-pockets that might have been bursting with toys for children in the little cabin at the head of the stream.

But not even he knew that it was Christmas Eve. He was thinking of Christmas Eve, but it was of Christmas Eve of the year before, when he sat in prison with a hundred other men in stripes, and listened to the chaplain talk of peace and good-will to all men upon earth, when he had forgotten all men upon earth but one, and had only hatred in his heart for him.

"Vengeance is mine!" saith the Lord.

That was what the chaplain had thundered at him. And then, as now, he thought of the enemy who had betrayed him to the law, and had sworn away his liberty, and had robbed him of everything in life except a fierce longing for the day when he could strike back and strike to kill. And then, while he looked back hard into the chaplain's eyes, and now, while he splashed through the yellow mud thinking of that Christmas Eve, Buck shook his head; and then, as now, his sullen heart answered, "Mine!"

The big flakes drifted to crotch and twig and limb. They gathered on the brim of Buck's slouch hat, filled out the wrinkles in his big coat, whitened his hair and his long mustache, and sifted into the yellow twisting path that guided his horse's feet.

High above he could see through the whirling snow now and then the gleam of a red star. He knew it was the light from his enemy's window; but somehow the chaplain's voice kept ringing in his ears, and every time he saw the light he couldn't help thinking of the story of the Star that the chaplain told that Christmas Eve, and he dropped his eyes by and by, so as not to see it again, and rode on until the light shone in his face.

Then he led his horse up a little ravine and hitched it among the snowy holly and rhododendrons, and slipped toward the light. There was a dog somewhere, of course; and like a thief he climbed over the low rail-fence and stole through the tall snow-wet grass until he leaned against an apple-tree with the sill of the window two feet above the level of his eyes.

Reaching above him, he caught a stout limb and dragged himself up to a crotch of the tree. A mass of snow slipped softly to the earth. The branch creaked above the light wind; around the corner of the house a dog growled and he sat still.

He had waited three long years and he had ridden two hard nights and lain out two cold days in the woods for this.

And presently he reached out very carefully, and noiselessly broke leaf and branch and twig until a passage was clear for his eye and for the point of the pistol that was gripped in his right hand.

A woman was just disappearing through the kitchen door, and he peered cautiously and saw nothing but darting shadows. From one corner a shadow loomed suddenly out in human shape. Buck saw the shadowed gesture of an arm, and he cocked his pistol. That shadow was his man, and in a moment he would be in a chair in the chimney-corner to smoke his pipe, maybe—his last pipe.

Buck smiled—pure hatred made him smile—but it was mean, a mean and sorry thing to shoot this man in the back, dog though he was; and now that the moment had come a wave of sickening shame ran through Buck. No one of his name had ever done that before; but this man and his people had, and with their own lips they had framed palliation for him. What was fair for one was fair for the other, they always said. A poor man couldn't fight money in the courts; and so they had shot from the brush, and that was why they were rich now and Buck was poor—why his enemy was safe at home, and he was out here, homeless, in the apple-tree.

Buck thought of all this, but it was no use. The shadow slouched suddenly and disappeared; and Buck was glad. With a gritting oath between his chattering teeth he pulled his pistol in and thrust one leg down to swing from the tree—he would meet him face to face next day and kill him like a man—and there he hung as rigid as though the cold had suddenly turned him, blood, bones, and marrow, into ice.

The door had opened, and full in the firelight stood the girl who he had heard was dead. He knew now how and why that word was sent him. And now she who had been his sweetheart stood before him—the wife of the man he meant to kill.

Her lips moved—he thought he could tell what she said: "Git up, Jim, git up!" Then she went back.

A flame flared up within him now that must have come straight from the devil's forge. Again the shadows played over the ceiling. His teeth grated as he cocked his pistol, and pointed it down the beam of light that shot into the heart of the apple-tree, and waited.

The shadow of a head shot along the rafters and over the fireplace. It was a madman clutching the butt of the pistol now, and as his eye caught the glinting sight and his heart thumped, there stepped into the square light of the window—a child!

It was a boy with yellow tumbled hair, and he had a puppy in his arms. In front of the fire the little fellow dropped the dog, and they began to play.

"Yap! yap! yap!"

Buck could hear the shrill barking of the fat little dog, and the joyous shrieks of the child as he made his playfellow chase his tail round and round or tumbled him head over heels on the floor. It was the first child Buck had seen for three years; it was *his* child and *hers*; and, in the apple-tree, Buck watched fixedly.

They were down on the floor now, rolling over and over together; and he watched them until the child grew tired and turned his face to the fire and lay still—looking into it. Buck could see his eyes close presently, and then the puppy crept closer, put his head on his playmate's chest, and the two lay thus asleep.

And still Buck looked—his clasp loosening on his pistol and his lips loosening under his stiff mustache—and kept looking until the door opened again and the woman crossed the floor. A flood of light flashed suddenly on the snow, barely touching the snow-hung tips of the apple-tree, and he saw her in the doorway—saw her look anxiously into the darkness—look and listen a long while.

Buck dropped noiselessly to the snow when she closed the door. He wondered what they would think when they saw his tracks in the snow next morning; and then he realized that they would be covered before morning.

As he started up the ravine where his horse was he heard the clink of metal down the road and the splash of a horse's hoofs in the soft mud, and he sank down behind a holly-bush.

Again the light from the cabin flashed out on the snow.

"That you, Jim?"

"Yep!"

And then the child's voice: "Has oo dot thum tandy?"

"Yep!"

The cheery answer rang out almost at Buck's ear, and Jim passed death waiting for him behind the bush which his left foot brushed, shaking the snow from the red berries down on the crouching figure beneath.

Once only—far down the dark jungled way, with the underlying streak of yellow that was leading him whither, God only knew—once only Buck looked back. There was the red light gleaming faintly through the moonlit flakes of snow. Once more he thought of the Star, and once more the chaplain's voice came back to him.

"Mine!" saith the Lord.

Just how, Buck could not see, with himself in the snow and *him* back there for life with her and the child, but some strange impulse made him bare his head.

"Yourn," said Buck grimly.

But nobody on Lonesome—not even Buck—knew that it was Christmas Eve.

THE CHRISTMAS MONKS

by Mary E. Wilkins Freeman

from *The Pot of Gold and Other Stories*

All children have wondered unceasingly from their very first Christmas up to their very last Christmas, where the Christmas presents come from. It is very easy to say that Santa Claus brought them. All well regulated people know that, of course; but the reindeer, and the sledge, and the pack crammed with toys, the chimney, and all the rest of it—that is all true, of course, and everybody knows about it; but that is not the question which puzzles. What children want to know is, where do these Christmas presents come from in the first place? Where does Santa Claus get them? Well the answer to that is, *In the garden of the Christmas Monks.* This has not been known until very lately; that is, it has not been known till very lately except in the immediate vicinity of the Christmas Monks. There, of course, it has been known for ages. It is rather an out-of-the-way place; and that accounts for our never hearing of it before.

The Convent of the Christmas Monks is a most charmingly picturesque pile of old buildings; there are towers and turrets, and peaked roofs and arches, and everything which could possibly be thought of in the architectural line, to make a convent picturesque. It is built of graystone; but it is only once in a while that you can see the graystone, for the walls are almost completely covered with mistletoe and ivy and evergreen. There are the most delicious little arched windows with diamond panes peeping out from the mistletoe and evergreen, and always at all times of the year, a little Christmas wreath of ivy and holly-berries is suspended in the center of every window. Over all the doors, which are likewise arched, are Christmas garlands, and over the main entrance *Merry Christmas* in evergreen letters.

The Christmas Monks are a jolly brethren; the robes of their order are white, gilded with green garlands, and they never are seen out at any time of the year without Christmas wreaths on their heads. Every morning they file in a long procession into the chapel, to sing a Christmas carol; and every evening they ring a Christmas chime on the convent bells. They eat roast turkey and plum pudding and mince-pie for dinner all the year round; and always carry what is left in baskets trimmed with evergreen, to the poor people. There are always wax candles lighted and set in every window of the convent at nightfall; and when the people in the country about get uncommonly blue and down-hearted, they always go for a cure to look at the Convent of the Christmas Monks after the candles are lighted and the chimes are ringing. It brings to mind things which never fail to cheer them.

But the principal thing about the Convent of the Christmas Monks is the garden; for that is where the Christmas presents grow. This garden extends over a large number of acres, and is divided into different departments, just as we divide our flower and vegetable gardens; one bed for onions, one for cabbages, and one for phlox, and one for verbenas, etc.

Every spring the Christmas Monks go out to sow the Christmas-present seeds after they have ploughed the ground and made it all ready.

There is one enormous bed devoted to rocking-horses. The rocking-horse seed is curious enough; just little bits of rocking-horses so small that they can only be seen through a very, very powerful microscope. The Monks drop these at quite a distance from each other, so that they will not interfere while growing; then they cover them up neatly with earth, and put up a sign-post with "Rocking-horses" on it in evergreen letters. Just so with the penny-trumpet seed, and the toy-furniture seed, the skate-seed, the sled-seed, and all the others.

Perhaps the prettiest and most interesting part of the garden is that devoted to wax dolls. There are other beds for the commoner dolls—for the rag dolls, and the china dolls, and the rubber dolls, but of course wax dolls would look much handsomer growing. Wax dolls have to be planted quite early in the season; for they need a good start before the sun is very high. The seeds are the loveliest bits of microscopic dolls imaginable. The Monks sow them pretty close together, and they begin to come up by the middle of May. There is first just a little glimmer of gold, or flaxen, or black, or brown as the case may be, above the soil. Then the snowy foreheads appear, and the blue eyes, and black eyes, and, later on, all those enchanting little heads are out of the ground, and are nodding and winking and smiling to each other the whole extent of the field; with their pinky cheeks and sparkling eyes and curly hair there is nothing so pretty as these little wax doll heads peeping out of the earth. Gradually, more and more of them come to light, and finally by Christmas they are all ready to gather. There they stand, swaying to and fro, and dancing lightly on their slender feet which are connected with the ground, each by a tiny green stem; their dresses of pink, or blue, or white—for their dresses grow with them—flutter in the air. Just about the prettiest sight in the world is the bed of wax dolls in the garden of the Christmas Monks at Christmas time.

Of course ever since this convent and garden were established (and that was so long ago that the wisest man can find no books about it) their glories have attracted a vast deal of admiration and curiosity from the young people in the surrounding country; but as the garden is enclosed on all sides by an immensely thick and high hedge, which no boy could climb, or peep over, they could only judge of the garden by the fruits which were parcelled out to them on Christmas-day.

You can judge, then, of the sensation among the young folks, and older ones, for that matter, when one evening there appeared hung upon a conspicuous place in the garden-hedge, a broad strip of white cloth trimmed with evergreen and printed with the following notice in evergreen letters:

WANTED: — *By Christmas Monks, two good boys to assist in garden work. Applicants will be examined by Fathers Anselmus and Ambrose, in the convent refectory, on April 10th.*

This notice was hung out about five o'clock in the evening, some time in the early part of February. By noon, the street was so full of boys staring at it with their mouths wide open, so as to see better, that the King was obliged to send his bodyguard before him to clear the way with brooms, when he wanted to pass on his way from his chamber of state to his palace.

There was not a boy in the country but looked upon this position as the height of human felicity. To work all the year in that wonderful garden, and see those wonderful things growing! and without doubt any boy who worked there could have all the toys he wanted, just as a boy who works in a candy-shop always has all the candy he wants!

But the great difficulty, of course, was about the degree of goodness requisite to pass the examination. The boys in this country were no worse than the boys in other countries, but there were not many of them that would not have done a little differently if he had only known beforehand of the advertisement of the Christmas Monks. However, they made the most of the time remaining, and were so good all over the kingdom that a very millennium seemed dawning. The school teachers used their ferrules for fire wood, and the King ordered all the birch-trees cut down and exported, as he thought there would be no more call for them in his own realm.

When the time for the examination drew near, there were two boys whom every one thought would obtain the situation, although some of the other boys had lingering hopes for themselves; if only the Monks would examine them on the last six weeks, they thought they might pass. Still all the older people had decided in their minds that the Monks would choose these two boys. One was the Prince, the King's oldest son; and the other was a poor boy named Peter. The Prince was no better than the other boys; indeed, to tell the truth, he was not so good; in fact, was the biggest rogue in the whole country; but all the lords and the ladies, and all the people who admired the lords and ladies, said it was their solemn belief that the Prince was the best boy in the whole kingdom; and they were prepared to give in their testimony, one and all, to that effect to the Christmas Monks.

Peter was really and truly such a good boy that there was no excuse for saying he was not. His father and mother were poor people; and Peter worked every minute out of school hours, to help them along. Then he had a sweet little crippled sister whom he was never tired of caring for. Then, too, he contrived to find time to do lots of little kindnesses for other people. He always studied his lessons faithfully, and never ran away from school. Peter was such a good boy, and so modest and unsuspicious that he was good, that everybody loved him. He had not the least idea that he could get the place with the Christmas Monks, but the Prince was sure of it.

When the examination day came all the boys from far and near, with their hair neatly brushed and parted, and dressed in their best clothes, flocked into the convent. Many of their relatives and friends went with them to witness the examination.

The refectory of the convent where they assembled was a very large hall with a delicious smell of roast turkey and plum pudding in it. All the little boys sniffed, and their mouths watered.

The two fathers who were to examine the boys were perched up in a high pulpit so profusely trimmed with evergreen that it looked like a bird's nest; they were remarkably pleasant-looking men, and their eyes twinkled merrily under their Christmas wreaths. Father Anselmus was a little the taller of the two, and Father Ambrose was a little the broader; and that was about all the difference between them in looks.

The little boys all stood up in a row, their friends stationed themselves in good places, and the examination began.

Then if one had been placed beside the entrance to the convent, he would have seen, one after another, a crestfallen little boy with his arm lifted up and crooked, and his face hidden in it, come out and walk forlornly away. He had failed to pass.

The two fathers found out that this boy had robbed birds' nests, and this one stolen apples. And one after another they walked disconsolately away till there were only two boys left: the Prince and Peter.

"Now, your Highness," said Father Anselmus, who always took the lead in the questions, "are you a good boy?"

"O holy Father!" exclaimed all the people—there were a good many fine folks from the court present. "He is such a good boy! such a wonderful boy! we never knew him to do a wrong thing."

"I don't suppose he ever robbed a bird's nest?" said Father Ambrose a little doubtfully.

"No, no!" chorused the people.

"Nor tormented a kitten?"

"No, no, no!" cried they all.

At last everybody being so confident that there could be no reasonable fault found with the Prince, he was pronounced competent to enter upon the Monks' service. Peter they knew a great deal about before—indeed a glance at his face was enough to satisfy any one of his goodness; for he did look more like one of the boy angels in the altar-piece than anything else. So after a few questions, they accepted him also; and the people went home and left the two boys with the Christmas Monks.

The next morning Peter was obliged to lay aside his homespun coat, and the Prince his velvet tunic, and both were dressed in some little white robes with evergreen girdles like the Monks. Then the Prince was set to sowing Noah's Ark seed, and Peter picture-book seed. Up and down they went scattering the seed. Peter sang a little psalm to himself, but the Prince grumbled because they had not given him gold-watch or gem seed to plant instead of the toy which he had outgrown long ago. By noon Peter had planted all his picture-books, and fastened up the card to mark them on the pole; but the Prince had dawdled so his work was not half done.

"We are going to have a trial with this boy," said the Monks to each other; "we shall have to set him a penance at once, or we cannot manage him at all."

So the Prince had to go without his dinner, and kneel on dried peas in the chapel all the afternoon. The next day he finished his Noah's Arks meekly; but the next day he rebelled again and had to go the whole length of the field where they planted jewsharps, on his knees. And so it was about every other day for the whole year.

One of the brothers had to be set apart in a meditating cell to invent new penances; for they had used up all on their list before the Prince had been with them three months.

The Prince became dreadfully tired of his convent life, and if he could have brought it about would have run away. Peter, on the contrary, had never been so happy in his life. He worked like a bee, and the pleasure he took in seeing the lovely things he had planted come up was unbounded, and the Christmas carols and chimes delighted his soul. Then, too, he had never fared so well in his life. He could never remember the time before when he had been a whole week without being hungry. He sent his wages every month to his parents; and he never ceased to wonder at the discontent of the Prince.

"They grow so slow," the Prince would say, wrinkling up his handsome forehead. "I expected to have a bushelful of new toys every month; and not one have I had yet. And these stingy old Monks say I can only have my usual Christmas share anyway, nor can I pick them out myself. I never saw such a stupid place to stay in in my life. I want to have my velvet tunic on and go home to the palace and ride on my white pony with the silver tail, and hear them all tell me how charming I am." Then the Prince would crook his arm and put his head on it and cry.

Peter pitied him, and tried to comfort him, but it was not of much use, for the Prince got angry because he was not discontented as well as himself.

Two weeks before Christmas everything in the garden was nearly ready to be picked. Some few things needed a little more December sun, but everything looked perfect. Some of the Jack-in-the-boxes would not pop out quite quick enough, and some of the jumping-Jacks were hardly as limber as they might be as yet; that was all. As it was so near Christmas the Monks were engaged in their holy exercises in the chapel for the greater part of the time, and only went over the garden once a day to see if everything was all right.

The Prince and Peter were obliged to be there all the time. There was plenty of work for them to do; for once in a while something would blow over, and then there were the penny-trumpets to keep in tune; and that was a vast sight of work.

One morning the Prince was at one end of the garden straightening up some wooden soldiers which had toppled over, and Peter was in the wax doll bed dusting the dolls. All of a sudden he heard a sweet little voice: "Oh, Peter!" He thought at first one of the dolls was talking, but they could not say anything but papa and mamma; and had the merest apologies for voices anyway. "Here I am, Peter!" and there was a little pull at his sleeve. There was his little sister. She was not any taller than the dolls around her, and looked uncommonly like the prettiest, pinkest-cheeked, yellowest-haired ones; so it was no wonder that Peter did not see her at first. She stood there poising herself on her crutches, poor little thing, and smiling lovingly up at Peter.

"Oh, you darling!" cried Peter, catching her up in his arms. "How did you get in here?"

"I stole in behind one of the Monks," said she. "I saw him going up the street past our house, and I ran out and kept behind him all the way. When he opened the gate I whisked in too, and then I followed him into the garden. I've been here with the dollies ever since."

"Well," said poor Peter, "I don't see what I am going to do with you, now you are here. I can't let you out again; and I don't know what the Monks will say."

"Oh, I know!" cried the little girl gayly. "I'll stay out here in the garden. I can sleep in one of those beautiful dolls' cradles over there; and you can bring me something to eat."

"But the Monks come out every morning to look over the garden, and they'll be sure to find you," said her brother, anxiously.

"No, I'll hide! Oh, Peter, here is a place where there isn't any doll!"

"Yes; that doll didn't come up."

"Well, I'll tell you what I'll do! I'll just stand here in this place where the doll didn't come up, and nobody can tell the difference."

"Well, I don't know but you can do that," said Peter, although he was still ill at ease. He was so good a boy he was very much afraid of doing wrong, and offending his kind friends the Monks; at the same time he could not help being glad to see his dear little sister.

He smuggled some food out to her, and she played merrily about him all day; and at night he tucked her into one of the dolls' cradles with lace pillows and quilt of rose-colored silk.

The next morning when the Monks were going the rounds, the father who inspected the wax doll bed was a bit nearsighted, and he never noticed the difference between the dolls and Peter's little sister, who swung herself on her crutches, and looked just as much like a wax doll as she possibly could. So the two were delighted with the success of their plan.

They went on thus for a few days, and Peter could not help being happy with his darling little sister, although at the same time he could not help worrying for fear he was doing wrong.

Something else happened now, which made him worry still more; the Prince ran away. He had been watching for a long time for an opportunity to possess himself of a certain long ladder made of twisted evergreen ropes, which the Monks kept locked up in the toolhouse. Lately, by some oversight, the toolhouse had been left unlocked one day, and the Prince got the ladder. It was the latter part of the afternoon, and the Christmas Monks were all in the chapel practicing Christmas carols. The Prince found a very large hamper, and picked as many Christmas presents for himself as he could stuff into it; then he put the ladder against the high gate in front of the convent, and climbed up, dragging the hamper after him. When he reached the top of the gate, which was quite broad, he sat down to rest for a moment before pulling the ladder up so as to drop it on the other side.

He gave his feet a little triumphant kick as he looked back at his prison, and down slid the evergreen ladder! The Prince lost his balance, and would inevitably have broken his neck if he had not clung desperately to the hamper which hung over on the convent side of the fence; and as it was just the same weight as the Prince, it kept him suspended on the other.

He screamed with all the force of his royal lungs; was heard by a party of noblemen who were galloping up the street; was rescued, and carried in state to the palace. But he was obliged to drop the hamper of presents, for with it all the ingenuity of the noblemen could not rescue him as speedily as it was necessary they should.

When the good Monks discovered the escape of the Prince they were greatly grieved, for they had tried their best to do well by him; and poor Peter could with difficulty be comforted. He had been very fond of the Prince, although the latter had done little except torment him for the whole year; but Peter had a way of being fond of folks.

A few days after the Prince ran away, and the day before the one on which the Christmas presents were to be gathered, the nearsighted father went out into the wax doll field again; but this time he had his spectacles on, and could see just as well as any one, and even a little better. Peter's little sister was swinging herself on her crutches, in the place where the wax doll did not come up, tipping her little face up, and smiling just like the dolls around her.

"Why, what is this!" said the father. "*Hoc credamo!* I thought that wax doll did not come up. Can my eyes deceive me? *Non verum est!* There is a doll there—and what a doll! on crutches, and in poor, homely gear!"

Then the nearsighted father put out his hand toward Peter's little sister. She jumped—she could not help it, and the holy father jumped too; the Christmas wreath actually tumbled off his head.

"It is a miracle!" exclaimed he when he could speak; "the little girl is alive! *parra puella viva est.* I will pick her and take her to the brethren, and we will pay her the honors she is entitled to."

Then the good father put on his Christmas wreath, for he dared not venture before his abbot without it, picked up Peter's little sister, who was trembling in all her little bones, and carried her into the chapel, where the Monks were just assembling to sing another carol. He went right up to the Christmas abbot, who was seated in a splendid chair, and looked like a king.

"Most holy abbot," said the nearsighted father, holding out Peter's little sister, "behold a miracle, *vide miraculum!* Thou wilt remember that there was one wax doll planted which did not come up. Behold, in her place I have found this doll on crutches, which is—alive!"

"Let me see her!" said the abbot; and all the other Monks crowded around, opening their mouths just like the little boys around the notice, in order to see better.

"*Verum est,*" said the abbot. "It is verily a miracle."

"Rather a lame miracle," said the brother who had charge of the funny picture-books and the toy monkeys; they rather threw his mind off its level of sobriety, and he was apt to make frivolous speeches unbecoming a monk.

The abbot gave him a reproving glance, and the brother who was the leach of the convent came forward. "Let me look at the miracle, most holy abbot," said he. He took up Peter's sister, and looked carefully at the small, twisted ankle. "I think I can cure this with my herbs and simples," said he.

"But I don't know," said the abbot doubtfully. "I never heard of curing a miracle."

"If it is not lawful, my humble power will not suffice to cure it," said the father who was the leach.

"True," said the abbot; "take her, then, and exercise thy healing art upon her, and we will go on with our Christmas devotions, for which we should now feel all the more zeal." So the father took away Peter's little sister, who was still too frightened to speak.

The Christmas Monk was a wonderful doctor, for by Christmas Eve the little girl was completely cured of her lameness. This may seem incredible, but it was owing in great part to the herbs and simples, which are of a species that our doctors have no knowledge of; and also to a wonderful lotion which has never been advertised on our fences.

Peter of course heard the talk about the miracle, and knew at once what it meant. He was almost heartbroken to think he was deceiving the Monks so, but at the same time he did not dare to confess the truth for fear they would put a penance upon his sister, and he could not bear to think of her having to kneel upon dried peas.

He worked hard picking Christmas presents, and hid his unhappiness as best he could. On Christmas Eve he was called into the chapel. The Christmas Monks were all assembled there. The walls were covered with green garlands and boughs and sprays of hollyberries, and branches of wax lights were gleaming brightly amongst them. The altar and the picture of the Blessed Child behind it were so bright as to almost dazzle one; and right up in the midst of it, in a lovely white dress, all wreaths and jewels, in a little chair with a canopy woven of green branches over it, sat Peter's little sister.

And there were all the Christmas Monks in their white robes and wreaths, going up in a long procession, with their hands full of the very showiest Christmas presents to offer them to her!

But when they reached her and held out the lovely presents—the first was an enchanting wax doll, the biggest beauty in the whole garden—instead of reaching out her hands for them, she just drew back, and said in her little sweet, piping voice: "Please, I ain't a millacle, I'm only Peter's little sister."

"Peter?" said the abbot, "the Peter who works in our garden?"

"Yes," said the little sister.

Now here was a fine opportunity for a whole convent full of monks to look foolish—filing up in procession with their hands full of gifts to offer to a miracle, and finding there was no miracle, but only Peter's little sister.

But the abbot of the Christmas Monks had always maintained that there were two ways of looking at all things; if any object was not what you wanted it to be in one light, that there was another light in which it would be sure to meet your views.

So now he brought this philosophy to bear.

"This little girl did not come up in the place of the wax doll, and she is not a miracle in that light," said he; "but look at her in another light and she is a miracle—do you not see?"

They all looked at her, the darling little girl, the very meaning and sweetness of all Christmas in her loving, trusting, innocent face.

"Yes," said all the Christmas Monks, "she is a miracle." And they all laid their beautiful Christmas presents down before her.

Peter was so delighted he hardly knew himself; and, oh! the joy there was when he led his little sister home on Christmas-day, and showed all the wonderful presents.

The Christmas Monks always retained Peter in their employ—in fact he is in their employ to this day. And his parents, and his little sister who was entirely cured of her lameness, have never wanted for anything.

As for the Prince, the courtiers were never tired of discussing and admiring his wonderful knowledge of physics which led to his adjusting the weight of the hamper of Christmas presents to his own so nicely that he could not fall. The Prince liked the talk and the admiration well enough, but he could not help, also, being a little glum; for he got no Christmas presents that year.

THE CHRISTMAS TREE

by Mary Austin

from *The Basket Woman: A Book of Fanciful Tales for Children*

Eastward from the Sierras rises a strong red hill known as Pinc Mountain, though the Indians call it The Hill of Summer Snow. At its foot stands a town of a hundred board houses, given over wholly to the business of mining. The noise of it goes on by day and night—the creak of the windlasses, the growl of the stamps in the mill, the clank of the cars running down to the dump, and from the open doors of the drinking saloons, great gusts of laughter and the sound of singing. Billows of smoke roll up from the tall stacks and by night are lit ruddily by the smelter fires all going at a roaring blast.

Whenever the charcoal-burner's son looked down on the red smoke, the glare, and the hot breath of the furnaces, it seemed to him like an exhalation from the wickedness that went on continually in the town; though all he knew of wickedness was the word, a rumor from passers-by, and a kind of childish fear. The charcoal-burner's cabin stood on a spur of Pine Mountain two thousand feet above the town, and sometimes the boy went down to it on the back of the laden burros when his father carried charcoal to the furnaces. All else that he knew were the wild creatures of the mountain, the trees, the storms, the small flowering things, and away at the back of his heart a pale memory of his mother like the faint forest odor that clung to the black embers of the pine. They had lived in the town when the mother was alive and the father worked in the mines. There were not many women or children in the town at that time, but mining men jostling with rude quick ways; and the young mother was not happy.

"Never let my boy grow up in such a place," she said as she lay dying; and when they had buried her in the coarse shallow soil, her husband looked for comfort up toward The Hill of Summer Snow shining purely, clear white and quiet in the sun. It swam in the upper air above the sooty reek of the town and seemed as if it called. Then he took the young child up to the mountain, built a cabin under the tamarack pines, and a pit for burning charcoal for the furnace fires.

No one could wish for a better place for a boy to grow up in than the slope of Pine Mountain. There was the drip of pine balm and a wind like wine, white water in the springs, and as much room for roaming as one desired. The charcoal-burner's son chose to go far, coming back with sheaves of strange bloom from the edge of snow banks on the high ridges, bright spar or peacock-painted ores, hatfuls of berries, or strings of shining trout. He played away whole mornings in glacier meadows where he heard the eagle scream; walking some- times in a mist of cloud, he came upon deer feeding, or waked them from their lair in the deep fern. On snow-shoes in winter he went over the deep drifts and spied among the pine tops on the sparrows, the grouse, and the chilly robins wintering under the green tents. The deep snow lifted him up and held him among the second stories of the trees. But that was not until he was a great lad, straight and springy as a young fir. As a little fellow he spent his days at the end of a long rope staked to a pine just out of reach of the choppers and the char- coal-pits. When he was able to go about alone, his father made him give three promises: never to follow a bear's trail nor meddle with the cubs, never to try to climb the eagle rocks after the young eagles, never to lie down nor to sleep on the sunny, south slope where the rattle- snakes frequented. After that he was free of the whole wood.

When Mathew, for so the boy was called, was ten years old, he began to be of use about the charcoal-pits, to mark the trees for cut- ting, to sack the coals, to keep the house, and cook his father's meals.

He had no companions of his own age nor wanted any, for at this time he loved the silver firs. A group of them grew in a swale below the cabin, tall and fine; the earth under them was slippery and brown with needles. Where they stood close together with overlapping boughs the light among the tops was golden green, but between the naked boles it was a vapor thin and blue. These were the old trees that had wagged their tops together for three hundred years. Around them stood a ring of saplings and seedlings scattered there by the parent firs, and a little apart from these was the one that Mathew loved. It was slender of trunk and silvery white, the branches spread out fanwise to the outline of a perfect spire. In the spring, when the young growth covered it as with a gossamer web, it gave out a pleasant odor, and it was to him like the memory of what his mother had been. Then he garlanded it with flowers and hung streamers of white clematis all heavy with bloom upon its boughs. He brought it berries in cups of bark and sweet water from the spring; always as long as he knew it, it seemed to him that the fir tree had a soul.

The first trip he had ever made on snow-shoes was to see how it fared among the drifts. That was always a great day when he could find the slender cross of its topmost bough above the snow. The fir was not very tall in those days, but the snows as far down on the slope as the charcoal-burner's cabin lay shallowly. There was a time when Mathew expected to be as tall as the fir, but after a while the boy did not grow so fast and the fir kept on adding its whorl of young branches every year.

Mathew told it all his thoughts. When at times there was a heaviness in his breast which was really a longing for his mother, though he did not understand it, he would part the low spreading branches and creep up to the slender trunk of the fir. Then he would put his arms around it and be quiet for a long beautiful time. The tree had its own way of comforting him; the branches swept the ground and shut him in dark and close. He made a little cairn of stones under it and kept his treasures there.

Often as he sat snuggled up to the heart of the tree, the boy would slip his hand over the smooth intervals between the whorls of boughs, and wonder how they knew the way to grow. All the fir trees are alike in this, that they throw out their branches from the main stem like the rays of a star, one added to another with the season's growth. They stand out stiffly from the trunk, and the shape of each new bough in the beginning and the shape of the last growing twig when they have spread out broadly with many branchlets, bending with the weight of their own needles, is the shape of a cross; and the topmost sprig that rises above all the star-built whorls is a long and slender cross, until by the springing of new branches it becomes a star. So the two forms go on running into and repeating each other, and each star is like all the stars, and every bough is another's twin. It is this trim and certain growth that sets out the fir from all the mountain trees, and gives to the young saplings a secret look as they stand straight and stiffly among the wild brambles on the hill. For the wood delights to grow abroad at all points, and one might search a summer long without finding two leaves of the oak alike, or any two trumpets of the spangled mimulus. So, as at that time, he had nothing better worth studying about, Mathew noticed and pondered the secret of the silver fir, and grew up with it until he was twelve years old and tall and strong for his age. By this time the charcoal-burner began to be troubled about the boy's schooling.

Meantime there was rioting and noise and coming and going of strangers in the town at the foot of Pine Mountain, and the furnace blast went on ruddily and smokily. Because of the things he heard Mathew was afraid, and on rare occasions when he went down to it he sat quietly among the charcoal sacks, and would not go far away from them except when he held his father by the hand. After a time it seemed life went more quietly there, flowers began to grow in the yards of the houses, and they met children walking in the streets with books upon their arms.

"Where are they going, father?" said the boy.

"To school," said the charcoal-burner.

"And may I go?" asked Mathew.

"Not yet, my son."

But one day his father pointed out the foundations of a new building going up in the town.

"It is a church," he said, "and when that is finished it will be a sign that there will be women here like your mother, and then you may go to school."

Mathew ran and told the fir tree all about it.

"But I will never forget you, never," he cried, and he kissed the trunk. Day by day, from the spur of the mountain, he watched the church building, and it was wonderful how much he could see in that clear, thin atmosphere; no other building in town interested him so much. He saw the walls go up and the roof, and the spire rise skyward with something that glittered twinkling on its top. Then they painted the church white and hung a bell in the tower. Mathew fancied he could hear it of Sundays as he saw the people moving along like specks in the streets.

"Next week," said the father, "the school begins, and it is time for you to go as I promised. I will come to see you once a month, and when the term is over you shall come back to the mountain." Mathew said good-by to the fir tree, and there were tears in his eyes though he was happy. "I shall think of you very often," he said, "and wonder how you are getting along. When I come back I will tell you everything that happens. I will go to church, and I am sure I shall like that. It has a cross on top like yours, only it is yellow and shines. Perhaps when I am gone I shall learn why you carry a cross, also." Then he went a little timidly, holding fast by his father's hand.

There were so many people in the town that it was quite as strange and fearful to him as it would be to you who have grown up in town to be left alone in the wood. At night, when he saw the charcoal-burner's fires glowing up in the air where the bulk of the mountain melted into the dark, he would cry a little under the blankets, but after he began to learn, there was no more occasion for crying. It was to the child as though there had been a candle lighted in a dark room. On Sunday he went to the church, and then it was both light and music, for he heard the minister read about God in the great book and believed it all, for everything that happens in the wood is true, and people who grow up in it are best at believing. Mathew thought it was all as the minister said, that there is nothing better than pleasing God. Then when he lay awake at night he would try to think how it would have been with him if he had never come to this place. In his heart he began to be afraid of the time when he would have to go back to the mountain, where there was no one to tell him about this most important thing in the world, for his father never talked to him of these things. It preyed upon his mind, but if any one noticed it, they thought that he pined for his father and wished himself at home.

It drew toward midwinter, and the white cap on The Hill of Summer Snow, which never quite melted even in the warmest weather, began to spread downward until it reached the charcoal-burner's home. There was a great stir and excitement among the children, for it had been decided to have a Christmas tree in the church. Every Sunday now the Christ-child story was told over and grew near and brighter like the Christmas star. Mathew had not known about it before, except that on a certain day in the year his father had bought him toys. He had supposed that it was because it was stormy and he had to be indoors. Now he was wrapped up in the story of love and sacrifice, and felt his heart grow larger as he breathed it in, looking upon clear windless nights to see if he might discern the Star of Bethlehem rising over Pine Mountain and the Christ-child come walking on the snow. It was not that he really expected it, but that the story was so alive in him. It is easy for those who have lived long in the high mountains to believe in beautiful things. Mathew wished in his heart that he might never go away from this place. He sat in his seat in church, and all that the minister said sank deeply into his mind.

When it came time to decide about the tree, because Mathew's father was a charcoal-burner and knew where the best trees grew, it was quite natural to ask him to furnish the tree for his part. Mathew fairly glowed with delight, and his father was pleased, too, for he liked to have his son noticed. The Saturday before Christmas, which fell on Tuesday that year, was the time set for going for the tree, and by that time Mathew had quite settled in his mind that it should be his silver fir. He did not know how otherwise he could bring the tree to share in his new delight, nor what else he had worth giving, for he quite believed what he had been told, that it is only through giving the best beloved that one comes to the heart's desire. With all his heart Mathew wished never to live in any place where he might not hear about God. So when his father was ready with the ropes and the sharpened axe, the boy led the way to the silver firs.

"Why, that is a little beauty," said the charcoal-burner, "and just the right size."

They were obliged to shovel away the snow to get at it for cutting, and Mathew turned away his face when the chips began to fly. The tree fell upon its side with a shuddering sigh; little beads of clear resin stood out about the scar of the axe. It seemed as if the tree wept. But how graceful and trim it looked when it stood in the church waiting for gifts! Mathew hoped that it would understand.

The charcoal-burner came to church on Christmas eve, the first time in many years. It makes a difference about these things when you have a son to take part in them. The church and the tree were alight with candles; to the boy it seemed like what he supposed the place of dreams might be. One large candle burned on the top of the tree and threw out pointed rays like a star; it made the charcoal-burner's son think of Bethlehem. Then he heard the minister talking, and it was all of a cross and a star; but Mathew could only look at the tree, for he saw that it trembled, and he felt that he had betrayed it. Then the choir began to sing, and the candle on top of the tree burned down quite low, and Mathew saw the slender cross of the topmost bough stand up dark before it. Suddenly he remembered his old puzzle about it, how the smallest twigs were divided off in each in the shape of a cross, how the boughs repeated the star form every year, and what was true of his fir was true of them all. Then it must have been that there were tears in his eyes, for he could not see plainly: the pillars of the church spread upward like the shafts of the trees, and the organ playing was like the sound of the wind in their branches, and the stately star-built firs rose up like spires, taller than the church tower, each with a cross on top. The sapling which was still before him trembled more, moving its boughs as if it spoke; and the boy heard it in his heart and believed, for it spoke to him of God. Then all the fear went out of his heart and he had no more dread of going back to the mountain to spend his days, for now he knew that he need never be away from the green reminder of hope and sacrifice in the star and the cross of the silver fir; and the thought broadened in his mind that he might find more in the forest than he had ever thought to find, now that he knew what to look for, since everything speaks of God in its own way and it is only a matter of understanding how.

It was very gay in the little church that Christmas night, with laughter and bonbons flying about, and every child had a package of candy and an armful of gifts. The charcoal-burner had his pockets bulging full of toys, and Mathew's eyes glowed like the banked fires of the charcoal-pits as they walked home in the keen, windless night.

"Well, my boy," said the charcoal-burner, "I am afraid you will not be wanting to go back to the mountain with me after this."

"Oh, yes, I will," said Mathew happily, "for I think the mountains know quite as much of the important things as they know here in the town."

"Right you are," said the charcoal-burner, as he clapped his boy's hand between both his own, "and I am pleased to think you have turned out such a sensible little fellow." But he really did not know all that was in his son's heart.

CHRISTMAS;
OR, THE GOOD FAIRY

by Harriet Beecher Stowe

from *Stories, Sketches and Studies*

"Oh, *dear!* Christmas is coming in a fortnight, and I have got to think up presents for everybody!" said young Ellen Stuart, as she leaned languidly back in her chair. "Dear me, it's so tedious! Everybody has got everything that can be thought of."

"Oh, no," said her confidential adviser, Miss Lester, in a soothing tone. "You have means of buying everything you can fancy; and when every shop and store is glittering with all manner of splendors, you cannot surely be at a loss."

"Well, now, just listen. To begin with, there's mamma. What can I get for her? I have thought of ever so many things. She has three card cases, four gold thimbles, two or three gold chains, two writing desks of different patterns; and then as to rings, brooches, boxes, and all other things, I should think she might be sick of the sight of them. I am sure I am," said she, languidly gazing on her white and jeweled fingers.

This view of the case seemed rather puzzling to the adviser, and there was silence for a few minutes, when Ellen, yawning, resumed:

"And then there's cousins Jane and Mary; I suppose they will be coming down on me with a whole load of presents; and Mrs. B. will send me something—she did last year; and then there's cousins William and Tom—I must get them something; and I would like to do it well enough, if I only knew what to get."

"Well," said Eleanor's aunt, who had been sitting quietly rattling her knitting needles during this speech, "it's a pity that you had not such a subject to practice on as I was when I was a girl. Presents did not fly about in those days as they do now. I remember, when I was ten years old, my father gave me a most marvelously ugly sugar dog for a Christmas gift, and I was perfectly delighted with it, the very idea of a present was so new to us."

"Dear aunt, how delighted I should be if I had any such fresh, unsophisticated body to get presents for! But to get and get for people that have more than they know what to do with now; to add pictures, books, and gilding when the centre tables are loaded with them now, and rings and jewels when they are a perfect drug! I wish myself that I were not sick, and sated, and tired with having everything in the world given me."

"Well, Eleanor," said her aunt, "if you really do want unsophisticated subjects to practice on, I can put you in the way of it. I can show you more than one family to whom you might seem to be a very good fairy, and where such gifts as you could give with all ease would seem like a magic dream."

"Why, that would really be worth while, aunt."

"Look over in that back alley," said her aunt. "You see those buildings?"

"That miserable row of shanties? Yes."

"Well, I have several acquaintances there who have never been tired of Christmas gifts or gifts of any other kind. I assure you, you could make quite a sensation over there."

"Well, who is there? Let us know."

"Do you remember Owen, that used to make your shoes?"

"Yes, I remember something about him."

"Well, he has fallen into a consumption, and cannot work any more; and he, and his wife, and three little children live in one of the rooms."

"How do they get along?"

"His wife takes in sewing sometimes, and sometimes goes out washing. Poor Owen! I was over there yesterday; he looks thin and wasted, and his wife was saying that he was parched with constant fever, and had very little appetite. She had, with great self-denial, and by restricting herself almost of necessary food, got him two or three oranges; and the poor fellow seemed so eager after them."

"Poor fellow!" said Eleanor, involuntarily.

"Now," said her aunt, "suppose Owen's wife should get up on Christmas morning and find at the door a couple of dozen of oranges, and some of those nice white grapes, such as you had at your party last week; don't you think it would make a sensation?"

"Why, yes, I think very likely it might; but who else, aunt? You spoke of a great many."

"Well, on the lower floor there is a neat little room, that is always kept perfectly trim and tidy; it belongs to a young couple who have nothing beyond the husband's day wages to live on. They are, nevertheless, as cheerful and chipper as a couple of wrens; and she is up and down half a dozen times a day, to help poor Mrs. Owen. She has a baby of her own about five months old, and of course does all the cooking, washing, and ironing for herself and husband; and yet, when Mrs. Owen goes out to wash, she takes her baby, and keeps it whole days for her."

"I'm sure she deserves that the good fairies should smile on her," said Eleanor; "one baby exhausts my stock of virtues very rapidly."

"But you ought to see her baby," said Aunt E.; "so plump, so rosy, and good-natured, and always clean as a lily. This baby is a sort of household shrine; nothing is too sacred or too good for it; and I believe the little thrifty woman feels only one temptation to be extravagant, and that is to get some ornaments to adorn this little divinity."

"Why, did she ever tell you so?"

"No; but one day, when I was coming down stairs, the door of their room was partly open, and I saw a peddler there with open box. John, the husband, was standing with a little purple cap on his hand, which he was regarding with mystified, admiring air, as if he didn't quite comprehend it, and trim little Mary gazing at it with longing eyes.

" 'I think we might get it,' said John.

" 'Oh, no,' said she, regretfully; 'yet I wish we could, it's so pretty!' "

"Say no more, aunt. I see the good fairy must pop a cap into the window on Christmas morning. Indeed, it shall be done. How they will wonder where it came from, and talk about it for months to come!"

"Well, then," continued her aunt, "in the next street to ours there is a miserable building, that looks as if it were just going to topple over; and away up in the third story, in a little room just under the eaves, live two poor, lonely old women. They are both nearly on to ninety. I was in there day before yesterday. One of them is constantly confined to her bed with rheumatism; the other, weak and feeble, with failing sight and trembling hands, totters about, her only helper; and they are entirely dependent on charity."

"Can't they do anything? Can't they knit?" said Eleanor.

"You are young and strong, Eleanor, and have quick eyes and nimble fingers; how long would it take you to knit a pair of stockings?"

"I?" said Eleanor. "What an idea! I never tried, but I think I could get a pair done in a week, perhaps."

"And if somebody gave you twenty-five cents for them, and out of this you had to get food, and pay room rent, and buy coal for your fire, and oil for your lamp—"

"Stop, aunt, for pity's sake!"

"Well, I will stop; but they can't: they must pay so much every month for that miserable shell they live in, or be turned into the street. The meal and flour that some kind person sends goes off for them just as it does for others, and they must get more or starve; and coal is now scarce and high priced."

"O aunt, I'm quite convinced, I'm sure; don't run me down and annihilate me with all these terrible realities. What shall I do to play good fairy to these old women?"

"If you will give me full power, Eleanor, I will put up a basket to be sent to them that will give them something to remember all winter."

"Oh, certainly I will. Let me see if I can't think of something myself."

"Well, Eleanor, suppose, then, some fifty or sixty years hence, if you were old, and your father, and mother, and aunts, and uncles, now so thick around you, lay cold and silent in so many graves—you have somehow got away off to a strange city, where you were never known—you live in a miserable garret, where snow blows at night through the cracks, and the fire is very apt to go out in the old cracked stove—you sit crouching over the dying embers the evening before Christmas—nobody to speak to you, nobody to care for you, except another poor old soul who lies moaning in the bed. Now, what would you like to have sent you?"

"O aunt, what a dismal picture!"

"And yet, Ella, all poor, forsaken old women are made of young girls, who expected it in their youth as little as you do, perhaps."

"Say no more, aunt. I'll buy—let me see—a comfortable warm shawl for each of these poor women; and I'll send them—let me see—oh, some tea—nothing goes down with old women like tea; and I'll make John wheel some coal over to them; and, aunt, it would not be a very bad thought to send them a new stove. I remember, the other day, when mamma was pricing stoves, I saw some such nice ones for two or three dollars."

"For a new hand, Ella, you work up the idea very well," said her aunt.

"But how much ought I to give, for any one case, to these women, say?"

"How much did you give last year for any single Christmas present?"

"Why, six or seven dollars for some; those elegant souvenirs were seven dollars; that ring I gave Mrs. B. was twenty."

"And do you suppose Mrs. B. was any happier for it?"

"No, really, I don't think she cared much about it; but I had to give her something, because she had sent me something the year before, and I did not want to send a paltry present to one in her circumstances."

"Then, Ella, give the same to any poor, distressed, suffering creature who really needs it, and see in how many forms of good such a sum will appear. That one hard, cold, glittering ring, that now cheers nobody, and means nothing, that you give because you must, and she takes because she must, might, if broken up into smaller sums, send real warm and heartfelt gladness through many a cold and cheerless dwelling, through many an aching heart."

"You are getting to be an orator, aunt; but don't you approve of Christmas presents, among friends and equals?"

"Yes, indeed," said her aunt, fondly stroking her head. "I have had some Christmas presents that did me a world of good—a little book mark, for instance, that a certain niece of mine worked for me, with wonderful secrecy, three years ago, when she was not a young lady with a purse full of money—that book mark was a true Christmas present; and my young couple across the way are plotting a profound surprise to each other on Christmas morning. John has contrived, by an hour of extra work every night, to lay by enough to get Mary a new calico dress; and she, poor soul, has bargained away the only thing in the jewelry line she ever possessed, to be laid out on a new hat for him.

"I know, too, a washerwoman who has a poor lame boy—a patient, gentle little fellow—who has lain quietly for weeks and months in his little crib, and his mother is going to give him a splendid Christmas present."

"What is it, pray?"

"A whole orange! Don't laugh. She will pay ten whole cents for it; for it shall be none of your common oranges, but a picked one of the very best going! She has put by the money, a cent at a time, for a whole month; and nobody knows which will be happiest in it, Willie or his mother. These are such Christmas presents as I like to think of —gifts coming from love, and tending to produce love; these are the appropriate gifts of the day."

"But don't you think that it's right for those who *have* money to give expensive presents, supposing always, as you say, they are given from real affection?"

"Sometimes, undoubtedly. The Saviour did not condemn her who broke an alabaster box of ointment—very precious—simply as a proof of love, even although the suggestion was made, 'This might have been sold for three hundred pence, and given to the poor.' I have thought he would regard with sympathy the fond efforts which human love sometimes makes to express itself by gifts, the rarest and most costly. How I rejoiced with all my heart, when Charles Elton gave his poor mother that splendid Chinese shawl and gold watch! because I knew they came from the very fulness of his heart to a mother that he could not do too much for—a mother that has done and suffered everything for him. In some such cases, when resources are ample, a costly gift seems to have a graceful appropriateness; but I cannot approve of it if it exhausts all the means of doing for the poor; it is better, then, to give a simple offering, and to do something for those who really need it."

Eleanor looked thoughtful; her aunt laid down her knitting, and said, in a tone of gentle seriousness, "Whose birth does Christmas commemorate, Ella?"

"Our Saviour's, certainly, aunt."

"Yes," said her aunt. "And when and how was he born? In a stable! laid in a manger; thus born, that in all ages he might be known as the brother and friend of the poor. And surely, it seems but appropriate to commemorate his birthday by an especial remembrance of the lowly, the poor, the outcast, and distressed; and if Christ should come back to our city on a Christmas day, where should we think it most appropriate to his character to find him? Would he be carrying splendid gifts to splendid dwellings, or would he be gliding about in the cheerless haunts of the desolate, the poor, the forsaken, and the sorrowful?"

And here the conversation ended.

"What sort of Christmas presents is Ella buying?" said Cousin Tom, as the servant handed in a portentous-looking package, which had been just rung in at the door.

"Let's open it," said saucy Will. "Upon my word, two great gray blanket shawls! These must be for you and me, Tom! And what's this? A great bolt of cotton flannel and gray yarn stockings!"

The door bell rang again, and the servant brought in another bulky parcel, and deposited it on the marble-topped centre table.

"What's here?" said Will, cutting the cord. "Whew! a perfect nest of packages! Oolong tea! oranges! grapes! white sugar! Bless me, Ella must be going to housekeeping!"

"Or going crazy!" said Tom; "and on my word," said he, looking out of the window, "there's a drayman ringing at our door, with a stove, with a teakettle set in the top of it!"

"Ella's cook stove, of course," said Will; and just at this moment the young lady entered, with her purse hanging gracefully over her hand.

"Now, boys, you are too bad!" she exclaimed, as each of the mischievous youngsters was gravely marching up and down, attired in a gray shawl.

"Didn't you get them for us? We thought you did," said both.

"Ella, I want some of that cotton flannel, to make me a pair of pantaloons," said Tom.

"I say, Ella," said Will, "when are you going to housekeeping? Your cooking stove is standing down in the street; 'pon my word, John is loading some coal on the dray with it."

"Ella, isn't that going to be sent to my office?" said Tom; "do you know I do so languish for a new stove with a teakettle in the top, to heat a fellow's shaving-water!"

Just then, another ring at the door, and the grinning servant handed in a small brown paper parcel for Miss Ella. Tom made a dive at it, and tearing off the brown paper, discovered a jaunty little purple velvet cap, with silver tassels.

"My smoking cap, as I live!" said he; "only I shall have to wear it on my thumb, instead of my head—too small entirely," said he, shaking his head gravely.

"Come, you saucy boys," said Aunt E., entering briskly. "What are you teasing Ella for?"

"Why, do see this lot of things, aunt! What in the world is Ella going to do with them?"

"Oh, I know!"

"You know! Then I can guess, aunt, it is some of your charitable works. You are going to make a juvenile Lady Bountiful of El, eh?"

Ella, who had colored to the roots of her hair at the *exposé* of her very unfashionable Christmas preparations, now took heart, and bestowed a very gentle and salutary little cuff on the saucy head that still wore the purple cap, and then hastened to gather up her various purchases.

"Laugh away," said she, gayly; "and a good many others will laugh, too, over these things. I got them to make people laugh—people that are not in the habit of laughing!"

"Well, well, I see into it," said Will; "and I tell you I think right well of the idea, too. There are worlds of money wasted, at this time of the year, in getting things that nobody wants, and nobody cares for after they are got; and I am glad, for my part, that you are going to get up a variety in this line; in fact, I should like to give you one of these stray leaves to help on," said he, dropping a ten dollar note into her paper. "I like to encourage girls to think of something besides breastpins and sugar candy."

But our story spins on too long. If anybody wants to see the results of Ella's first attempts at *good fairyism*, they can call at the doors of two or three old buildings on Christmas morning, and they shall hear all about it.

A CHRISTMAS EVE SURPRISE

by Lilian Quiller-Couch

from *The Canadian Magazine*
of Politics, Science, Art and Literature

"White silk, rich enough to stand by itself, my dear, with the loveliest pink roses all over it, and the beautifullest little pink shoes. 'Liza, hurry with that can of hot water."

Mrs. Bassom took the can from the flustered 'Liza and bustled upstairs to the imperious little lady who in the space of twenty-four hours had turned the sober farmhouse and farm minds upside down, and bewitched the lot of them.

Never had the guest-chamber of Wendry Farm been the scene of such feminine luxury and loveliness as on this bleak November evening; nor had it, probably, ever held a more brilliant young creature than the one standing before the mirror in a wonderful dressing-gown of lawn and lace. She was polishing her pretty nails with scented powder, as Mrs. Bassom bustled in with her relay of warm water.

"Thanks, Mrs. Bassom, you good soul!" exclaimed the impetuous young beauty. "I don't deserve one-half your pretty attention, coming here a stranger, and haymaking in your tidy home. Just tepid, please, with a dash of perfume from that biggest bottle. And about the carriage. Has Jenkins had luck?"

"No, miss, that he hasn't," said Mrs. Bassom, deprecatingly. "He says every mortal thing with a wheel to it is bespoke. And I misdoubt me if you'd get a fly even if you were to scour the country for a score of miles."

"I'd get it sure enough if 'twere only a score of miles stopping me," declared the young lady. "Well, Mrs. Bassom, to go to Sir Verlin Tranter's ball I'm determined, if I have to go in a wheelbarrow. Hasn't your good husband himself something better than that—a haycart, a threshing machine, anything with wheels?"

"Oh, miss, if you ain't set on having a fly, John, he shall drive you in our gig—"

"Bless your comforting heart! The gig, of course. There's a freezing, howling wind that will sear my complexion and nearly tear off my hair; but I'll put my head in a bandbox rather than stay away. Depend on it, Mrs. Bassom, this noble action will lift you and your good husband one rung farther up the ladder to Heaven—"

"Oh, miss! What things you do say!"

"Shocked? Never mind! Help me into my finery; and if ever you saw a lovelier sight than I shall be when I'm ready you'd better not tell me so."

As the blustering north wind tore round the house and wailed at the corners, and the road lay white and dry as bleached bones between Wendry Farm and Haselton Hall, Farmer Bassom harnessed his briskest horse to the gig. The young beauty upstairs put the last touches to her toilette, exclaiming at the finish, "I quite agree with your eyes, Mrs. Bassom. I do think I'm the handsomest thing I've seen for many a long day!"

She was right in her admiration if the opinion of the majority counts for anything; for not only could she read it in Mrs. Bassom's eyes, but in those of the gaping 'Liza, in those of Farmer Bassom too, and, with a thrill of excitement and triumph, in the many questioning eyes turned upon her when, her journey over and her wraps discarded, she followed an astonished footman to the brilliant reception room of Haselton Hall.

At the doorway there was a dramatic pause before the man, with an uncontrollable glance of questioning wonder at his master, announced: "Miss Evelyn Tranter!"

The name, when it did come, brought amazement deep on the faces near. It was as if the nerves in the room became tense as the brilliant figure, in its pink and white bravery, with waving black hair and sparkling dark eyes, stepped up to the fair, childish-looking hostess standing beside her father, Sir Verlin, and cordially took the hand which was instinctively, though hesitatingly, held out.

"I am pleased to meet you," said the newcomer, in a brisk, business-like voice. "I am your cousin from California—Evelyn—Tranter's daughter."

"My cousin!" repeated the amazed young hostess, not realizing the full importance of the words. A good-looking young man standing near unconsciously made a step forward, as if protectingly. Then both Mary Tranter and the Californian turned towards Sir Verlin.

For a short breathless period the baronet and the stranger, who had never met before, looked at one another as if measuring swords were more natural under the circumstances than shaking hands. The face of the beauty became stern and accusing; that of the aristocratic, dignified man remained unmoved in feature, but grew white to the lips. With the swiftness of a man of the world he realized the ruin which the words meant, if they were true; the insult to his guests, his entertainment and himself, if they were false.

"We have never met before, Sir Verlin," the girl said at last, with cool deliberateness, "but I thought I might venture to join your party by right of a relative in a strange land."

"All," replied Sir Verlin, with cold politeness, "who bear my name are welcome to my hospitality. Allow me to escort you to a seat." He offered his arm in courtesy instead of his hand in friendship, and, all eyes following them, they walked together down the long room.

"You won't shake hands with me, I see," began Evelyn Tranter bluntly. "Well, you must do as you like. You oughtn't to blame me for existing, but it seems to me I can blame you pretty thoroughly for sitting down quietly in my rightful home without taking the trouble to find out that I did, and do, exist. Ninety-nine out of a hundred would say that I've shown hideously bad taste in coming here tonight. But I do as I like; and I'd a fancy to see you before I begin to fight you."

She certainly did not veil her intentions, this outspoken young colonial. Sir Verlin bowed stiffly as he endeavoured to adapt his reserved nature to the awful truth and these unusual methods of conversational attack.

"Whoever you may be," he said, frigidly, "you have chosen to come here at a time ill-fitted for discussion. But all women, I trust, may count on courtesy at Haselton Hall." Then he indicated a chair, bowed again, and left her.

But the difficulties of Sir Verlin's position, even the immediate ones, were not to be so easily disposed of. The Californian was beautiful and alluring in a quite unusual style; and were young and impressionable men to leave these charms severely alone in a big chair? Introductions were sought, and Sir Verlin was harassed. The question of conduct was a delicate one. He knew nothing of this girl, and was he to undertake her introduction to his own circle? On the other hand, if she should prove to be his blood relation—!

Evelyn Tranter, sitting alone where he had left her, was keenly alive to the situation. Indeed her entire attention was occupied by four persons—Sir Verlin; his daughter Mary; the young man who had stepped forward as if to protect Mary Tranter from the newcomer who claimed cousinship; and another young man, well-dressed, talkative and handsome, who seemed to be all in all to the young hostess—so Evelyn Tranter thought—and did not object to the position. With quick eyes and brain, the Californian noted and weighed signs and facts, and was not altogether unprepared to see Sir Verlin, after ineffectual evasions and some inward debate, approach the first-mentioned man and bear him down the room towards herself.

"Allow me to introduce Mr. Hargrave," said Sir Verlin in his unbending manner. "He will escort you to the ball-room."

If Mr. Hargrave had feared there would be difficulty in conversing with this embarrassing young intruder, he was mistaken. She saved him all trouble.

"You are a friend of the family, and you have relieved Sir Verlin in an awkward predicament," she began.

Mr. Hargrave was taken aback, and tried to find words.

"Oh, don't mind me," she continued. "I understand Sir Verlin's trials. But—I've a heavy score against him."

"Indeed!"

"Yes, indeed!" she retorted. "We speak out plainer in California than you do in England, and I now feel that I have a right to ask why my father was left to die in poverty when this wealth was his, and why I am sitting here a stranger when the very chair is probably my own. I know you're thinking 'how unladylike' for me to talk so at once and to

you. How Californian! But I'm of English blood, and it has something to do with you, too, for I've taken a liking for Mary Tranter, and
you—you're in love with her."

"Really—!" he began, in angry protest.

"It's no use getting angry. You must just take it that I'm different
from you English-born, and that I've guessed a thing or two. We're
spry, you know, out there. Now, I can tell you that you won't be any
the worse for my coming. You're a bit poorish, aren't you?"

Mr. Hargrave's sense of humour came to his aid.

"Not rich enough," he answered.

"I saw that. But there's a man over there who is—and yet the lady
does not look the sort to be bought—"

"We will not discuss the lady, if you please."

"There's your English stiffness again. Bless your heart, I don't want
to say anything unkind of her. What I say is, you both want her at
present, and he has a better background, and the lady—"

"If you must mention the lady, I say she has a right to take a man if
she loves him."

"Yes, and she does think she loves him. Now, if you will help me—"

"Do you expect me—" he began hotly.

"I expect you to do nothing," she replied calmly, "but thank me
when you are engaged—which you will probably forget to do. If I read
Mr. Popinjay aright—"

"Whose name is Aredale," he interposed.

"Mr. Popinjay Aredale," she corrected herself—"my task won't be
difficult."

"Perhaps you wish me to introduce him to you," he suggested
rather bitterly.

"No, thanks," she answered. "There will be no need to trouble you,
you'll see. Now we will go to the ball-room, please, and I'll tell you, for
your comfort, that you wouldn't have been a bad sort if you'd had the
luck to be born our side the water—and without starch."

No one present ever forgot Mary Tranter's coming-of-age ball.
Looking back afterwards, it stood out as a turning point in many lives.
A witch in white silk and pink roses had danced among them—dancing the hearts and senses out of the men and wonder and pain into
the hearts of women. It was not all the witch's fault. There were but
two men occupying her attention—one, Sir Verlin, she wished to pain;
the other, Charles Aredale, merely to engage the attention of, to fur-

ther a new scheme for the future good of a girl whose face had attracted her, and who, for some time, at least, would certainly not thank her for her interference.

On Mary Tranter's face surprise turned to swift, keen pain. She could not quite realize that this night of nights was to hold the death-hour of her happiness—that the man who had heretofore sought her, whom she loved, had deserted her, but she knew that she was heart-sick and miserable as her eyes followed Aredale and the Californian. She asked herself in anguish—"What does it all mean?"

Many asked that question as they watched the trend of events, for the whisper quickly went from ear to ear that this girl was the daughter of Evelyn Tranter, Sir Verlin's elder brother, and there were many to shake their heads and declare they always felt sure that the efforts to trace Evelyn Tranter had been quite inadequate. Then the girl herself! She was enough to bewitch a nation. And Aredale! From the moment he had caught sight of her, entering the ball-room on Hargrave's arm, and had felt her dark eyes upon him, he had lost his head under the spell of her charm. The hours which to Mary Tranter —who should have been queen of the night, to whom he had paid marked devotion for months—were leaden-footed, intolerable, were to him as swift moments of delight. First the stranger's beauty had drawn him; then her well-told story had gripped his cautious nature. Charles Aredale was rich, but he was also bourgeois, and he knew the value of position. If Mary Tranter were to be penniless, if this girl were heiress in her own right—!

Of all the eager men, Aredale was the favoured one. Dance followed dance, and laughter mingled with low-toned confidences. "The man's bewitched," the others laughed enviously. "The girl is daringly unconventional," they suggested.

They were confirmed in their opinion. When the ball was over, those who were in the hall heard Aredale dismiss Farmer Bassom's gig, and himself insist upon driving the beautiful stranger back to her lodging. As the two drove from the lamplight into the darkness Mary Tranter's anguished eyes were following them, and the first flakes of snow were beginning to fall.

Next morning the news thrilled through the snow-covered village and country-side, and robbed the blizzard of all its importance. Who could think of a snow-storm in face of the tidings that Mr. Evelyn's own daughter had come, and that Sir Verlin was not the rightful master of the Hall?

As for Farmer Bassom and his good wife, they stared at one another in dismay. They, Sir Verlin's oldest tenants were harbouring the claimant to his property! It was terrible! Yet they had always loved Mr. Evelyn best as a lad—and if this should be his daughter— The facts overwhelmed them; they left words and fell to staring again.

On Evelyn Tranter's coming upon them in passing through the hall, Farmer Bassom fled in cowardly haste, and left his wife to face the outspoken young lady.

"Come, I know what it's all about, Mrs. Bassom. You've heard the tale; and you don't know whether to turn me into the snow or not. Look at that," she said, drawing the good woman to the window and pointing to the white world outside, "then come to my room and listen."

Seated before the blazing fire, wrapped in a bewitching morning-gown, Evelyn Tranter told her tale, and told it well. There were tears in her own eyes as well as in those of Mrs. Bassom, as the story of two sisters was unfolded, of their hardships, struggles, neglect and poverty, till worn out with the fight for existence, the younger sister had died.

"When I think of that," the girl cried out, all the laughter gone from her now, "when I think that if she had had her rights she might be with me this moment, I feel I must make the man suffer, in revenge for our sufferings. Do you wonder?"

No, Mrs. Bassom did not wonder, her motherly heart was too soft for that. "But it'll be a hard job to turn out Sir Verlin," she said.

"I begin to-day," said the claimant determinedly. "Meanwhile, do you mean to turn me out into that very cold garden, when I'm so happy here?"

No, Mrs. Bassom didn't see how she could. It would seem strange to Sir Verlin, she was afraid; but there really wasn't another place in the village where she liked to think of Miss Evelyn settling in.

"And I should die wandering about in the snow," said the beauty plaintively. Which remark seemed to settle the matter.

Except to Mr. Aredale and Mrs. Bassom, Evelyn Tranter did not tell her story, but while Mary Tranter sat in her boudoir with tragic, tear-stained eyes brooding over her heartache; while Sir Verlin sat in his study with gray-lined face, admitting, with inward groan and fear, the inadequacy of his enquiries as to his brother's death and heirship; while Percy Hargrave strode restlessly along snowy roads chafing under the pain which he knew was being inflicted on the girl he loved, and the pain yet in store for her—the cruelty of her lover and the threatened loss of her home; while the self-satisfied Mr. Aredale was lounging in a luxurious chair smoking cigarettes, rereading his ball programme, and planning a fresh meeting with the bewitching Californian, the bewitching Californian herself was writing to her lawyers, taking the first steps towards establishing her claim to Haselton Hall.

As the December days wore on, events moved quickly. For the outside world there were merely rumours for the imaginations to feed on, rumours which grew vastly in the telling; but for those more nearly concerned, things were far more serious. Miss Evelyn Tranter's papers and proofs wore a decidedly genuine appearance, her statements were straightforward and faithful in detail, and although Sir Verlin's solicitors smiled tolerantly as they listened, and took on the air of those who indulgently bear with fairy stories for the sake of humouring a child, they could bring no definite contradiction, and were forced to fall back at once upon the question of identification.

And Evelyn Tranter had her desire; she was making Sir Verlin suffer. Those who knew him best could note the suffering most keenly, though he strove to maintain his usual calm, and almost irritably desired no changes to be shown, no signs betrayed.

In this way the time wore on towards Christmas. "Such a happy Christmas it was to have been," sobbed Mary Tranter in girlish self-pity, as she and her friends had talked of skating, dancing and feasting for rich and poor, and Aredale had been always at her side seconding and suggesting, and Hargrave had worked to carry out her wishes. And now! "Why did she come!" she moaned with childish inconsistency, seeing only her own troubles, and not realizing that there might be right on the other side, too.

It was while she was in this mood that Sir Verlin sent for her. The news from his solicitors that morning had struck a warning note. The claimant's proofs were being followed up with somewhat disquieting results, and the sight of his daughter's tear-stained face, added to his gnawing anxiety, chafed him into irritability, and he spoke sharply. His mind was too full of the threatened loss of home and position for him to realize that his daughter had a private sorrow of her own.

"There must be no showing of the white feather, I beg," he began. "This strange young woman is putting me to great anxiety and expense, and indeed we have real difficulties before us. I—I will not deny that the news this morning is bad. But for Heaven's sake don't let us go about looking as if we had stolen Haselton. I sent for you to desire that you follow your ordinary occupations, that you do not mope and show the world we are afraid. Let everything go forward as we had planned. We are within a few days of Christmas; remember it is my especial wish that Christmas shall be kept up with more than usual merriment. Do you understand?"

"Yes, papa," the girl answered dully, even while her heart was crying out, "What do I care for appearances, or lands, or money when my heart is broken!"

When, the interview being over, she re-crossed the hall, she came face to face with Hargrave.

Mary Tranter was a very simple English girl, young and silly perhaps, wearing her heart on her sleeve, lacking dignity; but she was miserably unhappy, and Hargrave loved her so devotedly, that her white, hopeless face now broke down his reserve.

"Come out," he said, in a sudden, commanding voice which she scarcely recognized; and wrapping a big cloak about her, he led the way to the terrace, whither she followed without interest or protest.

"Mary dear, it isn't worth all this," he urged. She had known him so long and so well that she never doubted to what he referred. He, Percy, would understand that she cared little that the stranger should take her home; but her lover—!

"Can I help that?" she asked wildly.

"You love him, dear?"

She bowed her head. "He never asked me—" she began—"but I thought—"

"Of course you did. He's—"

"Don't, don't," she implored. "He is good; it is she— Oh, I'm tortured!"

"I know that torture," he said quietly.

"You know!" she shook her head, with a sad, incredulous smile.

"I have been tortured for many months," he persisted.

For a moment she forgot herself. "Who has tortured you?" she demanded.

"You have," he answered quietly. "—You and Aredale."

It was good for her to know this now, he knew; it would rouse her.

"Do you mean that you—"

"I love you; and I know every pang you are feeling; and I know it is so hard to bear, and I love you so dearly that I would gladly go on with the torture if you might be spared it."

She paused, trying to realize the sudden revelation.

"I like to feel that," she said at length, slowly, unconscious of her great selfishness. "Fancy your loving me—in that way, I never thought of it. You know—I can never—"

"Yes dear, I know."

"You are good, Percy," she said with a sigh; the sigh sounded heartbroken—nevertheless she felt somewhat comforted.

They had left the terrace and turned towards the lodge gate, walking slowly now, each thinking of the tangle of their lives. He, as usual, was thinking of her; she, as was unusual, was giving some of her thoughts to him.

The sound of merry voices at last roused them. They had unthinkingly neared the road, on the other side of which lay a big straggling pond, now frozen many inches thick.

With a swift return to the present, Mary Tranter's cheeks paled with foreboding, and hurrying up a little slope which commanded the scene, she looked eagerly, fearfully down at the merry-makers. As Hargrave reached her side, her wide, excited eyes had lighted on what she had dreaded to see. With a little moan, like that of a hurt child, she turned and held her hand to him, as Aredale and Evelyn Tranter skimmed over the ice before them, hand in hand.

"You are going to be brave," he whispered. "I want you to be brave."

For the few remaining days before Christmas, Mary Tranter tried to obey her father's commands and imitate Hargrave's fortitude. Under the latter's escort, she walked each morning, white-faced, but smiling, over the frozen snow to join the merry-making at the pond. Her teeth were set hard behind her lips, but her heart—! It was like exposing a raw wound to a goad, to skim by the couple on whom all her thoughts would dwell.

Above and beyond Aredale's infatuation for the vivacious, beautiful claimant, the cautiousness handed down to him by his forefathers warned him that to indulge his "little fancy," as he had come to term it, for Mary Tranter would be madness under the circumstances, even had he still wished to; while the heiress of Haselton Hall was a prudent choice. Whoever might slight Evelyn Tranter before her claim was proved, he, Charles Aredale, was not the man to do so. He had satisfied himself of the strength of her claim, and he followed her as a shadow; her somewhat cavalier treatment of him serving only to fire his passion.

On the morning of Christmas Eve, Mary Tranter, still striving for her new bravery, rose from table determined to be outwardly cheerful, if only for the sake of others. The gray anxiety which crept over Sir Verlin's face as he read his letters struck on her with some realization of his sorrow. He would need all her help these days.

There was much to be done, for many guests were to fill the house to overflowing this night—so many that the dinners were to be held in the hall and barn instead of the dining-room; for rich and poor were to feast at Haselton on this first Christmas of the heiress's coming of age. There were, too, gifts and alms to be set ready—so much had been neglected lately—decorations were to be organized, and rooms prepared.

The snow had ceased falling for many days; the ground was white and hard, the cold was exhilarating. In the huge fireplaces the logs were blazing, the walls gradually grew bright with holly and shining evergreens, the smell of good cheer from the kitchen regions was wafted to the more dignified passages whenever opportunity was allowed, which in the cheerful bustle of preparation was not infrequent.

So the hours passed, and the pain in Mary's heart fought for the mastery as she went about her work. Then the short day closed in, and the anguish tore her fictitious courage to tatters. Trembling in every limb, she turned to fly to the solitude of her own room, and caught sight of Sir Verlin, standing in silence in the glowing hall, looking round it with the look of a man stricken at heart. Then she saw him turn with a groan and enter his study.

Impulsively she ran to him; but he waved her back.

That action seemed to be the last straw in her burden. She did not guess that the strong, self-sufficient man was fearful of breaking down; she saw only the stern forbidding, and she shrank back quivering under the repulse.

No one wanted her—lover, happiness, home, father—nothing was left. Why should she strive and suffer and bear torture. No one cared. The world was empty, cold, bitter. With strained, glittering eyes she turned from the closed door, and leaving the brightness and merriment, went out into the snow. She knew—she would end it all. When he knew, perhaps he would be sorry.

Tears of misery and self-pity poured down her cheeks. Over the hard snow, the cracking ice-pool, across the road—she knew—it was in the near corner the ice had been broken for the cattle. Ugh! It would be cold and black, and—

"Mary Tranter! What are you going to do?"

Mary Tranter turned on the figure, which suddenly appeared beside her.

"I am going to do what you have driven me to," she cried wildly. "I am going to end it all, and you shall not stop me."

For long moments Evelyn Tranter stood there on the ice, in the darkening day, with the lonely white country round her, shaken to the very foundations of her nature, appalled by the work she had done, yet gripping with a grip of iron the desperate girl she had followed.

Evelyn Tranter, however, was not the girl to lose her self-possession at a crisis. Her voice when she next spoke was shaken and strained, but her tones were calm.

"You must tell me what you mean," she commanded; "there is some mistake."

"There is no mistake. You have taken my lover, my home, my happiness. What good is life to me?"

"Hush!" said Evelyn Tranter gently. "Listen. I have not taken your lover really, if you will but believe me. Your real lover is a brave gentleman, devoted to you, and worth your love. The man you are unhappy about—ah, let me tell you, you never loved him. You looked at his handsome face—"

"Oh!" angrily.

"No. I don't mean to insult you. You looked, and your good, pure heart gave him qualities he never had. You loved the man you thought Charles Aredale to be. You couldn't love the man he is— ready to fly to the latest face; ready to foreswear his love when it is prudent to do so. Think of him as dead, my dear; I swear to you he never lived. And I vow I never loved or wanted him."

The arm which had been straining under Evelyn's grip grew slack; the wild gleam died from Mary's eyes and a new light dawned in them as she strained to see her companion's face in the darkness.

"As to your home," continued Evelyn, "I have not taken that either. Go there now, and dress yourself in all your bravery for the night's feasting."

Puzzled, distracted, confused, Mary Tranter gazed in silence.

"You must," continued the other, "for I am coming again uninvited to Haselton Hall. And I shall have something to say to you and your father. Go straight back now and prepare, and in an hour's time I will come to you."

In an hour's time Sir Verlin, raising his bowed head, saw before him his daughter in her shining white gown and as he had first seen her, the Californian in her pink and white bravery. In wrath and amazement he rose.

"Sir Verlin," began the visitor, raising her hand as if to avert his wrath. "I have come to tell you a story—and a piece of news."

He bowed haughtily and waited.

"It is Christmas," she went on with a brave, ringing voice. "The season of peace and good-will. Will you bear that in mind and will you listen?"

"Yes," he said, wearily, the wrath dying somewhat and chiefly the old anxiety remaining.

Then Evelyn told her story—the story of an exiled heir, sent, wild, reckless, and extravagant, by a stern, unbending father to a wild, lawless country. The struggles, the hot, unforgiving pride, the growth in manliness and character, the sweetness of temper of this exile; of his work, his love, his marriage.

Of the two listeners one was eager-eyed and excited, the other as yet stern and untouched.

"Those were not unhappy days," continued the girl, "but when the adored wife died leaving two little girls to the heart-broken father, the world seemed black indeed. He strove to work on, but the light had gone out of his life. Far afield he wandered to seek work and distraction, faithfully sending back such small sums as he could earn for the maintenance of the children. But it soon ended; he had no wish to live, and he died."

There were tears in her voice as she went on to tell of the hardships of these little children, fallen among hard task-masters in a rough land; of the patience, the delicacy of the younger sister, the passionate anguish of the elder who watched her die.

"It was then—then, when a few days after her death the old, travel-stained papers proving Evelyn Tranter's heirship came back from his mates to my hands, that I vowed by all the sufferings of my dead sister, that I would bring to those who might have prevented it some of the pain they had made her bear. For a whole year I was forced to live on in poverty and helplessness; then money came to me, abundance of money, one of those turns of fortune we know more of in my country than you do in yours—from a rough gold-digging uncle, dying without wife or child; and I started, telling no one, on my mission of revenge."

Sir Verlin's face had pity on it by this time, mingling with his pride and resentment.

"Well," he said, at last, "you have fulfilled your vow. You are having your revenge. You have merely to prove the truth of your statements. What, then, do you want here to-night? To gloat over your success?"

"I came for two things—the story to explain my action, I have told you—but the piece of news—"

She moved close to them, her eyes were glittering. The listeners stood as if under her spell.

"I," she said, slowly, "was only a step-daughter of Evelyn Tranter. My mother was secretly married before, though no one knew it but her second husband. I have no right here whatever. Indeed, I am sorry now for my anger. It can do my sister no good. I have come to give you this knowledge now as my Christmas gift."

It was the brilliant stranger now who broke down, burying her face in her hands. It was Sir Verlin, helped by Mary Tranter, who comforted.

That night there was joy indeed at Haselton Hall, and not a little amazement, too; for in all the feasting and gladness the witch who had danced into their midst a month ago, danced again now with a happy face and a gay word for every one; and it was clear to all eyes that between herself and her host and hostess there was perfect goodwill and accord.

The only absentee was Mr. Charles Aredale, to whom Miss Evelyn had sent a letter of explanation earlier in the evening.

It was a Christmas to be long remembered. The night of gloom had lifted, the dawn of good-feeling was bright. Even Mary found that there was something comforting in Percy Hargrave's love and attention, which she had not noticed before it had been pointed out to her.

"But you, you yourself?" she asked, as she stood aside once with her new friend, looking out on the snow and listening to the clashing, clanging bells. "When you leave us, must you be lonely and sad?"

"Not a bit," declared Evelyn. "My own faithful lover has traced me out at last and followed me, and I have every hope that good Mrs. Bassom is at this moment declaring to him that hot negus is quite the best thing after a long journey. Let me dance out of your lives as I danced into them, feeling that I have done you no real harm but, perhaps, a little good." She looked at Mary with a question in her eyes.

"I believe you may have been right," replied Mary, gravely, but not sadly. "I think it is possible that I may have made a mistake. You will think me fickle, of course, but—"

"No, I don't think you fickle, my dear," declared the pink and white witch mischievously, "only suffering from a bad dream, and now awaking—awaking just in time, too, for a merry Christmas, and a New Year, the like of which you've never known before."

SHAKESPEARE'S CHRISTMAS

by "Q" (A. T. Quiller-Couch)

from *Shakespeare's Christmas and Other Stories*

> *And moreover, at this Fair there is at all times to be seen Jugglings, Cheats, Games, Plays, Fools, Apes, Knaves, and Rogues, and that of every kind. . . . Now, as I said, the way to the Celestial City lies just through this town, where this lusty Fair is kept; and he that will go to the City, and yet not go through this Town, must needs go out of the World.*
>
> —BUNYAN

I

At the theatre in Shoreditch, on Christmas Eve, 1598, the Lord Chamberlain's servants presented a new comedy. Never had the Burbages played to such a house. It cheered every speech—good, bad, or indifferent. To be sure, some of the *dramatis personæ*—Prince Hal and Falstaff, Bardolph and Mistress Quickly—were old friends; but this alone would not account for such a welcome. A cutpurse in the twopenny gallery who had been paid to lead the applause gave up toiling in the wake of it, and leaned back with a puzzled grin.

"Bravo, master!" said he to his left-hand neighbour, a burly, red-faced countryman well past middle age, whose laughter kept the bench rocking. "But have a care, lest they mistake you for the author!"

"The author? Ho-ho!" But here he broke off to leap to his feet and lead another round of applause. "The author?" he repeated, dropping back and glancing an eye sidelong from under his handkerchief while he mopped his brow. "You shoot better than you know, my friend: the bolt grazes. But a miss, they say, is as good as a mile."

The cutpurse kept his furtive grin, but was evidently mystified. A while before it had been the countryman who showed signs of bewilderment. Until the drawing of the curtains he had fidgeted nervously, then, as now, mopping his forehead in despite of the raw December air. The first shouts of applause had seemed to astonish as well as delight him. When, for example, a player stepped forward and flung an arm impressively towards heaven while he recited, "When we mean to build, We first survey the plot, then draw the model," and so paused with a smile, his voice drowned in thunder from every side of the house, our friend had rubbed his eyes and gazed around in amiable protest, as who should say, "Come, come . . . but let us discriminate!" By-and-by, however, as the indifferent applause grew warmer, he warmed with it. At the entrance of Falstaff he let out a bellowing laugh worthy of Olympian Jove, and from that moment led the house. The fops on the sixpenny stools began to mimic, the pit and lower gallery to crane necks for a sight of their fugleman; a few serious playgoers called to have him pitched out; but the mass of the audience backed him with shouts of encouragement. Some wag hailed him as "Burbage's Landlord," and apparently there was meaning, if not merit, in the jest. Without understanding it he played up to it royally, leaning forward for each tally-ho! and afterwards waving his hat as a huntsman laying on his hounds.

The pace of the performance (it had begun at one o'clock) dragged sensibly with all this, and midway in Act IV., as the edge of a grey river-fog overlapped and settled gradually upon the well of the unroofed theatre, voices began to cough and call for lanterns. Two lackeys ran with a dozen. Some they hung from the balcony at the back, others they disposed along both sides of the stage, in front of the sixpenny stools, the audience all the while chaffing them by their Christian names and affectionately pelting them with nuts. Still the fog gathered, until the lantern-rays criss-crossed the stage in separate shafts, and among them the actors moved through Act V. in a luminous haze, their figures looming large, their voices muffled and incredibly remote.

An idle apprentice, seated on the right of the cutpurse, began for a game to stop and unstop his ears. This gave the cutpurse an opportunity to search his pockets. *Cantat vacuus*: the apprentice felt him at it and went on with his game. Whenever he stopped his ears the steaming breath of the players reminded him of the painted figures he had seen carried in my Lord Mayor's Show, with labels issuing from their mouths.

He had stopped his ears during the scene of King Henry's reconciliation with Chief Justice Gascoigne, and unstopped them eagerly again when his old friends reappeared—Falstaff and Bardolph and Pistol, all agog and hurrying, hot-foot, boot-and-saddle, to salute the rising sun of favour. "Welcome these pleasant days!" He stamped and clapped, following his neighbours' lead, and also because his feet and hands were cold.

Eh? What was the matter? Surely the fog had taken hold of the rogues! What was happening to Mistress Quickly and Doll Tearsheet? Poor souls, they were but children: they had meant no harm. For certain this plaguy fog was infecting the play; and yet, for all the fog, the play was a play no longer, but of a sudden had become savagely real. Why was this man turning on his puppets and rending them? The worst was, they bled—not sawdust, but real blood.

The apprentice cracked a nut and peeled it meditatively, with a glance along the bench. The countryman still fugled; the cutpurse cackled, with lips drawn back like a wolf's, showing his yellow teeth.

"Hist, thou silly knave!" said the apprentice. "Canst not see 'tis a tragedy?"

The rascal peered at him for a moment, burst out laughing, and nudged the countryman.

"Hi, master! Breeds your common at home any such goose as this, that cannot tell tickling from roasting?"

The apprentice cracked another nut. "Give it time," he answered. "I said a tragedy. Yours, if you will, my friend; his too, may be"—with a long and curious stare at the countryman.

II

My tongue is weary: when my legs are too, I will bid you good night: and so kneel down before you; but indeed to pray for the Queen.

Play, epilogue, dance, all were over; the curtains drawn, the lanterns hidden behind them. The cutpurse had slipped away, and the countryman and apprentice found themselves side by side waiting while the gallery dissolved its crowd into the fog.

"A brisk fellow," remarked the one, nodding at the vacant seat as he stowed away his handkerchief. "But why should he guess me a rustic?"

"The fellow has no discernment," the apprentice answered dryly. "He even took the play for a merry one."

The countryman peered forward into the young-old face silhouetted against the glow which, cast upward and over the curtain-rod across the stage, but faintly reached the gallery.

"I love wit, Sir, wherever I meet it. For a pint of sack you shall prove me this play a sad one, and choose your tavern!"

"I thank you, but had liefer begin and discuss the epilogue: and the epilogue is 'Who's to pay?' "

"A gentleman of Warwickshire, Master What-d'ye-lack—will that content you? A gentleman of Warwickshire, with a coat-of-arms, or the College's promise—which, I take it, amounts to the same thing." The countryman puffed his cheeks.

"So-so?" The apprentice chuckled.

"When we mean to build, We first survey the plot, then search our pockets. How goes it? Either so, or to that effect."

"The devil!" The countryman, who had been fumbling in his breek pockets, drew forth two hands blankly, spreading empty fingers.

"That was your neighbour, Sir: a brisk fellow, as you were clever enough to detect, albeit unserviceably late. I wish we had made acquaintance sooner: 'twould have given me liberty to warn you."

"It had been a Christian's merest duty."

"La, la, master! In London the sneaking of a purse is no such rarity that a poor 'prentice pays twopence to gape at it. I paid to see the play, Sir, and fought hard for my seat. Before my master gave over beating me, in fear of my inches and his wife (who has a liking for me), he taught me to husband my time. For your purse, the back of my head had eyes enough to tell me what befalls when a lean dog finds himself alongside a bone."

He seated himself on the bench, unstrapped a shoe, slipped two fingers beneath his stocking, and drew forth a silver piece. "If a gentleman of Warwickshire will be beholden to a poor apprentice of Cheapside?"

"Put it up, boy; put it up! I need not your money, good lad: but I like the spirit of that offer, and to meet it will enlarge my promise. A pint of sack, did I say? You shall sup with me to-night, and of the best, or I am a Dutchman. We will go see the town together, the roaring, gallant town. I will make you free of great company: you shall hear the talk of gods! Lord, how a man rusts in the country!—for, I will confess it to you, lad, the rogue hit the mark: the country is my home."

"I cannot think how he guessed it."

"Nor I. And yet he was wrong, too: for that cannot be called home where a man is never at his ease. I had passed your years, lad, before ever I saw London; and ever since, when my boots have been deepest in Midland clay, I have heard her bells summon me, clear as ever they called to Whittington, 'London, thou art of townes *a per se.*' Nay, almost on that first pilgrimage I came to her as a son. *Urbem quam dicunt Romam*—I was no such clodpate as that rustic of Virgil's. I came expecting all things, and of none did she disappoint me. Give me the capital before all! 'Tis only there a man measures himself with men."

"And cutpurses?" the apprentice interjected.

"Good and bad, rough and smooth," the countryman assented, with a large and catholic smile. "'Tis no question of degrees, my friend, but of kind. I begin to think that, dwelling in London, you have not made her acquaintance. But you shall. As a father, lad—for I like you—I will open your eyes and teach your inheritance. What say you to the Bankside, for example?"

"The Bankside—hem!—and as a father!" scoffed the youth, but his eyes glistened. He was wise beyond his opportunities, and knew all about the Bankside, albeit he had never walked through that quarter but in daylight, wondering at the histories behind its house-fronts.

"As a father, I said; and evil be to him who evil thinks."

"I can tell you of one who will think evil; and that is my master. I can tell you of another; and that will be the sheriff, when I am haled before him."

"You said just now—or my hearing played a trick—that your mistress had a liking for you."

"And *you* said, 'Evil be to him that evil thinks.' She hath a double chin, and owns to fifty-five."

"What, chins!"

"Years, years, master. Like a grandmother she dotes on me and looks after my morals. Nathless when you talk of Bankside—" The apprentice hesitated: in the dusk his shrewd young eyes glistened. "Say that I risk it?" He hesitated again.

"Lads were not so cautious in my young days. I pay the shot, I tell you—a gentleman of Warwickshire and known to the College of Arms."

"It standeth on Paul's Wharf and handy for the ferry to Bankside: but the College closes early on Christmas Eve, and the Heralds be all at holiday. An you think of pawning your coat-of-arms with them to raise the wind, never say that I let you take that long way round without warning."

"Leave the cost to me, once more!" The countryman gazed down into the well of the theatre as if seeking an acquaintance among the figures below. "But what are they doing? What a plague means this hammering? A man cannot hear himself speak for it."

" 'Tis the play."

"The play?"

"The true play—the play you applauded: and writ by the same Will Shakespeare, they tell me—some share of it at least. Cometh he not, by the way, from your part of the world?"

The countryman's eyes glistened in their turn: almost in the dusk they appeared to shine with tears.

"Ay, I knew him, down in Warwickshire: a good lad he was, though his mother wept over him for a wild one. Hast ever seen a hen when her duckling takes to water? So it is with woman when, haply, she has hatched out genius."

The apprentice slapped his leg. "I could have sworn it!"

"Hey?"

"Nay, question me not, master, for I cannot bring it to words. You tell me that you knew him: and I—on the instant I clapped eyes on you it seemed that somehow you were part of his world and somehow had belonged to him. Nearer I cannot get, unless you tell me more."

"I knew him: to be sure, down in Warwickshire: but he has gone somedel beyond my ken, living in London, you see."

"He goes beyond any man's kenning: he that has taught us to ken the world with new eyes. I tell you, master"—the apprentice stretched out a hand—"I go seeking him like one seeking a father who has begotten him into a new world, seeking him with eyes derived from him. Tell me ——"

But the countryman was leaning over the gallery-rail and scanning the pit again. He seemed a trifle bored by a conversation if not of less, then certainly of other, wit than he had bargained for. Somebody had drawn the curtains back from the stage, where the two lackeys who had decked the balcony with lanterns were busy now with crowbars, levering its wooden supports from their sockets.

"Sure," said he, musing, "they don't lift and pack away the stage every night, do they? Or is this some new law to harass players?" He brought his attention back to the apprentice with an effort. "If you feel that way towards him, lad," he answered, "why not accost him? He walks London streets; and he has, if I remember, a courteous, easy manner."

"If the man and his secret were one! But they are not, and there lies the fear—that by finding one I shall miss the other and recover it never. I cannot dare either risk: I want them both. You saw, this afternoon, how, when the secret came within grasp, the man slipped away; how, having taught us to know Falstaff as a foot its old shoe, he left us wondering on a sudden why we laughed! And yet 'twas not sudden, but bred in the play from the beginning; no, nor cruel, but merely right: only he had persuaded us to forget it."

The countryman put up a hand to hide a yawn: and the yawn ended in a slow chuckle.

"Eh? that rogue Falstaff was served out handsomely: though, to tell the truth, I paid no great heed to the last scene, my midriff being sore with laughing."

The apprentice sighed.

"But what is happening below?" the other went on impatiently. "Are they taking the whole theatre to pieces?"

"That is part of the play."

"A whole regiment of workmen!"

"And no stage-army, neither. Yet they come into the play—not the play you saw without understanding, but the play you understood without seeing. They call it *The Phœnix*. Be seated, master, while I unfold the plot: this hammering deafens me. The Burbages, you must know—"

"I knew old James, the father. He brought me down a company of players to our town the year I was High Bailiff; the first that ever played in our Guildhall. Though a countryman, I have loved the arts —even to the length of losing much money by them. A boon fellow, old James! and yet dignified as any alderman. He died—let me see—was it two year agone? The news kept me sad for a week."

"A good player, too"—the apprentice nodded—"though not a patch upon his son Richard. Cuthbert will serve, in ripe sententious parts that need gravity and a good memory for the lines. But Richard bears the bell of the Burbages. Well, Sir, old James being dead, and suddenly, and (as you say) these two years come February, his sons must go suing to the ground landlord, the theatre being leased upon their dad's life. You follow me?"

The countryman nodded in his turn.

"Very well. The landlord, being a skinflint, was willing to renew the lease, but must raise the rent. If they refuse to pay it, the playhouse fell to him. You may fancy how the Burbages called gods and men to witness. Being acquainted with players, you must know how little they enjoy affliction until the whole town shares it. Never so rang Jerusalem with all the woes of Jeremy as did City and suburb—from north beyond Bishopsgate to south along the river, with the cursings of this landlord, who—to cap the humour of it—is a precisian, and never goes near a playhouse. Nevertheless, he patched up a truce for two years ending to-night, raising the rent a little, but not to the stretch of his demands. To-morrow—or, rather, the day after, since to-morrow is Christmas—the word is pay or quit. But in yielding this he yielded our friends the counterstroke. They have bought a plot across the water, in the Clink Liberty: and to-morrow, should he pass this way to church, no theatre will be here for him to smack his Puritan lips over. But for this hammering and the deep slush outside you might even now hear the rumbling of wagons; for wagons there be, a dozen of them, ready to cart the Muses over the bridge before midnight. 'Tis the proper vehicle of Thespis. See those dozen stout rascals lifting the proscenium—"

The countryman smote his great hands together, flung back his head, and let his lungs open in shout after shout of laughter.

"But, master—"

"Oh—oh—oh! Hold my sides, lad, or I start a rib. . . . Nay, if you keep st-staring at me with that s-sol-ol-ol-emn face. Don't—oh, don't!"

"Now I know," murmured the apprentice, "what kind of jest goes down in the country: and, by'r Lady, it goes deep!"

But an instant later the man had heaved himself upon his feet; his eyes expanded from their creases into great O's; his whole body towered and distended itself in gigantic indignation. "The villain! The nipcheese curmudgeonly villain! And we tarry here, talking, while such things are done in England! A Nabal, I say. Give me a hammer!" He heaved up an enormous thigh and bestrode the gallery-rail.

"Have a care, master: the rail—"

"A hammer! Below there. A hammer!" He leaned over, bellowing. The gang of workmen lifting the proscenium stared up open-mouthed into the foggy gloom—a ring of ghostly faces upturned in a luminous haze.

Already the man's legs dangled over the void. Twelve, fifteen feet perhaps, beneath him projected a lower gallery, empty but for three tiers of disordered benches. Plumb as a gannet he dropped, and an eloquent crash of timber reported his arrival below. The apprentice, craning over, saw him regain his feet, scramble over the second rail, and vanish. Followed an instant's silence, a dull thud, a cry from the workmen in the area. The apprentice ran for the gallery stairs and leapt down them, three steps at a time.

It took him, maybe, forty seconds to reach the area. There already, stripped to the shirt, in a whirl of dust and voices, stood his friend waving a hammer and shouting down the loudest. The man was possessed, transformed, a Boanerges; his hammer, a hammer of Thor! He had caught it from the hand of a douce, sober-looking man in a plum-colored doublet, who stood watching but taking no active share in the work.

"By your leave, Sir!"

"With or without my leave, good Sir, since you are determined to have it," said the quiet man, surrendering the hammer.

The countryman snatched and thrust it between his knees while he stripped. Then, having spat on both hands, he grasped the hammer and tried its poise. " 'Tis odd, now," said he, as if upon an afterthought, staring down on the quiet man, "but methinks I know your voice?"

"Marry and there's justice in that," the quiet man answered; "for 'tis the ghost of one you drowned erewhile."

III

"Tom! What, Tom! Where be the others? I tell thee, Tom, there have been doings . . ."

"Is that Dick Burbage?" A frail, thin windle-straw of a man came coughing across the foggy courtyard with a stable-lantern, holding it high. Its rays wavered on his own face, which was young but extraordinarily haggard, and on the piles of timber between and over which he picked his way—timbers heaped pell-mell in the slush of the yard or stacked against the boundary wall, some daubed with paint, others gilded wholly or in part, and twinkling as the lantern swung. "Dick Burbage already? Has it miscarried, then?"

"Miscarried? What in the world was there to miscarry? I tell thee, Tom—but where be the others?"

The frail man jerked a thumb at the darkness behind his shoulder. "Hark to them, back yonder, stacking the beams! Where should they be? and what doing but at work like galley-slaves, by the pace you have kept us going? Look around. I tell you from the first 'twas busy-all to get the yard clear between the wagons' coming, and at the fifth load we gave it up. My shirt clings like a dish-clout; a chill on this will be the death o' me. What a plague! How many scoundrels did you hire, that they take a house to pieces and cart it across Thames faster than we can unload it?"

"That's the kernel of the story, lad. I hired the two-score rogues agreed on, neither more nor less: but one descended out of heaven and raised the number to twelve-score. Ten-score extra, as I am a sinner; and yet but one man, for I counted him. His name, he told me, was Legion."

"Dick," said the other sadly, "when a sober man gives way to drinking—I don't blame you: and your pocket will be the loser more than all the rest if you've boggled to-night's work; but poor Cuthbert will take it to heart."

"There was a man, I tell you—"

"Tut, tut, pull yourself together and run back across bridge. Or let me go: take my arm now, before the others see you. You shall tell me on the way what's wrong at Shoreditch."

"There is naught wrong with Shoreditch, forby that it has lost a theatre: and I am not drunk, Tom Nashe—no, not by one-tenth as drunk as I deserve to be, seeing that the house is down, every stick of it, and the bells scarce yet tolling midnight. 'Twas all this man, I tell you!"

"Down? The Theatre down? Oh, go back, Dick Burbage!"

"Level with the ground, I tell you—his site a habitation for the satyr. *Cecidit, cecidit Babylon illa magna!* and the last remains of it, more by token, following close on my heels in six wagons. Hist, then, my Thomas, my Didymus, my doubting one! Canst not hear the rumble of their wheels? and—and—oh, good Lord!" Burbage caught his friend by the arm and leaned against him heavily. "*He's* there, and following!"

The wagons came rolling over the cobbles of the Clink along the roadway outside the high boundary-wall of the yard: and as they came, clear above their rumble and the slow clatter of hoofs a voice like a trumpet declaimed into the night:

> Above all ryvers thy Ryver bath renowne,
>   Whose beryall streamys, pleasaunt and preclare,
> Under thy lusty wallys renneth downe,
>   Where many a swan doth swymme with wyngis fair,
>   Where many a barge doth sail and row with are . . .

"We had done better—a murrain on their cobbles!—we had done better, lad, to step around by Paul's Wharf and take boat. . . . This jolting ill agrees with a man of my weight. . . . 'Where many a barge doth sail and row with are . . .' Gr-r-r! Did I not warn thee beware, master wagoner, of the kerbstones at the corners? We had done better by water, what though it be dark. . . . Lights of Bankside on the water . . . no such sight in Europe, they tell me. . . . My Lord of Surrey took boat one night from Westminster and fired into their windows with a stone-bow, breaking much glass . . . drove all the longshore queans screaming into the streets in their night-rails. . . . He went to the Fleet for it . . . a Privy Council matter. . . . I forgive the lad, for my part: for only think of it—all those windows aflame on the river, and no such river in Europe!

> Where many a barge doth sail and row with are;
>   Where many a ship doth rest with top-royall.
> O towne of townes! patrone and not compare,
>   London, thou art the flow'r of Cities all!

Who-oop!"

"In the name of—" stammered Nashe, as he listened, Burbage all the while clutching his arm.

"He dropped from the top gallery, I tell you—clean into the pit from the top gallery—and he weighs eighteen stone if an ounce. 'Your servant, Sir, and of all the Muses,' he says, picking himself up; and with that takes the hammer from my hand and plays Pyrrhus in Troy —Pyrrhus with all the ravening Danai behind him: for those hired scoundrels of mine took fire, and started ripping out the bowels of the poor old theatre as though it had been the Fleet and lodged all their cronies within! It went down before my eyes like a sand-castle before the tide. Within three hours they had wiped the earth of it. The Lord be praised that Philip Gosson had ne'er such an arm, nor could command such! Oh, but he's a portent! Troy's horse and Bankes's bay gelding together are a fool to him: he would harness them as Samson did the little foxes, and fire brushwood under their tails. . . ."

"Of a certainty you are drunk, Dick."

"Drunk? I?" Burbage gripped the other's thin arm hysterically. "If you want to see a man drunk come to the gate. Nay, then, stay where you are: for there's no escaping him."

Nor was there. Between them and the wagoners' lanterns at the gate a huge shadow thrust itself, the owner of it rolling like a ship in a seaway, while he yet recited, " 'Strong be thy wallis that about thee standis' (meaning the Clink, my son), 'Wise be the people that within thee dwellis' (which you may take for the inhabitants thereof), 'Fresh is thy ryver with his lusty strandis, Blith be thy chirches, wele sowning be thy bellis.' "

"Well sounding is my belly, master, any way," put in a high, thin voice; "and it calls on a gentleman of Warwickshire to redeem his promise."

"He shall, he shall, lad—in the fullness of time: 'but before dining ring at the bell,' says the proverb. Grope, lad, feel along the gate-posts if this yard, this courtlage, this base-court, hath any such thing as bell or knocker.

> And when they came to mery Carleile
> All in the mornyng tyde-a,
> They found the gates shut them until
> About on every syde-a.
>
> Then Adam Bell bete on the gates
> With strokes great and stronge-a . . .

"Step warely, lad. Plague of this forest! Have we brought timber to Sherwood?

> With strokes great and strong-a
> The porter marveiled who was thereat,
> And to the gates he thronge-a.

> *They called the porter to counsell,*
> *And wrange his necke in two-a,*
> *And caste him in a depe dungeon,*
> *And took hys keys hym fro-a.*

"Within! You rascal, there, with the lantern! . . . Eh? but these be two gentlemen, it appears? I cry your mercy, Sirs."

"For calling us rascals?" Nashe stepped forward. "'T hath been done to me before now, in print, upon as good evidence; and to my friend here by Act of Parliament."

"But seeing you with a common stable-lantern—"

"Yet Diogenes was a gentleman. Put it that, like him, I am searching for an honest man."

"Then we are well met. I' faith we are very well met," responded the countryman, recognising Burbage's grave face and plum-coloured doublet.

"Or, as one might better say, well overtaken," said Burbage.

"Marry, and with a suit. I have some acquaintance, Sir, with members of your honourable calling, as in detail and at large I could prove to you. Either I have made poor use of it or I guess aright, as I guess with confidence, that after the triumph will come the speech-making, and the supper's already bespoken."

"At Nance Witwold's, by the corner of Paris Garden, Sir, where you shall be welcome."

"I thank you, Sir. But my suit is rather for this young friend of mine, to whom I have pledged my word."

"He shall be welcome, too."

"He tells me, Sir, that you are Richard Burbage. I knew your father well, Sir—an honest Warwickshire man: he condescended to my roof and tasted my poor hospitality many a time; and belike you, too, Sir, being then a child, may have done the same: for I talk of prosperous days long since past—nay, so long since that 'twould be a wonder indeed had you remembered me. The more pleasure it gives me, Sir, to find James Burbage's sappy virtues flourishing in the young wood, and by the branch be reminded of the noble stock."

"The happier am I, Sir, to have given you welcome or ever I heard your claim."

"Faith!" said the apprentice to himself, "compliments begin to fly when gentlefolks meet." But he had not bargained to sup in this high company, and the prospect thrilled him with delicious terror. He glanced nervously across the yard, where some one was approaching with another lantern.

"My claim?" the countryman answered Burbage. "You have heard but a part of it as yet. Nay, you have heard none of it, since I use not past hospitalities with old friends to claim a return from their children. My claim, Sir, is a livelier one—"

"Tom Nashe! Tom Nashe!" called a voice, clear and strong and masculine, from the darkness behind the advancing lantern.

"Anon, anon, Sir," quoted Nashe, swinging his own lantern about and mimicking.

"Don't tell me there be yet more wagons arrived?" asked the voice.

"Six, lad—six, as I hope for mercy: and outside the gate at this moment."

"There they must tarry, then, till our fellows take breath to unload 'em. But—six? How is it managed, think you? Has Dick Burbage called out the train-bands to help him? Why, hullo, Dick! What means—" The newcomer's eyes, round with wonder as they rested a moment on Burbage, grew rounder yet as they travelled past him to the countryman. "Father?" he stammered, incredulous.

"Good evening, Will! Give ye good evening, my son! Set down that lantern and embrace me, like a good boy: a good boy, albeit a man of fame. Didst not see me, then, in the theatre this afternoon? Yet was I to the fore there, methinks, and proud to be called John Shakespeare."

"Nay, I was not there; having other fish to fry."

"Shouldst have heard the applause, lad; it warmed your old father's heart. Yet 'twas no more than the play deserved. A very neat, pretty drollery—upon my faith, no man's son could have written a neater!"

"But what hath fetched you to London?"

"Business, business: a touch, too, maybe, of the old homesickness: but business first. Dick Quiney—But pass me the lantern, my son, that I may take a look at thee. Ay, thou hast sobered, thou hast solidified: thy beard hath ta'en the right citizen's cut—'twould ha' been a cordial to thy poor mother to see thee wear so staid a beard. Rest her soul! There's nothing like property for filling out a man's frame, firming his eye, his frame, bearing, footstep. Talking of property, I have been none so idle a steward for thee. New Place I have made habitable— the house at least; patched up the roof, taken down and rebuilt the west chimney that was overleaning the road, repaired the launders, enlarged the parlour-window, run out the kitchen passage to a new back-entrance. The garden I cropped with peas this summer, and have set lettuce and winter-kale between the young apple-trees, whereof the whole are doing well, and the mulberry likewise I look for to thrive. Well, as I was saying, Dick Quiney—"

"—Is in trouble again, you need not tell."

"None so bad but it could be mended by the thirty pounds whereof I wrote. Mytton will be security with him, now that Bushell draws back. He offers better than those few acres at Shottery you dealt upon in January."

"Land is land."

"And ale is ale: you may take up a mortgage on the brewhouse. Hast ever heard, Mr. Burbage"—John Shakespeare swung about—"of a proverb we have down in our Warwickshire? It goes

> *Who buys land buys stones,*
> *Who buys meat buys bones,*
> *Who buys eggs buys shells,*
> *But who buys ale buys nothing else.*

"And that sets me in mind, Will, that these friends of yours have bidden me to supper: and their throats will be dry an we keep 'em gaping at our country discourse. Here come I with Thespis, riding on a wagon: but where tarries the vintage feast? Where be the spigots? Where be the roasted geese, capons, sucking-pigs? Where the hogs-puddings, the trifles, the custards, the frumenties? Where the minstrels? Where the dancing girls? I have in these three hours swallowed as many pecks of dust. I am for the bucket before the manger and for good talk after both—high, brave translunary talk with wine in the veins of it—Hippocras with hippocrene: with music too—some little kickshaw whatnots of the theorbo or viol da gamba pleasantly thrown in for interludes. 'Tis a fog-pated land I come from, with a pestilent rheumy drip from the trees and the country scarce recovered from last year's dearth—"

"Dick Quiney should have made the better prices for that dearth," put in his son, knitting his great brow thoughtfully. "With wheat at fifty shillings, and oats—"

"The malt, lad, the malt! His brewhouse swallowed malt at twenty-eight or nine which a short two years before had cost him twelve-and-threepence the quarter. A year of dearth, I say. It took poor Dick at unawares. But give him time: he will pull round. Sure, we be slow in the country, but you have some in this town that will beat us. How many years, lad, have I been battering the doors of Heralds' College for that grant of arms, promised ere my beard was grey and yours fully grown?"

"Malt at twenty-eight, you say?"

"Last year, lad—a year of dearth. Call it a good twenty in these bettering times, and wheat anything under forty-five shillings."

"Well, we will talk it over." His son seemed to come out of a brown study. "We will talk it over," he repeated briskly, and added, "How? The chimney overleaning the road? 'Twas a stout enough chimney, as I remember, and might have lasted another twenty years. Where did you draw the bricks?"

Nashe glanced at his friend with a puzzled smile. Burbage—better used, no doubt, to the businesslike ways of authors—betrayed no surprise. The apprentice stared, scarcely believing his ears. Was this the talk of Shakespeare? Nay, rather the talk of Justice Shallow himself—"How a good yoke of bullocks at Stamford Fair?" "How a score of ewes now?"

A heavy tread approached from the gateway.

"Are we to bide here all night, and on Christmas morn, too?" a gruff voice demanded. "Unpack, and pay us our wage, or we tip the whole load of it into Thames." Here the wagoner's shin encountered in the darkness with a plank, and he cursed violently.

"Go you back to your horses, my friend," answered Burbage. "The unloading shall begin anon. As for your wage, your master will tell you I settled it at the time I bargained for his wagons—ay, and paid. I hold his receipt."

"For tenpence a man—mowers' wages," growled the wagoner.

"I asked him his price and he fixed it. 'Tis the current rate, I understand, and a trifle over."

"Depends on the job. I've been talkin' with my mates, and we don't like it. We're decent labouring men, and shifting a lot of play-actors' baggage don't come in our day's work. I'd as lief wash dirty linen for my part. Therefore," the fellow wound up lucidly, "you'll make it twelvepence a head, master. We don't take a groat less."

"I see," said Burbage blandly: "twopence for salving your conscience, hey? And so, being a decent man, you don't stomach players?"

"No, nor the Bankside at this hour o' night. I live clean, I tell you."

"'Tis a godless neighbourhood and a violent." Burbage drew a silver whistle from his doublet and eyed it. "Listen a moment, master wagoner, and tell me what you hear."

"I hear music o' sorts. No Christmas carols, I warrant."

"Aught else?"

"Ay: a sound like a noise of dogs baying over yonder."

"Right again: it comes from the kennels by the Bear-Pit. Have you a wish, my friend, to make nearer acquaintance with these dogs? No? With the bears, then? Say the word, and inside of a minute I can whistle up your two-pennyworth."

The wagoner with a dropping jaw stared from one to another of the ring of faces in the lantern-light. They were quiet, determined. Only the apprentice stood with ears pricked, as it were, and shivered at the distant baying.

"No offence, Sir; I meant no offence, you'll understand," the wagoner stammered.

"Nay, call your mates, man!" spoke up William Shakespeare, sudden and sharp, and with a scornful ring in his voice which caused our apprentice to jump. "Call them in and let us hear you expound Master Burbage's proposal. I am curious to see how they treat you— having an opinion of my own on crowds and their leaders."

But the wagoner had swung about surlily on his heel.

"I'll not risk disputing it," he growled. "'Tis your own dunghill, and I must e'en take your word that 'tis worse than e'er a man thought. But one thing I'll not take back. You're a muck of play-actors, and a man that touches ye should charge for his washing. Grr!" he spat. "Ye're worse than Patty Ward's sow, and *she* was no lavender!"

IV

The Bankside was demure. But for the distant baying of dogs which kept him shivering, our apprentice had been disappointed in the wickedness of it.

He had looked to meet with roisterers, to pass amid a riot of taverns, to happen, belike, upon a street scuffle, to see swords drawn or perchance to come upon a body stretched across the roadway and hear the murderers' footsteps in the darkness, running. These were the pictures his imagination had drawn and shuddered at: for he was a youth of small courage.

But the Bankside was demure; demure as Chepe. The waterside lanes leading to Mistress Witwold's at the corner of Paris Gardens differed only from Chepe in this—that though the hour was past midnight, every other door stood open or at least ajar, showing a light through the fog. Through some of these doorways came the buzz and murmur of voices, the tinkling of stringed instrument. Others seemed to await their guests. But the lanes themselves were deserted.

From the overhanging upper storeys lights showed here and there through the chinks of shutters or curtains. Once or twice in the shadows beneath, our apprentice saw, or thought he saw, darker shadows draw back and disappear: and gradually a feeling grew upon him that all these shadows, all these lidded upper windows, were watching, following him with curious eyes. Again, though the open doorways were bright as for a fête, a something seemed to subdue the voices within—a constraint, perhaps an expectancy—as though the inmates whispered together in the pauses of their talk and between the soft thrumming of strings. He remarked, too, that his companions had fallen silent.

Mother Witwold's door, when they reached it, stood open like the rest. Her house overhung a corner where from the main street a short alley ran down to Paris Garden stairs. Nashe, who had been leading along the narrow pavement, halted outside the threshold to extinguish his lantern; and at the same moment jerked his face upward. Aloft, in one of the houses across the way, a lattice had flown open with a crash of glass.

"Jesu! help!"

The cry ended in a strangling sob. The hands that had thrust the lattice open projected over the sill. By the faint foggy light of Mother Witwold's doorway our apprentice saw them outstretched for a moment; saw them disappear, the wrists still rigid, as some one drew them back into the room. But what sent the horror crawling through the roots of his hair was the shape of these hands.

"You there!" called Nashe, snatching the second lantern from Burbage's hand and holding it aloft towards the dim house-front. "What's wrong within?"

A woman's hand came around the curtain and felt for the lattice stealthily, to close it. There was no other answer.

"What's wrong there?" demanded Nashe again.

"Go your ways!" The voice was a woman's, hoarse and angry, yet frightened withal. The curtain still hid her. "Haven't I trouble enough with these tetchy dwarfs, but you must add to it by waking the streets?"

"Dwarfs?" Nashe swung the lantern so that its rays fell on the house-door below: a closed door and stout, studded with iron nails. "Dwarfs?" he repeated.

"Let her be," said Burbage, taking his arm. "I know the woman. She keeps a brace of misbegotten monsters she picked up at Wapping off a ship's captain. He brought 'em home from the Isle of Serendib, or Cathay, or some such outlandish coast, or so she swears his word was."

"Swears, doth she? Didst hear the poor thing cry out?"

"Ay, like any Christian; as, for aught I know, it may be. There's another tale that she found 'em down in Gloucestershire, at a country fair, and keeps 'em pickled in walnut juice. But monsters they be, whether of Gloucester or Cathay, for I have seen 'em; and so hath the Queen, who sent for them the other day to be brought to Westminster, and there took much delight in their oddity."

While the others hesitated, William Shakespeare turned on his heel and walked past them into Mother Witwold's lighted doorway.

His father glanced after him. "Well, to be sure, the poor thing cried out like a Christian," he said. "But dwarfs and monsters be kittle cattle to handle, I am told." As the lattice closed on their debate he linked his arm in the apprentice's, and they too passed into the doorway.

From it a narrow passage led straight to a narrow staircase; and at the stairs' foot the apprentice had another glimpse into the life of this Bankside. A door stood wide there upon an ill-lighted room, and close within the door sat two men—foreigners by their black-avised faces—casting dice upon a drumhead. In a chair, beyond, a girl, low-bodiced, with naked gleaming shoulders, leaned back half asleep; and yet she did not seem to sleep, but to regard the gamesters with a lazy scorn from under her dropped lashes. A tambourine tied with bright ribbons rested in the lap of her striped petticoat, kept from sliding to the floor by the careless crook—you could see it was habitual—of her jewelled fingers. The two men looked up sharply, almost furtively, at the company mounting the stairs. The girl scarcely lifted her eyes. Scornful she looked, and sullen and infinitely weary, yet she was beautiful withal. The apprentice wondered while he climbed.

"Yes," his patron was saying, "'tis the very mart and factory of pleasure. Ne'er a want hath London in that way but the Bankside can supply it, from immortal poetry down to—to—"

"—Down to misshapen children. Need'st try no lower, my master."

"There be abuses, my son: and there be degrees of pleasure, the lowest of which (I grant you) be vile, sensual, devilish. Marry, I defend not such. But what I say is that a great city should have delights proportionate to her greatness; rich shows and pageants and processions by land and water; plays and masques and banquets with music; and the men who cater for these are citizens as worthy as the rest. Take away Bankside, and London would be the cleaner of much wickedness: yet by how much the duller of cheer, the poorer in all that colour, that movement which together be to cities the spirit of life! Where would be gone that glee of her that lifts a man's lungs and swells his port when his feet feel London stones? Is't of her money the country nurses think when to wondering children they fable of streets all paved with gold? Nay, lad: and this your decent, virtuous folk know well enough—your clergy, your aldermen—and use the poor players while abusing them. Doth the parish priest need a miracle-play for his church? Doth my Lord Mayor intend a show? To the Bankside they hie with money in their purses: and if his purse be long enough, my Lord Mayor shall have a fountain running with real wine, and Mass Thomas a Hell with flames of real cloth-in-grain, or at least a Lazarus with real sores. Doth the Court require a masque, the Queen a bull-baiting, the City a good roaring tragedy, full of blood and impugned innocence— Will! Will, I say! Tarry a moment!"

They had reached the landing, and looked down a corridor at the end of which, where a lamp hung, Shakespeare waited with his hand on a door-latch. From behind the door came a buzz of many voices.

"Lad, lad, let us go in together! Though the world's applause weary thee, 'tis sweet to thine old father."

As he pressed down the latch the great man turned for an instant with a quick smile, marvellously tender.

"He *can* smile, then?" thought the apprentice to himself. "And I was doubting that he kept it for his writing!"

Within the room, as it were with one shout, a great company leapt to its feet, cheering and lifting glasses. Shakespeare, pausing on the threshold, smiled again, but more reservedly, bowing to the homage as might a king.

V

Three hours the feast had lasted: and the apprentice had listened to many songs, many speeches, but scarcely to the promised talk of gods.

The poets, maybe, reserved such talk for the Mermaid. Here they were outnumbered by the players and by such ladies as the Bankside (which provided everything) furnished to grace the entertainment; and doubtless they subdued their discourse to the company. The Burbages, Dick and Cuthbert, John Heminge, Will Kempe—some half-a-dozen of the crew perhaps—might love good literature: but even these were pardonably more elate over the epilogue than over the play. For months they, the Lord Chamberlain's servants, had felt the eyes of London upon them: to-night they had triumphed, and to-morrow London would ring with appreciative laughter. It is not every day that your child of pleasure outwits your man of business at his own game: it is not once in a generation that he scores such a hit as had been scored to-day. The ladies, indeed, yawned without dissembling, while Master Jonson—an ungainly youth with a pimply face, a rasping accent, and a hard pedantic manner—proposed success to the new comedy and long life to its author; which he did at interminable length; spicing his discourse with quotations from Aristotle, Longinus, Quintilian, the Ars Poetica, Persius, and Seneca, authors less studied than the Aretine along Bankside. He loved Will Shakespeare. . . . A comedy of his own (as the company might remember) owed not a little to his friend Will Shakespeare's acting. . . . Here was a case in which love and esteem—yes, and worship—might hardly be dissociated. . . . In short, speaking as modestly as a young man might of his senior, Will Shakespeare was the age's ornament and, but for lack of an early gruelling in the classics, might easily have been an ornament for any age.

Cuthbert Burbage—it is always your quiet man who first succumbs on these occasions—slid beneath the table with a vacuous laugh and lay in slumber. Dick Burbage sat and drummed his toes impatiently. Nashe puffed at a pipe of tobacco. Kempe, his elbows on the board, his chin resting on his palms, watched the orator with amused interest, mischief lurking in every crease of his wrinkled face. Will Shakespeare leaned back in his chair and scanned the rafters, smiling gently the while. His speech, when his turn came to respond, was brief, almost curt. He would pass by (he said) his young friend's learned encomiums, and come to that which lay nearer to their thoughts than either the new play or the new play's author. Let them fill and drink in silence to the demise of an old friend, the vanished theatre, the first ever built in London. Then, happening to glance at Heminge as he poured out the wine—"Tut, Jack!" he spoke up sharply: "keep that easy rheum for the boards. Brush thine eyes, lad: we be all players here—or women—and know the trade."

It hurt. If Heminge's eyes had begun to water sentimentally, they flinched now with real pain. This man loved Shakespeare with a dog's love. He blinked, and a drop fell and rested on the back of his hand as it fingered the base of his wine-glass. The apprentice saw and noted it.

"And another glass, lads, to the Phœnix that shall arise! A toast, and this time not in silence!" shouted John Shakespeare, springing up, flask in one hand and glass in the other. Meat or wine, jest or sally of man or woman, dull speech or brisk—all came alike to him. His doublet was unbuttoned, he had smoked three pipes, drunk a quart of sack, and never once yawned. He was enjoying himself to the top of his bent. "Music, I say! Music!" A thought seemed to strike him; his eyes filled with happy inspiration. Still gripping his flask, he rolled to the door, flung it open, and bawled down the stairway, "Ahoy! Below, there!"

"Ahoy, then, with all my heart!" answered a voice, gay and youthful, pat on the summons. "What is't ye lack, my master?"

"Music, an' thou canst give it. If not—"

"My singing voice broke these four years past, I fear me."

"Your name, then, at least, young man, or ever you thrust yourself upon private company."

"William Herbert, at your service." A handsome lad—a boy, almost —stood in the doorway, having slipped past John Shakespeare's guard: a laughing, frank-faced boy, in a cloak slashed with orange-tawny satin. So much the apprentice noted before he heard a second voice, as jaunty and even more youthfully shrill, raised in protest upon the stairhead outside.

"And where the master goes," it demanded, "may not his page follow?"

John Shakespeare seemingly gave way to this second challenge as to the first. "Be these friends of thine, Will?" he called past them as a second youth appeared in the doorway, a pretty, dark-complexioned lad, cloaked in white, who stood a pace behind his companion's elbow and gazed into the supper-room with his eyes at once mischievous and timid.

"Good-evening, gentles! The taller lad comprehended the feasters and the disordered table in a roguish bow. Good-morning, Will!" He singled out Shakespeare, and nodded.

"My Lord Herbert!"

The apprentice's eye, cast towards Shakespeare at the salutation given, marked a dark flush rise to the great man's temples as he answered the nod.

"I called thee 'Will,' " answered Herbert lightly.

"You called us 'gentles,' " Shakespeare replied, the dark flush yet lingering on either cheek. "A word signifying bait for gudgeons, bred in carrion."

"Yet I called thee Will," insisted Herbert more gently. " 'Tis my name as well as thine, and we have lovingly exchanged it before now, or my memory cheats me."

" 'Tis a name lightly exchanged in love." With a glance at the white-cloaked page Shakespeare turned on his heel.

"La, Will, where be thy manners?" cried one of the women. "Welcome, my young Lord; and welcome the boy beside thee for his pretty face! Step in, child, that I may pass thee round to be kissed."

The page laughed and stepped forward with his chin defiantly tilted. His eyes examined the women curiously and yet with a touch of fear.

"Nay, never flinch, lad! I'll do thee no harm," chuckled the one who had invited him. "Mass o' me, how I love modesty in these days of scandal!"

"Music? Who called for music?" a foreign voice demanded: and now in the doorway appeared three newcomers, two men and a woman—the same three of whom the apprentice had caught a glimpse within the room at the stairs' foot. The spokesman, a heavily built fellow with a short bull-neck and small cunning eyes, carried a drum slung about his shoulders and beat a rub-a-dub on it by way of flourish. "Take thy tambourine and dance, Julitta. *"Julie, prends ton tambourin; Toi, prends ta flute, Robin,'* " he hummed, tapping his drum again.

"So? So? What foreign gabble is this?" demanded John Shakespeare, following and laying a hand on his shoulder.

"A pretty little carol for Christmas, Signore, that we picked up on our way through Burgundy, where they sing it to a jargon I cannot emulate. But the tune is as it likes you. *"Au son ces instruments— Turelurelu, patapatapan—Nous dirons Noël gaiment!'* Goes it not trippingly, Signore? You will say so when you see my Julitta dance to it."

"Eh—eh? Dance to a carol?" a woman protested. " 'Tis inviting the earth to open and swallow us."

"Why, where's the harm on 't?" John Shakespeare demanded. "A pretty little concomitant, and anciently proper to all religions, nor among the heathen only, but in England and all parts of Christendom.

> *In manger wrapped it was—*
> *So poorly happ'd my chance—*
> *Between an ox and a silly poor ass*
> *To call my true love to the dance!*
> *Sing O, my love, my love, my love. . . .*

"There's precedent for ye, Ma'am—good English precedent. Zooks! I'm a devout man, I hope; but I bear a liberal mind and condemn no form of mirth, so it be honest. The earth swallow us? Ay, soon or late it will, not being squeamish. Meantime, dance, I say! Clear back the tables there, and let the girl show her paces!"

Young Herbert glanced at Burbage with lifted eyebrow, as if to demand, "Who is this madman?" Burbage laughed, throwing out both hands.

"But he is gigantic!" lisped the page, as with a wave of his two great arms John Shakespeare seemed to catch up the company and fling them to work pell-mell, thrusting back tables, piling chairs, clearing the floor of its rushes. "He is a whirlwind of a man!"

"Come, Julitta!" called the man with the drum. "Francisco, take thy pipe, man! '*Au son de ces instruments—Turelurelu, patapatapan.*'"

As the music struck up, the girl, still with her scornful, impassive face, leapt like a panther from the doorway into the space cleared for her, and whirled down the room in a dance and the like of which our apprentice had never seen nor dreamed of. And yet his gaze at first was not for her, but for the younger foreigner, the one with the pipe. For if ever horror took visible form, it stood and stared from the windows of that man's eyes. They were handsome eyes, too, large and dark and passionate: but just now they stared blindly as though a hot iron had seared them. Twice they had turned to the girl, who answered by not so much as a glance; and twice with a shudder upon the man with the drum, who caught the look and blinked wickedly. Worst of all was it when the music began, to see that horror fixed and staring over a pair of cheeks ludicrously puffing at a flageolet. A face for a gargoyle! The apprentice shivered, and glanced from one to the other of the company: but they, one and all, were watching the dancer.

It was a marvellous dance, truly. The girl, her tambourine lifted high, and clashing softly to the beat of the music, whirled down the length of the room, while above the pipe's falsetto and rumble of the drum the burly man lifted his voice and trolled, "*Turelurelu, patapatapan—Au son de ces instruments Faisons la nique à Satan!*"

By the barricade of chairs and tables, under which lay Cuthbert Burbage in peaceful stupor, she checked her onward rush, whirling yet, but so lazily that she seemed for the moment to stand poised, her scarf outspread like the wings of a butterfly: and so, slowly, very slowly, she came floating back. Twice she repeated this, each time narrowing her circuit, until she reached the middle of the floor, and there began to spin on her toes as a top spins when (as children say) it goes to sleep. The tambourine no longer clashed. Balanced high on the point of her uplifted forefinger, it too began to spin, and span until its outline became a blur. Still, as the music rose shriller and wilder, she revolved more and more rapidly, yet apparently with less and less of effort. Her scarf had become a mere filmy disc rotating around a whorl of gleaming flesh and glancing jewels.

A roar of delight from John Shakespeare broke the spell. The company echoed it with round upon round of hand-clapping. The music ceased suddenly, and the dancer, dipping low until her knees brushed the floor, stood erect again, dropped her arms, and turned carelessly to the nearest table.

"Bravo! bravissimo!" thundered John Shakespeare. "A cup of wine for her, there!"

The girl had snatched up a crust of bread and was gnawing it ravenously. He thrust his way through the guests and poured out wine for her. She took the glass with a steady hand, scarcely pausing in her meal to thank him.

"But who is your master of ceremonies?" demanded the page's piping voice.

William Shakespeare heard it and turned. "He is my father," said he quietly.

But John Shakespeare had heard also. Wheeling about, wine-flask in hand, he faced the lad with a large and mock-elaborate bow. "That, young Sir, must be my chief title to your notice. For the rest, I am a plain gentleman of Warwickshire, of impaired but (I thank God) bettering fortune; my name John Shakespeare; my coat, or, a bend sable, charged with a lance proper. One of these fine days I may bring it to Court for you to recognise: but, alas! says Skelton,

> Age is a page
> For the Court full unmeet,
> For age cannot rage
> Nor buss her sweet sweet.

"I shall bide at home and kiss the Queen's hand, through my son, more like."

"Indeed," said the page, "I hear reports that her Majesty hath already a mind to send for him."

"Is that so, Will?" His father beamed, delighted.

"In some sort it is," answered Herbert, "and in some sort I am her messenger's forerunner. She will have a play of thee, Will."

"The Queen?" Shakespeare turned on him sharply. "This is a fool's trick you play on me, my Lord." Yet his face flushed in spite of himself.

"I tell thee, straight brow and true man, I heard the words fall from her very lips. 'He shall write us a play,' she said; 'and this Falstaff shall be the hero on't, with no foolish royalties to overlay and clog his mirth.'"

"And, you see," put in the page maliciously, "we have come express to the Boar's Head to seek him out."

"That," Herbert added, "is our suit to-night."

"Will, lad, thy fortune's made!" John Shakespeare clapped a hand on his son's shoulder. "I shall see thee Sir William yet afore I die!"

If amid the general laughter two lines of vexation wrote themselves for a moment on Shakespeare's brow they died out swiftly. He stood back a pace, eyed his father awhile with grave and tender humour, and answered the pair of courtiers with a bow.

"Her Majesty's gracious notion of a play," said he, "must needs be her poor subject's pattern. If then I come to Court in motley, you, Sirs, at least will be indulgent, knowing how much a suit may disguise." The page, meeting his eye, laughed uneasily. "'Tis but a frolic—" he began.

"Ay, there's the pity o't," interrupted a deep voice—Kempe's.

The page laughed again, yet more nervously. "I should have said the Queen—God bless her!—desires but a frolic. And I had thought"

—here he lifted his chin saucily and looked Kempe in the face—"that on Bankside they took a frolic less seriously."

"Why, no," answered Kempe: "they have to take it seriously, and the cost too—that being their business."

" 'Tis but a frolic, at any rate, that her Majesty proposes, with a trifling pageant or dance to conclude, in which certain of the Court may join."

A harsh laugh capped this explanation. It came from the dancing-girl, who, seated at the disordered table, had been eating like a hungry beast. She laid down her knife, rested her chin on her clasped hands, and, munching slowly, stared at the page from under her sullen, scornful brows.

"Wouldst learn to dance, child?" she demanded.

"With thee for teacher," the page answered modestly. "I have no skill, but a light foot only."

"A light foot!" the woman mimicked and broke into a laugh horrible to hear. "Wouldst achieve such art as mine with a light foot? I tell thee that to dance as I dance thy feet must go deep as hell!" She pushed back her plate, and, rising, nodded to the musicians. "Play, you!" she commanded.

This time she used no wild whirl down the room to give her impetus. She stood in the cleared space of floor, her arms hanging limp, and at the first shrill note of the pipe began to revolve on the points of her toes, her eyes, each time as they came full circle, meeting the gaze of the page, and slowly fascinating, freezing it. As slowly, deliberately, her hand went up, curved itself to the armpit of her bodice; and lo! as she straightened it aloft, a snake writhed itself around her upper arm, lifting its head to reach the shining bracelets, the jewelled fingers. A curving lift of the left arm, and on that too a snake began to coil and climb. Effortless, rigid as a revolving statue, she brought her finger-tips together overhead and dipped them to her bosom.

A shriek rang out, piercing high above the music.

"Catch her! She faints!" shouted Kempe, darting forward. But it was Shakespeare who caught the page's limp body as it dropped back on his arm. Bearing it to the window, he tore aside the curtain and thrust open a lattice to the dawn. The unconscious head drooped against his shoulder.

"My Lord"—he turned on Herbert as though the touch maddened him—"you are a young fool! God forgive me that I ever took you for better! Go, call a boat and take her out of this."

"Nay, but she revives," stammered Herbert, as the page's lips parted in a long, shuddering sigh.

"Go, fetch a boat, I say!—and make way there, all you by the door!"

VI

"Tut! tut!—the wench will come to fast enough in the fresh air. A dare-devil jade, too, to be sparking it on Bankside at this hour! But it takes more than a woman, they say, to kill a mouse, and with serpents her sex hath an ancient feud. What's her name, I wonder?"

The candles, burning low and guttering in the draught of the open window, showed a banquet-hall deserted, or all but deserted. A small crowd of the guests—our apprentice among them—had trooped downstairs after Shakespeare and his burden. Others, reminded by the grey dawn, had slipped away on their own account to hire a passage home from the sleepy watermen before Paris Garden Stairs.

"Can any one tell me her name, now?" repeated John Shakespeare, rolling to the table and pouring himself yet another glass of wine. But no one answered him. The snake-woman had folded back her pets within her bodice and resumed her meal as though nothing had happened. The burly drummer had chosen a chair beside her and fallen to on the remains of a pasty. Both were eating voraciously. Francisco, the pipe-player, sat sidesaddle-wise on a form at a little distance and drank and watched them, still with the horror in his eyes. One or two women lingered, and searched the tables, pocketing crusts—searched with faces such as on battlefields, at dawn, go peering among the dead and wounded.

"But hullo!" John Shakespeare swung round, glass in hand, as the apprentice stood panting in the doorway. "Faith, you return before I had well missed you."

The lad's eyes twinkled with mischief.

"An thou hasten not, master, I fear me thou may'st miss higher game; with our hosts—your son amongst 'em—even now departing by boat and, for aught I know, leaving thee to pay the shot."

"Michael and all his angels preserve us! I had forgot—"

John Shakespeare clapped a hand on his empty pocket, and ran for the stairhead. "Will!" he bawled. "Will! My son Will!"

The apprentice laughed and stepped toward the window, tittuping slightly; for (to tell the truth) he had drunk more wine than agreed with him. Standing by the window, he laughed again vacuously, drew a long breath, and so spun round on his heels at the sound of a choking cry and a rush of feet. With that he saw, as in a haze—his head being yet dizzy—the heavy man catch up his drum by its strap and, using it as a shield, with a backward sweep of the arm hurl off the youth Francisco, who had leapt on him knife in hand. Clutching the curtain, he heard the knife rip through the drum's parchment and saw the young man's face of hate as the swift parry flung him back staggering, upsetting a form, against the table's edge. He saw the glasses there leap and totter from the shock, heard their rims jar and ring together like a peal of bells.

The sound seemed to clear his brain. He could not guess what had provoked the brawl; but in one and the same instant he saw the drummer reach back an arm as if to draw the dancing woman on his knee; heard his jeering laugh as he slipped a hand down past her bare shoulder; saw her unmoved face, sullenly watching; saw Francisco, still clutching his knife, gather himself up for another spring. As he sprang the drummer's hand slid round from behind the woman's back, and it too grasped a knife. An overturned chair lay between the two, and the rail of it as Francisco leapt caught his foot, so that with a clutch he fell sideways against the table. Again the glasses jarred and rang, and yet again and more loudly as the drummer's hand went up and drove the dagger through the neck, pinning it to the board. The youth's legs contracted in a horrible kick, contracted again and fell limp. There was a gush of blood across the cloth, a sound of breath escaping and choked in its escape: and as the killer wrenched out his knife for a second stroke, the body slid with a thud to the floor.

The apprentice had feasted, and feasted well; yet throughout the feast (he bethought himself of this later), no serving-man and but one serving-maid had entered the room. Wines and dishes had come at call to a hatch in the wall at the far end of the room. One serving-maid had done all the rest, moving behind the guests' chairs with a face and mien which reminded him of a tall angel he had seen once borne in a car of triumph at a City show. But now as he left his curtain, twittering, crazed with fear, spreading out both hands toward the stain on the tablecloth, a door beside the hatch opened noiselessly, and swift and prompt as though they had been watching, two men entered, flung a dark coverlet over the body, lifted and bore it off, closing the door behind them. They went as they had come, swiftly, without a word. He had seen it as plainly as he saw now the murderer sheathing his knife, the woman sullenly watching him. The other women, too, had vanished—they that had been gleaning among the broken crusts. Had they decamped, scurrying, at the first hint of the brawl? He could not tell: they had been, and were not.

He stretched out both hands towards the man, the woman—would they, too, vanish?—and the damning stain? A cry worked in his throat, but would not come.

"Gone!" a voice called, hearty at once and disconsolate, from the doorway behind him. "Gone—given me the slip, as I am a Christian sinner. What? You three left alone here? But where is our friend the piper?"

The apprentice made a snatch at a flask of wine, and, turning, let its contents spill wildly over the bloodied tablecloth.

"Art drunk, lad—shamefully drunk," said John Shakespeare, lurching forward. "They have given me the slip, I say, and ne'er a groat have I to redeem my promises."

"They paid the score below—I saw them; and this thy son charged me to hand to thee." The apprentice drew a full purse from his pocket and flung it on the table. "I—I played thee a trick, master: but let me forth into fresh air. This room dizzies me. . . ."

"Go thy ways—go thy ways, child. For my part I was ever last at a feast to leave it, and would crack one more cup with these good folk. To your health, Madam!" He reached a hand for the wine-flask as the apprentice set it down and went forth, tottering yet.

VII

Dawn was breaking down the river; a grey dawn as yet, albeit above the mists rolling low upon the tide-way a clear sky promised gold to come—a golden Christmas Day. The mist, however, had a chill which searched the bones. The red-eyed waterman pulled as though his arms were numb. Tom Nashe coughed and huddled his cloak about him, as he turned for a last backward glance on Bankside, where a few lights yet gleamed, and the notes of a belated guitar tinkled on, dulled by the vapours, calling like a thin ghost above the deeper baying of the hounds.

"Take care of thyself, lad," said Shakespeare kindly, stretching out a hand to help his friend draw the cloak closer.

"Behoved me think of that sooner, I doubt," Nashe answered,

glancing up with a wry, pathetic smile, yet gratefully. He dropped his eyes to the cloak and quoted, " 'Sometime it was of cloth-in-grain, 'Tis now but a sigh-clout, as you may see; It will hold out neither wind nor rain . . .' and—and—I thank thee. Will. 'But I'll take my old cloak about me.' There's salt in the very warp of it, good Yarmouth salt. Will?"

"Ay, lad?"

"Is't true thou'rt become a landowner, down in my native shire?"

"In a small way, Tom."

"A man of estate? with coat-of-arms and all?"

"Even that too, with your leave."

"I know—I know. *Nescio qua natale solum*—those others did not understand: but I understood. Yes, and now I understand that fifth act of thine, which puzzled me afore, and yet had not puzzled me; but I fancied—poor fool!—that the feeling was singular in me. 'Twas a vile life, Will." He jerked a thumb back at Bankside.

"Ay, 'tis vile."

"My cough translates it into the past tense; but—then, or now, or hereafter—'tis vile. Count them up, Will—the lads we have drunk with aforetime. There was Greene, now—"

Shakespeare bent his head for tally.

"—I can see his poor corse staring up at the rafters: there on the shoemaker's bed, with a chaplet of laurel askew on the brow. The woman meant it kindly, poor thing! . . . She forgot to close his eyes, though. With my own fingers I closed 'em, and borrowed two penny pieces of her for weights. 'Twas the first dead flesh I had touched, and I feel it now. . . . But George Peele was worse, ten times worse. I forget if you saw him?"

Again Shakespeare bent his head.

"And poor Kit? You saw Kit, I know . . . with a hole below the eye, they told me, where the knife went through. And that was our Kit, our hope, pride, paragon, our Daphnis. Damnation, and this is art! Didst hear that blotch-faced youngster, that Scotchman, how he prated of it, laying down the law?"

"That Jonson, Tom, is a tall poet, or will be."

"The devil care I! Tall poet or not, he is no Englishman and understands not the race. Art is not for us. We have dreamed dreams, thou and I: and thy dreams are coming to glory. But the last dream of a true Englishman is to own a few good English acres and die respected in a dear, if narrow, round. Dear Will, there is more in this than greed. There is the call of the land, which is home. For me—thou knowest—I had ne'er the gift of saving. My bolt is shot, or almost: two years at farthest must see the end of me. But when thou rememberest, bethink thee that I understood the call. Wilt guess what I am writing, now at the last? a great book—a sound book—and all of the red-herring! Ay, the red-herring, staple of my own Yarmouth. Canst never, as an inland man, rise to the virtues of that fish nor to the merit of my handling. But I have read some pages of it to my neighbours there and I learn from their approving looks that I shall die respected. Yet I, too, forgot and dreamed of art. . . ."

On the Bankside at the foot of Paris Garden Stairs, deserted now of watermen, a youth sat with his teeth chattering.

Above, while he tried to clench his teeth, a window opened stealthily. There was a heavy splash on the tideway, and the window shut to, softly as it had opened. He watched. He was past fear. The body bobbed once to the surface, half a furlong below the spreading, fading circles thrown to the foot of Paris Garden Stairs. It did not rise again. The Bankside knew its business.

A heavy footfall came down the steps to the landing-stage.

"A glorious night!"

The apprentice watched the river.

"A glorious night! A night to remember! Tell me, lad, have I made good my promises, or have I not?"

"They rise thrice before sinking, I have always heard," twittered the lad.

"What the devil art talking of? Here, take my cloak, if thou feelest the chill. The watermen here ply by shifts, and we shall hail a boat anon to take us over. Meanwhile, if thou hast eyes, boy, look on the river—see the masts there, below bridge, the sun touching them!—see the towers yonder, in the gold of it! 'London, thou art the flower of cities all!' Eh, lad?"

The sun's gold drifted through the fog, touched the side of a small row-boat nearing the farther shore. Behind, and to right and left along Bankside, a few guitars yet tinkled. Across the tide came wafted the voices of London's Christmas bells.

THE BABY'S CHRISTMAS

by Joel Chandler Harris

from *Tales of the Home Folks in Peace and War*

I

Rockville ought to have been a harmonious community if there
ever was one. The same families had been living there for generations,
and they had intermarried until everybody was everybody else's
cousin. Those who were no kin at all called one another cousin in
public—such is the force of example and habit. Little children playing with other children would hear them call one another cousin, and
so the habit grew until even the few newcomers who took up their
abode in Rockville speedily became cousins.

There were different degrees of prosperity in the village before and
during the war, but everybody was comfortably well off, so that there
was no necessity for drawing social distinctions. Those who were com-
paratively poor boasted of good blood, and they made as nice cousins
as those who were richer. When the editor of the "Vade Mecum"
wished to impress on his subscribers the necessity of settling their accounts, he prefaced his remarks with this statement: "We are a

homogeneous people. We are united. What is the interest of one is the interest of all. We must continue to preserve our harmony."

But envy knows no race or clime, and it had taken up its abode among the cousins of Rockville. It was not even rooted out by the disastrous results of the war, which tended to bring each and every cousin down to the same level of hopeless poverty. When, therefore, Colonel Asbury announced in the streets that his wife had concluded to take boarders, and caused to be inserted in the "Vade Mecum" a notice to the effect that "a few select parties" could find accommodations at The Cedars, there were a good many smothered exclamations of affected surprise among the cousins, with no little secret satisfaction that "Cousin Becky T." had at last been compelled to "get off her high horse," to employ the vernacular of Rockville.

Such an announcement was certainly the next thing to a crash in the social fabric, and while some of the cousins were secretly pleased, there were others who shook their heads in sorrow, feeling that a deep and lasting humiliation had been visited on the community. For if ever a human being was seized and possessed by pride of family and position, that person was Cousin Becky T. Her pride was reënforced by a will as firm, and an individuality as strong, as ever woman had; and these characteristics were so marked that she was never known among her acquaintances as Mrs. Asbury, but always as Rebecca Tumlin or "Cousin Rebecca T." The colonel himself invariably referred to her, even in his most hilarious moments, as Rebecca Tumlin. Times were hard indeed when this gentlewoman could be induced to throw open to boarders the fine old mansion, with its massive white pillars standing out against a background of red brick.

The colonel had three plantations—one near Rockville, one in the low country, and one in the Cherokee region; but in 1868 these possessions were a burden to him to the extent of the taxes he was compelled to pay. There was no market for agricultural lands. The value they might have had was swallowed up in the poverty and depression that enveloped everything in the region where war had dropped its litter of furies. Colonel Asbury might have practiced law: he did practice it, in fact; but it was like building a windmill over a dry well.

Cousin Rebecca Tumlin finally solved the problem by announcing that she purposed to take boarders. No one ever knew what it cost her to make that announcement. Envious people suspected the nature of the struggle through which she passed—the hard and bitter struggle between pride and necessity—and some of them predicted it would do her good. The colonel, who was proud after his own fashion, and also sympathetic, was shocked at first and then grieved, But he made no remark. Comment was unnecessary. He walked back and forth on the colonnade, and measured many a mile before his agitation was allayed. More than once he went down the long graveled avenue, and turned and gazed fondly at the perspective that carried the eye to the fine old house. It seemed as if he were bidding farewell to the beauty and glory of it all. But he made no complaint. When he grew tired of walking, he went in with the intention of taking down some family pictures that adorned the walls of the wide hall. But his wife had forestalled him. The house, by a few deft changes, had been made as cheerless as the most fastidious boarder could wish.

And so the word went round that Cousin Rebecca Tumlin would be pleased to take boarders. The response was all that she could have desired. The young men—the bachelor storekeepers and their clerks— deserted the rickety old tavern and the smaller boardinghouses, and took up their abode at The Cedars, and soon the house was gay with a company that was profitable if not pleasant.

The advent of boarders—some of them transient traveling-men— opened a new world for Mary Asbury, Cousin Rebecca Tumlin's daughter, and she made the most of it. She followed the example of her father, the colonel, and made herself agreeable to the young men. She made herself especially agreeable to Laban Pierson, the young conductor of the daily train on the little branch railroad that con- nected Rockville with the outside world. Cousin Rebecca T. held her- self severely aloof from her boarders, but her attitude was so serene and graceful, so evidently the natural and correct thing, that it caused no ill-natured comment. Mary was sixteen, and when she sat at the head of the table, her mother was not missed. The young girl's manners were a rare combination of sweetness, grace, and dignity. She was affable, she was thoughtful, and she had a fair share of her father's humor. Above all, she was beautiful. Naturally, therefore, while her mother nursed her pride, and counted the money, Mary beamed on the boarders, and her father drew upon his vast fund of anecdote for their instruction and amusement.

Laban Pierson was not a very brilliant young man, but he was fairly good-looking, and he knew how to make himself agreeable. His train arrived at Rockville at half-past two in the afternoon, and left at five o'clock in the morning, so that he had plenty of time to make himself agreeable to Miss Mary Asbury, and he did so with only a vague notion of what the end would be. Mary made herself agreeable to Laban simply because it was her nature to be pleasant to everybody. As for any other reason—why, the idea of such a thing! If young Pierson had told himself that he was courting Mary Asbury, he would have blushed with alarm. Perhaps he would have left The Cedars and gone to the old tavern again. Who knows? Young men will do very desperate things at certain stages of their checkered careers.

It was the old story with its own particular variations. Mary loved Laban, and was too shy to know what she was about. Laban loved Mary, and never discovered it until the disease had become epidemic in his system, and spread over his heart and mind in every direction. Neither one of them discovered it. It was a beautiful dream, too good to be true, too sweet to last. Finally the discovery was made by old Aunt Mimy, the cook, who had never seen Mary and Laban together. The affair, if it can be called by so imposing a name, had been going on a year or more, and Mary was past seventeen, when one afternoon the train failed to arrive on time. The afternoon wore into evening, and still the train did not come. Mary had the habit of sitting in the kitchen with Aunt Mimy when anything troubled her, and on this particular afternoon, after waiting an hour for the train, she went to her old seat near the window. Aunt Mimy was beating biscuit. Mary looked out of the window toward the depot.

"Train ain't come yit, is she, honey?" asked Aunt Mimy.

"No, not yet," replied Mary. "What can be the matter?"

"Run off de trussle, I speck," said Aunt Mimy.

"Oh, mammy!" cried Mary, starting to her feet; "do you really think so? What have you heard?"

The girl stood with one hand against her bosom, her face pale, and her nether lip trembling. Aunt Mimy regarded her with astonishment for a moment, and then the shrewd old negro jumped to a conclusion. She paused with her arm uplifted.

"Is yo' ma on dat train? Is yo' pa on dat train? What de name er de Lord you got ter do wid dat train?"

She brought the beater down on the pliant dough with a resounding thwack. Mary hid her face in her hands. After a little she went out, leaving Aunt Mimy mumbling and talking to herself.

The cook lost no time in relating this incident to Cousin Rebecca T., and that lady lost just as little in making plain to her daughter the folly and futility of interesting herself in such a person as the young conductor. Cousin Rebecca T. gave Mary a brief but picturesque biography of Laban Pierson. His family belonged to the poor white trash before the war, and he was no better. Muddy well, muddy water. He had been a train-hand, a brakeman, baggage-master, and what not. The colonel was called in to verify these biographical details.

Mary's reply to it all was characteristic. She listened amd smiled, and tossed her head.

"What do I care about Laban Pierson? What have I to do with his affairs? Ought I to have jumped for joy when mammy told me the train had dropped through the trestle?"

The colonel accepted this logic without question, but Cousin Rebecca T. saw through it. She was a woman, and had a natural contempt for logic, especially a woman's logic. She simply realized that she had made a mistake. She had gone about the matter in the wrong way. As for Mary, she had found out her own secret. She hardened her heart against Aunt Mimy, and when the old woman sought an explanation, it was readily forthcoming.

"You got me into trouble," said Mary; "you won't get me into any more if I can help it." Aunt Mimy grieved over the situation to such an extent that she made herself disagreeable to everybody, especially to Cousin Rebecca T. She broke dishes, she burned the waffles, she flung the dish-water into the yard, and for a day or two she whipped the little negroes every time she got her hands on them.

Cousin Rebecca T. did not let the matter drop, as she might have done. The colonel used to tell his intimate friends that his wife had a fearful amount of misdirected energy, and the results that it wrought in this particular instance justified the colonel's description. Cousin Rebecca T. went straight to young Laban Pierson, and gave him to understand, without circumlocution or mincing of words, what she thought of any possible notion he had or might have of uniting his fortunes with those of her daughter. As might have been expected, Laban was thunderstruck. He blushed violently, turned pale, stammered, and, in short, acted just as any other young fellow would act when confronted with his own secret thoughts and desires, hardly acknowledged even to himself. To Cousin Rebecca T. all this was in the nature of a confession of guilt, and she congratulated herself on the promptness with which she had put an end to the whole miserable business. As a matter of fact, she did what many another hasty-tempered woman has done before her; she kindled into flame a spark that might have expired if let alone.

Young Mr. Pierson promptly took himself away from The Cedars, and it was not until after he was gone that the other guests discovered what an interesting companion he was at table and on the wide veranda. They began to talk about him and to discuss his good qualities. He was a clean, manly, bright, industrious, genial, generous young fellow. This was the verdict. The colonel, missing the cigars that Laban was in the habit of bringing him, and resenting the situation (inflamed, perhaps, by a little too much toddy), went further, and said that in the whole course of his career, sir, he had never seen a finer young man, sir. So that in spite of the fact that Laban sat at table no longer, he was more in evidence than ever.

Affairs went on without a break or a ripple. Occasionally Mary would walk in the direction of the depot in the afternoon, and whenever she saw Laban she made it a point to bow to him, and this salutation he always returned with marked emphasis. But Mary was not happy. She no longer went singing through the house. She was cheerful, but not in the old fashion. No one noticed the change but old Aunt Mimy, and perhaps she would have been blind to it if her conscience had not hurt her. The old woman's conscience was not specially active or sensitive, but her affections were set on Mary, and for many long weeks the girl had hardly deigned to speak to her. Conscience lives next door to the affections. Aunt Mimy rebelled against hers for a long time, but at last it roused her to action.

One afternoon, when dinner had been cleared away, she filled her pipe, adjusted her head-kerchief, and sallied out in the direction of the depot. The wheezy old locomotive was engaged in shifting the cars about, and Conductor Pierson was assisting the brakeman. Aunt Mimy seated herself on the depot platform, smoked her pipe, and patiently waited till the shunting was over. Then she placed herself in Pierson's way. He seemed to be preoccupied, but the old woman did not stand on ceremony.

"Look like our victuals wa'n't good 'nough fer you," she said bluntly.

"Why, this is Aunt Mimy!" He shook hands with her and asked about her health, and this pleased her very much. He asked about the family, and especially about Miss Mary. When it came to this, Aunt Mimy took her pipe out of her mouth, drew a long breath, and shook her head. She could have given points on the art of pantomime to any strolling company of players. The whole history of the sad case of Mary Asbury was in the lift of her eyebrows, the motions of her head, and in her sorrowful sigh; and Conductor Pierson seemed to be able to read a part of it, for he asked Aunt Mimy into the passenger-coach, and there the two sat and talked until it was time for Aunt Mimy to go home and see about supper.

That night, as Aunt Mimy sat on the kitchen steps smoking her pipe and resting herself, preparatory to going to bed, she saw Mary sitting at her room window looking out into the moonlight. It was not a very beautiful scene that fell under the young girl's eye. There was nothing romantic or picturesque in the view of the back yard, with the kitchen and the comical figure of the fat old cook in the foreground: but when a young girl is in love, it is wonderful what a mellowing influence the moonlight has on the most forbidding scene. It pushes the shadows into strange places, and softens and subdues all that is angular and ugly. Take the moon out of our scheme, and a good deal of our poetry and romance would vanish with it, and even true love would take on a prosiness that it does not now possess.

Aunt Mimy looked at Mary, and felt sorry for her. Mary looked at Aunt Mimy, and felt that she would be glad to be able to despise the old negro if she could. Aunt Mimy spoke to her presently in a subdued, insinuating tone.

"Is dat you, honey?"

"Yes."

"Better fling on yo' cape—"

"I'm not cold."

"An' come down here an' talk wid me."

"I don't feel like talking."

"Been long time sence you felt like talkin' wid me. Well, dem dat don't talk don't never hear tell."

She pulled from somewhere under her apron something white and oblong, dropped it on the ground purposely, picked it up, and put it back under her apron. Then she said, "Good-night, honey! I ain't tellin' you good-night des fer myse'f."

Aunt Mimy's tone was charged with information. Mary vanished from the window, and came tripping out to the kitchen. Then followed a whispered conversation between the cook and the young lady. At something or other that Aunt Mimy said to her—some quaint comment, or maybe a happy piece of intelligence—Mary laughed loudly. The sound of it reached the ears of Cousin Rebecca T., who was playing whist. The colonel was dealing. She slipped away from the table, peeped through the blinds of the dining-room, and was just in time to see Aunt Mimy hand Mary something that had the appearance of a letter. She returned to the whist-table, revoked on the first round, and trumped her partner's trick on the second. Such a thing had never been heard of before. Her partner shook his head, and buried his face in his cards. Her husband regarded her with amazement. She made no excuse or explanation, but in the next two hands more than made up in brilliant play for the advantage she had lost.

Meanwhile Mary was reading the letter that Laban Pierson had sent her. It was a frank, manly declaration of his love expressed in plain and simple language. He had written, he said, on the impulse of the moment, but he did not propose to engage in a clandestine correspondence. He did not invite or expect a reply, but would always—ah, well, the formula was the same old one that we are all familiar with.

Mary placed the letter where she could feel her heart beat against it, and went to bed happy, and was soon dreaming about Laban Pierson. Cousin Rebecca T. played whist fiercely and won continuously. After the game was over, she went upstairs, stirred a stiff toddy for the colonel, and put him to bed. Then she went into her daughter's room, shading the lamp with her hand so that the light would not arouse Innocence from its happy dreams. She moved as noiselessly as Lady Macbeth moves in the play; though not with the same intent. She searched everywhere for the letter, and at last found it where a more feminine woman would have hunted for it at first. One corner of this human document was peeping modestly forth from the virgin bosom of Innocence. Deftly, gently, even lovingly, Cousin Rebecca T. lifted the letter from its warm and shy covert.

It was a very simple thing to do, but there were hours and days and years when Cousin Rebecca T. would have given all her possessions to have left the letter nestling in her daughter's bosom; for, in lifting it out, Innocence was aroused from its sleep and caught Experience in the very act of making a fool of itself. Mary opened her wondering eyes, and found her mother with Laban's letter in her hand. The young lady sat bolt upright in bed. Cousin Rebecca T. was inwardly startled, but outwardly she was as calm as the moonlight that threw its slanting shadows eastward.

"I don't wonder that you blush," she cried, holding up the letter.

"Do you think I am blushing for myself?" asked Mary.

"If you know what shame is, you ought to feel it now," exclaimed her mother.

"I do—I do," said Mary, with rising indignation. "After to-night I shall always be ashamed of myself and of my family."

Cousin Rebecca T., stung by the tone and by this first sign of rebellion, turned upon her daughter; but her anger quickly died away, for she saw in her daughter's eyes her own courage and her own unconquerable will.

The scene did not end there, but the rest of it need not be described here. Innocence has as long a tongue as Experience when it feels itself wronged, and the result of this family quarrel was that Innocence went farther than Experience would have dared to go. When Laban Pierson's train went puffing out of Rockville at five o'clock the next morning, it carried among its few passengers Miss Mary Asbury and old Aunt Mimy. The colonel and Cousin Rebecca T. lost a daughter, and their boarders had to wait a long time for their breakfast or go without.

The next number of the "Vade Mecum" had a beautifully written account of the marriage of Mary Asbury to Laban Pierson, under the double heading: "LOVE LAUGHS AT LOCKSMITHS. A LOCAL ROMANCE WITH A HAPPY ENDING."

Cousin Rebecca T. turned up her nose at the newspaper account, but the colonel cut it out and hid it away in his large morocco pocketbook. That night, after he had taken his toddy and was sound asleep, Cousin Rebecca T. took the clipping from its hiding-place, and read it over carefully. Then she put out the light, and sat by the window and cried until far into the night. But she cried so softly that a little bird, sitting on its nest in the honeysuckle vine not two feet away from the lady's grief, did not take its head from under its wing.

II

This was at the beginning of 1870, and about this time Colonel Asbury's fortunes took a decided turn for the better. During the war, in a spirit of speculative recklessness, he had invested thirty thousand dollars in Confederate money in ten thousand acres of land in Texas. He thought so little of the investment then, and afterwards, that he did not take the trouble to pay the taxes. But the purchase of the land was a fortunate stroke for the colonel. In 1870 land-values in Texas were not what they were in Georgia. That vast southwestern empire (as the phrase goes) was just beginning to attract the attention of Northern and foreign capital. Railway promoters, British land syndicates, and native boomers, were combining to develop the material resources of the wonderful State.

In the early part of 1870, a powerful combination of railway promoters determined to build a line straight through the colonel's Texan possessions. His land there increased in value to thirty dollars, and then to forty dollars, an acre, at which figure the colonel was induced to part with his titles. Cousin Rebecca Tumlin thus found herself to be the wife of a very rich man, and her pride at last found something substantial to cling to. The Cedars ceased to be a boardinghouse. The old family pictures were brought down from the garret, dusted, and hung in their accustomed places. Great improvements were made in the place, and Cousin Rebecca and the colonel sat down to enjoy life as they thought it ought to be enjoyed.

But something was lacking. Life did not run as pleasantly as before. The dollar that brings content is at such a high premium among the nations of the earth that it can never be made the standard of value. That dollar was not among the four hundred thousand dollars the colonel received for his Texan lands. The old style did not fit the new times. The colonel's old friends did not fall away from him, but they were less friendly and more obsequious. His daughter did not come forward to ask his forgiveness and his blessing. Something was wrong somewhere. The colonel and Cousin Rebecca Tumlin fretted a good deal, and finally concluded to move to Atlanta. So they closed their house in Rockville, and built a mansion in Peachtree Street in the city whose name has come to be identified with all that is progressive in the South.

The building is on the left as you go out Peachtree. You can't mistake it. It is a queer mixture of summer cottage and feudal castle, with a great deal of fussy detail that bewilders the eye, and a serene stretch of roof broken by a delirious display of scrollwork. It is Rebecca Tumlin all over; pride—pride nailed to the grim walls, and vexation of spirit worked into the ornamentation. Yet it is a house that easily catches the eye. It is on a little elevation, and it has about it a certain suggestion of individuality. On the dome of the middle gable a smart and business-like dragon upholds the weather-vane with his curled and gilded tail.

The colonel prospered steadily. He was regarded as one of the most successful businessmen and financiers the South has ever produced. It is no wonder the Bible parable gives money the name of "talent." It *is* a talent. Give it half a chance, and it is the most active talent that man possesses. It is always in a state of fermentation; it grows; it accumulates. At any rate, the colonel thought so. His capital carried him into the inner circles of investment and speculation, and he found himself growing richer and richer, only vaguely realizing how the result was brought about.

The receptions at the Asbury mansion were conceded to be the most fashionable that Atlanta had ever seen; for along in the seventies Atlanta was merely experimenting with the social instinct. The "smart set" had no kind of organization. Society was engaged in disentangling itself from the furious business energy that has made Atlanta the best-known city in the South. It was at this juncture that Cousin Rebecca T., with her money, her taste, and her ambition to lead, appeared on the scene. She had all the requisites of a leader. Pride is a quickening quality, and it had made of Cousin Rebecca T. a most accomplished woman. There was something attractive and refreshing about her strong individuality. There was a simplicity about her methods that commended her to the social experimenters, who stood in great awe of forms and conventions.

Naturally, therefore, the Asbury mansion was the social centre. The younger set gathered there to be gay, and the married people went there to meet their friends. But many and many a night after the lights were out in the parlors, and the gas was turned low in the hall, Cousin Rebecca T. and the colonel sat and thought about their daughter Mary, each refraining from mentioning her name to the other—the colonel because he was afraid of irritating his wife, and Cousin Rebecca T. because she was afraid of exhibiting any weakness before her husband. Each, unknown to the other, had set on foot inquiries in regard to the whereabouts of Mary, and the fact that the inquiries elicited no response and no information gave the two old people a more valid excuse for misery than they had ever known.

The trouble was that their inquiries had begun too late. For a few months after her marriage the colonel had kept himself informed about his daughter. He expected her to write to him. He had a vague and unformed notion that in due season Mary would return and ask her mother's forgiveness, and then, if Cousin Rebecca T. showed any hardness of heart, he proposed to put his foot down, and show her that he was not a cipher in the family. The mother, for her part, fully expected that some day when she was going about the house, neither doing nor thinking of anything in particular, her daughter would rush suddenly in upon her and tell her between laughter and tears that there was no happiness away from home. Cousin Rebecca T. had her part all prepared. She would frown at first, and then throw her arms around Mary, and tell her what a naughty girl she had been.

But all this mental preparation was in vain. Weeks, months, and years passed by, but Mary never came. When the colonel and Cousin Rebecca T. woke up to their new prosperity, they were very busily engaged for some time in fitting themselves to it. It was during this period that Mary and her husband disappeared. The colonel heard in a vague way that Laban Pierson had moved to Atlanta, and that from Atlanta he had gone out West. All the rest was mystery.

But it was no mystery to Laban and Mary. For a little while their affairs went along comfortably. Laban became the conductor of a passenger-train on the main line of the Central of Georgia. Then he moved to Atlanta. Afterward he accepted a position on the Louisville and Nashville Railway, and there had the misfortune to lose a leg in a collision. This was the beginning of troubles that seemed to pursue Laban and Mary. Poverty laid its grim hand upon them at every turn. Mary did the best she could. She was indeed a helpmate and a comforter; she was brave and hopeful; yet she would have given up in despair but for old Aunt Mimy, who worked and slaved that her young mistress might be spared the bitterest pangs of poverty. Her faithfulness was without boundary or limit. Day and night she toiled, cooking, washing, and taking care of the toddling baby that had come to share the troubles of Laban and Mary. As soon as Laban could get about on his crutches, he tried to find work; but his efforts were fruitless. The time came when he was ready to say to his wife that he could do no more.

Finally the little family drifted back to Atlanta. Here Laban found employment in a small way as a solicitor of life insurance. He was doing so well in this business that a rival company sought his services, offering to pay a fixed salary instead of commissions. But no sooner had he given notice to his employers that he intended to accept the new position than a complication arose in his accounts. How it happened Laban never knew; he was as innocent as a lamb. The company was a new one, trying to establish a business in the Atlanta territory, and out of the funds he collected he used money to pay expenses incurred in the company's behalf. His vouchers showed it all; he had been careful to put down everything, even to the cost of a postal card. He turned over these vouchers and accounts to his employers. But when it was found that he had entered the service of a rival company, the charge of embezzlement was made against him. He found it impossible to give bonds, and was compelled to go to jail. A young lawyer took his case, and was sure he could clear him when the case came to trial. But meanwhile Laban was in jail, and to Mary this was the end of all things; for a time she was utterly prostrated. She refused to eat or sleep, but sat holding her child to her bosom, and crying over it. This went on for so long a time that Aunt Mimy thought it best to interfere. So she took the two-year-old child from its mother, and made some characteristic observations.

"You ain't gwine ter git Marse Laban out'n jail by settin' dar cryin', honey. Better git mad an' stir roun', an' hurt somebody's feelin's. Make you feel lots better, kaze I done tried it."

"O mammy! mammy!" moaned Mary.

"Day atter ter-morrer 'll be Chris'mus," Aunt Mimy continued, "an' Marse Laban got ter be here ter dinner. Dey ain't no two ways 'bout dat."

"Oh, what a Christmas!" cried Mary.

"Yes 'm; an' de cake done baked. Don't you fret, honey! De Lord ain't fur f'om whar folks is in trouble. I done notice dat. He may n't be right dar in de nex' room, an' maybe he ain't right roun' de cornder, but he ain't so mighty fur off. Now, I tell you dat."

Whereupon Aunt Mimy, carrying the child, went out of the house into the street, and was so disturbed in mind that she walked on and on with no thought of the distance. After a while she found herself on Peachtree Street, where the baby's attention was attracted by the jingling bells of the street-car horses. In front of one of the large mansions a fine carriage was standing. On the veranda a lady stood drawing on her gloves and giving some parting orders to a servant in the hall. Aunt Mimy knew at once that the lady was her old mistress. But she turned to the negro coachman, who sat on the box stiff and stolid in all the grandeur of a long coat and brass buttons.

"Who live' here?" she asked.

"Cun-nol Asbe'y," the coachman replied.

"Ain't dat Becky Tumlin yonder?" inquired Aunt Mimy, with some asperity.

"No, ma'am; dat is Missus Cun-nol Asbe'y."

"Well, de Lord he'p my soul!" exclaimed Aunt Mimy.

Then she turned and went back home as fast as she could, talking to herself and the child. Once she looked back, but Cousin Rebecca T. was sitting grandly in the carriage, and the carriage was going rapidly toward the business portion of the city. Cousin Rebecca T. bowed right and left to her acquaintances and smiled pleasantly as the carriage rolled along. She bowed and smiled, but she was thinking about her daughter.

Aunt Mimy hurried home as fast as she could go. She had intended at first to tell Mary of her discovery, but she thought better of it. She had another plan.

"You see me gwine 'long here?" she said, as much to herself as to the baby. "Well, ef I don't fix dat ar white 'oman you kin put me in de calaboose." She stood at the gate of the house Laban had rented, and compared its appearance with the magnificence of the mansion she had just left. The contrast was so startling that all the comment she could make was, "De Lord he'p my soul!" She took the child in, got its playthings, and then went about her business more briskly than she had gone in many a day. If Mary had not been so deeply engaged in contemplating her troubles, she would have discovered at once that something unusual had occurred. Aunt Mimy was agitated. Her mind was not in her work. She drew a bucket of water from the well when she intended to get wood for the little stove. Occasionally she would pause in her work and stand lost in thought. At last Mary remarked her agitation.

"What is the matter, mammy?" she asked. "Something has happened."

"Ah, Lord, honey! 'T ain't happen' yit, but it's gwine ter happen."

"Well," said Mary, shaking her head, "let it happen. Nothing can hurt me. The worst has already happened."

Aunt Mimy made no audible comment, but went about mumbling and talking to herself. Mary sat rocking and moaning, and the little child made the most of the situation by toddling from room to room, getting into all sorts of mischief without let or hindrance. After a while Aunt Mimy asked, "Honey, don't you know whar yo' pa an' ma is?"

"Yes," said Mary languidly; "they live in Atlanta."

"Right here in dis town?"

"Yes."

"Whar' bouts?"

"Oh, don't worry me, mammy! I don't know. They care nothing for me. See how they have treated Laban!"

"Why n't you hunt 'em up, an' tell 'em what kinder fix you in? I boun' dey'd he'p you out." Mary gazed at Aunt Mimy with open-eyed wonder. "Write a letter ter yo' ma. Here's what'll take it. I'll fin' out whar she live at."

Mary rose from her chair and took a step toward Aunt Mimy, not in anger, but by way of emphasis.

"Mammy," she cried, "don't speak of such a thing!"

"Humph!" Aunt Mimy grunted; "ef you ain't de ve'y spi't an' image er Becky Tumlin, I'm a saddle-hoss. Proud! consated! Dat ain't no name fer it. De nigger man what I got now ain't much, but ef he wuz in jail I'd be trottin' roun' right now tryin' ter git 'im out."

The next morning Aunt Mimy was up betimes. She cooked breakfast, and after that meal was over (it need not have been prepared so far as Mary was concerned), she dressed the baby in some of its commonest clothes, and put on its feet a pair of shoes that were worn at the toes. This done, she took the lively youngster in her arms and started out.

"Where arc you going?" Mary asked.

"Baby gwine ter walk," Aunt Mimy answered.

"Not in those clothes!" Mary protested.

"Now, honey," exclaimed Aunt Mimy, "does you speck I ain't got no better sense dan ter rig dis baby out, an' his pa down yonder in de dungeons?"

"Oh, what shall I do?" cried Mary, forgetting everything else but her own misery and her husband's disgrace.

"Stay right here, honey, tell I come back. I won't be gone so mighty long. Den you kin take dis precious baby down ter see his pa."

The day was clear and bright, and although it was Christmas, the soft breezes and the invigorating sunshine had the flavor and quality of spring. Aunt Mimy paid no attention to the auspicious weather, but made her way straight to the Asbury mansion on Peachtree Street. On her face there was a frown, and her "head-han'k'cher," which usually sat straight back from her forehead, had an upward tilt that gave her a warlike appearance.

She went up the tiled walk and rang the door-bell. A quadroon girl came to the door; the girl's voice was soft, and her manners gentle, but Aunt Mimy had a strong prejudice against mulattoes, and it came to the surface now.

"Is yo' mist'ess in?" she asked harshly.

"Mis' Asbury is in," said the girl softly.

"Ax her kin I see her."

The girl slipped away from the door, leaving it ajar. The glimpse of the magnificence within angered Aunt Mimy. Presently the girl returned.

"Has you got any message?" she asked.

"No, I ain't. Tell her dat a' ole nigger 'oman fum de country want to see her."

Cousin Rebecca T. was listening at the farther end of the hall, and thought she recognized the voice. The girl turned away with a smile to deliver the message, but her mistress was standing near. With a wave of her hand, Cousin Rebecca T. dismissed the servant, saw her safely out of hearing, and then opened wide the door.

"Come in, Mimy," she said in a voice as serene as a summer morning; "come into my room. I have n't seen you in a coon's age." She dropped easily into the vernacular of Rockville and the region round about. She took Aunt Mimy somewhat off her guard, but this only served to increase the agitation of the old negro. Cousin Rebecca T. led the way to her back parlor.

"Come in," she said kindly. "How have you been since I saw you last?" She shut the door and caught the thumb-bolt. "Sit in that chair. Now, what have you to tell me?"

Aunt Mimy saw that the thin white hand of her old mistress trembled as she raised it to her hair.

"Wellum," Aunt Mimy replied, "I des tuck er notion I'd drap by an' say 'Chris'mus Gif'.' You know how we use' ter do down dar at home. I ain't seed you so long, it's des de same ez sayin' howdy?"

Cousin Rebecca T. looked hard at the old darky, and drew a long breath.

"Do you mean to say you have nothing to tell me—nothing? What do you want?" She would have laid her hand on Aunt Mimy's shoulder, but the old woman shrunk away, exclaiming, "God knows dey ain't nothin' here I want! No, ma'am!"

Cousin Rebecca T. took a step toward her old servant.

"Where is Mary?" she asked, almost in a whisper.

"She down yander—down dar at de house." Aunt Mimy put the child down, faced Cousin Rebecca T., whose agitation was now extreme, and raised her strong right arm in the air. "I thank my God, I ain't got no chillun! I thank 'im day an' night. Ef I'd a' had 'em, maybe I'd 'a' done 'em like you done yone."

"You are impudent," said Cousin Rebecca T. The little child had gone to her, and her hand rested on its curly head.

"Wellum," Aunt Mimy rejoined, "ef you want ter call de trufe by some yuther name, let it go at dat."

"Whose child is this?"

"Heh!" the old negro grunted. "He look like he know who he kin ter."

Cousin Rebecca T. took the child in her arms and carried it into her bedroom, closing the door behind her. Aunt Mimy went to the door on tiptoe, and listened silently for a moment. Then she nodded her head vigorously, ejaculating at intervals, "Aha-a-a!" "What I tell you?" "Ah-yi!"

Cousin Rebecca T. placed the child on the floor and knelt beside it.

"Darling, what is your name?"

"Azzerbewy Tummerlin Pierson," replied the child solemnly.

"Oh, will the Lord ever forgive me?" cried Cousin Rebecca T., falling prone on the floor in her grief and humiliation.

"Yonner mudder!" said the child.

"Where?" exclaimed Cousin Rebecca T., starting up.

"Yonner." The youngster pointed to a picture of his mother hanging on the wall, an enlarged copy of a photograph taken before she was married. Seeing that the lady was crying, the child went to her, laid its soft face against hers, and gently patted her with one of its pretty hands.

"Mudder c'y—all, all'e time," said the child, by way of consolation.

"Oh, precious baby!" exclaimed Cousin Rebecca T., "she shall never cry any more if I can help it."

"Ah-yi!" responded Aunt Mimy on the other side.

At this juncture the colonel walked into the back parlor. "Well, my dear," he said, "what is the programme to-day? In my opinion—why, this is Mimy! Mimy"—his voice sank to a whisper—"where is your young mistress?"

"Ah, Lord! you been waitin' a mighty long time 'fo' you ax anybody dat quesht'on!"

"Mimy, is she dead?" The ruddy color had fled from his face.

"Go in dar, suh." Aunt Mimy pointed to the door leading into the bedroom.

The colonel found his wife weeping over the little child, and, being a tender-hearted man, he joined her. As Aunt Mimy said afterward, "Dey went on in dar mo' samer dan ef dey 'd'a' done got erligion sho 'nough, an' de Lord knows dey needed it mighty bad."

The colonel went on at a great rate over the baby. "Look at the little shoes with holes in them!" he cried. "Look at the torn frock!" Then he fairly blubbered.

In the midst of it all, Aunt Mimy opened the door and walked into the room, calm, cool, and indifferent. Ah, how wonderfully she could play the hypocrite! "Come on, honey," she said. "Mudder waitin' fer you. I tole 'er we wuz comin' right back. Come ter mammy." The baby ran away from its old nurse, and hid its face in its grandmother's bosom, then sought refuge between its grandfather's knees, and was otherwise as cute and as cunning as babies know so well how to be. But Aunt Mimy was persistent.

"Come on, honey; time ter go. Spile you ter stay here. Too much finery fer po' folks."

"Randall," said Cousin Rebecca T., calling her husband by his first name (something she had not done for years), "order the carriage."

"No, ma'am; no, ma'am!" Aunt Mimy cried. "You sha'n't be a-sailin' roun' my chile in a fine carriage wid a big nigger man settin' up dar grinnin'—no ma'am! I won't go wid you. I won't show you de way. I'm free, an' I'll die fust. I ain't gwine ter have no fine carriage sailin' roun' dar, and Marse Laban lyin' down town dar in jail."

"In jail!" cried the colonel. "What has he done?"

"Nothin' 't all," said Aunt Mimy. "De folks des put 'im in dar 'ca'se he wuz po'."

"Randall, go and get him out, and bring him here. Take the carriage." In this way Cousin Rebecca settled the trouble about the carriage. Then she went with Aunt Mimy to find her daughter, and the old woman had to walk rapidly to keep up with her. When they came to the door, Aunt Mimy paused and looked at her old mistress, and for the first time felt a little sympathy for her. Cousin Rebecca's hands were trembling, and her lips quivering.

"Des go an' knock at de door," said Aunt Mimy kindly. "De po' chile 's in dar some'r's. I'm gwine roun'."

She went round the corner of the house, and there paused to listen. Cousin Rebecca T. knocked, a little timidly at first, and then a little louder. Mary opened the door, and saw standing there a richly dressed lady crying as if her heart would break. For a moment she was appalled by this appearance of grief incarnate on her threshold, and stood with surprise and pity shining from her eyes.

"My precious child!" cried Cousin Rebecca T., "have you forgotten me?"

"Mother!" exclaimed Mary.

Then Aunt Mimy heard the door close. "Come on, honey," she said to the baby; "I'll turn you loose in dar wid 'em."

Cousin Rebecca T. took her daughter home, and not long afterward the colonel appeared with Laban, and the baby's Christmas was celebrated in grand style. Aunt Mimy was particularly conspicuous, taking charge of affairs in a high-handed way, and laughing and crying whenever she found herself alone.

"Nummine!" she said to herself, seeing Mary and Laban and the old folks laughing and carrying on like little children. "Nummine! You're all here now, an' dat's doin' mighty well atter so long a time. I b'lieve dat ar aig-nog done flew'd ter der heads. I know mighty well it's done flew'd ter mine, kaze how come I wanter cry one minute an' laugh de nex'?"

CHRISTMAS EVE

by Guy de Maupassant

from *Short Stories of the Tragedy and Comedy of Life*

"The Christmas-eve supper! Oh, no, I shall never go in for that again!" Stout Henri Templier said that in a furious voice, as if some-one had proposed some crime to him, while the others laughed and said, "What are you flying into a rage about?"

"Because a Christmas-eve supper played me the dirtiest trick in the world, and ever since I have felt an insurmountable horror for that night of imbecile gaiety."

"Tell us about it."

"You want to know what it was? Very well then, just listen.

"You remember how cold it was two years ago at Christmas, cold enough to kill poor people in the streets. The Seine was covered with ice, the pavements froze one's feet through the soles of one's boots, and the whole world seemed to be at the point of congealing.

"I had a big piece of work on and refused every invitation to supper, as I preferred to spend the night at my writing table. I dined alone and then began to work. But about ten o'clock I grew restless at the thought of the gay and busy life all over Paris, at the noise in the streets, which reached me in spite of everything, at my neighbors' preparations for supper, which I heard through the walls. I hardly knew any longer what I was doing; I wrote nonsense, and at last I came to the conclusion that I had better give up all hope of producing any good work that night.

"I walked up and down my room; I sat down and got up again. I was certainly under the mysterious influence of the enjoyment outside, and I resigned myself to it. So I rang for my servant and said to her, 'Angela, go and get a good supper for two: some oysters, a cold partridge, some crayfish, ham, and some cakes. Put out two bottles of champagne, lay the cloth, and go to bed.'

"She obeyed in some surprise, and when all was ready, I put on my greatcoat and went out. The great question remained: Whom was I going to bring in to supper? My female friends had all been invited elsewhere, and if I had wished to have one, I ought to have seen about it beforehand.

"So I thought that I would do a good action at the same time, and said to myself, Paris is full of poor and pretty girls who will have nothing on their table tonight, and who are on the lookout for some generous fellow. I will act the part of Providence to one of them this evening; I will find one if I have to go into every pleasure resort, and will hunt till I find one to my choice. So I started off on my search.

"I certainly found many poor girls who were on the lookout for some adventure, but they were ugly enough to give any man a fit of indigestion, or thin enough to freeze in their tracks if they stopped, and you all know that I have a weakness for stout women. The more flesh they have the better I like them, and a female colossus would be my ideal.

"Suddenly, opposite the Théâtre des Variétés, I saw a figure to my liking. I trembled with pleasure, and said, 'By Jove! What a fine girl!'

"It only remained for me to see her face, for a woman's face is the dessert.

"I hastened on, overtook her, and turned around suddenly under a gas lamp. She was charming, quite young, dark, with large black eyes, and I immediately made my proposition, which she accepted without any hesitation, and a quarter of an hour later we were sitting at supper in my lodgings. 'Oh! how comfortable it is here,' she said as she came in, and she looked about her with evident satisfaction at having found a supper and a bed on that bitter night. She was superb; so beautiful that she astonished me, and so stout that she fairly captivated me.

"She took off her cloak and hat, sat down and began to eat; but she seemed in low spirits, and sometimes her pale face twitched as if she were suffering from some hidden sorrow.

" 'Have you anything troubling you?' I asked her.

" 'Bah! Don't let us think of troubles!'

"And she began to drink. She emptied her champagne glass at a draft, filled it again, and emptied it again without stopping, and soon a little color came into her cheeks, and she began to laugh.

"I adored her already, kissed her continually, and discovered that she was neither stupid nor common nor coarse, as ordinary street-walkers are. I asked her for some details about her life, but she replied, 'My little fellow, that is no business of yours!' Alas! an hour later!

"At last it was time to retire, and while I was clearing the table, which had been laid in front of the fire, she undressed herself quickly, and got in. My neighbors were making a terrible din, singing and laughing like lunatics, and so I said to myself, I was quite right to go out and bring in this girl; I should never have been able to do any work.

"At that moment, however, a deep groan made me look round, and I said, 'What is the matter with you, my dear?'

"She did not reply, but continued to utter painful sighs, as if she were suffering horribly, and I continued: 'Do you feel ill?' And suddenly she uttered a cry, a heartrending cry, and I rushed up to the bed, with a candle in my hand.

"Her face was distorted with pain, and she was wringing her hands, panting and uttering long, deep groans, which sounded like a rattle in the throat and were painful to hear. I asked her in consternation, 'What is the matter with you? Do tell me what is the matter.'

" 'Oh! the pain! the pain!' she said. I pulled up the bedclothes, and I saw, my friends, that she was in labor.

"Then I lost my head and ran and knocked at the wall with my fists, shouting: 'Help! Help!'

"My door was opened almost immediately, and a crowd of people came in—men in evening clothes, women in full dress, harlequins, Turks, musketeers—and the inroad startled me so, that I could not explain myself, while they, who had thought that some accident had happened, or that a crime had been committed, could not understand what was the matter. At last, however, I managed to say, 'This—this—woman—is being confined.'

"Then they looked at her and gave their opinion. A friar, especially, declared that he knew all about it, and wished to assist nature, but as they were all as drunk as pigs, I was afraid that they would kill her. So I rushed downstairs without my hat to fetch an old doctor who lived in the next street. When I came back with him, the whole house was up; the gas on the stairs had been relighted, the lodgers from every floor were in my room, while four boatmen were finishing my champagne and crayfish.

"As soon as they saw me they raised a loud shout. A milkmaid presented me with a horrible little wrinkled specimen of humanity that was mewing like a cat, and said to me, 'It is a girl.'

"The doctor examined the woman, declared that she was in a dangerous state, as the event had occurred immediately after supper, and took his leave, saying he would immediately send a sick nurse and a wet nurse. An hour later the two women came, bringing all that was requisite with them.

"I spent the night in my armchair, too distracted to be able to think of the consequences, and almost as soon as it was light the doctor came again. He found his patient very ill, and said to me, 'Your wife, Monsieur—'

" 'She is not my wife,' I interrupted him.

" 'Very well then, your mistress; it does not matter to me.'

"He told me what must be done for her, what her diet must be, and then wrote a prescription.

"What was I to do? Could I send the poor creature to the hospital? I should have been looked upon as a brute in the house and in all the neighborhood. So I kept her in my rooms, and she had my bed for six weeks.

"I sent the child to some peasants at Poissy to be taken care of, and she still costs me fifty francs a month, for as I had paid at first, I shall be obliged to go on paying as long as I live. Later on, she will believe that I am her father. But to crown my misfortunes, when the girl had recovered, I found that she was in love with me, madly in love with me, the baggage!"

"Well?"

"Well, she had grown as thin as a homeless cat, and I turned the

skeleton out of doors. But she watches for me in the streets, hides herself, so that she may see me pass, stops me in the evening when I go
out, in order to kiss my hand, and, in fact, worries me enough to drive
me mad. That is why I never keep Christmas eve now."

CHAPTER IX

HOW SANTA CLAUS CAME TO SIMPSON'S BAR

by Bret Harte

from Mrs. Skagg's Husbands and Other Sketches

It had been raining in the valley of the Sacramento. The North Fork had overflowed its banks and Rattlesnake Creek was impassable. The few boulders that had marked the summer ford at Simpson's Crossing were obliterated by a vast sheet of water stretching to the foothills. The up stage was stopped at Grangers; the last mail had been abandoned in the *tules*, the rider swimming for his life. "An area," remarked the "Sierra Avalanche," with pensive local pride, "as large as the State of Massachusetts is now under water."

Nor was the weather any better in the foothills. The mud lay deep on the mountain road; wagons that neither physical force nor moral objurgation could move from the evil ways into which they had fallen, encumbered the track, and the way to Simpson's Bar was indicated by broken-down teams and hard swearing. And farther on, cut off and inaccessible, rained upon and bedraggled, smitten by high winds and threatened by high water, Simpson's Bar, on the eve of Christmas day,

1862, clung like a swallow's nest to the rocky entablature and splintered capitals of Table Mountain, and shook in the blast.

As night shut down on the settlement, a few lights gleamed through the mist from the windows of cabins on either side of the highway now crossed and gullied by lawless streams and swept by marauding winds. Happily most of the population were gathered at Thompson's store, clustered around a red-hot stove, at which they silently spat in some accepted sense of social communion that perhaps rendered conversation unnecessary. Indeed, most methods of diversion had long since been exhausted on Simpson's Bar; high water had suspended the regular occupations on gulch and on river, and a consequent lack of money and whiskey had taken the zest from most illegitimate recreation. Even Mr. Hamlin was fain to leave the Bar with fifty dollars in his pocket—the only amount actually realized of the large sums won by him in the successful exercise of his arduous profession. "Ef I was asked," he remarked somewhat later, "ef I was asked to pint out a purty little village where a retired sport as didn't care for money could exercise hisself, frequent and lively, I'd say Simpson's Bar; but for a young man with a large family depending on his exertions, it don't pay." As Mr. Hamlin's family consisted mainly of female adults, this remark is quoted rather to show the breadth of his humor than the exact extent of his responsibilities.

Howbeit, the unconscious objects of this satire sat that evening in the listless apathy begotten of idleness and lack of excitement. Even the sudden splashing of hoofs before the door did not arouse them. Dick Bullen alone paused in the act of scraping out his pipe, and lifted his head, but no other one of the group indicated any interest in, or recognition of, the man who entered.

It was a figure familiar enough to the company, and known in Simpson's Bar as "the Old Man." A man of perhaps fifty years; grizzled and scant of hair, but still fresh and youthful of complexion. A face full of ready but not very powerful sympathy, with a chameleon-like aptitude for taking on the shade and color of contiguous moods and feelings. He had evidently just left some hilarious companions, and did not at first notice the gravity of the group, but clapped the shoulder of the nearest man jocularly, and threw himself into a vacant chair.

"Jest heard the best thing out, boys! Ye know Smiley, over yar— Jim Smiley, funniest man in the Bar? Well, Jim was jest telling the richest yarn about—"

"Smiley's a————fool," interrupted a gloomy voice.

"A particular————skunk," added another in sepulchral accents.

A silence followed these positive statements. The Old Man glanced quickly around the group. Then his face slowly changed. "That's so," he said reflectively, after a pause, "certingly a sort of a skunk and suthin of a fool. In course." He was silent for a moment as in painful contemplation of the unsavoriness and folly of the unpopular Smiley. "Dismal weather, ain't it?" he added, now fully embarked on the current of prevailing sentiment. "Mighty rough papers on the boys, and no show for money this season. And tomorrow's Christmas."

There was a movement among the men at this announcement, but whether of satisfaction or disgust was not plain. "Yes," continued the Old Man in the lugubrious tone he had, within the last few moments, unconsciously adopted, "yes, Christmas, and to-night's Christmas eve. Ye see, boys, I kinder thought—that is, I sorter had an idee, jest passin' like, you know—that may be ye'd all like to come over to my house to-night and have a sort of tear round. But I suppose, now, you wouldn't? Don't feel like it, may be?" he added with anxious sympathy, peering into the faces of his companions.

"Well, I don't know," responded Tom Flynn with some cheerfulness. "P'r'aps we may. But how about your wife, Old Man? What does *she* say to it?"

The Old Man hesitated. His conjugal experience had not been a happy one, and the fact was known to Simpson's Bar. His first wife, a delicate, pretty little woman, had suffered keenly and secretly from the jealous suspicions of her husband, until one day he invited the whole Bar to his house to expose her infidelity. On arriving, the party found the shy, *petite* creature quietly engaged in her household duties, and retired abashed and discomfited. But the sensitive woman did not easily recover from the shock of this extraordinary outrage. It was with difficulty she regained her equanimity sufficiently to release her lover from the closet in which he was concealed and escape with him. She left a boy of three years to comfort her bereaved husband. The Old Man's present wife had been his cook. She was large, loyal, and aggressive.

Before he could reply, Joe Dimmick suggested with great directness that it was the "Old Man's house," and that, invoking the Divine Power, if the case were his own, he would invite whom he pleased, even if in so doing he imperilled his salvation. The Powers of Evil, he further remarked, should contend against him vainly. All this delivered with a terseness and vigor lost in this necessary translation.

"In course. Certainly. Thet's it," said the Old Man with a sympathetic frown. "Thar's no trouble about *thet*. It's my own house, built every stick on it myself. Don't you be afeard o' her, boys. She *may* cut up a trifle rough—ez wimmin do—but she'll come round." Secretly the Old Man trusted to the exaltation of liquor and the power of courageous example to sustain him in such an emergency.

As yet, Dick Bullen, the oracle and leader of Simpson's Bar, had not spoken. He now took his pipe from his lips. "Old Man, how's that yer Johnny gettin' on? Seems to me he didn't look so peart last time I seed him on the bluff heavin' rocks at Chinamen. Didn't seem to take much interest in it. Thar was a gang of 'em by yar yesterday—drownded out up the river—and I kinder thought o' Johnny, and how he'd miss 'em! May be now, we'd be in the way ef he wuz sick?"

The father, evidently touched not only by this pathetic picture of Johnny's deprivation, but by the considerate delicacy of the speaker, hastened to assure him that Johnny was better and that a "little fun might 'liven him up." Whereupon Dick arose, shook himself, and saying, "I'm ready. Lead the way, Old Man: here goes," himself led the way with a leap, a characteristic howl, and darted out into the night. As he passed through the outer room he caught up a blazing brand from the hearth. The action was repeated by the rest of the party, closely following and elbowing each other, and before the astonished proprietor of Thompson's grocery was aware of the intention of his guests, the room was deserted.

The night was pitchy dark. In the first gust of wind their temporary torches were extinguished, and only the red brands dancing and flitting in the gloom like drunken will-o'-the-wisps indicated their whereabouts. Their way led up Pine-Tree Cañon, at the head of which a broad, low, bark-thatched cabin burrowed in the mountainside. It was the home of the Old Man, and the entrance to the tunnel in which he worked when he worked at all. Here the crowd paused for a moment, out of delicate deference to their host, who came up panting in the rear.

"P'r'aps ye'd better hold on a second out yer, whilst I go in and see thet things is all right," said the Old Man, with an indifference he was far from feeling. The suggestion was graciously accepted, the door opened and closed on the host, and the crowd, leaning their backs against the wall and cowering under the eaves, waited and listened.

For a few moments there was no sound but the dripping of water from the eaves, and the stir and rustle of wrestling boughs above them. Then the men became uneasy, and whispered suggestion and suspicion passed from the one to the other. "Reckon she's caved in his head the first lick!" "Decoyed him inter the tunnel and barred him up, likely." "Got him down and sittin' on him." "Prob'ly bilin suthin to heave on us: stand clear the door, boys!" For just then the latch clicked, the door slowly opened, and a voice said, "Come in out o' the wet."

The voice was neither that of the Old Man nor of his wife. It was the voice of a small boy, its weak treble broken by that preternatural hoarseness which only vagabondage and the habit of premature self-assertion can give. It was the face of a small boy that looked up at theirs—a face that might have been pretty and even refined but that it was darkened by evil knowledge from within, and dirt and hard experience from without. He had a blanket around his shoulders and had evidently just risen from his bed. "Come in," he repeated, "and don't make no noise. The Old Man's in there talking to mar," he continued, pointing to an adjacent room which seemed to be a kitchen, from which the Old Man's voice came in deprecating accents. "Let me be," he added, querulously, to Dick Bullen, who had caught him up, blanket and all, and was affecting to toss him into the fire, "let go o' me, you d———d old fool, d'ye hear?"

Thus adjured, Dick Bullen lowered Johnny to the ground with a smothered laugh, while the men, entering quietly, ranged themselves around a long table of rough boards which occupied the centre of the room. Johnny then gravely proceeded to a cupboard and brought out several articles which he deposited on the table. "Thar's whiskey. And crackers. And red herons. And cheese." He took a bite of the latter on his way to the table. "And sugar." He scooped up a mouthful *en route* with a small and very dirty hand. "And terbacker. Thar's dried appils too on the shelf, but I don't admire 'em. Appils is swellin'. Thar," he concluded, "now wade in, and don't be afeard. I don't mind the old woman. She don't b'long to *me*. S'long."

He had stepped to the threshold of a small room, scarcely larger than a closet, partitioned off from the main apartment, and holding in its dim recess a small bed. He stood there a moment looking at the company, his bare feet peeping from the blanket, and nodded.

"Hello, Johnny! You ain't goin' to turn in agin, are ye?" said Dick.

"Yes, I are," responded Johnny, decidedly.

"Why, wot's up, old fellow?"

"I'm sick."

"How sick?"

"I've got a fevier. And childblains. And roomatiz," returned Johnny, and vanished within. After a moment's pause, he added in the dark, apparently from under the bedclothes, "And biles!"

There was an embarrassing silence. The men looked at each other, and at the fire. Even with the appetizing banquet before them, it seemed as if they might again fall into the despondency of Thompson's grocery, when the voice of the Old Man, incautiously lifted, came deprecatingly from the kitchen.

"Certainly! Thet's so. In course they is. A gang o' lazy drunken loafers, and that ar Dick Bullen's the ornariest of all. Didn't hev no more *sabe* than to come round yar with sickness in the house and no provision. Thet's what I said: 'Bullen,' sez I, 'it's crazy drunk you are, or a fool,' sez I, 'to think o' such a thing.' 'Staples,' I sez, 'be you a man, Staples, and 'spect to raise h——l under my roof and invalids lyin' round?' But they would come—they would. Thet's wot you must 'spect o' such trash as lays round the Bar."

A burst of laughter from the men followed this unfortunate exposure. Whether it was overheard in the kitchen, or whether the Old Man's irate companion had just then exhausted all other modes of expressing her contemptuous indignation, I cannot say, but a back door was suddenly slammed with great violence. A moment later and the Old Man reappeared, haply unconscious of the cause of the late hilarious outburst, and smiled blandly.

"The old woman thought she'd jest run over to Mrs. McFadden's for a sociable call," he explained, with jaunty indifference, as he took a seat at the board.

Oddly enough it needed this untoward incident to relieve the embarrassment that was beginning to be felt by the party, and their natural audacity returned with their host. I do not propose to record the convivialities of that evening. The inquisitive reader will accept the statement that the conversation was characterized by the same intellectual exaltation, the same cautious reverence, the same fastidious delicacy, the same rhetorical precision, and the same logical and coherent discourse somewhat later in the evening, which distinguish similar gatherings of the masculine sex in more civilized localities and under more favorable auspices. No glasses were broken in the absence of any; no liquor was uselessly spilt on floor or table in the scarcity of that article.

It was nearly midnight when the festivities were interrupted. "Hush," said Dick Bullen, holding up his hand. It was the querulous voice of Johnny from his adjacent closet: "Oh, dad!"

The Old Man arose hurriedly and disappeared in the closet. Presently he reappeared. "His rheumatiz is coming on agin bad," he explained, "and he wants rubbin'." He lifted the demijohn of whiskey from the table and shook it. It was empty. Dick Bullen put down his tin cup with an embarrassed laugh. So did the others. The Old Man examined their contents and said hopefully, "I reckon that's enough; he don't need much. You hold on all o' you for a spell, and I'll be back"; and vanished in the closet with an old flannel shirt and the whiskey. The door closed but imperfectly, and the following dialogue was distinctly audible:

"Now, sonny, whar does she ache worst?"

"Sometimes over yar and sometimes under yar; but it's most powerful from yer to yer. Rub yer, dad."

A silence seemed to indicate a brisk rubbing. Then Johnny:

"Hevin' a good time out yer, dad?"

"Yes, sonny."

"To-morrer's Chrismiss, ain't it?"

"Yes, sonny. How does she feel now?"

"Better. Rub a little furder down. Wot's Chrismiss, anyway? Wot's it all about?"

"Oh, it's a day."

This exhaustive definition was apparently satisfactory, for there was a silent interval of rubbing. Presently Johnny again: "Mar sez that everywhere else but yer everybody gives things to everybody Chrismiss, and then she jist waded inter you. She sez thar's a man they call Sandy Claws, not a white man, you know, but a kind o' Chinemin, comes down the chimbley night afore Chrismiss and gives things to chillern—boys like me. Puts 'em in their butes! Thet's what she tried to play upon me. Easy now, pop, whar are you rubbin' to—thet's a mile from the place. She jest made that up, didn't she, jest to aggrewate me and you? Don't rub thar. . . . Why, dad!"

In the great quiet that seemed to have fallen upon the house the sigh of the near pines and the drip of leaves without was very distinct. Johnny's voice, too, was lowered as he went on. "Don't you take on now, fur I'm gettin' all right fast. Wot's the boys doin' out thar?"

The Old Man partly opened the door and peered through. His guests were sitting there sociably enough, and there were a few silver coins and a lean buckskin purse on the table. "Bettin' on suthin— some little game or 'nother. They're all right," he replied to Johnny, and recommenced his rubbing.

"I'd like to take a hand and win some money," said Johnny, reflectively, after a pause.

The Old Man glibly repeated what was evidently a familiar formula, that if Johnny would wait until he struck it rich in the tunnel he'd have lots of money, etc., etc.

"Yes," said Johnny, "but you don't. And whether you strike it or I win it, it's about the same. It's all luck. But it's mighty cur'o's about Chrismiss, ain't it? Why do they call it Chrismiss?"

Perhaps from some instinctive deference to the overhearing of his guests, or from some vague sense of incongruity, the Old Man's reply was so low as to be inaudible beyond the room.

"Yes," said Johnny, with some slight abatement of interest, "I've heerd o' *him* before. Thar, that'll do, dad. I don't ache near so bad as I did. Now wrap me tight in this yer blanket. So. Now," he added in a muffled whisper, "sit down yer by me till I go asleep." To assure himself of obedience, he disengaged one hand from the blanket and, grasping his father's sleeve, again composed himself to rest.

For some moments the Old Man waited patiently. Then the unwonted stillness of the house excited his curiosity, and without moving from the bed, he cautiously opened the door with his disengaged hand, and looked into the main room. To his infinite surprise it was dark and deserted. But even then a smouldering log on the hearth broke, and by the upspringing blaze he saw the figure of Dick Bullen sitting by the dying embers.

"Hello!"

Dick started, rose, and came somewhat unsteadily toward him.

"Whar's the boys?" said the Old Man.

"Gone up the cañon on a little *pasear*. They're coming back for me in a minit. I'm waitin' round for 'em. What are you starin' at, Old Man?" he added with a forced laugh; "do you think I'm drunk?"

The Old Man might have been pardoned the supposition, for Dick's eyes were humid and his face flushed. He loitered and lounged back to the chimney, yawned, shook himself, buttoned up his coat and laughed. "Liquor ain't so plenty as that, Old Man. Now don't you git up," he continued, as the Old Man made a movement to release his sleeve from Johnny's hand. "Don't you mind manners. Sit jest whar you be; I'm goin' in a jiffy. Thar, that's them now."

There was a low tap at the door. Dick Bullen opened it quickly, nodded "Good night" to his host, and disappeared. The Old Man would have followed him but for the hand that still unconsciously grasped his sleeve. He could have easily disengaged it: it was small, weak, and emaciated. But perhaps because it *was* small, weak, and emaciated, he changed his mind, and, drawing his chair closer to the bed, rested his head upon it. In this defenceless attitude the potency of his earlier potations surprised him. The room flickered and faded before his eyes, reappeared, faded again, went out, and left him asleep.

Meantime Dick Bullen, closing the door, confronted his companions. "Are you ready?" said Staples. "Ready," said Dick; "what's the time?" "Past twelve," was the reply; "can you make it? It's nigh on fifty miles, the round trip hither and yon." "I reckon," returned Dick, shortly. "Whar's the mare?" "Bill and Jack's holdin' her at the crossin'." "Let 'em hold on a minit longer," said Dick.

He turned and re-entered the house softly. By the light of the guttering candle and dying fire he saw that the door of the little room was open. He stepped toward it on tiptoe and looked in. The Old Man had fallen back in his chair, snoring, his helpless feet thrust out in a line with his collapsed shoulders, and his hat pulled over his eyes. Beside him, on a narrow wooden bedstead, lay Johnny, muffled tightly in a blanket that hid all save a strip of forehead and a few curls damp with perspiration. Dick Bullen made a step forward, hesitated, and glanced over his shoulder into the deserted room. Everything was quiet. With a sudden resolution he parted his huge mustaches with both hands and stooped over the sleeping boy. But even as he did so a mischievous blast, lying in wait, swooped down the chimney, rekindled the hearth, and lit up the room with a shameless glow from which Dick fled in bashful terror.

His companions were already waiting for him at the crossing. Two of them were struggling in the darkness with some strange misshapen bulk, which as Dick came nearer took the semblance of a great yellow horse.

It was the mare. She was not a pretty picture. From her Roman nose to her rising haunches, from her arched spine hidden by the stiff *machillas* of a Mexican saddle, to her thick, straight, bony legs, there was not a line of equine grace. In her half-blind but wholly vicious white eyes, in her protruding under lip, in her monstrous color, there was nothing but ugliness and vice.

"Now then," said Staples, "stand cl'ar of her heels, boys, and up with you. Don't miss your first holt of her mane, and mind ye get your off stirrup *quick*. Ready!"

There was a leap, a scrambling struggle, a bound, a wild retreat of the crowd, a circle of flying hoofs, two springless leaps that jarred the earth, a rapid play and jingle of spurs, a plunge, and then the voice of Dick somewhere in the darkness, "All right!"

"Don't take the lower road back onless you're hard pushed for time! Don't hold her in down hill! We'll be at the ford at five. G'lang! Hoopa! Mula! GO!"

A splash, a spark struck from the ledge in the road, a clatter in the rocky cut beyond, and Dick was gone.

Sing, O Muse, the ride of Richard Bullen! Sing, O Muse of chivalrous men! the sacred quest, the doughty deeds, the battery of low churls, the fearsome ride and grewsome perils of the Flower of Simpson's Bar! Alack! she is dainty, this Muse! She will have none of this bucking brute and swaggering, ragged rider, and I must fain follow him in prose, afoot!

It was one o'clock, and yet he had only gained Rattlesnake Hill. For in that time Jovita had rehearsed to him all her imperfections and practised all her vices. Thrice had she stumbled. Twice had she thrown up her Roman nose in a straight line with the reins, and, resisting a bit and spur, struck out madly across country. Twice had she reared, and, rearing, fallen backward; and twice had the agile Dick, unharmed, regained his seat before she found her vicious legs again. And a mile beyond them, at the foot of a long hill, was Rattlesnake Creek. Dick knew that here was the crucial test of his ability to perform his enterprise, set his teeth grimly, put his knees well into her flanks, and changed his defensive tactics to brisk aggression. Bullied and maddened, Jovita began the descent of the hill. Here the artful Richard pretended to hold her in with ostentatious objurgation and well-feigned cries of alarm. It is unnecessary to add that Jovita instantly ran away. Nor need I state the time made in the descent; it is written in the chronicles of Simpson's Bar. Enough that in another moment, as it seemed to Dick, she was splashing on the overflowed banks of Rattlesnake Creek. As Dick expected, the momentum she had acquired carried her beyond the point of balking, and, holding her well together for a mighty leap, they dashed into the middle of the swiftly flowing current. A few moments of kicking, wading, and swimming, and Dick drew a long breath on the opposite bank.

The road from Rattlesnake Creek to Red Mountain was tolerably level. Either the plunge in Rattlesnake Creek had dampened her baleful fire, or the art which led to it had shown her the superior wickedness of her rider, for Jovita no longer wasted her surplus energy in wanton conceits. Once she bucked, but it was from force of habit; once she shied, but it was from a new freshly painted meeting-house at the crossing of the county road. Hollows, ditches, gravelly deposits, patches of freshly springing grasses, flew from beneath her rattling hoofs. She began to smell unpleasantly, once or twice she coughed slightly, but there was no abatement of her strength or speed. By two o'clock he had passed Red Mountain and begun the descent to the plain. Ten minutes later the driver of the fast Pioneer coach was overtaken and passed by a "man on a Pinto hoss"—an event sufficiently notable for remark. At half past two Dick rose in his stirrups with a great shout. Stars were glittering through the rifted clouds, and beyond him, out of the plain, rose two spires, a flagstaff, and a straggling line of black objects. Dick jingled his spurs and swung his *riata*, Jovita bounded forward, and in another moment they swept into Tuttleville and drew up before the wooden piazza of "The Hotel of All Nations."

What transpired that night at Tuttleville is not strictly a part of this record. Briefly I may state, however, that after Jovita had been handed over to a sleepy ostler, whom she at once kicked into unpleasant consciousness, Dick sallied out with the bar-keeper for a tour of the sleeping town. Lights still gleamed from a few saloons and gambling-houses; but, avoiding these, they stopped before several closed shops, and by persistent tapping and judicious outcry roused the proprietors from their beds, and made them unbar the doors of their magazines and expose their wares. Sometimes they were met by curses, but oftener by interest and some concern in their needs, and the interview was invariably concluded by a drink. It was three o'clock before this pleasantry was given over, and with a small waterproof bag of india-rubber strapped on his shoulders Dick returned to the hotel. But here he was waylaid by Beauty—Beauty opulent in charms, affluent in dress, persuasive in speech, and Spanish in accent! In vain she repeated the invitation in "Excelsior," happily scorned by all Alpine-climbing youth, and rejected by this child of the Sierras—a rejection softened in this instance by a laugh and his last gold coin. And then he sprang to the saddle and dashed down the lonely street and out into the lonelier plain, where presently the lights, the black line of houses, the spires, and the flagstaff sank into the earth behind him again and were lost in the distance.

The storm had cleared away, the air was brisk and cold, the outlines of adjacent landmarks were distinct, but it was half past four before Dick reached the meeting-house and the crossing of the county road. To avoid the rising grade he had taken a longer and more circuitous road, in whose viscid mud Jovita sank fetlock deep at every bound. It was a poor preparation for a steady ascent of five miles more; but Jovita, gathering her legs under her, took it with her usual blind, unreasoning fury, and a half-hour later reached the long level that led to Rattlesnake Creek. Another half-hour would bring him to the creek. He threw the reins lightly upon the neck of the mare, chirruped to her, and began to sing.

Suddenly Jovita shied with a bound that would have unseated a less practised rider. Hanging to her rein was a figure that had leaped from the bank, and at the same time from the road before her arose a shadowy horse and rider. "Throw up your hands," commanded this second apparition, with an oath.

Dick felt the mare tremble, quiver, and apparently sink under him. He knew what it meant and was prepared.

"Stand aside, Jack Simpson, I know you, you d——d thief. Let me pass or—"

He did not finish the sentence. Jovita rose straight in the air with a terrific bound, throwing the figure from her bit with a single shake of her vicious head, and charged with deadly malevolence down on the impediment before her. An oath, a pistol-shot, horse and highwayman rolled over in the road, and the next moment Jovita was a hundred yards away. But the good right arm of her rider, shattered by a bullet, dropped helplessly at his side.

Without slacking his speed he shifted the reins to his left hand. But a few moments later he was obliged to halt and tighten the saddle-girths that had slipped in the onset. This in his crippled condition took some time. He had no fear of pursuit, but looking up he saw that the eastern stars were already paling, and that the distant peaks had lost their ghostly whiteness, and now stood out blackly against a lighter sky. Day was upon him. Then completely absorbed in a single idea, he forgot the pain of his wound, and mounting again dashed on toward Rattlesnake Creek. But now Jovita's breath came broken by gasps, Dick reeled in his saddle, and brighter and brighter grew the sky.

Ride, Richard; run, Jovita; linger, O day!

For the last few rods there was a roaring in his ears. Was it exhaustion from loss of blood, or what? He was dazed and giddy as he swept down the hill, and did not recognize his surroundings. Had he taken the wrong road, or was this Rattlesnake Creek?

It was. But the brawling creek he had swam a few hours before had risen, more than doubled its volume, and now rolled a swift and resistless river between him and Rattlesnake Hill. For the first time that night Richard's heart sank within him. The river, the mountain, the quickening east, swam before his eyes. He shut them to recover his self-control. In that brief interval, by some fantastic mental process, the little room at Simpson's Bar and the figures of the sleeping father and son rose upon him. He opened his eyes widely, cast off his coat, pistol, boots, and saddle, bound his precious pack tightly to his shoulders, grasped the bare flanks of Jovita with his bared knees, and with a shout dashed into the yellow water. A cry rose from the opposite bank as the head of a man and horse struggled for a few moments against the battling current, and then were swept away amidst uprooted trees and whirling drift-wood.

The Old Man started and woke. The fire on the hearth was dead, the candle in the outer room flickering in its socket, and somebody was rapping at the door. He opened it, but fell back with a cry before the dripping, half-naked figure that reeled against the doorpost.

"Dick?"

"Hush! Is he awake yet?"

"No, but, Dick—"

"Dry up, you old fool! Get me some whiskey *quick!*" The Old Man flew and returned with—an empty bottle! Dick would have sworn, but his strength was not equal to the occasion. He staggered, caught at the handle of the door, and motioned to the Old Man.

"Thar's suthin' in my pack yer for Johnny. Take it off. I can't."

The Old Man unstrapped the pack and laid it before the exhausted man.

"Open it, quick!"

He did so with trembling fingers. It contained only a few poor toys —cheap and barbaric enough, goodness knows, but bright with paint and tinsel. One of them was broken; another, I fear, was irretrievably ruined by water; and on the third—ah me! there was a cruel spot. "It don't look like much, that's a fact," said Dick, ruefully. "But it's the best we could do. . . . Take 'em, Old Man, and put 'em in his stocking, and tell him—tell him, you know—hold me, Old Man—" The Old Man caught at his sinking figure. "Tell him," said Dick, with a weak little laugh, "tell him Sandy Claus has come."

And even so, bedraggled, ragged, unshaven, and unshorn, with one arm hanging helplessly at his side, Santa Claus came to Simpson's Bar and fell fainting on the first threshold. The Christmas dawn came slowly after, touching the remoter peaks with the rosy warmth of ineffable love. And it looked so tenderly on Simpson's Bar that the whole mountain, as if caught in a generous action, blushed to the skies.

CHRISTMAS PHANTOMS

by Maxim Gorky

from *Index of Current Literature*, Vol. XXXIX

My Christmas story was concluded. I flung down my pen, rose from the desk, and began to pace up and down the room.

It was night, and outside the snowstorm whirled through the air. Strange sounds reached my ears as of soft whispers, or of sighs, that penetrated from the street through the walls of my little chamber, three-fourths of which were engulfed in dark shadows. It was the snow driven by the wind that came crunching against the walls and lashed the windowpanes. A light, white, indefinite object scurried past my window and disappeared, leaving a cold shiver within my soul.

I approached the window, looked out upon the street, and leaned my head, heated with the strained effort of imagination, upon the cold frame. The street lay in deserted silence. Now and then the wind ripped up little transparent clouds of snow from the pavement and sent them flying through the air like shreds of a delicate white fabric. A lamp burned opposite my window. Its flame trembled and quivered in fierce struggle with the wind. The flaring streak of light projected like a broadsword into the air, and the snow that was drifted from the roof of the house into this streak of light became aglow for a moment like a scintillating robe of sparks. My heart grew sad and chill as I watched this play of the wind. I quickly undressed myself, put out the lamp, and lay down to sleep.

When the light was extinguished and darkness filled my room, the sounds grew more audible and the window stared at me like a great white spot. The ceaseless ticking of the clock marked the passing of the seconds. At times their swift onward rush was drowned in the wheezing and crunching of the snow, but soon I heard again the low beat of the seconds as they dropped into eternity. Occasionally their sound was as distinct and precise as if the clock stood in my own skull.

I lay in my bed and thought of the story that I had just completed, wondering whether it had come out a success.

In this story I told of two beggars, a blind old man and his wife, who in silent, timid retirement trod the path of life that offered them nothing but fear and humiliation. They had left their village on the morning before Christmas to collect alms in the neighboring settlements that they might on the day thereafter celebrate the birth of Christ in holiday fashion.

They expected to visit the nearest villages and to be back home for the early morning service, with their bags filled with all kinds of crumbs doled out to them for the sake of Christ.

Their hopes (thus I proceeded in my narration) were naturally disappointed. The gifts they received were scanty, and it was very late when the pair, worn out with the day's tramp, finally decided to return to their cold, desolate clay hut. With light burdens on their shoulders and with heavy grief in their hearts, they slowly trudged along over the snow-covered plain, the old woman walking in front and the old man holding fast to her belt and following behind. The night was dark, clouds covered the sky, and for two old people the way to the village was still very long. Their feet sank into the snow and the wind whirled it up and drove it into their faces. Silently and trembling with cold, they plodded on and on. Weary and blinded by the snow, the old woman had strayed from the path, and they were now wandering aimlessly across the valley out on the open field.

"Are we going to be home soon? Take care that we do not miss the early mass!" mumbled the blind man behind his wife's shoulders.

She said that they would soon be home, and a new shiver of cold passed through her body. She knew that she had lost the way, but she dared not tell her husband. At times it seemed to her as if the wind carried the sound of the barking dogs to her ears, and she turned in the direction whence those sounds came; but soon she heard the barking from the other side.

At length her powers gave way and she said to the old man, "Forgive me, father, forgive me for the sake of Christ. I have strayed from the road and I cannot go further. I must sit down."

"You will freeze to death," he answered.

"Let me rest only for a little while. And even if we do freeze to death, what matters it? Surely our life on this earth is not sweet."

The old man heaved a heavy sigh and consented.

They sat down on the snow with their backs against each other and looked like two bundles of rags—the sport of the wind. It drifted clouds of snow against them, covered them up with sharp, pointed crystals, and the old woman, who was more lightly dressed than her husband, soon felt herself in the embrace of a rare, delicious warmth.

"Mother," called the blind man, who shivered with violent cold, "stand up, we must be going!"

But she had dozed off and muttered but half-intelligible words through her sleep. He endeavored to raise her, but he could not for want of adequate strength.

"You will freeze!" he shouted, and then he called aloud for help into the wide open field.

But she felt so warm, so comfortable! After some vain endeavor the blind man sat down again on the snow in dumb desperation. He was now firmly convinced that all that happened to him was by the express will of God and that there was no escape for him and his aged wife. The wind whirled and danced around them in wanton frolic, playfully bestrewed them with snow and had a merry, roguish sport with the tattered garments that covered their old limbs, weary with a long life of pinching destitution. The old man also was now overcome with a feeling of delicious comfort and warmth.

Suddenly the wind wafted the sweet, solemn, melodious sounds of a bell to his ears.

"Mother!" he cried, starting back, "they are ringing for matins. Quick, let us go!"

But she had already gone whence there is no return.

"Do you hear? They are ringing, I say. Get up! Oh, we will be too late!"

He tried to rise, but he found that he could not move. Then he understood that his end was near and he began to pray silently: "Lord, be gracious unto the souls of your servants! We were sinners, both. Forgive us, O Lord! Have mercy upon us!"

Then it seemed to him that from across the field, enveloped in a bright, sparkling snow cloud, a radiant temple of God was floating toward him—a rare, wondrous temple. It was all made of flaming hearts of men and itself had the likeness of a heart, and in the midst of it, upon an elevated pedestal, stood Christ in his own person. At this vision the old man rose and fell upon his knees on the threshold of the temple. He regained his sight again and he looked at the Saviour and Redeemer. And from his elevated position Christ spoke in a sweet, melodious voice: "Hearts aglow with pity are the foundation of my temple. Enter thou into my temple, thou who in thy life hast thirsted for pity, thou who hast suffered misfortune and humiliation, go to thy Eternal Peace!"

"O Lord!" spoke the old man, restored to sight, weeping with rapturous joy, "is it Thou in truth O Lord!"

And Christ smiled benignly upon the old man and his life companion, who was awakened to life again by the smile of the Saviour.

And thus both the beggars froze to death out in the open snow-covered field.

I brought back to my mind the various incidents of the story and wondered whether it had come out smooth and touching enough to arouse the reader's pity. It seemed to me that I could answer the question in the affirmative, that it could not possibly fail to produce the effect at which I had aimed.

With this thought I fell asleep, well satisfied with myself. The clock continued to tick, and I heard in my sleep the chasing and roaring of the snowstorm, that grew more and more violent. The lantern was blown out. The storm outside produced ever new sounds. The window shutters clattered. The branches of the trees near the door knocked against the metal plate of the roof. There was a sighing, groaning, howling, roaring, and whistling, and all this was now united into a woeful melody that filled the heart with sadness, now into a soft, low strain like a cradle song. It had the effect of a fantastic tale that held the soul as if under a spell.

But suddenly—what was this? The faint spot of the window flamed up into a bluish phosphorescent light, and the window grew larger and larger until it finally assumed the proportions of the wall. In the blue light which filled the room there appeared of a sudden a thick white cloud in which bright sparks glowed as with countless eyes. As if whirled about by the wind, the cloud turned and twisted, began to dissolve, became more and more transparent, broke into tiny pieces, and breathed a frosty chill into my body that filled me with anxiety. Something like a dissatisfied angry mumble proceeded from the shreds of cloud that gained more and more definite shape and assumed forms familiar to my eye. Yonder in the corner were a swarm of children, or rather the shades of children, and behind them emerged a gray-bearded old man by the side of several female forms.

"Whence do these shades come? What do they wish?" were the questions that passed through my mind as I gazed affrighted at this strange apparition.

"Whence come we and whence are we?" was the solemn retort of a serious, stern voice. "Do you not know us? Think a little!"

I shook my head in silence. I did not know them. They kept floating through the air in rhythmic motion as if they led a solemn dance to the tune of the storm. Half transparent, scarcely discernible in their outlines, they wavered lightly and noiselessly around me, and suddenly I distinguished in their midst the blind old man who held on fast to the belt of his old wife. Deeply bent, they limped past me, their eyes fixed upon me with a reproachful look.

"Do you recognize them now?" asked the same solemn voice. I did not know whether it was the voice of the storm or the voice of my conscience, but there was in it a tone of command that brooked no contradiction.

"Yes, this is who they are," continued the Voice, "the sad heroes of your successful story. And all the others are also heroes of your Christmas stories—children, men, and women whom you made to freeze to death in order to amuse the public. See how many there are and how pitiful they look, the offspring of your fancy!"

A movement passed through the wavering forms and two children, a boy and a girl, appeared in the foreground. They looked like two flowers of snow or of the sheen of the moon.

"These children," spoke the Voice, "you have caused to freeze under the window of that rich house in which beamed the brilliant Christmas tree. They were looking at the tree—do you recollect?—and they froze."

Noiselessly my poor little heroes floated past me and disappeared.

They seemed to dissolve in the nebulous blue glare of light. In their place appeared a woman with a sorrowful, emaciated countenance.

"This is that poor woman who was hurrying to her village home on Christmas Eve to bring her children some cheap Christmas gifts. You have let her freeze to death also."

I gazed full of shame and fear at the shade of the woman. She also vanished, and new forms appeared in their turn. They were all sad, silent phantoms with an expression of unspeakable woe in their somber gaze.

And again I heard the solemn Voice speak in sustained, impassive accents:

"Why have you written these stories? Is there not enough of real, tangible and visible misery in the world that you must needs invent more misery and sorrow, and strain your imagination in order to paint pictures of thrilling, realistic effects? Why do you do this? What is your object? Do you wish to deprive man of all joy in life, do you wish to take from him the last drop of faith in the good by painting for him only the evil? Why is it that in your Christmas stories year after year you cause to freeze to death now children, now grown-up people? Why? What is your aim?"

I was staggered by this strange indictment. Everybody writes Christmas stories according to the same formula. You take a poor boy or a poor girl, or something of that sort, and let them freeze somewhere under a window, behind which there is usually a Christmas tree that throws its radiant splendor upon them. This has become the fashion, and I was following the fashion.

I answered accordingly.

"If I let these people freeze," I said, "I do it with the best object in the world. By painting their death struggle I stir up humane feelings in the public for these unfortunates. I want to move the heart of my reader, that is all."

A strange agitation passed through the throng of phantoms, as if they wished to raise a mocking protest against my words.

"Do you see how they are laughing?" said the mysterious Voice.

"Why are they laughing?" I asked in a scarcely audible tone.

"Because you speak so foolishly. You wish to arouse noble feelings in the hearts of men by your pictures of imagined misery, when real misery and suffering are nothing to them but a daily spectacle. Consider for how long a time people have endeavored to stir up noble feelings in the hearts of men, think of how many men before you have applied their genius to that end, and then cast a look into real life! Fool that you are! If the reality does not move them, and if their feelings are not offended by its cruel, ruthless misery, and by the fathomless abyss of actual wretchedness, then how can you hope that the fictions of your imagination will make them better? Do you really think that you can move the heart of a human being by telling him about a frozen child? The sea of misery breaks against the dam of heartlessness, it rages and surges against it, and you want to appease it by throwing a few peas into it!"

The phantoms accompanied these words with their silent laughter, and the storm laughed a shrill, cynical laugh; but the Voice continued to speak unceasingly. Each word that it spoke was like a nail driven into my brain. It became intolerable, and I could no longer hold out.

"It is all a lie, a lie!" I cried in a paroxysm of rage, and jumping from my bed, I fell headlong into the dark, and sank more and more quickly, more and more deeply, into the gaping abyss that suddenly opened before me. The whistling, howling, roaring, and laughing followed me downward, and the phantoms chased me through the dark, grinned in my face and mocked at me.

I awoke in the morning with a violent headache and in a very bad humor. The first thing I did was to read over my story of the blind beggar and his wife once more, and then I tore the manuscript into pieces.

THE GIFT OF THE MAGI

by O. Henry

from *The Four Million*

One dollar and eighty-seven cents. That was all. And sixty cents of it was in pennies. Pennies saved one and two at a time by bulldozing the grocer and the vegetable man and the butcher until one's cheeks burned with the silent imputation of parsimony that such close dealing implied. Three times Della counted it. One dollar and eighty-seven cents. And the next day would be Christmas.

There was clearly nothing to do but flop down on the shabby little couch and howl. So Della did it. Which instigates the moral reflection that life is made up of sobs, sniffles, and smiles, with sniffles predominating.

While the mistress of the home is gradually subsiding from the first stage to the second, take a look at the home. A furnished flat at $8 per week. It did not exactly beggar description, but it certainly had that word on the lookout for the mendicancy squad.

In the vestibule below was a letter-box into which no letter would go, and an electric button from which no mortal finger could coax a ring. Also appertaining thereunto was a card bearing the name "Mr. James Dillingham Young."

The "Dillingham" had been flung to the breeze during a former period of prosperity when its possessor was being paid $30 per week. Now, when the income was shrunk to $20, the letters of "Dillingham" looked blurred, as though they were thinking seriously of contracting to a modest and unassuming D. But whenever Mr. James Dillingham Young came home and reached his flat above he was called "Jim" and greatly hugged by Mrs. James Dillingham Young, already introduced to you as Della. Which is all very good.

Della finished her cry and attended to her cheeks with the powder rag. She stood by the window and looked out dully at a grey cat walking a grey fence in a grey backyard. To-morrow would be Christmas Day, and she had only $1.87 with which to buy Jim a present. She had been saving every penny she could for months, with this result. Twenty dollars a week doesn't go far. Expenses had been greater than she had calculated. They always are. Only $1.87 to buy a present for Jim. Her Jim. Many a happy hour she had spent planning for something nice for him. Something fine and rare and sterling—something just a little bit near to being worthy of the honour of being owned by Jim.

There was a pier-glass between the windows of the room. Perhaps you have seen a pier-glass in an $8 flat. A very thin and very agile person may, by observing his reflection in a rapid sequence of longitudinal strips, obtain a fairly accurate conception of his looks. Della, being slender, had mastered the art.

Suddenly she whirled from the window and stood before the glass. Her eyes were shining brilliantly, but her face had lost its colour within twenty seconds. Rapidly she pulled down her hair and let it fall to its full length.

Now, there were two possessions of the James Dillingham Youngs in which they both took a mighty pride. One was Jim's gold watch that had been his father's and grandfather's. The other was Della's hair. Had the Queen of Sheba lived in the flat across the airshaft, Della would have let her hair hang out the window some day to dry just to depreciate Her Majesty's jewels and gifts. Had King Solomon been the janitor, with all his treasures piled up in the basement, Jim would have pulled out his watch every time he passed, just to see him pluck at his beard from envy.

So now Della's beautiful hair fell about her, rippling and shining like a cascade of brown waters. It reached below her knee and made itself almost a garment for her. And then she did it up again nervously and quickly. Once she faltered for a minute and stood still while a tear or two splashed on the worn red carpet.

On went her old brown jacket; on went her old brown hat. With a whirl of skirts and with the brilliant sparkle still in her eyes, she fluttered out the door and down the stairs to the street.

Where she stopped the sign read: "Mme. Sofronie. Hair Goods of All Kinds." One flight up Della ran, and collected herself, panting. Madame, large, too white, chilly, hardly looked the "Sofronie."

"Will you buy my hair?" asked Della.

"I buy hair," said Madame. "Take yer hat off and let's have a sight at the looks of it."

Down rippled the brown cascade.

"Twenty dollars," said Madame, lifting the mass with a practised hand.

"Give it to me quick," said Della.

Oh, and the next two hours tripped by on rosy wings. Forget the hashed metaphor. She was ransacking the stores for Jim's present.

She found it at last. It surely had been made for Jim and no one else. There was no other like it in any of the stores, and she had turned all of them inside out. It was a platinum fob chain simple and chaste in design, properly proclaiming its value by substance alone and not by meretricious ornamentation—as all good things should do. It was even worthy of The Watch. As soon as she saw it she knew that it must be Jim's. It was like him. Quietness and value—the description applied to both. Twenty-one dollars they took from her for it, and she hurried home with the 87 cents. With that chain on his watch Jim might be properly anxious about the time in any company. Grand as the watch was, he sometimes looked at it on the sly on account of the old leather strap that he used in place of a chain.

When Della reached home her intoxication gave way a little to prudence and reason. She got out her curling irons and lighted the gas and went to work repairing the ravages made by generosity added to love. Which is always a tremendous task, dear friends—a mammoth task.

Within forty minutes her head was covered with tiny, close-lying curls that made her look wonderfully like a truant schoolboy. She looked at her reflection in the mirror long, carefully, and critically.

"If Jim doesn't kill me," she said to herself, "before he takes a second look at me, he'll say I look like a Coney Island chorus girl. But what could I do—oh! what could I do with a dollar and eighty-seven cents?"

At 7 o'clock the coffee was made and the frying-pan was on the back of the stove hot and ready to cook the chops.

Jim was never late. Della doubled the fob chain in her hand and sat on the corner of the table near the door that he always entered. Then she heard his step on the stair away down on the first flight, and she turned white for just a moment. She had a habit of saying little silent prayers about the simplest everyday things, and now she whispered: "Please God, make him think I am still pretty."

The door opened and Jim stepped in and closed it. He looked thin and very serious. Poor fellow, he was only twenty-two—and to be burdened with a family! He needed a new overcoat and he was without gloves.

Jim stopped inside the door, as immovable as a setter at the scent of quail. His eyes were fixed upon Della, and there was an expression in them that she could not read, and it terrified her. It was not anger, nor surprise, nor disapproval, nor horror, nor any of the sentiments that she had been prepared for. He simply stared at her fixedly with that peculiar expression on his face.

Della wriggled off the table and went for him.

"Jim, darling," she cried, "don't look at me that way. I had my hair cut off and sold it because I couldn't have lived through Christmas without giving you a present. It'll grow out again—you won't mind, will you? I just had to do it. My hair grows awfully fast. Say 'Merry Christmas!' Jim, and let's be happy. You don't know what a nice—what a beautiful, nice gift I've got for you."

"You've cut off your hair?" asked Jim, laboriously, as if he had not arrived at that patent fact yet even after the hardest mental labour.

"Cut it off and sold it," said Della. "Don't you like me just as well, anyhow? I'm me without my hair, ain't I?"

Jim looked about the room curiously.

"You say your hair is gone?" he said, with an air almost of idiocy.

"You needn't look for it," said Della. "It's sold, I tell you—sold and gone, too. It's Christmas Eve, boy. Be good to me, for it went for you. Maybe the hairs of my head were numbered," she went on with a sudden serious sweetness, "but nobody could ever count my love for you. Shall I put the chops on, Jim?"

Out of his trance Jim seemed quickly to wake. He enfolded his Della. For ten seconds let us regard with discreet scrutiny some inconsequential object in the other direction. Eight dollars a week or a million a year—what is the difference? A mathematician or a wit would give you the wrong answer. The magi brought valuable gifts, but that was not among them. This dark assertion will be illuminated later on.

Jim drew a package from his overcoat pocket and threw it upon the table.

"Don't make any mistake, Dell," he said, "about me. I don't think there's anything in the way of a haircut or a shave or a shampoo that could make me like my girl any less. But if you'll unwrap that package you may see why you had me going a while at first."

White fingers and nimble tore at the string and paper. And then an ecstatic scream of joy; and then, alas! a quick feminine change to hysterical tears and wails, necessitating the immediate employment of all the comforting powers of the lord of the flat.

For there lay The Combs—the set of combs, side and back, that Della had worshipped for long in a Broadway window. Beautiful combs, pure tortoise shell, with jeweled rims—just the shade to wear in the beautiful vanished hair. They were expensive combs, she knew, and her heart had simply craved and yearned over them without the least hope of possession. And now, they were hers, but the tresses that should have adorned the coveted adornments were gone.

But she hugged them to her bosom, and at length she was able to look up with dim eyes and a smile and say: "My hair grows so fast, Jim!"

And then Della leaped up like a little singed cat and cried, "Oh, oh!"

Jim had not yet seen his beautiful present. She held it out to him eagerly upon her open palm. The dull precious metal seemed to flash with a reflection of her bright and ardent spirit.

"Isn't it a dandy, Jim? I hunted all over town to find it. You'll have to look at the time a hundred times a day now. Give me your watch. I want to see how it looks on it."

Instead of obeying, Jim tumbled down on the couch and put his hands under the back of his head and smiled.

"Dell," said he, "let's put our Christmas presents away and keep 'em a while. They're too nice to use just at present. I sold the watch to get the money to buy your combs. And now suppose you put the chops on."

The magi, as you know, were wise men—wonderfully wise men—who brought gifts to the Babe in the manger. They invented the art of giving Christmas presents. Being wise, their gifts were no doubt wise ones, possibly bearing the privilege of exchange in case of duplication. And here I have lamely related to you the uneventful chronicle of two foolish children in a flat who most unwisely sacrificed for each other the greatest treasures of their house. But in a last word to the wise of these days let it be said that of all who give gifts these two were the wisest. Of all who give and receive gifts, such as they are wisest. Everywhere they are wisest. They are the magi.

THE SYMBOL AND THE SAINT

by Eugene Field

from *The Writings in Prose and Verse of Eugene Field,*
A *Little Book of Profitable Tales*

Once upon a time a young man made ready for a voyage. His name was Norss; broad were his shoulders, his cheeks were ruddy, his hair was fair and long, his body betokened strength, and good-nature shone from his blue eyes and lurked about the corners of his mouth.

"Where are you going?" asked his neighbor Jans, the forge-master.

"I am going sailing for a wife," said Norss.

"For a wife, indeed!" cried Jans. "And why go you to seek her in foreign lands? Are not our maidens good enough and fair enough, that you must need search for a wife elsewhere? For shame, Norss! for shame!"

But Norss said, "A spirit came to me in my dreams last night and said, 'Launch the boat and set sail to-morrow. Have no fear; for I will guide you to the bride that awaits you.' Then, standing there, all white and beautiful, the spirit held forth a symbol—such as I had never before seen—in the figure of a cross, and the spirit said: 'By this symbol shall she be known to you.' "

"If this be so, you must need go," said Jans. "But are you well victualled? Come to my cabin, and let me give you venison and bear's meat."

Norss shook his head. "The spirit will provide," said he. "I have no fear, and I shall take no care, trusting in the spirit."

So Norss pushed his boat down the beach into the sea, and leaped into the boat, and unfurled the sail to the wind. Jans stood wondering on the beach, and watched the boat speed out of sight.

On, on, many days on sailed Norss—so many leagues that he thought he must have compassed the earth. In all this time he knew no hunger nor thirst; it was as the spirit had told him in his dream— no cares nor dangers beset him. By day the dolphins and the other creatures of the sea gambolled about his boat; by night a beauteous Star seemed to direct his course; and when he slept and dreamed, he saw ever the spirit clad in white, and holding forth to him the symbol in the similitude of a cross.

At last he came to a strange country—a country so very different from his own that he could scarcely trust his senses. Instead of the rugged mountains of the North, he saw a gentle landscape of velvety green; the trees were not pines and firs, but cypresses, cedars, and palms; instead of the cold, crisp air of his native land, he scented the perfumed zephyrs of the Orient; and the wind that filled the sail of his boat and smote his tanned cheeks was heavy and hot with the odor of cinnamon and spices. The waters were calm and blue—very different from the white and angry waves of Norss's native fiord.

As if guided by an unseen hand, the boat pointed straight for the beach of this strangely beautiful land; and ere its prow cleaved the shallower waters, Norss saw a maiden standing on the shore, shading her eyes with her right hand, and gazing intently at him. She was the most beautiful maiden he had ever looked upon. As Norss was fair, so was this maiden dark; her black hair fell loosely about her shoulders in charming contrast with the white raiment in which her slender, graceful form was clad. Around her neck she wore a golden chain, and therefrom was suspended a small symbol, which Norss did not immediately recognize.

"Hast thou come sailing out of the North into the East?" asked the maiden.

"Yes," said Norss.

"And thou art Norss?" she asked.

"I am Norss; and I come seeking my bride," he answered.

"I am she," said the maiden. "My name is Faia. An angel came to me in my dreams last night, and the angel said: 'Stand upon the beach to-day, and Norss shall come out of the North to bear thee home a bride.' So, coming here, I found thee sailing to our shore."

Remembering then the spirit's words, Norss said: "What symbol have you, Faia, that I may know how truly you have spoken?"

"No symbol have I but this," said Faia, holding out the symbol that was attached to the golden chain about her neck. Norss looked upon it, and lo! it was the symbol of his dreams—a tiny wooden cross.

Then Norss clasped Faia in his arms and kissed her, and entering into the boat they sailed away into the North. In all their voyage neither care nor danger beset them; for as it had been told to them in their dreams, so it came to pass. By day the dolphins and the other creatures of the sea gambolled about them; by night the winds and the waves sang them to sleep; and, strangely enough, the Star which before had led Norss into the East, now shone bright and beautiful in the Northern sky!

When Norss and his bride reached their home, Jans, the forge-master, and the other neighbors made great joy, and all said that Faia was more beautiful than any other maiden in the land. So merry was Jans that he built a huge fire in his forge, and the flames thereof filled the whole Northern sky with rays of light that danced up, up, up to the Star, singing glad songs the while. So Norss and Faia were wed, and they went to live in the cabin in the fir-grove.

To these two was born in good time a son, whom they named Claus. On the night that he was born wondrous things came to pass. To the cabin in the fir-grove came all the quaint, weird spirits—the fairies, the elves, the trolls, the pixies, the fadas, the crions, the goblins, the kobolds, the moss-people, the gnomes, the dwarfs, the water-sprites, the courils, the bogles, the brownies, the nixies, the trows, the stille-volk—all came to the cabin in the fir-grove, and capered about and sang the strange, beautiful songs of the Mist-Land. And the flames of old Jans's forge leaped up higher than ever into the Northern sky, carrying the joyous tidings to the Star, and full of music was that happy night.

Even in infancy Claus did marvellous things. With his baby hands he wrought into pretty figures the willows that were given him to play with. As he grew older, he fashioned, with the knife old Jans had made for him, many curious toys—carts, horses, dogs, lambs, houses, trees, cats, and birds, all of wood and very like to nature. His mother taught him how to make dolls too—dolls of every kind, condition, temper, and color; proud dolls, homely dolls, boy dolls, lady dolls, wax dolls, rubber dolls, paper dolls, worsted dolls, rag dolls—dolls of every description and without end. So Claus became at once quite as popular with the little girls as with the little boys of his native village; for he was so generous that he gave away all these pretty things as fast as he made them.

Claus seemed to know by instinct every language. As he grew older he would ramble off into the woods and talk with the trees, the rocks, and the beasts of the greenwood; or he would sit on the cliffs overlooking the fiord, and listen to the stories that the waves of the sea loved to tell him; then, too, he knew the haunts of the elves and the stille-volk, and many a pretty tale he learned from these little people. When night came, old Jans told him the quaint legends of the North, and his mother sang to him the lullabies she had heard when a little child herself in the far-distant East. And every night his mother held out to him the symbol in the similitude of the cross, and bade him kiss it ere he went to sleep.

So Claus grew to manhood, increasing each day in knowledge and in wisdom. His works increased too; and his liberality dispensed everywhere the beauteous things which his fancy conceived and his skill executed. Jans, being now a very old man, and having no son of his own, gave to Claus his forge and workshop, and taught him those secret arts which he in youth had learned from cunning masters. Right joyous now was Claus; and many, many times the Northern sky glowed with the flames that danced singing from the forge while Claus moulded his pretty toys. Every color of the rainbow were these flames; for they reflected the bright colors of the beauteous things strewn round that wonderful workshop. Just as of old he had dispensed to all children alike the homelier toys of his youth, so now he gave to all children alike these more beautiful and more curious gifts. So little children everywhere loved Claus, because he gave them pretty toys, and their parents loved him because he made their little ones so happy.

But now Norss and Faia were come to old age. After long years of love and happiness, they knew that death could not be far distant. And one day Faia said to Norss: "Neither you nor I, dear love, fear death; but if we could choose, would we not choose to live always in this our son Claus, who has been so sweet a joy to us?"

"Ay, ay," said Norss; "but how is that possible?"

"We shall see," said Faia.

That night Norss dreamed that a spirit came to him, and that the spirit said to him: "Norss, thou shalt surely live forever in thy son Claus, if thou wilt but acknowledge the symbol."

Then when the morning was come Norss told his dream to Faia, his wife; and Faia said, "The same dream had I—an angel appearing to me and speaking these very words."

"But what of the symbol?" cried Norss.

"I have it here, about my neck," said Faia.

So saying, Faia drew from her bosom the symbol of wood—a tiny cross suspended about her neck by the golden chain. And as she stood there holding the symbol out to Norss, he—he thought of the time when first he saw her on the far-distant Orient shore, standing beneath the Star in all her maidenly glory, shading her beauteous eyes with one hand, and with the other clasping the cross—the holy talisman of her faith.

"Faia, Faia!" cried Norss, "it is the same—the same you wore when I fetched you a bride from the East!"

"It is the same," said Faia, "yet see how my kisses and my prayers have worn it away; for many, many times in these years, dear Norss, have I pressed it to my lips and breathed your name upon it. See now —see what a beauteous light its shadow makes upon your aged face!"

The sunbeams, indeed, streaming through the window at that moment, cast the shadow of the symbol on old Norss's brow. Norss felt a glorious warmth suffuse him, his heart leaped with joy, and he stretched out his arms and fell about Faia's neck, and kissed the symbol and acknowledged it. Then likewise did Faia; and suddenly the place was filled with a wondrous brightness and with strange music, and never thereafter were Norss and Faia beholden of men.

Until late that night Claus toiled at his forge; for it was a busy season with him, and he had many, many curious and beauteous things to make for the little children in the country round about. The colored flames leaped singing from his forge, so that the Northern sky seemed to be lighted by a thousand rainbows; but above all this voiceful glory beamed the Star, bright, beautiful, serene.

Coming late to the cabin in the fir-grove, Claus wondered that no sign of his father or of his mother was to be seen. "Father—mother!"

he cried, but he received no answer. Just then the Star cast its golden gleam through the latticed window, and this strange, holy light fell and rested upon the symbol of the cross that lay upon the floor. Seeing it, Claus stooped and picked it up, and kissing it reverently, he cried, "Dear talisman, be thou my inspiration evermore; and wheresoever thy blessed influence is felt, there also let my works be known henceforth forever!"

No sooner had he said these words than Claus felt the gift of immortality bestowed upon him; and in that moment, too, there came to him a knowledge that his parents' prayer had been answered, and that Norss and Faia would live in him through all time.

And lo! to that place and in that hour came all the people of Mist-Land and of Dream-Land to declare allegiance to him: yes, the elves, the fairies, the pixies—all came to Claus, prepared to do his bidding. Joyously they capered about him, and merrily they sang.

"Now haste ye all," cried Claus, "haste ye all to your homes and bring to my workshop the best ye have. Search, little hill-people, deep in the bowels of the earth for finest gold and choicest jewels; fetch me, O mermaids, from the bottom of the sea the treasures hidden there— the shells of rainbow tints, the smooth, bright pebbles, and the strange ocean flowers; go, pixies, and other water-sprites, to your secret lakes, and bring me pearls! Speed! speed you all! for many pretty things have we to make for the little ones of earth we love!"

But to the kobolds and the brownies Claus said, "Fly to every house on earth where the cross is known; loiter unseen in the corners, and watch and hear the children through the day. Keep a strict account of good and bad, and every night bring back to me the names of good and bad, that I may know them."

The kobolds and the brownies laughed gleefully, and sped away on noiseless wings; and so, too, did the other fairies and elves.

There came also to Claus the beasts of the forest and the birds of the air, and bade him be their master. And up danced the Four Winds, and they said, "May we not serve you, too?"

The snow-king came stealing along in his feathery chariot. "Oho!" he cried, "I shall speed over all the world and tell them you are coming. In town and country, on the mountain-tops and in the valleys— wheresoever the cross is raised—there will I herald your approach, and thither will I strew you a pathway of feathery white. Oho! oho!" So, singing softly, the snow-king stole upon his way.

But of all the beasts that begged to do him service, Claus liked the reindeer best. "You shall go with me in my travels; for henceforth I shall bear my treasures not only to the children of the North, but to the children in every land whither the Star points me and where the cross is lifted up!" So said Claus to the reindeer, and the reindeer neighed joyously and stamped their hoofs impatiently, as though they longed to start immediately.

Oh, many, many times has Claus whirled away from his far Northern home in his sledge drawn by the reindeer, and thousands upon thousands of beautiful gifts—all of his own making—has he borne to the children of every land; for he loves them all alike, and they all alike love him, I trow. So truly do they love him that they call him Santa Claus, and I am sure that he must be a saint; for he has lived these many hundred years, and we, who know that he was born of Faith and Love, believe that he will live forever.

THE OTHER WISE MAN

by Henry van Dyke

from *The Blue Flower*

You know the story of the Three Wise Men of the East, and how they traveled from far away to offer their gifts at the manger-cradle in Bethlehem. But have you ever heard the story of the Other Wise Man, who also saw the star in its rising, and set out to follow it, yet did not arrive with his brethren in the presence of the young child Jesus? Of the great desire of this fourth pilgrim, and how it was denied, yet accomplished in the denial; of his many wanderings and the probations of his soul; of the long way of his seeking and the strange way of his finding the One whom he sought—I would tell the tale as I have heard fragments of it in the Hall of Dreams, in the palace of the Heart of Man.

I

In the days when Augustus Caesar was master of many kings and Herod reigned in Jerusalem, there lived in the city of Ecbatana, among the mountains of Persia, a certain man named Artaban. His house stood close to the outermost of the walls which encircled the royal treasury. From his roof he could look over the seven-fold battlements of black and white and crimson and blue and red and silver and gold, to the hill where the summer palace of the Parthian emperors glittered like a jewel in a crown.

Around the dwelling of Artaban spread a fair garden, a tangle of flowers and fruit-trees, watered by a score of streams descending from the slopes of Mount Orontes, and made musical by innumerable birds. But all colour was lost in the soft and odorous darkness of the late September night, and all sounds were hushed in the deep charm of its silence, save the plashing of the water, like a voice half-sobbing and half-laughing under the shadows. High above the trees a dim glow of light shone through the curtained arches of the upper chamber, where the master of the house was holding council with his friends.

He stood by the doorway to greet his guests—a tall, dark man of about forty years, with brilliant eyes set near together under his broad brow, and firm lines graven around his fine, thin lips; the brow of a dreamer and the mouth of a soldier, a man of sensitive feeling but inflexible will—one of those who, in whatever age they may live, are born for inward conflict and a life of quest.

His robe was of pure white wool, thrown over a tunic of silk; and a white, pointed cap, with long lapels at the sides, rested on his flowing black hair. It was the dress of the ancient priesthood of the Magi, called the fire-worshippers.

"Welcome!" he said, in his low, pleasant voice, as one after another entered the room—"welcome, Abdus; peace be with you, Rhodaspes and Tigranes, and with you my father, Abgarus. You are all welcome. This house grows bright with the joy of your presence."

There were nine of the men, differing widely in age, but alike in the richness of their dress of many-coloured silks, and in the massive golden collars around their necks, marking them as Parthian nobles, and in the winged circles of gold resting upon their breasts, the sign of the followers of Zoroaster.

They took their places around a small black altar at the end of the room, where a tiny flame was burning. Artaban, standing beside it, and waving a barsom of thin tamarisk branches above the fire, fed it with dry sticks of pine and fragrant oils. Then he began the ancient chant of the Yasna, and the voices of his companions joined in the hymn to Ahura-Mazda:

We worship the Spirit Divine,
all wisdom and goodness possessing,
Surrounded by Holy Immortals,
the givers of bounty and blessing;
We joy in the work of His hands,
His truth and His power confessing.
We praise all the things that are pure,
for these are His only Creation;
The thoughts that are true, and the words
and the deeds that have won approbation;
These are supported by Him,
and for these we make adoration.
Hear us, O Mazda! Thou livest
in truth and in heavenly gladness;
Cleanse us from falsehood, and keep us
from evil and bondage to badness;
Pour out the light and the joy of Thy life
on our darkness and sadness.
Shine on our gardens and fields,
shine on our working and weaving;
Shine on the whole race of man,
believing and unbelieving;
Shine on us now through the night,
Shine on us now in Thy might,
The flame of our holy love
and the song of our worship receiving.

The fire rose with the chant, throbbing as if the flame responded to the music, until it cast a bright illumination through the whole apartment, revealing its simplicity and splendour.

The floor was laid with tiles of dark blue veined with white; pilasters of twisted silver stood out against the blue walls; the clearstory of round-arched windows above them was hung with azure silk; the vaulted ceiling was a pavement of blue stones, like the body of heaven in its clearness, sown with silver stars. From the four corners of the roof hung four golden magic-wheels, called the tongues of the gods. At the eastern end, behind the altar, there were two dark-red pillars of porphyry; above them a lintel of the same stone, on which was carved the figure of a winged archer, with his arrow set to the string and his bow drawn.

The doorway between the pillars, which opened upon the terrace of the roof, was covered with a heavy curtain of the colour of a ripe pomegranate, embroidered with innumerable golden rays shooting upward from the floor. In effect the room was like a quiet, starry night, all azure and silver, flushed in the east with rosy promise of the dawn. It was, as the house of a man should be, an expression of the character and spirit of the master.

He turned to his friends when the song was ended, and invited them to be seated on the divan at the western end of the room.

"You have come to-night," said he, looking around the circle, "at my call, as the faithful scholars of Zoroaster, to renew your worship and rekindle your faith in the God of Purity, even as this fire has been rekindled on the altar. We worship not the fire, but Him of whom it is the chosen symbol, because it is the purest of all created things. It speaks to us of one who is Light and Truth. Is it not so, my father?"

"It is well said, my son," answered the venerable Abgarus. "The enlightened are never idolaters. They lift the veil of form and go in to the shrine of reality, and new light and truth are coming to them continually through the old symbols."

"Hear me, then, my father and my friends," said Artaban, "while I tell you of the new light and truth that have come to me through the most ancient of all signs. We have searched the secrets of Nature together, and studied the healing virtues of water and fire and the plants. We have read also the books of prophecy in which the future is dimly foretold in words that are hard to understand. But the highest of all learning is the knowledge of the stars. To trace their course is to untangle the threads of the mystery of life from the beginning to the end. If we could follow them perfectly, nothing would be hidden from us. But is not our knowledge of them still incomplete? Are there not many stars still beyond our horizon—lights that are known only to the dwellers in the far south-land, among the spice-trees of Punt and the gold mines of Ophir?"

There was a murmur of assent among the listeners.

"The stars," said Tigranes, "are the thoughts of the Eternal. They are numberless. But the thoughts of man can be counted, like the years of his life. The wisdom of the Magi is the greatest of all wisdoms on earth, because it knows its own ignorance. And that is the secret of power. We keep men always looking and waiting for a new sunrise. But we ourselves understand that the darkness is equal to the light, and that the conflict between them will never be ended."

"That does not satisfy me," answered Artaban, "for, if the waiting must be endless, if there could be no fulfilment of it, then it would not be wisdom to look and wait. We should become like those new teachers of the Greeks, who say that there is no truth, and that the only wise men are those who spend their lives in discovering and exposing the lies that have been believed in the world. But the new sunrise will certainly appear in the appointed time. Do not our own books tell us that this will come to pass, and that men will see the brightness of a great light?"

"That is true," said the voice of Abgarus; "every faithful disciple of Zoroaster knows the prophecy of the Avesta, and carries the word in his heart. 'In that day Sosiosh the Victorious shall arise out of the number of the prophets in the east country. Around him shall shine a mighty brightness, and he shall make life everlasting, incorruptible, and immortal, and the dead shall rise again.'"

"This is a dark saying," said Tigranes, "and it may be that we shall never understand it. It is better to consider the things that are near at hand, and to increase the influence of the Magi in their own country, rather than to look for one who may be a stranger, and to whom we must resign our power."

The others seemed to approve these words. There was a silent feeling of agreement manifest among them; their looks responded with that indefinable expression which always follows when a speaker has uttered the thought that has been slumbering in the hearts of his listeners. But Artaban turned to Abgarus with a glow on his face, and said, "My father, I have kept this prophecy in the secret place of my soul. Religion without a great hope would be like an altar without a living fire. And now the flame has burned more brightly, and by the light of it I have read other words which also have come from the fountain of Truth, and speak yet more clearly of the rising of the Victorious One in his brightness."

He drew from the breast of his tunic two small rolls of fine parchment, with writing upon them, and unfolded them carefully upon his knee.

"In the years that are lost in the past, long before our fathers came into the land of Babylon, there were wise men in Chaldea, from whom the first of the Magi learned the secret of the heavens. And of these Balaam the son of Beor was one of the mightiest. Hear the words of his prophecy: 'There shall come a star out of Jacob, and a sceptre shall arise out of Israel.'"

The lips of Tigranes drew downward with contempt, as he said, "Judah was a captive by the waters of Babylon, and the sons of Jacob were in bondage to our kings. The tribes of Israel are scattered through the mountains like lost sheep, and from the remnant that dwells in Judea under the yoke of Rome neither star nor sceptre shall arise."

"And yet," answered Artaban, "it was the Hebrew Daniel, the mighty searcher of dreams, the counsellor of kings, the wise Belteshazzar, who was most honoured and beloved of our great King Cyrus. A prophet of sure things and a reader of the thoughts of the Eternal, Daniel proved himself to our people. And these are the words that he wrote."

Artaban read from the second roll: " 'Know, therefore, and understand that from the going forth of the commandment to restore Jerusalem, unto the Anointed One, the Prince, the time shall be seven and threescore and two weeks.' "

"But, my son," said Abgarus, doubtfully, "these are mystical numbers. Who can interpret them or who can find the key that shall unlock their meaning?"

Artaban answered, "It has been shown to me and to my three companions among the Magi—Caspar, Melchior, and Balthazar. We have searched the ancient tablets of Chaldea and computed the time. It falls in this year. We have studied the sky, and in the spring of the year we saw two of the greatest planets draw near together in the sign of the Fish, which is the house of the Hebrews. We also saw a new star there, which shone for one night and then vanished. Now again the two great planets are meeting. This night is their conjunction. My three brothers are watching by the ancient Temple of the Seven Spheres, at Borsippa, in Babylonia, and I am watching here. If the star shines again, they will wait ten days for me at the temple, and then we will set out together for Jerusalem, to see and worship the promised one who shall be born King of Israel. I believe the sign will come. I have made ready for the journey. I have sold my possessions, and bought these three jewels—a sapphire, a ruby, and a pearl—to carry them as tribute to the King. And I ask you to go with me on the pilgrimage, that we may have joy together in finding the Prince who is worthy to be served."

While he was speaking he thrust his hand into the inmost fold of his girdle and drew out three great gems—one blue as a fragment of the night sky, one redder than a ray of sunrise, and one as pure as the peak of a snow-mountain at twilight—and laid them on the out-spread scrolls before him.

But his friends looked on with strange and alien eyes. A veil of doubt and mistrust came over their faces, like a fog creeping up from the marshes to hide the hills. They glanced at each other with looks of wonder and pity, as those who have listened to incredible sayings, the story of a wild vision, or the proposal of an impossible enterprise.

At last Tigranes said, "Artaban, this is a vain dream. It comes from too much looking upon the stars and the cherishing of lofty thoughts. It would be wiser to spend the time in gathering money for the new fire-temple at Chala. No king will ever rise from the broken race of Israel, and no end will ever come to the eternal strife of light and darkness. He who looks for it is a chaser of shadows. Farewell."

And another said, "Artaban, I have no knowledge of these things, and my office as guardian of the royal treasure binds me here. The quest is not for me. But if thou must follow it, fare thee well."

And another said, "In my house there sleeps a new bride, and I cannot leave her nor take her with me on this strange journey. This quest is not for me. But may thy steps be prospered wherever thou goest. So, farewell."

And another said, "I am ill and unfit for hardship, but there is a man among my servants whom I will send with thee when thou goest, to bring me word how thou farest."

So, one by one, they left the house of Artaban. But Abgarus, the oldest and the one who loved him the best, lingered after the others had gone, and said, gravely, "My son, it may be that the light of truth is in this sign that has appeared in the skies, and then it will surely lead to the Prince and the mighty brightness. Or it may be that it is only a shadow of the light, as Tigranes has said, and then he who follows it will have a long pilgrimage and a fruitless search. But it is better to follow even the shadow of the best than to remain content with the worst. And those who would see wonderful things must often be ready to travel alone. I am too old for this journey, but my heart shall be a companion of thy pilgrimage day and night, and I shall know the end of thy quest. Go in peace."

Then Abgarus went out of the azure chamber with its silver stars, and Artaban was left in solitude.

He gathered up the jewels and replaced them in his girdle. For a long time he stood and watched the flame that flickered and sank upon the altar. Then he crossed the hall, lifted the heavy curtain, and passed out between the pillars of porphyry to the terrace on the roof.

The shiver that runs through the earth ere she rouses from her night-sleep had already begun, and the cool wind that heralds the daybreak was drawing downward from the lofty snow-traced ravines of Mount Orontes. Birds, half-awakened, crept and chirped among the rustling leaves, and the smell of ripened grapes came in brief wafts from the arbours.

Far over the eastern plain a white mist stretched like a lake. But where the distant peaks of Zagros serrated the western horizon the sky was clear. Jupiter and Saturn rolled together like drops of lambent flame about to blend in one.

As Artaban watched them, a steel-blue spark was born out of the darkness beneath, rounding itself with purple splendours to a crimson sphere, and spiring upward through rays of saffron and orange into a point of white radiance. Tiny and infinitely remote, yet perfect in every part, it pulsated in the enormous vault as if the three jewels in the Magian's girdle had mingled and been transformed into a living heart of light.

He bowed his head. He covered his brow with his hands.

"It is the sign," he said. "The King is coming, and I will go to meet him."

II

All night long, Vasda, the swiftest of Artaban's horses, had been waiting, saddled and bridled, in her stall, pawing the ground impatiently, and shaking her bit as if she shared the eagerness of her master's purpose, though she knew not its meaning.

Before the birds had fully roused to their strong, high, joyful chant of morning song, before the white mist had begun to lift lazily from the plain, the Other Wise Man was in the saddle, riding swiftly along the high-road, which skirted the base of Mount Orontes, westward.

How close, how intimate is the comradeship between a man and his favourite horse on a long journey. It is a silent, comprehensive friendship, an intercourse beyond the need of words.

They drink at the same way-side springs, and sleep under the same guardian stars. They are conscious together of the subduing spell of nightfall and the quickening joy of daybreak. The master shares his evening meal with his hungry companion, and feels the soft, moist lips caressing the palm of his hand as they close over the morsel of bread. In the gray dawn he is roused from his bivouac by the gentle stir of a warm, sweet breath over his sleeping face, and looks up into the eyes of his faithful fellow-traveller, ready and waiting for the toil of the day. Surely, unless he is a pagan and an unbeliever, by whatever name he calls upon his God, he will thank Him for this voiceless sympathy, this dumb affection, and his morning prayer will embrace a double blessing—God bless us both, the horse and the rider, and keep our feet from falling and our souls from death!

Then, through the keen morning air, the swift hoofs beat their tattoo along the road, keeping time to the pulsing of two hearts that are moved with the same eager desire—to conquer space, to devour the distance, to attain the goal of the journey.

Artaban must indeed ride wisely and well if he would keep the appointed hour with the other Magi; for the route was a hundred and fifty parasangs, and fifteen was the utmost that he could travel in a day. But he knew Vasda's strength, and pushed forward without anxiety, making the fixed distance every day, though he must travel late into the night, and in the morning long before sunrise.

He passed along the brown slopes of Mount Orontes, furrowed by the rocky courses of a hundred torrents.

He crossed the level plains of the Nisæans, where the famous herds of horses, feeding in the wide pastures, tossed their heads at Vasda's approach, and galloped away with a thunder of many hoofs, and flocks of wild birds rose suddenly from the swampy meadows, wheeling in great circles with a shining flutter of innumerable wings and shrill cries of surprise.

He traversed the fertile fields of Concabar, where the dust from the threshing-floors filled the air with a golden mist, half hiding the huge temple of Astarte with its four hundred pillars.

At Baghistan, among the rich gardens watered by fountains from the rock, he looked up at the mountain thrusting its immense rugged brow out over the road, and saw the figure of King Darius trampling upon his fallen foes, and the proud list of his wars and conquests graven high upon the face of the eternal cliff.

Over many a cold and desolate pass, crawling painfully across the wind-swept shoulders of the hills; down many a black mountain-gorge, where the river roared and raced before him like a savage guide; across many a smiling vale, with terraces of yellow limestone full of vines and fruit-trees; through the oak-groves of Carine and the dark Gates of Zagros, walled in by precipices; into the ancient city of Chala, where the people of Samaria had been kept in captivity long ago; and out again by the mighty portal, riven through the encircling hills, where he saw the image of the High Priest of the Magi sculptured on the wall of rock, with hand uplifted as if to bless the centuries of pilgrims; past the entrance of the narrow defile, filled from end to end with orchards of peaches and figs, through which the river Gyndes foamed down to meet him; over the broad rice-fields, where the autumnal vapours spread their deathly mists; following along the course of the river, under tremulous shadows of poplar and tamarind, among the lower hills; and out upon the flat plain, where the road ran straight as an arrow through the stubble-fields and parched meadows; past the city of Ctesiphon, where the Parthian emperors reigned, and the vast metropolis of Seleucia which Alexander built; across the swirling floods of Tigris and the many channels of Euphrates, flowing yellow through the corn-lands—Artaban pressed onward until he arrived, at nightfall on the tenth day, beneath the shattered walls of populous Babylon.

Vasda was almost spent, and Artaban would gladly have turned into the city to find rest and refreshment for himself and for her. But he knew that it was three hours' journey yet to the Temple of the Seven Spheres, and he must reach the place by midnight if he would find his comrades waiting. So he did not halt, but rode steadily across the stubble-fields.

A grove of date-palms made an island of gloom in the pale yellow sea. As she passed into the shadow Vasda slackened her pace, and began to pick her way more carefully.

Near the farther end of the darkness an access of caution seemed to fall upon her. She scented some danger or difficulty; it was not in her heart to fly from it—only to be prepared for it, and to meet it wisely, as a good horse should do. The grove was close and silent as the tomb; not a leaf rustled, not a bird sang.

She felt her steps before her delicately, carrying her head low, and sighing now and then with apprehension. At last she gave a quick breath of anxiety and dismay, and stood stock-still, quivering in every muscle, before a dark object in the shadow of the last palm-tree.

Artaban dismounted. The dim starlight revealed the form of a man lying across the road. His humble dress and the outline of his haggard face showed that he was probably one of the Hebrews who still dwelt in great numbers around the city. His pallid skin, dry and yellow as parchment, bore the mark of the deadly fever which ravaged the marsh-lands in autumn. The chill of death was in his lean hand, and, as Artaban released it, the arm fell back inertly upon the motionless breast.

He turned away with a thought of pity, leaving the body to that strange burial which the Magians deemed most fitting—the funeral of the desert, from which the kites and vultures rise on dark wings, and the beasts of prey slink furtively away. When they are gone there is only a heap of white bones on the sand.

But, as he turned, a long, faint, ghostly sigh came from the man's lips. The bony fingers gripped the hem of the Magian's robe and held him fast.

Artaban's heart leaped to his throat, not with fear, but with a dumb resentment at the importunity of this blind delay.

How could he stay here in the darkness to minister to a dying stranger? What claim had this unknown fragment of human life upon his compassion or his service? If he lingered but for an hour he could hardly reach Borsippa at the appointed time. His companions would think he had given up the journey. They would go without him. He would lose his quest.

But if he went on now, the man would surely die. If Artaban stayed, life might be restored. His spirit throbbed and fluttered with the urgency of the crisis. Should he risk the great reward of his faith for the sake of a single deed of charity? Should he turn aside, if only for a moment, from the following of the star, to give a cup of cold water to a poor, perishing Hebrew?

"God of truth and purity," he prayed, "direct me in the holy path, the way of wisdom which Thou only knowest."

Then he turned back to the sick man. Loosening the grasp of his hand, he carried him to a little mound at the foot of the palm-tree.

He unbound the thick folds of the turban and opened the garment above the sunken breast. He brought water from one of the small canals near by, and moistened the sufferer's brow and mouth. He mingled a draught of one of those simple but potent remedies which he carried always in his girdle—for the Magians were physicians as well as astrologers—and poured it slowly between the colourless lips. Hour after hour he laboured as only a skilful healer of disease can do. At last the man's strength returned; he sat up and looked about him.

"Who art thou?" he said, in the rude dialect of the country, "and why has thou sought me here to bring back my life?"

"I am Artaban the Magian, of the city of Ecbatana, and I am going to Jerusalem in search of one who is to be born King of the Jews, a great Prince and Deliverer of all men. I dare not delay any longer upon my journey, for the caravan that has waited for me may depart without me. But see, here is all that I have left of bread and wine, and here is a potion of healing herbs. When thy strength is restored thou canst find the dwellings of the Hebrews among the houses of Babylon."

The Jew raised his trembling hand solemnly to heaven.

"Now may the God of Abraham and Isaac and Jacob bless and prosper the journey of the merciful, and bring him in peace to his desired haven. Stay! I have nothing to give thee in return—only this: that I can tell thee where the Messiah must be sought. For our prophets have said that he should be born not in Jerusalem, but in Bethlehem of Judah. May the Lord bring thee in safety to that place, because thou hast had pity upon the sick."

It was already long past midnight. Artaban rode in haste, and Vasda, restored by the brief rest, ran eagerly through the silent plain and swam the channels of the river. She put forth the remnant of her strength, and fled over the ground like a gazelle.

But the first beam of the rising sun sent a long shadow before her as she entered upon the final stadium of the journey, and the eyes of Artaban, anxiously scanning the great mound of Nimrod and the Temple of the Seven Spheres, could discern no trace of his friends.

The many-coloured terraces of black and orange and red and yellow and green and blue and white, shattered by the convulsions of nature, and crumbling under the repeated blows of human violence, still glittered like a ruined rainbow in the morning light.

Artaban rode swiftly around the hill. He dismounted and climbed to the highest terrace, looking out toward the west.

The huge desolation of the marshes stretched away to the horizon and the border of the desert. Bitterns stood by the stagnant pools and jackals skulked through the low bushes; but there was no sign of the caravan of the Wise Men, far or near.

At the edge of the terrace he saw a little cairn of broken bricks, and under them a piece of papyrus. He caught it up and read: "We have waited past the midnight, and can delay no longer. We go to find the King. Follow us across the desert."

Artaban sat down upon the ground and covered his head in despair.

"How can I cross the desert," said he, "with no food and with a spent horse? I must return to Babylon, sell my sapphire, and buy a train of camels, and provision for the journey. I may never overtake my friends. Only God the merciful knows whether I shall not lose the sight of the King because I tarried to show mercy."

III

There was a silence in the Hall of Dreams, where I was listening to the story of the Other Wise Man. Through this silence I saw, but very dimly, his figure passing over the dreary undulations of the desert, high upon the back of his camel, rocking steadily onward like a ship over the waves.

The land of death spread its cruel net around him. The stony waste bore no fruit but briers and thorns. The dark ledges of rock thrust themselves above the surface here and there, like the bones of perished monsters. Arid and inhospitable mountain-ranges rose before him, furrowed with dry channels of ancient torrents, white and ghastly as scars on the face of nature. Shifting hills of treacherous sand were heaped like tombs along the horizon. By day, the fierce heat pressed its intolerable burden on the quivering air. No living creature moved on the dumb, swooning earth, but tiny jerboas scuttling through the parched bushes, or lizards vanishing in the clefts of the rock. By night the jackals prowled and barked in the distance, and the lion made the black ravines echo with his hollow roaring, while a bitter, blighting chill followed the fever of the day. Through heat and cold, the Magian moved steadily onward.

Then I saw the gardens and orchards of Damascus, watered by the streams of Abana and Pharpar, with their sloping swards inlaid with bloom, and their thickets of myrrh and roses. I saw the long, snowy ridge of Herman, and the dark groves of cedars, and the valley of the Jordan, and the blue waters of the Lake of Galilee, and the fertile plain of Esdraelon, and the hills of Ephraim, and the highlands of Judah. Through all these I followed the figure of Artaban moving steadily onward, until he arrived at Bethlehem. And it was the third day after the three Wise Men had come to that place and had found Mary and Joseph, with the young child, Jesus, and had laid their gifts of gold and frankincense and myrrh at his feet.

Then the Other Wise Man drew near, weary, but full of hope, bearing his ruby and his pearl to offer to the King. "For now at last," he said, "I shall surely find him, though I be alone, and later than my brethren. This is the place of which the Hebrew exile told me that the prophets had spoken, and here I shall behold the rising of the great light. But I must inquire about the visit of my brethren, and to what house the star directed them, and to whom they presented their tribute."

The streets of the village seemed to be deserted, and Artaban wondered whether the men had all gone up to the hill-pastures to bring down their sheep. From the open door of a cottage he heard the sound of a woman's voice singing softly. He entered and found a young mother hushing her baby to rest. She told him of the strangers from the far East who had appeared in the village three days ago, and how they said that a star had guided them to the place where Joseph of Nazareth was lodging with his wife and her new-born child, and how they had paid reverence to the child and given him many rich gifts.

"But the travellers disappeared again," she continued, "as suddenly as they had come. We were afraid at the strangeness of their visit. We could not understand it. The man of Nazareth took the child and his mother, and fled away that same night secretly, and it was whispered that they were going to Egypt. Ever since, there has been a spell upon the village; something evil hangs over it. They say that the Roman soldiers are coming from Jerusalem to force a new tax from us, and the men have driven the flocks and herds far back among the hills, and hidden themselves to escape it."

Artaban listened to her gentle, timid speech, and the child in her arms looked up in his face and smiled, stretching out its rosy hands to grasp at the winged circle of gold on his breast. His heart warmed to the touch. It seemed like a greeting of love and trust to one who had journeyed long in loneliness and perplexity, fighting with his own doubts and fears, and following a light that was veiled in clouds.

"Why might not this child have been the promised Prince?" he asked within himself, as he touched its soft cheek. "Kings have been born ere now in lowlier houses than this, and the favourite of the stars may rise even from a cottage. But it has not seemed good to the God of wisdom to reward my search so soon and so easily. The one whom I seek has gone before me; and now I must follow the King to Egypt."

The young mother laid the baby in its cradle, and rose to minister to the wants of the strange guest that fate had brought into her house. She set food before him, the plain fare of peasants, but willingly offered, and therefore full of refreshment for the soul as well as for the body. Artaban accepted it gratefully; and, as he ate, the child fell into a happy slumber, and murmured sweetly in its dreams, and a great peace filled the room.

But suddenly there came the noise of a wild confusion in the streets of the village, a shrieking and wailing of women's voices, a clangour of brazen trumpets and a clashing of swords, and a desperate cry: "The soldiers! the soldiers of Herod! They are killing our children."

The young mother's face grew white with terror. She clasped her child to her bosom, and crouched motionless in the darkest corner of the room, covering him with the folds of her robe, lest he should wake and cry.

But Artaban went quickly and stood in the doorway of the house. His broad shoulders filled the portal from side to side, and the peak of his white cap all but touched the lintel.

The soldiers came hurrying down the street with bloody hands and dripping swords. At the sight of the stranger in his imposing dress they hesitated with surprise. The captain of the band approached the threshold to thrust him aside. But Artaban did not stir. His face was as calm as though he were watching the stars, and in his eyes there burned that steady radiance before which even the half-tanned hunting leopard shrinks, and the bloodhound pauses in his leap. He held the soldier silently for an instant, and then said in a low voice, "I am all alone in this place, and I am waiting to give this jewel to the prudent captain who will leave me in peace."

He showed the ruby, glistening in the hollow of his hand like a great drop of blood.

The captain was amazed at the splendour of the gem. The pupils of his eyes expanded with desire, and the hard lines of greed wrinkled around his lips. He stretched out his hand and took the ruby.

"March on!" he cried to his men, "there is no child here. The house is empty."

The clamour and the clang of arms passed down the street as the headlong fury of the chase sweeps by the secret covert where the trembling deer is hidden. Artaban re-entered the cottage. He turned his face to the east and prayed: "God of truth, forgive my sin! I have said the thing that is not, to save the life of a child. And two of my gifts are gone. I have spent for man that which was meant for God. Shall I ever be worthy to see the face of the King?"

But the voice of the woman, weeping for joy in the shadow behind him, said very gently, "Because thou hast saved the life of my little one, may the Lord bless thee and keep thee; the Lord make His face to shine upon thee and be gracious upon thee; the Lord lift up His countenance upon thee and give thee peace."

IV

Again there was a silence in the Hall of Dreams, deeper and more mysterious than the first interval, and I understood that the years of Artaban were flowing very swiftly under the stillness, and I caught only a glimpse, here and there, of the river of his life shining through the mist that concealed its course.

I saw him moving among the throngs of men in populous Egypt, seeking everywhere for traces of the household that had come down from Bethlehem, and finding them under the spreading sycamore-trees of Heliopolis, and beneath the walls of the Roman fortress of New Babylon beside the Nile—traces so faint and dim that they vanished before him continually, as footprints on the wet river-sand glisten for a moment with moisture and then disappear.

I saw him again at the foot of the pyramids, which lifted their sharp points into the intense saffron glow of the sunset sky, changeless monuments of the perishable glory and the imperishable hope of man. He looked up into the face of the crouching Sphinx and vainly tried to read the meaning of the calm eyes and smiling mouth. Was it, indeed, the mockery of all effort and all aspiration, as Tigranes had said—the cruel jest of a riddle that has no answer, a search that never can succeed? Or was there a touch of pity and encouragement in that inscrutable smile—a promise that even the defeated should attain a victory, and the disappointed should discover a prize, and the ignorant should be made wise, and the blind should see, and the wandering should come into the haven at last?

I saw him again in an obscure house of Alexandria, taking counsel with a Hebrew rabbi. The venerable man, bending over the rolls of parchment on which the prophecies of Israel were written, read aloud the pathetic words which foretold the sufferings of the promised Messiah—the despised and rejected of men, the man of sorrows and acquainted with grief.

"And remember, my son," said he, fixing his eyes upon the face of Artaban, "the King whom thou seekest is not to be found in a palace, nor among the rich and powerful. If the light of the world and the glory of Israel had been appointed to come with the greatness of earthly splendour, it must have appeared long ago. For no son of Abraham will ever again rival the power which Joseph had in the palaces of Egypt, or the magnificence of Solomon throned between the lions in Jerusalem. But the light for which the world is waiting is a new light, the glory that shall rise out of patient and triumphant suffering. And the kingdom which is to be established forever is a new kingdom, the royalty of unconquerable love.

"I do not know how this shall come to pass, nor how the turbulent kings and peoples of earth shall be brought to acknowledge the Messiah and pay homage to him. But this I know. Those who seek him will do well to look among the poor and the lowly, the sorrowful and the oppressed."

So I saw the Other Wise Man again and again, travelling from place to place, and searching among the people of the dispersion, with whom the little family from Bethlehem might, perhaps, have found a refuge. He passed through countries where famine lay heavy upon the land, and the poor were crying for bread. He made his dwelling in plague-stricken cities where the sick were languishing in the bitter companionship of helpless misery. He visited the oppressed and the afflicted in the gloom of subterranean prisons, and the crowded wretchedness of slave-markets, and the weary toil of galley-ships. In all this populous and intricate world of anguish, though he found none to worship, he found many to help. He fed the hungry, and clothed the naked, and healed the sick, and comforted the captive; and his years passed more swiftly than the weaver's shuttle that flashes back and forth through the loom while the web grows and the pattern is completed.

It seemed almost as if he had forgotten his quest. But once I saw him for a moment as he stood alone at sunrise, waiting at the gate of a Roman prison. He had taken from a secret resting-place in his bosom the pearl, the last of his jewels. As he looked at it, a mellower lustre, a soft and iridescent light, full of shifting gleams of azure and rose, trembled upon its surface. It seemed to have absorbed some reflection of the lost sapphire and ruby. So the secret purpose of a noble life draws into itself the memories of past joy and past sorrow. All that has helped it, all that has hindered it, is transfused by a subtle magic into its very essence. It becomes more luminous and precious the longer it is carried close to the warmth of the beating heart.

Then, at last, while I was thinking of this pearl, and of its meaning, I heard the end of the story of the Other Wise Man.

V

Three-and-thirty years of the life of Artaban had passed away, and he was still a pilgrim and a seeker after light. His hair, once darker than the cliffs of Zagros, was now white as the wintry snow that covered them. His eyes, that once flashed like flames of fire, were dull as embers smouldering among the ashes.

Worn and weary and ready to die, but still looking for the King, he had come for the last time to Jerusalem. He had often visited the holy city before, and had searched all its lanes and crowded hovels and black prisons without finding any trace of the family of Nazarenes who had fled from Bethlehem long ago. But now it seemed as if he must make one more effort, and something whispered in his heart that, at last, he might succeed.

It was the season of the Passover. The city was thronged with strangers. The children of Israel, scattered in far lands, had returned to the Temple for the great feast, and there had been a confusion of tongues in the narrow streets for many days.

But on this day a singular agitation was visible in the multitude. The sky was veiled with a portentous gloom. Currents of excitement seemed to flash through the crowd. A secret tide was sweeping them all one way. The clatter of sandals and the soft, thick sound of thousands of bare feet shuffling over the stones, flowed unceasingly along the street that leads to the Damascus gate.

Artaban joined a group of people from his own country, Parthian Jews who had come up to keep the Passover, and inquired of them the cause of the tumult, and where they were going.

"We are going," they answered, "to the place called Golgotha, outside the city walls, where there is to be an execution. Have you not heard what has happened? Two famous robbers are to be crucified, and with them another, called Jesus of Nazareth, a man who has done many wonderful works among the people, so that they love him greatly. But the priests and elders have said that he must die, because he gave himself out to be the Son of God. And Pilate has sent him to the cross because he said that he was the 'King of the Jews.'"

How strangely these familiar words fell upon the tired heart of Artaban! They had led him for a lifetime over land and sea. And now they came to him mysteriously, like a message of despair. The King had arisen, but he had been denied and cast out. He was about to perish. Perhaps he was already dying. Could it be the same who had been born in Bethlehem thirty-three years ago, at whose birth the star had appeared in heaven, and of whose coming the prophets had spoken?

Artaban's heart beat unsteadily with that troubled, doubtful apprehension which is the excitement of old age. But he said within himself, "The ways of God are stranger than the thoughts of men, and it may be that I shall find the King, at last, in the hands of his enemies, and shall come in time to offer my pearl for his ransom before he dies."

So the old man followed the multitude with slow and painful steps toward the Damascus gate of the city. Just beyond the entrance of the guard-house a troop of Macedonian soldiers came down the street, dragging a young girl with torn dress and dishevelled hair. As the Magian paused to look at her with compassion, she broke suddenly from the hands of her tormentors, and threw herself at his feet, clasping him around the knees. She had seen his white cap and the winged circle on his breast.

"Have pity on me," she cried, "and save me, for the sake of the God of Purity! I also am a daughter of the true religion which is taught by the Magi. My father was a merchant of Parthia, but he is dead, and I am seized for his debts to be sold as a slave. Save me from worse than death!"

Artaban trembled.

It was the old conflict in his soul, which had come to him in the palm-grove of Babylon and in the cottage at Bethlehem—the conflict between the expectation of faith and the impulse of love. Twice the gift which he had consecrated to the worship of religion had been drawn to the service of humanity. This was the third trial, the ultimate probation, the final and irrevocable choice.

Was it his great opportunity, or his last temptation? He could not tell. One thing only was clear in the darkness of his mind—it was inevitable. And does not the inevitable come from God?

One thing only was sure to his divided heart—to rescue this helpless girl would be a true deed of love. And is not love the light of the soul?

He took the pearl from his bosom. Never had it seemed so luminous, so radiant, so full of tender, living lustre. He laid it in the hand of the slave.

"This is thy ransom, daughter! It is the last of my treasures which I kept for the King."

While he spoke, the darkness of the sky deepened, and shuddering tremors ran through the earth heaving convulsively like the breast of one who struggles with mighty grief.

The walls of the houses rocked to and fro. Stones were loosened and crashed into the street. Dust clouds filled the air. The soldiers fled in terror, reeling like drunken men. But Artaban and the girl whom he had ransomed crouched helpless beneath the wall of the Prætorium.

What had he to fear? What had he to hope? He had given away the last remnant of his tribute for the King. He had parted with the last hope of finding him. The quest was over, and it had failed. But, even in that thought, accepted and embraced, there was peace. It was not resignation. It was not submission. It was something more profound and searching. He knew that all was well, because he had done the best that he could from day to day. He had been true to the light that had been given to him. He had looked for more. And if he had not found it, if a failure was all that came out of his life, doubtless that was the best that was possible. He had not seen the revelation of "life everlasting, incorruptible and immortal." But he knew that even if he could live his earthly life over again, it could not be otherwise than it had been.

One more lingering pulsation of the earthquake quivered through the ground. A heavy tile, shaken from the roof, fell and struck the old man on the temple. He lay breathless and pale, with his gray head resting on the young girl's shoulder, and the blood trickling from the wound. As she bent over him, fearing that he was dead, there came a voice through the twilight, very small and still, like music sounding from a distance, in which the notes are clear but the words are lost. The girl turned to see if some one had spoken from the window above them, but she saw no one.

Then the old man's lips began to move, as if in answer, and she heard him say in the Parthian tongue: "Not so, my Lord! For when saw I thee and hungered and fed thee? Or thirsty, and gave thee drink? When saw I thee a stranger, and took thee in? Or naked, and clothed thee? When saw I thee sick or in prison, and came unto thee? Three-and-thirty years have I looked for thee; but I have never seen thy face, nor ministered to thee, my King."

He ceased, and the sweet voice came again. And again the maid heard it, very faint and far away. But now it seemed as though she understood the words:

"*Verily I say unto thee, Inasmuch as thou hast done it unto one of the least of these my brethren, thou hast done it unto me.*"

A calm radiance of wonder and joy lighted the pale face of Artaban like the first ray of dawn on a snowy mountain-peak. A long breath of relief exhaled gently from his lips.

His journey was ended. His treasures were accepted. The Other Wise Man had found the King.

THE LITTLE MATCH-GIRL

from the Danish of Hans Christian Andersen

from *Hans Andersen's Fairy Tales and Wonder Stories*

It was terribly cold; it snowed and was already almost dark, and evening came on, the last evening of the year. In the cold and gloom a poor little girl, bareheaded and barefoot, was walking through the streets. When she left her own house she certainly had had slippers on, but of what use were they? They were very big slippers, and her mother had used them till then, so big were they. The little maid lost them as she slipped across the road, where two carriages were rattling by terribly fast. One slipper was not to be found again, and a boy had seized the other and run away with it. He thought he could use it very well as a cradle some day when he had children of his own. So now the little girl went with her little naked feet, which were quite red and blue with the cold. In an old apron she carried a number of matches, and a bundle of them in her hand. No one had bought anything of her all day, and no one had given her a farthing.

Shivering with cold and hunger, she crept along, a picture of misery, poor little girl! The snowflakes covered her long fair hair, which fell in pretty curls over her neck; but she did not think of that now. In all the windows lights were shining, and there was a glorious smell of roast goose, for it was New Year's Eve. Yes, she thought of that!

In a corner formed by two houses, one of which projected beyond the other, she sat down, cowering. She had drawn up her little feet, but she was still colder, and she did not dare to go home, for she had sold no matches and did not bring a farthing of money. From her father she would certainly receive a beating; and, besides, it was cold at home, for they had nothing over them but a roof through which the wind whistled, though the largest rents had been stopped with straw and rags.

Her little hands were almost benumbed with the cold. Ah, a match might do her good, if she could only draw one from the bundle and rub it against the wall and warm her hands at it. She drew one out. R-r-atch! how it sputtered and burned! It was a warm, bright flame, like a little candle, when she held her hands over it; it was a wonderful little light! It really seemed to the little girl as if she sat before a great polished stove with bright brass feet and a brass cover. How the fire burned! How comfortable it was! But the little flame went out, the stove vanished, and she had only the remains of the burnt match in her hand.

A second was rubbed against the wall. It burned up, and when the light fell upon the wall it became transparent like a thin veil, and she could see through it into the room. On the table a snow-white cloth was spread; upon it stood a shining dinner service; the roast goose smoked gloriously, stuffed with apples and dried plums. And, what was still more splendid to behold, the goose hopped down from the dish and waddled along the floor, with a knife and fork in its breast, to the little girl. Then the match went out and only the thick, damp, cold wall was before her. She lighted another match. Then she was sitting under a beautiful Christmas tree; it was greater and more ornamented than the one she had seen through the glass door at the rich merchant's. Thousands of candles burned upon the green branches, and colored pictures like those in the print shops looked down upon them. The little girl stretched forth her hand toward them; then the match went out. The Christmas lights mounted higher. She saw them now as stars in the sky; one of them fell down, forming a long line of fire.

"Now someone is dying," thought the little girl, for her old grandmother, the only person who had loved her, and who was now dead, had told her that when a star fell down a soul mounted up to God.

She rubbed another match against the wall; it became bright again, and in the brightness the old grandmother stood clear and shining, mild and lovely.

"Grandmother!" cried the child. "Oh, take me with you! I know you will go when the match is burned out. You will vanish like the warm fire, the warm food, and the great, glorious Christmas tree!"

And she hastily rubbed the whole bundle of matches, for she wished to hold her grandmother fast. And the matches burned with such a glow that it became brighter than in the middle of the day; grandmother had never been so large or so beautiful. She took the little girl in her arms, and both flew in brightness and joy above the earth, very, very high, and up there was neither cold, nor hunger, nor care—they were with God.

But in the corner, leaning against the wall, sat the poor girl with red cheeks and smiling mouth, frozen to death on the last evening of the old year. The New Year's sun rose upon a little corpse! The child sat there, stiff and cold, with the matches, of which one bundle was burned. "She wanted to warm herself," the people said. No one imagined what a beautiful thing she had seen and in what glory she had gone in with her grandmother to the New Year's Day.

THE FIR-TREE

from the Danish of Hans Christian Andersen

from Hans Andersen's Fairy Tales and Wonder Stories

Out in the woods stood a nice little Fir-tree. The place he had was a very good one; the sun shone on him; as to fresh air, there was enough of that, and round him grew many large-sized comrades, pines as well as firs. But the little Fir wanted so very much to be a grown-up tree.

He did not think of the warm sun and of the fresh air; he did not care for the little cottage children that ran about and prattled when they were in the woods looking for wild strawberries. The children often came with a whole pitcherful of berries, or a long row of them threaded on a straw, and sat down near the young Tree and said, "Oh, how pretty he is! What a nice little Fir!" But this was what the Tree could not bear to hear.

At the end of a year he had shot up a good deal, and after another year he was another long bit taller; for with fir-trees one can always tell by the shoots how many years old they are.

"Oh, were I but such a high tree as the others are!" sighed he.

"Then I should be able to spread out my branches and with the tops look into the wide world! Then would the birds build nests among my branches; and when there was a breeze I could bend with as much stateliness as the others!"

Neither the sunbeams, nor the birds, nor the red clouds which morning and evening sailed above him gave the little Tree any pleasure.

In winter, when the snow lay glittering on the ground, a hare would often come leaping along and jump right over the little Tree. Oh, that made him so angry! But two winters were past, and in the third the Tree was so large that the hare was obliged to go round it. "To grow and grow, to get older and be tall," thought the Tree—"that, after all, is the most delightful thing in the world!"

In autumn the woodcutters always came and felled some of the largest trees. This happened every year; and the young Fir-tree, that had now grown to a very comely size, trembled at the sight; for the magnificent great trees fell to the earth with noise and cracking, the branches were lopped off, and the trees looked long and bare; they were hardly to be recognized; and then they were laid in carts, and the horses dragged them out of the wood.

Where did they go to? What became of them?

In spring, when the Swallows and the Storks came, the Tree asked them, "Don't you know where they have been taken? Have you not met them anywhere?"

The Swallows did not know anything about it; but the Stork looked musing, nodded his head, and said, "Yes, I think I know. I met many ships as I was flying hither from Egypt; on the ships were magnificent masts, and I venture to assert that it was they that smelt so of fir. I may congratulate you, for they lifted themselves on high most majestically!"

"Oh, were I but old enough to fly across the sea! But how does the sea look in reality? What is it like?"

"That would take a long time to explain," said the Stork; and with these words off he went.

"Rejoice in thy growth!" said the Sunbeams; "rejoice in thy vigorous growth and in the fresh life that moveth within thee!"

And the Wind kissed the Tree, and the Dew wept tears over him; but the Fir understood it not.

When Christmas came, quite young trees were cut down, trees which often were not even as large or of the same age as this Fir-tree who could never rest but always wanted to be off. These young trees, and they were always the finest-looking, retained their branches; they were laid on carts, and the horses drew them out of the wood.

"Where are they going to?" asked the Fir. "They are not taller than I; there was one indeed that was considerably shorter—and why do they retain all their branches? Whither are they taken?"

"We know! We know!" chirped the Sparrows. "We have peeped in at the windows in the town below! We know whither they are taken! The greatest splendor and the greatest magnificence one can imagine await them. We peeped through the windows and saw them planted in the middle of the warm room, and ornamented with the most splendid things—with gilded apples, with gingerbread, with toys and many hundred lights!"

"And then?" asked the Fir-tree, trembling in every bough. "And then? What happens then?"

"We did not see anything more; it was incomparably beautiful."

"I would fain know if I am destined for so glorious a career," cried the Tree, rejoicing. "That is still better than to cross the sea! What a longing do I suffer! Were Christmas but come! I am now tall, and my branches spread like the others that were carried off last year! Oh, were I but already on the cart! Were I in the warm room with all the splendor and magnificence! Yes; then something better, something still grander, will surely follow, or wherefore should they thus ornament me? Something better, something still grander, *must* follow—but what? Oh, how I long, how I suffer! I do not know myself what is the matter with me!"

"Rejoice in our presence!" said the Air and the Sunlight; "rejoice in thy own fresh youth!"

But the Tree did not rejoice at all; he grew and grew, and was green both winter and summer. People that saw him said, "What a fine tree!" and toward Christmas he was one of the first that was cut down. The ax struck deep into the very pith; the tree fell to the earth with a sigh; he felt a pang—it was like a swoon; he could not think of happiness, for he was sorrowful at being separated from his home, from the place where he had sprung up. He well knew that he should never see his dear old comrades, the little bushes and flowers around him, any more, perhaps not even the birds! The departure was not at all agreeable.

The Tree only came to himself when he was unloaded in a court-yard with the other trees, and heard a man say, "That one is splendid;

we don't want the others." Then two servants came in rich livery and carried the Fir-tree into a large and splendid drawing room. Portraits were hanging on the walls, and near the white porcelain stove stood two large Chinese vases with lions on the covers. There, too, were large easy chairs, silken sofas, large tables full of picture books and full of toys worth hundreds and hundreds of crowns—at least the children said so. And the Fir-tree was stuck upright in a cask that was filled with sand; but no one could see that it was a cask, for green cloth was hung all around it, and it stood on a large, gaily colored carpet. Oh, how the tree quivered! What was to happen? The servants as well as the young ladies decorated it. On one branch there hung little nets cut out of colored paper, and each net was filled with sugarplums; and among the other boughs gilded apples and walnuts were suspended, looking as though they had grown there, and little blue and white tapers were placed among the leaves. Dolls that looked for all the world like men—the Tree had never beheld such before—were seen among the foliage, and at the very top a large star of gold tinsel was fixed. It was really splendid—beyond description splendid.

"This evening!" said they all; "how it will shine this evening!"

"Oh," thought the Tree, "if the evening were but come! If the tapers were but lighted! And then I wonder what will happen! Perhaps the other trees from the forest will come to look at me! Perhaps the sparrows will beat against the windowpanes! I wonder if I shall take root here and winter and summer stand covered with ornaments!"

He knew very much about the matter! But he was so impatient that for sheer longing he got a pain in his back, and this with trees is the same thing as a headache with us.

The candles were now lighted. What brightness! What splendor! The Tree trembled so in every bough that one of the tapers set fire to the foliage. It blazed up splendidly.

"Help! help!" cried the young ladies, and they quickly put out the fire.

Now the Tree did not even dare tremble. What a state he was in! He was so uneasy lest he should lose something of his splendor that he was quite bewildered amid the glare and brightness, when suddenly both folding doors opened and a troop of children rushed in as if they would upset the Tree. The older persons followed quietly; the little ones stood quite still. But it was only for a moment; then they shouted

so that the whole place re-echoed with their rejoicing; they danced
round the Tree, and one present after the other was pulled off.

"What are they about?" thought the Tree. "What is to happen
now?" And the lights burned down to the very branches, and as they
burned down they were put out one after the other, and then the
children had permission to plunder the Tree. So they fell upon it with
such violence that all its branches cracked; if it had not been fixed
firmly in the cask it would certainly have tumbled down.

The children danced about with their beautiful playthings; no one
looked at the Tree except the old nurse, who peeped between the
branches; but it was only to see if there was a fig or an apple left that
had been forgotten.

"A story! A story!" cried the children, drawing a little fat man toward the Tree. He seated himself under it and said, "Now we are in
the shade, and the Tree can listen too. But I shall tell only one story.
Now which will you have: that about Ivedy-Avedy, or about Klumpy-
Dumpy who tumbled downstairs, and yet after all came to the throne
and married the princess?"

"Ivedy-Avedy," cried some; "Klumpy-Dumpy," cried the others.
There was such a bawling and screaming. The Fir-tree alone was
silent, and he thought to himself, "Am I not to bawl with the rest—
am I to do nothing whatever?" for he was one of the company and
had done what he had to do.

And the man told about Klumpy-Dumpy that tumbled down, who
notwithstanding came to the throne and at last married the princess.
And the children clapped their hands and cried out, "Oh, go on! Do
go on!" They wanted to hear about Ivedy-Avedy, too, but the little
man only told them about Klumpy-Dumpy. The Fir-tree stood quite
still and absorbed in thought; the birds in the wood had never related
the like of this. "Klumpy-Dumpy fell downstairs, and yet he married
the princess! Yes, yes! That's the way of the world!" thought the Fir-
tree, and believed it all, because the man who told the story was so
good-looking. "Well, well! Who knows, perhaps I may fall downstairs, too, and get a princess as wife!" And he looked forward with joy
to the morrow, when he hoped to be decked out again with lights,
playthings, fruits, and tinsel.

"I won't tremble tomorrow!" thought the Fir-tree. "I will enjoy to
the full all my splendor! Tomorrow I shall hear again the story of
Klumpy-Dumpy, and perhaps that of Ivedy-Avedy, too." And the
whole night the Tree stood still and in deep thought.

In the morning the servant and the housemaid came in.

"Now, then, the splendor will begin again," thought the Fir. But they dragged him out of the room, and up the stairs into the loft; and here in a dark corner, where no daylight could enter, they left him. "What's the meaning of this?" thought the Tree. "What am I to do here? What shall I hear now, I wonder?" And he leaned against the wall, lost in reverie. Time enough had he, too, for his reflections, for days and nights passed on, and nobody came up; and when at last somebody did come it was only to put some great trunks in a corner out of the way. There stood the Tree, quite hidden; it seemed as if he had been entirely forgotten.

" 'Tis now winter out-of-doors!" thought the Tree. "The earth is hard and covered with snow; men cannot plant me now, and therefore I have been put up here under shelter till the springtime comes! How thoughtful that is! How kind man is, after all! If it only were not so dark here and so terribly lonely! Not even a hare. And out in the woods it was so pleasant when the snow was on the ground, and the hare leaped by; yes, even when he jumped over me; but I did not like it then. It is really terribly lonely here!"

"Squeak! Squeak!" said a little Mouse, at the same moment peeping out of his hole. And then another little one came.

They snuffed about the Fir-tree and rustled among the branches.

"It is dreadfully cold," said the Mouse. "But for that it would be delightful here, old Fir, wouldn't it?"

"I am by no means old," said the Fir-tree. "There's many a one considerably older than I am."

"Where do you come from," asked the Mice, "and what can you do?" They were so extremely curious. "Tell us about the most beautiful spot on the earth. Have you never been there? Were you never in the larder where cheeses lie on the shelves and hams hang from above, where one dances about on tallow candles; that place where one enters lean and comes out again fat and portly?"

"I know no such place," said the Tree. "But I know the wood, where the sun shines, and where the little birds sing." And then he told all about his youth; and the little Mice had never heard the like before; and they listened and said, "Well, to be sure! How much you have seen! How happy you must have been!"

"I!" said the Fir-tree, thinking over what he had himself related. "Yes, in reality those were happy times." And then he told about Christmas Eve, when he was decked out with cakes and candles.

"Oh," said the little Mice, "how fortunate you have been, old Fir-tree!"

"I am by no means old," said he. "I came from the wood this winter; I am in my prime, and am only rather short for my age."

"What delightful stories you know!" said the Mice; and the next night they came with four other little Mice, who were to hear what the Tree recounted; and the more he related the more plainly he remembered all himself; and it appeared as if those times had really been happy times. "But they may still come—they may still come. Klumpy-Dumpy fell downstairs, and yet he got a princess!" And he thought at the moment of a nice little Birch-tree growing out in the wood; to the Fir that would be a real charming princess.

"Who is Klumpy-Dumpy?" asked the Mice. So then the Fir-tree told the whole fairy tale, for he could remember every single word of it; and the little Mice jumped for joy up to the very top of the Tree. Next night two more Mice came, and on Sunday two Rats, even; but they said the stories were not interesting, which vexed the little Mice; and they, too, now began to think them not so very amusing, either.

"Do you know only one story?" asked the Rats.

"Only that one," answered the Tree. "I heard it on my happiest evening; but I did not then know how happy I was."

"It is a very stupid story! Don't you know one about bacon and tallow candles? Can't you tell any larder stories?"

"No," said the Tree.

"Then good-by," said the Rats; and they went home.

At last the little Mice stayed away also; and the Tree sighed. "After all, it was very pleasant when the sleek little Mice sat round me and listened to what I told them. Now that, too, is over. But I will take good care to enjoy myself when I am brought out again."

But when was that to be? Why, one morning there came a quantity of people and set to work in the loft. The trunks were moved, the tree was pulled out and thrown—rather hard, it is true—down on the floor, but a man drew him toward the stairs, where the daylight shone.

"Now a merry life will begin again," thought the Tree. He felt the fresh air, the first sunbeam—and now he was out in the courtyard. All passed so quickly, there was so much going on around him, that the Tree quite forgot to look to himself. The court adjoined a garden, and all was in flower; the roses hung so fresh and odorous over the balustrade, the lindens were in blossom, the Swallows flew by and said,

"Quirre-vit! My husband is come!" but it was not the Fir-tree that they meant.

"Now, then, I shall really enjoy life," said he, exultingly, and spread out his branches; but, alas! they were all withered and yellow. It was in a corner that he lay, among weeds and nettles. The golden star of tinsel was still on the top of the Tree, and glittered in the sunshine.

In the courtyard some of the merry children were playing who had danced at Christmas round the Fir-tree and were so glad at the sight of him. One of the youngest ran and tore off the golden star.

"Only look what is still on the ugly old Christmas tree!" said he, trampling on the branches so that they all cracked beneath his feet.

And the Tree beheld all the beauty of the flowers and the freshness in the garden; he beheld himself and wished he had remained in his dark corner in the loft; he thought of his first youth in the wood, of the merry Christmas Eve, and of the little Mice who had listened with so much pleasure to the story of Klumpy-Dumpy.

"'Tis over! 'Tis past!" said the poor Tree. "Had I but rejoiced when I had reason to do so! But now 'tis past, 'tis past!"

And the gardener's boy chopped the Tree into small pieces; there was a whole heap lying there. The wood flamed up splendidly under the large brewing cauldron, and it sighed so deeply! Each sigh was like a shot.

The boys played about in the court, and the youngest wore the gold star on his breast which the Tree had had on the happiest evening of his life. However, that was over now—the Tree gone, the story at an end. All, all was over; every tale must end at last.

McALLISTER'S CHRISTMAS

by Arthur Train

from *Scribner's Magazine*, Vol. XXXVI

I

McAllister was out of sorts. All the afternoon he had sat in the club window and watched the Christmas shoppers hurrying by with their bundles. He thanked God *he* had no brats to buy moo-cows and bow-wows for! The very nonchalance of these victims of a fate that had given them families irritated him. McAllister was a club-man, pure and simple; that is to say, though neither simple nor pure, he was a clubman and nothing more. He had occupied the same seat by the same window during the greater part of his earthly existence, and they were the same seat and window that his father had filled before him. His select and exclusive circle called him "Chubby," and his five and forty years of terrapin and cocktails had given him a graceful rotundity of person that did not belie the name. They had also endowed him with a cheerful, though florid, countenance, a rather watery eye, and a permanent sense of well-being.

As the afternoon wore on and the pedestrians became fewer, McAllister sank deeper and deeper into gloom. The club was deserted. Everybody had gone out of town to spend Christmas with someone else, and the Winthrops, on whom he had counted for a certainty, had failed for some reason to invite him. He had waited confidently until the last minute, and now he was stranded, alone.

It began to snow softly, gently. McAllister grunted and threw himself disconsolately into a leathern arm-chair by the smouldering logs of the six-foot hearth. A servant in livery entered, pulled down the shades, and after touching a button that threw a subdued radiance over the room, withdrew noiselessly.

"Come back here, Peter!" growled McAllister. "Anybody in the club?"

"Only Mr. Tomlinson, sir."

McAllister swore under his breath.

"Yes, sir," replied Peter.

McAllister shot a quick glance at him.

"I didn't say anything. You may go."

This time Peter got almost to the door.

"Er—Peter! Ask Mr. Tomlinson if he will dine with me."

Peter returned with the intelligence that Mr. Tomlinson would be delighted.

"Of course," grumbled McAllister to himself. "No one ever knew Tomlinson to refuse *anything*."

He ordered dinner, and then took up an evening paper in which an effort had been made to conceal the absence of news by summarizing the achievements of the past year. Staring headlines invited his notice to: "A YEAR OF PROGRESS." "WHAT THE TENEMENT-HOUSE COMMISSION HAS ACCOMPLISHED." "FURTHUR NEED OF PRISON REFORM." He threw down the paper in disgust. This reform made him *sick!* Tenements and prisons! Why were the papers always talking about tenements and prisons? They were a great deal better than the people who lived in them deserved! He remembered Wilkins, his valet, who had stolen his black pearl scarf-pin. It increased his ill-humor. Hang Wilkins! The thief was probably "out" now and wearing the pin. It had been a matter of jest among his friends at the time, that the servant had looked not unlike his master. McAllister winced at the thought.

"Dinner is served," said Peter.

An hour and a half later Tomlinson and McAllister, having finished a sumptuous repast, stared stupidly at each other across their liqueurs. They were stuffed and bored. Tomlinson was a thin man who knew everything positively. McAllister hated him. He always felt when in his company like the woman who invariably answered her husband's remarks by " 'Tain't so! It's just the opposite!" Tomlinson was trying to make conversation by repeating assertively what he had read in the evening press.

"Now our prisons," he announced authoritatively. "Why, it is outrageous! The people are crowded in like cattle; the food is loathsome; it is a disgrace to a civilized city!"

This was the last straw to McAllister.

"Look here," he snarled back at Tomlinson, who shrank behind his cigar at the vehemence of the attack, "what do *you* know about it? I tell you it's all rot! It's all politics! Our tenements are all right, and so are our prisons. The law of supply and demand regulates the tenements, and *who pay* for the prisons, I'd like to know? *We* pay for 'em, and the scamps that *rob* us live in 'em for nothing. The 'Tombs' is a great deal better than most second-class hotels on the Continent. I *know*. I had a valet once that— Oh, what's the use! I'd be glad to spend Christmas in no worse place! Reform! Stuff! Don't tell *me!*" He sank back, purple in the face.

"Oh, of course—if you *know*." Tomlinson hesitated politely, remembering that McAllister had signed for the dinner.

"Well, I *do* know," grunted McAllister.

II

"No-el! No-el! No-el! No-el!" rang out the bells, as McAllister left the club at twelve o'clock and started down the Avenue.

"No-el! No-el!" McAllister hummed the tune. "Pretty old air!" he thought. He had almost forgotten after his game of Bridge that it was Christmas morning. As he felt his way gingerly over the stone sidewalks, the bells were ringing all around him. First one chime, then another. "Noel! Noel! No-e-el! No-el!" They ceased, leaving the melody floating on the moist night air.

Suddenly it began to rain. First a soft, wet mist, that dimmed the electric lights and shrouded the hotel windows; then a fine sprinkle; at last the chill rain of a winter's night. McAllister turned up his coat collar and looked about for a cab. It was too late. He hurried hastily down the Avenue. As he neared Twenty-eighth Street, a welcome sight met his eye—a coupé, a night hawk, crawling slowly down the block, on the lookout, no doubt, for belated Christmas revellers. Without superfluous introduction McAllister made a dive for the door, shouted his address, and jumped inside. The driver, but half roused from his lethargy, muttered something unintelligible and *pulled in* his horse. At the same moment the dark figure of a man swiftly emerged from a side street, ran up to the cab, opened the door, threw in a heavy object upon McAllister's feet, and followed it with himself.

"Let her go!" he cried, slamming the door. The driver, without hesitation, lashed his horse and started at a furious gallop down the slippery Avenue.

Then for the first time the stranger perceived McAllister. There was a muttered curse, a gleam of steel as they flashed by a street lamp, and the clubman felt the cold muzzle of a revolver against his cheek.

"Speak, and I'll blow yer head off!"

The cab swayed and swerved in all directions, and the driver retained his seat with difficulty. McAllister clinging to the sides of the rocking vehicle expected every moment to be either shot or thrown out and killed.

"Don't move!" hissed his companion.

McAllister tried with difficulty not to move.

Suddenly there came a shrill whistle, followed by the clatter of hoofs. A figure on horseback dashed by. The driver, trying to rein in his now maddened beast, lost his balance and pitched overboard. There was a confusion of shouts, a blue flash—a loud report. The horse sprang into the air and fell kicking upon the pavement; the cab crashed upon its side; amid a shower of glass, the door parted company with its hinges; and the stranger, placing his heel on McAllister's stomach, leaped quickly into the darkness. A moment later, having recovered a part of his scattered senses, our hero, thrusting himself through the shattered framework of the cab, staggered to his feet. He remembered dimly afterward having expected to create a mild sensation among the spectators by announcing in response to their polite inquiries as to his safety, that he was "quite uninjured." Instead, however, the glare of a policeman's lantern was turned upon his dishevelled countenance and a hoarse voice shouted, "Throw up your hands!"

He threw them up. Like the Phœnix rising from its ashes, McAllister emerged from the débris which surrounded him. On either side of the cab was a policeman with levelled revolver. A mounted officer stood sentinel beside the smoking body of the horse.

"No tricks, now!" continued the voice. "Pull your feet out of that mess and keep your hands *up!* Slip on the nippers, Tom. Better go through him *here*. They always manage to '*lose*' something goin' over."

McAllister wondered where "Over" was. Before he could protest he was unceremoniously seated upon the body of the dead horse and the officers were going rapidly through his clothes.

"Thought so!" muttered Tom, as he drew out of McAllister's coat pocket a revolver and a jimmy. "Just as well to unballast 'em at the start." A black calico mask and a bottle filled with a colorless liquid followed.

Tom drew a quick breath.

"So you're one of *those*, are ye?" and he kicked McAllister in the leg.

The victim of this astounding adventure had not yet spoken. Now he stammered:

"Look here! Who do you think I am? This is all a mistake. My name is McAllister."

Tom did not deign to reply.

The officer on horseback had dismounted and was poking among the pieces of cab.

"What's this here?" he inquired, as he kicked out the bottom of the vehicle. He dragged a large bundle covered with black cloth into the circle of light and, untying a bit of cord, poured the contents upon the pavement. A glittering silver service rolled out upon the asphalt and reflected the glow of the lanterns.

"Gee, look at all the swag!" exclaimed Tom. "I wonder where he melts it up."

Faintly at first, then nearer and nearer came the harsh clanging of the "hurry-up" wagon.

"Get up," directed Tom, punctuating his order with mild kicks. Then, as the driver reined up the panting horses alongside, the officer grabbed his prisoner by the coat collar and yanked him to his feet.

"Step in, 'Mr. McAllister,' " he said with grim sarcasm.

"My God!" exclaimed our friend half aloud, "where are they going to take me?"

"To the 'Tombs'—for Christmas!" answered Tom.

III

McAllister, hatless, stumbled into the wagon and was thrust forcibly into a corner. Above the steady drum of the rain upon the waterproof cover he could hear the officers outside packing up the silver ware and discussing their capture.

The wagon started and the officers swung on to the steps behind. McAllister, crouching in the straw by the driver's seat, maintained a gloomy silence. The ignominy of his position crushed him. Never again, should this disgrace become known, could he bring himself to enter the portals of the club. Explanation to these fools of officers was clearly impossible. With an official it would be different. He had once met a Police Commissioner at dinner, and remembered that he had seemed really almost like a gentleman.

The wagon drew up at Jefferson Market and presently McAllister found himself in a small room, at one end of which iron bars ran from floor to ceiling. A kerosene lamp cast a dim light over a weatherbeaten desk, behind which, half asleep, reclined an officer on night duty. A single other chair and four large octagonal stone receptacles were the only remaining furniture.

The man behind the desk opened his eyes, yawned, and stared stupidly at the officers. A clock directly overhead struck "one" with harsh, vibrant clang.

"Wot yer got?" inquired the sergeant.

"A second-story man," answered the guard.

"He took to a cab," explained Tom, "and him and his partner give us a fierce chase down the Avenoo. O'Halloran shot the horse, and the cab was all knocked to hell. The other fellow clawed out before we could nab him. But we got this one all right."

"Hi, there, McCarthy," shouted the sergeant to someone in the dim vast beyond. "Come and open up." He examined McAllister with a degree of interest. "Quite a *swell* guy!" he commented. "Them dress clothes must have been real pretty, onct."

McAllister stood with soaked and rumpled hair, hatless and collarless, his coat torn and splashed, and his shirt bosom bloody and covered with mud. He wanted to cry, for the first time in thirty-five years.

Suddenly the sergeant jumped to his feet and scrutinized the prisoner's face.

"Well, of all the luck!" he exclaimed. "Do you know who you've caught? It's '*Fatty Welch*'!"

IV

How he had managed to live through the night that followed, McAllister could never afterward understand. It was hardly light when he was awakened by the keeper rattling the door of his cell.

"Get up and take your grub," ordered that official. McAllister vaguely rubbed his eyes. The keeper shut and locked the door, leaving behind him on the cot a tin mug of scalding hot coffee and a half loaf of sour bread.

McAllister arose and felt his clothes. They were entirely dry, but had shrunk perceptibly. He was surprised to find that save for the dizziness in his head he felt not unlike himself. Moreover, he was most abominably hungry. He knelt down and smelt of the contents of the tin cup. It did not smell like coffee at all. It looked like a combination of hot water, tea, and molasses. He waited until it had cooled and drank it. The bread was not so bad. McAllister ate it all.

There was a good deal of noise in the cells now, and outside he could hear many feet coming and going. Occasionally a draught of cold air would flow in and an officer would tramp down the corridor and remove one of the occupants of the row. His watch showed that it was already eight o'clock. He fumbled in his waistcoat pocket and found a very warped and wrinkled cigar. His match box supplied the necessary light, and "Chubby" McAllister, seated upon the prison bed, smoked his after-breakfast Havana with appreciation.

"No smoking in the cells!" came the rough voice of the keeper. "Give us that cigar, Welch!"

McAllister started to his feet.

"Hand it over now! Quick!"

The clubman passed his cherished comforter through the bars, and the keeper, thrusting it still lighted into his own mouth, grinned at him, winked, and walked away.

"Merry Christmas, Fatty!" he remarked genially over his shoulder.

V

Half an hour later Tom and his "side-partner" came to the cell door. They were flushed with victory. Already the morning papers contained full accounts of the pursuit and startling arrest of "Fatty Welch," the well-known crook, who was wanted in Pennsylvania and half a dozen other States on various charges. Altogether, Tom was in a very genial frame of mind. Bidding his prisoner good-morning, he led him up a flight of iron stairs and through a door into the court room. But here McAllister shrank back. It was his first sight of that great cosmopolitan institution the "Police Court." Before him lay the scene of which he had so often read in the newspapers. The big room with its Gothic windows was filled to overflowing with every variety of the human species, who not only taxed the seating capacity of the benches to the utmost, but near the doors were packed into a solid, impenetrable mass. Upon a platform behind a desk a square-jawed man with chin whiskers disposed rapidly of the file of prisoners brought before him, while by his side the clerk was busily filling in their "pedigrees."

A long line of officers, each with one or more prisoners, stood upon the judge's left, and as fast as the business of one was concluded the next pushed forward. McAllister perceived that at best only a few moments could elapse before he was brought to face the charge against him, and that he must make up his mind quickly what course of action to pursue. As he stepped down from the doorway to take his place, there was a perceptible flutter among the spectators. Several hungry-looking men with note-books opened them and poised their pencils expectantly.

"I must get time," thought McAllister. "I must get time!"

One after another the victims of the varied delights of too much Christmas jubilation were disposed of. "Fatty" Welch was the only real "gun" that had been taken. He had the arena practically to himself. Now only one case intervened. He braced himself and tried to steady his nerves.

"Next! What's this?"

McAllister was thrust down below the bridge facing the bench, and Tom began to describe the circumstances of the arrest.

"'Fatty Welch'?" interrupted the Magistrate. "Oh, yes! I read

about it in the morning papers. Chased off in a cab, didn't he? You
shot the horse and his partner got away? Wanted in Pennsylvania and
Illinois, you say? That's enough." Then looking down at McAllister,
who stood before him in bespattered dress suit and fragmentary linen,
he inquired, "Have you counsel?"

McAllister made no answer. If he proclaimed who he was and
demanded an immediate hearing, the harpies of the press would fill
the papers with full accounts of his episode. His incognito must be
preserved at any cost. Whatever action he might decide to take, this
was not the time and place; a better opportunity would undoubtedly
present itself later in the day.

"You are charged with the crime of burglary," continued the judge,
"and it is further alleged that you are a fugitive from justice in two
other States. What have you to say for yourself?"

McAllister sought the judge's eye in vain.

"I have nothing to say," he replied faintly. There was a renewed
scratching of pens.

The judge conferred with the clerk for a moment.

"Any question of the prisoner's identity?" he asked.

"Oh, no," replied Tom conclusively. "The fact is, yer onner, we
took him by accident, as you may say. We laid a plant for a feller
doin' second-story work on the Avenoo, and when we nabbed him,
who should it be but Welch! Ye see, they wired on his description
from Philadelphia a couple of weeks ago, but we couldn't find hide or
hair of him in the city, and had about give up lookin'. Then quite
unexpected we scoops him in. Here's his identity," handing the judge
a soiled telegraph blank. "It's him, all right," he added with a grin.
"They didn't have no picture of him."

The Magistrate glanced at the form and at McAllister.

"Seems to fit," he commented. "Have you looked for the scar?"

Tom flushed.

"Well, no, yer onner, we didn't have no time last night, and of
course—"

"Turn around, Welch, and let's see your back," directed the Magistrate.

The clubman turned around and displayed his collarless neck.

"There it is!" exclaimed Tom.

McAllister mechanically put his hand to his neck and turned faint.
He had had a boil two years before, which had been lanced, and the
scar was still there. He experienced a genuine thrill of horror.

"Remanded to the 'Tombs' till Monday, pending examination," ordered the judge curtly. "Next!"

In the patrol wagon McAllister had ample time for reflection. A motley collection of tramps, "disorderlies," and petty law-breakers filled the seats and crowded the aisle. They all talked, joked, and swore. Thus the "Black Maria," with its cargo of criminals swinging from side to side and clutching at one another for support with harsh outbursts of profanity, rattled down the deserted streets toward New York's Bastille. Staggering for a foothold between four women of the town, McAllister was forced to breathe the fumes of alcohol, the odor of musk, and the aroma of foul linen. He no longer felt innocent. The sense of guilt was upon him. He seemed part and parcel of this load of miserable humanity.

The wagon clattered over the cobblestones of Elm Street, and whirling round, backed up to the door of the Tombs. The low, massive Egyptian structure, surrounded by a high stone wall, seemed like a gigantic mortuary vault waiting to receive the "civilly dead." Warden and keepers were ready for the prisoners, who were now unceremoniously bundled out and hustled inside. McAllister stood with the others in a small ante-room leading directly into the lowest tier. He could hear the ceaseless shuffling of feet and the subdued murmur of voices, rising and falling, but continuous, like the twittering of a multitude of birds, while through the bars came the fetid prison smell, with a new and disagreeable element—the odor of prison food.

"Mum, eh?" remarked the deputy to McAllister, as he scribbled the words "Prisoner refuses to answer," and blotted them.

"We're rather crowded just now," he added apologetically. "I guess I'll send you to 'Murderer's Row.' Holloa, there!" he called to someone above, "one for the first tier!"

A keeper seized him by the arm, opened a door in the steel grating, and pushed him through.

"Go 'long up!" he ordered. McAllister started wearily up the stairs. At the top of the flight he came to another door, behind which stood another keeper. In the background marched in ceaseless procession an irregular file of men. In the gloom they looked like ghosts. Aimlessly they walked on, one behind the other, most of them with eyes downcast, wordless, taking that exercise of the body which the law prescribed.

McAllister entered The Den of Beasts.

"All right, Jimmy!" yelled the keeper to the deputy warden below. Then, turning to McAllister, "I'm goin' to put you in with Davidson. He's quiet and won't bother you if you let him alone. Better give him whichever berth he feels like. Them 'double-decker' cots is just as good on top as they is below."

McAllister followed the keeper down the narrow gangway that ran around the prison. In the stone corridor below a great iron stove glowed red hot, and its fumes rose and mingled with the tainted air that floated out from every cell. Above him rose tier on tier, illuminated only by the gray light which filtered through a grimy window at one end of the prison. The arrangement of cells, the "bridges" that joined the tiers, and the murky atmosphere heightened the resemblance to the "'tween decks" of an enormous slaver, bearing them all away to some distant port of servitude.

"Get up there, Jake. Here's a bunkie for you."

McAllister bent his head and entered. He was standing beside a two-story cot bed, in a compartment about six by eight feet square. A faint light came from a narrow horizontal slit in the rear wall. A faucet with tin basin completed the contents of the room. On the top bunk lay a man's soiled coat and waistcoat, the feet of the owner being discernible below.

The keeper locked the door and departed while the occupant of the berth, rolling lazily over, peered up at the new-comer; then he sprang from the cot.

"*Mr. McAllister!*" he whispered hoarsely.

It was Wilkins—the old Wilkins, in spite of a new light-brown beard.

For a few moments neither spoke.

"Sorry to see you 'ere, sir," said Wilkins at length, in his old respectful tones. "Won't you sit down, sir?" McAllister seated himself upon the bed automatically.

"You here, Wilkins?" he managed to say.

Wilkins laughed rather bitterly.

"I've been 'in stir' most of the time since I left you, sir; an' two weeks ago I pleaded guilty to larceny and was sentenced to one year more. But I'm glad to see you lookin' so well, if you'll pardon me, sir."

"I'm sorry for you, Wilkins," he managed to reply. "I hope my severity in that matter of the pin did not bring you to this!"

Wilkins hesitated for a moment.

"It ain't your fault, sir. I was born crooked, I fancy, sir. It's all right.

You've got troubles of your own. Only—you'll excuse me, sir—I never suspected anything when I was in your service."

McAllister did not grasp the meaning of this remark; he only felt relief that Wilkins apparently bore him no ill will. Very few of his friends would have followed up a theft of that sort. They expected their "men" to steal their pins.

"Mebbe I might 'elp you. Wot's the charge, sir?"

With Wilkins listening sympathetically, McAllister poured out his whole story, omitting nothing. As he finished he leaned toward his former servant, searching his face eagerly.

"Now, what shall I do? What shall I do, Wilkins?"

The latter coughed deprecatingly.

"You'll pardon me, but that'll *never* go, sir! You'll have to get somethin' better than that, sir. The jury will never believe it."

McAllister sprang to his feet, in so doing knocking his head against the iron support of the upper cot.

"How dare you, Wilkins! What do you mean?"

"There, there, sir!" exclaimed the other. "Don't take on so. Of course I didn't mean you wouldn't tell the truth, sir. But don't you see, sir, it isn't *I* as am goin' to listen to it? Shall I fetch you some water to wash your face, sir?" He turned on the faucet.

The clubman, yielding to the force of ancient habit, allowed Wilkins to let it run for him, and having washed his face and combed his hair, felt somewhat refreshed.

"That feels good," he remarked, rubbing his hands together.

It was obvious that so long as he remained in prison he would be either "Fatty Welch" or someone else equally depraved; and since he could not make anyone understand, his best plan was to accept for the time, with equanimity, the personality that fate had thrust upon him.

"Well, Wilkins, my boy, we're in a tight place. But we'll do what we can to assist each other. If I get out first I'll help *you*, and vice versa. Now, what's the first thing to be done? You see, I've never been here before."

"That's the talk, sir," answered Wilkins. "Now, who's your lawyer?"

"Haven't any, yet."

"All depends on the lawyer," returned the valet judicially. "Now there's Ebstein and O'Sullivan and Kemp, all sharp fellows, but they're always after you for money, and then they're so clever that the jury is apt to distrust 'em. The best thing, I find, is to get the most respectable old solicitor you can—kind of genteel, 'family' variety, with the goodness just stickin' out all over 'im. 'E creates a hatmosphere of hinnocence, and that's wot you need. One as has white 'air and can talk about 'this boy 'ere' and put 'is 'and on yer shoulder and weep. That's the go, sir."

"I see," said McAllister.

Under the guidance of his valet our hero secured writing materials and indicted a pitiful appeal to his family lawyer.

A gong rang; the squad of prisoners who had been exercising went back to their cells, and the keeper came and unlocked the door.

McAllister stepped out and fell into line. His tight clothes proved very uncomfortable as he strode round the tiers, and the absence of a collar—yes, that was really the most unpleasant feature. His neck was not much to boast of, therefore he always wore his shirts low and his collars high. Now, as he stumbled along with the others, he was the object of considerable attention from his fellows.

At the end of an hour a gong sounded. In a moment the tiers were empty; fifty doors clanged to.

"Well, Wilkins?"

"Being as this is Sunday, sir, we 'ave a few hours of service. Church of England first—then City Mission. We're not allowed to talk, but if you don't mind the 'owlin' you can snatch a wink o' sleep. Christmas dinner at twelve. Old Burridge, the trusty, was a-tellin' me as 'ow it's hexcellent, sir!"

McAllister looked at his watch in despair. It was only a quarter past ten. He had not been to church for fifteen years, but evidently he was in for it now. Following his former valet's example he took off his shoes and stretched himself upon the cot.

On and on in never-varying tones dragged the service. The preacher held the key to the situation. His congregation could not escape; he had a full house, and he was bent on making the most of it.

The hands of McAllister's watch crept slowly round to five minutes of eleven.

When at last the preacher stopped, carefully folded his manuscript, and pronounced the benediction, a prolonged sigh of relief eddied through the Tombs. Men were waking on all sides; cots creaked; there was a general and contagious yawn.

Again the gong rang, and with it the smell of food floated up along the tiers. McAllister realized that he was hungry—not mildly as he was at the club, but ravenous as he had never been before. Presently the longed-for food came, borne by a "trusty" in new white uniform. Wilkins, who had been making a meagre toilet at the faucet, took in the dinner through the door—two tin plates piled high with turkey and chicken, flanked by heaps of potato and carrots, and one whole apple pie!

"Ha!" thought McAllister, "I was not so far wrong about this part of it!" The turkey and chicken were perhaps not of the variety known as "spring," but if they were somewhat dry, neither master nor man noticed it as they feasted, sitting side by side upon the cot.

"Carrots!" philosophized McAllister, looking regretfully at his empty tin plate. "Now, I thought only *horses* eat carrots; and really, they're not bad at all. I should like some more. Er—Wilkins! Can we get some more carrots?"

Wilkins shook his head mournfully.

"Message for 134! Message for 134!"

A letter was thrust through the bars.

McAllister tore it open with feverish haste and recognized the crabbed hand of old Mr. Potter.

> *2 East Seventy-first Street*
>
> F. Welch, Esq.,
> Sir:
>
> *The remarkable letter just delivered to me, signed by a name which you request me not to use in my reply, has received my careful consideration. I telephoned to Mr. McA——'s rooms and was informed by his valet that that gentleman had gone to the country to visit friends over Christmas. I have therefore directed the messenger to collect from yourself his fee for delivering this answer.*
>
> *Yours, etc.,*
> *Ebenezer Potter*

"That fool Morton!" groaned McAllister. "How the devil could he have thought I had gone away?" Then he remembered that he had directed the valet to pack his bags and send them to the station, in anticipation of the Winthrops' invitation.

He was at his wits' end.

"How do you get bail, Wilkins?"

"You 'ave to find someone as owns real estate in the city, sir, to go on your bond. 'Ow much is it?"

"Five thousand dollars," replied McAllister.

"'Oly Moses!" ejaculated the valet. He regarded his former master with renewed interest.

But the dinner had wrought a change in that hitherto subdued individual. With a valet and running water he was beginning to "feel his oats" a little. He checked off mentally the names of his acquaintances. There was not one left in town.

He repressed a yawn and looked at his watch. One o'clock. Just then the gong rang again.

"What in thunder is this, now?"

"*Afternoon* service, sir. City Mission from one to two-thirty."

"Ye gods!" ejaculated McAllister.

A band of young girls came and stood with their hymn books along the opposite tier, while a Presbyterian clergyman took the place on the bridge recently vacated by his Episcopal brother. Prayers alternated with hymns until the sermon, which lasted sixty-five minutes.

McAllister, almost desperate, fretted and fumed until half-past two, when the choir and missionary finally departed.

"Only a 'arf 'our, sir, an' we can get some more exercise," said Wilkins encouragingly.

But McAllister did not want exercise. He swung to his feet, and peering disconsolately through the bars was suddenly confronted by a slender young woman holding an armful of flowers. Before he could efface himself she smiled sweetly at him.

"My poor man," she began confidently, "how sorry I am for you this beautiful Christmas *Day!* Please take some of these; they will brighten up your cell wonderfully; and they are so fragrant." She pushed a dozen carnations and asters through the bars.

McAllister, utterly dumbfounded, took them.

"What is your name?" continued the maiden.

"*Welch!*" blurted out our bewildered friend.

There was a stifled snort from the bunk behind.

"Good-by, Welch. I know you are not *really* bad. Won't you shake hands with me?"

She thrust her hand through the bars and McAllister gave it a perfunctory shake. "Good-by," she murmured, and passed on.

"Lawd!" exploded Wilkins, rolling from side to side upon his cot. "Oh, Lawd! Oh, Lawd! Oh—" and he held his sides while McAllister stuck the carnations into the wash basin.

The gong again, and once more that endless tramp along the hot tiers. The prison grew darker. Gas jets were lighted here and there, and the air became more and more oppressive. With five o'clock came supper; then the long, weary night.

Next morning the valet seemed nervous and excited, eating little breakfast and smiling from time to time vaguely to himself. Having fumbled in his pocket he at last pulled out a dirty pawn ticket, which he held toward his master.

"'Ere, sir," he said, with averted head. "It's for the pin. I'm sorry I took it."

McAllister's eyes were a little blurred as he mechanically received the card-board.

"Shake hands, Wilkins," was all he said.

A keeper came walking along the tier rattling the doors and telling those who were wanted in court to get ready.

"Good-by," said McAllister. "I'm sorry you felt obliged to plead guilty. I might have helped you if I'd only known. Why didn't you stand your trial?"

"I 'ad my reasons," replied the valet. "I wanted to get my case disposed of as quick as possible. You see, I'd been livin' in Philadelphia and 'ad just come to New York when I was arrested. I didn't want 'em to find out who I was or where I come from, so I just gives the name of Davidson, and takes my dose."

"Well," said McAllister, "you're taking your *own* dose; I'm taking somebody else's. That hardly seems a fair deal, now does it, Wilkins? But of course *you* don't know but that I *am* Welch."

"Oh, yes I do, sir," returned the valet. "You won't never be punished for what *he* done."

"*How* do you know?" exclaimed McAllister, visions of a speedy release crowding into his mind. "And *if* you knew, why didn't you say so *before?* Why, you might have got me out. *How* do you know?" he repeated.

Wilkins looked around cautiously. The keeper was at the other end of the tier. Then he came close to McAllister and whispered, "*Because I'm 'Fatty' Welch myself!*"

VI

Downstairs, across the sun-lit prison yard, past the spot where the hangings had taken place in the old days, up an inclosed staircase, a half turn, and the clubman was marched across the "Bridge of Sighs." Most of the prisoners with him seemed in good spirits, but McAllister, who was oppressed with the foreboding of imminent peril, felt that he could no longer take any chances. His fatal resemblance to Fatty Welch, alias Wilkins, his former valet, the circumstances of his arrest, the scar on his neck, would seem to make conviction certain unless he followed one of two alternatives—either that of disclosing Welch's identity or his own. He dismissed the former instantly. Now that he knew something of the real sufferings of men, his own life seemed contemptible. What mattered the laughter of his friends or sarcastic paragraphs in the society columns of the papers? What did the fellows at the club know of the game of life and death going on around them? of the misery and vice to which they contributed? of the hopelessness of those wretched souls who had been crushed down by fate into the gutters of life? Determined to declare himself, he entered the court room and tramped with the others to the rail.

There, to his amazement, sat old Mr. Potter beside the judge. Tom and his partner stood at one side.

"Welch, step up here."

Mr. Potter nodded very slightly, and McAllister, taking the hint, stepped forward.

"Is this your prisoner, officer?"

"Shure, that's him, right enough," answered Tom.

"Discharged," said the Magistrate.

Mr. Potter shook hands with his honor, who smiled good humoredly and winked at McAllister.

"Now, Welch, try and behave yourself. I'll let you off this time, but if it happens again I won't answer for the consequences. *Go home.*"

Mr. Potter whispered something to the baffled officers, who touched their hats and grinned sheepishly, and then, seizing McAllister's arm, led our astonished friend out of the court room.

As they whirled uptown in the closed automobile which had been waiting for them around the corner, Mr. Potter explained. After sending the letter he had felt far from satisfied, and had bethought him of calling up Mrs. Winthrop on the telephone. Her polite surprise at the lawyer's inquiries had fully convinced him of his error, and after evading her questions with his usual caution, he had taken immediate steps for his client's release—steps which, by reason of the lateness of the hour, he could not communicate to the unhappy McAllister.

"What has become of the fugitive Welch," he ended, "remains a mystery. The police cannot imagine where he has hidden himself."

"I wonder," said McAllister.

It was just seven o'clock when McAllister, arrayed, as usual, in immaculate evening dress, sauntered into the club. Most of the men were back from their Christmas outing; half a dozen of them were engaged in ordering dinner.

"Hello, Chubby," shouted someone. "Come and have a drink. Had a pleasant Christmas? You were at the Winthrops', weren't you?"

"No," answered McAllister; "had to stay right in New York. Couldn't get away. Yes, I'll take a dry Martini and a cherry—er, waiter, make that two Martinis. I want you all to have dinner with me. How would terrapin and canvasback do? Fill it out to suit yourselves, while I just take a look at the *Post*."

He picked up a paper, glanced at the headlines, threw it down with a sigh of relief, and lighted a cigarette. At the same moment two policemen in civilian dress were leaving McAllister's apartments, each having received at the hands of the impassive Morton a bundle containing a silver-mounted revolver and a large bottle full of an unknown brown liquid.

McAllister's dinner was a great success. The boys all said afterward that they had never seen Chubby in such good form. Only one incident marred the serenity of the occasion, and that was a mere trifle. Charlie Bush had been staying over Christmas with an ex-Chairman of the Prison Reform Association, and being in a communicative mood insisted on talking about it.

"Only fancy," he remarked, as he took a gulp of champagne, "he says the prisons in the city are in an abominable condition—that they're a disgrace to a civilized community."

Tomlinson paused in lifting his glass. He remembered his host's opinion, expressed on a previous occasion, and desired to show his appreciation of an excellent meal.

"That's all rot!" he interrupted a little thickly. "'S all politics. The Tombs is a lot better than most second-class hotels on the Continent. Our prisons are all right I tell you!" His eye swept the circle militantly.

"Look here Tomlinson," remarked McAllister sternly, "don't be so sure. What do *you* know about it?"

SOLOMON CROW'S CHRISTMAS POCKETS

by Ruth McEnery Stuart

from *Solomon Crow's Christmas Pockets and Other Tales*

His mother named him Solomon because, when he was a baby, he looked so wise; and then she called him Crow because he was so black. True, she got angry when the boys caught it up, but then it was too late. They knew more about crows than they did about Solomon, and the name suited.

His twin-brother, who died when he was a day old, his mother had called Grundy—just because, as she said, "Solomon an' Grundy b'longs together in de books."

When the wee black boy began to talk, he knew himself equally as Solomon or Crow, and so, when asked his name, he would answer, "Sol'mon Crow," and Solomon Crow he thenceforth became.

Crow was ten years old now, and he was so very black and polished and thin, and had so peaked and bright a face, that no one who had any sense of humor could hear him called Crow without smiling.

Crow's mother, Tempest, had been a worker in her better days, but she had grown fatter and fatter until now she was so lazy and broad that her chief pleasure seemed to be sitting in her front door and gossiping with her neighbors over the fence, or in abusing or praising little Solomon, according to her mood.

Tempest had never been very honest. When, in the old days, she had hired out as cook and carried "her dinner" home at night, the basket on her arm had usually held enough for herself and Crow and a pig and the chickens—with some to give away. She had not meant Crow to understand, but the little fellow was wide awake, and his mother was his pattern.

Crow's mother loved him very much—she thought. She would knock down anyone who even blamed him for anything. Indeed, when things went well, she would sometimes go sound asleep in the door with her fat arm around him—very much as the mother-cat beside her lay half dozing while she licked her baby kitten.

But if Crow was awkward or forgot anything—or didn't bring home money enough—her abuse was worse than any mother-cat's claws.

One of her worst taunts on such occasions was about like this: "Well, you is a low-down nigger, I must say. Nobody, to look at you, would b'lieve you was twin to a angel!"

Or, "How you reckon yo' angel-twin feels ef he's a-lookin' at you now?"

Crow had great reverence for his little lost mate. Indeed, he feared the displeasure of this other self, who, he believed, watched him from the skies, quite as much as the anger of God. Sad to say, the good Lord, whom most children love as a kind, heavenly Father, was to poor little Solomon Crow only a terrible, terrible punisher of wrong, and the little boy trembled at His very name. He seemed to hear God's anger in the thunder or the wind; but in the blue sky, the faithful stars, the opening flowers and singing birds—in all loving-kindness and friendship—he never saw a heavenly Father's love.

He knew that some things were right and others wrong. He knew that it was right to go out and earn dimes to buy the things needed in the cabin, but he equally knew it was wrong to get this money dishonestly. Crow was a very shrewd little boy, and he made money honestly in a number of ways that only a wide-awake boy would think about.

When fig season came, in hot summer-time, he happened to notice that beautiful ripe figs were drying up on the tip-tops of some great trees in a neighboring yard, where a stout old gentleman and his old wife lived alone, and he began to reflect.

"If I could des git a-holt o' some o' dem fine sugar figs dat's a-swivelin' up every day on top o' dem trees, I'd meck a heap o' money peddlin' 'em on de street." And even while he thought this thought he licked his lips. There were, no doubt, other attractions about the figs for a very small boy with a very sweet tooth.

On the next morning after this, Crow rang the front gate-bell of the yard where the figs were growing.

"Want a boy to pick figs on sheers?" That was all he said to the fat old gentleman who had stepped around the house in answer to his ring.

Crow's offer was timely.

Old Mr. Cary was red in the face and panting even yet from reaching up into the mouldy, damp lower limbs of his fig-trees, trying to gather a dishful for breakfast.

"Come in," he said, mopping his forehead as he spoke. "Pick on shares, will you?"

"Yassir."

"Even?"

"Yassir."

"Promise never to pick any but the very ripe figs?"

"Yassir."

"Honest boy?"

"Yassir."

"Turn in, then; but wait a minute."

He stepped aside into the house, returning presently with two baskets.

"Here," he said, presenting them both. "These are pretty nearly of a size. Go ahead, now, and let's see what you can do."

Needless to say, Crow proved a great success as a fig-picker. The very sugary figs that old Mr. Cary had panted for and reached for in vain lay bursting with sweetness on top of both baskets.

The old gentleman and his wife were delighted, and the boy was quickly engaged to come every morning.

And this was how Crow went into the fig business.

Crow was a likable boy—"so bright and handy and nimble"—and the old people soon became fond of him.

They noticed that he always handed in the larger of the two

baskets, keeping the smaller for himself. This seemed not only honest, but generous.

And generosity is a winning virtue in the very needy—as winning as it is common. The very poor are often great of heart.

But this is not a safe fact upon which to found axioms.

All God's poor are not educated up to the point of even small, fine honesties, and the so-called "generous" are not always "just" or honest.

And—

Poor little Solomon Crow! It is a pity to have to write it, but his weak point was exactly that he was not quite honest. He wanted to be, just because his angel-twin might be watching him, and he was afraid of thunder. But Crow was so anxious to be "smart" that he had long ago begun doing "tricky" things. Even the men working the roads had discovered this. In eating Crow's "fresh-boiled crawfish" or "shrimps," they would often come across one of the left-overs of yesterday's supply, mixed in with the others; and a yesterday's shrimp is full of stomach-ache and indigestion. So that business suffered.

In the fig business the ripe ones sold well; but when one of Crow's customers offered to buy all he would bring of green ones for preserving, Crow began filling his basket with them and distributing a top layer of ripe ones carefully over them. His lawful share of the very ripe he also carried away—in his little bread-basket.

This was all very dishonest, and Crow knew it. Still he did it many times.

And then—and this shows how one sin leads to another—and then, one day—oh, Solomon Crow, I'm ashamed to tell it on you!—one day he noticed that there were fresh eggs in the hen-house nests, quite near the fig-trees. Now, if there was anything Crow liked, it was a fried egg—two fried eggs. He always said he wanted two on his plate at once, looking at him like a pair of round eyes, "an' when dey reco'nizes me," he would say, "den I eats 'em up."

Why not slip a few of these tempting eggs into the bottom of the basket and cover them up with ripe figs?"

And so—

One day, he did it.

He had stopped at the dining-room door that day and was handing in the larger basket, as usual, when old Mr. Cary, who stood there, said, smiling, "No, give us the smaller basket to-day, my boy. It's our turn to be generous."

He extended his hand as he spoke.

Crow tried to answer, but he could not. His mouth felt as dry and stiff and hard as a chip, and he suddenly began to open it wide and shut it slowly, like a chicken with the gapes.

Mr. Cary kept his hand out waiting, but still Crow stood as if paralyzed, gaping and swallowing.

Finally, he began to blink. And then he stammered, "I ain't p-p-p-ertic'lar b-b-bout de big basket. D-d-d-de best figs is in y'all's pickin'—in dis, de big basket."

Crow's appearance was conviction itself. Without more ado, Mr. Cary grasped his arm firmly and fairly lifted him into the room.

"Now, set those baskets down." He spoke sharply.

The boy obeyed.

"Here! Empty the larger one on this tray. That's it. All fine, ripe figs. You've picked well for us. Now turn the other one out."

At this poor Crow had a sudden relapse of the dry gapes. His arm fell limp and he looked as if he might tumble over.

"Turn 'em out!" The old gentleman shrieked in so thunderous a tone that Crow jumped off his feet, and, seizing the other basket with his little shaking paws, he emptied it upon the heap of figs.

Old Mrs. Cary had come in just in time to see the eggs roll out of the basket, and for a moment she and her husband looked at each other. And then they turned to the boy.

When she spoke her voice was so gentle that Crow, not understanding, looked quickly into her face:

"Let me take him into the library, William. Come, my boy."

Her tone was so soft, so sorrowful and sympathetic, that Crow felt as he followed her as if, in the hour of his deepest disgrace, he had found a friend; and when presently he stood in a great square room before a high arm-chair, in which a white-haired old lady sat looking at him over her gold-rimmed spectacles and talking to him as he had never been spoken to in all his life before, he felt as if he were in a great court before a judge who didn't understand half how very bad little boys were.

She asked him a good many questions—some very searching ones, too—all of which Crow answered as best he could, with his very short breath.

His first feeling had been of pure fright. But when he found he was not to be abused, not beaten or sent to jail, he began to wonder.

Little Solomon Crow, ten years old, in a Christian land, was hearing for the first time in his life that God loved him—loved him even now in his sin and disgrace, and wanted him to be good.

He listened with wandering eyes at first, half expecting the old gentleman, Mr. Cary, to appear suddenly at the door with a whip or a policeman with a club. But after a while he kept his eyes steadily upon the lady's face.

"Has no one ever told you, Solomon"—she had always called him Solomon, declaring that Crow was not a fit name for a boy who looked as he did—it was altogether "too personal"—"has no one ever told you, Solomon," she said, "that God loves all His little children, and that you are one of these children?"

"No, ma'am," he answered, with difficulty. And then, as if catching at something that might give him a little standing, he added, quickly —so quickly that he stammered again: "B-b-b-but I knowed I was twin to a angel. I know dat. An' I knows ef my angel-twin seen me steal dem aigs he'll be mighty ap' to tell Gord to strike me down daid."

Of course he had to explain then about the "angel-twin," and the old lady talked to him for a long time. And then together they knelt down. When at last they came out of the library she held the boy's hand and led him to her husband.

"Are you willing to try him again, William?" she asked. "He has promised to do better."

Old Mr. Cary cleared his throat and laid down his paper.

"Don't deserve it," he began; "dirty little thief." And then he turned to the boy: "What have you got on, sir?"

His voice was really quite terrible.

"N-n-n-nothin'; only but des my b-b-b-briches an' jacket, an'—an'— an' skin," Crow replied, between gasps.

"How many pockets?"

"Two," said Crow.

"Turn 'em out!"

Crow drew out his little rust-stained pockets, dropping a few old nails and bits of twine upon the floor as he did so.

"Um—h'm! Well, now, I'll tell you. *You're a dirty little thief*, as I said before. And I'm going to treat you as one. If you wear those pockets hanging out, or rip 'em out, and come in here before you leave every day dressed just as you are—pants and jacket and skin—and empty out your basket for us before you go, until I'm satisfied you'll do better, you can come."

The old lady looked at her husband as if she thought him pretty hard on a very small boy. But she said nothing.

Crow glanced appealingly at her before answering. And then he said, seizing his pocket:

"Is you got air pair o' scissors, lady?"

Mrs. Cary wished her husband would relent even while she brought the scissors, but he only cried, "Out with 'em!"

"Suppose you cut them out yourself, Solomon," she interposed, kindly, handing him the scissors. "You'll have all this work to do yourself. We can't make you good."

When, after several awkward efforts, Crow finally put the coarse little pockets in her hands, there were tears in her eyes, and she tried to hide them as she leaned over and gathered up his treasures—three nails, a string, a broken top, and a half-eaten chunk of cold cornbread. As she handed them to him she said, "And I'll lay the pockets away for you, Solomon, and when we see that you are an honest boy I'll sew them back for you myself."

As she spoke she rose, divided the figs evenly between the two baskets, and handed one to Crow.

If there ever was a serious little black boy on God's beautiful earth it was little Solomon Crow as he balanced his basket of figs on his head that day and went slowly down the garden walk and out the great front gate.

The next few weeks were not without trial to the boy. Old Mr. Cary continued very stern, even following him daily to the *banquette*, as if he dare not trust him to go out alone. And when he closed the iron gate after him he would say in a tone that was awfully solemn, "Good-mornin', sir!"

That was all.

Little Crow dreaded that walk to the gate more than all the rest of the ordeal. And yet, in a way, it gave him courage. He was at least worth while, and with time and patience he would win back the lost faith of the friends who were kind to him even while they could not trust him. They were, indeed, kind and generous in many ways, both to him and his unworthy mother.

Fig-time was soon nearly over, and, of course, Crow expected a dismissal; but it was Mr. Cary himself who set these fears at rest by proposing to him to come daily to blacken his boots and to keep the garden-walk in order for regular wages.

"But," he warned him, in closing, "don't you show your face here with a pocket on you. If your heavy pants have any in 'em, rip 'em out." And then he added, severely, "You've been a very bad boy."

"Yassir," answered Crow, "I know I is. I been a heap wusser boy'n you knowed I was, too."

"What's that you say, sir?"

Crow repeated it. And then he added, for full confession, "I picked green figs heap o' days, and kivered 'em up wid ripe ones, an' sol' 'em to a white 'oman fur perserves." There was something desperate in the way he blurted it all out.

"The dickens you did! And what are you telling me for?" He eyed the boy keenly as he put the question.

At this Crow fairly wailed aloud, " 'Caze I ain't gwine do it no mo'." And throwing his arms against the door-frame he buried his face in them, and he sobbed as if his little heart would break.

For a moment old Mr. Cary seemed to have lost his voice, and then he said, in a voice quite new to Crow, "I don't believe you will, sir—I don't believe you will." And in a minute he said, still speaking gently, "Come here, boy."

Still weeping aloud, Crow obeyed.

"Tut, tut! No crying!" he began. "Be a man—be a man. And if you stick to it, before Christmas comes, we'll see about those pockets, and you can walk into the new year with your head up. But look sharp! Good-bye, now!"

For the first time since the boy's fall Mr. Cary did not follow him to the gate. Maybe this was the beginning of trust. Slight a thing as it was, the boy took comfort in it.

At last it was Christmas eve. Crow was on the back "gallery" putting a final polish on a pair of boots. He was nearly done, and his heart was beginning to sink, when the old lady came and stood near him. There was a very hopeful twinkle in her eye as she said, presently, "I wonder what our little shoeblack, who has been trying so hard to be good, would like to have for his Christmas gift?"

But Crow only blinked while he polished the faster.

"Tell me, Solomon," she insisted. "If you had one wish to-day, what would it be?"

The boy wriggled nervously. And then he said, "You knows, lady. Needle—an' thrade—an'—an'—you knows, lady. Pockets."

"Well, pockets it shall be. Come into my room when you get through."

Old Mrs. Cary sat beside the fire reading as he went in. Seeing him, she nodded, smiling, towards the bed, upon which Crow saw a brand-new suit of clothes—coat, vest, and breeches—all spread out in a row.

"There, my boy," she said; "there are your pockets."

Crow had never in all his life owned a full new suit of clothes. All his "new" things had been second-hand, and for a moment he could not quite believe his eyes; but he went quickly to the bed and began passing his hands over the clothes. Then he ventured to take up the vest—and to turn it over. And now he began to find pockets.

"Three pockets in de ves'—two in de pants—an'—an' fo', no five, no six—six pockets in de coat!"

He giggled nervously as he thrust his little black fingers into one and then another. And then, suddenly overcome with a sense of the situation, he turned to Mrs. Cary, and, in a voice that trembled a little, said, "Is you sho' you ain't 'feerd to trus' me wid all deze pockets, lady?"

It doesn't take a small boy long to slip into a new suit of clothes. And when a ragged urchin disappeared behind the head of the great old "four-poster" to-day, it seemed scarcely a minute before a trig, "tailor-made boy" strutted out from the opposite side, hands deep in pockets—breathing hard.

As Solomon Crow strode up and down the room, radiant with joy, he seemed for the moment quite unconscious of anyone's presence. But presently he stopped, looked involuntarily upward a minute, as if he felt himself observed from above. Then, turning to the old people, who stood together before the mantel, delightedly watching him, he said, "Bet you my angel-twin ain't ashamed, ef he's a-lookin' down on me to-day."

A KIDNAPPED SANTA CLAUS

by L. Frank Baum

from *The Delineator*, Vol. LXIV

Santa Claus lives in the Laughing Valley, where stands the big rambling castle in which his toys are manufactured. His workmen, selected from the ryls, knooks, pixies and fairies, live with him, and every one is as busy as can be from one year's end to another.

It is called the Laughing Valley because everything there is happy and gay. The brook chuckles to itself as it leaps rollicking between its green banks; the wind whistles merrily in the trees; the sunbeams dance lightly over the soft grass, and the violets and wildflowers look smilingly up from their green nests. To laugh one needs to be happy; to be happy one needs to be content. And throughout the Laughing Valley of Santa Claus contentment reigns supreme.

On one side is the mighty Forest of Burzee. At the other side stands the huge mountain that contains the Caves of the Daemons. And between them the Valley lies smiling and peaceful.

One would think that our good old Santa Claus, who devotes his days to making children happy, would have no enemies on all the earth; and, as a matter of fact, for a long period of time he encountered nothing but love wherever he might go.

But the Daemons who live in the mountain caves grew to hate Santa Claus very much, and all for the simple reason that he made children happy.

The Caves of the Daemons are five in number. A broad pathway leads up to the first cave, which is a finely arched cavern at the foot of the mountain, the entrance being beautifully carved and decorated. In it resides the Daemon of Selfishness. Back of this is another cavern inhabited by the Daemon of Envy. The cave of the Daemon of Hatred is next in order, and through this, one passes to the home of the Daemon of Malice—situated in a dark and fearful cave in the very heart of the mountain. I do not know what lies beyond this. Some say there are terrible pitfalls leading to death and destruction, and this may very well be true. However, from each one of the four caves mentioned there is a small, narrow tunnel leading to the fifth cave—a cozy little room occupied by the Daemon of Repentance. And as the rocky floors of these passages are well worn by the track of passing feet, I judge that many wanderers in the Caves of the Daemons have escaped through the tunnels to the abode of the Daemon of Repentance, who is said to be a pleasant sort of fellow who gladly opens for one a little door admitting you into fresh air and sunshine again.

Well, these Daemons of the Caves, thinking they had great cause to dislike old Santa Claus, held a meeting one day to discuss the matter.

"I'm really getting lonesome," said the Daemon of Selfishness. "For Santa Claus distributes so many pretty Christmas gifts to all the children that they become happy and generous, through his example, and keep away from my cave."

"I'm having the same trouble." rejoined the Daemon of Envy. "The little ones seem quite content with Santa Claus, and there are few, indeed, that I can coax to become envious."

"And that makes it bad for me!" declared the Daemon of Hatred. "For if no children pass through the caves of Selfishness and Envy, none can get to *my* cavern."

"Or to mine," added the Daemon of Malice.

"For my part," said the Daemon of Repentance, "it is easily seen that if children do not visit your caves they have no need to visit mine; so I am quite as neglected as you are."

"And all because of this person they call Santa Claus!" exclaimed the Daemon of Envy. "He is simply ruining our business, and something must be done at once."

To this they readily agreed; but what to do was another and more difficult matter to settle. They knew that Santa Claus worked all through the year at his castle in the Laughing Valley, preparing the gifts he was to distribute on Christmas Eve; and at first they resolved to try to tempt him into their caves, that they might lead him on to the terrible pitfalls that ended in destruction.

So the very next day, while Santa Claus was busily at work, surrounded by his little band of assistants, the Daemon of Selfishness came to him and said, "These toys are wonderfully bright and pretty. Why do you not keep them for yourself? It's a pity to give them to those noisy boys and fretful girls, who break and destroy them so quickly."

"Nonsense!" cried the old graybeard, his bright eyes twinkling merrily as he turned toward the tempting Daemon; "the boys and girls are never so noisy and fretful after receiving my presents, and if I can make them happy for one day in the year I am quite content."

So the Daemon went back to the others, who awaited him in their caves, and said, "I have failed, for Santa Claus is not at all selfish."

The following day the Daemon of Envy visited Santa Claus. Said he, "The toy-shops are full of playthings quite as pretty as these you are making. What a shame it is that they should interfere with your business! They make toys by machinery much quicker than you can make them by hand; and they sell them for money, while you get nothing at all for your work."

But Santa Claus refused to be envious of the toy-shops.

"I can supply the little ones but once a year—on Christmas Eve," he answered; "for the children are many, and I am but one. And as my work is one of love and kindness I would be ashamed to receive money for my little gifts. But throughout all the year the children must be amused in some way, and so the toy-shops are able to bring much happiness to my little friends. I like the toy-shops, and am glad to see them prosper."

In spite of this second rebuff, the Daemon of Hatred thought he would try to influence Santa Claus. So the next day he entered the busy workshop and said, "Good morning, Santa! I have bad news for you."

"Then run away, like a good fellow," answered Santa Claus. "Bad news is something that should be kept secret and never told."

"You cannot escape this, however," declared the Daemon; "for in the world are a good many who do not believe in Santa Claus, and these you are bound to hate bitterly, since they have so wronged you."

"Stuff and rubbish!" cried Santa.

"And there are others who resent your making children happy and who sneer at you and call you a foolish old rattlepate! You are quite right to hate such base slanderers, and you ought to be revenged upon them for their evil words."

"But I *don't* hate 'em!" exclaimed Santa Claus, positively. "Such people do me no real harm, but merely render themselves and their children unhappy. Poor things! I'd much rather help them any day than injure them."

Indeed, the Daemons could not tempt old Santa Claus in any way. On the contrary, he was shrewd enough to see that their object in visiting him was to make mischief and trouble. So the Daemons abandoned honeyed words and determined to use force.

It is well known that no harm can come to Santa Claus while he is in the Laughing Valley, for the fairies, and ryls, and knooks all protect him. But on Christmas Eve he drives his reindeer out into the big world, carrying a sleigh-load of toys and pretty gifts to the children; and this was the time and the occasion when his enemies had the best chance to injure him. So the Daemons laid their plans and awaited the arrival of Christmas Eve.

The moon shone big and white in the sky, and the snow lay crisp and sparkling on the ground as Santa Claus cracked his whip and sped away out of the Valley into the great world beyond. The roomy sleigh was packed full with huge sacks of toys, and as the reindeer dashed onward our jolly old Santa laughed and whistled and sang for very joy. For in all his merry life this was the one day in the year when he was happiest—the day he lovingly bestowed the treasures of his workshop upon the little children.

It would be a busy night for him, he well knew. As he whistled and shouted and cracked his whip again, he reviewed in mind all the towns and cities and farm-houses where he was expected, and figured that he had just enough presents to go around and make every child happy. The reindeer knew exactly what was expected of them, and dashed along so swiftly that their feet scarcely seemed to touch the snow-covered ground.

Suddenly a strange thing happened: a rope shot through the moonlight and a big noose that was in the end of it settled over the arms and body of Santa Claus and drew tight. Before he could resist or even cry out he was jerked from the seat of the sleigh and tumbled head foremost into a snowbank, while the reindeer rushed onward with the load of toys and carried it quickly out of sight and sound.

Such a surprising experience confused old Santa for a moment, and when he had collected his senses he found that the wicked Daemons had pulled him from the snowdrift and bound him tightly with many coils of the stout rope. And then they carried the kidnapped Santa Claus away to their mountain, where they thrust the prisoner into a secret cave and chained him to the rocky wall so that he could not escape.

"Ha, ha!" laughed the Daemons, rubbing their hands together with cruel glee. "What will the children do now? How they will cry and scold and storm when they find there are no toys in their stockings and no gifts on their Christmas trees! And what a lot of punishment they will receive from their parents, and how they will flock to our caves of Selfishness, and Envy, and Hatred, and Malice! We have done a mighty clever thing, we Daemons of the Caves!"

Now it so chanced that on this Christmas Eve the good Santa Claus had taken with him in his sleigh Nuter the Ryl, Peter the Knook, Kilter the Pixie, and a small fairy named Wisk—his four favorite assistants. These little people he had often found very useful in helping him to distribute his gifts to the children, and when their master was so suddenly dragged from the sleigh they were all snugly tucked underneath the seat, where the sharp wind could not reach them.

The tiny immortals knew nothing of the capture of Santa Claus until some time after he had disappeared. But finally they missed his cheery voice, and as their master always sang or whistled on his journeys, the silence warned them that something was wrong.

Little Wisk stuck out his head from underneath the seat and found Santa Claus gone and no one to direct the flight of the reindeer.

"Whoa!" he called out, and the deer obediently slackened speed and came to a halt.

Peter and Nuter and Kilter all jumped upon the seat and looked back over the track made by the sleigh. But Santa Claus had been left miles and miles behind.

"What shall we do?" asked Wisk, anxiously, all the mirth and mischief banished from his wee face by this great calamity.

"We must go back at once and find our master," said Nuter the Ryl, who thought and spoke with much deliberation.

"No, no!" exclaimed Peter the Knook, who, cross and crabbed though he was, might always be depended upon in an emergency. "If we delay, or go back, there will not be time to get the toys to the children before morning; and that would grieve Santa Claus more than anything else."

"It is certain that some wicked creatures have captured him," added Kilter, thoughtfully; "and their object must be to make the children unhappy. So our first duty is to get the toys distributed as carefully as if Santa Claus were himself present. Afterward we can search for our master and easily secure his freedom."

This seemed such good and sensible advice that the others at once resolved to adopt it. So Peter the Knook called to the reindeer, and the faithful animals again sprang forward and dashed over hill and valley, through forest and plain, until they came to the houses wherein children lay sleeping and dreaming of the pretty gifts they would find on Christmas morning.

The little immortals had set themselves a difficult task; for although they had assisted Santa Claus on many of his journeys, their master had always directed and guided them and told them exactly what he wished them to do. But now they had to distribute the toys according to their own judgment, and they did not understand children as well as did old Santa. So it is no wonder they made some laughable errors.

Mamie Brown, who wanted a doll, got a drum instead; and a drum is of no use to a girl who loves dolls. And Charlie Smith, who delights to romp and play out of doors, and who wanted some new rubber boots to keep his feet dry, received a sewing-box filled with colored worsteds and threads and needles, which made him so provoked that he thoughtlessly called our dear Santa Claus a fraud.

Had there been many such mistakes the Daemons would have accomplished their evil purpose and made the children unhappy. But the little friends of the absent Santa Claus labored faithfully and intelligently to carry out their master's ideas, and they made fewer errors than might be expected under such unusual circumstances.

And, although they worked as swiftly as possible, day had begun to break before the toys and other presents were all distributed; so for the first time in many years the reindeer trotted into the Laughing Valley, on their return, in broad daylight, with the brilliant sun peeping over the edge of the forest to prove they were far behind their accustomed hour.

Having put the deer in the stable, the little folk began to wonder how they might rescue their master; and they realized they must discover, first of all, what had happened to him and where he was.

So Wisk the Fairy transported himself to the bower of the Fairy Queen, which was located deep in the heart of the Forest of Burzee; and once there, it did not take him long to find out all about the naughty Daemons and how they had kidnapped the good Santa Claus to prevent his making children happy. The Fairy Queen also promised her assistance, and then, fortified by this powerful support, Wisk flew back to where Nuter and Peter and Kilter awaited him, and the four counselled together and laid plans to rescue their master from his enemies.

It is possible that Santa Claus was not as merry as usual during the night that succeeded his capture. For although he had faith in the judgment of his little friends he could not avoid a certain amount of worry, and an anxious look would creep at times into his kind old eyes as he thought of the disappointment that might await his dear little children. And the Daemons, who guarded him by turns, one after another, did not neglect to taunt him with contemptuous words in his helpless condition.

When Christmas Day dawned the Daemon of Malice was guarding the prisoner, and his tongue was sharper than that of any of the others.

"The children are waking up, Santa!" he cried; "they are waking up to find their stockings empty! Ho, ho! How they will quarrel, and wail, and stamp their feet in anger! Our caves will be full to-day, old Santa! Our caves are sure to be full!"

But to this, as to other like taunts, Santa Claus answered nothing. He was much grieved by his capture, it is true; but his courage did not forsake him. And, finding that the prisoner would not reply to his jeers, the Daemon of Malice presently went away, and sent the Daemon of Repentance to take his place.

This last personage was not so disagreeable as the others. He had gentle and refined features, and his voice was soft and pleasant in tone.

"My brother Daemons do not trust me overmuch," said he, as he entered the cavern; "but it is morning, now, and the mischief is done. You cannot visit the children again for another year."

"That is true," answered Santa Claus, almost cheerfully; "Christmas Eve is past, and for the first time in centuries I have not visited my children."

"The little ones will be greatly disappointed," murmured the Daemon of Repentance, almost regretfully, "but that cannot be helped now. Their grief is likely to make the children selfish and envious and hateful, and if they come to the Caves of the Daemons to-day I shall get a chance to lead some of them to my Cave of Repentance."

"Do you never repent, yourself?" asked Santa Claus, curiously.

"Oh, yes, indeed," answered the Daemon. "I am even now repenting that I assisted in your capture. Of course it is too late to remedy the evil that has been done; but repentance, you know, can come only after an evil thought or deed, for in the beginning there is nothing to repent of."

"So I understand," said Santa Claus. "Those who avoid evil need never visit your cave."

"As a rule, that is true," replied the Daemon; "yet you, who have done no evil, are about to visit my cave at once; for to prove that I sincerely regret my share in your capture I am going to permit you to escape."

This speech greatly surprised the prisoner, until he reflected that it was just what might be expected of the Daemon of Repentance. The fellow at once busied himself untying the knots that bound Santa Claus and unlocking the chains that fastened him to the wall. Then he led the way through a long tunnel until they both emerged in the Cave of Repentance.

"I hope you will forgive me," said the Daemon, pleadingly. "I am not really a bad person, you know; and I believe I accomplish a great deal of good in the world."

With this he opened a back door that let in a flood of sunshine, and Santa Claus sniffed the fresh air gratefully.

"I bear no malice," said he to the Daemon, in a gentle voice; "and I am sure the world would be a dreary place without you. So, good morning, and a Merry Christmas to you!"

With these words he stepped out to greet the bright morning, and a moment later he was trudging along, whistling softly to himself, on his way to his home in the Laughing Valley.

Marching over the snow toward the mountain was a vast army,

made up of the most curious creatures imaginable. There were numberless knooks from the forest, as rough and crooked in appearance as the gnarled branches of the trees they ministered to. And there were dainty ryls from the fields, each one bearing the emblem of the flower or plant it guarded. Behind these were many ranks of pixies, gnomes and nymphs, and in the rear a thousand beautiful fairies floating along in gorgeous array.

This wonderful army was led by Wisk, Peter, Nuter and Kilter, who had assembled it to rescue Santa Claus from captivity and to punish the Daemons who had dared to take him away from his beloved children.

And, although they looked so bright and peaceful, the little immortals were armed with powers that would be very terrible to those who had incurred their anger. Woe to the Daemons of the Caves if this mighty army of vengeance ever met them!

But lo! coming to meet his loyal friends appeared the imposing form of Santa Claus, his white beard floating in the breeze and his bright eyes sparkling with pleasure at this proof of the love and veneration he had inspired in the hearts of the most powerful creatures in existence.

And while they clustered around him and danced with glee at his safe return, he gave them earnest thanks for their support. But Wisk, and Nuter, and Peter, and Kilter, he embraced affectionately.

"It is useless to pursue the Daemons," said Santa Claus to the army. "They have their place in the world, and can never be destroyed. But that is a great pity, nevertheless," he continued, musingly.

So the fairies, and knooks, and pixies, and ryls all escorted the good man to his castle, and there left him to talk over the events of the night with his little assistants.

Wisk had already rendered himself invisible and flown through the big world to see how the children were getting along on this bright Christmas morning; and by the time he returned, Peter had finished telling Santa Claus of how they had distributed the toys.

"We really did very well," cried the Fairy, in a pleased voice; "for I found little unhappiness among the children this morning. Still, you must not get captured again, my dear master, for we might not be so fortunate another time in carrying out your ideas."

He then related the mistakes that had been made, and which he had not discovered until his tour of inspection. And Santa Claus at once sent him with rubber boots for Charlie Smith, and a doll for

Mamie Brown; so that even those two disappointed ones became happy.

As for the wicked Daemons of the Caves, they were filled with anger and chagrin when they found that their clever capture of Santa Claus had come to naught. Indeed, no one on that Christmas Day appeared to be at all selfish, or envious, or hateful. And, realizing that while the children's saint had so many powerful friends it was folly to oppose him, the Daemons never again attempted to interfere with his journeys on Christmas Eve.

ROCK CRYSTAL

from the German of Adalbert Stifter

from *The German Classics*

Story Translated by Lee M. Hollander

Among the high mountains of our fatherland there lies a little village with a small but very pointed church tower which emerges with red shingles from the green of many fruit trees, and by reason of its red color is to be seen far and away amid the misty bluish distances of the mountains. The village lies right in the center of a rather broad valley which has about the shape of a longish circle. Besides the church it contains a school, a town hall, and several other houses of no mean appearance, which form a square on which stand four linden trees surrounding a stone cross. These buildings are not mere farms but house within them those handicrafts which are indispensable to the human race and furnish the mountaineers with all the products of industry which they require. In the valley and along the mountain-sides many other huts and cottages are scattered, as is very often the case in mountain regions. These habitations belong to the parish and school district and pay tribute to the artisans we mentioned by purchasing their wares. Still other more distant huts belong to the village, but are so deeply ensconced in the recesses of the mountains that one cannot see them at all from the valley. Those who live in them rarely come down to their fellow parishioners and in winter frequently must keep their dead until after the snows have melted away in order to give them a burial. The greatest personage whom the villagers get to see in the course of the year is the priest. They greatly honor him, and usually he himself through a longer sojourn becomes so accustomed to the solitude of the valley that he not unwillingly stays and simply lives on there. At least, it has not happened in the memory of man that the priest of the village had been a man hankering to get away or unworthy of his vocation.

No roads lead through the valley. People use their double-track cart paths, upon which they bring in the products of their fields in carts drawn by one horse. Hence, few people come into the valley, among them sometimes a solitary pedestrian who is a lover of nature and dwells for some little time in the upper room of the inn and admires the mountains; or perhaps a painter who sketches the small pointed spire of the church and the beautiful summits of the rocky peaks. For this reason the villagers form a world by themselves. They all know each other by name and their several histories down from the time of grandfather and great-grandfather; they all mourn when one of them dies; know what name the new-born will receive; they have a language differing from that of the plains; they have their quarrels, which they settle among themselves; they assist one another and flock together when something extraordinary has happened.

They are conservative, and things are left to remain as they were. Whenever a stone drops out of a wall, the same stone is put back again; the new houses are built like the old ones; the dilapidated roofs are repaired with the same kind of shingles; and if there happen to be brindled cows on a farm, calves of the same color are raised always, so that the color stays on the farm.

To the south of the village one sees a snow mountain which seems to lift up its shining peaks right above the roofs of the houses. Yet it is not quite so near. Summer and winter it dominates the valley with its beetling crags and snowy sides. Being the most remarkable object in the landscape, this mountain is of main interest to the inhabitants and has become the central feature of many a story. There is not a young man or graybeard in the village but can tell of the crags and crests of the mountain, of its crevasses and caves, of its torrents and screes, whether now he knows it from his own experience or from hearsay. The mountain is the boast of the villagers, as if it were a work of theirs, and one is not so sure, however high one may esteem the plain-spokenness and reputation for truthtelling of the natives, whether they do not fib, now and then, to the honor and glory of their mountain. Besides being the wonder of the valley, the mountain affords actual profit; for whenever a company of tourists arrives to ascend the mountain the natives serve as guides; and to have been a guide, to have experienced this or that, to know this or that spot, is a distinction everyone likes to gain for himself. The mountain often is the object of their conversation at the inn, when they sit together and tell of their feats and wonderful experiences; nor do they omit to relate what this or that traveler had said and what reward they had received from him for their labor. Furthermore, the snowy sides of the mountain feed a lake among its heavily forested recesses, from which a merry brook runs through the valley, drives the sawmill and the flour mill, cleanses the village, and waters the cattle. The forests of the mountain furnish timber and form a bulwark against the avalanches.

The annual history of the mountain is as follows: In winter the two pinnacles of its summit, which they call horns, are snow-white and, when visible on bright days, tower up into the blackish blue of the sky in dazzling splendor; and all its shoulders are white, too, and all slopes. Even the perpendicular precipices, called walls by the natives, are covered with white frost delicately laid on, or with thin ice adhering to them like varnish, so that the whole mass looms up like an enchanted castle from out of the hoary gray of the forests which lie spread out heavily about its base. In summer, when the sun and warm winds melt the snow from their steep sides, the peaks soar up black into the sky and have only beautiful veins and specks of white on their flanks—as the natives say. But the fact is, the peaks are of a delicate, distant blue, and what they call veins and specks are not white, but have the lovely milk-blue color of distant snow against the darker blue of the rocks. When the weather is hot, the more elevated slopes about the peaks do not lose their covering of eternal snow. On the contrary, it then gleams with double resplendence down upon the green of the trees in the valley, but the winter's snow is melted off their lower parts. Then becomes visible the bluish or greenish iridescence of the glaciers, which are bared and gleam down upon the valley below. At the edge of this iridescence, there where it seems from the distance like a fringe of gems, a nearer view reveals confused masses of wild and monstrous boulders, slabs, and fragments piled up in chaotic fashion. In very hot and long summers, the ice fields are denuded even in the higher regions, and then a much greater amount of blue-green glacier ice glances down into the valley, many knobs and depressions are laid bare which one otherwise sees only covered with white, the muddy edge of the ice comes to view with its deposit of rocks, silt, and slime, and far greater volumes of water than usual rush into the valley. This continues until it gradually becomes autumn again, the waters grow less, and one day a gray continuous gentle rain spreads over all the valley. Then, after the mists have dispersed about the summits, the mountain is seen to have draped itself again in its soft robe of snow, and all crags, cones, and pinnacles are vested in white. Thus it goes on, year after year, with but slight divergences; and thus it will go on so long as nature remains the same and there is snow upon the heights and people live in the valleys. But to the natives these changes seem great; they pay much attention to them and calculate the progress of the seasons by them.

The ascent of the mountain is made from our valley. One follows a fine road which leads south to another valley over a so-called "neck." "Neck" is what they call a moderately high mountain ridge which connects two mountain ranges of considerable magnitude and over which one can pass from one valley to another between the mountains. The "neck" which connects our snow mountain with another great mountain mass is altogether covered with pine forests. At its greatest elevation, where the road begins gradually to descend into the valley beyond, there stands a post erected to commemorate a calamity. Once upon a time a baker carrying bread in a basket slung around his neck was found dead on that spot. They painted a picture of the dead baker with his basket and the pine trees round about, and beneath it an explanation with a request for prayer from the passer-by; and this picture they fastened to a wooden post painted red, and erected it at the spot where the accident occurred. At this post, then, one leaves the road and continues along the ridge of the "neck" instead of crossing it and descending into the valley beyond. There is an opening among the pine trees at that spot, as if there were a road between them. In fact, a path is sometimes made in that direction which then serves to bring down timber from the higher regions, but which is afterward overgrown again with grass. Proceeding along this way, which gently ascends, one arrives at last at a bare, treeless region. It is barren heath where grows nothing but heather, mosses, and lichens. It grows ever steeper the farther one ascends; but one always follows a gully resembling a rounded-out ditch, which is convenient, as one cannot then miss one's way in this extensive, treeless, monotonous region. After a while rocks as large as churches rise out of the grassy soil, between whose walls one climbs up still farther. Then there are again bleak ridges, with hardly any vegetation, which reach up into the thinner air of higher altitudes and lead straight to the ice. At both sides of this path, steep ledges plunge down, and by this natural causeway the snow mountain is joined to the "neck." In order to surmount the ice, one skirts it for some distance where it is surrounded by rock walls, until one comes to the old hard snow which bridges the crevasses and at most seasons of the year bears the weight of the climber. From the highest point of this snowfield, two peaks tower up, of which the one is higher and, therefore, the summit of the mountain. These pinnacles are very hard to climb. As they are surrounded by a chasm of varying width—the bergschrund—which one must leap over, and as their precipitous escarpments afford but small footholds, most of the tourists climbing the mountain content themselves with reaching the bergschrund and from there enjoying the panorama. Those who mean to climb to the top must use climbing irons, ropes, and iron spikes.

Besides this mountain there are still others south of the valley, but none as high. Even if the snow begins to lie on them early in fall and stays till late in spring, midsummer always removes it, and then the rocks gleam pleasantly in the sunlight, and the forests at their base have their soft green intersected by the broad blue shadows of these peaks which are so beautiful that one never tires of looking at them.

On the opposite, northern, eastern, and western sides of the valley the mountains rise in long ridges and are of lower elevation. Scattered fields and meadows climb up along their sides till rather high up, and above them one sees clearings, chalets, and the like, until at their edge they are silhouetted against the sky with their delicately serrated forest —which is indicative of their inconsiderable height—whereas the mountains toward the south, though also magnificently wooded, cut off the shining horizon with entirely smooth lines.

When one stands about in the center of the valley, it would seem as if there were no way out or into the basin; but people who have often been in the mountains are familiar with this illusion. The fact is, diverse roads lead through the folds of the mountains to the plains to the north, some of them with hardly a rise; and to the south, where the valley seems shut in by precipitous mountain walls, a road leads over the "neck" mentioned above.

The village is called Gschaid and the snow mountain looking down upon it, Gars.

On the other side of the "neck" there lies a valley by far more beautiful and fertile than that of Gschaid. At its entrance there lies a country town of considerable size named Millsdorf which has several industrial enterprises and carries on almost urban trade and business. Its inhabitants are much more well-to-do than those of Gschaid, and, although only three hours away, which for these labor-loving mountaineers used to great distances is only a bagatelle, manners and customs are so different in the two valleys and even their external appearance is so unlike that one might suppose a great number of miles lay between. This is of common occurrence in the mountains and due not only to the more or less favored position of the valleys but also to the spirit of the natives, who by reason of their differing occupations are inclined this way or that. But in this they all agree, that they adhere to established customs and the usages of their forefathers, lightly bear the absence of great traffic, cling to their native valley with an extraordinary love; in fact, can hardly live out of it.

Months, aye a whole year, may pass without a native of Gschaid setting foot into the valley beyond and visiting the town of Millsdorf. The same is true of the people of Millsdorf, although they have more intercourse with the country beyond and hence live in less seclusion than the villagers of Gschaid. A road which might be called a highroad leads through the length of their valley, and many a traveler passes through it without suspecting in the least that to the north of him, on the other side of the snow mountain towering high above him, there is another valley with many scattered houses and the village with its pointed church tower.

Among the trades of the village which supply the necessities of the valley is that of the shoemaker, indispensable indeed to man excepting in his most primitive condition. But the natives are so high raised above that condition that they stand in need of very good and durable footgear for the mountains. The shoemaker is the only one of his trade in the valley—with one inconsiderable exception. His house stands on the public square of Gschaid, where most of the larger dwellings are situated, and its gray walls, white window frames, and green shutters face the four linden trees. On the ground floor are the workshop, the workmen's room, a larger and a smaller sitting room, the shop, and then the kitchen and pantry; the first story, or, more properly, the attic space, contains the "upper room," which is also the "best room." In it there stand two beds of state, beautifully polished clothes presses; there is a china closet with dishes, a table with inlaid work, upholstered easy chairs, a strongbox for the savings. Furthermore there hang on the walls pictures of saints, two handsome watches, being prizes won in shooting matches, and finally there are some rifles both for target firing and hunting, with all the necessary paraphernalia, carefully hung up in a special case with a glass door.

Added to the shoemaker's house there is a smaller house, built exactly like it and, though separated from it by an arched gateway, belonging to it like part of a whole. It has only one large room with some closets. Its purpose is to serve the owner of the larger house as habitation for the remainder of his days, after having left the property to his son or successor, there to dwell with his wife until both are dead and the little house stands empty again and is ready for another occupant. To the rear of the shoemaker's house are stable and barn, for every dweller in the valley carries on farming along with his regular occupation and makes a good living from it. Behind these buildings, finally, is the garden which is lacking to none of the better houses of Gschaid and from which the villagers obtain their vegetables, their fruit, and the flowers necessary for festive occasions. And, as quite commonly in the mountains, apiculture is pursued also in the gardens of Gschaid.

The small exception alluded to, and the only competitor of the shoemaker, is a man of the same trade, old Tobias, who is not a real rival, though, because he only cobbles and is kept quite busy with that. Nor would he ever think of competing with the gentleman shoemaker of the township, especially as the latter frequently provides him gratuitously with leather cuttings, sole strips, and the like. In summertime old Tobias sits under a clump of elder bushes at the end of the village and works away. All about him are shoes and lace-boots, all of them, however, gray, muddy, and torn. There are no high boots, because these are not worn in the village and its surroundings; only two personages own such boots, the priest and the schoolteacher, both of whom have their new work and repairing done by the shoemaker. In winter old Tobias sits in his cottage behind the elder bushes and has it comfortably warm, because wood is not dear in Gschaid.

Before entering into possession of his house, the shoemaker had been a chamois poacher—in fact, had not exactly been a model in

504 PEARL S. BUCK'S BOOK OF CHRISTMAS

youth, so the people of Gschaid said. In school he had always been one of the brightest scholars. Afterward he had learned his father's trade and had gone on his journeyman wanderings, finally returning to the village. Instead of wearing a black hat, as befits a tradesman, and as his father had done all his life, he put on a green one, decorated it with all the feathers obtainable, and strutted around in the very shortest homespun coat to be found in all the valley; whereas his father always had worn a coat of dark, even black, cloth with very long tails to indicate his station as tradesman. The young shoemaker was to be seen on all dancing floors and bowling alleys. Whenever anyone gave him a piece of good advice, he merely whistled. He attended all shooting matches in the neighborhood with his target rifle and often brought back a prize, which he considered a great victory. The prize generally consisted of coins artistically set. To win them he frequently had to spend more coins of the same value than the prize was worth— especially as he was very generous with his money. He also participated in all the chases of the surrounding country and won a name as a marksman. Sometimes, however, he issued alone with his double-barreled gun and climbing irons, and once, it is said, returned with an ugly wound in his head.

In Millsdorf there lived a dyer who carried on a very notable industry. His works lay right at the entrance of the town at the side toward Gschaid. He employed many people and even worked with machines, which was an unheard of thing in the valley. Besides, he did extensive farming. The shoemaker frequently crossed the mountain to win the daughter of this wealthy dyer. Because of her beauty, but also because of her modesty and domesticity, she was praised far and near. Nevertheless the shoemaker, it is said, attracted her attention. The dyer did not permit him to enter his house; and whereas his beautiful daughter had, even before that, never attended public places and merry-makings, and was rarely to be seen outside the house of her parents, now she became even more retiring in her habits and was to be seen only in church, in her garden, or at home.

Some time after the death of his parents, by which the paternal house which he inhabited all alone became his, the shoemaker became an altogether different man. Boisterous as he had been before, he now sat in his shop and hammered away day and night. Boastingly, he set a prize on it that there was no one who could make better shoes and footgear. He took none but the best workmen and kept after them when they worked in order that they should do as he told them.

And really he accomplished his desire, so that not only the whole village of Gschaid, which for the most part had got its shoes from neighboring valleys, had their work done by him, but the whole valley also. And finally he had some customers even from Millsdorf and other valleys. Even down into the plains his fame spread, so that a good many who intended to climb in the mountains had their shoes made by him for that purpose.

He ordered his house very neatly and in his shop the shoes, lace-boots, and high boots shone upon their several shelves; and when on Sundays the whole population of the valley came into the village, gathering under the four linden trees of the square, people liked to go over to the shoemaker's shop and look through the panes to watch the customers.

On account of the love he bore to the mountains, even now he devoted his best endeavor to the making of mountain lace-shoes. In the inn he used to say that there was no one who could show him any-one else's mountain boots that could compare with his own. "They don't know," he was accustomed to add, "and they have never learned it in all their life, how such a shoe is to be made so that the firmament of the nails shall fit well on the soles and contain the proper amount of iron, so as to render the shoe hard on the outside, so that no flint, however sharp, can be felt through, and so that on its inside it fits the foot as snug and soft as a glove."

The shoemaker had a large ledger made for himself in which he entered all goods he had manufactured, adding the names of those who had furnished the materials and of those who had bought the finished goods, together with a brief remark about the quality of the product. Footgear of the same kind bore their continuous numbers, and the book lay in the large drawer of his shop.

Even if the beautiful daughter of the Millsdorf dyer did not take a step outside her parents' home, and even though she visited neither friends nor relatives, yet the shoemaker of Gschaid knew how to ar-range it so that she saw him from afar when she walked to church, when she was in her garden, and when she looked out upon the mead-ows from the windows of her room. On account of this unceasing spy-ing the dyer's wife by dint of her long and persevering prayers had brought it about that her obstinate husband yielded and that the shoemaker—as he had, in fact, become a better man—led the beauti-ful and wealthy Millsdorf girl home to Gschaid as his wife. However, the dyer was a man who meant to have his own way. The right sort of man, he said, ought to ply his trade in a manner to prosper and ought, therefore, to be able to maintain his wife, children, himself, and his servants, to keep house and home in good condition, and yet save a goodly amount—which savings were, after all, the main aids to honor and dignity in the world. Therefore, he said, his daughter would receive nothing from home but an excellent outfit; all else it was and remained the duty of the husband to provide. The dyeing works in Millsdorf and the farming he carried on were a dignified and honorable business by themselves which had to exist for their own sake. All property belonging to them had to serve as capital, for which reason he would not give away any part of them. But when he, the dyer, and his wife were deceased, then both the dye works and the farm in Millsdorf would fall to their only daughter, the shoemaker's wife in Gschaid, and she and her husband could do with the property what they pleased: they would inherit it, however, only if worthy of inheriting it; if unworthy, it would go to their children, and if there were none, to other relatives, with the exception of the lawful portion. Neither did the shoemaker demand anything, but proudly gave the dyer to understand that he had cared but for his beautiful daughter and that he was able to maintain her as she had been maintained at home. And when she was his wife, he gave her clothes not only finer than those the women of Gschaid and the Gschaid valley owned, but also than she had ever worn at home. And as to food and drink, he insisted on having it better and her treatment more considerate than she had enjoyed in her own father's house. Moreover, in order to show his independence of his father-in-law, he bought more and more land with his savings, so that he came to own a goodly property.

Now, the natives of Gschaid rarely leave their valley, as has been remarked, hardly even traveling to Millsdorf, from which they are separated by customs as well as by mountain ridges; besides, it never happens that a man leaves his valley to settle in a neighboring one, though settlements at greater distances do take place; neither does a woman or a girl like to emigrate from one valley into another, except in the rather rare cases when she follows her love and as wife joins her husband in another valley. So it happened that the dyer's daughter from Millsdorf was ever considered a stranger by all the people of Gschaid, even after she had become the shoemaker's wife; and although they never did her any ill, aye, even loved her on account of her beautiful ways, yet they always seemed to keep their distance, or, if you will, showed marked consideration for her, and never became intimate or treated her as their equal, as men and women of Gschaid did men and women of their own valley. Thus matters stood and remained, and were not mended by the better dress and the lighter domestic duties of the shoemaker's wife.

At the end of the first year, she had born to her husband a son, and several years afterward, a daughter. She believed, however, that he did not love his children as she thought he ought to, and as she knew she loved them herself; for his face was mostly serious and he was chiefly concerned with his work. He rarely fondled or played with the children and always spoke seriously to them as one does to adults. With regard to food and clothes and other material things, his care for them was above reproach.

At first the dyer's wife frequently came over to Gschaid, and the young couple in their turn visited Millsdorf on occasion of country fairs and other festivities. But when the children came, circumstances were altered. If mothers love their children and long for them, this is frequently, and to a much higher degree, the case with grandmothers; they occasionally long for their grandchildren with an intensity that borders on morbidness. The dyer's wife very frequently came over to Gschaid now, in order to see the children and to bring them presents. Then she would depart again after giving them kindly advice. But when her age and health did not any longer permit of these frequent journeys and the dyer for this reason objected to them, they bethought themselves of another plan; they changed about, and now the children visited their grandmother. Frequently the mother herself took them over in their carriage; at other times they were bundled up warmly and driven over the "neck" under the care of a servant girl. But when they were a little older, they went to Millsdorf on foot, either in the company of their mother or of some servant; indeed, when the boy had become strong, clever, and self-reliant, they let him travel the well-known road over the "neck" by himself; and when the weather was especially beautiful and he begged them, they permitted his little sister to accompany him. This is customary in Gschaid, as the people are hardy pedestrians, and because parents—especially a man like the shoemaker—like to see their children able to take care of themselves.

Thus it happened that the two children made the way over the pass more frequently than all the other villagers together; and inasmuch as their mother had always been treated as half a stranger in Gschaid, the children, by this circumstance, grew up to be strangers' children to

the village folks; they hardly were Gschaid children, but belonged half
to Millsdorf.

The boy, Conrad, had already something of the earnest ways of his
father, and the girl, Susanna, named so after her mother, or Sanna for
brevity, had great faith in his knowledge, understanding, and
strength, and unquestioningly followed where he led, just as her
mother absolutely trusted her husband, whom she credited with all
possible insight and ability.

On beautiful mornings, one could see the children walk southward
through the valley and traverse the meadows toward the point where
the forest of the "neck" looks down on them. They would enter the
forest, gain the height on the road, and before noon come to the open
meadows on the side toward Millsdorf. Conrad then showed Sanna
the pastures that belonged to grandfather, then they walked through
his fields, in which he explained to her the various kinds of grain, then
they saw the long cloths wave in the wind and blow into antic shapes
as they hung to dry on poles under the eaves, then they heard the
noises of the fullery and of the tannery which the dyer had built by
the brook, then they rounded a corner of the fields, and very soon entered the garden of the dyer's establishment by the back gate, where
they were received by grandmother. She always had a presentiment
when the children were coming, looked out of the windows, and
recognized them from afar, whenever Sanna's red kerchief shone
brightly in the sun.

She led the children through the laundry and the press into the living room and had them sit down, not letting them take off their
neckcloths or coats lest they should catch cold, and then kept them
for dinner. After the meal, they were allowed to go into the open and
play, and to walk about in the house of their grandparents, or do
whatever else they cared to, provided it was not improper or forbidden. The dyer, who always ate with them, questioned them about
school and impressed upon them what they ought to learn. In the afternoon they were urged by their grandmother to depart even before it
was time, so that they should in no case reach home too late. Although the dyer had given his daughter no dowry and had vowed not
to give away anything of his fortune before his death, his wife did not
hold herself so strictly bound. She not only frequently made the
children presents of pieces of money, sometimes of considerable value,
but also invariably tied two bundles for them to carry in which there
were things she believed were necessary or would give the children

pleasure. And even if the same things were to be found in the shoe-maker's house and as good as one might wish, yet grandmother made presents of them in her joy of giving, and the children carried them home as something especially fine. Thus it happened that the children on the day before Christmas unwittingly carried home the presents—well sealed and packed in pasteboard boxes—which were intended for them as their Christmas presents the very same night.

Grandmother's pressing the children to go before it was time, so that they should not get home late, had only the effect that they tarried on the way, now here, now there. They liked to sit by the hazelwoods on the "neck" and open nuts with stones; or, if there were no nuts, they played with leaves or pegs or the soft brown cones that crop from the branches of fir trees in the beginning of spring. Some-times Conrad told his little sister stories or, when arrived at the red memorial post, would lead her a short distance up the side road and tell her that here one could get on the Snow Mountain, that up there were great rocks and stones, that the chamois gamboled and great birds circled about up there. He often led her out beyond the forest, when they would look at the dry grass and the small bushes of the heather; but then he returned with her, invariably bringing her home before twilight, which always earned him praise.

One winter, on the morning before Christmas, when the first dawn had passed into day, a thin dry veil was spread over the whole sky, so that one could see the low and distant sun only as an indistinct red spot; moreover, the air that day was mild, almost genial, and absolute calm reigned in the entire valley as well as in the heavens, as was in-dicated by the unchanging and immobile forms of the clouds. So the shoemaker's wife said to her children, "As today is pleasant and it has not rained for a long time and the roads are hard, and as father gave you permission yesterday, if the weather continued fine, you may go to visit grandmother in Millsdorf; but ask father once more."

The children, who were still standing there in their little night-gowns, ran into the adjoining room where their father was speaking with a customer and asked him again for his permission because it was such a fine day. It was given and they ran back to their mother.

The shoemaker's wife now dressed the children carefully, or rather she dressed the little girl in snug-fitting warm dresses; for the boy began to dress himself and was finished long before his mother had the little girl straightened out. When they were both ready she said, "Now, Conrad, be nice and careful. As I let your little sister go with you, you must leave betimes and not remain standing anywhere, and when you have eaten at grandmother's you must return at once and come home; for the days are very short now and the sun sets very soon."

"Yes, I know, mother," said Conrad.

"And take good care of Sanna that she does not fall or get overheated."

"Yes, mother."

"Well, then, God bless you. Now go to father and tell him you are leaving."

The boy slung a bag of calfskin, artfully sewed by his father, about his shoulders by a strap, and the children went into the adjoining room to say farewell to their father. Soon they issued again and merrily skipped along the village street, after their mother had once more made the sign of the cross over them.

Quickly they passed over the square and along the rows of houses, and finally between the railings of the orchards out into the open. The sun already stood above the wooded heights that were woven through with milky wisps of cloud, and its dim reddish disk proceeded along with them through the leafless branches of the crabapple trees.

There was no snow in the whole valley, but the higher mountains that had been glistening with it for many weeks already were thoroughly covered. The lower ridges, however, remained snowless and silent in the mantle of their pine forests and the fallow red of their bare branches. The ground was not frozen yet and would have been entirely dry, after the long dry period that had been prevailing, if the cold of the season had not covered it with a film of moisture. This did not render the ground slippery, however, but rather firm and resilient so that the children made good progress. The scanty grass still standing on the meadows and especially along the ditches in them bore the colors of autumn. There was no frost on the ground, and a closer inspection did not reveal any dew, either, which signifies rain, according to the country people.

Toward the edge of the meadows there was a mountain brook over which led a high, narrow wooden bridge. The children walked over it and looked down. There was hardly any water in the brook, only a thin streak of intensely blue color wound through the dry white pebbles of its stony bed, and both the small amount and the color of the water indicated that cold was prevailing in the greater altitudes; for this rendered the soil on the mountains dry, so that it did not make the water of the brook turbid and hardened the ice so that it could give off but a few clear drops.

From the bridge, the children passed through the valleys in the hills and came closer and closer to the woods.

Finally they reached the edge of the woods and walked on through them.

When they had climbed up into the higher woodlands of the "neck," the long furrows of the road were no longer soft, as had been the case in the valley, but were firm, not from dryness, but, as the children soon perceived, because they were frozen over. In some places, the frost had rendered them so hard that they could bear the weight of their bodies. From now on they did not persist any longer in the slippery path beside the road, but in the ruts, as children will, try-ing whether this or that furrow would carry them. When, after an hour's time, they had arrived at the height of the "neck," the ground was so hard that their steps resounded on it and the clods were hard like stones.

Arrived at the location of the memorial post, Sanna was the first to notice that it no longer stood there. They went up to the spot and saw that the round red-painted post which carried the picture was lying in the dry grass which stood there like thin straw and concealed the fallen post from view. They could not understand, to be sure, why it had toppled over—whether it had been knocked down or fallen of it-self; but they did see that the wood was much decayed at the place where it emerged from the ground and that the post might therefore easily have fallen of itself. Since it was lying there, however, they were pleased that they could get a closer look at the picture and the inscrip-tion than they had ever had before. When they had examined all—the basket with the rolls, the whitish hands of the baker, his closed eyes, his gray coat and the pine trees surrounding him—and when they had spelled out and read aloud the inscription, they proceeded on their way.

After another hour, the dark forest on either side receded, scattered trees, some of them isolated oaks, others birches, and clumps of bushes received them and accompanied them onward, and after a short while the children were running down through the meadows of the valley of Millsdorf.

Although this valley is not as high, by far, as the valley of Gschaid and so much warmer that they could begin harvesting two weeks ear-lier than in Gschaid, the ground was frozen here, too; and when the children had come to the tannery and the fulling mill of their grandfather, pretty little cakes of ice were lying on the road where it was frequently spattered by drops from the wheels. That is usually a great pleasure for children.

Grandmother had seen them coming and had gone to meet them. She took Sanna by her cold little hands and led her into the room.

She made them take off their heavy outer garments, ordered more wood to be put in the stove, and asked them what had happened on the way over.

When they had told her she said, "That's nice and good, and I am very glad that you have come again; but today you must be off early. The day is short and it is growing colder. Only this morning there was no frost in Millsdorf."

"Not in Gschaid, either," said the boy.

"There you see. On that account you must hurry so that you will not grow too cold in the evening," said grandmother.

Then she asked how mother was and how father was, and whether anything particular had happened in Gschaid.

After having questioned them, she devoted herself to the preparation of dinner, made sure that it would be ready at an earlier time than usual, and herself prepared tidbits for the children which she knew would give them pleasure. Then the master dyer was called. Covers were set on the table for the children as for grown-up people and then they ate with grandfather and grandmother, and the latter helped them to particularly good things. After the meal she stroked Sanna's cheeks, which had grown quite red meanwhile.

Thereupon she went busily to and fro packing the boy's knapsack till it was full and, besides, stuffed all kinds of things into his pockets. Also in Sanna's little pockets she put all manner of things. She gave each a piece of bread to eat on the way, and in the knapsack, she said, there were two more pieces of wheat bread, in case they should grow too hungry.

"For mother, I have given you some well-roasted coffee," she said, "and in the little bottle that is stoppered and tightly wrapped up there is also some black coffee, better than mother usually makes over at your house. Just let her taste it; it is a veritable medicine tonic, so strong that one swallow of it will warm up the stomach so that the body will not grow cold on the coldest of winter days. The other things in the pasteboard box and those that are wrapped up in paper in the knapsack you are to bring home without touching."

After having talked with the children a little while longer, she bade them go.

"Take good care, Sanna," she said, "that you don't get chilled; you mustn't get overheated. And don't you run up along the meadows and under the trees. Probably there will be some wind toward evening, and then you must walk more slowly. Greet father and mother and wish them a right merry Christmas."

Grandmother kissed both children on their cheeks and pushed them through the door. Nevertheless she herself went along, accompanied them through the garden, let them out by the back gate, closed it behind them, and went back into the house.

The children walked past the cakes of ice beside grandfather's mill, passed through the fields of Millsdorf, and turned upward toward the meadows.

When they were passing along the heights where, as has been said, stood scattered trees and clumps of bushes, there fell, quite slowly, some few snowflakes.

"Do you see, Sanna," said the boy, "I had thought right away that we would have snow; do you remember, when we left home, how the sun was a bloody red like the lamp hanging at the Holy Sepulcher; and now nothing is to be seen of it any more, and only the gray mist is above the treetops. That always means snow."

The children walked on more gladly, and Sanna was happy whenever she caught a falling flake on the dark sleeve of her coat and the flake stayed there a long time before melting. When they had finally arrived at the outermost edge of the Millsdorf heights where the road enters the dark pines of the "neck," the solid front of the forest was already prettily sprinkled by the flakes falling ever more thickly. They now entered the dense forest which extended over the longest part of the journey still ahead of them.

From the edge of the forest the ground continues to rise up to the point where one reaches the red memorial post, when the road leads downward toward the valley of Gschaid. In fact, the slope of the forest from the Millsdorf side is so steep that the road does not gain the height by a straight line but climbs up in long serpentines from west to east and from east to west. The whole length of the road up to the post and down to the meadows of Gschaid leads through tall, dense woods without a clearing, which grow less heavy as one comes down on the level again, and issues from them near the meadows of the valley of Gschaid. Indeed, the "neck," though being only a small ridge connecting two great mountain masses, is yet large enough to appear a considerable mountain itself if it were placed in the plain.

The first observation the children made when entering the woods was that the frozen ground appeared gray, as though powdered with flour, and that the beards of the dry grass stalks standing here and there between the trees by the roadside were weighted down with snowflakes; while on the many green twigs of the pines and firs, opening up like hands, there sat little white flames.

"Is it snowing at home, too, I wonder?" asked Sanna.

"Of course," answered the boy, "and it is growing colder, too, and you will see that the whole pond is frozen over by tomorrow."

"Yes, Conrad," said the girl.

She hastened her steps to keep up with the boy striding along.

They now continued steadily up along the serpentines, now from west to east and again from east to west. The wind predicted by grandmother did not come; on the contrary, the air was so still that not a branch or twig was moving. In fact, it seemed warmer in the forest, as, in general, loose bodies with air spaces between, such as a forest, are in winter. The snowflakes descended ever more copiously, so that the ground was altogether white already and the woods began to appear dappled with gray, while snow lay on the garments of the children.

Both were overjoyed. They stepped upon the soft down and looked for places where there was a thicker layer of it in order to tread on them and make it appear as if they were wading in it already. They did not shake off the snow from their clothes.

A great stillness had set in. There was nothing to be seen of any bird, although some do flit to and fro through the forest in wintertime and the children on their way to Millsdorf had even heard some twitter. The whole forest seemed deserted.

As theirs were the only tracks and the snow in front of them was untrod and immaculate, they understood that they were the only ones crossing the "neck" that day.

They proceeded onward, now approaching, now leaving the trees. Where there was dense undergrowth they could see the snow lying upon it.

Their joy was still growing, for the flakes descended ever more densely, and after a short time they needed no longer to search for places to wade in the snow, for it was so thick already that they felt it soft under their soles and up around their shoes. And when all was so silent and peaceful, it seemed to them that they could hear the swish of the snow falling upon the needles.

"Shall we see the post today?" asked the girl. "Because it has fallen down, you know, and then the snow will fall on it and the red color will be white."

"We shall be able to see it though, for that matter," replied the boy. "Even if the snow falls upon it and it becomes white all over, we are bound to see it, because it is a thick post, and because it has the black iron cross on its top which will surely stick out."

"Yes, Conrad."

Meanwhile, as they had proceeded still farther, the snowfall had become so dense that they could see only the very nearest trees.

No hardness of the road, not to mention its ruts, was to be felt, the road was everywhere equally soft with snow and was, in fact, recognizable only as an even white band running on through the forest. On all the branches there lay already the beautiful white covering.

The children now walked in the middle of the road, furrowing the snow with their little feet and proceeding more slowly as the walking became more tiresome. The boy pulled up his jacket about his throat so that no snow should fall in his neck, and he pulled down his hat so as to be more protected. He also fastened his little sister's neckerchief which her mother had given her to wear over her shoulders, pulling it forward over her forehead so that it formed a roof.

The wind predicted by grandmother still had not come; on the other hand, the snowfall gradually became so dense that not even the nearest trees were to be recognized, but stood there like misty sacks.

The children went on. They drew up their shoulders and walked on.

Sanna took hold of the strap by which Conrad had his calfskin bag fastened about his shoulders and thus they proceeded on their way.

They still had not reached the post. The boy was not sure about the time, because the sun was not shining and all was a monotonous gray.

"Shall we reach the post soon?" asked the girl.

"I don't know," said the boy. "I can't see the trees today and recognize the way, because it is so white. We shall not see the post at all, perhaps, because there is so much snow that it will be covered up and scarcely a blade of grass or an arm of the black cross will show. But never mind. We just continue on our road, and the road goes between the trees, and when it gets to the spot where the post stands it will go down, and we shall keep on it, and when it comes out of the trees we are already on the meadows of Gschaid; then comes the path, and then we shall not be far from home."

"Yes, Conrad," said the girl.

They proceeded along their road, which still led upward.

The footprints they left behind them did not remain visible long, for the extraordinary volume of the descending snow soon covered them up. The snow no longer rustled, in falling upon the needles, but hurriedly and peacefully added itself to the snow already there. The children gathered their garments still more tightly about them in order to keep the steadily falling snow from coming in on all sides.

They walked on very fast, and still the road led upward.

After a long time they still had not reached the height on which the post was supposed to be, and from where the road was to descend toward Gschaid.

Finally the children came to a region where there were no more trees.

"I see no more trees," said Sanna.

"Perhaps the road is so broad that we cannot see them on account of the snow," answered the boy.

"Yes, Conrad," said the girl.

After a while the boy remained standing and said, "I don't see any trees now myself, we must have got out of the woods, and also the road keeps on rising. Let us stand still a while and look about; perhaps we may see something."

But they perceived nothing. They saw the sky only through a dim space. Just as in a hailstorm gloomy fringes hang down over the white or greenish swollen clouds, thus it was here, and the noiseless falling continued. On the ground they saw only a round spot of white and nothing else.

"Do you know, Sanna," said the boy, "we are on the dry grass I often led you up to in summer, where we used to sit and look at the pastureland that leads up gradually and where the beautiful herbs grow. We shall now at once go down there on the right."

"Yes, Conrad."

"The day is short, as grandmother said, and as you well know yourself, and so we must hurry."

"Yes, Conrad," said the girl.

"Wait a little and I will fix you a little better," replied the boy.

He took off his hat, put it on Sanna's head and fastened it with both ribbons under her chin. The kerchief she had worn protected her too little, while on his head there was such a mass of dense curls that the snow could fall on it for a long time before the wet and cold would penetrate. Then he took off his little fur jacket and drew it over her little arms. About his own shoulders and arms, which now showed the bare shirt, he tied the little kerchief Sanna had worn over her chest and the larger one she had had over her shoulders. That was enough for himself, he thought, and if he only stepped briskly he should not be cold.

He took the little girl by her hand, and they marched on.

The girl with her docile little eyes looked out into the monotonous gray round about and gladly followed him, only her little hurrying feet could not keep up with his, for he was striding onward like one who wanted to decide a matter once for all.

Thus they proceeded with the unremitting energy children and animals have when they do not realize how far their strength will carry them and when their supply of it will give out.

But as they went on, they did not notice whether they were going down or up. They had turned down to the right at once, but they came again to places that led up. Often they encountered steep places which they were forced to avoid, and a trench in which they continued led them about in a curve. They climbed heights which grew ever steeper as they proceeded, and what they thought led downward was level ground, or it was a depression, or the way went on in an even stretch.

"Where are we, I wonder, Conrad?" asked the girl.

"I don't know," he answered. "If I only could see something with my eyes," he continued, "that I could take my direction from."

But there was nothing about them but the blinding white, white everywhere, which drew an ever narrowing circle about them, passing beyond it into a luminous mist descending in bands which consumed and concealed all objects beyond, until there was nothing but the unceasingly descending snow.

"Wait, Sanna," said the boy, "let us stand still for a moment and listen; perhaps we might hear a sound from the valley, a dog, or a bell, or the mill, or a shout, something we must hear, and then we shall know which way to go."

So they remained standing, but they heard nothing. They remained standing a little longer, but nothing came, not a single sound, not the faintest noise beside their own breath; aye, in the absolute stillness they thought they could hear the snow as it fell on their eyelashes.

The prediction of grandmother had still not come true; no wind had arisen. In fact, what is rare in those regions, not a breath of air was stirring.

After having waited for a long time they went on again.

"Never mind, Sanna," said the boy, "don't be afraid. Just follow me and I shall lead you down yet. If only it would stop snowing!"

The little girl was not faint-hearted, but lifted her little feet as well as she could and followed him. He led her on in the white, bright, living, opaque space.

After a time they saw rocks. Darkling and indistinct they loomed up out of the white opaque light. As the children approached, they almost bumped against them. They rose up like walls and were quite perpendicular, so that scarcely a flake of snow could settle on them.

"Sanna, Sanna," he said, "there are the rocks. Just let us keep on, let us keep on."

They went on, had to enter in between the rocks and push on at their base. The rocks would let them escape neither to left nor right and led them on in a narrow path. After a while the children lost sight of them. They got away from the rocks as unexpectedly as they had got among them. Again nothing surrounded them but white; no more dark forms interposed. They moved in what seemed a great brightness and yet could not see three feet ahead, everything being, as it were, enveloped in a white darkness; and as there were no shadows no opinion about the size of objects was possible. The children did not know whether they were to descend or ascend until some steep slope compelled their feet to climb.

"My eyes smart," said Sanna.

"Don't look on the snow," answered the boy, "but into the clouds. Mine have hurt a long time already; but it does not matter, because I must watch our way. But don't be afraid. I shall lead you safely down to Gschaid."

"Yes, Conrad."

They went on; but wheresoever they turned, whichever way they turned, there never showed a chance to descend. On either side steep acclivities hemmed them in, and also made them constantly ascend. Whenever they turned downward, the slopes proved so precipitous that they were compelled to retreat. Frequently they met obstacles and often had to avoid steep slopes.

They began to notice that whenever their feet sank in through the new snow they no longer felt the rocky soil underneath but something else which seemed like older, frozen snow; but still they pushed onward and marched fast and perseveringly. Whenever they made a halt, everything was still, unspeakably still. When they resumed their march, they heard the shuffling of their feet and nothing else; for the veils of heaven descended without a sound, and so abundantly that one might have seen the snow grow. The children themselves were covered with it, so that they did not contrast with the general whiteness and would have lost each other from sight had they been separated but a few feet.

A comfort it was that the snow was as dry as sand, so that it did not adhere to their boots and stockings or cling and wet them.

At last they approached some other objects. They were gigantic fragments lying in wild confusion and covered with snow sifting everywhere into the chasms between them. The children almost touched them before seeing them. They went up to them to examine what they were.

It was ice—nothing but ice.

There were snow-covered slabs on whose lateral edges the smooth green ice became visible; there were hillocks that looked like heaped-up foam, but whose inward-looking crevasses had a dull sheen and luster as if bars and beams of gems had been flung pellmell. There rose rounded hummocks that were entirely enveloped in snow, slabs and other forms that stood inclined or in a perpendicular position, towering as high as houses or the church of Gschaid. In some, cavities were hollowed out through which one could insert an arm, a head, a body, a whole big wagon full of hay. All these were jumbled together and tilted so that they frequently formed roofs or eaves whose edges the snow overlaid and over which it reached down like long white paws. Nay, even a monstrous black boulder as large as a house lay stranded among the blocks of ice and stood on end so that no snow could stick to its sides. And even larger ones which one saw only later were fast in the ice and skirted the glacier like a wall of debris.

"There must have been very much water here, because there is so much ice," remarked Sanna.

"No, that did not come from any water," replied her brother. "That is the ice of the mountain which is always on it, because that is the way things are."

"Yes, Conrad," said Sanna.

"We have come to the ice now," said the boy; "we are on the mountain, you know, Sanna, that one sees so white in the sunshine from our garden. Now keep in mind what I shall tell you. Do you remember how often we used to sit in the garden in the afternoon, how beautiful it was, how the bees hummed about us, how the linden trees smelled sweet, and how the sun shone down on us?"

"Yes, Conrad, I remember."

"And then we also used to see the mountain. We saw how blue it was, as blue as the sky; we saw the snow that is up there even when we had summer weather, when it was hot and the grain ripened."

"Yes, Conrad."

"And below it where the snow stopped one sees all sorts of colors if one looks close—green, blue, and whitish. That is the ice; but it only looks so small from below because it is so very far away. Father said the ice will not go away before the end of the world. And then I also often saw that there was blue color below the ice and thought it was stones, or soil and pastureland, and then come the woods, and they go down farther and farther, and there are some boulders in them, too, and then come meadows that are already green, and then the green leafy woods, and then our meadowlands and fields in the valley of Gschaid. Do you see now, Sanna, as we are at the ice we shall go down over the blue color, and through the forests in which are the boulders, and then over the pastureland, and through the green leafy forests, and then we shall be in the valley of Gschaid and easily find our way to the village."

"Yes, Conrad," said the girl.

The children now entered upon the glacier where it was accessible. They were like wee little specks wandering among the huge masses.

As they were peering in under the overhanging slabs, moved as it were by an instinct to seek some shelter, they arrived at a trench, broad and deeply furrowed, which came right out of the ice. It looked like the bed of some torrent now dried up and everywhere covered with fresh snow. At the spot where it emerged from the ice there yawned a vault of ice beautifully arched above it. The children continued in the trench and, entering the vault, went in farther and farther. It was quite dry and there was smooth ice under their feet. All the cavern, however, was blue, bluer than anything else in the world, more profoundly and more beautifully blue than the sky, as blue as azure glass through which a bright glow is diffused. There were more or less heavy flutings, icicles hung down pointed and tufted, and the passage led inward still farther, they knew not how far; but they did not go on. It would also have been pleasant to stay in this grotto; it was warm and no snow could come in, but it was so fearfully blue that the children took fright and ran out again. They went on awhile in the trench and then clambered over its side.

They passed along the ice, as far as it was possible to edge through that chaos of fragments and boulders.

"We shall now have to pass over this, and then we shall run down away from the ice," said Conrad.

"Yes," said Sanna and clung to him.

From the ice they took a direction downward over the snow which was to lead them into the valley. But they were not to get far. Another river of ice traversed the soft snow like a gigantic wall bulging up and towering aloft and, as it were, reaching out with its arms to the right and the left. It was covered by snow on top, but at its sides there were gleams of blue and green and drab and black, aye, even of yellow and red. They could now see to larger distances, as the enormous and unceasing snowfall had abated somewhat and was only as heavy as on ordinary snowy days. With the audacity of ignorance, they clambered up on the ice in order to cross the interposing tongue of the glacier and to descend farther behind it. They thrust their little bodies into every opening; they put their feet on every projection covered by a white snow hood, whether ice or rock; they aided their progress with their hands; they crept where they could not walk, and with their light bodies worked themselves up until they had finally gained the top of the wall.

They had intended to climb down its other side.

There was no other side.

As far as the eyes of the children reached there was only ice. Hummocks, slabs, and spires of ice rose about them, all covered with snow. Instead of being a wall which one might surmount and which would be followed by an expanse of snow, as they had thought, new walls of ice lifted up out of the glacier, shattered and fissured and variegated with innumerable blue sinuous lines; and behind them were other walls of the same nature, and behind them others again, until the falling snow veiled the distance with its gray.

"Sanna, we cannot make our way here," said the boy.

"No," answered his sister.

"Then we will turn back and try to get down somewhere else."

"Yes, Conrad."

The children now tried to climb down from the ice wall where they had clambered up, but they did not succeed. There was ice all about them, as if they had mistaken the direction from which they had come. They turned hither and thither and were not able to extricate themselves from the ice. It was as if they were entangled in it. At last, when the boy followed the direction they had, as he thought, come, they reached more scattered boulders, but they were also larger and more awe-inspiring, as is usually the case at the edge of the glacier. Creeping and clambering, the children managed to issue from the ice. At the rim of the glacier there were enormous boulders, piled in huge heaps, such as the children had never yet seen. Many were covered all over with snow, others showed their slanting undersides, which were very smooth and finely polished as if they had been shoved along on them, many were inclined toward one another like huts and roofs, many lay upon one another like mighty clods. Not far from where the children stood, several boulders were inclined together, and over them lay broad slabs like a roof. The little house they thus formed was open in front, but protected in the rear and on both sides. The interior was dry, as not a single snowflake had drifted in. The children were very glad that they were no longer in the ice but stood on the ground again.

But meanwhile it had been growing dark.

"Sanna," said the boy, "we shall not be able to go down today, because it has become night, and because we might fall or even drop into some pit. We will go in under those stones where it is so dry and warm, and there we will wait. The sun will soon rise again, and then we shall run down from the mountain. Don't cry, please, don't cry, and I shall give you all the things to eat which grandmother has given us to take along."

The little girl did not weep. After they had entered under the stone roof, where they could not only sit comfortably but also stand and walk about, she seated herself close to him and kept very quiet.

"Mother will not be angry," said Conrad. "We shall tell her of the heavy snow that has kept us, and she will say nothing; father will not, either. And if we grow cold, why then we must slap our hands to our bodies as the woodcutters did, and then we shall grow warm again."

"Yes, Conrad," said the girl.

Sanna was not at all so inconsolable because they could not run down the mountain and get home as he might have thought; for the immense exertion, of whose severity the children hardly had any conception, made the very sitting down seem sweet to them, unspeakably sweet, and they did not resist.

But now hunger asserted itself imperiously. Almost at the same time, both took their pieces of bread from their pockets and began to eat. They ate also the other things, such as little pieces of cake, almonds, raisins, and other trifles which grandmother had put into their pockets.

"Sanna, now we must clean the snow from our clothes," said the boy, "so that we shall not become wet."

"Yes, Conrad," replied Sanna.

The children went before their little house. Conrad first brushed off his little sister. He grasped the corners of her coat and shook them, took off the hat he had put on her head, emptied it of snow, and wiped off the snow that remained in it. Then he rid himself as best he could of the snow that lay on him.

At that time it had entirely stopped snowing. The children could not feel one flake descending.

They returned into their stone hut and sat down. Getting up had showed them how tired they really were, and they were glad to sit down again. Conrad laid down the calfskin bag which he had strapped on his shoulders. He took out the cloth in which grandmother had wrapped a pasteboard box and several paper packages and put it about his shoulders for greater warmth. He also took the two pieces of wheat bread out of his wallet and gave Sanna both. The child ate them most eagerly. A part of them, however, she gave back to Conrad, as she saw he was not eating anything. He accepted it and ate it.

From that time on, the children merely sat and looked.

As far as the eye could reach in the twilight there was nothing but snow, whose minute crystals began to scintillate in a strange manner as if they had absorbed the light of day and were emitting it again now.

Night fell with the rapidity usual in high altitudes. Soon it was dark all about, only the snow continued to glimmer faintly. Not only had it stopped snowing but the clouds began to grow thin and to part, for the children saw the gleam of a star. As the snow really emitted light, as it were, and the clouds no longer hung down from the sky, they could see from their cave how the snowy hillocks round about were sharply outlined against the dark sky. The cave was warmer than it had been at any other place during the day, and so the children rested, clinging closely to each other and even forgot to be afraid of the darkness. Soon the stars multiplied, they gleamed forth, now here, now there, until it seemed that there was not a single cloud left in the whole sky.

This was the moment when people in the valleys are accustomed to light their candles. At first, only one is kindled in order to make light in the room, or possibly only a pine splinter; or the fire is burning in the hearth, and all windows of human habitations grow bright and shed luster into the snowy night; but all the more tonight, Christmas eve, when many more lights were kindled in order to shine full upon the presents for the children which lay upon the tables or hung on the trees. Innumerable candles were lit; for in nearly every house, every cottage, every room, there were children for whom the Christ-child had brought presents which had to be shown by the light of candles. The boy had thought one could very quickly come down from the mountain, and yet not a single one of the lights burning that night in the valley shone up to them. They saw nothing but the pale snow and the dark sky; all else was rendered invisible by the distance. At this hour the children in all valleys were receiving their Christmas presents. These two alone sat up there by the edge of the glacier, and the finest presents meant for them on this day lay in little sealed packages in the calfskin bag in the rear of the cave.

The snow clouds had sunk below the mountains on all sides, and a vault entirely dark-blue, almost black, full of densely clustered burning stars, extended above the children; and through the midst of them was woven a shimmering broad milky band which they had, indeed, seen also below in the valley, but never so distinctly. The night was advancing. The children did not know that the stars change their position and move toward the west, else they might have recognized the hour of night by their progress. New stars came and the old ones disappeared, but they believed them to be always the same. It grew somewhat brighter about the children by the radiance of the stars; but they saw no valley, no known places, but everywhere white—only white. Only some dark peak, some dark knob became visible looming up out of the shimmering waste. The moon was nowhere to be seen in the heavens, perhaps it had set early with the sun, or it had not yet risen.

After a long time the boy said, "Sanna, you must not sleep; for do you remember what father said, that if one sleeps in the mountains one will freeze to death, as the old hunter slept and sat four months dead on that stone and no one had known where he was."

"No, I shall not sleep," said the little girl feebly.

Conrad had shaken her by a corner of her coat in order to make her listen to his words.

Then there was silence again.

After a little while the boy felt a soft pressure against his arm, which became ever heavier. Sanna had fallen asleep and had sunk over toward him.

"Sanna, don't sleep, please, don't sleep!" he said.

"No," she mumbled drowsily, "I shall not sleep."

He moved farther away from her in order to make her move; she toppled over and would have continued sleeping on the ground. He took hold of her shoulder and shook her. As he moved a little more, he noticed that he was feeling cold himself and that his arm had grown numb. He was frightened and jumped up. He seized his sister, shook her more vigorously, and said, "Sanna, get up a little; we want to stand up a little so that we shall feel better."

"I am not cold, Conrad," she answered.

"Yes indeed you are, Sanna; get up," he cried.

"My fur jacket is warm," she said.

"I shall help you up," he said.

"No," she replied and lay still.

Then something else occurred to the boy. Grandmother had said, "Just one little mouthful of it will warm the stomach so that one's body will not be cold on the coldest winter day."

He reached for his little calfskin knapsack, opened it, and groped around in it until he found the little flask into which grandmother had put the black coffee for mother. He took away the wrappings from the bottle and with some exertion uncorked it. Then he bent down to Sanna and said, "Here is the coffee that grandmother sends mother. Taste a little of it; it will make you feel warm. Mother would give it to us if she knew what we needed it for."

The little girl, who was by nature inclined to be passive, answered, "I am not cold."

"Just take a little," urged the boy, "and then you may go to sleep again."

This expectation tempted Sanna, and she mastered herself so far that she took a swallow of the liquor. Then the boy drank a little, too.

The exceedingly strong extract took effect at once, and all the more powerfully as the children had never in their life tasted coffee. Instead of going to sleep, Sanna became more active and acknowledged that she was cold, but that she felt nice and warm inside, and that the warmth was already passing into her hands and feet. The children even spoke a while together.

In this fashion they drank ever more of the liquor in spite of its bitter taste, as the effect of it began to die away and roused their nerves to a fever heat which was able to counteract their utter weariness.

It had become midnight, meanwhile. As they still were so young, and because on every Christmas eve in the excess of their joy they went to bed very late and only after being overcome by sleep, they never had heard the midnight tolling, and never the organ of the church when holy mass was being celebrated, although they lived close by. At this moment of the Holy Night, all bells were being rung, the bells of Millsdorf were ringing, the bells of Gschaid were ringing, and behind the mountain there was still another church whose three bells were pealing brightly. In the distant lands outside the valley there were innumerable churches and bells, and all of them were ringing at this moment. From village to village the wave of sound traveled, from one village to another one could hear the peal through the bare branches of the trees; but up to the children there came not a sound. Nothing was heard here, for nothing was to be announced here. In the winding valleys the lights of lanterns gleamed along the mountain slopes, and from many a farm came the sound of the farm bell to rouse the hands. But far less could all this be seen and heard up here. Only the stars gleamed and calmly twinkled and shone.

Even though Conrad kept before his mind the fate of the huntsman who was frozen to death, and even though the children had almost emptied the bottle of black coffee—which necessarily would bring on a corresponding relaxation afterward—they would not have been able to conquer their desire for sleep, whose seductive sweetness outweighs all arguments against it, had not nature itself in all its grandeur assisted them and in its own depths awakened a force which was able to cope with sleep.

In the enormous stillness that reigned about them, a silence in which no snow crystal seemed to move, the children heard three times the bursting of the ice. That which seems the most rigid of all things and yet is most flexible and alive, the glacier, had produced these sounds. Thrice they heard behind them a crash, terrific as if the earth were rent asunder, a sound that ramified through the ice in all directions and seemed to penetrate all its veins. The children remained sitting open-eyed and looked out upon the stars.

Their eyes also were kept busy. As the children sat there, a pale light began to blossom forth on the sky before them among the stars and extended a flat arc through them. It had a greenish tinge which gradually worked downward. But the arc became ever brighter until the stars paled in it. It sent a luminosity also into other regions of the heavens, which shed greenish beams softly and actively among the stars. Then, sheaves of varicolored light stood in burning radiance on the height of the arc like the spikes of a crown. Mildly it flowed through the neighboring regions of the heavens; it flashed and showered softly, and in gentle vibrations extended through vast spaces. Whether now the electric matter of the atmosphere had become so tense by the unexampled fall of snow that it resulted in this silent, splendid efflorescence of light, or whether some other cause of unfathomable nature may be assigned as reason for the phenomenon, however that be, gradually the light grew weaker and weaker. First the sheaves died down, until by unnoticeable degrees it grew ever less and there was nothing in the heavens but the thousands upon thousands of simple stars.

The children never exchanged a word but remained sitting and gazed open-eyed into the heavens.

Nothing particular happened afterward. The stars gleamed and shone and twinkled, only an occasional shooting star traversed them.

At last, after the stars had shone alone for a long time and nothing had been seen of the moon, something else happened. The sky began to grow brighter, slowly but recognizably brighter; its color became visible. The faintest stars disappeared, and the others were not clustered so densely any longer. Finally, the bigger stars also faded away, and the snow on the heights became more distinct. Now one region of the heavens grew yellow, and a strip of cloud floating in it was inflamed to a glowing line. All things became clearly visible, and the remote snow hills assumed sharp outlines.

"Sanna, day is breaking," said the boy.

"Yes, Conrad," answered the girl.

"After it grows just a bit brighter, we shall go out of the cave and run down from the mountain."

It grew brighter. No star was visible any longer, and all things stood out clear in the dawn.

"Well, then, let us go," said the boy.

"Yes, let us go," answered Sanna.

The children rose and tried their limbs, which only now felt their tiredness. Although they had not slept, the morning had reinvigorated them. The boy slung the calfskin bag around his shoulder and fastened Sanna's fur jacket about her. Then he led her out of the cave.

As they had believed it would be an easy matter to run down from the mountain, they had not thought of eating and had not searched the bag to see whether it contained any wheat bread or other eatables.

The sky being clear, Conrad had wanted to look down from the mountain into the valleys in order to recognize the valley of Gschaid and descend to it. But he saw no valleys whatever. He seemed not to stand on any mountain from which one can look down, but in some strange, curious country in which there were only unknown objects. Today they saw awful rocks stand up out of the snow at some distance which they had not seen the day before; they saw the glacier, they saw hummocks and slanting snowfields, and behind these either the sky or the blue peak of some very distant mountain above the edge of the snowy horizon.

At this moment the sun rose.

A gigantic bloody red disk emerged above the white horizon, and immediately the snow about the children blushed as if it had been strewn with millions of roses. The knobs and pinnacles of the mountain cast very long and greenish shadows along the snow.

"Sanna, we shall go on here, until we come to the edge of the mountain and can look down," said the boy.

They went farther into the snow. In the clear night, it had become still drier and easily yielded to their steps. They waded stoutly on. Their limbs became even more elastic and strong as they proceeded, but they came to no edge and could not look down. Snowfield succeeded snowfield, and at the end of each always shone the sky.

They continued nevertheless.

Before they knew it, they were on the glacier again. They did not know how the ice had got there, but they felt the ground smooth under foot, and although there were not such awful boulders as in the moraine where they had passed the night, yet they were aware of the glacier being underneath them. They saw the blocks growing ever larger and coming ever nearer, forcing them to clamber again.

Yet they kept on in the same direction.

Again they were clambering up some boulders; again they stood on the glacier. Only today, in the bright sunlight, could they see what it was like. It was enormously large, and beyond it again black rocks soared aloft. Wave heaved behind wave, as it were; the snowy ice was crushed, raised up, swollen, as if it pressed onward and were flowing toward the children. In the white of it they perceived innumerable advancing wavy blue lines. Between those regions where the icy masses rose up, as if shattered against each other, there were lines like paths, and these were strips of firm ice or places where the blocks of ice had not been screwed up very much. The children followed these paths, as they intended to cross part of the glacier at least in order to get to the edge of the mountain and at last have a glimpse down. They said not a word. The girl followed in the footsteps of the boy. The place where they had meant to cross grew ever broader, it seemed. Giving up their direction, they began to retreat. Where they could not walk they broke with their hands through the masses of snow which often gave way before their eyes, revealing the intense blue of a crevasse where all had been pure white before. But they did not mind this and labored on until they again emerged from the ice somewhere.

"Sanna," said the boy, "we shall not go into the ice again at all, because we cannot make our way in it. And because we cannot look down into our valley anyway, we want to go down from the mountain in a straight line. We must come into some valley, and there we shall tell people that we are from Gschaid and they will show us the way home."

"Yes, Conrad," said the girl.

So they began to descend on the snow in the direction which its slope offered them. The boy led the little girl by her hand. However, after having descended some distance, the slope no longer followed that direction and the snowfield rose again. The children, therefore, changed their direction and descended toward a shallow basin. But there they struck ice again. So they climbed up along the side of the basin in order to seek a way down in some other direction. A slope led them downward, but that gradually became so steep that they could scarcely keep a footing and feared lest they should slide down. So they retraced their steps upward to find some other way down. After having clambered up the snowfield a long time and then continuing along an even ridge, they found it to be as before: either the snow sloped so steeply that they would have fallen, or it ascended so that they feared it would lead to the very peak of the mountain. And thus it continued to be.

Then they had the idea of finding the direction from which they had come and of descending to the red post. As it is not snowing and the sky is bright, thought the boy, we should be able, after all, to see the spot where the post ought to be, and to descend down from it to Gschaid.

The boy told his little sister his thought, and she followed him.

But the way down to the "neck" was not to be found.

However clear the sun shone, however beautifully the snowy heights stood there, and the fields of snow lay there, yet they could not recognize the places over which they had come the day before. Yesterday all had been veiled by the immense snowfall, so they had scarcely seen a couple of feet ahead of them, and then all had been a mingled white and gray. They had seen only the rocks along and between which they had passed; but today they had also seen many rocks and they all resembled those they had seen the day before. Today they left fresh tracks behind them in the snow; yesterday all tracks had been obliterated by the falling snow. Neither could they gather from the aspect of things which way they had to return to the "neck," since all places looked alike. Snow and snow again. But on they marched and hoped to succeed in the end. They avoided the declivities and did not attempt to climb steep slopes.

Today also they frequently stood still to listen; but they heard nothing, not the slightest sound. Neither was anything to be seen excepting the dazzling snow from which emerged, here and there, black peaks and ribs of rock.

At last the boy thought he saw a flame skipping over a faraway snow slope. It bobbed up and dipped down again. Now they saw it, and then again they did not. They remained standing and steadfastly gazed in that direction. The flame kept on skipping up and down and seemed to be approaching, for they saw it growing bigger and skipping more plainly. It did not disappear so often and for so long a time as before. After a while they heard in the still blue air faintly, very faintly, something like the long note of a shepherd's horn. As if from instinct, both children shouted aloud. A little while and they heard the sound again. They shouted again and remained standing on the same spot. The flame also came nearer. The sound was heard for the third time, and this time more plainly. The children answered again by shouting loudly. After some time they also recognized that it was no flame they had seen but a red flag which was being swung. At the same time, the shepherd's horn resounded closer to them, and the children made reply.

"Sanna," cried the boy, "there come people from Gschaid. I know the flag; it is the red flag that the stranger gentleman planted on the peak when he had climbed the Gars with the young hunter, so that the reverend father could see it with his spyglass, and that was to be the sign that they had reached the top, and the stranger gentleman gave him the flag afterward as a present. You were a real small child, then."

"Yes, Conrad."

After a while the children could also see the people near the flag, like little black dots that seemed to move. The call of the horn came again and again, and ever nearer. Each time the children made answer.

Finally they saw on the snow slope opposite them several men with the flag in their midst coast down on their Alpenstocks. When they had come closer, the children recognized them. It was the shepherd Philip with his horn, his two sons, the young hunter, and several men of Gschaid.

"God be blessed," cried Philip, "why here you are. The whole mountain is full of people. Let one of you run down at once to the Sideralp chalet and ring the bell, that they down below may hear that we have found them; and one must climb the Krebsstein and plant the flag there so that they in the valley may see it and fire off the mortars, so that the people searching in the Millsdorf forest may hear it and that they may kindle the smudge fires in Gschaid, and all those on the mountain may come down to the Sideralp chalet. This is a Christmas for you!"

"I shall climb down to the chalet," one said.

"And I shall carry the flag to the Krebsstein," said another.

"And we will get the children down to the Sideralp chalet as well as we can, if God help us," said Philip.

One of Philip's sons made his way downward, and the other went his way with the flag.

The hunter took the little girl by her hand, and the shepherd Philip the boy. The others helped as they could. Thus they started out. They turned this way and that. Now they followed one direction, now they took the opposite course, now they climbed up, now down, always through snow, and the surroundings seemed to remain the same. On very steep inclines they fastened climbing irons to their feet and carried the children. Finally, after a long time, they heard the ringing of a little bell that sounded up to them soft and thin, which was the first sign the lower regions sent to them again. They must really have descended quite far; for now they saw a snowy bluish peak lift up its head to a great height above them. The bell, however, which they had heard was that of the Sideralp chalet, which was being rung because there the meeting was to be. As they proceeded farther they also heard in the still atmosphere the faint report of the mortars which were fired at the sight of the flag; and still later they saw thin columns of smoke rising into the still air.

When they, after a little while, descended a gentle slope, they caught sight of the Sideralp chalet. They approached. In the hut a fire was burning, the mother of the children was there, and with a terrible cry she sank in the snow as she saw her children coming with the hunter.

Then she ran up, looked them all over, wanted to give them something to eat, wanted to warm them, and bed them in the hay that was there; but soon she convinced herself that the children were more stimulated by their rescue than she had thought and only required some warm food and a little rest, both of which they now obtained.

When, after some time of rest, another group of men descended the snow slope while the little bell continued tolling, the children themselves ran out to see who they were. It was the shoemaker, the former mountaineer, with Alpenstock and climbing irons, accompanied by friends and comrades.

"Sebastian, here they are!" cried the woman.

He, however, remained speechless, shaking with emotion, and then ran up to her. Then his lips moved as if he wanted to say something, but he said nothing, caught the children in his embrace, and held them long. Thereupon he turned to his wife, embraced her, and cried, "Sanna, Sanna!"

After a while he picked up his hat, which had fallen on the snow, and stepped among the men as if to speak. But he only said, "Neighbors and friends, I thank you!"

After waiting awhile, until the children had recovered from their excitement, he said, "If we are all together we may start, in God's name."

"We are not all together yet, I believe," said the shepherd Philip, "but those who are still missing will know from the smoke that we have found the children and will go home when they find the chalet empty."

All got ready to depart.

The Sideralp chalet is not so very far from Gschaid, from whose windows one can in summertime very well see the green pasture on which stands the gray hut with its small belfry; but below it there is a perpendicular wall with a descent of many fathoms, which one could climb in summer with the help of climbing irons, but which was not to be scaled in winter. They were, therefore, compelled to go by way of the "neck" in order to get down to Gschaid. On their way they came to the Sider meadow, which is still nearer to Gschaid, so that from it one could see the windows in the village.

As they were crossing these meadows, the bell of the Gschaid church sounded up to them bright and clear, announcing the Holy Transubstantiation.

On account of the general commotion that obtained in Gschaid that morning, the celebration of the high mass had been deferred, as the priest thought the children would soon be found. Finally, however, as still no news came, the holy mass had to be celebrated.

When they heard the bell announcing the Holy Transubstantiation, all those crossing the Sider meadow sank upon their knees in the snow and prayed. When the tolling had ceased, they rose and marched on.

The shoemaker was carrying his little girl for the most part and made her tell him all.

When they were descending toward the forest of the "neck," they saw tracks which, he declared, came not from shoes of his make.

The explanation came soon. Attracted probably by the many voices they heard, another body of men joined them. It was the dyer—ash-gray in the face from fright—descending at the head of his workmen, apprentices, and several men of Millsdorf.

"They climbed over the glacier and the crevasses without knowing it," the shoemaker shouted to his father-in-law.

"There they are. There they are. Praised be the Lord," answered the dyer. "I knew already that they had been on the mountain when your messenger came to us in the night, and we had searched through the whole forest with lanterns and had not found anything. And then, when it dawned, I observed that on the road which leads on the left up toward the snow mountain, on the spot where the post stands, that there some twigs and stalks were broken off, as children like to do on their way, and then I knew they could not get away, because they walked in the hollow and then between the rocks onto the ridge, which is so steep on either side that they could not get down. They just had to ascend. After making this observation, I sent a message to Gschaid, but the woodcutter Michael who carried it told us at his return, when he joined us up there near the ice, that you had found them already, and so we came down again."

"Yes," said Michael, "I told you so because the red flag is hung out on the Krebsstein, and this was the sign agreed upon in Gschaid. And I told you that they all would come down this way, as one cannot climb down the precipice."

"And kneel down and thank God on your knees, my son-in-law," continued the dyer, "that there was no wind. A hundred years will pass before there will be another such fall of snow that will come down straight like wet cords hanging from a pole. If there had been any wind the children would have perished."

"Yes, let us thank God, let us thank God," said the shoemaker.

The dyer, who since the marriage of his daughter had never been in Gschaid, decided to accompany the men to the village.

When they approached the red post where the side road began, they saw the sleigh waiting for them which the shoemaker had ordered there, whatever the outcome. They let mother and children get into it, covered them well up in the rugs and furs provided for them, and let them ride ahead to Gschaid.

The others followed and arrived in Gschaid by afternoon.

Those who still were on the mountain, and had only learned through the smoke that the signal for returning had been given, gradually also found their way into the valley. The last to appear in the evening was the son of the shepherd Philip who had carried the red flag to the Krebsstein and planted it there.

In Gschaid there was also grandmother waiting for them who had driven across the "neck."

"Never, never," she cried, "will I permit the children to cross the 'neck' in winter!"

The children were confused by all this commotion. They received something more to eat and were put to bed then. Late in the evening, when they had recovered somewhat, and some neighbors and friends had assembled in the living room and were talking about the event, their mother came into the bedroom. As she sat by Sanna's bed and caressed her, the little girl said, "Mother, last night, when we sat on the mountain, I saw the holy Christ-child."

"Oh, my dear, darling child," answered her mother. "He sent you some presents, too, and you shall get them right soon."

The pasteboard boxes had been unpacked and the candles lit, and now the door into the living room was opened, and from their bed the children could behold their belated, brightly gleaming, friendly Christmas tree. Notwithstanding their utter fatigue, they wanted to be dressed partly, so that they could go into the room. They received their presents, admired them, and finally fell asleep over them.

In the inn at Gschaid it was more lively than ever this evening. All who had not been to church were there, and the others, too. Each related what he had seen and heard, what he had done or advised, and the experiences and dangers he had gone through. Special stress was laid on how everything could have been done differently and better.

This occurrence made an epoch in the history of Gschaid. It furnished material for conversation for a long time; and for many years to come people will speak about it on bright days when the mountain is seen with special clearness, or when they tell strangers of the memorable events connected with it.

Only from this day on the children were really felt to belong to the village and were not any longer regarded as strangers in it but as natives whom the people had fetched down to them from the mountain.

Their mother, Sanna, also now was a native of Gschaid.

The children, however, will not forget the mountain and will look up to it more attentively when they are in the garden; when, as in the past, the sun is shining beautifully and the linden tree is sending forth its fragrance, when the bees are humming, and the mountain looks down upon them beautifully blue, like the soft sky.

THE CHRISTMAS BANQUET

by Nathaniel Hawthorne

from *Mosses from an Old Manse*

"I have here attempted," said Roderick, unfolding a few sheets of manuscript, as he sat with Rosina and the sculptor in the summerhouse—"I have attempted to seize hold of a personage who glides past me, occasionally, in my walk through life. My former sad experience, as you know, has gifted me with some degree of insight into the gloomy mysteries of the human heart, through which I have wandered like one astray in a dark cavern, with his torch fast flickering to extinction. But this man—this class of men—is a hopeless puzzle."

"Well, but propound him," said the sculptor. "Let us have an idea of him, to begin with."

"Why, indeed," replied Roderick, "he is such a being as I could conceive you to carve out of marble, and some yet unrealized perfection of human science to endow with an exquisite mockery of intellect; but still there lacks the last inestimable touch of a divine Creator. He looks like a man, and, perchance, like a better specimen of man than you ordinarily meet. You might esteem him wise—he is capable of cultivation and refinement, and has at least an external conscience—but the demands that spirit makes upon spirit, are precisely those to which he cannot respond. When, at last, you come close to him, you find him chill and unsubstantial—a mere vapor."

"I believe," said Rosina, "I have a glimmering idea of what you mean."

"Then be thankful," answered her husband, smiling; "but do not anticipate any further illumination from what I am about to read. I have here imagined such a man to be—what, probably, he never is— conscious of the deficiency in his spiritual organization. Methinks the result would be a sense of cold unreality, wherewith he would go shivering through the world, longing to exchange his load of ice for any burthen of real grief that fate could fling upon a human being."

Contenting himself with this preface, Roderick began to read.

In a certain old gentleman's last will and testament, there appeared a bequest, which, as his final thought and deed, was singularly in keeping with a long life of melancholy eccentricity. He devised a considerable sum for establishing a fund, the interest of which was to be expended, annually for ever, in preparing a Christmas Banquet for ten of the most miserable persons that could be found. It seemed not to be the testator's purpose to make these half-a-score of sad hearts merry, but to provide that the stern or fierce expression of human discontent should not be drowned, even for that one holy and joyful day, amid the acclamations of festal gratitude which all Christendom sends up. And he desired, likewise, to perpetuate his own remonstrance against the earthly course of Providence, and his sad and sour dissent from those systems of religion or philosophy which either find sunshine in the world, or draw it down from heaven.

The task of inviting the guests, or of selecting among such as might advance their claims to partake of his dismal hospitality, was confided to the two trustees or stewards of the fund. These gentlemen, like their deceased friend, were sombre humorists, who made it their principal occupation to number the sable threads in the web of human life, and drop all the golden ones out of the reckoning. They performed their present office with integrity and judgment. The aspect of the assembled company, on the day of the first festival, might not, it is true, have satisfied every beholder that these were especially the individuals, chosen forth from all the world, whose griefs were worthy to stand as indicators of the mass of human suffering. Yet, after due consideration, it could not be disputed that here was a variety of hopeless discomfort, which, if it sometimes arose from causes apparently inadequate, was thereby only the shrewder imputation against the nature and mechanism of life.

The arrangements and decorations of the banquet were probably intended to signify that death-in-life which had been the testator's definition of existence. The hall, illuminated by torches, was hung round with curtains of deep and dusky purple, and adorned with branches of cypress and wreaths of artificial flowers, imitative of such as used to be strewn over the dead. A sprig of parsley was laid by every plate. The main reservoir of wine was a sepulchral urn of silver, whence the liquor was distributed around the table in small vases, accurately copied from those that held the tears of ancient mourners. Neither had the stewards—if it were their taste that arranged these details—forgotten the fantasy of the old Egyptians, who seated a skeleton at every festive board, and mocked their own merriment with the imperturbable grin of a death's-head. Such a fearful guest, shrouded in a black mantle, sat now at the head of the table. It was whispered, I know not with what truth, that the testator himself had once walked the visible world with the machinery of that same skeleton, and that it was one of the stipulations of his will, that he should thus be permitted to sit, from year to year, at the banquet which he had instituted. If so, it was perhaps covertly implied that he had cherished no hopes of bliss beyond the grave, to compensate for the evils which he felt or imagined here. And if, in their bewildered conjectures as to the purpose of earthly existence, the banqueters should throw aside the veil, and cast an inquiring glance at this figure of death, as seeking thence the solution otherwise unattainable, the only reply would be a stare of the vacant eye-caverns, and a grin of the skeleton-jaws. Such was the response that the dead man had fancied himself to receive, when he asked of Death to solve the riddle of his life; and it was his desire to repeat it, when the guests of his dismal hospitality should find themselves perplexed with the same question.

"What means that wreath?" asked several of the company, while viewing the decorations of the table.

They alluded to a wreath of cypress, which was held on high by a skeleton-arm, protruding from within the black mantle.

"It is a crown," said one of the stewards, "not for the worthiest, but for the wofullest, when he shall prove his claim to it."

The guest earliest bidden to the festival, was a man of soft and gentle character, who had not energy to struggle against the heavy despondency to which his temperament rendered him liable; and therefore with nothing outwardly to excuse him from happiness, he had spent a life of quiet misery, that made his blood torpid, and weighed upon his breath, and sat like a ponderous night-fiend upon every throb of his unresisting heart. His wretchedness seemed as deep as his original nature, if not identical with it. It was the misfortune of a second guest to cherish within his bosom a diseased heart, which had become so wretchedly sore, that the continual and unavoidable rubs of the world, the blow of an enemy, the careless jostle of a stranger, and even the faithful and loving touch of a friend, alike made ulcers in it. As is the habit of people thus afflicted, he found his chief employment in exhibiting these miserable sores to any who would give themselves the pain of viewing them. A third guest was a hypochondriac, whose imagination wrought necromancy in his outward and inward world, and caused him to see monstrous faces in the household fire, and dragons in the clouds of sun-set, and fiends in the guise of beautiful women, and something ugly or wicked beneath all the pleasant surfaces of nature. His neighbor at table was one who, in his early youth, had trusted mankind too much, and hoped too highly in their behalf, and, meeting with many disappointments, had become desperately soured. For several years back, this misanthrope had employed himself in accumulating motives for hating and despising his race—such as murder, lust, treachery, ingratitude, faithlessness of trusted friends, instinctive vices of children, impurity of women, hidden guilt in men of saintlike aspect—and, in short, all manner of black realities that sought to decorate themselves with outward grace or glory. But, at every atrocious fact that was added to his catalogue— at every increase of the sad knowledge which he spent his life to collect—the native impulses of the poor man's loving and confiding heart made him groan with anguish. Next, with his heavy brow bent downward, there stole into the hall a man naturally earnest and impassioned, who, from his immemorial infancy, had felt the consciousness of a high message to the world, but, essaying to deliver it, had found either no voice or form of speech, or else no ears to listen. Therefore his whole life was a bitter questioning of himself—"Why have not men acknowledged my mission? Am I not a self-deluding fool? What business have I on earth? Where is my grave?" Throughout the festival, he quaffed frequent draughts from the sepulchral urn of wine, hoping thus to quench the celestial fire that tortured his own breast, and could not benefit his race.

Then there entered—having flung away a ticket for a ball—a gay gallant of yesterday, who had found four or five wrinkles in his brow, and more grey hairs than he could well number, on his head. Endowed with sense and feeling, he had nevertheless spent his youth in folly, but had reached at last that dreary point in life, where Folly quits us of her own accord, leaving us to make friends with Wisdom if we can. Thus, cold and desolate, he had come to seek Wisdom at the banquet, and wondered if the skeleton were she. To eke out the company, the stewards had invited a distressed poet from his home in the alms-house, and a melancholy idiot from the street corner. The latter had just the glimmering of sense that was sufficient to make him conscious of a vacancy, which the poor fellow, all his life long, had mistily sought to fill up with intelligence, wandering up and down the streets, and groaning miserably, because his attempts were ineffectual. The only lady in the hall was one who had fallen short of absolute and perfect beauty, merely by the trifling defect of a slight cast in her left eye. But this blemish, minute as it was, so shocked the pure ideal of her soul, rather than her vanity, that she passed her life in solitude, and veiled her countenance even from her own gaze. So the skeleton sat shrouded at one end of the table, and this poor lady at the other.

One other guest remains to be described. He was a young man of smooth brow, fair cheek, and fashionable mien. So far as his exterior developed him, he might much more suitably have found a place at some merry Christmas table, than have been numbered among the blighted, fate-stricken, fancy-tortured set of ill-starred banqueters. Murmurs arose among the guests, as they noted the glance of general scrutiny which the intruder threw over his companions. What had he to do among them? Why did not the skeleton of the dead founder of the feast unbend its rattling joints, arise, and motion the unwelcome stranger from the board?

"Shameful!" said the morbid man, while a new ulcer broke out in his heart. "He comes to mock us!—we shall be the jest of his tavern friends!—he will make a farce of our miseries, and bring it out upon the stage!"

"Oh, never mind him!" said the hypochondriac, smiling sourly. "He shall feast from yonder tureen of viper soup; and if there is a fricassee of scorpions on the table, pray let him have his share of it.

For the dessert, he shall taste the apples of Sodom. Then, if he like our Christmas fare, let him return again next year!"

"Trouble him not," murmured the melancholy man, with gentleness. "What matters it whether the consciousness of misery comes a few years sooner or later? If this youth deem himself happy now, yet let him sit with us, for the sake of the wretchedness to come."

The poor idiot approached the young man, with that mournful aspect of vacant inquiry which his face continually wore, and which caused people to say that he was always in search of his missing wits. After no little examination, he touched the stranger's hand, but immediately drew back his own, shaking his head and shivering.

"Cold, cold, cold!" muttered the idiot.

The young man shivered too—and smiled.

"Gentlemen—and you, madam," said one of the stewards of the festival, "do not conceive so ill, either of our caution or judgment, as to imagine that we have admitted this young stranger—Gervayse Hastings by name—without a full investigation and thoughtful balance of his claims. Trust me, not a guest at the table is better entitled to his seat."

The steward's guarantee was perforce satisfactory. The company, therefore, took their places, and addressed themselves to the serious business of the feast, but were soon disturbed by the hypochondriac, who thrust back his chair, complaining that a dish of stewed toads and vipers was set before him, and that there was green ditch-water in his cup of wine. This mistake being amended, he quietly resumed his seat. The wine, as it flowed freely from the sepulchral urn, seemed to come imbued with all gloomy inspirations; so that its influence was not to cheer, but either to sink the revellers into a deeper melancholy, or elevate their spirits to an enthusiasm of wretchedness. The conversation was various. They told sad stories about people who might have been worthy guests at such a festival as the present. They talked of grisly incidents in human history; of strange crimes, which, if truly considered, were but convulsions of agony; of some lives that had been altogether wretched, and of others, which, bearing a general semblance of happiness, had yet been deformed, sooner or later, by misfortune, as by the intrusion of a grim face at a banquet; of death-bed scenes, and what dark intimations might be gathered from the words of dying men; of suicide, and whether the more eligible mode were by halter, knife, poison, drowning, gradual starvation, or the fumes of charcoal. The majority of the guests, as is the custom with people thoroughly and profoundly sick at heart, were anxious to make their own woes the theme of discussion, and prove themselves most excellent in anguish. The misanthropist went deep into the philosophy of evil, and wandered about in the darkness, with now and then a gleam of discolored light hovering on ghastly shapes and horrid scenery. Many a miserable thought, such as men have stumbled upon from age to age, did he now rake up again, and gloat over it as an inestimable gem, a diamond, a treasure far preferable to those bright, spiritual revelations of a better world, which are like precious stones from heaven's pavement. And then, amid his lore of wretchedness, he hid his face and wept.

It was a festival at which the woful man of Uz might suitably have been a guest, together with all, in each succeeding age, who have tasted deepest of the bitterness of life. And be it said, too, that every son or daughter of woman, however favored with happy fortune, might at one sad moment or another, have claimed the privilege of a stricken heart, to sit down at this table. But, throughout the feast, it was remarked that the young stranger, Gervayse Hastings, was unsuccessful in his attempts to catch its pervading spirit. At any deep, strong thought that found utterance, and which was torn out, as it were, from the saddest recesses of human consciousness, he looked mystified and bewildered; even more than the poor idiot, who seemed to grasp at such things with his earnest heart, and thus occasionally to comprehend them. The young man's conversation was of a colder and lighter kind, often brilliant, but lacking the powerful characteristics of a nature that had been developed by suffering.

"Sir," said the misanthropist, bluntly, in reply to some observation by Gervayse Hastings, "pray do not address me again. We have no right to talk together. Our minds have nothing in common. By what claim you appear at this banquet, I cannot guess; but methinks, to a man who could say what you have just now said, my companions and myself must seem no more than shadows, flickering on the wall. And precisely such a shadow are you to us!"

The young man smiled and bowed, but drawing himself back in his chair, he buttoned his coat over his breast, as if the banqueting-hall were growing chill. Again the idiot fixed his melancholy stare upon the youth, and murmured, "Cold! cold! cold!"

The banquet drew to its conclusion, and the guests departed. Scarcely had they stepped across the threshold of the hall, when the scene that had there passed seemed like the vision of a sick fancy, or an exhalation from a stagnant heart. Now and then, however, during the year that ensued, these melancholy people caught glimpses of one another, transient, indeed, but enough to prove that they walked the earth with the ordinary allotment of reality. Sometimes, a pair of them came face to face, while stealing through the evening twilight, enveloped in their sable cloaks. Sometimes, they casually met in church-yards. Once, also, it happened, that two of the dismal banqueters mutually started, at recognizing each other in the noon-day sunshine of a crowded street, stalking there like ghosts astray. Doubtless, they wondered why the skeleton did not come abroad at noonday, too!

But, whenever the necessity of their affairs compelled these Christmas guests into the bustling world, they were sure to encounter the young man, who had so unaccountably been admitted to the festival. They saw him among the gay and fortunate; they caught the sunny sparkle of his eye; they heard the light and careless tones of his voice—and muttered to themselves, with such indignation as only the aristocracy of wretchedness could kindle, "The traitor! The vile impostor! Providence, in its own good time, may give him a right to feast among us!" But the young man's unabashed eye dwelt upon their gloomy figures, as they passed him, seeming to say, perchance with somewhat of a sneer, "First, know my secret; then, measure your claims with mine!"

The step of Time stole onward, and soon brought merry Christmas round again, with glad and solemn worship in the churches, and sports, games, festivals, and everywhere the bright face of Joy beside the household fire. Again, likewise, the hall, with its curtains of dusky purple, was illuminated by the death-torches, gleaming on the sepulchral decorations of the banquet. The veiled skeleton sat in state, lifting the cypress-wreath above its head, as the guerdon of some guest, illustrious in the qualifications which there claimed precedence. As the stewards deemed the world inexhaustible in misery, and were desirous of recognizing it in all its forms, they had not seen fit to reassemble the company of the former year. New faces now threw their gloom across the table.

There was a man of nice conscience, who bore a blood-stain in his heart—the death of a fellow-creature—which, for his more exquisite torture, had chanced with such a peculiarity of circumstances, that he could not absolutely determine whether his will had entered into the deed or not. Therefore, his whole life was spent in the agony of an inward trial for murder, with a continual sifting of the details of his terrible calamity, until his mind had no longer any thought, nor his soul any emotion, disconnected with it. There was a mother, too—a mother once, but a desolation now—who, many years before, had gone out on a pleasure-party, and, returning, found her infant smothered in its little bed. And ever since she has been tortured with the fantasy, that her buried baby lay smothering in its coffin. Then there was an aged lady, who had lived from time immemorial with a constant tremor quivering through her frame. It was terrible to discern her dark shadow tremulous upon the wall; her lips, likewise, were tremulous; and the expression of her eye seemed to indicate that her soul was trembling too. Owing to the bewilderment and confusion which made almost a chaos of her intellect, it was impossible to discover what dire misfortune had thus shaken her nature to its depths; so that the stewards had admitted her to the table, not from any acquaintance with her history, but on the safe testimony of her miserable aspect. Some surprise was expressed at the presence of a bluff, red-faced gentleman, a certain Mr. Smith, who had evidently the fat of many a rich feast within him, and the habitual twinkle of whose eye betrayed a disposition to break forth into uproarious laughter, for little cause or none. It turned out, however, that, with the best possible flow of spirits, our poor friend was afflicted with a physical disease of the heart, which threatened instant death on the slightest cachinnatory indulgence, or even that titillation of the bodily frame, produced by merry thoughts. In this dilemma, he had sought admittance to the banquet, on the ostensible plea of his irksome and miserable state, but, in reality, with the hope of imbibing a life-preserving melancholy.

A married couple had been invited, from a motive of bitter humor; it being well understood, that they rendered each other unutterably miserable whenever they chanced to meet, and therefore must necessarily be fit associates at the festival. In contrast with these, was another couple, still unmarried, who had interchanged their hearts in early life, but had been divided by circumstances as impalpable as morning mist, and kept apart so long, that their spirits now found it impossible to meet. Therefore, yearning for communion, yet shrinking from one another, and choosing none beside, they felt themselves companionless in life, and looked upon eternity as a boundless desert. Next to the skeleton sat a mere son of earth—a hunter of the Exchange—a gatherer of shining dust—a man whose life's record was in his ledger, and whose soul's prison-house, the vaults of the bank where he kept his deposits. This person had been greatly perplexed at his invitation, deeming himself one of the most fortunate men in the city; but the stewards persisted in demanding his presence, assuring him that he had no conception how miserable he was.

And now appeared a figure, which we must acknowledge as our acquaintance of the former festival. It was Gervayse Hastings, whose presence had then caused so much question and criticism, and who now took his place with the composure of one whose claims were satisfactory to himself, and must needs be allowed by others. Yet his easy and unruffled face betrayed no sorrow. The well-skilled beholders gazed a moment into his eyes, and shook their heads, to miss the unuttered sympathy—the countersign, never to be falsified—of those whose hearts are cavern-mouths, through which they descend into a region of illimitable woe, and recognize other wanderers there.

"Who is this youth?" asked the man with a blood-stain on his conscience. "Surely he has never gone down into the depths! I know all the aspects of those who have passed through the dark valley. By what right is he among us?"

"Ah, it is a sinful thing to come hither without a sorrow," murmured the aged lady, in accents that partook of the eternal tremor which pervaded her whole being. "Depart, young man! Your soul has never been shaken; and therefore I tremble so much the more to look at you."

"His soul shaken! No; I'll answer for it," said bluff Mr. Smith, pressing his hand upon his heart, and making himself as melancholy as he could, for fear of a fatal explosion of laughter. "I know the lad well; he has as fair prospects as any young man about town, and has no more right among us, miserable creatures, than the child unborn. He never was miserable, and probably never will be!"

"Our honored guests," interposed the stewards, "pray have patience with us, and believe, at least, that our deep veneration for the sacredness of this solemnity would preclude any wilful violation of it. Receive this young man to your table. It may not be too much to say, that no guest here would exchange his own heart for the one that beats within that youthful bosom!"

"I'd call it a bargain, and gladly too," muttered Mr. Smith with a perplexing mixture of sadness and mirthful conceit. "A plague upon their nonsense! My own heart is the only really miserable one in the company—it will certainly be the death of me at last!"

Nevertheless, as on the former occasion, the judgment of the stewards being without appeal, the company sat down. The obnoxious guest made no more attempt to obtrude his conversation on those about him, but appeared to listen to the table-talk with peculiar assiduity, as if some inestimable secret, otherwise beyond his reach, might be conveyed in a casual word. And, in truth, to those who could understand and value it, there was rich matter in the upgushings and outpourings of these initiated souls, to whom sorrow had been a talisman, admitting them into spiritual depths which no other spell can open. Sometimes, out of the midst of densest gloom, there flashed a momentary radiance, pure as crystal, bright as the flame of stars, and shedding such a glow upon the mysteries of life, that the guests were ready to exclaim, "Surely the riddle is on the point of being solved!" At such illuminated intervals, the saddest mourners felt it to be revealed, that mortal griefs are but shadowy and external; no more than the sable robes, voluminously shrouding a certain divine reality, and thus indicating what might otherwise be altogether invisible to mortal eye.

"Just now," remarked the trembling old woman, "I seemed to see beyond the outside. And then my everlasting tremor passed away!"

"Would that I could dwell always in these momentary gleams of light!" said the man of stricken conscience. "Then the blood-stain in my heart would be washed clean away."

This strain of conversation appeared so unintelligibly absurd to good Mr. Smith, that he burst into precisely the fit of laughter which his physicians had warned him against, as likely to prove instantaneously fatal. In effect, he fell back in his chair, a corpse with a broad grin upon his face; while his ghost, perchance, remained beside it, bewildered at its unpremeditated exit. This catastrophe, of course, broke up the festival.

"How is this? You do not tremble?" observed the tremulous old woman to Gervayse Hastings, who was gazing at the dead man with singular intentness. "Is it not awful to see him so suddenly vanish out of the midst of life—this man of flesh and blood, whose earthly nature was so warm and strong? There is a never-ending tremor in my soul; but it trembles afresh at this! And you are calm!"

"Would that he could teach me somewhat!" said Gervayse Hastings, drawing a long breath. "Men pass before me like shadows on the wall—their actions, passions, feelings, are flickerings of the light

—and then they vanish! Neither the corpse, nor yonder skeleton, nor this old woman's everlasting tremor, can give me what I seek."

And then the company departed.

We cannot linger to narrate, in such detail, more circumstances of these singular festivals, which, in accordance with the founder's will, continued to be kept with the regularity of an established institution. In process of time, the stewards adopted the custom of inviting, from far and near, those individuals whose misfortunes were prominent above other men's, and whose mental and moral development might, therefore, be supposed to possess a corresponding interest. The exiled noble of the French Revolution, and the broken soldier of the Empire, were alike represented at the table. Fallen monarchs, wandering about the earth, have found places at that forlorn and miserable feast. The statesman, when his party flung him off, might, if he chose it, be once more a great man for the space of a single banquet. Aaron Burr's name appears on the record, at a period when his ruin—the profoundest and most striking, with more of moral circumstance in it than that of almost any other man—was complete, in his lonely age. Stephen Girard, when his wealth weighed upon him like a mountain, once sought admittance of his own accord. It is not probable, however, that these men had any lesson to teach in the lore of discontent and misery, which might not equally well have been studied in the common walks of life. Illustrious unfortunates attract a wider sympathy, not because their griefs are more intense, but because, being set on lofty pedestals, they the better serve mankind as instances and bywords of calamity.

It concerns our present purpose to say that, at each successive festival, Gervayse Hastings showed his face, gradually changing from the smooth beauty of his youth to the thoughtful comeliness of manhood, and thence to the bald, impressive dignity of age. He was the only individual invariably present. Yet, on every occasion, there were murmurs, both from those who knew his character and position, and from them whose hearts shrank back, as denying his companionship in their mystic fraternity.

"Who is this impassive man?" had been asked a hundred times. "Has he suffered? Has he sinned? There are no traces of either. Then wherefore is he here?"

"You must inquire of the stewards, or of himself," was the constant reply. "We seem to know him well, here in our city, and know nothing of him but what is creditable and fortunate. Yet hither he comes, year after year, to this gloomy banquet, and sits among the guests like a marble statue. Ask yonder skeleton—perhaps that may solve the riddle!"

It was, in truth, a wonder. The life of Gervayse Hastings was not merely a prosperous, but a brilliant one. Everything had gone well with him. He was wealthy, far beyond the expenditure that was required by habits of magnificence, a taste of rare purity and cultivation, a love of travel, a scholar's instinct to collect a splendid library, and, moreover, what seemed a munificent liberality to the distressed. He had sought domestic happiness, and not vainly, if a lovely and tender wife, and children of fair promise, could insure it. He had, besides, ascended above the limit which separates the obscure from the distinguished, and had won a stainless reputation in affairs of the widest public importance. Not that he was a popular character, or had within him the mysterious attributes which are essential to that species of success. To the public, he was a cold abstraction, wholly destitute of those rich hues of personality, that living warmth, and the peculiar faculty of stamping his own heart's impression on a multitude of hearts, by which the people recognize their favorites. And it must be owned that, after his most intimate associates had done their best to know him thoroughly, and love him warmly, they were startled to find how little hold he had upon their affections. They approved—they admired—but still, in those moments when the human spirit most craves reality, they shrank back from Gervayse Hastings, as powerless to give them what they sought. It was the feeling of distrustful regret, with which we should draw back the hand, after extending it, in an illusive twilight, to grasp the hand of a shadow upon the wall.

As the superficial fervency of youth decayed, this peculiar effect of Gervayse Hastings' character grew more perceptible. His children, when he extended his arms, came coldly to his knees, but never climbed them of their own accord. His wife wept secretly, and almost adjudged herself a criminal, because she shivered in the chill of his bosom. He, too, occasionally appeared not unconscious of the chillness of his moral atmosphere, and willing, if it might be so, to warm himself at a kindly fire. But age stole onward, and benumbed him more and more. As the hoar-frost began to gather on him, his wife went to her grave, and was doubtless warmer there; his children either died, or were scattered to different homes of their own; and old Gervayse Hastings, unscathed by grief—alone, but needing no companionship—continued his steady walk through life, and still, on every

Christmas-day, attended at the dismal banquet. His privilege as a guest had become prescriptive now. Had he claimed the head of the table, even the skeleton would have been ejected from its seat.

Finally, at the merry Christmas-tide, when he had numbered fourscore years complete, this pale, high-browed, marble-featured old man once more entered the long-frequented hall, with the same impassive aspect that had called forth so much dissatisfied remark at his first attendance. Time, except in matters merely external, had done nothing for him, either of good or evil. As he took his place he threw a calm, inquiring glance around the table, as if to ascertain whether any guest had yet appeared, after so many unsuccessful banquets, who might impart to him the mystery—the deep, warm secret—the life within the life—which, whether manifested in joy or sorrow, is what gives substance to a world of shadows.

"My friends," said Gervayse Hastings, assuming a position which his long conversance with the festival caused to appear natural, "you are welcome! I drink to you in this cup of sepulchral wine."

The guests replied courteously, but still in a manner that proved them unable to receive the old man as a member of their sad fraternity. It may be well to give the reader an idea of the present company at the banquet.

One was formerly a clergyman, enthusiastic in his profession, and apparently of the genuine dynasty of those old puritan divines, whose faith in their calling, and stern exercise of it, had placed them among the mighty of the earth. But yielding to the speculative tendency of the age, he had gone astray from the firm foundation of an ancient faith, and wandered into a cloud region, where everything was misty and deceptive, ever mocking him with a semblance of reality, but still dissolving when he flung himself upon it for support and rest. His instinct and early training demanded something steadfast; but, looking forward, he beheld vapors piled on vapors, and behind him, an impassable gulf between the man of yesterday and to-day; on the borders of which he paced to and fro, sometimes wringing his hands in agony, and often making his own woe a theme of scornful merriment. This surely was a miserable man. Next, there was a theorist—one of a numerous tribe, although he deemed himself unique since the creation—a theorist, who had conceived a plan by which all the wretchedness of earth, moral and physical, might be done away, and the bliss of the millennium at once accomplished. But, the incredulity of mankind debarring him from action, he was smitten with as much grief as if the whole mass of woe which he was denied the opportunity to remedy, were crowded into his own bosom. A plain old man in black attracted much of the company's notice, on the supposition that he was no other than Father Miller, who, it seemed, had given himself up to despair at the tedious delay of the final conflagration. Then there was a man distinguished for native pride and obstinacy, who, a little while before, had possessed immense wealth, and held the control of a vast moneyed interest, which he had wielded in the same spirit as a despotic monarch would wield the power of his empire, carrying on a tremendous moral warfare, the roar and tremor of which was felt at every fireside in the land. At length came a crushing ruin— a total overthrow of fortune, power, and character—the effect of which on his imperious, and, in many respects, noble and lofty nature, might have entitled him to a place, not merely at our festival, but among the peers of Pandemonium.

There was a modern philanthropist, who had become so deeply sensible of the calamities of thousands and millions of his fellow creatures, and of the impracticableness of any general measures for their relief, that he had no heart to do what little good lay immediately within his power, but contented himself with being miserable for sympathy. Near him sat a gentleman in a predicament hitherto unprecedented, but of which the present epoch, probably, affords numerous examples. Ever since he was of capacity to read a newspaper, this person had prided himself on his consistent adherence to one political party, but, in the confusion of these latter days, had got bewildered, and knew not whereabouts his party was. This wretched condition, so morally desolate and disheartening to a man who has long accustomed himself to merge his individuality in the mass of a great body, can only be conceived by such as have experienced it. His next companion was a popular orator who had lost his voice, and—as it was pretty much all that he had to lose—had fallen into a state of hopeless melancholy. The table was likewise graced by two of the gentler sex— one, a half-starved, consumptive seamstress, the representative of thousands just as wretched; the other, a woman of unemployed energy, who found herself in the world with nothing to achieve, nothing to enjoy, and nothing even to suffer. She had, therefore, driven herself to the verge of madness by dark broodings over the wrongs of her sex, and its exclusion from a proper field of action. The roll of guests being thus complete, a side-table had been set for three or four disappointed office-seekers, with hearts as sick as death, whom the stewards had admitted, partly because their calamities really entitled them to entrance here, and partly that they were in especial need of a good dinner. There was likewise a homeless dog, with his tail between his legs, licking up the crumbs and gnawing the fragments of the feast —such a melancholy cur as one sometimes sees about the streets, without a master, and willing to follow the first that will accept his service.

In their own way, these were as wretched a set of people as ever had assembled at the festival. There they sat, with the veiled skeleton of the founder, holding aloft the cypress wreath, at one end of the table; and at the other, wrapt in furs, the withered figure of Gervayse Hastings, stately, calm and cold, impressing the company with awe, yet so little interesting their sympathy, that he might have vanished into thin air, without their once exclaiming, "Whither is he gone?"

"Sir," said the philanthropist, addressing the old man, "you have been so long a guest at this annual festival, and have thus been conversant with so many varieties of human affliction, that, not improbably, you have thence derived some great and important lessons. How blessed were your lot, could you reveal a secret by which all this mass of woe might be removed!"

"I know of but one misfortune," answered Gervayse Hastings, quietly, "and that is my own."

"Your own!" rejoined the philanthropist. "And, looking back on your serene and prosperous life, how can you claim to be the sole unfortunate of the human race?"

"You will not understand it," replied Gervayse Hastings feebly, and with a singular inefficiency of pronunciation, and sometimes putting one word for another. "None have understood it—not even those who experience the like. It is a chilliness—a want of earnestness—a feeling as if what should be my heart were a thing of vapor—a haunting perception of unreality! Thus seeming to possess all that other men have —all that men aim at—I have really possessed nothing, neither joy nor griefs. All things—all persons—as was truly said to me at this table long and long ago—have been like shadows flickering on the wall. It was so with my wife and children—with those who seemed my friends: it is so with yourselves, whom I see now before me. Neither have I myself any real existence, but am a shadow like the rest!"

"And how is it with your views of a future life?" inquired the speculative clergyman.

"Worse than with you," said the old man, in a hollow and feeble tone; "for I cannot conceive it earnestly enough to feel either hope or fear. Mine—mine is the wretchedness! This cold heart—this unreal life! Ah! it grows colder still."

It so chanced, that at this juncture the decayed ligaments of the skeleton gave way, and the dry bones fell together in a heap, thus causing the dusty wreath of cypress to drop upon the table. The attention of the company being thus diverted, for a single instant, from Gervayse Hastings, they perceived, on turning again towards him, that the old man had undergone a change. His shadow had ceased to flicker on the wall.

"Well, Rosina, what is your criticism?" asked Roderick, as he rolled up the manuscript.

"Frankly, your success is by no means complete," replied she. "It is true, I have an idea of the character you endeavor to describe; but it is rather by dint of my own thought than your expression."

"That is unavoidable," observed the sculptor, "because the characteristics are all negative. If Gervayse Hastings could have imbibed one human grief at the gloomy banquet, the task of describing him would have been infinitely easier. Of such persons—and we do meet with these moral monsters now and then—it is difficult to conceive how they came to exist here, or what there is in them capable of existence hereafter. They seem to be on the outside of everything; and nothing wearies the soul more than an attempt to comprehend them within its grasp."

Biographical Notes

HANS CHRISTIAN ANDERSEN (1805–1875), born into poverty in Odense, Denmark, went to Copenhagen at the age of fourteen. He tried being an actor but without success. Turning to writing, in 1829 he wrote a fantasy, followed a year later by a collection of poems. His first novel, *Improvisatoren* (1835), finally brought him some critical attention, but it was with the publication of his first book of fairy tales that same year that he hit upon the form that was to bring him fame. Similar volumes followed almost annually. Among his best-known tales are "The Ugly Duckling," "The Brave Tin Soldier," "The Little Mermaid," and "The Red Shoes." His autobiography, *The Story of My Life* (1855), was translated into English in 1871.

MARY AUSTIN (1868–1934) was born in Carlinville, Illinois, and graduated from Blackburn College in 1888. She is primarily noted for her realistic renderings of Indian and Spanish cultures in the United States. These works were the outgrowth of her long residence in California and Sante Fe, New Mexico, resulting in her conviction that an important culture existed there. Her works include *The Land of Little Rain* (1903); the play *The Arrow Maker* (1911); a chapter on aboriginal literature in *The Cambridge History of American Literature*; a study of Amerindian poetry, *The American Rhythm* (1923); and *The Children Sing in the Far West* (1928). *Earth Horizon* (1932) is an autobiographical work.

JAMES M. BARRIE (1860–1937), novelist and playwright, was born in Scotland. As a young man he wrote for newspapers in Nottingham and in London. His third published book, *The Little Minister* (1891), firmly established him as a successful novelist, and the book's subsequent dramatization led the way to a career as a playwright. Although he wrote several more novels, after 1902 his output was almost entirely dramatic. Some of his most important full-length plays are *Quality Street* (1901), *The Admirable Crichton* (1902), *Peter Pan* (1904), *Alice-Sit-by-the-Fire* (1905), *What Every Woman Knows* (1908), and *Dear Brutus* (1917). His one-act play *The Twelve-Pound Look* (1911) is also highly regarded.

L. FRANK BAUM (1856–1919) was born in Chittenango, New York. As a young man he did editorial work for newspapers and magazines in the midwest. It was his need for a higher income that made him turn to writing children's stories. He became famous as the author of the Oz books, of which he wrote fourteen in all. The first one was *The Wonderful Wizard of Oz* (1900), and it provided the book for a most successful musical comedy in 1902. In 1939, twenty years after Baum's death at the age of sixty-three, it was adapted into the well-beloved film starring Judy Garland and Bert Lahr.

FRANÇOIS COPPÉE (1842–1908) was a French poet and dramatist. A member of the poets' group called the Parnassians, he first attracted notice with *Le Passant* (1869; English translation, 1881), a one-act verse play staged by Sarah Bernhardt. His poetry, concerned mostly with the problems of the underprivileged classes, includes *Le Reliquaire* (1866), *Intimités* (1868), *Les Humbles* (1872), and *La Bonne Souffrance* (1898). Two political dramas, *Severo Torelli* (1883) and *Pour la Couronne* (1895), received great acclaim. He was elected to the French Academy in 1884, when he was only forty-two years old.

ALPHONSE DAUDET (1840–1897) was born in Nîmes, France. At the early age of sixteen he taught in a school at Cévennes. Later, after he went to Paris, he published a slim volume of verse, *Les Amoureuses* (1857). It was followed by the highly successful *Lettres de Mon Moulin* (1866), a collection of short stories. Other works include *Tartarin de Tarascon* (1872), *Le Nabab* (1877), *Sappho* (1884), *Trente Ans de Paris* (1888) and *Souvenirs d'un Homme de Lettres* (1888).

CHARLES DICKENS (1812–1870), born in Portsmouth, England, suffered a childhood of humiliations and hardships similar to those of the hero of *David Copperfield*. Dickens began his literary career as a journalist, and most of his great novels were first published in serial form in various magazines. At the age of twenty-four he achieved both fame and financial success with the publication of *The Pickwick Papers* (1836). He continued throughout his lifetime to produce a remarkable number of important works, including *Oliver Twist* (1837), *A Christmas Carol* (1843), *Dombey and Son* (1848), *David Copperfield* (1849), *Bleak House* (1852), *A Tale of Two Cities* (1859), and *Great Expectations* (1860).

FEODOR DOSTOYEVSKY (1821–1881), one of Russia's greatest novelists, was born in Moscow. His first work, *Poor Folk* (1846), a deep psychological study of poor, unhappy people, won critical acclaim for its innovative nature. He was later involved in a political conspiracy and sentenced to death. Reprieved by the Czar, he spent four years at hard labor in Siberia, followed by four years as a common soldier. *The House of the Dead* (1862) describes these bitter experiences. Always poverty-stricken, he barely escaped debtors' prison many times. After *Notes from Underground* (1864), an extraordinary study of a spiritual and intellectual misfit, he again won popular acclaim with the great novel *Crime and Punishment* (1866). But his generosity and poor handling of money kept him virtually destitute. While living abroad, he wrote *The Idiot* (1868) and *The Possessed* (1871). After returning to Russia, he completed *The Brothers Karamazov* (1880) one year before his death. His novels deal with complex characters fiercely struggling between good and evil in an effort to achieve salvation through suffering.

ANTOINE GUSTAVE DROZ (1832–1895) was born in Paris, the son of a noted sculptor, Jules Antoine Droz. Young Droz devoted himself to painting from 1857 to 1865. Then he turned to journalism and contributed to the *Revue des Deux Mondes* and *La Vie Parisienne*, assuring the latter's success with a series of light, sentimental sketches on the intimacies of family life, entitled *Monsieur, Madame et Bébé*. These were published in book form in 1866, followed by a similar series, *Entre Nous* (1867). His novels *Autour d'une Source* (1869) and *Un Paquet de Lettres* (1870) were more ambitious. Later novels include *Tristesses et Sourires* (1884) and *L'Enfant* (1885).

MAXIME DU CAMP (1822–1894) was born and educated in Paris. He is remembered largely for his association with Flaubert, whom he accompanied on a trip to the Near East, and by his *Souvenirs Littéraires* (1882–83). He also edited the *Revue des Deux Mondes* and wrote books on travel, history, art, and some novels: *Souvenirs et Paysages d'Orient* (1848), *Les Six Aventures* (1857), *Les Buveurs de Cendres* (1866), *Les Convulsions de Paris* (1878–79) is a narrative of the insurrections of 1871. He is noted more for his brilliance as a journalist than as a novelist.

EUGENE FIELD (1850–1895), poet and journalist, was born in St. Louis. After attending various colleges he went abroad for one year. Back in the United States in 1873, he worked as a journalist for various newspapers, finally joining the Chicago *Daily News* in 1883. Here he wrote a column called "Sharps and Flats," which became nationally famous. Field's poems of childhood include "Little Boy Blue" and "Wynken, Blynken, and Nod." His books include *A Little Book of Western Verse* (1889) and *With Trumpet and Drum* (1892).

JOHN FOX, JR. (1862–1919) was born in Paris, Kentucky. He graduated from Harvard in 1883 as the youngest of his class. For brief periods he was a journalist, then he went into the mining business in Big Stone Gap, Virginia. His short stories and novels were a direct outgrowth of his contact with, and accurate perception of, the then little-known mountaineers of Kentucky, Tennessee, and West Virginia. *The Little Shepherd of Kingdom Come* (1903) and *The Trail of the Lonesome Pine* (1908) made his name a household word throughout America. He died at fifty-seven from pneumonia contracted on a fishing trip in the mountains.

MARY WILKINS FREEMAN (1852–1930), American novelist and short story writer, was born in Randolph, Massachusetts. She lived there or in Brattleboro, Vermont, until her marriage to Dr. Charles Freeman, after which she moved to Metuchen, New Jersey. She is mainly known for her stories of rural New England, which are honest, realistic depictions of an austere and frustrating way of life. The best of these are collected in *A Humble Romance and Other Stories* (1887) and *A New England Nun and Other Stories* (1891). Other works include volumes of stories, a play, and several novels.

MAXIM GORKY (1868–1936) is a pen name meaning "Maxim the bitter one." Gorky was born Alexei Maximovich Peshkov in Nizhni Novgorod, Russia. Beginning his literary career at the age of twenty-four, he was noted for realistic writings depicting the lives of the poor and downtrodden. The revolutionary nature of his works as well as his political activities led to his exile. He returned to support the Bolshevik revolution, and he became the central figure of Soviet literature, blending romanticism with realistic observation. Some of his most noted works include the play *The Lower Depths* (1903), the novel *Mother* (1907), and three widely read autobiographical novels: *Childhood* (1913), *In the World* (1916), and *My Universities* (1923).

JOEL CHANDLER HARRIS (1848–1908) was born in Eatonton, Georgia. He is famous for his Uncle Remus stories, which were first published in the Atlanta *Constitution*. His first collection, *Uncle Remus: His Songs and His Sayings* (1881), received international acclaim, especially the Tar Baby story. Demand for more Uncle Remus stories resulted in *Nights with Uncle Remus* (1883), and the series continued to appear for many years thereafter. Harris was the first author to give literary form to Negro folklore, and his stories accurately represent the Negro dialect of middle Georgia. His depictions of the white Georgia cracker are equally vivid, in works such as *Mingo and Other Sketches in Black and White* (1884) and *Free Joe and Other Georgian Sketches* (1887). His home in Atlanta is now an Uncle Remus memorial.

BRET HARTE (1836–1902) was famous for his colorful stories of the California gold-rush days. Born in Albany, New York, he moved to California at the age of eighteen and in 1859 joined a small newspaper, the *Northern Californian*. After writing an editorial criticizing white Californians for their part in an Indian massacre he was forced to resign. From 1868 until 1871 Harte then served as editor of the *Overland Monthly*, a San Francisco magazine for which he wrote many short stories, including "The Luck of Roaring Camp" (1868) and "The Outcasts of Poker Flat" (1869), which won him a nationwide reputation. These later appeared in his collection, *The Luck of Roaring Camp and Other Sketches* (1870). His reputation ultimately declined after he moved back East in 1871. Discouraged, he went abroad in 1878, spending seven years as a United States diplomat in Germany and Scotland. He lived in London from 1885 until his death.

NATHANIEL HAWTHORNE (1804–1864) was born in Salem, Massachusetts. He attended Bowdoin College, where he became a friend of future United States President Franklin Pierce. Hawthorne later lived in Boston and Concord, but returned to Salem in 1846, where he worked as a port surveyor until 1849. However, between 1825 and 1850 he had contributed more than a hundred short stories to various periodicals, and these were later compiled in *Twice-Told Tales* (1837, 1842, 1851) and other collections. Two of his most impressive stories are "The Minister's Black Veil" and "Ethan Brand." In 1850 his brilliant novel *The Scarlet Letter* brought him international acclaim, followed a year later by *The House of the Seven Gables*. His works, noted for their deep insight, dealt mainly with the themes of morality, sin and redemption, against the somber background of Puritan New England. He also wrote popular children's books, *A Wonder Book for Boys and Girls* (1852) and *Tanglewood Tales* (1853). In 1853 President Pierce appointed him as United States consul in Liverpool, England. After 1857 Hawthorne resided in Italy and England, returning to Concord in 1860.

O. HENRY, pseudonym of WILLIAM SYDNEY PORTER (1862–1910), was born in Greensboro, North Carolina. He went to Texas in 1882, where he worked at various jobs including teller in an Austin bank. In 1896 an unexplained shortage in the bank was charged to him. He fled to Honduras but returned and served three years in prison, during which time he began to write. In 1903 he went to New York and contributed short stories to magazines. Each story was short, simple, and with an unexpected and often ironic ending. The color and movement of New York City were caught in his collections *The Four Million* (1906), *The Voice of the City* (1908), and others. His collection *Cabbages and Kings* (1904) is set in Honduras.

WILLIAM DEAN HOWELLS (1837–1920), born in Martins Ferry, Ohio, learned the printer's trade from his father before he turned to writing. In 1858 he became editor of the *Ohio State Journal*. He served as the American consul in Venice from 1861 to 1865 and drew on that experience to write the first of many travel books, *Venetian Life* (1866). He then began a fifteen-year association with the *Atlantic Monthly*; the essays and criticisms he contributed stressed the appreciation of European writers. With his novel *The Rise of Silas Lapham* (1885) he emerged as a leading realistic portrayer of life in America. His humanitarian sympathies are stressed in other works; and his encouragement of younger writers, including Hamlin Garland and Thorstein Veblen, stimulated outstanding achievements by later Americans.

WASHINGTON IRVING (1783–1859) was born in New York City, the last of eleven children. He left school at the age of sixteen and worked for a law office, but his restlessness finally found an outlet in traveling and writing. In 1802, under the pen name of Jonathan Oldstyle, he wrote a series of letters for the New York *Morning Chronicle*. Then, because of ill health, he went abroad for two years. Back in the United States, he wrote *A History of New York from the Beginning of the World to the End of the Dutch Dynasty* (1809), and retold tales of Dutch New York in *The Sketch Book of Geoffrey Crayon, Gent.*, such as "Rip Van Winkle" and "The Legend of Sleepy Hollow." He lived abroad for more than twenty years, at one time serving as minister to Spain for four years. His last years were spent in the Sleepy Hollow region on the Hudson River, where he wrote *Oliver Goldsmith* (1849) and his monumental *Life of George Washington* (1859).

GUY DE MAUPASSANT (1850–1893) was born and educated in Normandy. He later served in the army and worked as a government clerk. Ultimately he became a disciple of Flaubert and joined an eminent literary circle that included Turgenev, Daudet, and Zola, among others. Under Flaubert's guidance, de Maupassant developed a remarkable technique of objectivity and stylistic precision. In 1880, with the publication of his short story "Boule de Suif," he became an overnight celebrity. His output during the next ten years amounted to three hundred stories, six novels, and some dramatic works. He is regarded as an unequaled master of the short story.

MARCEL PRÉVOST (1862–1941) was born in Paris. He worked as a civil engineer in the tobacco industry, then turned to writing. His novels deal chiefly with feminine psychology and show a censorious attitude toward what he considered the moral looseness of women. An early novel was *Les Demi-Vierges* (1894; English translation *The Demi-Virgins*, 1895). His approach was essentially French and often shocking to English readers. His *Lettres à Françoise*, begun in 1902 and appearing at intervals, are perceptive letters to a girl during various stages of her life. A new, more restrained style was apparent in *Sa Maîtresse et Moi* (1925; English translation *His Mistress and I*, 1927). He was elected to the French Academy in 1909.

("Q") ARTHUR THOMAS QUILLER-COUCH (1863–1944), English scholar and man of letters, was born in Fowey, Cornwall. After graduating from Trinity College, Oxford, he lectured there in the classics from 1886 to 1887 and was later appointed an honorary fellow. He held many honorary doctorates and fellowships elsewhere. Though an intellectual, he was never pedantic, and in his youth he was a fine athlete. Some of his more than twenty works of fiction include *Ship of Stars* (1899), *The Laird's Luck* (1902), and *Q's Mystery Stories* (1937). He was the editor of many noted literary anthologies, including the *Oxford Book of English Verse* (1900). He is also highly regarded as a writer of short stories and of literary criticism. He died at the age of eighty, in the same village where he was born.

SIR WALTER SCOTT (1771–1832) was born in Edinburgh, Scotland. Though lame from a childhood illness, he was an enthusiastic outdoorsman. He practiced law for many years before turning to writing. First-hand knowledge of the rural Scots resulted in his first major publication, *Minstrelsy of the Scottish Border* (1802), a collection of popular songs and ballads. This work was followed by narrative poems, including "Lochinvar" (1808) and "The Lady of the Lake" (1810). After publication of his novel *Waverley* (1814), he devoted himself mainly to fiction. His novels, which include *The Heart of Midlothian* (1818) and *Ivanhoe* (1819), are generally referred to as the *Waverley* novels, since Scott preferred to be identified on the title page as "The Author of *Waverley*." His works display great tolerance for all classes and cultures and he had a unique genius for re-creating social history, drawing his readers into the lives of both great and ordinary characters caught up in dramatic historical events. Scott's output numbers twenty-eight novels, four plays, and much nonfiction.

ADALBERT STIFTER (1805–1868) was an Austrian author who was widely read in his time. His novels and poetic tales of the Bohemian forest were vivid and powerful in their descriptions of nature, and they placed him in the high regard of critics. Nietzsche considered Stifter to be one of the great German stylists. Most of his tales were collected in *Studien* (six volumes, 1844–50), of which six were retitled and published in *Bunte Steine* (*Colored Stones*) (1853). His novels include *Der Nachsommer* (1857) and *Witiko* (1867).

FRANK R. STOCKTON (1834–1902), humorist and story writer, was born in Philadelphia. He worked as a wood engraver until writing became his career. He wrote several children's books, including *Ting-a-Ling* (1870), *The Floating Prince and Other Fairy Tales* (1881), and was the assistant editor (1873–81) of *St. Nicholas* magazine. Most notable of his many humorous works for adults include *Rudder Grange* (1879) and its sequels *The Rudder Grangers Abroad* (1884) and *Pomona's Travels*

(1894). He became famous for the title story of his collection *The Lady or the Tiger?* (1884), which was followed by *The Casting Away of Mrs. Lecks and Mrs. Aleshine* in 1886. His novels and stories were collected in twenty-three volumes between 1899 and 1904.

HARRIET BEECHER STOWE (1811–1896), born in Litchfield, Connecticut, was a minister's daughter. In 1836 she married Calvin Stowe, a faculty member of the Lane Theological Seminary in Cincinnati, Ohio, where her father then served as president. She is remembered chiefly for her antislavery novel *Uncle Tom's Cabin* (1851). In it she not only created characters and scenes with humor and realism but also analyzed the slavery issue during the days of the Fugitive Slave Law. The book intensified the disagreement between the North and the South which led to the Civil War. Many of her other works deal with Puritanical New England life in the late 1700s and early 1800s. *Lady Byron Vindicated* (1870), considered shocking at the time, dealt with Lady Byron's separation from the famous poet Lord Byron. Mrs. Stowe was the mother of seven children and the sister of clergyman Henry Ward Beecher and reformer-educator Catherine Beecher.

RUTH McENERY STUART (1849–1917) was born in Marksville, Louisiana. In 1879 she married A. O. Stuart, a cotton planter. After his death four years later, she moved to New Orleans and began contributing to several magazines. Early in the 1890s she moved to New York, and from then until her death she published over twenty books. Her works display an extraordinary knowledge of Southern types, including Creoles, plantation Negroes, and poor whites. She is especially noted for her ability to accurately present the various dialects of these people. Some of her principal works include *A Golden Wedding and Other Tales* (1893), *Sonny* (1896), and *In Simpkinsville: Character Tales* (1897).

ARTHUR CHENEY TRAIN (1875–1945) was born in Boston's Back Bay area, the son of Charles Russell Train, Attorney-General for Massachusetts for seventeen years, and Sarah M. Cheney. Such notables as Emerson, Lowell, and Holmes were family friends. Young Train graduated from Harvard Law School in 1899. He thereafter practiced law, ultimately serving as New York City's assistant district attorney (1901–08) and later entering private practice. His first short story, "The Maximilian Diamond" (1904), was followed by *The Prisoner at the Bar* (1906) and *True Stories of Crime* (1908). *Mr. Tutt's Case Book* (1937) is required reading in some law schools. Combining two careers, Train managed an output of nearly 250 short stories and novels.

ANTHONY TROLLOPE (1815–1882) was born in London. He became a post office inspector, was sent to Ireland, and later wrote novels of Irish life. His travels also provided him with much of the background for the imaginary county of Barset, which he utilized in a highly successful series of novels known as the "Barsetshire Chronicles," written between 1855 and 1867. Other popular novels include *Phineas Finn, the Irish Member* (1869) and *The American Senator* (1877). A trip to the United States resulted in a travel book, *North America* (1862). He retired from the English postal department in 1867. His tremendous output included more than fifty novels as well as travel books and biographies. He is noted for his ability to display the unfolding of character by the use of commonplace scenes.

ARMANDO PALACIO VALDÉS (1853–1938) studied law at the University of Madrid, but he soon turned to writing. His first publications were critical works: *Los Oradores del Ateneo* (*The Orators of the Athenaeum*) (1878) and *Los Novelistas Españoles* (*The Spanish Novelists*) (1878). However, he mainly owes his fame to his psychological novels, suffused with an upbeat outlook on life. Some of the best known are *Marta y María* (1883; English translation, *The Marquis of Peñalta*, 1886); *La Alegría del Capitán Ribot* (1899; English translation, *The Joy of Captain Ribot*, 1900); and the series in which Dr. Angélico appears, including *Años de Juventud del Doctor Angélico* and *La Hija de Natalia* (1924). In 1935 an English collection of his short stories appeared.

HENRY VAN DYKE (1852–1933), American clergyman and writer, was born in Germantown, Pennsylvania. He graduated from Princeton in 1873 and Princeton Theological Seminary in 1874. From 1883 to 1899 he served as pastor of the Brick Presbyterian Church in New York City, and then he taught English literature at Princeton from 1899 to 1923, with time out for diplomatic service in the Netherlands from 1913 to 1916 and service as a chaplain in the U.S. Navy during World War I. "The Other Wise Man" (1896), included in this collection, is one of his most popular stories. His other works include poems; essays in the collections *Little Rivers* (1895) and *Fisherman's Luck* (1899); *The Unknown Quantity* (1912); and his translation from Novalis, *The Blue Flower* (1902).

ISRAEL ZANGWILL (1864–1926), born in London, got his start as a journalist when he edited *Ariel*, a comic journal. He enhanced his reputation with his novel *Children of the Ghetto* (1892), which was followed by *Dreamers of the Ghetto* (1898), a series of biographical studies. Among his other works are *Merely Mary Ann* (1893) and *The Melting Pot* (1914), both of which were later dramatized. Politically active, he was a prominent Territorialist leader in the Zionist movement. In this vein, his writings include *The Principle of Nationalities* (1917) and *Chosen Peoples* (1918).